INSTITUTES OF THE CHRISTIAN RELIGION

BOOK III

INSTITUTES OF THE CHRISTIAN RELIGION

BOOK III: THE MODE OF OBTAINING THE GRACE OF CHRIST, THE BENEFIT IT CONFERS, AND THE EFFECTS RESULTING FROM IT

JOHN CALVIN

Translated by Henry Beveridge
with an Introduction by Toby Sumpter
& Discussion Questions and Answers by Douglas Wilson

The Christian Heritage Series
Published by Canon Press
P.O. Box 8729, Moscow, Idaho 83843
800.488.2034 | www.canonpress.com

CONTENTS

INTRODUCTION

Perhaps one of the most surprising experiences in reading John Calvin's *Institutes of the Christian Religion* is the warmth that fills them. Calvin is not at all soft or overly emotional; he is rigorous, sturdy, even rough (in all the right ways). But if you have picked up on any of the caricatures of John Calvin, you may be surprised to find him describing faith and repentance, justification and election, and holiness and heaven in ways that are startlingly moving. Do not let me mislead you, Calvin was a theologian and an academic. Calvin was a stern spiritual general of the church. His work is at war with the world, the flesh, and the devil, and he does not take the battle lightly. Paragraph after paragraph consists of volley after volley in which Calvin meticulously aims and fires the Word of God at sinful hearts, lofty arguments, and arrogant corruptions in the world and the church. Just when you think he's laid low an enemy with the last six chapters on repentance, he adjusts his aim and fires off six more. Just when you think there can't possibly be anything left of the Roman doctrines of indulgences or purgatory or private confession or meritorious works, Calvin a few more stones still standing. And yet, through the meticulous barrage, just when you might be tempted to think him some kind of Biblical or theological machine, his words crest again with an unmistakable light and warmth.

Book Three is entitled "The way in which we receive the grace of
Christ: What benefits come to us from it, and what effects follow."
Recall that Calvin's Institutes roughly follows the outline of the Apostles' Creed, which is broadly Trinitarian in structure, tracing the work
of the Father, Son, and Holy Spirit. While the First Book focused
on God the Father and Book Two focused on the work of Christ the
Son, Book Three takes up the ministry of God the Spirit, and Book
Four continues that same theme as Calvin takes up the doctrine of
the church. Here in Book Three Calvin begins with the ministry of
the Spirit granting the gift of saving faith and distinguishes Christian
repentance from various errors. He continues, describing the Christian life as fundamentally a path of self-denial under God's blessing,
and then arrives at the doctrine of justification by faith alone. Finally,
Calvin explains Christian freedom and the vital role of prayer, both
grounded in God's eternal election, and he closes with a meditation
on the final resurrection.

If there is a common element, a thread wound through Calvin's
work holding his warmth of expression together, I would argue that
it is Calvin's unrelenting grasp of God's gracious sovereignty. Man
contributes nothing but sin and corruption to his salvation; God is
the source of all goodness, righteousness, and glory. All is mercy. All
is grace, freely given, and for nothing found in man. This is the touch-
stone of his work. It's what he comes back to again and again. In other
words, what fires Calvin's theology is a deep and abiding conviction
and experience of God's goodness planning, pursuing, initiating, saving, caring for Christians throughout their lives, and as the Good
Shepherd, carrying them home and to the final resurrection.

It might come as surprise to some, though he is so universally famous for it now, but Calvin's work on the doctrine of election and
predestination comes here, towards the end of his work on the Holy
Spirit and the Christian life – since the Holy Spirit is the "Spirit
of adoption" and the Spirit seals in our hearts our certain salvation.

For Calvin the thing that rises above all else through his treatment of election is the glory of God's mercy and kindness (III.24.1). In fact, the doctrine of election flows directly from his understanding of evangelical faith: "Now we shall possess a right definition of faith if we call it a firm and certain knowledge of God's benevolence toward us, founded upon the truth of the freely given promise in Christ, both revealed to our minds and sealed upon our hearts through the Holy Spirit" (III.2.7). That benevolence of God is what drives everything, and rightly understood ought to drive everyone to Christ: "First, if we seek God's fatherly mercy and kindly heart, we should turn our eyes to Christ, on whom alone God's Spirit rests... Accordingly, those whom God has adopted as sons are said to have been chosen not in themselves but in his Christ" (III.24.5).

Election is in Christ, and Christ is the revelation of God's goodness and kindness and mercy. Even weak faith in Christ is likened to "a man who, shut up in a prison, into which the sun's rays shine obliquely and half obscured through a rather narrow window, is indeed deprived of the full sight of the sun. Yet his eyes dwell on its steadfast brightness, and he receives its benefits. Thus, bound with the fetters of an earthly body, however much we are shadowed on every side with great darkness, we are nevertheless illumined as much as need be for firm assurance when, to show forth his mercy, the light of God sheds even a little of its radiance" (III.2.18). If something shines through Calvin's sometimes grim and painstaking theological precision, it is this light of God's goodness in Christ permeating all things, ruling all things, upholding all things. And none of it originates from us. All of it is a gift from Him. "For in Christ he offers all happiness in place of our misery, all wealth in place of our neediness; in him he opens to us the heavenly treasures that our whole faith may contemplate his beloved Son, our whole expectation depend upon him, and our whole hope cleave to and rest in Him" (III.20.1).

We might call this a thoroughly evangelical theology. Calvin's theology is robust, solid, philosophical and biblical marble, but it shines with gospel light, grasped by faith alone. His theological project is a fireplace built out of biblical bricks and theological steel, but it's filled with an evangelical fire. "Unbelief does not hold sway within believers' hearts, but assails them from without. It does not mortally wound them with its weapons, but merely harasses them, or at most so injures them that the wound is curable. Faith, then, as Paul teaches, serves as our shield" (III.2.21).

This evangelical faith is the sovereign gift of God the Spirit that calls the dead to life, enabling believers to receive all things from God with patience and joy. "Thus it will come to pass that, by whatever kind of cross we may be troubled, even in the greatest tribulations of mind, we shall firmly keep our patience... the conclusion will always be: the Lord so willed, therefore let us follow his will. Indeed, amid the very pricks of pain, amid groaning and tears, this thought must intervene: to incline our heart to bear cheerfully those things which have so moved it" (III.8.10). As Calvin meticulously examines the doctrines of faith and repentance and justification and prayer, election and heaven, he is no hypocrite. His own Spirit-wrought joy and patience shine through his work.

It is this warmth that Calvin brings to the battlefield. "However great are the devices, as Augustine says, that the devil throws up against us, while he holds no lodgement in the heart, where faith dwells, he is cast out. Thus, if we may judge from the outcome, believers not only emerge safely from every battle, so that, having received fresh strength, they are shortly after ready to descend again into the arena; but, besides, what John says in his canonical letter is also fulfilled: 'This is the victory that overcomes the world, your faith' (1 Jn. 5:4). And he affirms that our faith will be victor not only in one battle, or a few, or against any particular assault; but that, though it be assailed a thousand times, it will prevail over the entire world" (III.2.21).

Notice that language at the end of that quotation in particular: not only in one battle, or a few... but though it be assailed a thousand times, it will prevail over the entire world. This is the tenor of Calvin's pastoral and theological heart. He comes to these great themes of theology with this battle cry of evangelical faith, ready to descend into the arena again and again, even a thousand times, confident this faith will prevail over the entire world.

If there is one thing I might pray for all who read these pages, it is that men, and pastors in particular, would imitate Calvin's warm and persistent warfare against the flesh, the world, and the devil. When Elisha was dying, Joash King of Israel came to visit him, and when Elisha would encourage Joash in his struggle with the Syrians, the prophet instructed the king to strike the ground with his arrows. The king struck the ground three times, and Elisha was very angry and said, "Thou shouldest have smitten five or six times; then hadst thou smitten Syria till thou hadst consumed it: whereas now thou shalt smite Syria but thrice" (2 Kgs. 13:19).

The best of modern Christian men strike the ground three times. We identify two or three modern evils and take our stands, often rightly so, and then we judge our faithfulness by those who will not stand for anything or have chosen relatively less important or even wicked things to stand for. But men of God will not be graded on a curve at the last day. We will not stand before God relative to our peers. We will stand before His holiness alone. Calvin's Institutes is a glorious example of a faithful man of God striking the ground five or six times.

Too often we have believed the lies of the world and the devil that being that kind of spiritual warrior means we must become belligerent and boorish. But Calvin is a wonderful counterexample – not to mention the apostles, patriarchs, prophets, and our Lord Jesus. We really could do with a generation of warm warriors, jovial cavaliers – stern men full of love, rough and faithful men, determined to overcome the world. As Calvin says of the scholastics, minions of Satan, that seek to overthrow justification by faith, "But because, as we said, they assail us with still other devices, come, let us keep beating them back!" (III.27.1) Do you have that Spirit of courage and patience and joy? Will you keep at the battle, when many think striking the ground three times really is quite enough? Come, let us keep beating them back!

The only thing that will do for such conviction and assurance is the confidence of an evangelical faith clinging to Christ: "Surely it is terrifying to walk in the darkness of death; and believers, whatever their strength may be, cannot but be frightened by it. But since the thought prevails that they have God beside them, caring for their safety, fear at once yields to assurance…" (III.2.21). Whatever dangers, whatever enemies, whatever sin assails the believer, even death itself is faced by a Christian with the certain knowledge that God walks beside them. He will never leave them or forsake them. The Lion of the Tribe of Judah walks with His soldiers. He is in our midst. He breathes His Spirit on His saints and they are filled with His fire and they fear no evil. They walk with Him and talk with Him and rest in His exhaustive care until He leads them home and to the final resurrection.

> "Let us, however, consider this settled: that no one has made progress in the school of Christ who does not joyfully await the day of death and final resurrection… and even though the blind and stupid desire of the flesh resists, let us not hesitate to await the Lord's coming… He will come to us as Redeemer, and rescuing us from this boundless abyss of all evils and miseries, he will lead us into that blessed inheritance of his life and glory" (III.9.5).

Even this charge to joyfully await the day of death and final resurrection is not at all at odds with Calvin's martial spirit. This is no escapist vision. Even as he closes Book III meditating on heaven and the resurrection, he reminds us that the joy in our labors is fed by this fervent desire: "Let us always have in mind the eternal happiness, the goal of resurrection – a happiness of whose excellence the minutest part would scarce be told if all were said that the tongues of all men can say" (III.25.10). For even that eternal happiness wells up with a godly ambition, recognizing that "just as God, variously distributing his gifts to the saints in this world, beams upon them unequally, so there will not be an equal measure of glory in heaven, where God shall crown his gifts" (III.25.10). Channeling Augustine's famous line, "God shall crown his gifts," Calvin proclaims with a happy heart what Scripture clearly teaches, and what faith longs for: that God is the rewarder of those who diligently seek Him (Heb. 11:6).

Calvin certainly guards against undue speculations and harmful questions about last things, but he nevertheless insists that the simple, biblical truth of the final resurrection and our rewards ought to continually drive us back into the fray, back into the arena, for yet another victory. "Almost all are lazy and loath to do battle, while already picturing themselves imaginary victories" (III.25.11). The faithful fight for goodness and truth on earth precisely because their greatest love is God in Heaven. This is the warmth that fills Calvin's work, the fire that filled his life. His had no imaginary vision of victory, but rather the certain victory of an evangelical faith in an infinitely gracious God, overcoming the world.

~Toby Sumpter

SUMMARY

The two former Books treated of God the Creator and Redeemer. This Book, which contains a full exposition of the Third Part of the Apostles' Creed, treats of the mode of procuring the grace of Christ, the benefits which we derive and the effects which follow from it, or of the operations of the Holy Spirit in regard to our salvation.

The subject is comprehended under seven principal heads, which almost all point to the same end, namely, the doctrine of faith.

I. As it is by the secret and special operation of the Holy Spirit that we enjoy Christ and all his benefits, the First Chapter treats of this operation, which is the foundation of faith, new life, and all holy exercises.

II. Faith being, as it were, the hand by which we embrace Christ the Redeemer, offered to us by the Holy Spirit, Faith is fully considered in the Second Chapter.

III. In further explanation of Saving Faith, and the benefits derived from it, it is mentioned that true repentance always flows from true faith. The doctrine of Repentance is considered generally in the Third Chapter, Popish Repentance in the Fourth Chapter, Indulgences and Purgatory in the Fifth Chapter. Chapters Sixth to Tenth are devoted to a special consideration of the different parts of true Repentance—viz. mortification of the flesh, and quickening of the Spirit.

IV. More clearly to show the utility of this Faith, and the effects resulting from it, the doctrine of Justification by Faith is explained in the Eleventh Chapter, and certain questions connected with it explained from the Twelfth to the Eighteenth Chapter. Christian liberty a kind of accessory to Justification, is considered in the Nineteenth Chapter.

V. The Twentieth Chapter is devoted to Prayer, the principal exercise of faith, and, as it were, the medium or instrument through which we daily procure blessings from God.

VI. As all do not indiscriminately embrace the fellowship of Christ offered in the Gospel, but those only whom the Lord favors with the effectual and special grace of his Spirit, lest any should impugn this arrangement, Chapters Twenty-First to Twenty-Fourth are occupied with a necessary and apposite discussion of the subject of Election.

VII. Lastly, As the hard warfare which the Christian is obliged constantly to wage may have the effect of disheartening him, it is shown how it may be alleviated by meditating on the final resurrection. Hence the subject of the Resurrection is considered in the Twenty-Fifth Chapter.

CHAPTER 1

The benefits of Christ made available to us by the secret operation of the Spirit.

The three divisions of this chapter are—I. The secret operation of the Holy Spirit, which seals our salvation, should be considered first in Christ the Mediator as our Head, sec. 1 and 2.

II. The titles given to the Holy Spirit show that we become members of Christ by his grace and energy, sec. 3.

III. As the special influence of the Holy Spirit is manifested in the gift of faith, the former is a proper introduction to the latter, and thus prepares for the second chapter, sec. 4.

Outline:

1. The Holy Spirit the bond which unites us with Christ. This the result of faith produced by the secret operation of the Holy Spirit. This obvious from Scripture.

2. In Christ the Mediator, the gifts of the Holy Spirit are to be seen in all their fullness. To what end. Why the Holy Spirit is called the Spirit of the Father and the Son.

3. Titles of the Spirit—1. The Spirit of adoption. 2. An earnest and seal. 3. Water. 4. Life. 5. Oil and unction. 6. Fire. 7. A fountain. 8. The word of God. Use of these titles.

4. Faith being the special work of the Holy Spirit, the power and efficacy of the Holy Spirit usually ascribed to it.

We must now see in what way we become possessed of the blessings which God has bestowed on his only-begotten Son, not for private use, but to enrich the poor and needy. And the first thing to be attended to is, that so long as we are without Christ and separated from him, nothing which he suffered and did for the salvation of the human race is of the least benefit to us. To communicate to us the blessings which he received from the Father, he must become ours and dwell in us. Accordingly, he is called our Head, and the first-born among many brethren, while, on the other hand, we are said to be ingrafted into him and clothed with him, all which he possesses being, as I have said, nothing to us until we become one with him. And although it is true that we obtain this by faith, yet since we see that all do not indiscriminately embrace the offer of Christ which is made by the gospel, the very nature of the case teaches us to ascend higher, and inquire into the secret efficacy of the Spirit, to which it is owing that we enjoy Christ and all his blessings. I have already treated of the eternal essence and divinity of the Spirit (Book 1, chap. 13, sect. 14-15); let us at present attend to the special point, that Christ came by water and blood, as the Spirit testifies concerning him, that we might not lose the benefits of the salvation which he has purchased. For as there are said to be three witnesses in heaven, the Father, the Word, and the Spirit, so there are also three on the earth, namely, water, blood, and Spirit. It is not without cause that the testimony of the Spirit is twice mentioned, a testimony which is engraven on our hearts by way of seal, and thus seals the cleansing and sacrifice of Christ. For which reason, also, Peter says, that believers are "elect" "through sanctification of the Spirit, unto obedience and sprinkling of the blood of Jesus Christ" (1 Pet. 1:2). By these words he reminds us, that if the shedding of his sacred blood is not to be in vain, our souls must be washed in it by the secret cleansing of the Holy Spirit. For which reason, also, Paul, speaking of cleansing and purification, says, "but ye are washed, but ye are sanctified, but ye are justified in the name of the Lord Jesus and by the Spirit of our God" (1 Cor. 6:11). The whole comes to this that the Holy Spirit is the bond by which Christ effectually binds us to himself. Here we may refer to what was said in the last Book concerning his anointing.

2. But in order to have a clearer view of this most important subject, we must remember that Christ came provided with the Holy Spirit after a peculiar manner, namely, that he might separate us from the world, and unite us in the hope of an eternal inheritance. Hence the Spirit is called the Spirit of sanctification, because he quickens and cherishes us, not merely by the general energy which is seen in the human race, as well as other animals, but because he is the seed and root of heavenly life in us. Accordingly, one of the highest commendations which the prophets give to the kingdom of Christ is, that under it the Spirit would be poured out in richer abundance. One of the most remarkable passages is that of Joel, "It shall come to pass afterward, that I will pour out my Spirit upon all flesh" (Joel 2:28). For although the prophet seems to confine the gifts of the Spirit to the office of prophesying, he yet intimates under a figure, that God will, by the illumination of his Spirit, provide himself with disciples who had previously been altogether ignorant of heavenly doctrine. Moreover, as it is for the sake of his Son that God bestows the Holy Spirit upon us, and yet has deposited him in all his fullness with the Son, to be the minister and dispenser of his liberality, he is called at one time the Spirit of the Father, at another the Spirit of the Son: "Ye are not in the flesh but in the Spirit, if so be that the Spirit of God dwell in you. Now, if any man have not the Spirit of Christ, he is none

of his" (Rom. 8:9); and hence he encourages us to hope for complete renovation: "If the Spirit of him that raised up Jesus from the dead dwell in you, he that raised up Christ from the dead shall also quicken your mortal bodies by his Spirit that dwelleth in you" (Rom. 8:11). There is no inconsistency in ascribing the glory of those gifts to the Father, inasmuch as he is the author of them, and, at the same time, ascribing them to Christ, with whom they have been deposited, that he may bestow them on his people. Hence he invites all the thirsty to come unto him and drink (John 7:37). And Paul teaches, that "unto every one of us is given grace, according to the measure of the gift of Christ" (Eph. 4:7). And we must remember, that the Spirit is called the Spirit of Christ, not only inasmuch as the eternal Word of God is with the Father united with the Spirit, but also in respect of his office of Mediator; because, had he not been endued with the energy of the Spirit, he had come to us in vain. In this sense he is called the "last Adam," and said to have been sent from heaven "a quickening Spirit" (1 Cor. 15:45), where Paul contrasts the special life which Christ breathes into his people, that they may be one with him with the animal life which is common even to the reprobate. In like manner, when he prays that believers may have "the grace of our Lord Jesus Christ, and the love of God," he at the same time adds, "the communion of the Holy Ghost," without which no man shall ever taste the paternal favor of God, or the benefits of Christ. Thus, also, in another passage he says, "The love of God is shed abroad in our hearts by the Holy Ghost, which is given unto us" (Rom. 5:5).

3. Here it will be proper to point out the titles which the Scripture bestows on the Spirit, when it treats of the commencement and entire renewal of our salvation. First, he is called the "Spirit of adoption," because he is witness to us of the free favor with which God the Father embraced us in his well-beloved and only-begotten Son, so as to become our Fathers and give us boldness of access to him; nays he dictates the very words, so that we can boldly cry, "Abba, Father." For

the same reason, he is said to have "sealed us, and given the earnest of the Spirit in our hearts," because, as pilgrims in the world, and persons in a manner dead, he so quickens us from above as to assure us that our salvation is safe in the keeping of a faithful God. Hence, also, the Spirit is said to be "life because of righteousness." But since it is his secret irrigation that makes us bud forth and produce the fruits of righteousness, he is repeatedly described as water. Thus in Isaiah "Ho, every one that thirsteth, come ye to the waters." Again, "I will pour water upon him that is thirsty, and floods upon the dry ground." Corresponding to this are the words of our Savior, to which I lately referred, "If any man thirst, let him come unto me and drink." Sometimes, indeed, he receives this name from his energy in cleansing and purifying, as in Ezekiel, where the Lord promises, "Then will I sprinkle you with clean water, and ye shall be clean." As those sprinkled with the Spirit are restored to the full vigor of life, he hence obtains the names of "Oil" and "Unction." On the other hand, as he is constantly employed in subduing and destroying the vices of our concupiscence, and inflaming our hearts with the love of God and piety, he hence receives the name of Fire. In fine, he is described to us as a Fountain, whence all heavenly riches flow to us; or as the Hand by which God exerts his power, because by his divine inspiration he so breathes divine life into us, that we are no longer acted upon by ourselves, but ruled by his motion and agency, so that everything good in us is the fruit of his grace, while our own endowments without him are mere darkness of mind and perverseness of heart. Already, indeed, it has been clearly shown, that until our minds are intent on the Spirit, Christ is in a manner unemployed, because we view him coldly without us, and so at a distance from us. Now we know that he is of no avail save only to those to whom he is a head and the first-born among the brethren, to those, in fine, who are clothed with him. To this union alone it is owing that, in regard to us, the Savior has not come in vain. To this is to be referred that sacred marriage, by which we become bone of his bone, and flesh of his flesh, and so one with him (Eph. 5:30), for it is by the Spirit alone that he unites himself to us. By the same grace and energy of the Spirit we become his members, so that he keeps us under him, and we in our turn possess him.

4. But as faith is his principal work, all those passages which express his power and operations are, in a great measure, referred to it, as it is, only by faith that he brings us to the light of the Gospel, as John teaches, that to those who believe in Christ is given the privilege "to become the sons of God, even to them that believe in his name, which were born not of blood, nor of the will of the flesh, nor of the will of man, but of God" (John 1:12). Opposing God to flesh and blood, he declares it to be a supernatural gift, that those who would otherwise remain in unbelief, receive Christ by faith. Similar to this is our Savior's reply to Peter, "Flesh and blood has not revealed it unto thee, but my Father which is in heaven" (Matt. 16:17). These things I now briefly advert to, as I have fully considered them elsewhere. To the same effect Paul says to the Ephesians, "Ye were sealed with that Holy Spirit of promise" (Eph. 1:13); thus showing that he is the internal teacher, by whose agency the promise of salvation, which would otherwise only strike the air or our ears, penetrates into our minds. In like manner, he says to the Thessalonians, "God has from the beginning chosen you to salvation, through sanctification of the Spirit and belief of the truth" (2 Thess. 2:13); by this passage briefly reminding us, that faith itself is produced only by the Spirit. This John explains more distinctly, "We know that he abideth in us, by the Spirit which he has given us;" again, "Hereby know we that we dwell in him and he in us, because he has given us of his Spirit" (1 John 3:24; 4:13). Accordingly to make his disciples capable of heavenly wisdom, Christ promised them "the Spirit of truth, whom the world cannot receive" (John 14:17). And he assigns it to him, as his proper office, to bring to remembrance the things which he had verbally taught; for in vain would light be offered to the blind, did not that Spirit of

understanding open the intellectual eye; so that he himself may be properly termed the key by which the treasures of the heavenly kingdom are unlocked, and his illumination, the eye of the mind by which we are enabled to see: hence Paul so highly commends the ministry of the Spirit (2 Cor. 3:6), since teachers would cry aloud to no purpose, did not Christ, the internal teacher, by means of his Spirit, draw to himself those who are given him of the Father. Therefore, as we have said that salvation is perfected in the person of Christ, so, in order to make us partakers of it, he baptizes us "with the Holy Spirit and with fire" (Luke 3:16), enlightening us into the faith of his Gospel, and so regenerating us to be new creatures. Thus cleansed from all pollution, he dedicates us as holy temples to the Lord.

Study Guide Questions

Section 1

1. What has to happen before all Christ's benefits become ours?
2. What is the bond that unites us to Christ?

Section 2

1. What does the Spirit do for all living creatures?
2. But what does He do for the believers?
3. Does the Spirit belong to the Father or the Son?

Section 3

1. What are some of the titles or names given to the Spirit that Calvin records here?

Section 4

1. What is the principal work of the Holy Spirit?

CHAPTER 2

Of faith. The definition of it. Its peculiar properties.

This chapter consists of three principal parts.

I. A brief explanation of certain matters pertaining to the doctrine of Faith, sec. 1-14. First, of the object of faith, sec. 1. Second, of Implicit Faith, sec. 2-6. Third, Definition of Faith, sec. 7. Fourth, the various meanings of the term Faith, sec. 8-13.

II. A full exposition of the definition given in the seventh section, sec. 14-40.

III. A brief confirmation of the definition by the authority of an Apostle. The mutual relation between faith, hope, and charity, sec. 41-43.

Outline:

A brief recapitulation of the leading points of the whole discussion. The scope of this chapter. The necessity of the doctrine of faith. This doctrine obscured by the Schoolmen, who make God the object of faith, without referring to Christ. The Schoolmen refuted by various passages.

2. The dogma of implicit faith refuted. It destroys faith, which consists in a knowledge of the divine will. What this will is, and how necessary the knowledge of it.

3. Many things are and will continue to be implicitly believed. Faith, however, consists in the knowledge of God and Christ, not in a reverence for the Church. Another refutation from the absurdities to which this dogma leads.

4. In what sense our faith may be said to be implicit. Examples in the Apostles, in the holy women, and in all believers.

5. In some, faith is implicit, as being a preparation for faith. This, however, widely different from the implicit faith of the Schoolmen.

6. The word of God has a similar relation to faith, the word being, as it were, the source and basis of faith, and the mirror in which it beholds God. Confirmation from various passages of Scripture. Without the knowledge of the word there can be no faith. Sum of the discussion of the Scholastic doctrine of implicit faith.

7. What faith properly has respect to in the word of God, namely, the promise of grace offered in Christ, provided it be embraced with faith. Proper definition of faith.

8. Scholastic distinction between faith formed and unformed, refuted by a consideration of the nature of faith, which, as the gift of the Spirit, cannot possibly be disjoined from pious affection.

9. Objection from a passage of Paul. Answer to it. Error of the Schoolmen in giving only one meaning to faith, whereas it has many meanings. The testimony of faith improperly ascribed to two classes of men.

10. View to be taken of this. Who those are that believe for a time. The faith of hypocrites. With whom they may be compared.

11. Why faith attributed to the reprobate. Objection. Answer. What perception of grace in the reprobate. How the elect are distinguished from the reprobate.

12. Why faith is temporary in the reprobate, firm and perpetual in the elect. Reason in the case of the reprobate. Example. Why God is angry with his children. In what sense many are said to fall from faith. 13. Various meanings of the term faith. 1. Taken for soundness in the faith. 2. Sometimes restricted to a particular object. 3. Signifies the ministry or testimony by which we are instructed in the faith.

14. Definition of faith explained under six principal heads. 1. What meant by Knowledge in the definition.

15. Why this knowledge must be sure and firm. Reason drawn from the consideration of our weakness. Another reason from the certainty of the promises of God.

16. The leading point in this certainty. Its fruits. A description of the true believer.

17. An objection to this certainty. Answer. Confirmation of the answer from the example of David. This enlarged upon from the opposite example of Ahab. Also from the uniform experience and the prayers of believers.

18. For this reason the conflict between the flesh and the Spirit in the soul of the believer described. The issue of this conflict, the victory of faith.

19. On the whole, the faith of the elect certain and indubitable. Conformation from analogy.

20. Another confirmation from the testimony of an Apostle, making it apparent, that, though the faith of the elect is as yet imperfect, it is nevertheless firm and sure.

21. A fuller explanation of the nature of faith. 1. When the believer is shaken with fear, he retakes himself to the bosom of a merciful God. 2. He does not even shun God when angry, but hopes in him. 3. He does not suffer unbelief to reign in his heart. 4. He opposes unbelief, and is never finally lost. 5. Faith, however often assailed, at length comes off victorious.

22. Another species of fear, arising from a consideration of the judgment of God against the wicked. This also faith overcomes. Examples of this description, placed before the eyes of believers, repress presumption, and fix their faith in God.

23. Nothing contrary to this in the exhortation of the Apostle to work out our salvation with fear and trembling. Fear and faith mutually connected. Confirmation from the words of a Prophet.

24. This doctrine gives no countenance to the error of those who dream of a confidence mingled with incredulity. Refutation of this error, from a consideration of the dignity of Christ dwelling in us. The argument retorted. Refutation confirmed by the authority of an Apostle. What we ought to hold on this question.

25. Confirmation of the preceding conclusion by a passage from Bernard.

26. True fear caused in two ways—viz. when we are required to reverence God as a Father, and also to fear him as Lord.

27. Objection from a passage in the Apostle John. Answer founded on the distinction between filial and servile fear.

28. How faith is said to have respect to the divine benevolence. What comprehended under this benevolence. Confirmation from David and Paul.

29. Of the Free Promise which is the foundation of Faith. Reason. Confirmation.

30. Faith not divided in thus seeking a Free Promise in the Gospel. Reason. Conclusion confirmed by another reason.

31. The word of God the prop and root of faith. The word attests the divine goodness and mercy. In what sense faith has respect to the power of God. Various passages of Isaiah, inviting the godly to behold the power of God, explained. Other passages from David. We must beware of going beyond the limits prescribed by the word, lest false zeal lead us astray, as it did Sarah, Rebekah, and Isaac. In this way

faith is obscured, though not extinguished. We must not depart one iota from the word of God.

32. All the promises included in Christ. Two objections answered. A third objection drawn from example. Answer explaining the faith of Naaman, Cornelius, and the Eunuch.

33. Faith revealed to our minds, and sealed on our hearts, by the Holy Spirit. 1. The mind is purified so as to have a relish for divine truth. 2. The mind is thus established in the truth by the agency of the Holy Spirit.

34. Proof of the former. 1. By reason. 2. By Scripture. 3. By example. 4. By analogy.

35. 5. By the excellent qualities of faith. 6. By a celebrated passage from Augustine.

36. Proof of the latter by the argument *a minore ad majus.* Why the Spirit is called a seal, an earnest, and the Spirit of promise.

37. Believers sometimes shaken, but not so as to perish finally. They ultimately overcome their trials, and remain steadfast. Proofs from Scripture.

38. Objection of the Schoolmen. Answer. Attempt to support the objection by a passage in Ecclesiastes. Answer, explaining the meaning of the passage.

39. Another objection, charging the elect in Christ with rashness and presumption. Answer. Answer confirmed by various passages from the Apostle Paul. Also from John and Isaiah.

40. A third objection, impugning the final perseverance of the elect. Answer by an Apostle. Summary of the refutation.

41. The definition of faith accords with that given by the Apostle in Hebrews. Explanation of this definition. Refutation of the scholastic error, that charity is prior to faith and hope.

42. Hope the inseparable attendant of true faith. Reason. Connection between faith and hope. Mutually support each other. Obvious

from the various forms of temptation, that the aid of hope necessary
to establish faith.

43. The terms faith and hope sometimes confounded. Refutation of
the Schoolmen, who attribute a twofold foundation to hope—viz. the
grace of God and the merit of works.

All these things will be easily understood after we have given a
clearer definition of faith, so as to enable the readers to apprehend its nature and power. Here it is of importance to call to mind
what was formerly taught, first, That since God by his Law prescribes
what we ought to do, failure in any one respect subjects us to the
dreadful judgment of eternal death, which it denounces. Secondly,
Because it is not only difficult, but altogether beyond our strength
and ability, to fulfill the demands of the Law, if we look only to ourselves and consider what is due to our merits, no ground of hope
remains, but we lie forsaken of God under eternal death. Thirdly, That
there is only one method of deliverance which can rescue us from
this miserable calamity—viz. when Christ the Redeemer appears, by
whose hand our heavenly Father, out of his infinite goodness and
mercy, has been pleased to succor us, if we with true faith embrace
this mercy, and with firm hope rest in it. It is now proper to consider
the nature of this faith, by means of which, those who are adopted
into the family of God obtain possession of the heavenly kingdom.
For the accomplishment of so great an end, it is obvious that no mere
opinion or persuasion is adequate. And the greater care and diligence
is necessary in discussing the true nature of faith, from the pernicious
delusions which many, in the present day, labor under with regard
to it. Great numbers, on hearing the term, think that nothing more
is meant than a certain common assent to the Gospel History; nay,
when the subject of faith is discussed in the Schools, by simply representing God as its object, they by empty speculation, as we have
elsewhere said (Book 2, chap. 6, sec. 4), hurry wretched souls away

from the right mark instead of directing them to it. For seeing that God dwells in light that is inaccessible, Christ must intervene. Hence he calls himself "the light of the world;" and in another passage, "the way, the truth, and the life." None cometh to the Father (who is the fountain of life) except by him; for "no man knoweth who the Father is but the Son, and he to whom the Son will reveal him." For this reason, Paul declares, "I count all things as loss for the excellency of the knowledge of Christ Jesus my Lord." In the twentieth chapter of the Acts, he states that he preached "faith towards our Lord Jesus Christ;" and in another passage, he introduces Christ as thus addressing him: "I have appeared unto thee for this purpose, to make thee a minister and a witness;" "delivering thee from the people, and from the Gentiles, unto whom now I send thee,": "that they may receive forgiveness of sins, and inheritance among them which are sanctified through faith which is in me." Paul further declares, that in the person of Christ the glory of God is visibly manifested to us, or, which is the same thing, we have "the light of the knowledge of the glory of God in the face of Jesus Christ." It is true, indeed, that faith has respect to God only; but to this we should add, that it acknowledges Jesus Christ whom he has sent. God would remain far off, concealed from us, were we not irradiated by the brightness of Christ. All that the Father had, he deposited with his only begotten Son, in order that he might manifest himself in him, and thus by the communication of blessings express the true image of his glory. Since, as has been said, we must be led by the Spirit, and thus stimulated to seek Christ, so must we also remember that the invisible Father is to be sought nowhere but in this image. For which reason Augustine treating of the object of faith (*De Civitate Dei*, lib. 11, ch. 2), elegantly says, "The thing to be known is, whither we are to go, and by what way;" and immediately after infers, that "the surest way to avoid all errors is to know him who is both God and man. It is to God we tend, and it is by man we go, and both of these are found only in Christ." Paul, when he

preaches faith towards God, surely does not intend to overthrow what
he so often inculcates—viz. that faith has all its stability in Christ. Peter most appropriately connects both, saying, that by him "we believe
in God" (1 Pet. 1:21).

2. This evil, therefore, must, like innumerable others, be attributed
to the Schoolmen, who have in a manner drawn a veil over Christ,
to whom, if our eye is not directly turned, we must always wander
through many labyrinths. But besides impairing, and almost annihilating, faith by their obscure definition, they have invented the fiction
of implicit faith, with which name decking the grossest ignorance,
they delude the wretched populace to their great destruction. Nay,
to state the fact more truly and plainly, this fiction not only buries
true faith, but entirely destroys it. Is it faith to understand nothing,
and merely submit your convictions implicitly to the Church? Faith
consists not in ignorance, but in knowledge—knowledge not of God
merely, but of the divine will. We do not obtain salvation either because we are prepared to embrace every dictate of the Church as true,
or leave to the Church the province of inquiring and determining; but
when we recognize God as a propitious Father through the reconciliation made by Christ, and Christ as given to us for righteousness,
sanctification, and life. By this knowledge, I say, not by the submission
of our understanding, we obtain an entrance into the kingdom of
heaven. For when the Apostle says, "With the heart man believeth
unto righteousness; and with the mouth confession is made unto salvation" (Rom. 10:10); he intimates, that it is not enough to believe
implicitly without understanding, or even inquiring. The thing requisite is an explicit recognition of the divine goodness, in which our
righteousness consists.

3. I indeed deny not (so enveloped are we in ignorance), that to us
very many things now are and will continue to be completely involved
until we lay aside this weight of flesh, and approach nearer to the presence of God. In such cases the fittest course is to suspend our judgment,

and resolve to maintain unity with the Church. But under this pretext, to honor ignorance tempered with humility with the name of faith, is most absurd. Faith consists in the knowledge of God and Christ (John 17:3), not in reverence for the Church. And we see what a labyrinth they have formed out of this implicit faith—every thing, sometimes even the most monstrous errors, being received by the ignorant as oracles without any discrimination, provided they are prescribed to them under the name of the Church. This inconsiderate facility, though the surest precipice to destruction, is, however, excused on the ground that it believes nothing definitely, but only with the appended condition, if such is the faith of the Church. Thus they pretend to find truth in error, light in darkness, true knowledge in ignorance. Not to dwell longer in refuting these views, we simply advise the reader to compare them with ours. The clearness of truth will itself furnish a sufficient refutation. For the question they raise is not, whether there may be an implicit faith with many remains of ignorance, but they maintain, that persons living and even indulging in a stupid ignorance duly believe, provided, in regard to things unknown, they assent to the authority and judgment of the Church: as if Scripture did not uniformly teach, that with faith understanding is conjoined.

4. We grant, indeed, that so long as we are pilgrims in the world faith is implicit, not only because as yet many things are hidden from us, but because, involved in the mists of error, we attain not to all. The highest wisdom, even of him who has attained the greatest perfection, is to go forward, and endeavor in a calm and teachable spirit to make further progress. Hence Paul exhorts believers to wait for further illumination in any matter in which they differ from each other, Phil. 3:15). And certainly experience teaches, that so long as we are in the flesh, our attainments are less than is to be desired. In our daily reading we fall in with many obscure passages which convict us of ignorance. With this curb God keeps us modest, assigning to each a measure of faith, that every teacher, however excellent, may still

be disposed to learn. Striking examples of this implicit faith may be observed in the disciples of Christ before they were fully illuminated. We see with what difficulty they take in the first rudiments, how they hesitate in the minutest matters, how, though hanging on the lips of their Master, they make no great progress; nay, even after running to the sepulcher on the report of the women, the resurrection of their Master appears to them a dream. As Christ previously bore testimony to their faith, we cannot say that they were altogether devoid of it; nay, had they not been persuaded that Christ would rise again, all their zeal would have been extinguished. Nor was it superstition that led the women to prepare spices to embalm a dead body of whose revival they had no expectation; but, although they gave credit to the words of one whom they knew to be true, yet the ignorance which still possessed their minds involved their faith in darkness, and left them in amazement. Hence they are said to have believed only when, by the reality, they perceive the truth of what Christ had spoken; not that they then began to believe, but the seed of a hidden faith, which lay as it were dead in their hearts, then burst forth in vigor. They had, therefore, a true but implicit faith, having reverently embraced Christ as the only teacher. Then, being taught by him, they felt assured that he was the author of salvation: in fine, believed that he had come from heaven to gather disciples, and take them thither through the grace of the Father. There cannot be a more familiar proof of this, than that in all men faith is always mingled with incredulity.

5. We may also call their faith implicit, as being properly nothing else than a preparation for faith. The Evangelists describe many as having believed, although they were only roused to admiration by the miracles, and went no farther than to believe that Christ was the promised Messiah, without being at all imbued with Evangelical doctrine. The reverence which subdued them, and made them willingly submit to Christ, is honored with the name of faith, though it was nothing but the commencement of it. Thus the nobleman who

believed in the promised cure of his son, on returning home, is said by
the Evangelist (John 4:53) to have again believed; that is, he had first
received the words which fell from the lips of Christ as an oracular
response, and thereafter submitted to his authority and received his
doctrine. Although it is to be observed that he was docile and disposed to learn, yet the word "believed" in the former passage denotes
a particular faith, and in the latter gives him a place among those
disciples who had devoted themselves to Christ. Not unlike this is
the example which John gives of the Samaritans who believed the
women, and eagerly hastened to Christ; but, after they had heard
him, thus express themselves, "Now we believe, not because of thy
saying, for we have heard him ourselves, and know that this is indeed
the Christ, the Savior of the world" (John 4:42). From these passages
it is obvious, that even those who are not yet imbued with the first
principles, provided they are disposed to obey, are called believers,
not properly indeed, but inasmuch as God is pleased in kindness so
highly to honor their pious feeling. But this docility, with a desire
of further progress, is widely different from the gross ignorance in
which those sluggishly indulge who are contented with the implicit
faith of the Papists. If Paul severely condemns those who are "ever
learning, and never able to come to the knowledge of the truth," how
much more sharply ought those to be rebuked who avowedly affect
to know nothing?

6. The true knowledge of Christ consists in receiving him as he is
offered by the Father, namely, as invested with his Gospel. For, as he is
appointed as the end of our faith, so we cannot directly tend towards
him except under the guidance of the Gospel. Therein are certainly
unfolded to us treasures of grace. Did these continue shut, Christ
would profit us little. Hence Paul makes faith the inseparable attendant of doctrine in these words, "Ye have not so learned Christ; if so
be that ye have heard him, and have been taught by him, as the truth
is in Jesus" (Eph. 4:20-21). Still I do not confine faith to the Gospel

in such a sense as not to admit that enough was delivered to Moses and the Prophets to form a foundation of faith; but as the Gospel exhibits a fuller manifestation of Christ, Paul justly terms it the doctrine of faith (1 Tim. 4:6). For which reason, also he elsewhere says, that, by the coming of faith, the Law was abolished (Rom. 10:4), including under the expression a new and unwonted mode of teaching, by which Christ, from the period of his appearance as the great Master, gave a fuller illustration of the Father's mercy, and testified more surely of our salvation. But an easier and more appropriate method will be to descend from the general to the particular. First, we must remember, that there is an inseparable relation between faith and the word, and that these can no more be disconnected from each other than rays of light from the sun. Hence in Isaiah the Lord exclaims, "Hear, and your soul shall live" (Isa. 4:3). And John points to this same fountain of faith in the following words, "These are written that ye might believe" (John 20:31). The Psalmist also exhorting the people to faith says, "To-day, if ye will hear his voice" (Ps. 95:7), "to hear" being uniformly taken for "to believe." In fine, in Isaiah the Lord distinguishes the members of the Church from strangers by this mark, "All thy children shall be taught of the Lord" (Isa. 54:13); for if the benefit was indiscriminate, why should he address his words only to a few? Corresponding with this, the Evangelists uniformly employ the terms "believers" and "disciples" as synonymous. This is done especially by Luke in several passages of the Acts. He even applies the term "disciple" to a woman (Acts 9:36). Wherefore, if faith declines in the least degree from the mark at which it ought to aim, it does not retain its nature, but becomes uncertain credulity and vague wandering of mind. The same word is the basis on which it rests and is sustained. Declining from it, it falls. Take away the word, therefore, and no faith will remain. We are not here discussing, whether, in order to propagate the word of God by which faith is engendered, the ministry of man is necessary (this will be considered elsewhere); but we say that the word itself, whatever be the way in which it is conveyed to us, is a kind of mirror in which faith beholds God. In this, therefore, whether God uses the agency of man, or works immediately by his own power, it is always by his word that he manifests himself to those whom he designs to draw to himself. Hence Paul designates faith as the obedience which is given to the Gospel (Rom. 1:5); and writing to the Philippians, he commends them for the obedience of faith (Phil. 2:17). For faith includes not merely the knowledge that God is, but also, nay chiefly, a perception of his will toward us. It concerns us to know not only what he is in himself, but also in what character he is pleased to manifest himself to us. We now see, therefore, that faith is the knowledge of the divine will in regard to us, as ascertained from his word. And the foundation of it is a previous persuasion of the truth of God. So long as your mind entertains any misgivings as to the certainty of the word, its authority will be weak and dubious, or rather it will have no authority at all. Nor is it sufficient to believe that God is true, and cannot lie or deceive, unless you feel firmly persuaded that every word which him is sacred, inviolable truth.

7. But since the heart of man is not brought to faith by every word of God, we must still consider what it is that faith properly has respect to in the word. The declaration of God to Adam was, "Thou shalt surely die" (Gen. 2:17); and to Cain, "The voice of thy brother's blood crieth unto me from the ground" (Gen. 4:10); but these, so far from being fitted to establish faith, tend only to shake it. At the same time, we deny not that it is the office of faith to assent to the truth of God whenever, whatever, and in whatever way he speaks: we are only inquiring what faith can find in the word of God to lean and rest upon. When conscience sees only wrath and indignation, how can it but tremble and be afraid? and how can it avoid shunning the God whom it thus dreads? But faith ought to seek God, not shun him. It is evident, therefore, that we have not yet obtained a full definition of faith, it being impossible to give the name to every kind of

knowledge of the divine will. Shall we, then, for "will", which is often
the messenger of bad news and the herald of terror, substitute the benevolence or mercy of God? In this way, doubtless, we make a nearer
approach to the nature of faith. For we are allured to seek God when
told that our safety is treasured up in him; and we are confirmed in
this when he declares that he studies and takes an interest in our welfare. Hence there is need of the gracious promise, in which he testifies
that he is a propitious Father; since there is no other way in which
we can approach to him, the promise being the only thing on which
the heart of man can recline. For this reason, the two things, mercy
and truth, are uniformly conjoined in the Psalms as having a mutual
connection with each other. For it were of no avail to us to know that
God is true, did He not in mercy allure us to himself; nor could we
of ourselves embrace his mercy did not He expressly offer it. "I have
declared thy faithfulness and thy salvation: I have not concealed thy
loving-kindness and thy truth. Withhold not thy tender mercies from
me, O Lord: let thy loving-kindness and thy truth continually preserve me" (Ps. 40:10-11). "Thy mercy, O Lord, is in the heavens; and
thy faithfulness reacheth unto the clouds" (Ps. 36:5). "All the paths
of the Lord are mercy and truth unto such as keep his covenant and
his testimonies" (Ps. 25:10). "His merciful kindness is great toward
us: and the truth of the Lord endureth for ever" (Ps. 117:2). "I will
praise thy name for thy loving-kindness and thy truth" (Ps. 138:2). I
need not quote what is said in the Prophets, to the effect that God
is merciful and faithful in his promises. It were presumptuous in us
to hold that God is propitious to us, had we not his own testimony,
and did he not prevent us by his invitation, which leaves no doubt or
uncertainty as to his will. It has already been seen that Christ is the
only pledge of love, for without him all things, both above and below
speak of hatred and wrath. We have also seen, that since the knowledge of the divine goodness cannot be of much importance unless it
leads us to confide in it, we must exclude a knowledge mingled with

doubt—a knowledge which, so far from being firm, is continually wavering. But the human mind, when blinded and darkened, is very far from being able to rise to a proper knowledge of the divine will; nor can the heart, fluctuating with perpetual doubt, rest secure in such knowledge. Hence, in order that the word of God may gain full credit, the mind must be enlightened, and the heart confirmed, from some other quarter. We shall now have a full definition of faith if we say that it is a firm and sure knowledge of the divine favor toward us, founded on the truth of a free promise in Christ, and revealed to our minds, and sealed on our hearts, by the Holy Spirit.

8. But before I proceed farther, it will be necessary to make some preliminary observations for the purpose of removing difficulties which might otherwise obstruct the reader. And first, I must refute the nugatory distinction of the Schoolmen as to formed and un-formed faith. For they imagine that persons who have no fear of God, and no sense of piety, may believe all that is necessary to be known for salvation; as if the Holy Spirit were not the witness of our adop-tion by enlightening our hearts unto faith. Still, however, though the whole Scripture is against them, they dogmatically give the name of faith to a persuasion devoid of the fear of God. It is unnecessary to go farther in refuting their definition, than simply to state the nature of faith as declared in the word of God. From this it will clearly appear how unskillfully and absurdly they babble, rather than discourse, on this subject. I have already done this in part, and will afterwards add the remainder in its proper place. At present, I say that nothing can be imagined more absurd than their fiction. They insist that faith is an assent with which any despiser of God may receive what is delivered by Scripture. But we must first see whether any one can by his own strength acquire faith, or whether the Holy Spirit, by means of it, becomes the witness of adoption. Hence it is childish trifling in them to inquire whether the faith formed by the supervening quality of love be the same, or a different and new faith. By talking in this style,

they show plainly that they have never thought of the special gift of the Spirit; since one of the first elements of faith is reconciliation implied in man's drawing near to God. Did they duly ponder the saying of Paul, "With the heart man believeth unto righteousness" (Rom. 10:10), they would cease to dream of that frigid quality. There is one consideration which ought at once to put an end to the debate—viz. that assent itself (as I have already observed, and will afterwards more fully illustrate) is more a matter of the heart than the head, of the affection than the intellect. For this reason, it is termed "the obedience of faith" (Rom. 1:5), which the Lord prefers to all other service, and justly, since nothing is more precious to him than his truth, which, as John Baptist declares, is in a manner signed and sealed by believers (John 3:33). As there can be no doubt on the matter, we in one word conclude, that they talk absurdly when they maintain that faith is formed by the addition of pious affection as an accessory to assent, since assent itself, such at least as the Scriptures describe, consists in pious affection. But we are furnished with a still clearer argument. Since faith embraces Christ as he is offered by the Father, and he is offered not only for justification, for forgiveness of sins and peace, but also for sanctification, as the fountain of living waters, it is certain that no man will ever know him aright without at the same time receiving the sanctification of the Spirit; or, to express the matter more plainly, faith consists in the knowledge of Christ; Christ cannot be known without the sanctification of his Spirit: therefore faith cannot possibly be disjoined from pious affection.

9. In their attempt to mar faith by divesting it of love, they are wont to insist on the words of Paul, "Though I have all faith, so that I could remove mountains, and have not charity, I am nothing" (1 Cor. 13:2). But they do not consider what the faith is of which the Apostle there speaks. Having, in the previous chapter, discoursed of the various gifts of the Spirit (1 Cor. 12:10), including diversity of tongues, miracles, and prophecy, and exhorted the Corinthians to follow the

better gifts, in other words, those from which the whole body of the Church would derive greater benefit, he adds, "Yet show I unto you a more excellent way" (1 Cor. 12:30). All other gifts, how excellent soever they may be in themselves, are of no value unless they are subservient to charity. They were given for the edification of the Church, and fail of their purpose if not so applied. To prove this he adopts a division, repeating the same gifts which he had mentioned before, but under different names. Miracles and faith are used to denote the same thing—viz. the power of working miracles. Seeing, then, that this miraculous power or faith is the particular gift of God, which a wicked man may possess and abuse, as the gift of tongues, prophecy, or other gifts, it is not strange that he separates it from charity. Their whole error lies in this, that while the term faith has a variety of meanings, overlooking this variety, they argue as if its meaning were invariably one and the same. The passage of James, by which they endeavor to defend their error, will be elsewhere discussed (infra, chap. 17, sec. 11). Although, in discoursing of faith, we admit that it has a variety of forms; yet, when our object is to show what knowledge of God the wicked possess, we hold and maintain, in accordance with Scripture, that the pious only have faith. Multitudes undoubtedly believe that God is, and admit the truth of the Gospel History, and the other parts of Scripture, in the same way in which they believe the records of past events, or events which they have actually witnessed. There are some who go even farther: they regard the Word of God as an infallible oracle; they do not altogether disregard its precepts, but are moved to some degree by its threatening and promises. To such the testimony of faith is attributed, but by catachresis; because they do not with open impiety impugn, reject, or condemn, the Word of God, but rather exhibit some semblance of obedience.

10. But as this shadow or image of faith is of no moment, so it is unworthy of the name. How far it differs from true faith will shortly be explained at length. Here, however, we may just indicate it in

passing. Simon Magus is said to have believed, though he soon after gave proof of his unbelief (Acts 8:13-18). In regard to the faith
attributed to him, we do not understand with some, that he merely pretended a belief which had no existence in his heart: we rather
think that, overcome by the majesty of the Gospel, he yielded some
kind of assent, and so far acknowledged Christ to be the author of
life and salvation, as willingly to assume his name. In like manner, in
the Gospel of Luke, those in whom the seed of the word is choked
before it brings forth fruit, or in whom, from having no depth of
earth, it soon withers away, are said to believe for a time. Such, we
doubt not, eagerly receive the word with a kind of relish, and have
some feeling of its divine power, so as not only to impose upon men
by a false semblance of faith, but even to impose upon themselves.
They imagine that the reverence which they give to the word is genuine piety, because they have no idea of any impiety but that which
consists in open and avowed contempt. But whatever that assent may
be, it by no means penetrates to the heart, so as to have a fixed seat
there. Although it sometimes seems to have planted its roots, these
have no life in them. The human heart has so many recesses for vanity, so many lurking places for falsehood, is so shrouded by fraud and
hypocrisy, that it often deceives itself. Let those who glory in such
semblances of faith know that, in this respect, they are not a whit
superior to devils. The one class, indeed, is inferior to them, inasmuch
as they are able without emotion to hear and understand things, the
knowledge of which makes devils tremble (James 2:19). The other
class equals them in this, that whatever be the impression made upon
them, its only result is terror and consternation.

11. I am aware it seems unaccountable to some how faith is attributed to the reprobate, seeing that it is declared by Paul to be one
of the fruits of election; and yet the difficulty is easily solved: for
though none are enlightened into faith, and truly feel the efficacy
of the Gospel, with the exception of those who are foreordained to

salvation, yet experience shows that the reprobate are sometimes affected in a way so similar to the elect, that even in their own judgment
there is no difference between them. Hence it is not strange, that by
the Apostle a taste of heavenly gifts, and by Christ himself a temporary faith, is ascribed to them. Not that they truly perceive the power
of spiritual grace and the sure light of faith; but the Lord, the better
to convict them, and leave them without excuse, instills into their
minds such a sense of his goodness as can be felt without the Spirit of
adoption. Should it be objected, that believers have no stronger testimony to assure them of their adoption, I answer, that though there is
a great resemblance and affinity between the elect of God and those
who are impressed for a time with a fading faith, yet the elect alone
have that full assurance which is extolled by Paul, and by which they
are enabled to cry, Abba, Father. Therefore, as God regenerates the
elect only forever by incorruptible seed, as the seed of life once sown
in their hearts never perishes, so he effectually seals in them the grace
of his adoption, that it may be sure and steadfast. But in this there is
nothing to prevent an inferior operation of the Spirit from taking its
course in the reprobate. Meanwhile, believers are taught to examine
themselves carefully and humbly, lest carnal security creep in and take
the place of assurance of faith. We may add, that the reprobate never
have any other than a confused sense of grace, laying hold of the
shadow rather than the substance, because the Spirit properly seals
the forgiveness of sins in the elect only, applying it by special faith to
their use. Still it is correctly said, that the reprobate believe God to be
propitious to them, inasmuch as they accept the gift of reconciliation,
though confusedly and without due discernment; not that they are
partakers of the same faith or regeneration with the children of God;
but because, under a covering of hypocrisy, they seem to have a principle of faith in common with them. Nor do I even deny that God
illumines their minds to this extent, that they recognize his grace; but
that conviction he distinguishes from the peculiar testimony which

he gives to his elect in this respect, that the reprobate never attain to
the full result or to fruition. When he shows himself propitious to
them, it is not as if he had truly rescued them from death, and taken
them under his protection. He only gives them a manifestation of his
present mercy. In the elect alone he implants the living root of faith,
so that they persevere even to the end. Thus we dispose of the objection, that if God truly displays his grace, it must endure forever. There
is nothing inconsistent in this with the fact of his enlightening some
with a present sense of grace, which afterwards proves evanescent.

12. Although faith is a knowledge of the divine favor towards us,
and a full persuasion of its truth, it is not strange that the sense of the
divine love, which though akin to faith differs much from it, vanishes
in those who are temporarily impressed. The will of God is, I confess,
immutable, and his truth is always consistent with itself; but I deny that
the reprobate ever advance so far as to penetrate to that secret revelation
which Scripture reserves for the elect only. I therefore deny that they
either understand his will considered as immutable, or steadily embrace
his truth, inasmuch as they rest satisfied with an evanescent impression;
just as a tree not planted deep enough may take root, but will in process
of time wither away, though it may for several years not only put forth
leaves and flowers, but produce fruit. In short, as by the revolt of the
first man, the image of God could be effaced from his mind and soul, so
there is nothing strange in His shedding some rays of grace on the reprobate, and afterwards allowing these to be extinguished. There is nothing to prevent His giving some a slight knowledge of his Gospel, and
imbuing others thoroughly. Meanwhile, we must remember that however feeble and slender the faith of the elect may be, yet as the Spirit of
God is to them a sure earnest and seal of their adoption, the impression
once engraven can never be effaced from their hearts, whereas the light
which glimmers in the reprobate is afterwards quenched. Nor can it be
said that the Spirit therefore deceives, because he does not quicken the
seed which lies in their hearts so as to make it ever remain incorruptible

as in the elect. I go farther: seeing it is evident, from the doctrine of Scripture and from daily experience, that the reprobate are occasionally impressed with a sense of divine grace, some desire of mutual love must necessarily be excited in their hearts. Thus for a time a pious affection prevailed in Saul, disposing him to love God. Knowing that he was treated with paternal kindness, he was in some degree attracted by it. But as the reprobate have no rooted conviction of the paternal love of God, so they do not in return yield the love of sons, but are led by a kind of mercenary affection. The Spirit of love was given to Christ alone, for the express purpose of conferring this Spirit upon his members; and there can be no doubt that the following words of Paul apply to the elect only: "The love of God is shed abroad in our hearts, by the Holy Ghost which is given unto us" (Rom. 5:5); namely, the love which begets that confidence in prayer to which I have above adverted. On the other hand, we see that God is mysteriously offended with his children, though he ceases not to love them. He certainly hates them not, but he alarms them with a sense of his anger, that he may humble the pride of the flesh, arouse them from lethargy, and urge them to repentance. Hence they, at the same instant, feel that he is angry with them or their sins, and also propitious to their persons. It is not from fictitious dread that they deprecate his anger, and yet they retake themselves to him with tranquil confidence. It hence appears that the faith of some, though not true faith, is not mere pretense. They are borne along by some sudden impulse of zeal, and erroneously impose upon themselves, sloth undoubtedly preventing them from examining their hearts with due care. Such probably was the case of those whom John describes as believing on Christ; but of whom he says, "Jesus did not commit himself unto them, because he knew all men, and needed not that any should testify of man: for he knew what was in man" (John 2:24-25). Were it not true that many fall away from the common faith (I call it common, because there is a great resemblance between temporary and living, everduring faith), Christ would not have said to his disciples, "If ye continue in my word, then are ye my disciples indeed; and ye shall know the truth, and the truth shall make you free" (John 8:31-32). He is addressing those who had embraced his doctrine, and urging them to progress in the faith, lest by their sluggishness they extinguish the light which they have received. Accordingly, Paul claims faith as the peculiar privilege of the elect, intimating that many, from not being properly rooted, fall away (Tit. 1:1). In the same way, in Matthew, our Savior says, "Every plant which my heavenly Father has not planted shall be rooted up" (Matt. 16:13). Some who are not ashamed to insult God and man are more grossly false. Against this class of men, who profane the faith by impious and lying pretense, James inveighs (James 2:14). Nor would Paul require the faith of believers to be unfeigned (1 Tim. 1:5), were there not many who presumptuously arrogate to themselves what they have not, deceiving others, and sometimes even themselves, with empty show. Hence he compares a good conscience to the ark in which faith is preserved, because many, by falling away, have in regard to it made shipwreck.

13. It is necessary to attend to the ambiguous meaning of the term: for faith is often equivalent in meaning to sound doctrine, as in the passage which we lately quoted, and in the same epistle where Paul enjoins the deacons to hold "the mystery of the faith in a pure conscience;" in like manner, when he denounces the defection of certain ones from the faith. The meaning again is the same, when he says that Timothy had been brought up in the faith; and in like manner, when he says that profane babblings and oppositions of science, falsely so called, lead many away from the faith. Such persons he elsewhere calls reprobate as to the faith. On the other hand, when he enjoins Titus, "Rebuke them sharply, that they may be sound in the faith;" by soundness he means purity of doctrine, which is easily corrupted, and degenerates through the fickleness of men. And indeed, since in Christ, as possessed by faith, are "hid all the treasures of wisdom and knowledge" (Col. 1:2-3), the term "faith" is justly extended to the

whole sum of heavenly doctrine, from which it cannot be separated. On the other hand, it is sometimes confined to a particular object, as when Matthew says of those who let down the paralytic through the roof, that Jesus saw their faith (Matt. 9:2); and Jesus himself exclaims in regard to the centurion, "I have not found so great faith, no, not in Israel" (Matt. 8:10). Now, it is probable that the centurion was thinking only of the cure of his son, by whom his whole soul was engrossed; but because he is satisfied with the simple answer and assurance of Christ, and does not request his bodily presence, this circumstance calls forth the eulogium on his faith. And we have lately shown how Paul uses the term faith for the gift of miracles—a gift possessed by persons who were neither regenerated by the Spirit of God, nor sincerely reverenced him. In another passage, he uses faith for the doctrine by which we are instructed in the "faith." For when he says, that "that which is in part shall be done away" (1 Cor. 13:10), there can be no doubt that reference is made to the ministry of the Church, which is necessary in our present imperfect state; in these forms of expression the analogy is obvious. But when the name of faith is improperly transferred to a false profession or lying assumption, the catachresis ought not to seem harsher than when the fear of God is used for vicious and perverse worship; as when it is repeatedly said in sacred history, that the foreign nations which had been transported to Samaria and the neighboring districts, feared false gods and the God of Israel: in other words, confounded heaven with earth. But we have now been inquiring what the faith is, which distinguishes the children of God from unbelievers, the faith by which we invoke God the Father, by which we pass from death unto life, and by which Christ our eternal salvation and life dwells in us. Its power and nature have, I trust, been briefly and clearly explained.

14. Let us now again go over the parts of the definition separately: I should think that, after a careful examination of them, no doubt will remain. By knowledge we do not mean comprehension, such as that

which we have of things falling under human sense. For that knowledge is so much superior, that the human mind must far surpass and go beyond itself in order to reach it. Nor even when it has reached it does it comprehend what it feels, but persuaded of what it comprehends not, it understands more from mere certainty of persuasion than it could discern of any human matter by its own capacity. Hence it is elegantly described by Paul as ability "to comprehend with all saints what is the breadth, and length, and depth, and height; and to know the love of Christ, which passeth knowledge" (Eph. 3:18-19). His object was to intimate, that what our mind embraces by faith is every way infinite, that this kind of knowledge far surpasses all understanding. But because the "mystery which has been hid from ages and from generations" is now "made manifest to the saints" (Col. 1:26), faith is, for good reason, occasionally termed in Scripture understanding (Col. 2:2); and knowledge, as by John (1 John 3:2), when he declares that believers know themselves to be the sons of God. And certainly they do know, but rather as confirmed by a belief of the divine veracity than taught by any demonstration of reason. This is also indicated by Paul when he says, that "whilst we are at home in the body, we are absent from the Lord: (For we walk by faith, not by sight)" (2 Cor. 5:6-7) thus showing, that what we understand by faith is yet distant from us and escapes our view. Hence we conclude that the knowledge of faith consists more of certainty than discernment.

15. We add, that it is sure and firm, the better to express strength and constancy of persuasion. For as faith is not contented with a dubious and fickle opinion, so neither is it contented with an obscure and ill-defined conception. The certainty which it requires must be full and decisive, as is usual in regard to matters ascertained and proved. So deeply rooted in our hearts is unbelief, so prone are we to it, that while all confess with the lips that God is faithful, no man ever believes it without an arduous struggle. Especially when brought to the test, we by our wavering betray the vice which lurked within.

Nor is it without cause that the Holy Spirit bears such distinguished testimony to the authority of God, in order that it may cure the disease of which I have spoken, and induce us to give full credit to the divine promises: "The words of the Lord" (says David, Ps. 12:6) "are pure words, as silver tried in a furnace of earth purified seven times:" "The word of the Lord is tried: he is a buckler to all those that trust in him" (Ps. 18:30). And Solomon declares the same thing almost in the same words, "Every word of God is pure" (Prov. 30:5). But further quotation is superfluous, as the 119th Psalm is almost wholly occupied with this subject. Certainly, whenever God thus recommends his word, he indirectly rebukes our unbelief, the purport of all that is said being to eradicate perverse doubt from our hearts. There are very many also who form such an idea of the divine mercy as yields them very little comfort. For they are harassed by miserable anxiety while they doubt whether God will be merciful to them. They think, indeed, that they are most fully persuaded of the divine mercy, but they confine it within too narrow limits. The idea they entertain is, that this mercy is great and abundant, is shed upon many, is offered and ready to be bestowed upon all; but that it is uncertain whether it will reach to them individually, or rather whether they can reach to it. Thus their knowledge stopping short leaves them only mid-way; not so much confirming and tranquilizing the mind as harassing it with doubt and disquietude. Very different is that feeling of full assurance (πληροφορια) which the Scriptures uniformly attribute to faith—an assurance which leaves no doubt that the goodness of God is clearly offered to us. This assurance we cannot have without truly perceiving its sweetness, and experiencing it in ourselves. Hence from faith the Apostle deduces confidence, and from confidence boldness. His words are, "In whom (Christ) we have boldness and access with confidence by the faith of him" (Eph. 3:12) thus undoubtedly showing that our faith is not true unless it enables us to appear calmly in the presence of God. Such boldness springs only from confidence in the divine favor and salvation. So true is this, that the term "faith" is often used as equivalent to "confidence."

16. The principal hinge on which faith turns is this: We must not suppose that any promises of mercy which the Lord offers are only true out of us, and not at all in us: we should rather make them ours by inwardly embracing them. In this way only is engendered that confidence which he elsewhere terms "peace" (Rom. 5:1); though perhaps he rather means to make peace follow from it. This is the security which quiets and calms the conscience in the view of the judgment of God, and without which it is necessarily vexed and almost torn with tumultuous dread, unless when it happens to slumber for a moment, forgetful both of God and of itself. And verily it is but for a moment. It never long enjoys that miserable obliviousness, for the memory of the divine judgment, ever and anon recurring, stings it to the quick. In one word, he only is a true believer who, firmly persuaded that God is reconciled, and is a kind Father to him, hopes everything from his kindness, who, trusting to the promises of the divine favor, with undoubting confidence anticipates salvation; as the Apostle shows in these words, "We are made partakers of Christ, if we hold the beginning of our confidence steadfast unto the end" (Heb. 3:14). He thus holds, that none hope well in the Lord save those who confidently glory in being the heirs of the heavenly kingdom. No man, I say, is a believer but he who, trusting to the security of his salvation, confidently triumphs over the devil and death, as we are taught by the noble exclamation of Paul, "I am persuaded, that neither death, nor life, nor angels, nor principalities, nor powers, nor things present, nor things to come, nor height, nor depth, nor any other creature, shall be able to separate us from the love of God, which is in Christ Jesus our Lord" (Rom. 8:38). In like manner, the same Apostle does not consider that the eyes of our understanding are enlightened unless we know what is the hope of the eternal inheritance to which we are called (Eph. 1:18). Thus he uniformly intimates throughout his

writings, that the goodness of God is not properly comprehended when security does not follow as its fruit.

17. But it will be said that this differs widely from the experience of believers, who, in recognizing the grace of God toward them, not only feel disquietude (this often happens), but sometimes tremble, overcome with terror, so violent are the temptations which assail their minds. This scarcely seems consistent with certainty of faith. It is necessary to solve this difficulty, in order to maintain the doctrine above laid down. When we say that faith must be certain and secure, we certainly speak not of an assurance which is never affected by doubt, nor a security which anxiety never assails; we rather maintain that believers have a perpetual struggle with their own distrust, and are thus far from thinking that their consciences possess a placid quiet, uninterrupted by perturbation. On the other hand, whatever be the mode in which they are assailed, we deny that they fall off and abandon that sure confidence which they have formed in the mercy of God. Scripture does not set before us a brighter or more memorable example of faith than in David, especially if regard be had to the constant tenor of his life. And yet how far his mind was from being always at peace is declared by innumerable complaints, of which it will be sufficient to select a few. When he rebukes the turbulent movements of his soul, what else is it but a censure of his unbelief? "Why art thou cast down, my soul? and why art thou disquieted in me? hope thou in God" (Ps. 42:6). His alarm was undoubtedly a manifest sign of distrust, as if he thought that the Lord had forsaken him. In another passage we have a fuller confession: "I said in my haste, I am cut off from before thine eyes" (Ps. 31:22). In another passage, in anxious and wretched perplexity, he debates with himself, nay, raises a question as to the nature of God: "Has God forgotten to be gracious? has he in anger shut up his tender mercies?" (Psalm 77:9). What follows is still harsher: "I said this is my infirmity; but I will remember the years of the right hand of the Most High." As if desperate, he adjudges himself to destruction.

He not only confesses that he is agitated by doubt, but as if he had
fallen in the contest, leaves himself nothing in reserve—God having
deserted him, and made the hand which was wont to help him the
instrument of his destruction. Wherefore, after having been tossed
among tumultuous waves, it is not without reason he exhorts his soul
to return to her quiet rest (Ps. 116:7). And yet (what is strange) amid
those commotions, faith sustains the believer's heart, and truly acts
the part of the palm tree, which supports any weights laid upon it, and
rises above them; thus David, when he seemed to be overwhelmed,
ceased not by urging himself forward to ascend to God. But he who
anxiously contending with his own infirmity has recourse to faith,
is already in a great measure victorious. This we may infer from the
following passage, and others similar to it: "Wait on the Lord: be of
good courage, and he shall strengthen thine heart: wait, I say, on the
Lord" (Ps. 27:14). He accuses himself of timidity, and repeating the
same thing twice, confesses that he is ever and anon exposed to agi-
tation. Still he is not only dissatisfied with himself for so feeling, but
earnestly labors to correct it. Were we to take a nearer view of his case,
and compare it with that of Ahaz, we should find a great difference
between them. Isaiah is sent to relieve the anxiety of an impious and
hypocritical king, and addresses him in these terms: "Take heed, and
be quiet; fear not," &c. (Isa. 7:4). How did Ahab act? As has already
been said, his heart was shaken as a tree is shaken by the wind: though
he heard the promise, he ceased not to tremble. This, therefore, is the
proper hire and punishment of unbelief, so to tremble as in the day of
trial to turn away from God, who gives access to himself only by faith.
On the other hand, believers, though weighed down and almost overwhelmed with the burden of temptation, constantly rise up, though
not without toil and difficulty; hence, feeling conscious of their own
weakness, they pray with the Prophet, "Take not the word of truth
utterly out of my mouths" (Ps. 119:43). By these words, we are taught
that they at times become dumb, as if their faith were overthrown,

and yet that they do not withdraw or turn their backs, but persevere in the contest, and by prayer stimulate their sluggishness, so as not to fall into stupor by giving way to it (See *Calv. in Psalm 88:16*).

18. To make this intelligible, we must return to the distinction between flesh and spirit, to which we have already adverted, and which here becomes most apparent. The believer finds within himself two principles: the one filling him with delight in recognizing the divine goodness, the other filling him with bitterness under a sense of his fallen state; the one leading him to recline on the promise of the Gospel, the other alarming him by the conviction of his iniquity; the one making him exult with the anticipation of life, the other making him tremble with the fear of death. This diversity is owing to imperfection of faith, since we are never so well in the course of the present life as to be entirely cured of the disease of distrust, and completely replenished and engrossed by faith. Hence those conflicts: the distrust cleaving to the remains of the flesh rising up to assail the faith enlisting in our hearts. But if in the believer's mind certainty is mingled with doubt, must we not always be carried back to the conclusion, that faith consists not of a sure and clear, but only of an obscure and confused, understanding of the divine will in regard to us? By no means. Though we are distracted by various thoughts, it does not follow that we are immediately divested of faith. Though we are agitated and carried to and fro by distrust, we are not immediately plunged into the abyss; though we are shaken, we are not therefore driven from our place. The invariable issue of the contest is, that faith in the long run surmounts the difficulties by which it was beset and seemed to be endangered.

19. The whole, then, comes to this: As soon as the minutest particle of faith is instilled into our minds, we begin to behold the face of God placid, serene, and propitious; far off, indeed, but still so distinctly as to assure us that there is no delusion in it. In proportion to the progress we afterwards make (and the progress ought to be uninterrupted), we

obtain a nearer and surer view, the very continuance making it more familiar to us. Thus we see that a mind illumined with the knowledge of God is at first involved in much ignorance—ignorance, however, which is gradually removed. Still this partial ignorance or obscure discernment does not prevent that clear knowledge of the divine favor which holds the first and principal part in faith. For as one shut up in a prison, where from a narrow opening he receives the rays of the sun indirectly and in a manner divided, though deprived of a full view of the sun, has no doubt of the source from which the light comes, and is benefited by it; so believers, while bound with the fetters of an earthly body, though surrounded on all sides with much obscurity, are so far illumined by any slender light which beams upon them and displays the divine mercy as to feel secure.

20. The Apostle elegantly adverts to both in different passages. When he says, "We know in part, and we prophesy in part;" and "Now we see through a glass darkly" (1 Cor. 13:9, 12), he intimates how very minute a portion of divine wisdom is given to us in the present life. For although those expressions do not simply indicate that faith is imperfect so long as we groan under a height of flesh, but that the necessity of being constantly engaged in learning is owing to our imperfection, he at the same time reminds us, that a subject which is of boundless extent cannot be comprehended by our feeble and narrow capacities. This Paul affirms of the whole Church, each individual being retarded and impeded by his own ignorance from making so near an approach as were to be wished. But that the foretaste which we obtain from any minute portion of faith is certain, and by no means fallacious, he elsewhere shows, when he affirms that "We all, with open face beholding as in a glass the glory of the Lord, are changed into the same image, from glory to glory, even as by the Spirit of the Lord" (2 Cor. 3:18). In such degrees of ignorance much doubt and trembling is necessarily implied, especially seeing that our heart is by its own natural bias prone to unbelief. To this we must

add the temptations which, various in kind and infinite in number, are ever and anon violently assailing us. In particular, conscience itself, burdened with an incumbent load of sins, at one time complains and groans, at another accuses itself; at one time murmurs in secret, at another openly rebels. Therefore, whether adverse circumstances betoken the wrath of God, or conscience finds the subject and matter within itself, unbelief thence draws weapons and engines to put faith to flight, the aim of all its efforts being to make us think that God is adverse and hostile to us, and thus, instead of hoping for any assistance from him, to make us dread him as a deadly foe.

21. To withstand these assaults, faith arms and fortifies itself with the word of God. When the temptation suggested is, that God is an enemy because he afflicts, faith replies, that while he afflicts he is merciful, his chastening proceeding more from love than anger. To the thought that God is the avenger of wickedness, it opposes the pardon ready to be bestowed on all offenses whenever the sinner retakes himself to the divine mercy. Thus the pious mind, how much soever it may be agitated and torn, at length rises superior to all difficulties, and allows not its confidence in the divine mercy to be destroyed. Nay, rather, the disputes which exercise and disturb it tend to establish this confidence. A proof of this is, that the saints, when the hand of God lies heaviest upon them, still lodge their complaints with him, and continue to invoke him, when to all appearance he is least disposed to hear. But of what use were it to lament before him if they had no hope of solace? They never would invoke him did they not believe that he is ready to assist them. Thus the disciples, while reprimanded by their Master for the weakness of their faith in crying out that they were perishing, still implored his aid (Matt. 8:25). And he, in rebuking them for their want of faith, does not disown them or class them with unbelievers, but urges them to shake off the vice. Therefore, as we have already said, we again maintain, that faith remaining fixed in the believer's breast never can be eradicated from it.

However it may seem shaken and bent in this direction or in that, its flame is never so completely quenched as not at least to lurk under the embers. In this way, it appears that the word, which is an incorruptible seed, produces fruit similar to itself. Its germ never withers away utterly and perishes. The saints cannot have a stronger ground for despair than to feel, that, according to present appearances, the hand of God is armed for their destruction; and yet Job thus declares the strength of his confidence: "Though he slay me, yet will I trust in him." The truth is, that unbelief reigns not in the hearts of believers, but only assails them from without; does not wound them mortally with its darts, but annoys them, or, at the utmost, gives them a wound which can be healed. Faith, as Paul declares (Eph. 6:16), is our shield, which receiving these darts, either wards them off entirely, or at least breaks their force, and prevents them from reaching the vitals. Hence when faith is shaken, it is just as when, by the violent blow of a javelin, a soldier standing firm is forced to step back and yield a little; and again when faith is wounded, it is as if the shield were pierced, but not perforated by the blow. The pious mind will always rise, and be able to say with David, "Yea, though I walk through the valley of the shadow of death, I will fear no evil: for thou art with me" (Ps. 23:4). Doubtless it is a terrific thing to walk in the darkness of death, and it is impossible for believers, however great their strength may be, not to shudder at it; but since the prevailing thought is that God is present and providing for their safety, the feeling of security overcomes that of fear. As Augustine says, whatever be the engines which the devil erects against us, as he cannot gain the heart where faith dwells, he is cast out. Thus, if we may judge by the event, not only do believers come off safe from every contest so as to be ready, after a short repose, to descend again into the arena, but the saying of John, in his Epistle, is fulfilled, "This is the victory that overcometh the world, even our faith" (1 John 5:4). It is not said that it will be victorious in a single fight, or a few, or some one assault, but that it will be victorious over the whole world, though it should be a thousand times assailed.

22. There is another species of fear and trembling, which, so far from impairing the security of faith, tends rather to establish it; namely, when believers, reflecting that the examples of the divine vengeance on the ungodly are a kind of beacons warning them not to provoke the wrath of God by similar wickedness keep anxious watch, or, taking a view of their own inherent wretchedness, learn their entire dependence on God, without whom they feel themselves to be fleeting and evanescent as the wind. For when the Apostle sets before the Corinthians the scourges which the Lord in ancient times inflicted on the people of Israel, that they might be afraid of subjecting themselves to similar calamities, he does not in any degree destroy the ground of their confidence; he only shakes off their carnal torpor which suppresses faith, but does not strengthen it. Nor when he takes occasion from the case of the Israelites to exhort, "Let him that thinketh he standeth take heed lest he fall" (1 Cor. 10:12), he does not bid us waver, as if we had no security for our steadfastness: he only removes arrogance and rash confidence in our strength, telling the Gentiles not to presume because the Jews had been cast off, and they had been admitted to their place (Rom. 11:20). In that passage, indeed, he is not addressing believers only, but also comprehends hypocrites, who gloried merely in external appearance; nor is he addressing individuals, but contrasting the Jews and Gentiles, he first shows that the rejection of the former was a just punishment of their ingratitude and unbelief, and then exhorts the latter to beware lest pride and presumption deprive them of the grace of adoption which had lately been transferred to them. For as in that rejection of the Jews there still remained some who were not excluded from the covenant of adoptions, so there might be some among the Gentiles who, possessing no true faith, were only puffed up with vain carnal confidence, and so abused the goodness of God to their own destruction. But though

you should hold that the words were addressed to elect believers, no inconsistency will follow. It is one thing, in order to prevent believers from indulging vain confidence, to repress the temerity which, from the remains of the flesh, sometimes gains upon them, and it is another thing to strike terror into their consciences, and prevent them from feeling secure in the mercy of God.

23. Then, when he bids us work out our salvation with fear and trembling, all he requires is, that we accustom ourselves to think very meanly of our own strength, and confide in the strength of the Lord. For nothing stimulates us so strongly to place all our confidence and assurance on the Lord as self-diffidence, and the anxiety produced by a consciousness of our calamitous condition. In this sense are we to understand the words of the Psalmist: "I will come into thy house in the multitude of thy mercy: and in thy fear will I worship toward thy holy temple," (Ps. 5:7). Here he appropriately unites confident faith leaning on the divine mercy with religious fear, which of necessity we must feel whenever coming into the presence of the divine majesty, we are made aware by its splendor of the extent of our own impurity. Truly also does Solomon declare: "Happy is the man that feareth alway; but he that hardeneth his heart falleth into mischief" (Prov. 28:14). The fear he speaks of is that which renders us more cautious, not that which produces despondency, the fear which is felt when the mind confounded in itself resumes its equanimity in God, downcast in itself, takes courage in God, distrusting itself, breathes confidence in God. Hence there is nothing inconsistent in believers being afraid, and at the same time possessing secure consolation as they alternately behold their own vanity, and direct their thoughts to the truth of God. How, it will be asked, can fear and faith dwell in the same mind? Just in the same way as sluggishness and anxiety can so dwell. The ungodly court a state of lethargy that the fear of God may not annoy them; and yet the judgment of God so urges that they cannot gain their desire. In the same way God can train his people to humility,

and curb them by the bridle of modesty, while yet fighting bravely. And it is plain, from the context, that this was the Apostle's meaning, since he states, as the ground of fear and trembling, that it is God who worketh in us to will and to do of his good pleasure. In the same sense must we understand the words of the Prophet, "The children of Israel" "shall fear the Lord and his goodness in the latter days" (Hos. 3:5). For not only does piety beget reverence to God, but the sweet attractiveness of grace inspires a man, though desponding of himself, at once with fear and admiration, making him feel his dependence on God, and submit humbly to his power.

24. Here, however, we give no countenance to that most pestilential philosophy which some semi-papists are at present beginning to broach in corners. Unable to defend the gross doubt inculcated by the Schoolmen, they have recourse to another fiction, that they may compound a mixture of faith and unbelief. They admit, that whenever we look to Christ we are furnished with full ground for hope; but as we are ever unworthy of all the blessings which are offered us in Christ, they will have us to fluctuate and hesitate in the view of our unworthiness. In short, they give conscience a position between hope and fear, making it alternate, by successive turns, to the one and the other. Hope and fear, again, they place in complete contrast—the one falling as the other rises, and rising as the other falls. Thus Satan, finding the devices by which he was wont to destroy the certainty of faith too manifest to be now of any avail, is endeavoring, by indirect methods, to undermine it. But what kind of confidence is that which is ever and anon supplanted by despair? They tell you, if you look to Christ salvation is certain; if you return to yourself damnation is certain. Therefore, your mind must be alternately ruled by diffidence and hope; as if we were to imagine Christ standing at a distance, and not rather dwelling in us. We expect salvation from him—not because he stands aloof from us, but because ingrafting us into his body he not only makes us partakers of all his benefits, but also of

himself. Therefore, I thus retort the argument, If you look to yourself damnation is certain: but since Christ has been communicated to you with all his benefits, so that all which is his is made yours, you become a member of him, and hence one with him. His righteousness covers your sins—his salvation extinguishes your condemnation; he interposes with his worthiness, and so prevents your unworthiness from coming into the view of God. Thus it truly is. It will never do to separate Christ from us, nor us from him; but we must, with both hands, keep firm hold of that alliance by which he has riveted us to himself. This the Apostle teaches us: "The body is dead because of sin; but the spirit is life because of righteousness" (Rom. 8:10). According to the frivolous trifling of these objectors, he ought to have said, Christ indeed has life in himself, but you, as you are sinners, remain liable to death and condemnation. Very different is his language. He tells us that the condemnation which we of ourselves deserve is annihilated by the salvation of Christ; and to confirm this he employs the argument to which I have referred—viz. that Christ is not external to us, but dwells in us; and not only unites us to himself by an undivided bond of fellowship, but by a wondrous communion brings us daily into closer connection, until he becomes altogether one with us. And yet I deny not, as I lately said, that faith occasionally suffers certain interruptions when, by violent assault, its weakness is made to bend in this direction or in that; and its light is buried in the thick darkness of temptation. Still happen what may, faith ceases not to long after God.

25. The same doctrine is taught by Bernard when he treats professedly on this subject in his Fifth Homily on the Dedication of the Temple:

> By the blessing of God, sometimes meditating on the soul, methinks, I find in it as it were two contraries. When I look at it as it is in itself and of itself, the truest thing I can say of it is, that it has been reduced to nothing. What need is there to enu-

merate each of its miseries? how burdened with sin, obscured with darkness, ensnared by allurements, teeming with lusts, ruled by passion, filled with delusions, ever prone to evil, inclined to every vice; lastly, full of ignominy and confusion. If all its righteousnesses, when examined by the light of truth, are but as filthy rags (Isa. 64:6), what must we suppose its unrighteousness to be? If, therefore, the light that is in thee be darkness, how great is that darkness?' (Matt. 6:23). What then? Man doubtless has been made subject to vanity—man has been reduced to nothing—man is nothing. And yet how is he whom God exalts utterly nothing? How is he nothing to whom a divine heart has been given? Let us breathe again, brethren. Although we are nothing in our hearts, perhaps something of us may lurk in the heart of God. O Father of mercies! O Father of the miserable! how plantest thou thy heart in us? Where thy heart is, there is thy treasure also. But how are we thy treasure if we are nothing? All nations before thee are as nothing. Observe, before thee; not within thee. Such are they in the judgment of thy truth, but not such in regard to thy affection. Thou callest the things which be not as though they were; and they are not, because thou callest them things that be not; and yet they are because thou callest them. For though they are not as to themselves, yet they are with thee according to the declaration of Paul: 'Not of works, but of him that calleth,' (Rom. 9:11).

He then goes on to say that the connection is wonderful in both points of view. Certainly things which are connected together do not mutually destroy each other. This he explains more clearly in his conclusion in the following terms: "If, in both views, we diligently consider what we are—in the one view our nothingness, in the other our greatness—I presume our glorying will seem restrained; but perhaps it is rather increased and confirmed, because we glory not in ourselves, but in the Lord. Our thought is, if he determined to save us we shall be delivered; and here we begin again to breathe. But, ascending to a loftier height, let us seek the city of God, let us seek the temple, let us seek our home, let us seek our spouse. I have not forgotten myself when, with fear and reverence, I say, We are—are in the heart of God. We are, by his dignifying, not by our own dignity."

26. Moreover, the fear of the Lord, which is uniformly attributed to all the saints, and which, in one passage, is called "the beginning of wisdom," in another wisdom itself, although it is one, proceeds from a twofold cause. God is entitled to the reverence of a Father and a Lord. Hence he who desires duly to worship him, will study to act the part both of an obedient son and a faithful servant. The obedience paid to God as a Father he by his prophet terms "honor;" the service performed to him as a master he terms "fear." "A son honoreth his father, and a servant his master. If then I be a father, where is mine honor? and if I be a master, where is my fear?" But while he thus distinguishes between the two, it is obvious that he at the same time confounds them. The fear of the Lord, therefore, may be defined reverence mingled with honor and fear. It is not strange that the same mind can entertain both feelings; for he who considers with himself what kind of a father God is to us, will see sufficient reason, even were there no hell, why the thought of offending him should seem more dreadful than any death. But so prone is our carnal nature to indulgence in sin, that, in order to curb it in every way, we must also give place to the thought that all iniquity is abomination to the Master under whom we live; that those who, by wicked lives, provoke his anger, will not escape his vengeance.

27. There is nothing repugnant to this in the observation of John: "There is no fear in love; but perfect love casteth out fear: because fear has torment" (1 John 4:18). For he is speaking of the fear of unbelief, between which and the fear of believers there is a wide difference. The wicked do not fear God from any unwillingness to offend him, provided they could do so with impunity; but knowing that he is armed with power for vengeance, they tremble in dismay on hearing of his anger. And they thus dread his anger, because they think

it is impending over them, and they every moment expect it to fall upon their heads. But believers, as has been said, dread the offense even more than the punishment. They are not alarmed by the fear of punishment, as if it were impending over them, but are rendered the more cautious of doing anything to provoke it. Thus the Apostle addressing believers says, "Let no man deceive you with vain words; for because of these things, the wrath of God cometh upon the children of disobedience" (Eph. 5:6; Col. 3:6). He does not threaten that wrath will descend upon them; but he admonishes them, while they think how the wrath of God is prepared for the wicked, on account of the crimes which he had enumerated, not to run the risk of provoking it. It seldom happens that mere threatenings have the effect of arousing the reprobate; nay, becoming more callous and hardened when God thunders verbally from heaven, they obstinately persist in their rebellion. It is only when actually smitten by his hand that they are forced, whether they will or not, to fear. This fear the sacred writers term "servile," and oppose to the free and voluntary fear which becomes sons. Some, by a subtle distinction, have introduced an intermediate species, holding that that forced and servile fear sometimes subdues the mind, and leads spontaneously to proper fear.

28. The divine favor to which faith is said to have respect, we understand to include in it the possession of salvation and eternal life. For if, when God is propitious, no good thing can be wanting to us, we have ample security for our salvation when assured of his love. "Turn us again, O God, and cause thy face to shine," says the Prophet, "and we shall be saved" (Ps. 80:3). Hence the Scriptures make the sum of our salvation to consist in the removal of all enmity, and our admission into favor; thus intimating, that when God is reconciled all danger is past, and every thing good will befall us. Wherefore, faith apprehending the love of God has the promise both of the present and the future life, and ample security for all blessings (Eph. 2:14). The nature of this must be ascertained from the word. Faith does not promise us length of

days, riches and honors (the Lord not having been pleased that any of these should be appointed us); but is contented with the assurance, that however poor we may be in regard to present comforts, God will never fail us. The chief security lies in the expectation of future life, which is placed beyond doubt by the word of God. Whatever be the miseries and calamities which await the children of God in this world, they cannot make his favor cease to be complete happiness. Hence, when we were desirous to express the sum of blessedness, we designated it by the favor of God, from which, as their source, all kinds of blessings flow. And we may observe throughout the Scriptures, that they refer us to the love of God, not only when they treat of our eternal salvation, but of any blessing whatever. For which reason David sings, that the loving-kindness of God experienced by the pious heart is sweeter and more to be desired than life itself (Ps. 63:3). In short, if we have every earthly comfort to a wish, but are uncertain whether we have the love or the hatred of God, our felicity will be cursed, and therefore miserable. But if God lift on us the light of his fatherly countenance, our very miseries will be blessed, inasmuch as they will become helps to our salvation. Thus Paul, after bringing together all kinds of adversity, boasts that they cannot separate us from the love of God: and in his prayers he uniformly begins with the grace of God as the source of all prosperity. In like manner, to all the terrors which assail us, David opposes merely the favor of God—"Yea, though I walk through the valley of the shadow of death, I will fear no evil: for thou art with me" (Ps. 23:4). And we feel that our minds always waver until, contented with the grace of God, we in it seek peace, and feel thoroughly persuaded of what is said in the psalm, "Blessed is the nation whose God is the Lord, and the people whom he has chosen for his own inheritance" (Ps. 33:12).

29. Free promise we make the foundation of faith, because in it faith properly consists. For though it holds that God is always true, whether in ordering or forbidding, promising or threatening; though it obediently receive his commands, observe his prohibitions, and give

heed to his threatening; yet it properly begins with promise, continues with it, and ends with it. It seeks life in God, life which is not
found in commands or the denunciations of punishment, but in the
promise of mercy. And this promise must be gratuitous; for a conditional promise, which throws us back upon our works, promises life
only insofar as we find it existing in ourselves. Therefore, if we would
not have faith to waver and tremble, we must support it with the
promise of salvation, which is offered by the Lord spontaneously and
freely, from a regard to our misery rather than our worth. Hence the
Apostle bears this testimony to the Gospel, that it is the word of faith
(Rom. 10:8). This he concedes not either to the precepts or the promises of the Law, since there is nothing which can establish our faith,
but that free embassy by which God reconciles the world to himself.
Hence he often uses "faith" and "the Gospel" as correlative terms, as
when he says, that the ministry of the Gospel was committed to him
for "obedience to the faith;" that "it is the power of God unto salvation to every one that believeth;" that "therein is the righteousness of
God revealed from faith to faith" (Rom. 1:5, 16-17). No wonder: for
seeing that the Gospel is "the ministry of reconciliation" (2 Cor. 5:18),
there is no other sufficient evidence of the divine favor, such as faith
requires to know. Therefore, when we say, that faith must rest on a
free promise, we deny not that believers accept and embrace the word
of God in all its parts, but we point to the promise of mercy as its
special object. Believers, indeed, ought to recognize God as the judge
and avenger of wickedness; and yet mercy is the object to which they
properly look, since he is exhibited to their contemplation as "good
and ready to forgive," "plenteous in mercy," "slow to anger," "good to
all," and shedding "his tender mercies over all his works" (Ps. 86:5;
103:8; 145:8-9).

30. I stay not to consider the rabid objections of Pighius, and others like-minded, who inveigh against this restriction, as rending faith,
and laying hold of one of its fragments. I admit, as I have already

said, that the general object of faith (as they express it) is the truth
of God, whether he threatens or gives hope of his favor. Accordingly,
the Apostle attributes it to faith in Noah, that he feared the destruction of the world, when as yet it was not seen (Heb. 11:17). If fear of
impending punishment was a work of faith, threatening ought not
to be excluded in defining it. This is indeed true; but we are unjustly
and calumniously charged with denying that faith has respect to the
whole word of God. We only mean to maintain these two points—
that faith is never decided until it attain to a free promise; and that
the only way in which faith reconciles us to God is by uniting us with
Christ. Both are deserving of notice. We are inquiring after a faith
which separates the children of God from the reprobate, believers
from unbelievers. Shall every man, then, who believes that God is just
in what he commands, and true in what he threatens, be on that account classed with believers? Very far from it. Faith, then, has no firm
footing until it stand in the mercy of God. Then what end have we in
view in discoursing of faith? Is it not that we may understand the way
of salvation? But how can faith be saving, unless insofar as it engrafts
us into the body of Christ? There is no absurdity, therefore, when, in
defining it, we thus press its special object, and, by way of distinction,
add to the generic character the particular mark which distinguishes
the believer from the unbeliever. In short, the malicious have nothing
to carp at in this doctrine, unless they are to bring the same censure
against the Apostle Paul, who specially designates the Gospel as "the
word of faith" (Rom. 10:8).

31. Hence again we infer, as has already been explained, that faith
has no less need of the word than the fruit of a tree has of a living
root; because, as David testifies, none can hope in God but those who
know his name (Ps. 9:10). This knowledge, however, is not left to
every man's imagination, but depends on the testimony which God
himself gives to his goodness. This the same Psalmist confirms in
another passage, "Thy salvation according to thy word" (Ps. 119:41).

Again, "Save me," "I hoped in thy word" (Ps. 119:146-147). Here we must attend to the relation of faith to the word, and to salvation as its consequence. Still, however, we exclude not the power of God. If faith cannot support itself in the view of this power, it never will give Him the honor which is due. Paul seems to relate a trivial or very ordinary circumstance with regard to Abraham, when he says, that he believed that God, who had given him the promise of a blessed seed, was able also to perform it (Rom. 4:21). And in like manner, in another passage, he says of himself, "I know whom I have believed, and am persuaded that he is able to keep that which I have committed unto him against that day" (2 Tim. 1:12). But let anyone consider with himself, how he is ever and anon assailed with doubts in regard to the power of God, and he will readily perceive, that those who duly magnify it have made no small progress in faith. We all acknowledge that God can do whatsoever he pleases; but while every temptation, even the most trivial, fills us with fear and dread, it is plain that we derogate from the power of God, by attaching less importance to his promises than to Satan's threatenings against them.

This is the reason why Isaiah, when he would impress on the hearts of the people the certainty of faith, discourses so magnificently of the boundless power of God. He often seems, after beginning to speak of the hope of pardon and reconciliation, to digress, and unnecessarily take a long circuitous course, describing how wonderfully God rules the fabric of heaven and earth, with the whole course of nature; and yet he introduces nothing which is not appropriate to the occasion; because unless the power of God, to which all things are possible is presented to our eye, our ears malignantly refuse admission to the word, or set no just value upon it. We may add, that an effectual power is here meant; for piety, as it has elsewhere been seen, always makes a practical application of the power of God; in particular, keeps those works in view in which he has declared himself to be a Father. Hence the frequent mention in Scripture of redemption; from which the

Israelites might learn, that he who had once been the author of salvation would be its perpetual guardian. By his own example, also, David reminds us, that the benefits which God has bestowed privately on any individual, tend to confirm his faith for the time to come; nay, that when God seems to have forsaken us, we ought to extend our view farther, and take courage from his former favors, as is said in another psalm, "I remember the days of old: I meditate on all thy works" (Ps. 143:5). Again "I will remember the works of the Lord; surely I will remember thy wonders of old" (Ps. 77:11). But because all our conceptions of the power and works of God are evanescent without the word, we are not rash in maintaining, that there is no faith until God present us with clear evidence of his grace.

Here, however, a question might be raised as to the view to be taken of Sarah and Rebekah, both of whom, impelled as it would seem by zeal for the faith, went beyond the limits of the word. Sarah, in her eager desire for the promised seed, gave her maid to her husband. That she sinned in many respects is not to be denied; but the only fault to which I now refer is her being carried away by zeal, and not confining herself within the limits prescribed by the word. It is certain, however, that her desire proceeded from faith. Rebekah, again, divinely informed of the election of her son Jacob, procures the blessing for him by a wicked stratagem; deceives her husband, who was a witness and minister of divine grace; forces her son to lie; by various frauds and impostures corrupts divine truth; in fine, by exposing his promise to scorn, does what in her lies to make it of no effect. And yet this conduct, however vicious and reprehensible, was not devoid of faith. She must have overcome many obstacles before she obtained so strong a desire of that which, without any hope of earthly advantage, was full of difficulty and danger. In the same way, we cannot say that the holy patriarch Isaac was altogether void of faith, in that, after he had been similarly informed of the honor transferred to the younger son, he still continues his predilection in favor of his first-born, Esau.

These examples certainly show that error is often mingled with faith; and yet that when faith is real, it always obtains the preeminence. For as the particular error of Rebekah did not render the blessing of no effect, neither did it nullify the faith which generally ruled in her mind, and was the principle and cause of that action. In this, nevertheless, Rebekah showed how prone the human mind is to turn aside whenever it gives itself the least indulgence. But though defect and infirmity obscure faith, they do not extinguish it. Still they admonish us how carefully we ought to cling to the word of God, and at the same time confirm what we have taught—viz. that faith gives way when not supported by the word, just as the minds of Sarah, Isaac, and Rebekah, would have lost themselves in devious paths, had not the secret restraint of Providence kept them obedient to the word.

32. On the other hand, we have good ground for comprehending all the promises in Christ, since the Apostle comprehends the whole Gospel under the knowledge of Christ, and declares that all the promises of God are in him yea, and amen. The reason for this is obvious. Every promise which God makes is evidence of his good will. This is invariably true, and is not inconsistent with the fact, that the large benefits which the divine liberality is constantly bestowing on the wicked are preparing them for heavier judgment. As they neither think that these proceed from the hand of the Lord, nor acknowledge them as his, or if they do so acknowledge them, never regard them as proofs of his favor, they are in no respect more instructed thereby in his mercy than brute beasts, which, according to their condition, enjoy the same liberality, and yet never look beyond it. Still it is true, that by rejecting the promises generally offered to them, they subject themselves to severer punishment. For though it is only when the promises are received in faith that their efficacy is manifested, still their reality and power are never extinguished by our infidelity or ingratitude. Therefore, when the Lord by his promises invites us not only to enjoy the fruits of his kindness, but also to meditate upon

them, he at the same time declares his love. Thus we are brought back to our statement, that every promise is a manifestation of the divine favor toward us. Now, without controversy, God loves no man out of Christ. He is the beloved Son, in whom the love of the Father dwells, and from whom it afterwards extends to us. Thus Paul says "In whom he has made us accepted in the Beloved" (Eph. 1:6). It is by his intervention, therefore, that love is diffused so as to reach us. Accordingly, in another passage, the Apostle calls Christ "our peace" (Eph. 2:14), and also represents him as the bond by which the Father is united to us in paternal affection (Rom. 8:3). It follows, that whenever any promise is made to us, we must turn our eyes toward Christ. Hence, with good reasons Paul declares that in him all the promises of God are confirmed and completed (Rom. 15:8). Some examples are brought forward as repugnant to this view. When Naaman the Syrian made inquiry at the prophet as to the true mode of worshiping God, we cannot (it is said) suppose that he was informed of the Mediator, and yet he is commended for his piety (2 Kings 5:17-19). Nor could Cornelius, a Roman heathen, be acquainted with what was not known to all the Jews, and at best known obscurely. And yet his alms and prayers were acceptable to God (Acts 10:31), while the prophet by his answer approved of the sacrifices of Naaman. In both, this must have been the result of faith. In like manner, the eunuch to whom Philip was sent, had he not been endued with some degree of faith, never would have incurred the fatigue and expense of a long and difficult journey to obtain an opportunity of worship (Acts 8:27, 31); and yet we see how, when interrogated by Philip, he betrays his ignorance of the Mediator. I admit that, in some respect, their faith was not explicit either as to the person of Christ, or the power and office assigned him by the Father. Still it is certain that they were imbued with principles which might give some, though a slender, foretaste of Christ. This should not be thought strange; for the eunuch would not have hastened from a distant country to Jerusalem to an unknown

God; nor could Cornelius, after having once embraced the Jewish religion, have lived so long in Judea without becoming acquainted with the rudiments of sound doctrine. In regard to Naaman, it is absurd to suppose that Elisha, while he gave him many minute precepts, said nothing of the principal matter. Therefore, although their knowledge of Christ may have been obscure, we cannot suppose that they had no such knowledge at all. They used the sacrifices of the Law, and must have distinguished them from the spurious sacrifices of the Gentiles, by the end to which they referred—viz. Christ.

33. A simple external manifestation of the word ought to be amply sufficient to produce faith, did not our blindness and perverseness prevent. But such is the proneness of our mind to vanity, that it can never adhere to the truth of God, and such its dullness, that it is always blind even in his light. Hence without the illumination of the Spirit the word has no effect; and hence also it is obvious that faith is something higher than human understanding. Nor were it sufficient for the mind to be illumined by the Spirit of God unless the heart also were strengthened and supported by his power. Here the Schoolmen go completely astray, dwelling entirely in their consideration of faith, on the bare simple assent of the understanding, and altogether overlooking confidence and security of heart. Faith is the special gift of God in both ways—in purifying the mind so as to give it a relish for divine truth, and afterwards in establishing it therein. For the Spirit does not merely originate faith, but gradually increases it, until by its means he conducts us into the heavenly kingdom. "That good thing which was committed unto thee," says Paul, "keep by the Holy Ghost which dwelleth in us" (2 Tim. 1:14). In what sense Paul says (Gal. 3:2), that the Spirit is given by the hearing of faith, may be easily explained. If there were only a single gift of the Spirit, he who is the author and cause of faith could not without absurdity be said to be its effect; but after celebrating the gifts with which God adorns his church, and by successive additions of faith leads it to perfection,

there is nothing strange in his ascribing to faith the very gifts which faith prepares us for receiving. It seems to some paradoxical, when it is said that none can believe Christ save those to whom it is given; but this is partly because they do not observe how recondite and sublime heavenly wisdom is, or how dull the mind of man in discerning divine mysteries, and partly because they pay no regard to that firm and stable constancy of heart which is the chief part of faith.

34. But as Paul argues, "What man knoweth the things of a man, save the spirit of man which is in him? even so the things of God knoweth no man but the Spirit of God" (1 Cor. 2:11). If in regard to divine truth we hesitate even as to those things which we see with the bodily eye, how can we be firm and steadfast in regard to those divine promises which neither the eye sees nor the mind comprehends? Here human discernment is so defective and lost, that the first step of advancement in the school of Christ is to renounce it (Matt. 11:25; Luke 10:21). Like a veil interposed, it prevents us from beholding divine masteries, which are revealed only to babes. "Flesh and blood" does not reveal them (Matt. 16:17). "The natural man receiveth not the things of the Spirit of God: for they are foolishness unto him; neither can he know them, for they are spiritually discerned" (1 Cor. 2:14). The supplies of the Holy Spirit are therefore necessary, or rather his agency is here the only strength. "For who has known the mind of the Lord? or who has been his counselor?" (Rom. 11:34); but "The Spirit searcheth all things, yea, the deep things of God" (1 Cor. 2:10). Thus it is that we attain to the mind of Christ: "No man can come to me, except the Father which has sent me draw him: and I will raise him up at the last day." "Every man therefore that has heard, and learned of the Father, cometh unto me. Not that any man has seen the Father, save he which is of God, he has seen the Father" (John 6:44-46). Therefore, as we cannot possibly come to Christ unless drawn by the Spirit, so when we are drawn we are both in mind and spirit exalted far above our own understanding. For the soul, when illumined

by him, receives as it were a new eye, enabling it to contemplate heavenly mysteries, by the splendor of which it was previously dazzled. And thus, indeed, it is only when the human intellect is irradiated by the light of the Holy Spirit that it begins to have a taste of those things which pertain to the kingdom of God; previously it was too stupid and senseless to have any relish for them. Hence our Savior, when clearly declaring the mysteries of the kingdom to the two disciples, makes no impression till he opens their minds to understand the Scriptures (Luke 24:27, 45). Hence also, though he had taught the Apostles with his own divine lips, it was still necessary to send the Spirit of truth to instill into their minds the same doctrine which they had heard with their ears. The word is, in regard to those to whom it is preached, like the sun which shines upon all, but is of no use to the blind. In this matter we are all naturally blind; and hence the word cannot penetrate our mind unless the Spirit, that internal teacher, by his enlightening power make an entrance for it.

35. Having elsewhere shown more fully, when treating of the corruption of our nature, how little able men are to believe (Book 2, chap. 2-3), I will not fatigue the reader by again repeating it. Let it suffice to observe, that the spirit of faith is used by Paul as synonymous with the very faith which we receive from the Spirit, but which we have not naturally (2 Cor. 4:13). Accordingly, he prays for the Thessalonians, "that our God would count you worthy of this calling, and fulfill all the good pleasure of his goodness, and the work of faith with power" (2 Thess. 1:2). Here, by designating faith the work of God, and distinguishing it by way of epithet, appropriately calling it his good pleasure, he declares that it is not of man's own nature; and not contented with this, he adds, that it is an illustration of divine power. In addressing the Corinthians, when he tells them that faith stands not "in the wisdom of man, but in the power of God" (1 Cor. 2:4), he is no doubt speaking of external miracles; but as the reprobate are blinded when they behold them, he also includes that internal seal

of which he elsewhere makes mention. And the better to display his liberality in this most excellent gift, God does not bestow it upon all promiscuously, but, by special privilege, imparts it to whom he will. To this effect we have already quoted passages of Scripture, as to which Augustine, their faithful expositor, exclaims (*De Verbo Apost.* Serm. 2) "Our Savior, to teach that faith in him is a gift, not a merit, says, 'No man can come to me, except the Father, which has sent me, draw him' (John 6:44). It is strange when two persons hear, the one despises, the other ascends. Let him who despises impute it to himself; let him who ascends not arrogate it to himself." In another passage he asks, "Wherefore is it given to the one, and not to the other? I am not ashamed to say, This is one of the deep things of the cross. From some unknown depth of the judgments of God, which we cannot scrutinize, all our ability proceeds. I see that I am able; but how I am able I see not:—this far only I see, that it is of God. But why the one, and not the other? This is too great for me: it is an abyss a depth of the cross. I can cry out with wonder; not discuss and demonstrate." The whole comes to this, that Christ, when he produces faith in us by the agency of his Spirit, at the same time engrafts us into his body, that we may become partakers of all blessings.

36. The next thing necessary is, that what the mind has imbibed be transferred into the heart. The word is not received in faith when it merely flutters in the brain, but when it has taken deep root in the heart, and become an invincible bulwark to withstand and repel all the assaults of temptation. But if the illumination of the Spirit is the true source of understanding in the intellect, much more manifest is his agency in the confirmation of the heart; inasmuch as there is more distrust in the heart than blindness in the mind; and it is more difficult to inspire the soul with security than to imbue it with knowledge. Hence the Spirit performs the part of a seal, sealing upon our hearts the very promises, the certainty of which was previously impressed upon our minds. It also serves as an earnest in establishing

and confirming these promises. Thus the Apostle says, "In whom also, after that ye believed, ye were sealed with that Holy Spirit of promise, which is the earnest of our inheritance" (Eph. 1:13-14). You see how he teaches that the hearts of believers are stamped with the Spirit as with a seal, and calls it the Spirit of promise, because it ratifies the gospel to us. In like manner he says to the Corinthians, "God has also sealed us, and given the earnest of the Spirit in our hearts" (2 Cor. 1:22). And again, when speaking of a full and confident hope, he founds it on the "earnest of the Spirit" (2 Cor. 5:5).

37. I am not forgetting what I formerly said, and experience brings daily to remembrance—viz. that faith is subject to various doubts, so that the minds of believers are seldom at rest, or at least are not always tranquil. Still, whatever be the engines by which they are shaken, they either escape from the whirlpool of temptation, or remain steadfast in their place. Faith finds security and protection in the words of the Psalm, "God is our refuge and strength, a very present help in trouble; therefore will not we fear, though the earth be removed, and the mountains be carried into the midst of the sea" (Ps. 46:1-2). This delightful tranquility is elsewhere described: "I laid me down and slept; I awaked, for the Lord sustained me" (Ps. 3:5). Not that David was uniformly in this joyful frame; but insofar as the measure of his faith made him sensible of the divine favor, he glories in intrepidly despising everything that could disturb his peace of mind. Hence the Scripture, when it exhorts us to faith, bids us be at peace. In Isaiah it is said, "In quietness and in confidence shall be your strength" (Isa. 30:15); and in the psalm, "Rest in the Lord, and wait patiently for him." Corresponding to this is the passage in the Hebrews, "Ye have need of patience," &c. (Heb. 10:36).

38. Hence we may judge how pernicious is the scholastic dogma, that we can have no stronger evidence of the divine favor toward us than moral conjecture, according as each individual deems himself not unworthy of it. Doubtless, if we are to determine by our works in

what way the Lord stands affected towards us, I admit that we cannot even get the length of a feeble conjecture: but since faith should
accord with the free and simple promise, there is no room left for
ambiguity. With what kind of confidence, pray, shall we be armed if
we reason in this way—God is propitious to us, provided we deserve
it by the purity of our lives? But since we have reserved this subject for
discussion in its proper place, we shall not prosecute it farther at present, especially seeing it is already plain that nothing is more adverse to
faith than conjecture, or any other feeling akin to doubt. Nothing can
be worse than their perversion of the passage of Ecclesiastes, which
is ever in their mouths: "No man knoweth either love or hatred by all
that is before them" (Eccl. 9:1). For without insisting that the passage
is erroneously rendered in the common version—even a child cannot
fail to perceive what Solomon's meaning is—viz. that any one who
would ascertain, from the present state of things, who are in the favor
or under the displeasure of God, labors in vain, and torments himself
to no useful purpose, since "All things come alike to all;" "to him that
sacrificeth, and to him that sacrificeth not:" and hence God does not
always declare his love to those on whom he bestows uninterrupted
prosperity, nor his hatred against those whom he afflicts. And it tends
to prove the vanity of the human intellect, that it is so completely in
the dark as to matters which it is of the highest importance to know.
Thus Solomon had said a little before, "That which befalleth the sons
of men befalleth beasts; even one thing befalleth them: as the one dieth, so dieth the other" (Eccl. 3:19). Were anyone thence to infer that
we hold the immortality of the soul by conjecture merely, would he
not justly be deemed insane? Are those then sane who cannot obtain
any certainty of the divine favor, because the carnal eye is now unable
to discern it from the present appearance of the world?

39. But, they say, it is rash and presumptuous to pretend to an un-
doubted knowledge of the divine will. I would grant this, did we hold
that we were able to subject the incomprehensible counsel of God

to our feeble intellect. But when we simply say with Paul, "We have received not the spirit of the world, but the Spirit which is of God; that we might know the things that are freely given to us of God" (1 Cor. 2:12), what can they oppose to this, without offering insult to the Spirit of God? But if it is Sacrilege to charge the revelation which he has given us with falsehood, or uncertainty, or ambiguity, how can we be wrong in maintaining its certainty? But they still exclaim, that there is great temerity in our presuming to glory in possessing the Spirit of God. Who could believe that these men, who desire to be thought the masters of the world, could be so stupid as to err thus grossly in the very first principles of religion? To me, indeed, it would be incredible, did not their own writings make it manifest. Paul declares that those only are the sons of God who are led by his Spirit (Rom. 8:14); these men would have those who are the sons of God to be led by their own, and void of the divine Spirit. He tells us that we call God our Father in terms dictated by the Spirit, who alone bears witness with our spirit that we are the sons of God (Rom. 8:16); they, though they forbid us not to invoke God, withdraw the Spirit, by whose guidance he is duly invoked. He declares that those only are the servants of Christ who are led by the Spirit of Christ (Rom. 8:9); they imagine a Christianity which has no need of the Spirit of Christ. He holds out the hope of a blessed resurrection to those only who feel His Spirit dwelling in them (Rom. 8:11); they imagine hope when there is no such feeling. But perhaps they will say, that they deny not the necessity of being endued with the Spirit, but only hold it to be the part of modesty and humility not to recognize it. What, then, does Paul mean, when he says to the Corinthians, "Examine yourselves whether ye be in the faith: prove your own selves. Know ye not your own selves, that Jesus Christ is in you, except ye be reprobates?" (2 Cor. 13:5). John, moreover, says, "Hereby we know that he abideth in us by the Spirit which he has given us" (1 John 3:24). And what else is it than to bring the promises of Christ into doubt, when we would

be deemed servants of Christ without having his Spirit, whom he
declared that he would pour out on all his people? (Isa. 44:3). What!
do we not insult the Holy Spirit, when we separate faith, which is
his peculiar work, from himself? These being the first rudiments of
religion, it is the most wretched blindness to charge Christians with
arrogance, for presuming to glory in the presence of the Holy Spirit;
a glorying without which Christianity itself does not exist. The example of these men illustrates the truth of our Savior's declaration, that
his Spirit "the world cannot receive, because it seeth him not, neither
knoweth him; but ye know him, for he dwelleth with you, and shall
be in you" (John 14:17).

40. That they may not attempt to undermine the certainty of faith
in one direction only, they attack it in another—viz. that though it be
lawful for the believer, from his actual state of righteousness, to form
a judgment as to the favor of God, the knowledge of final perseverance still remains in suspense. An admirable security, indeed, is left us,
if, for the present moment only, we can judge from moral conjecture
that we are in grace, but know not how we are to be tomorrow! Very
different is the language of the Apostle, "I am persuaded that neither
death, nor life, nor angels, nor principalities, nor powers, nor things
present, nor things to come, nor height, nor depth, nor any other
creature, shall be able to separate us from the love of God, which is in
Christ Jesus our Lord" (Rom. 8:38). They endeavor to evade the force
of this by frivolously pretending that the Apostle had this assurance
by special revelation. They are too well caught thus to escape; for in
that passage he is treating not of his individual experience, but of the
blessings which all believers in common derive from faith. But then
Paul in another passage alarms us by the mention of our weakness
and inconstancy, "Let him that thinketh he standeth take heed lest he
fall" (1 Cor. 10:12). True; but this he says not to inspire us with terror,
but that we may learn to humble ourselves under the mighty hand
of God, as Peter explains (1 Pet. 5:6). Then how preposterous is it to

limit the certainty of faith to a point of time; seeing it is the property of faith to pass beyond the whole course of this life, and stretch forward to a future immortality? Therefore since believers owe it to the favor of God, that, enlightened by his Spirit, they, through faith, enjoy the prospect of heavenly life; there is so far from an approach to arrogance in each glorying, that anyone ashamed to confess it, instead of testifying modesty or submission, rather betrays extreme ingratitude, by maliciously suppressing the divine goodness.

41. Since the nature of faith could not be better or more clearly evinced than by the substance of the promise on which it leans as its proper foundation, and without which it immediately falls or rather vanishes away, we have derived our definition from it—a definition, however, not at all at variance with that definition, or rather description, which the Apostle accommodates to his discourse, when he says that faith is "the substance of things hoped for, the evidence of things not seen" (Heb. 11:1). For by the term "substance" (υποστασις), he means a kind of prop on which the pious mind rests and leans. As if he had said, that faith is a kind of certain and secure possession of those things which are promised to us by God; unless we prefer taking υποστασις for "confidence." I have no objection to this, though I am more inclined to adopt the other interpretation, which is more generally received. Again, to intimate that until the last day, when the books will be opened (Dan. 7:10; Rev. 20:12), the things pertaining to our salvation are too lofty to be perceived by our sense, seen by our eyes, or handled by our hands, and that in the meantime there is no possible way in which these can be possessed by us, unless we can transcend the reach of our own intellect, and raise our eye above all worldly objects; in short, surpass ourselves, he adds that this certainty of possession relates to things which are only hoped for, and therefore not seen. For as Paul says (Rom. 8:24), "A hope that is seen is not hope," that we "hope for that we see not." When he calls it the evidence or proof, or, as Augustine repeatedly renders it (see

Hom. in Joann. 79 and 95), the conviction of things not present, the Greek term being *elennchos*, it is the same as if he had called it the appearance of things not apparent, the sight of things not seen, the clearness of things obscure, the presence of things absent, the manifestation of things hid. For the mysteries of God (and to this class belong the things which pertain to our salvation) cannot be discerned in themselves, or, as it is expressed, in their own nature; but we behold them only in his word, of the truth of which we ought to be as firmly persuaded as if we held that every thing which it says were done and completed. But how can the mind rise to such a perception and foretaste of the divine goodness, without being at the same time wholly inflamed with love to God? The abundance of joy which God has treasured up for those who fear him cannot be truly known without making a most powerful impression. He who is thus once affected is raised and carried entirely towards him. Hence it is not strange that no sinister perverse heart ever experiences this feeling, by which, transported to heaven itself, we are admitted to the most hidden treasures of God, and the holiest recesses of his kingdom, which must not be profaned by the entrance of a heart that is impure. For what the Schoolmen say as to the priority of love to faith and hope is a mere dream (see *Sent.* Lib. 3 Dist. 25, &c.) since it is faith alone that first engenders love. How much better is Bernard, "The testimony of conscience, which Paul calls the rejoicing' of believers, I believe to consist in three things. It is necessary, first of all, to believe that you cannot have remission of sins except by the indulgence of God; secondly, that you cannot have any good work at all unless he also give it; lastly, that you cannot by any works merit eternal life unless it also be freely given" (Bernard, Serm. 1 in *Annuntiatione*). Shortly after he adds, "These things are not sufficient, but are a kind of commencement of faith; for while believing that your sins can only be forgiven by God, you must also hold that they are not forgiven until persuaded by the testimony of the Holy Spirit that salvation is treasured up for us; that as God pardons sins, and gives merits, and after merits rewards, you cannot halt at that beginning." But these and other topics will be considered in their own place; let it suffice at present to understand what faith is.

42. Wherever this living faith exists, it must have the hope of eternal life as its inseparable companion, or rather must of itself beget and manifest it; where it is wanting, however clearly and elegantly we may discourse of faith, it is certain we have it not. For if faith is (as has been said) a firm persuasion of the truth of God—a persuasion that it can never be false, never deceive, never be in vain—those who have received this assurance must at the same time expect that God will perform his promises, which in their conviction are absolutely true; so that in one word hope is nothing more than the expectation of those things which faith previously believes to have been truly promised by God. Thus, faith believes that God is true; hope expects that in due season he will manifest his truth. Faith believes that he is our Father; hope expects that he will always act the part of a Father towards us. Faith believes that eternal life has been given to us; hope expects that it will one day be revealed. Faith is the foundation on which hope rests; hope nourishes and sustains faith. For as no man can expect anything from God without previously believing his promises, so, on the other hand, the weakness of our faith, which might grow weary and fall away, must be supported and cherished by patient hope and expectation. For this reason Paul justly says, "We are saved by hope" (Rom. 8:24). For while hope silently waits for the Lord, it restrains faith from hastening on with too much precipitation, confirms it when it might waver in regard to the promises of God or begin to doubt of their truth, refreshes it when it might be fatigued, extends its view to the final goal, so as not to allow it to give up in the middle of the course, or at the very outset. In short, by constantly renovating and reviving, it is ever and anon furnishing more vigor for perseverance. On the whole, how necessary the reinforcements of hope are to establish faith will better appear if we reflect on the numerous forms

of temptation by which those who have embraced the word of God are assailed and shaken. First, the Lord often keeps us in suspense, by delaying the fulfillment of his promises much longer than we could wish. Here the office of hope is to perform what the prophet enjoins, "Though it tarry, wait for it" (Hab. 2:3). Sometimes he not only permits faith to grow languid, but even openly manifests his displeasure. Here there is still greater necessity for the aid of hope, that we may be able to say with another prophet, "I will wait upon the Lord that hideth his face from the house of Jacob, and I will look for him" (Isa. 8:17). Scoffers also rise up, as Peter tells us, and ask, "Where is the promise of his coming? For since the fathers fell asleep, all things continue as they were from the beginning of the creation" (2 Pet. 3:4). Nay, the world and the flesh insinuate the same thing. Here faith must be supported by the patience of hope, and fixed on the contemplation of eternity, consider that "one day is with the Lord as a thousand years, and a thousand years as one day" (2 Pet. 3:8; Ps. 90:4).

43. On account of this connection and affinity Scripture sometimes confounds the two terms "faith" and "hope." For when Peter says that we are "kept by the power of God through faith until salvation, ready to be revealed in the last times" (1 Pet. 1:5), he attributes to faith what more properly belongs to hope. And not without cause, since we have already shown that hope is nothing else than the food and strength of faith. Sometimes the two are joined together, as in the same Epistle, "That your faith and hope might be in God" (1 Pet. 1:21). Paul, again, in the Epistle to the Philippians, from hope deduces expectation (Phil. 1:20), because in hoping patiently we suspend our wishes until God manifest his own time. The whole of this subject may be better understood from the tenth chapter of the Epistle to the Hebrews, to which I have already adverted. Paul, in another passage, though not in strict propriety of speech, expresses the same thing in these words, "For we through the Spirit wait for the hope of righteousness by faith" (Gal. 5:5); that is, after embracing the testimony

of the Gospel as to free love, we wait till God openly manifest what is now only an object of hope. It is now obvious how absurdly Peter Lombard lays down a double foundation of hope—viz. the grace of God and the merit of works (*Sent.* Lib. 3, Dist. 26). Hope cannot have any other object than faith has. But we have already shown clearly that the only object of faith is the mercy of God, to which, to use the common expression, it must look with both eyes. But it is worthwhile to listen to the strange reason which he adduces. If you presume, says he, to hope for anything without merit, it should be called not hope, but presumption. Who, dear reader, does not execrate the gross stupidity which calls it rashness, and presumption to confide in the truth of God? The Lord desires us to expect everything from his goodness and yet these men tell us, it is presumption to rest in it. O teacher, worthy of the pupils, whom you found in these insane raving schools! Seeing that, by the oracles of God, sinners are enjoined to entertain the hope of salvation, let us willingly presume so far on his truth as to cast away all confidence in our works, and trusting in his mercy, venture to hope. He who has said, "According to your faith be it unto you" (Matt. 9:29), will never deceive.

Study Guide Questions

Section 1

1. Is it hard for us to keep the law?
2. What inadequate notion of faith does Calvin address first?
3. What two things must we know?
4. How does Christ the God/man help us in this?

Section 2

1. What fiction does Calvin reject?

Section 3

1. Does Calvin believe that ignorance should be tempered by humility?

2. What does Scripture regularly teach about this?

Section 4

1. Does Calvin believe that there is such a thing as implicit faith?

Section 5

1. Is there something else that we may call implicit faith?
2. Are there believers who are not yet believers in an exact sense?

Section 6

1. How must we receive Christ?
2. How does Paul define faith?

Section 7

1. Does the word of God automatically build faith?
2. Should we decide that God is well disposed toward us?

Section 8

1. What does Calvin think of the scholastic distinction between formed and unformed faith?
2. How does the assent of faith work?
3. What can faith not be separated from?

Section 9

1. How does Calvin answer the proof from 1 Corinthians 13 that argues that if faith is described as being without love, there must be something like unformed faith?
2. What mistake is made by Calvin's adversaries here?

Section 10

1. What common explanation of Simon Magus' behavior does Calvin reject?

2. What kind of faith did he have then?

3. What is the human heart like, such that it makes self-deception possible?

Section 11

1. What is hard to some?

2. Yet what do the reprobate sometimes experience?

3. What does Calvin call the effecting of this kind of transitory faith?

Section 12

1. In what way are the reprobate in this sense compared to a tree?

2. What is common faith?

Section 13

1. What must we understand about the meaning of the word "faith"?

2. Does the Bible use the word in ways that allow the reprobate to have "faith"?

Section 14

1. Does faith comprehend what it knows?

Section 15

1. According to Calvin, what does genuine faith require?

2. What is God's intention with regard to us?

Section 16

2. What does the man who hopes in the Lord do?

Section 17

1. If faith is essentially certain, then what must we explain in the believer's experience?

2. Who does Calvin use as a prime example of this?

Section 18

1. How does this variation arise within us?

2. What does this imperfect faith do?

Section 19

1. What illustration of weak but real faith does Calvin use?

Section 20

1. In this life, what must we put up with?

Section 21

1. Although believers have to deal with unbelief, where does it come from?

2. What illustration of shaken faith does Calvin give?

Section 22

1. What are the two kinds of fear?

2. What might happen among the Gentiles that had happened among the Jews?

Section 23

1. What kind of man does Solomon pronounce a blessing on?

Section 24

1. What does Calvin call those who believe that we have assurance so long as we look to Christ (over there)?

2. What is the basis for our assurance in Christ?

Section 25

1. What medieval father does Calvin quote extensively and with approval on this subject of faith?

Section 26
1. What do our duties of fear and honor relate to?

Section 27
1. What distinguishes childlike and servile fear?

Section 28
1. Does God guarantee believers earthly prosperity?
2. What does He promise then?

Section 29
1. What is the foundation of faith?

Section 30
1. What must a man attain to in the first place to have faith?
2. What must also happen in order for this faith to reconcile us to God?

Section 31
1. Can faith latch on to nothing?
2. What must God do to bring about faith?

Section 32
1. What is the testimony of God's love toward us?
2. Did the ancient Jews know of Christ?

Section 33
1. How do the Schoolmen go completely astray on the question of faith?

Section 34
1. Can we find our way unless someone leads us?

2. What does Calvin compare the word to?

Section 35
1. What does our corruption of nature do to our capacity for faith?
2. Can man initiate faith?
3. What then is necessary for belief?

Section 36
1. What is not true faith?
2. What is greater than the mind's blindness?

Section 37
1. Can true faith be shaken?

Section 38
1. According to the Schoolmen, how do we discern the grace of God toward us?
2. What does Calvin say faith should correspond to?

Section 39
1. Is it a small error the Schoolmen have fallen into?
2. Do the Schoolmen deny that we have the Spirit?
3. What is to charge with arrogance those Christians who dare to glory in the presence of the Holy Spirit?

Section 40
1. What other argument against assurance is brought?
2. Did Paul say what he did in Romans 8:38–39 by special revelation in his own case?
3. What does doubt about our future reveal instead of modesty?

Section 41

1. What translation of *hypostasis* in Hebrews 11:1 does Calvin prefer?
2. What teaching of the Schoolmen does Calvin dismiss as mere madness?
3. What three things does Bernard teach about the glory of the pious?
4. Does Calvin approve of this?

Section 42

1. What is the foundation of hope?
2. How does faith look forward to our future blessedness?

Section 43

1. What common foundation do faith and hope share?

CHAPTER 3

Regeneration. Of repentance.

This chapter is divided into five parts.

I. The title of the chapter seems to promise a treatise on Faith, but the only subject here considered is Repentance, the inseparable attendant of faith. And, first, various opinions on the subject of repentance are stated, sec. 1-4.

II. An exposition of the orthodox doctrine of Repentance, sec. 5-9.

III. Reasons why repentance must be prolonged to the last moment of life, sec. 10-14.

IV. Of the fruits of repentance, or its object and tendency, sec. 15-20.

V. The source whence repentance proceeds, sec. 21-24. Of the sin against the Holy Spirit, and the impenitence of the reprobate, sec. 25.

Outline:

1. Connection of this chapter with the previous one and the subsequent chapters. Repentance follows faith, and is produced by it. Reason. Error of those who take a contrary view.

2. Their First Objection. Answer. In what sense the origin of Repentance ascribed to Faith. Cause of the erroneous idea that faith is

77

produced by repentance. Refutation of it. The hypocrisy of Monks and Anabaptists in assigning limits to repentance exposed.

3. A second opinion concerning repentance considered.

4. A third opinion, assigning two forms to repentance, a legal and an Evangelical. Examples of each.

5. The orthodox doctrine of Repentance. 1. Faith and Repentance to be distinguished, not confounded or separated. 2. A consideration of the name. 3. A definition of the thing, or what repentance is. Doctrine of the Prophets and Apostles.

6. Explanation of the definition. This consists of three parts. 1. Repentance is a turning of our life unto God. This described and enlarged upon.

7. 2. Repentance produced by fear of God. Hence the mention of divine judgment by the Prophets and Apostles. Example. Exposition of the second branch of the definition from a passage in Paul. Why the fear of God is the first part of Repentance.

8. 3. Repentance consists in the mortification of the flesh and the quickening of the Spirit. These required by the Prophets. They are explained separately.

9. How this mortification and quickening are produced. Repentance just a renewal of the divine image in us. Not completed in a moment, but extends to the last moment of life.

10. Reasons why repentance must so extend. Augustine's opinion as to concupiscence in the regenerate examined. A passage of Paul which seems to confirm that opinion.

11. Answer. Confirmation of the answer by the Apostle himself. Another confirmation from a precept of the law. Conclusion.

12. Exception, that those desires only are condemned which are repugnant to the order of God. Desires not condemned insofar as natural, but insofar as inordinate. This held by Augustine.

13. Passages from Augustine to show that this was his opinion. Objection from a passage in James.

14. Another objection of the Anabaptists and Libertines to the continuance of repentance throughout the present life. An answer disclosing its impiety. Another answer, founded on the absurdities to which it leads. A third answer, contrasting sincere Christian repentance with the erroneous view of the objectors. Confirmation from the example and declaration of an Apostle.

15. Of the fruits of repentance. Carefulness. Excuse. Indignation. Fear. Desire. Zeal. Revenge. Moderation to be observed, as most sagely counseled by Bernard.

16. Internal fruits of Repentance. 1. Piety towards God. 2. Charity towards man. 3. Purity of life. How carefully these fruits are commended by the Prophets. External fruits of repentance. Bodily exercises too much commended by ancient writers. Twofold excess in regard to them.

17. Delusion of some who consider these external exercises as the chief part of Repentance. Why received in the Jewish Church. The legitimate use of these exercises in the Christian Church.

18. The principal part of repentance consists in turning to God. Confession and acknowledgment of sins. What their nature should be. Distinction between ordinary and special repentance. Use of this distinction.

19. End of Repentance. Its nature shown by the preaching of John the Baptist, our Savior, and his Apostles. The sum of this preaching.

20. Christian repentance terminates with our life.

21. Repentance has its origin in the grace of God, as communicated to the elect, whom God is pleased to save from death. The hardening and final impenitence of the reprobate. A passage of an Apostle as to voluntary reprobates, gives no countenance to the Novatians.

22. Of the sin against the Holy Ghost. The true definition of this sin as proved and explained by Scripture. Who they are that sin against the Holy Spirit. Examples: 1. The Jews resisting Stephen. 2. The Pharisees. Definition confirmed by the example of Paul.

23. Why that sin unpardonable. The paralogism of the Novatians in wresting the words of the Apostle examined. Two passages from the same Apostle.

24. First objection to the above doctrine. Answer. Solution of a difficulty founded on the example of Esau and the threatening of a Prophet. Second objection.

25. Third objection, founded on the seeming approval of the feigned repentance of the ungodly, as Ahab. Answer. Confirmation from the example of Esau. Why God bears for a time with the ungodly, pretending repentance. Exception.

Although we have already in some measure shown how faith possesses Christ, and gives us the enjoyment of his benefits, the subject would still be obscure were we not to add an exposition of the effects resulting from it. The sum of the Gospel is, not without good reason, made to consist in repentance and forgiveness of sins; and, therefore, where these two heads are omitted, any discussion concerning faith will be meager and defective, and indeed almost useless. Now, since Christ confers upon us, and we obtain by faith, both free reconciliation and newness of life, reason and order require that I should here begin to treat of both. The shortest transition, however, will be from faith to repentance; for repentance being properly understood it will better appear how a man is justified freely by faith alone, and yet that holiness of life, real holiness, as it is called, is inseparable from the free imputation of righteousness. That repentance not only always follows faith, but is produced by it, ought to be without controversy (see *Calvin in Joann. 1:13*). For since pardon and forgiveness are offered by the preaching of the Gospel, in order that the sinner, delivered from the tyranny of Satan, the yoke of sin, and the miserable bondage of iniquity, may pass into the kingdom of God, it is certain that no man can embrace the grace of the Gospel without retaking himself from the errors of his former life into the right path, and making it his whole study to practice repentance. Those who think that repentance precedes faith instead of flowing from, or being produced by it, as the fruit by the tree, have never understood its nature, and are moved to adopt that view on very insufficient grounds.

2. Christ and John, it is said, in their discourses first exhort the people to repentance, and then add, that the kingdom of heaven is at hand (Matt. 3:2; 4:17). Such too, is the message which the Apostles received and such the course which Paul followed, as is narrated by Luke (Acts 20:21). But clinging superstitiously to the juxtaposition of the syllables, they attend not to the coherence of meaning in the words. For when our Lord and John begin their preaching thus "Repent, for the kingdom of heaven is at hand" (Matt. 3:2), do they not deduce repentance as a consequence of the offer of grace and promise of salvation? The force of the words, therefore, is the same as if it were said, as the kingdom of heaven is at hand, for that reason repent. For Matthew, after relating that John so preached, says that therein was fulfilled the prophecy concerning the voice of one crying in the desert, "Prepare ye the way of the Lord, make straight in the desert a highway for our God" (Isa. 40:3). But in the Prophet that voice is ordered to commence with consolation and glad tidings. Still, when we attribute the origin of repentance to faith, we do not dream of some period of time in which faith is to give birth to it: we only wish to show that a man cannot seriously engage in repentance unless he know that he is of God. But no man is truly persuaded that he is of God until he has embraced his offered favor. These things will be more clearly explained as we proceed. Some are perhaps misled by this, that not a few are subdued by terror of conscience, or disposed to obedience before they have been imbued with a knowledge, nay, before they have had any taste of the divine favor (see *Calvin in Acts 20:21*). This is that initial fear which some writers class among the virtues, because they think it approximates to true and genuine obedience. But we are not here considering the various modes in which

Christ draws us to himself, or prepares us for the study of piety: All I say is, that no righteousness can be found where the Spirit, whom Christ received in order to communicate it to his members, reigns not. Then, according to the passage in the Psalms, "There is forgiveness with thee, that thou mayest be feared" (Psalm 130:4), no man will ever reverence God who does not trust that God is propitious to him, no man will ever willingly set himself to observe the Law who is not persuaded that his services are pleasing to God. The indulgence of God in tolerating and pardoning our iniquities is a sign of paternal favor. This is also clear from the exhortation in Hosea, "Come, and let us return unto the Lord: for he has torn, and he will heal us; he has smitten, and he will bind us up" (Hos. 6:1); the hope of pardon is employed as a stimulus to prevent us from becoming reckless in sin. But there is no semblance of reason in the absurd procedure of those who, that they may begin with repentance, prescribe to their neophytes certain days during which they are to exercise themselves in repentance, and after these are elapsed, admit them to communion in Gospel grace. I allude to great numbers of Anabaptists, those of them especially who plume themselves on being spiritual, and their associates the Jesuits, and others of the same stamp. Such are the fruits which their giddy spirit produces, that repentance, which in every Christian man lasts as long as life, is with them completed in a few short days.

3. Certain learned men, who lived long before the present days and were desirous to speak simply and sincerely according to the rule of Scripture, held that repentance consists of two parts, mortification and quickening. By mortification they mean, grief of soul and terror, produced by a conviction of sin and a sense of the divine judgment. For when a man is brought to a true knowledge of sin, he begins truly to hate and abominate sin. He also is sincerely dissatisfied with himself, confesses that he is lost and undone, and wishes he were different from what he is. Moreover, when he is touched with some sense

of the divine justice (for the one conviction immediately follows the other), he lies terror-struck and amazed, humbled and dejected, desponds and despairs. This, which they regarded as the first part of repentance, they usually termed "contrition." By quickening they mean, the comfort which is produced by faith, as when a man prostrated by a consciousness of sin, and smitten with the fear of God, afterwards beholding his goodness, and the mercy, grace, and salvation obtained through Christ, looks up, begins to breathe, takes courage, and passes, as it were, from death unto life. I admit that these terms, when rightly interpreted, aptly enough express the power of repentance; only I cannot assent to their using the term "quickening," for the joy which the soul feels after being calmed from perturbation and fear. It more properly means, that desire of pious and holy living which springs from the new birth; as if it were said, that the man dies to himself that he may begin to live unto God.

4. Others seeing that the term is used in Scripture in different senses, have set down two forms of repentance, and, in order to distinguish them, have called the one Legal repentance; or that by which the sinner, stung with a sense of his sin, and overwhelmed with fear of the divine anger, remains in that state of perturbation, unable to escape from it. The other they term Evangelical repentance; or that by which the sinner, though grievously downcast in himself, yet looks up and sees in Christ the cure of his wound, the solace of his terror; the haven of rest from his misery. They give Cain, Saul, and Judas, as examples of legal repentance. Scripture, in describing what is called their repentance, means that they perceived the heinousness of their sins, and dreaded the divine anger; but, thinking only of God as a judge and avenger, were overwhelmed by the thought. Their repentance, therefore, was nothing better than a kind of threshold to hell, into which having entered even in the present life, they began to endure the punishment inflicted by the presence of an offended God. Examples of evangelical repentance we see in all those who,

first stung with a sense of sin, but afterwards raised and revived by confidence in the divine mercy, turned unto the Lord. Hezekiah was frightened on receiving the message of his death, but praying with tears, and beholding the divine goodness, regained his confidence. The Ninevites were terrified at the fearful announcement of their destruction; but clothing themselves in sackcloth and ashes, they prayed, hoping that the Lord might relent and avert his anger from them. David confessed that he had sinned greatly in numbering the people, but added "Now, I beseech thee, O Lord, take away the iniquity of thy servant." When rebuked by Nathan, he acknowledged the crime of adultery, and humbled himself before the Lord; but he, at the same time, looked for pardon. Similar was the repentance of those who, stung to the heart by the preaching of Peter, yet trusted in the divine goodness, and added, "Men and brethren, what shall we do?" Similar was the case of Peter himself, who indeed wept bitterly, but ceased not to hope.

5. Though all this is true, yet the term "repentance" (insofar as I can ascertain from Scripture) must be differently taken. For in comprehending faith under repentance, they are at variance with what Paul says in the Acts, as to his "testifying both to the Jews and also to the Greeks, repentance toward God, and faith toward our Lord Jesus Christ" (Acts 20:21). Here he mentions faith and repentance as two different things. What then? Can true repentance exist without faith? By no means. But although they cannot be separated, they ought to be distinguished. As there is no faith without hope, and yet faith and hope are different, so repentance and faith, though constantly linked together, are only to be united, not confounded. I am not unaware that under the term "repentance is comprehended the whole work of turning to God, of which not the least important part is faith; but in what sense this is done will be perfectly obvious, when its nature and power shall have been explained. The term "repentance" is derived in the Hebrew from "conversion," or "turning again;" and in the Greek

from a change of mind and purpose; nor is the thing meant inappropriate to both derivations, for it is substantially this, that withdrawing from ourselves we turn to God, and laying aside the old, put on a new mind. Wherefore, it seems to me, that repentance may be not inappropriately defined thus: A real conversion of our life unto God, proceeding from sincere and serious fear of God; and consisting in the mortification of our flesh and the old man, and the quickening of the Spirit. In this sense are to be understood all those addresses in which the prophets first, and the apostles afterwards, exhorted the people of their time to repentance. The great object for which they labored was, to fill them with confusion for their sins and dread of the divine judgment, that they might fall down and humble themselves before him whom they had offended, and, with true repentance, retake themselves to the right path. Accordingly, they use indiscriminately in the same sense, the expressions turning, or returning to the Lord; repenting, doing repentance. Whence, also, the sacred history describes it as repentance towards God, when men who disregarded him and wantoned in their lusts begin to obey his word, and are prepared to go whithersoever he may call them. And John the Baptist and Paul, under the expression, bringing forth fruits meet for repentance, described a course of life exhibiting and bearing testimony, in all its actions, to such a repentance.

6. But before proceeding farther, it will be proper to give a clearer exposition of the definition which we have adopted. There are three things, then, principally to be considered in it. First, in the conversion of the life to God, we require a transformation not only in external works, but in the soul itself, which is able only after it has put off its old habits to bring forth fruits conformable to its renovation. The prophet, intending to express this, enjoins those whom he calls to repentance to make them "a new heart and a new spirit" (Ezek. 18:31). Hence Moses, on several occasions, when he would show how the Israelites were to repent and turn to the Lord, tells them that it

must be done with the whole heart, and the whole soul (a mode of expression of frequent recurrence in the prophets), and by terming it the circumcision of the heart, points to the internal affections. But there is no passage better fitted to teach us the genuine nature of repentance than the following: "If thou wilt return, O Israel, saith the Lord, return unto me." "Break up your fallow ground, and sow not among thorns. Circumcise yourselves to the Lord, and take away the foreskins of your heart" (Jer. 4:1-4). See how he declares to them that it will be of no avail to commence the study of righteousness unless impiety shall first have been eradicated from their inmost heart. And to malice the deeper impression, he reminds them that they have to do with God, and can gain nothing by deceit, because he hates a double heart. For this reason Isaiah derides the preposterous attempts of hypocrites, who zealously aimed at an external repentance by the observance of ceremonies, but in the meanwhile cared not "to loose the bands of wickedness, to undo the heavy burdens, and to let the oppressed go free" (Isa. 58:6). In these words he admirably shows wherein the acts of unfeigned repentance consist.

7. The second part of our definition is, that repentance proceeds from a sincere fear of God. Before the mind of the sinner can be inclined to repentance, he must be aroused by the thought of divine judgment; but when once the thought that God will one day ascend his tribunal to take an account of all words and actions has taken possession of his mind, it will not allow him to rest, or have one moment's peace, but will perpetually urge him to adopt a different plan of life, that he may be able to stand securely at that judgment seat. Hence the Scripture, when exhorting to repentance, often introduces the subject of judgment, as in Jeremiah, "Lest my fury come forth like fire, and burn that none can quench it, because of the evil of your doings" (Jer. 4:4). Paul, in his discourse to the Athenians says, "The times of this ignorance God winked at; but now commandeth all men everywhere to repent: because he has appointed a day in the which he will judge

the world in righteousness" (Acts 17:30-31). The same thing is repeated in several other passages. Sometimes God is declared to be a judge, from the punishments already inflicted, thus leading sinners to reflect that worse awaits them if they do not quickly repent. There is an example of this in the 29th chapter of Deuteronomy. As repentance begins with dread and hatred of sin, the Apostle sets down godly sorrow as one of its causes (2 Cor. 7:10). By godly sorrow he means when we not only tremble at the punishment, but hate and abhor the sin, because we know it is displeasing to God. It is not strange that this should be, for unless we are stung to the quick, the sluggishness of our carnal nature cannot be corrected; nay, no degree of pungency would suffice for our stupor and sloth, did not God lift the rod and strike deeper. There is, moreover, a rebellious spirit which must be broken as with hammers. The stern threatening which God employs are extorted from him by our depraved dispositions. For while we are asleep it were in vain to allure us by soothing measures. Passages to this effect are everywhere to be met with, and I need not quote them. But there is another reason why the fear of God lies at the root of repentance—viz. that though the life of man were possessed of all kinds of virtue, still if they do not bear reference to God, how much soever they may be lauded in the world, they are mere abomination in heaven, inasmuch as it is the principal part of righteousness to render to God that service and honor of which he is impiously defrauded, whenever it is not our express purpose to submit to his authority.

8. We must now explain the third part of the definition, and show what is meant when we say that repentance consists of two parts—viz. the mortification of the flesh, and the quickening of the Spirit. The prophets, in accommodation to a carnal people, express this in simple and homely terms, but clearly, when they say, "Depart from evil, and do good" (Ps. 34:14). "Wash you, make you clean, put away the evil of your doings from before mine eyes; cease to do evil; learn to do well; seek judgment; relieve the oppressed," &c. (Isa. 1:16-17).

In dissuading us from wickedness they demand the entire destruction of the flesh, which is full of perverseness and malice. It is a most difficult and arduous achievement to renounce ourselves, and lay aside our natural disposition. For the flesh must not be thought to be destroyed unless everything that we have of our own is abolished. But seeing that all the desires of the flesh are enmity against God (Rom. 8:7), the first step to the obedience of his law is the renouncement of our own nature. Renovation is afterwards manifested by the fruits produced by it—viz. justice, judgment, and mercy. Since it were not sufficient duly to perform such acts, were not the mind and heart previously endued with sentiments of justice, judgment, and mercy this is done when the Holy Spirit, instilling his holiness into our souls, so inspired them with new thoughts and affections, that they may justly be regarded as new. And, indeed, as we are naturally averse to God, unless self-denial precede, we shall never tend to that which is right. Hence we are so often enjoined to put off the old man, to renounce the world and the flesh, to forsake our lusts, and be renewed in the spirit of our mind. Moreover, the very name mortification reminds us how difficult it is to forget our former nature, because we hence infer that we cannot be trained to the fear of God, and learn the first principles of piety, unless we are violently smitten with the sword of the Spirit and annihilated, as if God were declaring, that to be ranked among his sons there must be a destruction of our ordinary nature.

9. Both of these we obtain by union with Christ. For if we have true fellowship in his death, our old man is crucified by his power, and the body of sin becomes dead, so that the corruption of our original nature is never again in full vigor (Rom. 6:5-6). If we are partakers in his resurrection, we are raised up by means of it to newness of life, which conforms us to the righteousness of God. In one word, then, by repentance I understand regeneration, the only aim of which is to form in us anew the image of God, which was sullied, and all but effaced by the transgression of Adam. So the Apostle teaches when

he says, "We all with open face beholding as in a glass the glory of the Lord, are changed into the same image from glory to glory, as by the Spirit of the Lord." Again, "Be renewed in the spirit of your minds" and "put ye on the new man, which after God is created in righteousness and true holiness." Again, "Put ye on the new man, which is renewed in knowledge after the image of him that created him." Accordingly through the blessing of Christ we are renewed by that regeneration into the righteousness of God from which we had fallen through Adam, the Lord being pleased in this manner to restore the integrity of all whom he appoints to the inheritance of life. This renewal, indeed, is not accomplished in a moment, a day, or a year, but by uninterrupted, sometimes even by slow progress God abolishes the remains of carnal corruption in his elect, cleanses them from pollution, and consecrates them as his temples, restoring all their inclinations to real purity, so that during their whole lives they may practice repentance, and know that death is the only termination to this warfare. The greater is the effrontery of an impure raver and apostate, named Staphylus, who pretends that I confound the condition of the present life with the celestial glory, when, after Paul, I make the image of God to consist in righteousness and true holiness; as if in every definition it were not necessary to take the thing defined in its integrity and perfection. It is not denied that there is room for improvement; but what I maintain is, that the nearer anyone approaches in resemblance to God, the more does the image of God appear in him. That believers may attain to it, God assigns repentance as the goal towards which they must keep running during the whole course of their lives.

10. By regeneration the children of God are delivered from the bondage of sin, but not as if they had already obtained full possession of freedom, and no longer felt any annoyance from the flesh. Materials for an unremitting contest remain, that they may be exercised, and not only exercised, but may better understand their weakness. All

writers of sound judgment agree in this, that, in the regenerate man, there is still a spring of evil which is perpetually sending forth desires that allure and stimulate him to sin. They also acknowledge that the saints are still so liable to the disease of concupiscence, that, though opposing it, they cannot avoid being ever and anon prompted and incited to lust, avarice, ambition, or other vices. It is unnecessary to spend much time in investigating the sentiments of ancient writers. Augustine alone may suffice, as he has collected all their opinions with great care and fidelity. Any reader who is desirous to know the sense of antiquity may obtain it from him. There is this difference apparently between him and us, that while he admits that believers, so long as they are in the body, are so liable to concupiscence that they cannot but feel it, he does not venture to give this disease the name of sin. He is contented with giving it the name of infirmity, and says, that it only becomes sin when either external act or consent is added to conception or apprehension; that is, when the will yields to the first desire. We again regard it as sin whenever man is influenced in any degree by any desire contrary to the law of God; nay, we maintain that the very gravity which begets in us such desires is sin. Accordingly, we hold that there is always sin in the saints until they are freed from their mortal frame, because depraved concupiscence resides in their flesh, and is at variance with rectitude. Augustine himself does not always refrain from using the name of sin, as when he says, "Paul gives the name of sin to that carnal concupiscence from which all sins arise. This in regard to the saints loses its dominion in this world, and is destroyed in heaven." In these words he admits that believers, insofar as they are liable to carnal concupiscence, are chargeable with sin.

11. When it is said that God purifies his Church, so as to be "holy and without blemish" (Eph. 5:26-27), that he promises this cleansing by means of baptism, and performs it in his elect, I understand that reference is made to the guilt rather than to the matter of sin. In regenerating his people God indeed accomplishes this much for

them; he destroys the dominion of sin, by supplying the agency of the Spirit, which enables them to come off victorious from the contest. Sin, however, though it ceases to reign, ceases not to dwell in them. Accordingly, though we say that the old man is crucified, and the law of sin is abolished in the children of God (Rom. 6:6), the remains of sin survive, not to have dominion, but to humble them under a consciousness of their infirmity. We admit that these remains, just as if they had no existence, are not imputed, but we, at the same time, contend that it is owing to the mercy of God that the saints are not charged with the guilt which would otherwise make them sinners before God. It will not be difficult for us to confirm this view, seeing we can support it by clear passages of Scripture. How can we express our view more plainly than Paul does in Romans 7:6? We have else-where shown and Augustine by solid reasons proves, that Paul is there speaking in the person of a regenerated man. I say nothing as to his use of the words evil and sin. However those who object to our view may quibble on these words, can any man deny that aversion to the law of God is an evil, and that hindrance to righteousness is sin? In short, who will not admit that there is guilt where there is spiritual misery? But all these things Paul affirms of this disease. Again, the law furnishes us with a clear demonstration by which the whole ques-tion may be quickly disposed of. We are enjoined to love God with all our heart, with all our soul, with all our strength. Since all the fac-ulties of our soul ought thus to be engrossed with the love of God, it is certain that the commandment is not fulfilled by those who receive the smallest desire into their heart, or admit into their minds any thought whatever which may lead them away from the love of God to vanity. What then? Is it not through the faculties of mind that we are assailed with sudden motions, that we perceive sensual, or form conceptions of mental objects? Since these faculties give admission to vain and wicked thoughts, do they not show that to that extent they are devoid of the love of God? He, then, who admits not that all the desires of the flesh are sins, and that that disease of concupiscence, which they call a stimulus, is a fountain of sin, must of necessity deny that the transgression of the law is sin.

12. If any one thinks it absurd thus to condemn all the desires by which man is naturally affected, seeing they have been implanted by God the author of nature, we answer, that we by no means condemn those appetites which God so implanted in the mind of man at his first creation, that they cannot be eradicated without destroying human nature itself, but only the violent lawless movements which war with the order of God. But as, in consequence of the corruption of nature, all our faculties are so vitiated and corrupted, that a perpetual disorder and excess is apparent in all our actions, and as the appetites cannot be separated from this excess, we maintain that therefore they are vicious; or, to give the substance in fewer words, we hold that all human desires are evil, and we charge them with sin not in as far as they are natural, but because they are inordinate, and inordinate because nothing pure and upright can proceed from a corrupt and polluted nature. Nor does Augustine depart from this doctrine in reality so much as in appearance. From an excessive dread of the invidious charge with which the Pelagians assailed him, he sometimes refrains from using the term sin in this sense; but when he says (*ad Bonif.*). that the law of sin remaining in the saints, the guilt only is taken away, he shows clearly enough that his view is not very different from ours.

13. We will produce some other passages to make it more apparent what his sentiments were. In his second book against Julian, he says, "This law of sin is both remitted in spiritual regeneration and remains in the mortal flesh; remitted, because the guilt is forgiven in the sacrament by which believers are regenerated, and yet remains, inasmuch as it produces desires against which believers fight." Again, "Therefore the law of sin (which was in the members of this great Apostle also) is forgiven in baptism, not ended." Again, "The law of sin, the guilt of which, though remaining, is forgiven in baptism, Ambrose called

iniquity, for it is iniquitous for the flesh to lust against the Spirit." Again, "Sin is dead in the guilt by which it bound us; and until it is cured by the perfection of burial, though dead it rebels." In the fifth book he says still more plainly, "As blindness of heart is the sin by which God is not believed; and the punishment of sin, by which a proud heart is justly punished; and the cause of sin, when through the error of a blinded heart any evil is committed: so the lust of the flesh, against which the good Spirit wars, is also sin, because disobedient to the authority of the mind; and the punishment of sin, because the recompense rendered for disobedience; and the cause of sin, consenting by revolt or springing up through contamination." He here without ambiguity calls it sin, because the Pelagian heresy being now refuted, and the sound doctrine confirmed, he was less afraid of calumny. Thus, also, in his forty-first Homily on John, where he speaks his own sentiments without controversy, he says, "If with the flesh you serve the law of sin, do what the Apostle himself says, 'Let not sin, therefore, reign in your mortal body, that ye should obey it in the lusts thereof,' (Rom. 6:12). He does not say, 'Let it not be,' but 'Let it not reign.' As long as you live there must be sin in your members; but at least let its dominion be destroyed; do not what it orders." Those who maintain that concupiscence is not sin, are wont to found on the passage of James, "Then, when lust has conceived, it bringeth forth sin" (James 1:15). But this is easily refuted: for unless we understand him as speaking only of wicked works or actual sins, even a wicked inclination will not be accounted sin. But from his calling crimes and wicked deeds the fruits of lust, and also giving them the name of sins, it does not follow that the lust itself is not an evil, and in the sight of God deserving of condemnation.

14. Some Anabaptists in the present age mistake some indescribable sort of frenzied excess for the regeneration of the Spirit, holding that the children of God are restored to a state of innocence, and, therefore, need give themselves no anxiety about curbing the

lust of the flesh; that they have the Spirit for their guide, and under
his agency never err. It would be incredible that the human mind
could proceed to such insanity, did they not openly and exultingly
give utterance to their dogma. It is indeed monstrous, and yet it is
just, that those who have resolved to turn the word of God into a lie,
should thus be punished for their blasphemous audacity. Is it indeed
true, that all distinction between base and honorable, just and unjust,
good and evil, virtue and vice, is abolished? The distinction, they say,
is from the curse of the old Adam, and from this we are exempted
by Christ. There will be no difference, then, between whoredom and
chastity, sincerity and craft, truth and falsehood, justice and robbery.
Away with vain fear! (they say), the Spirit will not bid you do any
thing that is wrong, provided you sincerely and boldly leave yourself to his agency. Who is not amazed at such monstrous doctrines?
And yet this philosophy is popular with those who, blinded by insane lusts, have thrown off common sense. But what kind of Christ,
pray, do they fabricate? what kind of Spirit do they belch forth? We
acknowledge one Christ, and his one Spirit, whom the prophets foretold and the Gospel proclaims as actually manifested, but we hear
nothing of this kind respecting him. That Spirit is not the patron of
murder, adultery, drunkenness, pride, contention, avarice, and fraud,
but the author of love, chastity, sobriety, modesty, peace, moderation,
and truth. He is not a Spirit of giddiness, rushing rashly and precip-
itately, without regard to right and wrong, but full of wisdom and
understanding, by which he can duly distinguish between justice and
injustice. He instigates not to lawless and unrestrained licentiousness,
but, discriminating between lawful and unlawful, teaches temperance
and moderation. But why dwell longer in refuting that brutish frenzy? To Christians the Spirit of the Lord is not a turbulent phantom,
which they themselves have produced by dreaming, or received ready-
made by others; but they religiously seek the knowledge of him from
Scripture, where two things are taught concerning him; first, that he

is given to us for sanctification, that he may purge us from all iniquity and defilement, and bring us to the obedience of divine righteousness, an obedience which cannot exist unless the lusts to which these men would give loose reins are tamed and subdued; secondly that though purged by his sanctification, we are still beset by many vices and much weakness, so long as we are enclosed in the prison of the body. Thus it is, that placed at a great distance from perfection, we must always be endeavoring to make some progress, and daily struggling with the evil by which we are entangled. Hence, too, it follows, that, shaking off sloth and security, we must be intently vigilant, so as not to be taken unawares in the snares of our flesh; unless, indeed, we presume to think that we have made greater progress than the Apostle, who was buffeted by a messenger of Satan, in order that his strength might be perfected in weakness, and who gives in his own person a true, not a fictitious representation, of the strife between the Spirit and the flesh (2 Cor. 12:7, 9; Rom. 7:6).

15. The Apostle, in his description of repentance (2 Cor. 7:2), enumerates seven causes, effects, or parts belonging to it, and that on the best grounds. These are carefulness, excuse, indignation, fear, desire, zeal, revenge. It should not excite surprise that I venture not to determine whether they ought to be regarded as causes or effects: both views may be maintained. They may also be called affections conjoined with repentance; but as Paul's meaning may be ascertained without entering into any of these questions, we shall be contented with a simple exposition. He says then that godly sorrow produces carefulness. He who is really dissatisfied with himself for sinning against his God, is, at the same time, stimulated to care and attention, that he may completely disentangle himself from the chains of the devil, and keep a better guard against his snares, so as not afterwards to lose the guidance of the Holy Spirit, or be overcome by security. Next comes excuse, which in this place means not defense, in which the sinner to escape the judgment of God either denies his fault or extenuates it, but apologizing,

which trusts more to intercession than to the goodness of the cause; just as children not altogether abandoned, while they acknowledge and confess their errors, yet employ deprecation; and to make room for it, testify, by every means in their power, that they have by no means cast off the reverence which they owe to their parents; in short, endeavor by excuse not to prove themselves righteous and innocent, but only to obtain pardon. Next follows indignation, under which the sinner inwardly murmurs, expostulates, and is offended with himself on recognizing his perverseness and ingratitude to God. By the term "fear" is meant that trepidation which takes possession of our minds whenever we consider both what we have deserved, and the fearful severity of the divine anger against sinners. Accordingly, the exceeding disquietude which we must necessarily feel, both trains us to humility and makes us more cautious for the future. But if the carefulness or anxiety which he first mentioned is the result of fear, the connection between the two becomes obvious. Desire seems to me to be used as equivalent to diligence in duty, and alacrity in doing service, to which the sense of our misdeeds ought to be a powerful stimulus. To this also pertains zeal, which immediately follows; for it signifies the ardor with which we are inflamed when such goads as these are applied to us. "What have I done? Into what abyss had I fallen had not the mercy of God prevented?" The last of all is revenge, for the stricter we are with ourselves, and the severer the censure we pass upon our sins, the more ground we have to hope for the divine favor and mercy. And certainly when the soul is overwhelmed with a dread of divine judgment, it cannot but act the part of an avenger in inflicting punishment upon itself. Pious men, doubtless, feel that there is punishment in the shame, confusion, groans, self-displeasure, and other feelings produced by a serious review of their sins. Let us remember, however, that moderation must be used, so that we may not be overwhelmed with sadness, there being nothing to which trembling consciences are more prone than to rush into despair. This, too, is one of Satan's artifices. Those whom he sees thus overwhelmed with fear he plunges deeper and deeper into the abyss of sorrow, that they may never again rise. It is true that the fear which ends in humility without relinquishing the hope of pardon cannot be in excess. And yet we must always beware, according to the apostolic injunction, of giving way to extreme dread, as this tends to make us shun God while he is calling us to himself by repentance. Wherefore, the advice of Bernard is good, "Grief for sins is necessary, but must not be perpetual. My advice is to turn back at times from sorrow and the anxious remembrance of your ways, and escape to the plain, to a calm review of the divine mercies. Let us mingle honey with wormwood, that the salubrious bitter may give health when we drink it tempered with a mixture of sweetness: while you think humbly of yourselves, think also of the goodness of the Lord" (Bernard *in Cant.* Serm. 11).

16. We can now understand what are the fruits of repentance—viz. offices of piety towards God, and love towards men, general holiness and purity of life. In short, the more a man studies to conform his life to the standard of the divine law, the surer signs he gives of his repentance. Accordingly, the Spirit, in exhorting us to repentance, brings before us at one time each separate precept of the law; at another the duties of the second table; although there are also passages in which, after condemning impurity in its fountain in the heart, he afterwards descends to external marks, by which repentance is proved to be sincere. A portraiture of this I will shortly set before the eye of the reader when I come to describe the Christian life (infra, chapter 6). I will not here collect the passages from the prophets in which they deride the frivolous observances of those who labor to appease God with ceremonies, and show that they are mere mockery; or those in which they show that outward integrity of conduct is not the chief part of repentance, seeing that God looks at the heart. Anyone moderately versant in Scripture will understand by himself, without being reminded by others, that when he has to do with God, nothing is gained without beginning with the internal affections of the heart. There is a passage

of Joel which will avail not a little for the understanding of others: "Rend your heart, and not your garments" (Joel 2:13). Both are also briefly expressed by James in these words: "Cleanse your hands, ye sinners; and purify your hearts, ye double-minded" (James 4:8). Here, indeed, the accessory is set down first; but the source and principle is afterwards pointed out—viz. that hidden defilements must be wiped away, and an altar erected to God in the very heart. There are, moreover, certain external exercises which we employ in private as remedies to humble us and tame our flesh, and in public, to testify our repentance. These have their origin in that revenge of which Paul speaks (2 Cor. 7:2), for when the mind is distressed, it naturally expresses itself in sackcloth, groans, and tears, shuns ornament and every kind of show, and abandons all delights. Then he who feels how great an evil the rebellion of the flesh is, tries every means of curbing it. Besides, he who considers aright how grievous a thing it is to have offended the justice of God, cannot rest until, in his humility, he has given glory to God. Such exercises are often mentioned by ancient writers when they speak of the fruits of repentance. But although they by no means place the power of repentance in them, yet my readers must pardon me for saying what I think—they certainly seem to insist on them more than is right. Anyone who judiciously considers the matter will, I trust, agree with me that they have exceeded in two ways; first, by so strongly urging and extravagantly commending that corporal discipline, they indeed succeeded in making the people embrace it with greater zeal; but they in a manner obscured what they should have regarded as of much more serious moment. Secondly, the inflictions which they enjoined were considerably more rigorous than ecclesiastical mildness demands, as will be elsewhere shown.

17. But as there are some who, from the frequent mention of sackcloth, fasting, and tears, especially in Joel (2:12), think that these constitute the principal part of repentance, we must dispel their delusion. In that passage the proper part of repentance is described by the

words, "turn ye even to me with your whole heart;" "rend your heart, and not your garments." The "fastings," "weeping," and "mourning," are introduced not as invariable or necessary effects, but as special circumstances. Having foretold that most grievous disasters were impending over the Jews, he exhorts them to turn away the divine anger not only by repenting, but by giving public signs of sorrow. For as a criminal, to excite the commiseration of the judge, appears in a supplicating posture, with a long beard, uncombed hair, and coarse clothing, so should those who are charged at the judgment seat of God deprecate his severity in a garb of wretchedness. But although sackcloth and ashes were perhaps more conformable to the customs of these times, yet it is plain that weeping and fasting are very appropriate in our case whenever the Lord threatens us with any defeat or calamity. In presenting the appearance of danger, he declares that he is preparing, and, in a manner, arming himself for vengeance. Rightly, therefore, does the Prophet exhort those, on whose crimes he had said a little before that vengeance was to be executed, to weeping and fasting—that is, to the mourning habit of criminals. Nor in the present day do ecclesiastical teachers act improperly when, seeing ruin hanging over the necks of their people, they call aloud on them to hasten with weeping and fasting: only they must always urge, with greater care and earnestness, "rend your hearts, and not your garments." It is beyond doubt that fasting is not always a concomitant of repentance, but is specially destined for seasons of calamity. Hence our Savior connects it with mourning (Matt. 9:15), and relieves the Apostles of the necessity of it until, by being deprived of his presence, they were filled with sorrow. I speak of formal fasting. For the life of Christians ought ever to be tempered with frugality and sobriety, so that the whole course of it should present some appearance of fasting. As this subject will be fully discussed when the discipline of the Church comes to be considered, I now dwell less upon it.

18. This much, however, I will add: when the name repentance is applied to the external profession, it is used improperly, and not in the genuine meaning as I have explained it. For that is not so much a turning unto God as the confession of a fault accompanied with deprecation of the sentence and punishment. Thus to repent in sackcloth and ashes (Matt. 11:21; Luke 10:13), is just to testify self-dissatisfaction when God is angry with us for having grievously offended him. It is, indeed, a kind of public confession by which, condemning ourselves before angels and the world, we prevent the judgment of God. For Paul, rebuking the sluggishness of those who indulge in their sins, says, "If we would judge ourselves, we should not be judged" (1 Cor. 11:31). It is not always necessary, however, openly to inform others, and make them the witnesses of our repentance; but to confess privately to God is a part of true repentance which cannot be omitted. Nothing were more incongruous than that God should pardon the sins in which we are flattering ourselves, and hypocritically cloaking that he may not bring them to light. We must not only confess the sins which we daily commit, but more grievous lapses ought to carry us farther, and bring to our remembrance things which seemed to have been long ago buried. Of this David sets an example before us in his own person (Ps. 51). Filled with shame for a recent crime he examines himself, going back to the womb, and acknowledging that even then he was corrupted and defiled. This he does not to extenuate his fault, as many hide themselves in the crowd, and catch at impunity by involving others along with them. Very differently does David, who ingenuously makes it an aggravation of his sin, that being corrupted from his earliest infancy he ceased not to add iniquity to iniquity. In another passage, also, he takes a survey of his past life, and implores God to pardon the errors of his youth (Ps. 25:7). And, indeed, we shall not prove that we have thoroughly shaken off our stupor until, groaning under the burden, and lamenting our sad condition, we seek relief from God. It is, moreover, to be observed, that the repentance which we are enjoined

assiduously to cultivate, differs from that which raises, as it were, from death those who had fallen more shamefully, or given themselves up to sin without restraint, or by some kind of open revolt, had thrown off the authority of God. For Scripture, in exhorting to repentance, often speaks of it as a passage from death unto life, and when relating that a people had repented, means that they had abandoned idolatry, and other forms of gross wickedness. For which reason Paul denounces woe to sinners, "who have not repented of the uncleanness, and fornication, and lasciviousness which they have committed" (2 Cor. 12:21). This distinction ought to be carefully observed, lest when we hear of a few individuals having been summoned to repent we indulge in supine security, as if we had nothing to do with the mortification of the flesh; whereas, in consequence of the depraved desires which are always enticing us, and the iniquities which are ever and anon springing from them, it must engage our unremitting care. The special repentance enjoined upon those whom the devil has entangled in deadly snares, and withdrawn from the fear of God, does not abolish that ordinary repentance which the corruption of nature obliges us to cultivate during the whole course of our lives.

19. Moreover if it is true, and nothing can be more certain, than that a complete summary of the Gospel is included under these two heads—viz. repentance and the remission of sins, do we not see that the Lord justifies his people freely, and at the same time renews them to true holiness by the sanctification of his Spirit? John, the messenger sent before the face of Christ to prepare his ways, proclaimed, "repent, for the kingdom of heaven is at hand" (Matt. 11:10; 3:2). By inviting them to repentance, he urged them to acknowledge that they were sinners, and in all respects condemned before God, that thus they might be induced earnestly to seek the mortification of the flesh, and a new birth in the Spirit. By announcing the kingdom of God he called for faith, since by the kingdom of God which he declared to be at hand, he meant forgiveness of sins, salvation, life, and every

other blessing which we obtain in Christ; wherefore we read in the other Evangelists, "John did baptize in the wilderness, and preach the baptism of repentance for the remission of sins" (Mark 1:4; Luke 3:3). What does this mean, but that, weary and oppressed with the burden of sin, they should turn to the Lord, and entertain hopes of forgiveness and salvation? Thus, too, Christ began his preaching, "The kingdom of God is at hand: repent ye, and believe the Gospel" (Mark 1:10). First, he declares that the treasures of the divine mercy were opened in him; next, he enjoins repentance; and, lastly, he encourages confidence in the promises of God. Accordingly, when intending to give a brief summary of the whole Gospel, he said that he behaved "to suffer, and to rise from the dead the third day, and that repentance and remission of sins should be preached in his name among all nations" (Luke 24:26, 46). In like manner, after his resurrection the Apostles preached, "Him has God exalted with his right hand, to be a Prince and a Savior, for to give repentance to Israel and forgiveness of sins" (Acts 5:31). Repentance is preached in the name of Christ, when men learn, through the doctrines of the Gospel, that all their thoughts, affections, and pursuits, are corrupt and vicious; and that, therefore, if they would enter the kingdom of God they must be born again. Forgiveness of sins is preached when men are taught that Christ "is made unto us wisdom, and righteousness, and sanctification, and redemption" (1 Cor. 1:30), that on his account they are freely deemed righteous and innocent in the sight of God. Though both graces are obtained by faith (as has been shown elsewhere), yet as the goodness of God, by which sins are forgiven, is the proper object of faith, it was proper to carefully distinguish it from repentance.

20. Moreover, as hatred of sin, which is the beginning of repentance, first gives us access to the knowledge of Christ, who manifests himself to none but miserable and afflicted sinners, groaning, laboring, burdened, hungry, and thirsty, pining away with grief and wretchedness, so if we would stand in Christ, we must aim at repentance,

cultivate it during our whole lives, and continue it to the last. Christ came to call sinners, but to call them to repentance. He was sent to bless the unworthy, but by "turning away every one" "from his iniquities." The Scripture is full of similar passages. Hence, when God offers forgiveness of sins, he in return usually stipulates for repentance, intimating that his mercy should induce men to repent. "Keep ye judgment," saith he, "and do justice: for my salvation is near to come." Again, "The Redeemer shall come to Zion, and unto them that turn from transgression in Jacob." Again, "Seek ye the Lord while he may be found, call ye upon him while he is near. Let the wicked forsake his way, and the unrighteous man his thoughts, and let him return unto the Lord, and he will have mercy upon him." "Repent ye, therefore, and be converted, that your sins may be blotted out." Here, however, it is to be observed, that repentance is not made a condition in such a sense as to be a foundation for meriting pardon; nay, it rather indicates the end at which they must aim if they would obtain favor, God having resolved to take pity on men for the express purpose of leading them to repent. Therefore, so long as we dwell in the prison of the body, we must constantly struggle with the vices of our corrupt nature, and so with our natural disposition. Plato sometimes says, that the life of the philosopher is to meditate on death. More truly may we say, that the life of a Christian man is constant study and exercise in mortifying the flesh, until it is certainly slain, and the Spirit of God obtains dominion in us. Wherefore, he seems to me to have made most progress who has learned to be most dissatisfied with himself. He does not, however, remain in the miry clay without going forward; but rather hastens and sighs after God, that, ingrafted both into the death and the life of Christ, he may constantly meditate on repentance. Unquestionably those who have a genuine hatred of sin cannot do otherwise: for no man ever hated sin without being previously enamored of righteousness. This view, as it is the simplest of all, seemed to me also to accord best with Scripture truth.

21. Moreover, that repentance is a special gift of God, I trust is too well understood from the above doctrine to require any lengthened discourse. Hence the Church extols the goodness of God, and looks on in wonder, saying, "Then has God also to the Gentiles granted repentance unto life" (Acts 11:18); and Paul enjoining Timothy to deal meekly and patiently with unbelievers, says, "If God per adventure will give them repentance to the acknowledging of the truth, and that they may recover themselves out of the snare of the devil" (2 Tim. 2:25-26). God indeed declares, that he would have all men to repent, and addresses exhortations in common to all; their efficacy, however, depends on the Spirit of regeneration. It were easier to create us at first, than for us by our own strength to acquire a more excellent nature. Wherefore, in regard to the whole process of regeneration, it is not without cause we are called God's "workmanship, created in Christ Jesus unto good works, which God has before ordained that we should walk in them" (Eph. 2:10). Those whom God is pleased to rescue from death, he quickens by the Spirit of regeneration; not that repentance is properly the cause of salvation, but because, as already seen, it is inseparable from the faith and mercy of God; for, as Isaiah declares, "The Redeemer shall come to Zion, and unto them that turn from transgression in Jacob." This, indeed, is a standing truth, that wherever the fear of God is in vigor, the Spirit has been carrying on his saving work. Hence, in Isaiah, while believers complain and lament that they have been forsaken of God, they set down the supernatural hardening of the heart as a sign of reprobation. The Apostle, also, intending to exclude apostates from the hope of salvation, states, as the reason, that it is impossible to renew them to repentance (Heb. 6:6); that is, God by renewing those whom he wills not to perish, gives them a sign of paternal favor, and in a manner attracts them to himself, by the beams of a calm and reconciled countenance; on the other hand, by hardening the reprobate, whose impiety is not to be forgiven, he thunders against them. This kind of vengeance the

Apostle denounces against voluntary apostates (Heb. 10:29), who, in falling away from the faith of the gospel, mock God, insultingly reject his favor, profane and trample under foot the blood of Christ, nay, as far as in them lies, crucify him afresh. Still, he does not, as some austere persons preposterously insist, leave no hope of pardon to voluntary sins, but shows that apostasy being altogether without excuse, it is not strange that God is inexorably rigorous in punishing sacrilegious contempt thus shown to himself. For, in the same Epistle, he says, that "it is impossible for those who were once enlightened, and have tasted of the heavenly gift, and were made partakers of the Holy Ghost, and have tasted the good word of God, and the powers of the world to come, if they shall fall away to renew them again to repentance, seeing they crucify the Son of God afresh, and put him to an open shame" (Heb. 7:4-6). And in another passage, "If we sin willingly, after that we have received the knowledge of the truth, there remaineth no more sacrifice for sins, but a certain fearful looking for of judgment," &c. (Heb. 11:25-26). There are other passages, from a misinterpretation of which the Novatians of old extracted materials for their heresy; so much so, that some good men taking offense at their harshness, have deemed the Epistle altogether spurious, though it truly savors in every part of it of the apostolic spirit. But as our dispute is only with those who receive the Epistle, it is easy to show that those passages give no support to their error. First, the Apostle must of necessity agree with his Master, who declares, that "all manner of sin and blasphemy shall be forgiven unto men, but the blasphemy against the Holy Ghost shall not be forgiven unto men," "neither in this world, neither in the world to come" (Matt. 12:31; Luke 12:10). We must hold that this was the only exception which the Apostle recognized, unless we would set him in opposition to the grace of God. Hence it follows, that to no sin is pardon denied save to one, which proceeding from desperate fury cannot be ascribed to infirmity, and plainly shows that the man guilty of it is possessed by the devil.

22. Here, however, it is proper to consider what the dreadful iniquity is which is not to be pardoned. The definition which Augustine somewhere gives—viz. that it is obstinate perverseness, with distrust of pardon, continued till death—scarcely agrees with the words of Christ, that it shall not be forgiven in this world. For either this is said in vain, or it may be committed in this world. But if Augustine's definition is correct, the sin is not committed unless persisted in till death. Others say, that the sin against the Holy Spirit consists in envying the grace conferred upon a brother; but I know not on what it is founded. Here, however, let us give the true definition, which, when once it is established by sound evidence, will easily of itself overturn all the others. I say therefore that he sins against the Holy Spirit who, while so constrained by the power of divine truth that he cannot plead ignorance, yet deliberately resists, and that merely for the sake of resisting. For Christ, in explanation of what he had said, immediately adds, "Whosoever speaketh a word against the Son of man, it shall be forgiven him; but whosoever speaketh against the Holy Ghost, it shall not be forgiven him" (Matt. 12:31). And Matthew uses the term "spirit of blasphemy" for blasphemy against the Spirit. How can anyone insult the Son, without at the same time attacking the Spirit? In this way. Those who in ignorance assail the unknown truth of God, and yet are so disposed that they would be unwilling to extinguish the truth of God when manifested to them, or utter one word against him whom they knew to be the Lord's Anointed, sin against the Father and the Son. Thus there are many in the present day who have the greatest abhorrence to the doctrine of the Gospel, and yet, if they knew it to be the doctrine of the Gospel, would be prepared to venerate it with their whole heart. But those who are convinced in conscience that what they repudiate and impugn is the word of God, and yet cease not to impugn it, are said to blaspheme against the Spirit, inasmuch as they struggle against the illumination which is the work of the Spirit. Such were some of the Jews, who, when they could

not resist the Spirit speaking by Stephen, yet were bent on resisting (Acts 6:10). There can be no doubt that many of them were carried away by zeal for the law; but it appears that there were others who maliciously and impiously raged against God himself, that is, against the doctrine which they knew to be of God. Such, too, were the Pharisees, on whom our Lord denounced woe. To depreciate the power of the Holy Spirit, they defamed him by the name of Beelzebub (Matt. 9:3-4; 12:24). The spirit of blasphemy, therefore, is, when a man audaciously, and of set purpose, rushes forth to insult his divine name. This Paul intimates when he says, "but I obtained mercy, because I did it ignorantly in unbelief;" otherwise he had deservedly been held unworthy of the grace of God. If ignorance joined with unbelief made him obtain pardon, it follows, that there is no room for pardon when knowledge is added to unbelief.

23. If you attend properly, you will perceive that the Apostle speaks not of one particular lapse or two, but of the universal revolt by which the reprobate renounce salvation. It is not strange that God should be implacable to those whom John, in his Epistle, declares not to have been of the elect, from whom they went out (1 John 2:19). For he is directing his discourse against those who imagined that they could return to the Christian religion though they had once revolted from it. To divest them of this false and pernicious opinion, he says, as is most true, that those who had once knowingly and willingly cast off fellowship with Christ, had no means of returning to it. It is not, however, so cast off by those who merely, by the dissoluteness of their lives, transgress the word of the Lord, but by those who avowedly reject his whole doctrine. There is a paralogism in the expressions "casting off" and "sinning." Casting off, as interpreted by the Novatians, is when anyone, notwithstanding of being taught by the Law of the Lord not to steal or commit adultery, refrains not from theft or adultery. On the contrary, I hold that there is a tacit antithesis, in which all the things, contrary to those which had been said, must be

held to be repeated, so that the thing expressed is not some particular vice, but universal aversion to God, and (so to speak) the apostasy of the whole man. Therefore, when he speaks of those falling away "who were once enlightened, and have tasted of the heavenly gift, and were made partakers of the Holy Ghost, and have tasted of the good word of God, and the powers of the world to come," we must understand him as referring to those who, with deliberate impiety, have quenched the light of the Spirit, tasted of the heavenly word and spurned it, alienated themselves from the sanctification of the Spirit, and trampled under foot the word of God and the powers of the world to come. The better to show that this was the species of impiety intended, he afterwards expressly adds the term "willfully." For when he says, "If we sin willfully, after that we have received the knowledge of the truth, there remaineth no more sacrifice for sins," he denies not that Christ is a perpetual victim to expiate the transgressions of saints (this the whole Epistle, in explaining the priesthood of Christ, distinctly proclaims), but he says that there remains no other sacrifice after this one is abandoned. And it is abandoned when the truth of the Gospel is professedly abjured.

24. To some it seems harsh, and at variance with the divine mercy, utterly to deny forgiveness to any who retake themselves to it. This is easily disposed of. It is not said that pardon will be refused if they turn to the Lord, but it is altogether denied that they can turn to repentance, inasmuch as for their ingratitude they are struck by the just judgment of God with eternal blindness. There is nothing contrary to this in the application which is afterwards made of the example of Esau, who tried in vain, by crying and tears, to recover his lost birthright; nor in the denunciation of the Prophet, "They cried, and I would not hear." Such modes of expression do not denote true conversion or calling upon God, but that anxiety with which the wicked, when in calamity, are compelled to see what they before securely disregarded—viz. that nothing can avail but the assistance of the Lord.

This, however, they do not so much implore as lament the loss of. Hence all that the Prophet means by crying, and the Apostle by tears, is the dreadful torment which stings and excruciates the wicked in despair. It is of consequence to carefully observe this: for otherwise God would be inconsistent with himself when he proclaims through the Prophet, that "If the wicked will turn from all his sins that he has committed," "he shall surely live, he shall not die" (Ezek. 18:21-22). And (as I have already said) it is certain that the mind of man cannot be changed for the better unless by his preventing grace. The promise as to those who call upon him will never fail; but the names of conversion and prayer are improperly given to that blind torment by which the reprobate are distracted when they see that they must seek God if they would find a remedy for their calamities, and yet shun to approach him.

25. But as the Apostle declares that God is not appeased by feigned repentance, it is asked how Ahab obtained pardon, and averted the punishment denounced against him (1 Kings 21:28-29), seeing, it appears, he was only amazed on the sudden, and afterwards continued his former course of life. He, indeed, clothed himself in sackcloth, covered himself with ashes, lay on the ground, and (as the testimony given to him bears) humbled himself before God. It was a small matter to rend his garments while his heart continued obstinate and swollen with wickedness, and yet we see that God was inclined to mercy. I answer, that though hypocrites are thus occasionally spared for a time, the wrath of God still lies upon them, and that they are thus spared not so much on their own account as for a public example. For what did Ahab gain by the mitigation of his punishment except that he did not suffer it alive on the earth? The curse of God, though concealed, was fixed on his house, and he himself went to eternal destruction. We may see the same thing in Esau (Gen. 27:38-39). For though he met with a refusal, a temporal blessing was granted to his tears. But as, according to the declaration of God, the spiritual

inheritance could be possessed only by one of the brothers, when Jacob was selected instead of Esau, that event excluded him from the divine mercy; but still there was given to him, as a man of a groveling nature, this consolation, that he should be filled with the fullness of the earth and the dew of heaven. And this, as I lately said, should be regarded as done for the example of others, that we may learn to apply our minds, and exert ourselves with greater alacrity, in the way of sincere repentance, as there cannot be the least doubt that God will be ready to pardon those who turn to him truly and with the heart, seeing his mercy extends even to the unworthy though they bear marks of his displeasure. In this way also, we are taught how dreadful the judgment is which awaits all the rebellious who with audacious brow and iron heart make it their sport to despise and disregard the divine threatening. God in this way often stretched forth his hand to deliver the Israelites from their calamities, though their cries were pretended, and their minds double and perfidious, as he himself complains in the Psalms, that they immediately returned to their former course (Psalm 78:36-37). But he designed thus by kindness and forbearance to bring them to true repentance, or leave them without excuse. And yet by remitting the punishment for a time, he does not lay himself under any perpetual obligation. He rather at times rises with greater severity against hypocrites, and doubles their punishment, that it may thereby appear how much hypocrisy displeases him. But, as I have observed, he gives some examples of his inclination to pardon, that the pious may thereby be stimulated to amend their lives, and the pride of those who petulantly kick against the pricks be more severely condemned.

Study Guide Questions

Section 1

1. According to Calvin, does true repentance follow faith or precede it?

Section 2

1. How does he deal with the objection that in Scripture, the command to repent comes first?

Section 3

1. What two aspects of repentance does Calvin discuss?

2. How does Calvin define them?

Section 4

1. What are the two kinds of repentance?

2. Unless it comes to the latter, what does repentance of the law accomplish?

Section 5

1. What is the relationship of faith and repentance?

2. What does Calvin draw from the Hebrew and Greek meanings of their words for repentance?

Section 6

1. What is the first of three heads in Calvin's understanding of repentance?

Section 7

1. What is the second of these three heads?

Section 8

1. What simple expression of mortification and vivification is used by the prophets?

2. Is mortification easy?

Section 9

1. How does Calvin sum up his understanding of repentance?

2. Does this regeneration take place at one moment in time?

3. How does Calvin interpret the image of God?

Section 10

1. In this life, do we receive entire freedom from sin?

2. What remains within every believer?

3. Where does Calvin differ with Augustine on this point?

Section 11

1. What is the believer's relation to sin?

2. Do we have to worry about our salvation because of this remaining sin?

Section 12

1. Did God create these corruptions?

Section 13

1. Does Calvin think there is a substantive difference between himself and Augustine on this?

Section 14

1. According to Calvin, what is the cause of certain Anabaptists claiming an antinomian perfection?

2. What does the Spirit not do in leading us?

Section 15

1. How many aspects of repentance does Paul outline in 2 Corinthians 7:11?

2. In repentance, what must we exercise?

Section 16

1. In order to keep the signs of repentance sure, what must a man measure his life by?

2. What are the two dangers of "exercises" to aid repentance?

Section 17

1. When fasting is necessary, what proviso does Calvin urge pastors to teach?

Section 18

1. What is the difference between special repentance and ordinary repentance?

Section 19

1. Under what two headings is the whole gospel contained?
2. Where do these two things come from?

Section 20

1. Is repentance the *basis* for our receiving pardon?

Section 21

1. Why does Calvin believe that repentance is a gift of God?
2. What does the efficacy of this gift depend on?
3. In passing, who does Calvin believe to be the author of Hebrews?

Section 22

1. Where does Calvin differ with Augustine on the unpardonable sin?
2. How does Calvin define the unpardonable sin?
3. What is a brief way of summarizing this sin?

Section 23

1. Is this a sin that a man can fall into accidentally one day?

Section 24

1. Is this teaching consistent with the tender mercies of God?

Section 25

1. Does God ever show mercy short of eternal mercy?

CHAPTER 4

Penitence, as explained in the sophistical jargon of the schoolmen, widely different from the purity required by the Gospel. Of the confession and satisfaction.

The divisions of this chapter are—

I. The orthodox doctrine of repentance being already expounded, the false doctrine is refuted in the present chapter; a general summary survey being at the same time taken of the doctrine of the Schoolmen, sec. 1-2.

II. Its separate parts are afterwards examined. Contrition, sec. 2 and 3. Confession, sec. 4-20. Sanctification, from sec. 20 to the end of the chapter.

Outline:

1. Errors of the Schoolmen in delivering the doctrine of repentance. 1. Errors in defining it. Four different definitions considered. 2. Absurd division. 3. Vain and puzzling questions. 4. Mode in which they entangle themselves.

2. The false doctrine of the Schoolmen necessary to be refuted. Of contrition. Their view of it examined.

3. True and genuine contrition.

4. Auricular confession. Whether or not of divine authority. Arguments of Canonists and Schoolmen. Allegorical argument founded on Judaism. Two answers. Reason why Christ sent the lepers to the priests.

5. Another allegorical argument. Answer.

6. A third argument from two passages of Scripture. These passages expounded.

7. Confession proved not to be of divine authority. The use of it free for almost twelve hundred years after Christ. Its nature. When enacted into a law. Confirmation from the history of the Church. A representation of the ancient auricular confession still existing among the Papists, to bear judgment against them. Confession abolished in the Church of Constantinople.

8. This mode of confession disapproved by Chrysostom, as shown by many passages.

9. False confession being thus refuted, the confession enjoined by the word of God is considered. Mistranslation in the old version. Proof from Scripture that confession should be directed to God alone.

10. Effect of secret confession thus made to God. Another kind of confession made to men.

11. Two forms of the latter confession—viz. public and private. Public confession either ordinary or extraordinary. Use of each. Objection to confession and public prayer. Answer.

12. Private confession of two kinds. 1. On our own account. 2. On account of our neighbor. Use of the former. Great assistance to be obtained from faithful ministers of the Church. Mode of procedure. Caution to be used.

13. The use of the latter recommended by Christ. What comprehended under it. Scripture sanctions no other method of confession.

14. The power of the keys exercised in these three kinds of confession. The utility of this power in regard to public confession and absolution. Caution to be observed.

15. Popish errors respecting confession. 1. In enjoining on all the necessity of confessing every sin. 2. Fictitious keys. 3. Pretended mandate to loose and bind. 4. To whom the office of loosing and binding committed.

16. Refutation of the first error, from the impossibility of so confessing, as proved by the testimony of David.

17. Refuted farther from the testimony of conscience. Impossible to observe this most rigid obligation. Necessarily leads to despair or indifference. Confirmation of the preceding remarks by an appeal to conscience.

18. Another refutation of the first error from analogy. Sum of the whole refutation. Third refutation, laying down the surest rule of confession. Explanation of the rule. Three objections answered.

19. Fourth objection—viz. that auricular confession does no harm, and is even useful. Answer, unfolding the hypocrisy, falsehood, impiety, and monstrous abominations of the patrons of this error.

20. Refutation of the second error. 1. Priests not successors of the Apostles. 2. They have not the Holy Spirit, who alone is arbiter of the keys.

21. Refutation of the third error. 1. They are ignorant of the command and promise of Christ. By abandoning the word of God they run into innumerable absurdities.

22. Objection to the refutation of the third error. Answers, reducing the Papists to various absurdities.

23. Refutation of the fourth error. 1. Petitio principii. 2. Inversion of ecclesiastical discipline. Three objections answered.

24. Conclusion of the whole discussion against this fictitious confession.

25. Of satisfaction, to which the Sophists assign the third place in repentance. Errors and falsehoods. These views opposed by the terms—1. Forgiveness. 2. Free forgiveness. 3. God destroying iniquities. 4. By and on account of Christ. No need of our satisfaction.

26. Objection, confining the grace and efficacy of Christ within narrow limits. Answers by both John the Evangelist and John the Baptist. Consequence of these answers.

27. Two points violated by the fiction of satisfaction. First, the honor of Christ impaired. Secondly, the conscience cannot find peace. Objection, confining the forgiveness of sins to Catechumens, refuted.

28. Objection, founded on the arbitrary distinction between venial and mortal sins. This distinction insulting to God and repugnant to Scripture. Answer, showing the true distinction in regard to venial sin.

29. Objection, founded on a distinction between guilt and the punishment of it. Answer, illustrated by various passages of Scripture. Admirable saying of Augustine.

30. Answer, founded on a consideration of the efficacy of Christ's death, and the sacrifices under the law. Our true satisfaction.

31. An objection, perverting six passages of Scripture. Preliminary observations concerning a twofold judgment on the part of God. 1. For punishment. 2. For correction.

32. Two distinctions hence arising. Objection, that God is often angry with his elect. Answer, God in afflicting his people does not take his mercy from them. This confirmed by his promise, by Scripture, and the uniform experience of the Church. Distinction between the reprobate and the elect in regard to punishment.

33. Second distinction. The punishment of the reprobate a commencement of the eternal punishment awaiting them; that of the elect designed to bring them to repentance. This confirmed by passages of Scripture and of the Fathers.

34. Two uses of this doctrine to the believer. In affliction he can believe that God, though angry, is still favorable to him. In the punishment of the reprobate, he sees a prelude to their final doom.

35. Objection, as to the punishment of David, answered. Why all men here subjected to chastisement.

36. Objections, founded on five other passages, answered.

37. Answer continued.

38. Objection, founded on passages in the Fathers. Answer, with passages from Chrysostom and Augustine.

39. These satisfactions had reference to the peace of the Church, and not to the throne of God. The Schoolmen have perverted the meaning of some absurd statements by obscure monks.

I come now to an examination of what the scholastic sophists teach concerning repentance. This I will do as briefly as possible; for I leave no intention to take up every point, lest this work, which I am desirous to frame as a compendium of doctrine, should exceed all bounds. They have managed to envelop a matter, otherwise not much involved, in so many perplexities, that it will be difficult to find an outlet if once you get plunged but a little way into their mire. And, first, in giving a definition, they plainly show they never understood what repentance means. For they fasten on some expressions in the writings of the Fathers which are very far from expressing the nature of repentance. For instance, that to repent is to deplore past sins and not commit what is to be deplored. Again that it is to bewail past evils and not to sin to do what is to be bewailed. Again, that it is a kind of grieving revenge, punishing in itself what it grieves to have committed. Again, that it is sorrow of heart and bitterness of soul for the evils which the individual has committed, or to which he has consented. Supposing we grant that these things were well said by the Fathers (though, if one were inclined to dispute, it were not difficult to deny it), they were not, however, said with the view of describing repentance but only of exhorting penitents not again to fall into the same faults from which they had been delivered. But if all descriptions of this kind are to be converted into definitions, there are others which have as good a title to be added. For instance, the following sentence of Chrysostom: "Repentance is a medicine for the cure of sin, a gift bestowed from above, an admirable virtue, a grace

surpassing the power of laws." Moreover, the doctrine which they afterwards deliver is somewhat worse than their definition. For they are
so keenly bent on external exercises, that all you can gather from immense volumes is, that repentance is a discipline, and austerity, which
serves partly to subdue the flesh, partly to chasten and punish sins: of
internal renovation of mind, bringing with it true amendment of life,
there is a strange silence. No doubt, they talk much of contrition and
attrition, torment the soul with many scruples, and involve it in great
trouble and anxiety; but when they seem to have deeply wounded the
heart, they cure all its bitterness by a slight sprinkling of ceremonies.
Repentance thus shrewdly defined, they divide into contrition of the
heart, confession of the mouth, and satisfaction of works. This is not
more logical than the definition, though they would be thought to
have spent their whole lives in framing syllogisms. But if any one
argues from the definition (a mode of argument prevalent with di-
alecticians) that a man may weep over his past sins and not commit
things that cause weeping; may bewail past evils, and not commit
things that are to be bewailed; may punish what he is grieved for having committed, though he does not confess it with the mouth—how
will they defend their division? For if he may be a true penitent and
not confess, repentance can exist without confession. If they answer,
that this division refers to repentance regarded as a sacrament, or is
to be understood of repentance in its most perfect form, which they
do not comprehend in their definitions, the mistake does not rest
with me: let them blame themselves for not defining more purely and
clearly. When any matter is discussed, I certainly am dull enough to
refer everything to the definition as the hinge and foundation of the
whole discussion. But granting that this is a license which masters
have, let us now survey the different parts in their order. In omitting
as frivolous several things which they vend with solemn brow as mysteries, I do it not from ignorance. It were not very difficult to dispose
of all those points which they plume themselves on their acuteness

and subtlety in discussing; but I consider it a sacred duty not to trouble the reader to no purpose with such absurdities. It is certainly easy to see from the questions which they move and agitate, and in which they miserably entangle themselves, that they are pealing of things they know not. Of this nature are the following: Whether repentance of one sin is pleasing to God, while there is an obstinate adherence to other sins. Again, whether punishments divinely indicted are available for satisfaction. Again, whether repentance can be several times repeated for mortal sins, whereas they grossly and wickedly define that daily repentance has to do with none but venial sins. In like manner, with gross error, they greatly torment themselves with a saying of Jerome, that repentance is a second plank after shipwreck. Herein they show that they have never awoke from brutish stupor, so as to obtain a distant view of the thousandth part of their sins.

2. I would have my readers to observe, that the dispute here relates not to a matter of no consequence; but to one of the most important of all—viz. the forgiveness of sins. For while they require three things in repentance—viz. compunction of heart, confession of the mouth, and satisfaction of work —they at the same time teach that these are necessary to obtain the pardon of sins. If there is anything in the whole compass of religion which it is of importance to us to know, this certainly is one of the most important—viz. to perceive and rightly hold by what means, what rule, what terms, with what facility or difficulty, forgiveness of sins may be obtained. Unless our knowledge here is clear and certain, our conscience can have no rest at all, no peace with God, no confidence or security, but is continually trembling, fluctuating, boiling, and distracted; dreads, hates, and shuns the presence of God. But if forgiveness of sins depends on the conditions to which they bind it, nothing can be more wretched and deplorable than our situation. Contrition they represent as the first step in obtaining pardon; and they exact it as due, that is, full and complete: meanwhile, they decide not when one may feel secure of

having performed this contrition in due measure. I admit that we are bound strongly and incessantly to urge every man bitterly to lament his sins, and thereby stimulate himself more and more to dislike and hate them. For this is the "repentance to salvation not to be repented of" (2 Cor. 7:10). But when such bitterness of sorrow is demanded as may correspond to the magnitude of the offense, and be weighed in the balance with confidence of pardon, miserable consciences are sadly perplexed and tormented when they see that the contrition due for sin is laid upon them, and yet that they have no measure of what is due, so as to enable them to determine that they have made full payment. If they say, we are to do what in us lies, we are always brought back to the same point; for when will any man venture to promise himself that he has done his utmost in bewailing sin? Therefore, when consciences, after a lengthened struggle and long contests with themselves, find no haven in which they may rest, as a means of alleviating their condition in some degree, they extort sorrow and wring out tears, in order to perfect their contrition.

3. If they say that this is calumny on my part, let them come forward and point out a single individual who, by this doctrine of contrition, has not either been driven to despair, or has not, instead of true, opposed pretended fear to the justice of God. We have elsewhere observed, that forgiveness of sins never can be obtained without repentance, because none but the afflicted, and those wounded by a consciousness of sins, can sincerely implore the mercy of God; but we, at the same time, added, that repentance cannot be the cause of the forgiveness of sins: and we also did away with that torment of souls— the dogma that it must be performed as due. Our doctrine was, that the soul looked not to its own compunction or its own tears, but fixed both eyes on the mercy of God alone. Only we observed, that those who labor and are heavy laden are called by Christ, seeing he was sent "to preach good tidings to the meek;" "to bind up the broken-hearted; to proclaim liberty to the captives, and the opening of the prison to

them that are bound;" "to comfort all that mourn." Hence the Pharisees were excluded, because, full of their own righteousness, they acknowledged not their own poverty; and despisers, because, regardless of the divine anger, they sought no remedy for their wickedness. Such persons neither labor nor are heavy-laden, are not broken-hearted, bound, nor in prison. But there is a great difference between teaching that forgiveness of sins is merited by a full and complete contrition (which the sinner never can give), and instructing him to hunger and thirst after the mercy of God, that recognizing his wretchedness, his turmoil, weariness, and captivity, you may show him where he should seek refreshment, rest, and liberty; in fine, teach him in his humility to give glory to God.

4. Confession has ever been a subject of keen contest between the Canonists and the Scholastic Theologians; the former contending that confession is of divine authority—the latter insisting, on the contrary, that it is merely enjoined by ecclesiastical constitution. In this contest great effrontery has been displayed by the Theologians, who have corrupted and violently wrested every passage of Scripture they have quoted in their favor. And when they saw that even thus they could not gain their object, those who wished to be thought particularly acute had recourse to the evasion that confession is of divine authority in regard to the substance, but that it afterwards received its form from positive enactment. Thus the silliest of these quibblers refer the citation to divine authority, from its being said, "Adam, where art thou?" (Gen. 3:9, 12); and also the exception from Adam having replied as if excepting, "The women whom thou gavest to be with me," &c.; but say that the form of both was appointed by civil law. Let us see by what arguments they prove that this confession, formed or unformed, is a divine commandment. The Lord, they say, sent the lepers to the priests (Matt. 8:4). What? did he send them to confession? Who ever heard tell that the Levitical priests were appointed to hear confession? Here they resort to allegory. The priests

were appointed by the Mosaic law to discern between leper and leper: sin is spiritual leprosy; therefore it belongs to the priests to decide upon it. Before I answer, I would ask, in passing, why, if this passage makes them judges of spiritual leprosy, they claim the cognizance of natural and carnal leprosy? This, forsooth, is not to play upon Scripture! The law gives the cognizance of leprosy to the Levitical priests: let us usurp this to ourselves. Sin is spiritual leprosy: let us also have cognizance of sin. I now give my answer: There being a change of the priesthood, there must of necessity be a change of the law. All the sacerdotal functions were transferred to Christ, and in him fulfilled and ended (Heb. 7:12). To him alone, therefore, all the rights and honors of the priesthood have been transferred. If they are so fond then of hunting out allegories, let them set Christ before them as the only priest, and place full and universal jurisdiction on his tribunal: this we will readily admit. Besides, there is an incongruity in their allegory: it classes a merely civil enactment among ceremonies. Why, then, does Christ send the lepers to the priests? Lest the priests should be charged with violating the law, which ordained that the person cured of leprosy should present himself before the priest, and be purified by the offering of a sacrifice, he orders the lepers who had been cleansed to do what the law required. "Go and show thyself to the priest, and offer for thy cleansing according as Moses commanded for a testimony unto them." (Luke 5:17). And assuredly this miracle would be a testimony to them: they had pronounced them lepers; they now pronounce them cured. Whether they would or not, they are forced to become witnesses to the miracles of Christ. Christ allows them to examine the miracle, and they cannot deny it: yet, as they still quibble, they have need of a testimony. So it is elsewhere said, "This gospel of the kingdom shall be preached in all the world, for a witness unto all nations" (Matt. 24:14). Again, "Ye shall be brought before governors and kings for my sake, for a testimony against them and the Gentiles" (Matt. 10:18); that is, in order that, in the judgment of God, they might be more filly convicted. But if they prefer taking the view of Chrysostom (Hom. 12 *de Muliere Cananæa*), he shows that this was done by Christ for the sake of the Jews also, that he might not be regarded as a violator of the law. But we are ashamed to appeal to the authority of any man in a matter so clear, when Christ declares that he left the legal right of the priests entire, as professed enemies of the Gospel, who were always intent on making a clamor if their mouths were not stopped. Wherefore, let the Popish priests, in order to retain this privilege, openly make common cause with those whom it was necessary to restrain, by forcible means, from speaking evil of Christ. For there is here no reference to his true ministers.

5. They draw their second argument from the same fountain—I mean allegory; as if allegories were of much avail in confirming any doctrine. But, indeed, let them avail, if those which I am able to produce are not more specious than theirs. They say, then, that the Lord, after raising Lazarus, commanded his disciples to "loose him and let him go" (John 11:44). Their first statement is untrue: we nowhere read that the Lord said this to the disciples; and it is much more probable that he spoke to the Jews who were standing by, that from there being no suspicion of fraud the miracle might be more manifest, and his power might be the more conspicuous from his raising the dead without touching him, by a mere word. In the same way, I understand that our Lord, to leave no ground of suspicion to the Jews, wished them to roll back the stone, feel the stench, perceive the sure signs of death, see him rise by the mere power of a word, and first handle him when alive. And this is the view of Chrysostom (Serm. *C. Jud. Gent. et Haeret*). But granting that it was said to the disciples, what can they gain by it? That the Lord gave the apostles the power of loosing? How much more aptly and dexterously might we allegorize and say, that by this symbol the Lord designed to teach his followers to loose those whom he raises up; that is, not to bring to remembrance the sins which he himself had forgotten, not to condemn as

sinners those whom he had acquitted, not still to upbraid those whom
he had pardoned, not to be stern and severe in punishing, while he
himself was merciful and ready to forgive. Certainly nothing should
more incline us to pardon than the example of the Judge who threatens that he will be inexorable to the rigid and inhumane. Let them go
now and vend their allegories.

6. They now come to closer quarters, while they support their view
by passages of Scripture which they think clearly in their favor. Those
who came to John's baptism confessed their sins, and James bids us
confess our sins one to another (James 5:16). It is not strange that
those who wished to be baptized confessed their sins. It has already
been mentioned, that John preached the baptism of repentance, baptized with water unto repentance. Whom then could he baptize, but
those who confessed that they were sinners? Baptism is a symbol of
the forgiveness of sins; and who could be admitted to receive the
symbol but sinners acknowledging themselves as such? They therefore
confessed their sins that they might be baptized. Nor without good
reason does James enjoin us to confess our sins one to another. But if
they would attend to what immediately follows, they would perceive
that this gives them little support. The words are, "Confess your sins
one to another, and pray one for another." He joins together mutual
confession and mutual prayer. If, then, we are to confess to priests
only, we are also to pray for them only. What? It would even follow
from the words of James, that priests alone can confess. In saying that
we are to confess mutually, he must be addressing those only who can
hear the confession of others. He says, αλληλους, mutually, by turns,
or, if they prefer it, reciprocally. But those only can confess reciprocally who are fit to hear confession. This being a privilege which they
bestow upon priests only, we also leave them the office of confessing
to each other. Have done then with such frivolous absurdities, and let
us receive the true meaning of the apostle, which is plain and simple; first, That we are to deposit our infirmities in the breasts of each

other, with the view of receiving mutual counsel, sympathy, and comfort; and, secondly, That mutually conscious of the infirmities of our brethren we are to pray to the Lord for them. Why then quote James against us who so earnestly insist on acknowledgment of the divine mercy? No man can acknowledge the mercy of God without previously confessing his own misery. Nay, we pronounce every man to be anathema who does not confess himself a sinner before God, before his angels, before the Church; in short, before all men. "The Scripture has concluded all under sin," "that every mouth may be stopped, and all the world may become guilty before God," that God alone may be justified and exalted (Gal. 3:22; Rom. 3:9, 19).

7. I wonder at their effrontery in venturing to maintain that the confession of which they speak is of divine authority. We admit that the use of it is very ancient; but we can easily prove that at one time it was free. It certainly appears, from their own records, that no law or constitution respecting it was enacted before the days of Innocent III. Surely if there had been a more ancient law they would have fastened on it, instead of being satisfied with the decree of the Council of Lateral, and so making themselves ridiculous even to children. In other matters, they hesitate not to coin fictitious decrees, which they ascribe to the most ancient Councils, that they may blind the eyes of the simple by veneration for antiquity. In this instance it has not occurred to them to practice this deception, and hence, themselves being witnesses, three centuries have not yet elapsed since the bridle was put, and the necessity of confession imposed by Innocent III. And to say nothing of the time, the mere barbarism of the terms used destroys the authority of the law. For when these worthy fathers enjoin that every person of both sexes (*utriusque sexus*) must once a year confess his sins to his own priest, men of wit humorously object that the precept binds hermaphrodites only, and has no application to any one who is either a male or a female. A still grosser absurdity has been displayed by their disciples, who are unable to explain what is meant by

one's own priest (*proprius sacerdos*). Let all the hired ravers of the Pope babble as they may, we hold that Christ is not the author of this law, which compels men to enumerate their sins; nay, that twelve hundred years elapsed after the resurrection of Christ before any such law was made, and that, consequently, this tyranny was not introduced until piety and doctrine were extinct, and pretended pastors had usurped to themselves unbridled license. There is clear evidence in historians, and other ancient writers, to show that this was a politic discipline introduced by bishops, not a law enacted by Christ or the Apostles. Out of many I will produce only one passage, which will be no obscure proof. Sozomen relates, that this constitution of the bishops was carefully observed in the Western churches, but especially at Rome; thus intimating that it was not the universal custom of all churches. He also says, that one of the presbyters was specially appointed to take charge of this duty. This abundantly confutes their falsehood as to the keys being given to the whole priesthood indiscriminately for this purpose, since the function was not common to all the priests, but specially belonged to the one priest whom the bishop had appointed to it. He it was (the same who at present in each of the cathedral churches has the name of penitentiary) who had cognizance of offenses which were more heinous, and required to be rebuked for the sake of example. He afterwards adds, that the same custom existed at Constantinople, until a certain matron, while pretending to confess, was discovered to have used it as a cloak to cover her intercourse with a deacon. In consequence of that crime, Nectarius, the bishop of that church—a man famous for learning and sanctity—abolished the custom of confessing. Here, then, let these asses prick up their ears. If auricular confession was a divine law, how could Nectarius have dared to abolish or remodel it? Nectarius, a holy man of God, approved by the suffrage of all antiquity, will they charge with heresy and schism? With the same vote they will condemn the church of Constantinople, in which Sozomen affirms that the custom of confessing was not only disguised for a time, but even in his own memory abolished. Nay, let them charge with defections not only Constantinople but all the Eastern churches, which (if they say true) disregarded an inviolable law enjoined on all Christians.

8. This abrogation is clearly attested in so many passages by Chrysostom, who lived at Constantinople, and was himself prelate of the church, that it is strange they can venture to maintain the contrary: "Tell your sins", says he, "that you may efface them: if you blush to tell another what sins you have committed, tell them daily in your soul. I say not, tell them to your fellow-servant who may upbraid you, but tell them to God who cures them. Confess your sins upon your bed, that your conscience may there daily recognize its iniquities." Again, "Now, however, it is not necessary to confess before witnesses; let the examination of your faults be made in your own thought: let the judgment be without a witness: let God alone see you confessing." Again, "I do not lead you publicly into the view of your fellow servants; I do not force you to disclose your sins to men; review and lay open your conscience before God. Show your wounds to the Lord, the best of physicians, and seek medicine from him. Show to him who upbraids not, but cures most kindly." Again, "Certainly tell it not to man lest he upbraid you. Nor must you confess to your fellow servant, who may make it public; but show your wounds to the Lord, who takes care of you, who is kind and can cure." He afterwards introduces God speaking thus: "I oblige you not to come into the midst of a theatre, and have many witnesses; tell your sins to me alone in private, that I may cure the ulcer." Shall we say that Chrysostom, in writing these and similar passages, carried his presumption so far as to free the consciences of men from those chains with which they are bound by the divine law? By no means; but knowing that it was not at all prescribed by the word of God, he dares not exact it as necessary.

9. But that the whole matter may be more plainly unfolded, we shall first honestly state the nature of confession as delivered in the word of

God, and thereafter subjoin their inventions—not all of them indeed (who could drink up that boundless sea?) but those only which contain summary of their secret confession. Here I am grieved to mention how frequently the old interpreter has rendered the word "confess" instead of "praise," a fact notorious to the most illiterate, were it not fitting to expose their effrontery in transferring to their tyrannical edict what was written concerning the praises of God. To prove that confession has the effect of exhilarating the mind, they obtrude the passage in the psalm, "with the voice of joy and praise" (Vulgate, *confessionis*) (Ps. 42:4). But if such a metamorphosis is valid, anything may be made of anything. But, as they have lost all shame, let pious readers reflect how, by the just vengeance of God, they have been given over to a reprobate mind, that their audacity may be the more detestable. If we are disposed to acquiesce in the simple doctrine of Scripture, there will be no danger of our being misled by such glosses. There one method of confessing is prescribed; since it is the Lord who forgives, forgets, and wipes away sins, to him let us confess them, that we may obtain pardon. He is the physician, therefore let us show our wounds to him. He is hurt and offended, let us ask peace of him. He is the discerner of the heart, and knows all our thoughts; let us hasten to pour out our hearts before him. He it is, in fine, who invites sinners; let us delay not to draw near to him. "I acknowledge my sin unto thee," says David; "and mine iniquity have I not hid. I said, I will confess my transgressions unto the Lord; and thou forgavest the iniquity of my sin" (Ps. 32:5). Another specimen of David's confessions is as follows: "Have mercy upon me, O God, according to thy loving kindness" (Ps. 51:1). The following is Daniel's confession: "We have sinned, and have committed iniquity, and have done wickedly, and have rebelled, even by departing from thy precepts and thy judgments" (Dan. 9:5). Other examples everywhere occur in Scripture: the quotation of them would almost fill a volume. "If we confess our sins," says John, "he is faithful and just to forgive us our sins" (1 John 1:9). To whom are we to confess? to Him surely;—that is, we are to fall down before him with a grieved and humbled heart, and sincerely accusing and condemning ourselves, seek forgiveness of his goodness and mercy.

10. He who has adopted this confession from the heart and is in the presence of God, will doubtless have a tongue ready to confess whenever there is occasion among men to publish the mercy of God. He will not be satisfied to whisper the secret of his heart for once into the ear of one individual, but will often, and openly, and in the hearing of the whole world, ingenuously make mention both of his own ignominy, and of the greatness and glory of the Lord. In this way David, after he was accused by Nathan, being stung in his conscience, confesses his sin before God and men. "I have sinned unto the Lord," says he (2 Sam. 12:13); that is, I have now no excuse, no evasion; all must judge me a sinner; and that which I wished to be secret with the Lord must also be made manifest to men. Hence the secret confession which is made to God is followed by voluntary confession to men, whenever that is conducive to the divine glory or our humiliation. For this reason the Lord anciently enjoined the people of Israel that they should repeat the words after the priest, and make public confession of their iniquities in the temple; because he foresaw that this was a necessary help to enable each one to form a just idea of himself. And it is proper that by confession of our misery, we should manifest the mercy of our God both among ourselves and before the whole world.

11. It is proper that this mode of confession should both be ordinary in the Church, and also be specially employed on extraordinary occasions, when the people in common happen to have fallen into any fault. Of this latter description we have an example in the solemn confession which the whole people made under the authority and guidance of Ezra and Nehemiah (Neh. 1:6-7). For their long captivity, the destruction of the temple, and suppression of their religion, having been the common punishment of their defection, they

could not make meet acknowledgment of the blessing of deliverance without previous confession of their guilt. And it matters not though in one assembly it may sometimes happen that a few are innocent, seeing that the members of a languid and sickly body cannot boast of soundness. Nay, it is scarcely possible that these few have not contracted some taint, and so bear part of the blame. Therefore, as often as we are afflicted with pestilence, or war, or famine, or any other calamity whatsoever, if it is our duty to retake ourselves to mourning, fasting, and other signs of guiltiness, confession also, on which all the others depend, is not to be neglected. That ordinary confession which the Lord has moreover expressly commended, no sober man, who has reflected on its usefulness, will venture to disapprove. Seeing that in every sacred assembly we stand in the view of God and angels, in what way should our service begin but in acknowledging our own unworthiness? But this you will say is done in every prayer; for as often as we pray for pardon, we confess our sins. I admit it. But if you consider how great is our carelessness, or drowsiness, or sloth, you will grant me that it would be a salutary ordinance if the Christian people were exercised in humiliation by some formal method of confession. For though the ceremony which the Lord enjoined on the Israelites belonged to the tutelage of the Law, yet the thing itself belongs in some respect to us also. And, indeed, in all well ordered churches, in observance of an useful custom, the minister, each Lord's day, frames a formula of confession in his own name and that of the people, in which he makes a common confession of iniquity, and supplicates pardon from the Lord. In short, by this key a door of prayer is opened privately for each, and publicly for all.

12. Two other forms of private confession are approved by Scripture. The one is made on our own account, and to it reference is made in the passage in James, "Confess your sins one to another" (James 5:16); for the meaning is, that by disclosing our infirmities to each other, we are to obtain the aid of mutual counsel and consolation.

The other is to be made for the sake of our neighbor, to appease and reconcile him if by our fault he has been in any respect injured. In the former, although James, by not specifying any particular individual into whose bosom we are to disburden our feelings, leaves us the free choice of confessing to any member of the church who may seem fittest; yet as for the most part pastors are to be supposed better qualified than others, our choice ought chiefly to fall upon them. And the ground of preference is, that the Lord, by calling them to the ministry, points them out as the persons by whose lips we are to be taught to subdue and correct our sins, and derive consolation from the hope of pardon. For as the duty of mutual admonition and correction is committed to all Christians, but is specially enjoined on ministers, so while we ought all to console each other mutually and confirm each other in confidence in the divine mercy, we see that ministers, to assure our consciences of the forgiveness of sins, are appointed to be the witnesses and sponsors of it, so that they are themselves said to forgive sins and loose souls (Matt. 16:19; 18:18). When you hear this attributed to them, reflect that it is for your use. Let every believer, therefore, remember, that if in private he is so agonized and afflicted by a sense of his sins that he cannot obtain relief without the aid of others, it is his duty not to neglect the remedy which God provides for him—viz. to have recourse for relief to a private confession to his own pastor, and for consolation privately implore the assistance of him whose business it is, both in public and private, to solace the people of God with Gospel doctrine. But we are always to use moderation, lest in a matter as to which God prescribes no certain rule, our consciences be burdened with a certain yoke. Hence it follows first, that confession of this nature ought to be free so as not to be exacted of all, but only recommended to those who feel that they have need of it; and, secondly, even those who use it according to their necessity must neither be compelled by any precept, nor artfully induced to enumerate all their sins, but only insofar as they shall deem it for their interest, that they may obtain the full benefit of consolation. Faithful pastors, as they would both eschew tyranny in their ministry, and superstition in the people, must not only leave this liberty to churches, but defend and strenuously vindicate it.

13. Of the second form of confession, our Savior speaks in Matthew. "If thou bring thy gift to the altar, and there remember that thy brother has ought against thee; leave there thy gift before the altar; first be reconciled to thy brother, and then come and offer thy gift" (Matt. 5:23-24). Thus love, which has been interrupted by our fault, must be restored by acknowledging and asking pardon for the fault. Under this head is included the confession of those who by their sin have given offense to the whole Church (supra, sec. 10). For if Christ attaches so much importance to the offense of one individual, that he forbids the sacrifice of all who have sinned in any respect against their brethren, until by due satisfaction they have regained their favor, how much greater reason is there that he, who by some evil example has offended the Church should be reconciled to it by the acknowledgment of his fault? Thus the member of the Church of Corinth was restored to communion after he had humbly submitted to correction (2 Cor. 2:6). This form of confession existed in the ancient Christian Church, as Cyprian relates: "They practice repentance," says he, "for a proper time, then they come to confession, and by the laying on of the hands of the bishop and clergy, are admitted to communion." Scripture knows nothing of any other form or method of confessing, and it belongs not to us to bind new chains upon consciences which Christ most strictly prohibits from being brought into bondage. Meanwhile, that the flock present themselves before the pastor whenever they would partake of the Holy Supper, I am so far from disapproving, that I am most desirous it should be everywhere observed. For both those whose conscience is hindered may thence obtain singular benefit, and those who require admonition thus afford an opportunity for it; provided always no countenance is given to tyranny and superstition.

14. The power of the keys has place in the three following modes of confession—either when the whole Church, in a formal acknowledgment of its defects, supplicates pardon; or when a private individual, who has given public offense by some notable delinquency, testifies his repentance; or when he who from disquiet of conscience needs the aid of his minister, acquaints him with his infirmity. With regard to the reparation of offense, the case is different. For though in this also provision is made for peace of conscience, yet the principal object is to suppress hatred, and reunite brethren in the bond of peace. But the benefit of which I have spoken is by no means to be despised, that we may the more willingly confess our sins. For when the whole Church stands as it were at the bar of God, confesses her guilt, and finds her only refuge in the divine mercy, it is no common or light solace to have an ambassador of Christ present, invested with the mandate of reconciliations by whom she may hear her absolution pronounced. Here the utility of the keys is justly commended when that embassy is duly discharged with becoming order and reverence. In like manner, when he who has as it were become an alien from the Church receives pardon, and is thus restored to brotherly unity, how great is the benefit of understanding that he is pardoned by those to whom Christ said, "Whose soever sins ye remit, they are remitted unto them" (John 20:23). Nor is private absolution of less benefit or efficacy when asked by those who stand in need of a special remedy for their infirmity. It not seldom happens, that he who hears general promises which are intended for the whole congregation of the faithful, nevertheless remains somewhat in doubt, and is still disquieted in mind, as if his own remission were not yet obtained. Should this individual lay open the secret wound of his soul to his pastor, and hear these words of the Gospel specially addressed to him, "Son, be of good cheer, thy sins be forgiven thee" (Matt. 9:2), his mind will feel secure, and escape from the trepidation with which it was previously agitated. But when we treat of the keys, we must always beware of

dreaming of any power apart from the preaching of the Gospel. This subject will be more fully explained when we come to treat of the government of the Church (Book 4, chap. 11-12). There we shall see, that whatever privilege of binding and loosing Christ has bestowed on his Church is annexed to the word. This is especially true with regard to the ministry of the keys, the whole power of which consists in this, that the grace of the Gospel is publicly and privately sealed on the minds of believers by means of those whom the Lord has appointed; and the only method in which this can be done is by preaching.

15. What say the Roman theologians? That all persons of both sexes, so soon as they shall have reached the years of discretion, must, once a year at least, confess all their sins to their own priest; that the sin is not discharged unless the resolution to confess has been firmly conceived; that if this resolution is not carried into effect when an opportunity offers, there is no entrance into Paradise; that the priest, moreover, has the power of the keys, by which he can loose and bind the sinner; because the declaration of Christ is not in vain: "Whatsoever ye shall bind on earth shall be bound in heaven" (Matt. 18:18). Concerning this power, however, they wage a fierce war among themselves. Some say there is only one key essentially—viz. the power of binding and loosing; that knowledge, indeed, is requisite for the proper use of it, but only as an accessory, not as essentially inherent in it. Others seeing that this gave too unrestrained license, have imagined two keys—viz. discernment and power. Others, again, seeing that the license of priests was curbed by such restraint, have forged other keys (infra, sec. 21), the authority of discerning to be used in defining, and the power to carry their sentences into execution; and to these they add knowledge as a counselor. This binding and loosing, however, they do not venture to interpret simply, to forgive and wipe away sins, because they hear the Lord proclaiming by the prophet, "I, even I, am the Lord; and beside me there is no savior." "I, even I, am he that blotteth out thy transgressions" (Isa. 43:11, 25). But they

say it belongs to the priest to declare who are bound or loosed, and whose sins are remitted or retained; to declare, moreover, either by confession, when he absolves and retains sins, or by sentence, when he excommunicates or admits to communion in the Sacraments. Lastly, perceiving that the knot is not yet untied, because it may always be objected that persons are often undeservedly bound and loosed, and therefore not bound or loosed in heaven; as their ultimate resource, they answer, that the conferring of the keys must be taken with limitations because Christ has promised that the sentence of the priest, properly pronounced, will be approved at his judgment seat according as the bound or loosed asked what they merited. They say, moreover, that those keys which are conferred by bishops at ordination were given by Christ to all priests but that the free use of them is with those only who discharge ecclesiastical functions; that with priests excommunicated or suspended the keys themselves indeed remain, but tied and rusty. Those who speak thus may justly be deemed modest and sober compared with others, who on a new anvil have forged new keys, by which they say that the treasury of heaven is locked up: these we shall afterwards consider in their own place (chap. 5 sec. 2).

16. To each of these views I will briefly reply. As to their binding the souls of believers by their laws, whether justly or unjustly, I say nothing at present, as it will be seen at the proper place; but their enacting it as a law, that all sins are to be enumerated; their denying that sin is discharged except under the condition that the resolution to confess has been firmly conceived; their pretense that there is no admission into Paradise if the opportunity of confession has been neglected, are things which it is impossible to bear. Are all sins to be enumerated? But David, who, I presume, had honestly pondered with himself as to the confession of his sins, exclaimed, "Who can understand his errors? Cleanse thou me from secret faults" (Ps. 19:12); and in another passage, "Mine iniquities are gone over my head: as a heavy burden they are too heavy for me" (Ps. 38:4). He knew how deep was

the abyss of our sins, how numerous the forms of wickedness, how many heads the hydra carried, how long a tail it drew. Therefore, he did not sit down to make a catalogue, but from the depth of his distress cried unto the Lord, "I am overwhelmed, and buried, and sore vexed; the gates of hell have encircled me: let thy right hand deliver me from the abyss into which I am plunged, and from the death which I am ready to die." Who can now think of a computation of his sins when he sees David's inability to number his?

17. By this ruinous procedure, the souls of those who were affected with some sense of God have been most cruelly racked. First, they retook themselves to calculation, proceeding according to the formula given by the Schoolmen, and dividing their sins into boughs, branches, twigs, and leaves; then they weighed the qualities, quantities, and circumstances; and in this way, for some time, matters proceeded. But after they had advanced farther, when they looked around, naught was seen but sea and sky; no road, no harbor. The longer the space they ran over, a longer still met the eye; nay, lofty mountains began to rise, and there seemed no hope of escape; none at least till after long wanderings. They were thus brought to a dead halt, till at length the only issue was found in despair. Here these cruel murderers, to ease the wounds which they had made, applied certain fomentations. Everyone was to do his best. But new cares again disturbed, nay, new torments excruciated their souls. "I have not spent enough of time; I have not exerted myself sufficiently: many things I have omitted through negligence: forgetfulness proceeding from want of care is not excusable." Then new drugs were supplied to alleviate their pains. "Repent of your negligence; and provided it is not done supinely, it will be pardoned." All these things, however, could not heal the wound, being not so much alleviations of the sore as poison besmeared with honey, that its bitterness might not at once offend the taste, but penetrate to the vitals before it could be detected. The dreadful voice, therefore, was always heard pealing in their ears, "Confess all your sins," and the

dread thus occasioned could not be pacified without sure consolation. Here let my readers consider whether it be possible to take an account of the actions of a whole year, or even to collect the sins committed in a single day, seeing every man's experience convinces him that at evening, in examining the faults of that single day, memory gets confused, so great is the number and variety presented. I am not speaking of dull and heartless hypocrites, who, after animadverting on three or four of their grosser offenses, think the work finished; but of the true worshipers of God, who, after they have performed their examination, feeling themselves overwhelmed, still add the words of John: "If our heart condemn us, God is greater than our heart, and knoweth all things" (1 John 3:20); and, therefore, tremble at the thought of that Judge whose knowledge far surpasses our comprehension.

18. Though a good part of the world rested in these soothing suggestions, by which this fatal poison was somewhat tempered, it was not because they thought that God was satisfied, or they had quite satisfied themselves; it was rather like an anchor cast out in the middle of the deep, which for a little interrupts the navigation, or a weary, worn-out traveler, who lies down by the way. I give myself no trouble in proving the truth of this fact. Everyone can be his own witness. I will mention generally what the nature of this law is. First, the observance of it is simply impossible; and hence its only results to destroy, condemn, confound, to plunge into ruin and despair. Secondly, By withdrawing sinners from a true sense of their sins, it makes them hypocritical, and ignorant both of God and themselves. For, while they are wholly occupied with the enumeration of their sins, they lose sight of that lurking hydra, their secret iniquities and internal defilements, the knowledge of which would have made them sensible of their misery. But the surest rule of confession is, to acknowledge and confess our sins to be an abyss so great as to exceed our comprehension. On this rule we see the confession of the publican was formed, "God be merciful to me, a sinner" (Luke 18:13); as if he had

said, How great, how very great a sinner, how utterly sinful I am! The extent of my sins I can neither conceive nor express. Let the depth of thy mercy engulf the depth of sin! What! you will say, are we not to confess every single sin? Is no confession acceptable to God but that which is contained in the words, "I am a sinner"? Nay, our endeavor must rather be, as much as in us lies, to pour out our whole heart before the Lord. Nor are we only in one word to confess ourselves sinners, but truly and sincerely acknowledge ourselves as such; to feel with our whole soul how great and various the pollutions of our sins are; confessing not only that we are impure, but what the nature of our impurity is, its magnitude and its extent; not only that we are debtors, but what the debts are which burden us, and how they were incurred; not only that we are wounded, but how numerous and deadly are the wounds. When thus recognizing himself, the sinner shall have poured out his whole heart before God, let him seriously and sincerely reflect that a greater number of sins still remains, and that their recesses are too deep for him thoroughly to penetrate. Accordingly, let him exclaim with David, "Who can understand his errors? Cleanse thou me from secret faults" (Ps. 19:12). But when the Schoolmen affirm that sins are not forgiven, unless the resolution to confess has been firmly conceived, and that the gate of Paradise is closed on him who has neglected the opportunity of confessing when offered, far be it from us to concede this to them. The remission of sins is not different now from what it has ever been. In all the passages in which we read that sinners obtained forgiveness from God, we read not that they whispered into the ear of some priest. Indeed, they could not then confess, as priests were not then confessionaries, nor did the confessional itself exist. And for many ages afterwards, this mode of confession, by which sins were forgiven on this condition, was unheard of: But not to enter into a long discussion, as if the matter were doubtful, the word of God, which abideth forever, is plain, "When the wicked shall turn away from all his sins that he has committed, and keep all my statutes, and do that which is lawful and right, he shall surely live, he shall not die" (Ezek. 18:21). He who presumes to add to this declaration binds not sins, but the mercy of God. When they contend that judgment cannot be given unless the case is known, the answer is easy, that they usurp the right of judging, being only self-created judges. And it is strange, how confidently they lay down principles, which no man of sound mind will admit. They give out, that the office of binding and loosing has been committed to them, as a kind of jurisdiction annexed to the right of inquiry. That the jurisdiction was unknown to the Apostles their whole doctrine proclaims. Nor does it belong to the priest to know for certainty whether or not a sinner is loosed, but to Him from whom acquittal is asked; since he who only hears can ever know whether or not the enumeration is full and complete. Thus there would be no absolution, without restricting it to the words of him who is to be judged. We may add, that the whole system of loosing depends on faith and repentance, two things which no man can know of another, so as to pronounce sentence. It follows, therefore, that the certainty of binding and loosing is not subjected to the will of an earthly judge, because the minister of the word, when he duly executes his office, can only acquit conditionally, when, for the sake of the sinner, he repeats the words, "Whose soever sins ye remit;" lest he should doubt of the pardon, which, by the command and voice of God, is promised to be ratified in heaven.

19. It is not strange, therefore, that we condemn that auricular confession, as a thing pestilent in its nature, and in many ways injurious to the Church, and desire to see it abolished. But if the thing were in itself indifferent, yet, seeing it is of no use or benefit, and has given occasion to so much impiety, blasphemy, and error, who does not think that it ought to be immediately abolished? They enumerate some of its uses, and boast of them as very beneficial, but they are either fictitious or of no importance. One thing they specially commend, that the blush of shame in the penitent is a severe punishment, which

makes him more cautious for the future, and anticipates divine punishment, by his punishing himself. As if a man was not sufficiently
humbled with shame when brought under the cognizance of God
at his supreme tribunal. Admirable proficiency—if we cease to sin
because we are ashamed to make one man acquainted with it, and
blush not at having God as the witness of our evil conscience! The
assertion, however, as to the effect of shame, is most unfounded, for
we may everywhere see, that there is nothing which gives men greater
confidence and license in sinning than the idea, that after making
confession to priests, they can wipe their lips and say, "I have not done
it." And not only do they during the whole year become bolder in sin,
but, secure against confession for the remainder of it, they never sigh
after God, never examine themselves, but continue heaping sins upon
sins, until, as they suppose, they get rid of them all at once. And when
they have got rid of them, they think they are disburdened of their
load, and imagine they have deprived God of the right of judging, by
giving it to the priest; have made God forgetful, by making the priest
conscious. Moreover, who is glad when he sees the day of confession
approaching? Who goes with a cheerful mind to confess, and does
not rather, as if he were dragged to prison with a rope about his neck,
go unwillingly, and, as it were, struggling against it? with the exception, perhaps, of the priests themselves, who take a fond delight in
the mutual narrative of their own misdeeds, as a kind of merry tales.
I will not pollute my page by retailing the monstrous abominations
with which auricular confession teems; I only say, that if that holy
man (Nectarius, of whom supra, sec. 7) did not act unadvisedly when
for one rumor of whoredom he banished confession from his church,
or rather from the memory of his people, the innumerable acts of
prostitution, adultery, and incest, which it produces in the present day,
warn us of the necessity of abolishing it.

20. As to the pretense of the confessionaries respecting the power
of the keys, and their placing in it, so to speak, the sum and substance

of their kingdom, we must see what force it ought to have. Were the keys then (they ask), given without a cause? Was it said without a cause, "Whatsoever ye shall bind on earth shall be bound in heaven, and whatsoever ye shall loose on earth shall be loosed in heaven?" (Matt. 18:18). Do we make void the word of Christ? I answer, that there was a weighty reason for giving the keys, as I lately explained, and will again show at greater length when I come to treat of Excommunication (Book 4, chap. 12). But what if I should cut off the handle for all such questions with one sword—viz. that priests are neither vicars nor successors of the Apostles? But that also will be elsewhere considered (Book 4, chap. 6). Now, at the very place where they are most desirous to fortify themselves, they erect a battering ram, by which all their own machinations are overthrown. Christ did not give his Apostles the power of binding and loosing before he endued them with the Holy Spirit. I deny, therefore, that any man, who has not previously received the Holy Spirit, is competent to possess the power of the keys. I deny that anyone can use the keys, unless the Holy Spirit precede, teaching and dictating what is to be done. They pretend, indeed, that they have the Holy Spirit, but by their works deny him; unless, indeed, we are to suppose that the Holy Spirit is some vain thing of no value, as they certainly do feign, but we will not believe them. With this engine they are completely overthrown; whatever be the door of which they boast of having the key, we must always ask, whether they have the Holy Spirit, who is arbiter and ruler of the keys? If they reply, that they have, we must again ask, whether the Holy Spirit can err? This they will not venture to say distinctly, although by their doctrine they indirectly insinuate it. Therefore, we must infer, that no priestlings have the power of the keys, because they everywhere and indiscriminately loose what the Lord was pleased should be bound, and bind what he has ordered to be loosed.

21. When they see themselves convicted on the clearest evidence, of loosing and binding worthy and unworthy without distinction, they

lay claim to power without knowledge. And although they dare not
deny that knowledge is requisite for the proper use, they still affirm
that the power itself has been given to bad administrators. This, however, is the power, "Whatsoever ye shall bind on earth shall be bound
in heaven, and whatsoever ye shall loose on earth shall be loosed in
heaven." Either the promise of Christ must be false, or those who are
endued with this power bind and loose properly. There is no room for
the evasion, that the words of Christ are limited, according to the merits of him who is loosed or bound. We admit, that none can be bound
or loosed but those who are worthy of being bound or loosed. But
the preachers of the Gospel and the Church have the word by which
they can measure this worthiness. By this word preachers of the Gospel can promise forgiveness of sins to all who are in Christ by faith,
and can declare a sentence of condemnation against all, and upon all,
who do not embrace Christ. In this word the Church declares, that
"neither fornicators, nor idolaters, nor adulterers," "nor thieves, nor
covetous, nor drunkards, nor revilers, nor extortioners shall inherit the
kingdom of God" (1 Cor. 6:9-10). Such it binds in sure fetters. By the
same word it looses and consoles the penitent. But what kind of power is it which knows not what is to be bound or loosed? You cannot
bind or loose without knowledge. Why, then, do they say, that they
absolve by authority given to them, when absolution is uncertain? As
regards us, this power is merely imaginary, if it cannot be used. Now,
I hold either that there is no use, or one so uncertain as to be virtually
no use at all. For when they confess that a good part of the priests do
not use the keys duly, and that power without the legitimate use is
ineffectual, who is to assure me, that the one by whom I am loosed is
a good dispenser of the keys? But if he is a bad one, what better has
he given me than this nugatory dispensation—What is to be bound
or loosed in you I know not, since I have not the proper use of the
keys; but if you deserve it, I absolve you? As much might be done, I
say not by a laic (since they would scarcely listen to such a statement),

but by the Turk or the devil. For it is just to say, I have not the word of God, the sure rule for loosing, but authority has been given me to absolve you, if you deserve it. We see, therefore, what their object was, when they defined (see sec. 16) the keys as authority to discern and power to execute; and said, that knowledge is added as a counselor, and counsels the proper use; their object was to reign libidinously and licentiously, without God and his word.

22. Should any one object, first, that the lawful ministers of Christ will be no less perplexed in the discharge of their duty, because the absolution, which depends on faith, will always be equivocal; and, secondly, that sinners will receive no comfort at all, or cold comfort, because the minister, who is not a fit judge of their faith, is not certain of their absolution, we are prepared with an answer. They say that no sins are remitted by the priest, but such sins as he is cognizant of; thus, according to them, remission depends on the judgment of the priest, and unless he accurately discriminate as to who are worthy of pardon, the whole procedure is null and void. In short, the power of which they speak is a jurisdiction annexed to examination, to which pardon and absolution are restricted. Here no firm footing can be found, nay, there is a profound abyss; because, where confession is not complete, the hope of pardon also is defective; next, the priest himself must necessarily remain in suspense, while he knows not whether the sinner gives a faithful enumeration of his sins; lastly, such is the rudeness and ignorance of priests, that the greater part of them are in no respect fitter to perform this office than a cobbler to cultivate the fields, while almost all the others have good reason to suspect their own fitness. Hence the perplexity and doubt as to the Popish absolution, from their choosing to found it on the person of the priest, and not on his person only, but on his knowledge, so that he can only judge of what is laid before him investigated, and ascertained. Now, if any should ask at these good doctors, whether the sinner is reconciled to God when some sins are remitted? I know not what answer they

could give, unless that they should be forced to confess, that whatever the priest pronounces with regard to the remission of sins which have been enumerated to him will be unavailing, so long as others are not exempted from condemnation. On the part of the penitent, again, it is hence obvious in what a state of pernicious anxiety his conscience will be held; because, while he leans on what they call the discernment of the priest, he cannot come to any decision from the word of God. From all these absurdities the doctrine which we deliver is completely free. For absolution is conditional, allowing the sinner to trust that God is propitious to him, provided he sincerely seek expiation in the sacrifice of Christ, and accept of the grace offered to him. Thus, he cannot err who, in the capacity of a herald, promulgates what has been dictated to him from the word of God. The sinner, again, can receive a clear and sure absolution when, in regard to embracing the grace of Christ, the simple condition annexed is in terms of the general rule of our Master himself—a rule impiously spurned by the Papacy: "According to your faith be it unto you" (Matt. 9:29).

23. The absurd jargon which they make of the doctrine of Scripture concerning the power of the keys, I have promised to expose elsewhere; the proper place will be in treating of the Government of the Church (Book 4, chap. 12). Meanwhile, let the reader remember how absurdly they wrest to auricular and secret confession what was said by Christ partly of the preaching of the Gospel, and partly of excommunication. Wherefore, when they object that the power of loosing was given to the Apostles, and that this power priests exercise by remitting sins acknowledged to them, it is plain that the principle which they assume is false and frivolous: for the absolution which is subordinate to faith is nothing else than an evidence of pardon, derived from the free promise of the Gospel, while the other absolution, which depends on the discipline of the Church, has nothing to do with secret sins; but is more a matter of example for the purpose of removing the public offense given to the Church. As to their diligence

in searching up and down for passages by which they may prove that it is not sufficient to confess sins to God alone, or to laymen, unless the priest take cognizance, it is vile and disgraceful. For when the ancient fathers advise sinners to disburden themselves to their pastor, we cannot understand them to refer to a recital which was not then in use. Then, so unfair are Lombard and others like-minded, that they seem intentionally to have devoted themselves to spurious books, that they might use them as a cloak to deceive the simple. They, indeed, acknowledge truly, that as forgiveness always accompanies repentance, no obstacle properly remains after the individual is truly penitent, though he may not have actually confessed; and, therefore, that the priest does not so much remit sins, as pronounce and declare that they are remitted; though in the term "declaring," they insinuate a gross error, surrogating ceremony in place of doctrine. But in pretending that he who has already obtained pardon before God is acquitted in the face of the Church, they unseasonably apply to the special use of every individual, that which we have already said was designed for common discipline when the offense of a more heinous and notorious transgression was to be removed. Shortly after they pervert and destroy their previous moderation, by adding that there is another mode of remission, namely, by the infliction of penalty and satisfaction, in which they arrogate to their priests the right of dividing what God has everywhere promised to us entire. While He simply requires repentance and faith, their division or exception is altogether blasphemous. For it is just as if the priest, assuming the office of tribune, were to interfere with God, and try to prevent him from admitting to his favor by his mere liberality anyone who had not previously lain prostrate at the tribunicial bench, and there been punished.

24. The whole comes to this, when they wish to make God the author of this fictitious confession their vanity is proved, as I have shown their falsehood in expounding the few passages which they cite. But while it is plain, that the law was imposed by men, I say that it is both

tyrannical and insulting to God, who, in binding consciences to his word, would have them free from human rule. Then when confession is prescribed as necessary to obtain pardon, which God wished to be free, I say that the sacrilege is altogether intolerable, because nothing belongs more peculiarly to God than the forgiveness of sins, in which our salvation consists. I have, moreover, shown that this tyranny was introduced when the world was sunk in shameful barbarism. Besides, I have proved that the law is pestiferous, inasmuch as when the fear of God exists, it plunges men into despair, and when there is security soothing itself with vain flattery, it blunts it the more. Lastly, I have explained that all the mitigations which they employ have no other tendency than to entangle, obscure, and corrupt the pure doctrine, and cloak their iniquities with deceitful colors.

25. In repentance they assign the third place to satisfaction, all their absurd talk as to which can be refuted in one word. They say, that it is not sufficient for the penitent to abstain from past sins, and change his conduct for the better, unless he satisfy God for what he has done; and that there are many helps by which we may redeem sins, such as tears, fastings oblations, and offices of charity; that by them the Lord is to be propitiated; by them the debts due to divine justice are to be paid; by them our faults are to be compensated; by them pardon is to be deserved: for though in the riches of his mercy he has forgiven the guilt, he yet, as a just discipline, retains the penalty, and that this penalty must be bought off by satisfaction. The sum of the whole comes to this: that we indeed obtain pardon of our sins from the mercy of God, but still by the intervention of the merit of works, by which the evil of our sins is compensated, and due satisfaction made to divine justice. To such false views I oppose the free forgiveness of sins, one of the doctrines most clearly taught in Scripture. First, what is forgiveness but a gift of mere liberality? A creditor is not said to forgive when he declares by granting a discharge, that the money has been paid to him; but when, without any payment, through

voluntary kindness, he expunges the debt. And why is the term "gra-tis" (free) afterwards added, but to take away all idea of satisfaction? With what confidence, then, do they still set up their satisfactions, which are thus struck down as with a thunderbolt? What? When the Lord proclaims by Isaiah, "I, even I, am he that blotteth out thy trans-gressions for mine own sake, and will not remember thy sins," does he not plainly declare, that the cause and foundation of forgiveness is to be sought from his goodness alone? Besides, when the whole of Scripture bears this testimony to Christ, that through his name the forgiveness of sins is to be obtained (Acts 10:43), does it not plainly exclude all other names? How then do they teach that it is obtained by the name of satisfaction? Let them not deny that they attribute this to satisfactions, though they bring them in as subsidiary aids. For when Scripture says, by the name of Christ, it means, that we are to bring nothing, pretend nothing of our own, but lean entirely on the recommendation of Christ. Thus Paul, after declaring that "God was in Christ reconciling the world unto himself, not imputing their tres-passes unto them," immediately adds the reason and the method, "For he has made him to be sin for us who knew no sin" (2 Cor. 5:19-20).

26. But with their usual perverseness, they maintain that both the forgiveness of sins and reconciliation take place at once when we are received into the favor of God through Christ in baptism; that in lapses after baptism we must rise again by means of satisfactions; that the blood of Christ is of no avail unless insofar as it is dispensed by the keys of the Church. I speak not of a matter as to which there can be any doubt; for this impious dogma is declared in the plainest terms, in the writings not of one or two, but of the whole Schoolmen. Their master (*Sent.* Lib. 3, Dist. 9), after acknowledging, according to the doctrine of Peter, that Christ "bare our sins in his own body on the tree" (1 Pet. 2:24), immediately modifies the doctrine by in-troducing the exception, that in baptism all the temporal penalties of sin are relaxed; but that after baptism they are lessened by means of

repentance, the cross of Christ and our repentance thus co-operating together. St. John speaks very differently, "If any man sin, we have an advocate with the Father, Jesus Christ the righteous; and he is the propitiation for our sins." "I write unto you, little children, because your sins are forgiven you for his name's sake" (1 John 2:1-2, 12). He certainly is addressing believers, and while setting forth Christ as the propitiation for sins, shows them that there is no other satisfaction by which an offended God can be propitiated or appeased. He says not: God was once reconciled to you by Christ; now, seek other methods; but he makes him a perpetual advocate, who always, by his intercession, reinstates us in his Fathered favor—a perpetual propitiation by which sins are expiated. For what was said by another John will ever hold true, "Behold the Lamb of God, which taketh away the sins of the world" (John 1:29). He, I say, took them away, and no other; that is, since he alone is the Lamb of God, he alone is the offering for our sins; he alone is expiation; he alone is satisfaction. For though the right and power of pardoning properly belongs to the Father, when he is distinguished from the Son, as has already been seen, Christ is here exhibited in another view, as transferring to himself the punishment due to us, and wiping away our guilt in the sight of God. Whence it follows that we could not be partakers of the expiation accomplished by Christ, were he not possessed of that honor of which those who try to appease God by their compensations seek to rob him.

27. Here it is necessary to keep two things in view: that the honor of Christ be preserved entire and unimpaired, and that the conscience, assured of the pardon of sin, may have peace with God. Isaiah says that the Father "has laid on him the iniquity of us all;" that "with his stripes we are healed" (Isa. 53:5-6). Peter repeating the same thing, in other words says, that he "bare our sins in his own body on the tree" (1 Pet. 2:24). Paul's words are, "God sending his own Son in the likeness of sinful flesh, and for sin condemned sin in the flesh," "being made a curse for us" (Rom. 8:3; Gal. 3:13); in other words, the power and curse of sin

was destroyed in his flesh when he was offered as a sacrifice, on which the whole weight of our sins was laid, with their curse and execration, with the fearful judgment of God, and condemnation to death. Here there is no mention of the vain dogma, that after the initial cleansing no man experiences the efficacy of Christ's passion in any other way than by means of satisfying penance: we are directed to the satisfaction of Christ alone for every fall. Now call to mind their pestilential dogma: that the grace of God is effective only in the first forgiveness of sins; but if we afterwards fall, our works co-operate in obtaining the second pardon. If these things are so, do the properties above attributed to Christ remain entire? How immense the difference between the two propositions—that our iniquities were laid upon Christ, that in his own person he might expiate them, and that they are expiated by our works; that Christ is the propitiation for our sins, and that God is to be propitiated by works. Then, in regard to pacifying the conscience, what pacification will it be to be told that sins are redeemed by satisfactions? How will it be able to ascertain the measure of satisfaction? It will always doubt whether God is propitious; will always fluctuate, always tremble. Those who rest satisfied with petty satisfactions form too contemptible an estimate of the justice of God, and little consider the grievous heinousness of sin, as shall afterwards be shown. Even were we to grant that they can buy off some sins by due satisfaction, still what will they do while they are overwhelmed with so many sins that not even a hundred lives, though wholly devoted to the purpose, could suffice to satisfy for them? We may add, that all the passages in which the forgiveness of sins is declared refer not only to catechumens, but to the regenerate children of God; to those who have long been nursed in the bosom of the Church. That embassy which Paul so highly extols, "we pray you in Christ's stead, be ye reconciled to God" (2 Cor. 5:20), is not directed to strangers, but to those who had been regenerated long before. Setting satisfactions altogether aside, he directs us to the cross of Christ. Thus when he writes to the Colossians that Christ had "made peace through the blood of his cross," "to reconcile all things unto himself," he does not restrict it to the moment at which we are received into the Church but extends it to our whole course. This is plain from the context, where he says that in him "we have redemption by his blood, even the forgiveness of sins" (Col. 1:14). It is needless to collect more passages, as they are ever occurring.

28. Here they take refuge in the absurd distinction that some sins are venial and others mortal; that for the latter a weighty satisfaction is due, but that the former are purged by easier remedies; by the Lord's Prayer, the sprinkling of holy water, and the absolution of the Mass. Thus they insult and trifle with God. And yet, though they have the terms venial and mortal sin continually in their mouth, they have not yet been able to distinguish the one from the other, except by making impiety and impurity of heart to be venial sin. We, on the contrary, taught by the Scripture, the standard of righteousness and unrighteousness, declare that "the wages of sin is death;" and that "the soul that sinneth, it shall die" (Rom. 6:23; Ezek. 18:20). The sins of believers are venial, not because they do not merit death, but because by the mercy of God there is "now no condemnation to those which are in Christ Jesus" their sin being not imputed, but effaced by pardon. I know how unjustly they calumniate this our doctrine; for they say it is the paradox of the Stoics concerning the equality of sins: but we shall easily convict them out of their own mouths. I ask them whether, among those sins which they hold to be mortal, they acknowledge a greater and a less? If so, it cannot follow, as a matter of course, that all sins which are mortal are equal. Since Scripture declares that the wages of sin is death—that obedience to the law is the way to life—the transgression of it the way to death—they cannot evade this conclusion. In such a mass of sins, therefore, how will they find an end to their satisfactions? If the satisfaction for one sin requires one day, while preparing it they involve themselves in more sins; since no man, however righteous, passes one day without

falling repeatedly. While they prepare themselves for their satisfactions, number, or rather numbers without number, will be added. Confidence in satisfaction being thus destroyed, what more would they have? How do they still dare to think of satisfying?

29. They endeavor, indeed, to disentangle themselves, but it is impossible. They pretend a distinction between penalty and guilt, holding that the guilt is forgiven by the mercy of God; but that though the guilt is remitted, the punishment which divine justice requires to be paid remains. Satisfactions then properly relate to the remission of the penalty. How ridiculous this levity! They now confess that the remission of guilt is gratuitous; and yet they are ever and anon telling us to merit it by prayers and tears, and other preparations of every kind. Still the whole doctrine of Scripture regarding the remission of sins is diametrically opposed to that distinction. But although I think I have already done more than enough to establish this, I will subjoin some other passages, by which these slippery snakes will be so caught as to be afterwards unable to writhe even the tip of their tail: "Behold, the days come, saith the Lord, that I will make a new covenant with the house of Israel, and with the house of Judah." "I will forgive their iniquity, and I will remember their sin no more" (Jer. 31:31, 34). What this means we learn from another Prophet, when the Lord says, "When the righteous turneth away from his righteousness" "all his righteousness that he has done shall not be mentioned." "Again, when the wicked man turneth away from his wickedness that he has committed, and does that which is lawful and right, he shall save his soul alive" (Ezek. 18:24, 27). When he declares that he will not remember righteousness, the meaning is, that he will take no account of it to reward it. In the same way, not to remember sins is not to bring them to punishment. The same thing is denoted in other passages, by casting them behind his back, blotting them out as a cloud, casting them into the depths of the sea, not imputing them, hiding them. By such forms of expression the Holy Spirit has explained his meaning

not obscurely, if we would lend a willing ear. Certainly if God punishes sins, he imputes them; if he avenges, he remembers; if he brings them to judgment, he has not hid them; if he examines, he has not cast them behind his back; if he investigates, he has not blotted them out like a cloud; if he exposes them, he has not thrown them into the depths of the sea. In this way Augustine clearly interprets: "If God has covered sins, he willed not to advert to them; if he willed not to advert, he willed not to animadvert; if he willed not to animadvert, he willed not to punish: he willed not to take knowledge of them, he rather willed to pardon them. Why then did he say that sins were hid? Just that they might not be seen. What is meant by God seeing sins but punishing them?" (*August. in Ps. 32:1*). But let us hear from another prophetical passage on what terms the Lord forgives sins: "Though your sins be as scarlet, they shall be white as snow; though they be red like crimson, they shall be as wool" (Isa. 1:18). In Jeremiah again we read: "In those days, and in that time, saith the Lord, the iniquity of Israel shall be sought for, and there shall be none; and the sins of Judah, they shall not be found: for I will pardon them whom I reserve" (Jer. 50:20). Would you briefly comprehend the meaning of these words? Consider what, on the contrary, is meant by these expressions, "that transgression is sealed up in a bag;" "that the iniquity of Ephraim is bound up; his sin is hid;" that "the sin of Judah is written with a pen of iron, and with the point of a diamond." If they mean, as they certainly do, that vengeance will be recompensed, there can be no doubt that, by the contrary passages, the Lord declares that he renounces all thought of vengeance. Here I must entreat the reader not to listen to any glosses of mine, but only to give some deference to the word of God.

30. What, pray, did Christ perform for us if the punishment of sin is still exacted? For when we say that he "bare our sins in his own body on the tree" (1 Pet. 2:24), all we mean is, that he endured the penalty and punishment which was due to our sins. This is more significantly

declared by Isaiah, when he says that the "chastisement (or correction) of our peace was upon him" (Is. 53:5). But what is the correction of our peace, unless it be the punishment due to our sins, and to be paid by us before we could be reconciled to God, had he not become our substitute? Thus you clearly see that Christ bore the punishment of sin that he might thereby exempt his people from it. And whenever Paul makes mention of the redemption procured by him, he calls it απολυτρωσις, by which he does not simply mean redemption, as it is commonly understood, but the very price and satisfaction of redemption. For which reason, he also says, that Christ gave himself an αντιλυτρν (ransom) for us. "What is propitiation with the Lord (says Augustine) but sacrifice? And what is sacrifice but that which was offered for us in the death of Christ?" But we have our strongest argument in the injunctions of the Mosaic Law as to expiating the guilt of sin. The Lord does not there appoint this or that method of satisfying, but requires the whole compensation to be made by sacrifice, though he at the same time enumerates all the rites of expiation with the greatest care and exactness. How comes it that he does not at all enjoin works as the means of procuring pardon, but only requires sacrifices for expiation, unless it were his purpose thus to testify that this is the only kind of satisfaction by which his justice is appeased? For the sacrifices which the Israelites then offered were not regarded as human works, but were estimated by their antitype, that is, the sole sacrifice of Christ. The kind of compensation which the Lord receives from us is elegantly and briefly expressed by Hosea: "Take with you words, and turn to the Lord: say unto him, Take away all iniquity, and receive us graciously," here is remission: "so will we render the calves of our lips," here is satisfaction (Hos. 14:2). I know that they have still a more subtle evasion, by making a distinction between eternal and temporal punishment; but as they define temporal punishment to be any kind of infliction with which God visits either the body or the soul, eternal death only excepted, this restriction avails them little.

The passages which we have quoted above say expressly that the terms
on which God receives us into favor are these—viz. he remits all the
punishment which we deserved by pardoning our guilt. And whenever
David or the other prophets ask pardon for their sins, they deprecate
punishment. Nay, a sense of the divine justice impels them to this.
On the other hand, when they promise mercy from the Lord, they
almost always discourse of punishments and the forgiveness of them.
Assuredly, when the Lord declares in Ezekiel, that he will put an end
to the Babylonian captivity, not "for your sakes, O house of Israel, but
for mine holy name's sake" (Ezek. 36:22), he sufficiently demonstrates
that both are gratuitous. In short, if we are freed from guilt by Christ,
the punishment consequent upon guilt must cease with it.

31. But since they also arm themselves with passages of Scripture,
let us see what the arguments are which they employ. David, they say,
when upbraided by Nathan the Prophet for adultery and murder, receives pardon of the sin, and yet by the death of the son born of adultery is afterwards punished (2 Sam. 12:13-14). Such punishments
which were to be inflicted after the remission of the guilt, we are
taught to ransom by satisfactions. For Daniel exhorted Nebuchadnezzar: "Break off thy sins by righteousness, and thine iniquities by
showing mercy to the poor" (Dan. 4:27). And Solomon says, "by mercy and truth iniquity is purged" (Prov. 16:6); and again, "love covereth
all sins" (Prov. 10:12). This sentiment is confirmed by Peter (1 Pet.
4:8). Also in Luke, our Lord says of the woman that was a sinner,
"Her sins, which are many, are forgiven; for she loved much" (Luke
7:47). How perverse and preposterous the judgment they ever form
of the doings of God! Had they observed, what certainly they ought
not to have overlooked, that there are two kinds of divine judgment,
they would have seen in the correction of David a very different form
of punishment from that which must be thought designed for vengeance. But since it in no slight degree concerns us to understand the
purpose of God in the chastisements by which he animadverts upon

our sins and how much they differ from the exemplary punishments which he indignantly inflicts on the wicked and reprobate, I think it will not be improper briefly to glance at it. For the sake of distinction, we may call the one kind of judgment punishment, the other chastisement. In judicial punishment, God is to be understood as taking vengeance on his enemies, by displaying his anger against them, confounding, scattering, and annihilating them. By divine punishment, properly so called, let us then understand punishment accompanied with indignation. In judicial chastisement, he is offended, but not in wrath; he does not punish by destroying or striking down as with a thunderbolt. Hence it is not properly punishment or vengeance, but correction and admonition. The one is the act of a judge, the other of a father. When the judge punishes a criminal, he animadverts upon the crime, and demands the penalty. When a father corrects his son sharply, it is not to mulct or avenge, but rather to teach him, and make him more cautious for the future. Chrysostom in his writings employs a simile which is somewhat different, but the same in purport. He says, "A son is whipt, and a slave is whipt, but the latter is punished as a slave for his offense: the former is chastised as a freeborn son, standing in need of correction." The correction of the latter is designed to prove and amend him; that of the former is scourging and punishment.

32. To have a short and clear view of the whole matter, we must make two distinctions. First, whenever the infliction is designed to avenge, then the curse and wrath of God displays itself. This is never the case with believers. On the contrary, the chastening of God carries his blessing with it, and is an evidence of love, as Scripture teaches. This distinction is plainly marked throughout the word of God. All the calamities which the wicked suffer in the present life are depicted to us as a kind of anticipation of the punishment of hell. In these they already see, as from a distance, their eternal condemnation; and so far are they from being thereby reformed, or deriving any

benefit, that by such preludes they are rather prepared for the fearful doom which finally awaits them. The Lord chastens his servants sore, but does not give them over unto death (Ps. 118:18). When afflicted, they acknowledge it is good for them, that they may learn his statutes (Ps. 119:71). But as we everywhere read that the saints received their chastisements with placid mind, so inflictions of the latter kind they always most earnestly deprecated. "O Lord, correct me," says Jeremiah, "but with judgment; not in thine anger, lest thou bring me to nothing. Pour out thy fury upon the heathen that know thee not, and upon the families that call not on thy name" (Jer. 10:24-25). David says "O Lord, rebuke me not in thine anger, neither chasten me in thy hot displeasure" (Ps. 6:1). There is nothing inconsistent with this in its being repeatedly said, that the Lord is angry with his saints when he chastens them for their sins (Ps. 38:7). In like manner, in Isaiah, "And in that day thou shalt say, O Lord, I will praise thee: though thou wast angry with me, thine anger is turned away, and thou comfortedst me" (Isa. 12:1). Likewise in Habakkuk, "In wrath remember mercy" (Hab. 3:2); and in Micah, "I will bear the indignation of the Lord, because I have sinned against him" (Mic. 7:9). Here we are reminded not only that those who are justly punished gain nothing by murmuring, but that believers obtain a mitigation of their pain by reflecting on the divine intention. For the same reason, he is said to profane his inheritance; and yet we know that he will never profane it. The expression refers not to the counsel or purpose of God in punishing, but to the keen sense of pain, endured by those who are visited with any measure of divine severity. For the Lord not only chastens his people with a slight degree of austerity, but sometimes so wounds them, that they seem to themselves on the very eve of perdition. He thus declares that they have deserved his anger, and it is fitting so to do, that they may be dissatisfied with themselves for their sins, may be more careful in their desires to appease God, and anxiously hasten to seek his pardon; still, at this very time, he gives clearer evidence of his mercy than of his anger. For He who cannot deceive has declared, that the covenant made with us in our true Solomon stands fast and will never be broken, "If his children forsake my law, and walk not in my judgments; if they break my statutes, and keep not my commandments; then will I visit their transgressions with the rod, and their iniquity with stripes. Nevertheless, my loving-kindness will I not utterly take from him, nor suffer my faithfulness to fail" (Ps. 89:31-34). To assure us of this mercy, he says, that the rod with which he will chastise the posterity of Solomon will be the "rod of men," and "the stripes of the children of men" (2 Sam. 7:14). While by these terms he denotes moderation and levity, he, at the same time, intimates, that those who feel the hand of God opposed to them cannot but tremble and be confounded. How much regard he has to this levity in chastening his Israel he shows by the Prophet, "Behold, I have refined thee, but not with silver; I have chosen thee in the furnace of affliction" (Isa. 48:10). Although he tells them that they are chastisements with a view to purification, he adds, that even these are so tempered, that they are not to be too much crushed by them. And this is very necessary, for the more a man reveres God, and devotes himself to the cultivation of piety, the more tender he is in bearing his anger (Ps. 90:11; and ibid. Calv.). The reprobate, though they groan under the lash, yet because they weigh not the true cause, but rather turn their back, as well upon their sins as upon the divine judgment, become hardened in their stupor; or, because they murmur and kick, and so rebel against their judge, their infatuated violence fills them with frenzy and madness. Believers, again, admonished by the rod of God, immediately begin to reflect on their sins, and, struck with fear and dread, retake themselves as suppliants to implore mercy. Did not God mitigate the pains by which wretched souls are excruciated, they would give way a hundred times, even at slight signs of his anger.

33. The second distinction is, that when the reprobate are brought under the lash of God, they begin in a manner to pay the punishment

due to his justice; and though their refusal to listen to these proofs of the divine anger will not escape with impunity, still they are not punished with the view of bringing them to a better mind, but only to teach them by dire experience that God is a judge and avenger. The sons of God are beaten with rods, not that they may pay the punishment due to their faults, but that they may thereby be led to repent. Accordingly, we perceive that they have more respect to the future than to the past. I prefer giving this in the words of Chrysostom rather than my own: "His object in imposing a penalty upon us, is not to inflict punishment on our sins but to correct us for the future" (Chrysost. *Serm. de Poenit. et Confess.*). So also Augustine, "The suffering at which you cry, is medicine, not punishment; chastisement, not condemnation. Do not drive away the rod, if you would not be driven away from the inheritance. Know, brethren, that the whole of that misery of the human race, under which the world groans, is a medicinal pain, not a penal sentence" (*August. in Ps. 102*, circa finem). It seemed proper to quote these passages, lest anyone should think the mode of expression which I have used to be novel or uncommon. To the same effect are the indignant terms in which the Lord expostulates with his people, for their ingratitude in obstinately despising all his inflictions. In Isaiah he says, "Why should ye be stricken any more? ye will revolt more and more. The whole head is sick and the whole heart faint" (Isa. 1:5-6). But as such passages abound in the Prophets, it is sufficient briefly to have shown, that the only purpose of God in punishing his Church is to subdue her to repentance. Thus, when he rejected Saul from the kingdoms he punished in vengeance (1 Sam. 15:23); when he deprived David of his child, he chastised for amendment (2 Sam. 12:18). In this sense Paul is to be understood when he says, "When we are judged, we are chastened of the Lord, that we should not be condemned with the world" (1 Cor. 11:32); that is, while we as sons of God are afflicted by our heavenly Father's hand, it is not punishment to confound, but only chastisement to train us. On this subject Augustine is plainly with us (*De Peccator. Meritis ac Remiss.* Lib. 2 cap. 33-34). For he shows that the punishments with which men are equally chastened by God are to be variously considered; because the saints after the forgiveness of their sins have struggles and exercises, the reprobate without forgiveness are punished for their iniquity. Enumerating the punishments inflicted on David and other saints, he says, it was designed, by thus humbling them, to prove and exercise their piety. The passage in Isaiah, in which it is said, "Speak ye comfortably to Jerusalem, and cry unto her, that her warfare is accomplished, that her iniquity is pardoned; for she has received of the Lord's hands double for all her sins" (Isa. 40:2), proves not that the pardon of sin depends on freedom from punishment. It is just as if he had said, Sufficient punishment has now been exacted; as for their number and heinousness you have long been oppressed with sorrow and mourning, it is time to send you a message of complete mercy, that your minds may be filled with joy on feeling me to be a Father. For God there assumes the character of a father who repents even of the just severity which he has been compelled to us, towards his son.

34. These are the thoughts with which the believer ought to be provided in the bitterness of affliction, "The time is come that judgment must begin at the house of God," "the city which is called by my name" (1 Pet. 4:17; Jer. 25:29). What could the sons of God do, if they thought that the severity which they feel was vengeance? He who, smitten by the hand of God, thinks that God is a judge inflicting punishment, cannot conceive of him except as angry and at enmity with him; cannot but detest the rod of God as curse and condemnation; in short, Can never persuade himself that he is loved by God, while he feels that he is still disposed to inflict punishment upon him. He only profits under the divine chastening who considers that God, though offended with his sins, is still propitious and favorable to him. Otherwise, the feeling must necessarily be what the Psalmist complains that he had experienced, "Thy wrath lieth hard upon me, and thou hast afflicted me with all thy waves." Also what Moses

says, "For we are consumed by thine anger, and by thy wrath we are troubled. Thou hast set our iniquities before thee, our secret sins in the light of thy countenance. For all our days are passed away in thy wrath; we spend our years as a tale that is told" (Ps. 90:7-9). On the other hand, David speaking of fatherly chastisements, to show how believers are more assisted than oppressed by them, thus sings "Blessed is the man whom thou chastenest, O Lord, and teachest him out of thy law; that thou mayest give him rest from the days of adversity, until the pit be digged for the wicked" (Ps. 94:12-13). It is certainly a sore temptation, when God, sparing unbelievers and overlooking their crimes, appears more rigid towards his own people. Hence, to solace them, he adds the admonition of the law which teaches them, that their salvation is consulted when they are brought back to the right path, whereas the wicked are borne headlong in their errors, which ultimately lead to the pit. It matters not whether the punishment is eternal or temporary. For disease, pestilence, famine, and war, are curses from God, as much as even the sentence of eternal death, whenever their tendency is to operate as instruments of divine wrath and vengeance against the reprobate.

35. All, if I mistake not, now see what view the Lord had in chastening David, namely, to prove that murder and adultery are most offensive to God, and to manifest this offensiveness in a beloved and faithful servant, that David himself might be taught never again to dare to commit such wickedness; still, however, it was not a punishment designed in payment of a kind of compensation to God. In the same way are we to judge of that other correction, in which the Lord subjects his people to a grievous pestilence, for the disobedience of David in forgetting himself so far as to number the people. He indeed freely forgave David the guilt of his sin; but because it was necessary, both as a public example to all ages and also to humble David himself, not to allow such an offense to go unpunished, he chastened him most sharply with his whip. We ought also to keep

this in view in the universal curse of the human race. For since after obtaining grace we still continue to endure the miseries denounced to our first parent as the penalty of transgression, we ought thereby to be reminded, how offensive to God is the transgression of his law, that thus humbled and dejected by a consciousness of our wretched condition, we may aspire more ardently to true happiness. But it were most foolish in any one to imagine, that we are subjected to the calamities of the present life for the guilt of sin. This seems to me to have been Chrysostom's meaning when he said, "If the purpose of God in inflicting punishment is to bring those persisting in evil to repentance, when repentance is manifested punishment would be superfluous" (Chrysos. Homily. 3 *de Provid.*). Wherefore, as he knows what the disposition of each requires, he treats one with greater harshness and another with more indulgence. Accordingly, when he wishes to show that he is not excessive in exacting punishment, he upbraids a hard-hearted and obstinate people, because, after being smitten, they still continued in sin (Jer. 5:3). In the same sense he complains, that "Ephraim is a cake not turned" (Hos. 7:8), because chastisement did not make a due impression on their minds, and, correcting their vices, make them fit to receive pardon. Surely he who thus speaks shows, that as soon as anyone repents he will be ready to receive him, and that the rigor which he exercises in chastising faults is wrung from him by our perverseness, since we should prevent him by a voluntary correction. Such, however, being the hardness and rudeness of all hearts, that they stand universally in need of castigation, our infinitely wise Parent has seen it meet to exercise all without exception, during their whole lives, with chastisement. It is strange how they fix their eyes so intently on the one example of David, and are not moved by the many examples in which they might have beheld the free forgiveness of sins. The publican is said to have gone down from the temple justified (Luke 18:14); no punishment follows. Peter obtained the pardon of his sin (Luke 22:61). "We read of his tears," says

Ambrose (Serm. 46, *De Poenit. Petri*), "we read not of satisfaction." To the paralytic it is said, "Son, be of good cheer; thy sins be forgiven thee" (Matt. 9:2); no penance is enjoined. All the acts of forgiveness mentioned in Scripture are gratuitous. The rule ought to be drawn from these numerous examples, rather than from one example which contains a kind of specialty.

36. Daniel, in exhorting Nebuchadnezzar to break off his sins by righteousness, and his iniquities by showing mercy to the poor (Dan. 4:27), meant not to intimate, that righteousness and mercy are able to propitiate God and redeem from punishment (far be it from us to suppose that there ever was any other *apolutrosis* (ransom) than the blood of Christ); but the breaking off referred to in that passage has reference to man rather than to God: as if he had said, O king, you have exercised an unjust and violent domination, you have oppressed the humble, spoiled the poor, treated your people harshly and unjustly; instead of unjust exaction, instead of violence and oppression, now practice mercy and justice. In like manner, Solomon says, that love covers a multitude of sins; not, however, with God, but among men. For the whole verse stands thus, "Hatred stirreth up strifes; but love covereth all sins" (Prov. 10:12). Here, after his manner, he contrasts the evils produced by hatred with the fruits of charity, in this sense, Those who hate are incessantly biting, carping at, upbraiding, lacerating each other, making every thing a fault; but those who love mutually conceal each other's faults, wink at many, forgive many: not that the one approves the vices of the other, but tolerates and cures by admonishing, rather than exasperates by assailing. That the passage is quoted by Peter (1 Pet. 4:8) in the same sense we cannot doubt, unless we would charge him with corrupting or craftily wresting Scripture. When it is said, that "by mercy and truth iniquity is purged" (Prov. 16:6), the meaning is, not that by them compensation is made to the Lord, so that he being thus satisfied remits the punishment which he would otherwise have exacted; but intimation is made after the

3eedabitur

familiar manner of Scripture, that those who, forsaking their vices and iniquities turn to the Lord in truth and piety, will find him propitious: as if he had said, that the wrath of God is calmed, and his judgment is at rest, whenever we rest from our wickedness. But, indeed, it is not the cause of pardon that is described, but rather the mode of true conversion; just as the Prophets frequently declare, that it is in vain for hypocrites to offer God fictitious rites instead of repentance, seeing his delight is in integrity and the duties of charity. In like manner, also, the author of the Epistle to the Hebrews, commending kindness and humanity, reminds us, that "with such sacrifices God is well pleased" (Heb. 13:16). And indeed when Christ, rebuking the Pharisees because, intent merely on the outside of the cup and platter, they neglected purity of heart, enjoins them, in order that they may be clean in all respects, to give alms, does he exhort them to give satisfaction thereby? He only tells them what the kind of purity is which God requires. Of this mode of expression we have treated elsewhere (Matt. 23:25; Luke 11:39-41; see *Calv. In Harm. Evang.*).

37. In regard to the passage in Luke (Luke 7:36, sq), no man of sober judgment, who reads the parable there employed by our Lord, will raise any controversy with us. The Pharisee thought that the Lord did not know the character of the woman whom he had so easily admitted to his presence. For he presumed that he would not have admitted her if he had known what kind of a sinner she was; and from this he inferred, that one who could be deceived in this way was not a prophet. Our Lord, to show that she was not a sinner, inasmuch as she had already been forgiven, spake this parable: "There was a certain creditor which had two debtors; the one owed five hundred pence, and the other fifty. And when they had nothing to pay, he frankly forgave them both. Tell me, therefore, which of them will love him most?" The Pharisee answers: "I suppose that he to whom he forgave most." Then our Savior rejoins: "Her sins, which are many, are forgiven; for she loved much." By these words it is plain he does not make love the

cause of forgiveness, but the proof of it. The similitude is borrowed from the case of a debtor, to whom a debt of five hundred pence had been forgiven. It is not said that the debt is forgiven because he loved much, but that he loved much because it was forgiven. The similitude ought to be applied in this way: You think this woman is a sinner; but you ought to have acknowledged her as not a sinner, in respect that her sins have been forgiven her. Her love ought to have been to you a proof of her having obtained forgiveness, that love being an expression of gratitude for the benefit received. It is an argument *a posteriori*, by which something is demonstrated by the results produced by it. Our Lord plainly attests the ground on which she had obtained forgiveness, when he says, "Thy faith has saved thee." By faith, therefore, we obtain forgiveness: by love we give thanks, and bear testimony to the loving-kindness of the Lord.

38. I am little moved by the numerous passages in the writings of the Fathers relating to satisfaction. I see indeed that some (I will frankly say almost all whose books are extant) have either erred in this matter, or spoken too roughly and harshly; but I cannot admit that they were so rude and unskillful as to write these passages in the sense in which they are read by our new satisfactionaries. Chrysostom somewhere says, "When mercy is implored interrogation ceases; when mercy is asked, judgment rages not; when mercy is sought, there is no room for punishment; where there is mercy, no question is asked; where there is mercy, the answer gives pardon" (Chrysos. *Hom. 2* in Ps. 50). How much soever these words may be twisted, they can never be reconciled with the dogmas of the Schoolmen. In the book *De Dogmatibus Ecclesiasticis*, which is attributed to Augustine, you read (chap. 54), "The satisfaction of repentance is to cut off the causes of sins, and not to indulge an entrance to their suggestions." From this it appears that the doctrine of satisfaction, said to be paid for sins committed, was everywhere derided in those ages; for here the only satisfaction referred to is caution, abstinence from sin for the future.

I am unwilling to quote what Chrysostom says (Hom. 10 in *Genes*) that God requires nothing more of us than to confess our faults before him with tears, as similar sentiments abound both in his writings and those of others. Augustine indeed calls works of mercy remedies for obtaining forgiveness of sins (*Enchir. ad Laur.*); but lest anyone should stumble at the expression, he himself, in another passage, obviates the difficulty. "The flesh of Christ," says he, "is the true and only sacrifice for sins—not only for those which are all effaced in baptism, but those into which we are afterwards betrayed through infirmity, and because of which the whole Church daily cries, 'Forgive us our debts,' (Matt. 6:12). And they are forgiven by that special sacrifice."

39. By satisfaction, however, they, for the most part, meant not compensation to be paid to God, but the public testimony, by which those who had been punished with excommunication, and wished again to be received into communion, assured the Church of their repentance. For those penitents were enjoined certain fasts and other things, by which they might prove that they were truly, and from the heart, weary of their former life, or rather might obliterate the remembrance of their past deeds: in this way they were said to give satisfaction, not to God, but to the Church. The same thing is expressed by Augustine in a passage in his *Enchiridion ad Laurentium*, chap. 65. From that ancient custom the satisfactions and confessions now in use took their rise. It is indeed a viperish progeny, not even a vestige of the better form now remaining. I know that ancient writers sometimes speak harshly; nor do I deny, as I lately said, that they have perhaps erred; but dogmas, which were tainted with a few blemishes now that they have fallen into the unwashed hands of those men, are altogether defiled. And if we were to decide the contest by authority of the Fathers, what kind of Fathers are those whom they obtrude upon us? A great part of those, from whom Lombard their Coryphaeus framed his centos, are extracted from the absurd dreams of certain monks passing under the names of Ambrose, Jerome, Augustine, and

Chrysostom. On the present subject almost all his extracts are from the book of Augustine *De Paenitentia*, a book absurdly compiled by some rhapsodist, alike from good and bad authors—a book which indeed bears the name of Augustine, but which no person of the least learning would deign to acknowledge as his. Wishing to save my readers trouble, they will pardon me for not searching minutely into all their absurdities. For myself it were not very laborious, and might gain some applause, to give a complete exposure of dogmas which have hitherto been vaunted as mysteries; but as my object is to give useful instruction, I desist.

Study Guide Questions

Section 1

1. What are the three elements of repentance, according to the Scholastics?
2. And according to Calvin, how do they heal all the bitterness?

Section 2

1. Why does Calvin say that this is not a dispute "matter of no consequence"?

Section 3

1. When someone follows the Scholastics in this, what are the two possible responses?

Section 4

1. How does Calvin respond to the Scholastics' allegorical argument from the ten lepers?
2. And how does Calvin explain why Christ sent the lepers to the priests?

Section 5

1. What does Calvin say about allegorical interpretation and dogma?

Section 6

1. How does Calvin handle the argument for confession from the baptism of John the Baptist?

2. What about James' requirement that we confess our sins to one another (Jas. 5:16)?

Section 7

1. When was auricular confession made a matter of canon law?

2. What other historical argument does Calvin use?

Section 8

1. What did Chrysostom teach on the subject of confession of sin?

Section 9

1. What mistake in interpretation did the defenders of auricular confession make?

2. Calvin then cites a number of passages to prove what?

Section 10

1. If we have confessed to God, what are the two circumstances that would require confession to men?

2. What passage in the Old Testament urges public confession?

Section 11

1. When should people confess all together?

2. What other circumstance should lead us to confess our sins corporately?

Section 12

1. Scripture approves two forms of private confession to others. What are they?

2. What role do ministers have in this?

3. To whom do we commend private confession?

Section 13

1. What does Calvin ardently wish was observed everywhere?

2. If this were observed, Calvin would desire two things to be avoided. What are they?

Section 14

1. What are the three occasions, according to Calvin, when the power of the keys is to be used?

2. What must we not "dream up" with regard to the power of the keys?

Section 15

1. What Roman practice is Calvin opposing?

Section 16

1. What does Calvin see as one problem with this?

Section 17

1. What does Calvin call this requirement?

2. How do Roman theologians categorize sins?

3. And what did they discover when they were done?

Section 18

1. Does Calvin agree that sins should be confessed singly?

2. What promise from the prophet Ezekiel does he quote?

Section 19

1. What is the problem with the requirement that Catholics make confession once a year?

Section 20

1. According to Calvin, what is necessary in order to hold the power of the keys?

Section 21
1. What is the central problem with auricular confession?

Section 22
1. Why is the Protestant practice free of "these absurdities"?

Section 23
1. Why do passages like Matthew 18:15–18 have nothing to do with auricular confession?

Section 24
1. What are the twin errors that arise when the Roman doctrine is practiced?

Section 25
1. What doctrine was Calvin countering here?

Section 26
1. What do our duties of fear and honor relate to?

Section 27
1. What two things is Calvin concerned to press home in this section?

Section 28
1. What does Calvin do with the distinction between venial and mortal sin?
2. What objection does he dismiss?

Section 29
1. What distinction does the Roman position attempt?
2. How does Calvin respond?

Section 30

1. What must a man attain to in the first place to have faith?

2. What must also happen in order for this faith to reconcile us to God?

Section 31

1. What are the two kinds of judgment, according to Calvin?

2. What role does God have in each?

Section 32

1. What is characteristic of the judgment of vengeance?

2. What is the characteristic of the judgment of teaching?

3. What is the difference between how two classes of people receive these respective judgments?

Section 33

1. What is the difference between discipline and punishment with respect to time?

2. When we as children of God are afflicted, what is it for?

Section 34

1. Why must believers be exhorted not to lose heart?

Section 35

1. Why was David disciplined with various calamities?

Section 36

1. What is Solomon referring to when he says that love covers a multitude of sins?

Section 37

1. How does Calvin prove that the woman who was forgiven much because she loved much did not earn her forgiveness?

Sections 38–39

1. What is Calvin's view of the church fathers on this subject?

CHAPTER 5

Of the modes of supplementing satisfaction—viz. indulgences and purgatory.

Divisions of the chapter—I. A summary description and refutation of Popish indulgences, sec. 1-2.

II. Confutation by Leo and Augustine. Answer to two objections urged in support of them, sec. 3-4. A profane love of filthy lucre on the part of the Pope. The origin of indulgences unfolded, sec. 5.

III. An examination of Popish purgatory. Its horrible impiety, sec. 6. An explanation of five passages of Scripture by which Sophists endeavor to support that dream, sec. 7-8. Sentiments of the ancient Theologians concerning purgatory, sec. 10.

Outline:

1. The dogma of satisfaction the parent of indulgences. Vanity of both. The reason of it. Evidence of the avarice of the Pope and the Romish clergy: also of the blindness with which the Christian world was smitten.

2. View of indulgences given by the Sophists. Their true nature. Refutation of them. Refutation confirmed by seven passages of Scripture.

3. Confirmed also by the testimony of Leo, a Roman Bishop, and by Augustine. Attempts of the Popish doctors to establish the monstrous doctrine of indulgences, and even support it by Apostolical authority. First answer.

4. Second answer to the passage of an Apostle adduced to support the dogma of indulgences. Answer confirmed by a comparison with other passages, and from a passage in Augustine, explaining the Apostle's meaning. Another passage from the same Apostle confirming this view.

5. The Pope's profane thirst for filthy lucre exposed. The origin of indulgences.

6. Examination of the fictitious purgatory of the Papists. 1. From the nature of the thing itself. 2. From the authority of God. 3. From the consideration of the merit of Christ, which is destroyed by this fiction. Purgatory, what it is. 4. From the impiety teeming from this fountain.

7. Exposition of the passages of Scripture quoted in support of purgatory. 1. Of the Impardonable sin, from which it is inferred that there are some sins afterwards to be forgiven. 2. Of the passage as to paying the last farthing.

8. 3. The passage concerning the bending of the knee to Christ by things under the earth. 4. The example of Judas Maccabeus in sending an oblation for the dead to Jerusalem.

9. 5. Of the fire which shall try every man's work. The sentiment of the ancient theologians. Answer, containing a *reductio ad absurdum.* Confirmation by a passage of Augustine. The meaning of the Apostle. What to be understood by "fire." A clear exposition of the metaphor. The day of the Lord. How those who suffer loss are saved by fire.

10. The doctrine of purgatory ancient, but refuted by a more ancient Apostle. Not supported by ancient writers, by Scripture, or solid argument. Introduced by custom and a zeal not duly regulated by the word of God. Ancient writers, as Augustine, speak doubtfully in

commending prayer for the dead. At all events, we must hold by the word of God, which rejects this fiction. A vast difference between the more ancient and the more modern builders of purgatory. This shown by comparing them.

From this dogma of satisfaction that of indulgences takes its rise. For the pretense is, that what is wanting to our own ability is hereby supplied; and they go the insane length of defining them to be a dispensation of the merits of Christ, and the martyrs which the Pope makes by his bulls. Though they are fitter for hellebore than for argument—and it is scarcely worthwhile to refute these frivolous errors, which, already battered down, begin of their own accord to grow antiquated, and totter to their fall—yet, as a brief refutation may be useful to some of the unlearned, I will not omit it. Indeed, the fact that indulgences have so long stood safe and with impunity, and wantoned with so much fury and tyranny, may be regarded as a proof into how deep a night of ignorance mankind were for some ages plunged. They saw themselves insulted openly, and without disguise, by the Pope and his bull-bearers; they saw the salvation of the soul made the subject of a lucrative traffic, salvation taxed at a few pieces of money, nothing given gratuitously; they saw what was squeezed from them in the form of oblations basely consumed on strumpets, pimps and gluttony, the loudest trumpeters of indulgences being the greatest despisers; they saw the monster stalking abroad, and every day luxuriating with greater license, and that without end, new bulls being constantly issued, and new sums extracted. Still indulgences were received with the greatest reverence, worshiped, and bought. Even those who saw more clearly than others deemed them pious frauds, by which, even in deceiving, some good was gained. Now, at length, that a considerable portion of the world have begun to re-think themselves, indulgences grow cool, and gradually even begin to freeze, preparatory to their final extinction.

2. But since very many who see the vile imposture, theft, and rapine (with which the dealers in indulgences have hitherto deluded and sported with us), are not aware of the true source of the impiety, it may be proper to show not only what indulgences truly are, but also that they are polluted in every part. They give the name of treasury of the Church to the merits of Christ, the holy Apostles and Martyrs. They pretend, as I have said, that the radical custody of the granary has been delivered to the Roman bishop, to whom the dispensation of these great blessings belongs in such a sense, that he can both exercise it by himself, and delegate the power of exercising it to others. Hence we have from the Pope at one time plenary indulgences, at another for certain years; from the cardinals for a hundred days, and from the bishops for forty. These, to describe them truly, are a profanation of the blood of Christ, and a delusion of Satan, by which the Christian people are led away from the grace of God and the life which is in Christ, and turned aside from the true way of salvation. For how could the blood of Christ be more shamefully profaned than by denying its sufficiency for the remission of sins, for reconciliation and satisfaction, unless its defects, as if it were dried up and exhausted, are supplemented from some other quarter? Peter's words are: "To him give all the prophets witness, that through his name whosoever believeth in him shall receive remission of sins" (Acts 10:43); but indulgences bestow the remission of sins through Peter, Paul, and the Martyrs. "The blood of Jesus Christ his Son cleanseth us from all sin," says John (1 John 1:7). Indulgences make the blood of the martyrs an ablution of sins. "He has made him to be sin (i.e., a satisfaction for sin) for us who knew no sin," says Paul (2 Cor. 5:21), "that we might be made the righteousness of God in him." Indulgences make the satisfaction of sin to depend on the blood of the martyrs. Paul exclaimed and testified to the Corinthians, that Christ alone was crucified, and died for them (1 Cor. 1:13). Indulgences declare that Paul and others died for us. Paul elsewhere says that Christ purchased the Church with his own blood (Acts 20:28). Indulgences

assign another purchase to the blood of martyrs. "By one offering he has perfected for ever them that are sanctified," says the Apostle (Heb. 10:14). Indulgences, on the other hand, insist that sanctification, which would otherwise be insufficient, is perfected by martyrs. John says that all the saints "have washed their robes, and made them white in the blood of the Lamb" (Rev. 7:14). Indulgences tell us to wash our robes in the blood of saints.

3. There is an admirable passage in opposition to their blasphemies in Leo, a Roman Bishop (*ad Palaestinos*, Ep. 81). "Although the death of many saints was precious in the sight of the Lord (Ps. 116:15), yet no innocent man's slaughter was the propitiation of the world. The just received crowns but did not give them; and the fortitude of believers produced examples of patience, not gifts of righteousness: for their deaths were for themselves; and none by his final end paid the debt of another, except Christ our Lord, in whom alone all are crucified—all dead, buried, and raised up." This sentiment, as it was of a memorable nature, he has elsewhere repeated (Epist. 95). Certainly one could not desire a clearer confutation of this impious dogma. Augustine introduces the same sentiment not less appositely: "Although brethren die for brethren, yet no martyr's blood is shed for the remission of sins: this Christ did for us, and in this conferred upon us not what we should imitate, but what should make us grateful" (August. *Tract. in Joann. 84*). Again, in another passage: "As he alone became the Son of God and the Son of man, that he might make us to be with himself sons of God, so he alone, without any ill desert, undertook the penalty for us, that through him we might, without good desert, obtain undeserved favor" (*ad Bonif.* Lib. 4, cap. 4). Indeed, as their whole doctrine is a patchwork of sacrilege and blasphemy, this is the most blasphemous of the whole. Let them acknowledge whether or not they hold the following dogmas: That the martyrs, by their death, performed more to God, and merited more than was necessary for themselves, and that they have a large surplus of merits which may

be applied to others; that in order that this great good may not prove superfluous, their blood is mingled with the blood of Christ, and out of both is formed the treasury of the Church, for the forgiveness and satisfaction of sins; and that in this sense we must understand the words of Paul: "Who now rejoice in my sufferings, and fill up that which is behind of the afflictions of Christ in my flesh for his body's sake, which is the Church" (Col. 1:24). What is this but merely to leave the name of Christ, and at the same time make him a vulgar saintling, who can scarcely be distinguished in the crowd? He alone ought to be preached, alone held forth, alone named, alone looked to, whenever the subject considered is the obtaining of the forgiveness of sins, expiation, and sanctification. But let us hear their propositions. That the blood of martyrs may not be shed without fruit, it must be employed for the common good of the Church. Is it so? Was there no fruit in glorifying God by death? in sealing his truth with their blood? in testifying, by contempt of the present life, that they looked for a better? in confirming the faith of the Church, and at the same time disabling the pertinacity of the enemy by their constancy? But thus it is. They acknowledge no fruit if Christ is the only propitiation, if he alone died for our sins, if he alone was offered for our redemption. Nevertheless, they say, Peter and Paul would have gained the crown of victory though they had died in their beds a natural death. But as they contended to blood, it would not accord with the justice of God to leave their doing so barren and unfruitful. As if God were unable to augment the glory of his servants in proportion to the measure of his gifts. The advantage derived in common by the Church is great enough, when, by their triumphs, she is inflamed with zeal to fight.

4. How maliciously they wrest the passage in which Paul says, that he supplies in his body that which was lacking in the sufferings of Christ! (Col. 1:24). That defect or supplement refers not to the work of redemption, satisfaction, or expiation, but to those afflictions with which the members of Christ, in other words, all believers, behave

to be exercised, so long as they are in the flesh. He says, therefore, that part of the sufferings of Christ still remains—viz. that what he suffered in himself he daily suffers in his members. Christ so honors us as to regard and count our afflictions as his own. By the additional words—for the Church, Paul means not for the redemptions or reconciliations or satisfaction of the Church, but for edification and progress. As he elsewhere says, "I endure all things for the elect's sakes, that they may also obtain the salvation which is in Christ Jesus with eternal glory" (2 Tim. 2:10). He also writes to the Corinthians: "Whether we be afflicted, it is for your consolation and salvation, which is effectual in the enduring of the same sufferings which we also suffer" (2 Cor. 1:6). In the same place he immediately explains his meaning by adding, that he was made a minister of the Church, not for redemption, but according to the dispensation which he received to preach the gospel of Christ. But if they still desire another interpreter, let them hear Augustine: "The sufferings of Christ are in Christ alone, as in the head; in Christ and the Church as in the whole body. Hence Paul, being one member says, 'I fill up in my body that which is behind of the sufferings of Christ.' Therefore, O hearers whoever you be, if you are among the members of Christ, whatever you suffer from those who are not members of Christ, was lacking to the sufferings of Christ" (August. *in Ps. 16*). He elsewhere explains the end of the sufferings of the Apostles undertaken for Christ: "Christ is my door to you, because ye are the sheep of Christ purchased by his blood: acknowledge your price, which is not paid by me, but preached by me" (August. *Tract. in Joann. 47*). He afterwards adds, "As he laid down his life, so ought we to lay down our lives for the brethren, to build up peace and maintain faith." Thus far Augustine. Far be it from us to imagine that Paul thought anything was wanting to the sufferings of Christ in regard to the complete fullness of righteousness, salvation, and life, or that he wished to make any addition to it, after showing so clearly and eloquently that the grace of Christ was poured out in such rich abundance as far to exceed all the power of sin (Rom. 5:15). All saints have been saved by it alone, not by the merit of their own life or death, as Peter distinctly testifies (Acts 15:11); so that it is an insult to God and his Anointed to place the worthiness of any saint in anything save the mercy of God alone. But why dwell longer on this, as if the matter were obscure, when to mention these monstrous dogmas is to refute them?

5. Moreover, to say nothing of these abominations, who taught the Pope to enclose the grace of Jesus Christ in lead and parchment, grace which the Lord is pleased to dispense by the word of the Gospel? Undoubtedly either the Gospel of God or indulgences must be false. That Christ is offered to us in the Gospel with all the abundance of heavenly blessings, with all his merits, all his righteousness, wisdom, and grace, without exception, Paul bears witness when he says, "Now then we are ambassadors for Christ, as though God did beseech you by us: we pray you in Christ's stead, be ye reconciled to God. For he has made him to be sin for us, who knew no sin; that we might be made the righteousness of God in him" (2 Cor. 5:20-21). And what is meant by the fellowship (κοινωνια) of Christ, which according to the same Apostle (1 Cor. 1:9) is offered to us in the Gospel, all believers know. On the contrary, indulgences, bringing forth some portion of the grace of God from the armory of the Pope, fix it to lead, parchment, and a particular place, but dissever it from the word of God. When we inquire into the origin of this abuse, it appears to have arisen from this, that when in old times the satisfactions imposed on penitents were too severe to be borne, those who felt themselves burdened beyond measure by the penance imposed, petitioned the Church for relaxation. The remission so given was called indulgence. But as they transferred satisfactions to God, and called them compensations by which men redeem themselves from the justice of God, they in the same way transferred indulgences, representing them as expiatory remedies which free us from merited punishment. The

blasphemies to which we have referred have been feigned with so much effrontery that there is not the least pretext for them.

6. Their purgatory cannot now give us much trouble, since with this ax we have struck it, thrown it down, and overturned it from its very foundations. I cannot agree with some who think that we ought to dissemble in this matter, and make no mention of purgatory, from which (as they say) fierce contests arise, and very little edification can be obtained. I myself would think it right to disregard their follies did they not tend to serious consequences. But since purgatory has been reared on many, and is daily propped up by new blasphemies; since it produces many grievous offenses, assuredly it is not to be connived at, however it might have been disguised for a time, that without any authority from the word of God, it was devised by prying audacious rashness, that credit was procured for it by fictitious revelations, the wiles of Satan, and that certain passages of Scripture were ignorantly wrested to its support. Although the Lord bears not that human presumption should thus force its way to the hidden recesses of his judgments; although he has issued a strict prohibition against neglecting his voice, and making inquiry at the dead (Deut. 18:11), and permits not his word to be so erroneously contaminated. Let us grant, however, that all this might have been tolerated for a time as a thing of no great moment; yet when the expiation of sins is sought elsewhere than in the blood of Christ, and satisfaction is transferred to others, silence were most perilous. We are bound, therefore, to raise our voice to its highest pitch, and cry aloud that purgatory is a deadly device of Satan; that it makes void the cross of Christ; that it offers intolerable insult to the divine mercy; that it undermines and overthrows our faith. For what is this purgatory but the satisfaction for sin paid after death by the souls of the dead? Hence when this idea of satisfaction is refuted, purgatory itself is forthwith completely overturned. But if it is perfectly clear, from what was lately said, that the blood of Christ is the only satisfaction, expiation, and cleansing for the sins of believers, what remains but to hold

that purgatory is mere blasphemy, horrid blasphemy against Christ? I say nothing of the sacrilege by which it is daily defended, the offenses which it begets in religion, and the other innumerable evils which we see teeming forth from that fountain of impiety.

7. Those passages of Scripture on which it is their wont falsely and iniquitously to fasten, it may be worthwhile to wrench out of their hands. When the Lord declares that the sin against the Holy Ghost will not be forgiven either in this world or the world to come, he thereby intimates (they say) that there is a remission of certain sins hereafter. But who sees not that the Lord there speaks of the guilt of sin? But if this is so, what has it to do with their purgatory, seeing they deny not that the guilt of those sins, the punishment of which is there expiated, is forgiven in the present life? Lest, however, they should still object, we shall give a plainer solution. Since it was the Lord's intention to cut off all hope of pardon from this flagitous wickedness, he did not consider it enough to say, that it would never be forgiven, but in the way of amplification employed a division by which he included both the judgment which every man's conscience pronounces in the present life, and the final judgment which will be publicly pronounced at the resurrection; as if he had said, Beware of this malignant rebellion, as you would of instant destruction; for he who of set purpose endeavors to extinguish the offered light of the Spirit, shall not obtain pardon either in this life, which has been given to sinners for conversion, or on the last day when the angels of God shall separate the sheep from the goats, and the heavenly kingdom shall be purged of all that offends. The next passage they produce is the parable in Matthew: "Agree with thine adversary quickly, whiles thou art in the way with him; lest at any time the adversary deliver thee to the judge, and the judge deliver thee to the officer, and thou be cast into prison. Verily, I say unto thee, Thou shalt by no means come out thence, till thou hast paid the uttermost farthing" (Matt. 5:25-26). If in this passage the judge means God, the adversary the devil,

the officer an angel, and the prison purgatory, I give in at once. But if every man sees that Christ there intended to show to how many perils and evils those expose themselves who obstinately insist on their utmost right, instead of being satisfied with what is fair and equitable, that he might thereby the more strongly exhort his followers to concord, where, I ask, are we to find their purgatory?

8. They seek an argument in the passage in which Paul declares, that all things shall bow the knee to Christ, "things in heaven, and things in earth, and things under the earth" (Phil. 2:10). They take it for granted, that by "things under the earth," cannot be meant those who are doomed to eternal damnation, and that the only remaining conclusion is, that they must be souls suffering in purgatory. They would not reason very ill if, by the bending of the knee, the Apostle designated true worship; but since he simply says that Christ has received a dominion to which all creatures are subject, what prevents us from understanding those "under the earth" to mean the devils, who shall certainly be sisted before the judgment seat of God, there to recognize their Judge with fear and trembling? In this way Paul himself elsewhere interprets the same prophecy: "We shall all stand before the judgment seat of Christ. For it is written, As I live, saith the Lord, every knee shall bow to me, and every tongue shall confess to God" (Rom. 14:10-11). But we cannot in this way interpret what is said in the Apocalypse: "Every creature which is in heaven, and on the earth, and under the earth, and such as are in the sea, heard I saying, Blessing, and honor, and glory, and power, be unto him that sitteth upon the throne, and unto the Lamb, for ever and ever" (Rev. 5:13). This I readily admit; but what kinds of creatures do they suppose are here enumerated? It is absolutely certain, that both irrational and inanimate creatures are comprehended. All, then, which is affirmed is, that every part of the universe, from the highest pinnacle of heaven to the very center of the earth, each in its own way proclaims the glory of the Creator.

To the passage which they produce from the history of the Maccabees (1 Macc. 12:43), I will not deign to reply, lest I should seem to include that work among the canonical books. But Augustine holds it to be canonical. First, with what degree of confidence? "The Jews," says he, "do not hold the book of the Maccabees as they do the Law, the Prophets, and the Psalms, to which the Lord bears testimony as to his own witnesses, saying, Ought not all things which are written in the Law, and the Psalms, and the Prophets, concerning me be fulfilled? (Luke 24:44). But it has been received by the Church not uselessly, if it be read or heard with soberness." Jerome, however, unhesitatingly affirms, that it is of no authority in establishing doctrine; and from the ancient little book, *De Expositione Symboli*; which bears the name of Cyprian, it is plain that it was in no estimation in the ancient Church. And why do I here contend in vain? As if the author himself did not sufficiently show what degree of deference is to be paid him, when in the end he asks pardon for anything less properly expressed (2 Macc. 15:38). He who confesses that his writings stand in need of pardon, certainly proclaims that they are not oracles of the Holy Spirit. We may add, that the piety of Judas is commended for no other reason than for having a firm hope of the final resurrection, in sending his oblation for the dead to Jerusalem. For the writer of the history does not represent what he did as furnishing the price of redemption, but merely that they might be partakers of eternal life, with the other saints who had fallen for their country and religion. The act, indeed, was not free from superstition and misguided zeal; but it is mere fatuity to extend the legal sacrifice to us, seeing we are assured that the sacrifices then in use ceased on the advent of Christ.

9. But, it seems, they find in Paul an invincible support, which cannot be so easily overthrown. His words are, "Now if any man build upon this foundation gold, silver, precious stones, wood, hay, stubble; every man's work shall be made manifest: for the day shall declare it, because it shall be revealed by fire; and the fire shall try every man's

work of what sort it is. If any man's work shall be burnt, he shall suffer loss: but he himself shall be saved; yet so as by fire" (1 Cor. 3:12-15). What fire (they ask) can that be but the fire of purgatory, by which the defilements of sin are wiped away, in order that we may enter pure into the kingdom of God? But most of the Fathers give it a different meaning—viz. the tribulation or cross by which the Lord tries his people, that they may not rest satisfied with the defilements of the flesh. This is much more probable than the fiction of a purgatory. I do not, however, agree with them, for I think I see a much surer and clearer meaning to the passage. But, before I produce it, I wish they would answer me, whether they think the Apostle and all the saints have to pass through this purgatorial fire? I am aware they will say, no; for it were too absurd to hold that purification is required by those whose superfluous merits they dream of as applicable to all the members of the Church. But this the Apostle affirms; for he says, not that the works of certain persons, but the works of all will be tried. And this is not my argument, but that of Augustine, who thus impugns that interpretation. And (what makes the thing more absurd) he says, not that they will pass through fire for certain works, but that even if they should have edified the Church with the greatest fidelity, they will receive their reward after their works shall have been tried by fire. First, we see that the Apostle used a metaphor when he gave the names of wood, hay, and stubble, to doctrines of man's device. The ground of the metaphor is obvious—viz. that as wood when it is put into the fire is consumed and destroyed, so neither will those doctrines be able to endure when they come to be tried. Moreover, everyone sees that the trial is made by the Spirit of God. Therefore, in following out the thread of the metaphor, and adapting its parts properly to each other, he gave the name of fire to the examination of the Holy Spirit. For, just as silver and gold, the nearer they are brought to the fire, give stronger proof of their genuineness and purity, so the Lord's truth, the more thoroughly it is submitted to spiritual examination, has its authority the better confirmed. As hay,

wood, and stubble, when the fire is applied to them, are suddenly consumed, so the inventions of man, not founded on the word of God,
cannot stand the trial of the Holy Spirit, but forthwith give way and
perish. In fine, if spurious doctrines are compared to wood, hay, and
stubble, because, like wood, hay, and stubble, they are burned by fire
and fitted for destruction, though the actual destruction is only completed by the Spirit of the Lord, it follows that the Spirit is that fire by
which they will be proved. This proof Paul calls the day of the Lord;
using a term common in Scripture. For the day of the Lord is said to
take place whenever he in some way manifests his presence to men, his
face being specially said to shine when his truth is manifested. It has
now been proved, that Paul has no idea of any other fire than the trial
of the Holy Spirit. But how are those who suffer the loss of their works
saved by fire? This it will not be difficult to understand, if we consider of
what kind of persons he speaks. For he designates them builders of the
Church, who, retaining the proper foundation, build different materials
upon it; that is, who, not abandoning the principal and necessary articles of faith, err in minor and less perilous matters, mingling their own
fictions with the word of God. Such, I say, must suffer the loss of their
work by the destruction of their fictions. They themselves, however, are
saved, yet so as by fire; that is, not that their ignorance and delusions are
approved by the Lord, but they are purified from them by the grace and
power of the Holy Spirit. All those, accordingly, who have tainted the
golden purity of the divine word with the pollution of purgatory must
necessarily suffer the loss of their work.

10. But the observance of it in the Church is of the highest antiquity. This objection is disposed of by Paul, when, including even
his own age in the sentence, he declares, that all who in building the
Church have laid upon it something not conformable to the foundation, must suffer the loss of their work. When, therefore, my opponents object, that it has been the practice for thirteen hundred years
to offer prayers for the dead, I, in return, ask them, by what word of

God, by what revelation, by what example it was done? For here not only are passages of Scripture wanting, but in the examples of all the saints of whom we read, nothing of the kind is seen. We have numerous, and sometimes long narratives, of their mourning and sepulchral rites, but not one word is said of prayers. But the more important the matter was, the more they ought to have dwelt upon it. Even those who in ancient times offered prayers for the dead, saw that they were not supported by the command of God and legitimate example. Why then did they presume to do it? I hold that herein they suffered the common lot of man, and therefore maintain, that what they did is not to be imitated. Believers ought not to engage in any work without a firm conviction of its propriety, as Paul enjoins (Rom. 14:23); and this conviction is expressly requisite in prayer. It is to be presumed, however, that they were influenced by some reason; they sought a solace for their sorrow, and it seemed cruel not to give some attestation of their love to the dead, when in the presence of God. All know by experience how natural it is for the human mind thus to feel.

Received custom too was a kind of torch, by which the minds of many were inflamed. We know that among all the Gentiles, and in all ages, certain rites were paid to the dead, and that every year lustrations were performed for their manes. Although Satan deluded foolish mortals by these impostures, yet the means of deceiving were borrowed from a sound principle—viz. that death is not destruction, but a passage from this life to another. And there can be no doubt that superstition itself always left the Gentiles without excuse before the judgment seat of God, because they neglected to prepare for that future life which they professed to believe. Thus, that Christians might not seem worse than heathens, they felt ashamed of paying no office to the dead, as if they had been utterly annihilated. Hence their ill-advised assiduity; because they thought they would expose themselves to great disgrace, if they were slow in providing funeral feasts and oblations. What was thus introduced by perverse rivalship, ever and anon received new additions, until the highest holiness of the Papacy consisted in giving assistance to the suffering dead. But far better and more solid comfort is furnished by scripture when it declares, "Blessed are the dead that die in the Lord;" and adds the reason, "for they rest from their labors" (Rev. 14:13). We ought not to indulge our love so far as to set up a perverse mode of prayer in the Church. Surely every person possessed of the least prudence easily perceives, that whatever we meet with on this subject in ancient writers, was in deference to public custom and the ignorance of the vulgar. I admit they were themselves also carried away into error, the usual effect of rash credulity being to destroy the judgment. Meanwhile the passages themselves show, that when they recommended prayer for the dead it was with hesitation. Augustine relates in his Confessions, that his mother, Monica, earnestly entreated to be remembered when the solemn rites at the altar were performed; doubtless an old woman's wish, which her son did not bring to the test of Scripture, but from natural affection wished others to approve. His book, *De Cura pro Mortals Agenda*, On showing Care for the Dead, is so full of doubt, that its coldness may well extinguish the heat of a foolish zeal. Should anyone, in pretending to be a patron of the dead, deal merely in probabilities, the only effect will be to make those indifferent who were formerly solicitous.

The only support of this dogma is, that as a custom of praying for the dead prevailed, the duty ought not to be despised. But granting that ancient ecclesiastical writers deemed it a pious thing to assist the dead, the rule which can never deceive is always to be observed—viz. that we must not introduce anything of our own into our prayers, but must keep all our wishes in subordination to the word of God, because it belongs to Him to prescribe what he wishes us to ask. Now, since the whole Law and Gospel do not contain one syllable which countenances the right of praying for the dead, it is a profanation of prayer to go one step farther than God enjoins. But, lest our opponents boast of sharing their error with the ancient Church, I say, that there is a wide difference between the two. The latter made a commemoration of the dead, that they might not seem to have cast off all concern for them; but they, at the same time, acknowledged that they were doubtful as to their state; assuredly they made no such assertion concerning purgatory as implied that they did not hold it to be uncertain. The former insist, that their dream of purgatory shall be received without question as an article of faith. The latter sparingly and in a perfunctory manner only commended their dead to the Lord, in the communion of the holy supper. The former are constantly urging the care of the dead, and by their importunate preaching of it, make out that it is to be preferred to all the offices of charity. But it would not be difficult for us to produce some passages from ancient writers, which clearly overturn all those prayers for the dead which were then in use. Such is the passage of Augustine, in which he shows that the resurrection of the flesh and eternal glory is expected by all, but that rest which follows death is received by everyone who is worthy of it when he dies. Accordingly, he declares that all the righteous, not less than the Apostles, Prophets, and Martyrs, immediately after death enjoy blessed rest. If such is their condition, what, I ask, will our prayers contribute to them? I say nothing of those grosser superstitions by which they have fascinated the minds of the simple; and yet they are innumerable, and most of them so monstrous, that they cannot cover them with any cloak of decency. I say nothing, moreover, of those most shameful traffickings, which they plied as they listed while the world was stupefied. For I would never come to an end; and, without enumerating them, the pious reader will here find enough to establish his conscience.

Study Guide Questions

Section 1

1. From which doctrine does the practice of granting indulgences flow?

2. Does Calvin want to argue with the men who advance these notions?

Section 2

1. What do many people see, and what do they miss?

2. What do indulgences establish?

Section 3

1. What two fathers does Calvin cite against the practice?

2. According to this doctrine, does the merit of Christ mingle with the merit of the saints in the treasury of the church?

Section 4

1. What then does the apostle Paul mean in Colossians 1:24?

Section 5

1. What does the practice of offering indulgences do to the redemption of Christ?

Section 6

1. What destroys the notion of purgatory before it is even discussed?

2. Could the idea of purgatory be a trifle not worth discussing at all?

Sections 7–8

1. What proofs of purgatory were offered from the gospels?

2. What proofs are offered from Philippians and Revelation?

3. How does he handle the proof from Maccabees?

Section 9

1. What passage in Paul was considered by Calvin to be crucial to the purgatory debate?
2. How does Calvin handle this passage?
3. And what class of men does this testing come upon?

Section 10

1. Does Calvin acknowledge that many of the fathers went along with prayers for the dead?

CHAPTER 6

The life of a Christian man. Scriptural arguments exhorting to it.

This and the four following chapters treat of the Life of the Christian, and are so arranged as to admit of being classed under two principal heads.

First, it must be held to be a universally acknowledged point, that no man is a Christian who does not feel some special love for righteousness (cap. 6). Secondly, in regard to the standard by which every man ought to regulate his life, although it seems to be considered in cap. 7 only, yet the three following chapters also refer to it. For it shows that the Christian has two duties to perform. First, the observance being so arduous, he needs the greatest patience. Hence cap. 8 treats professedly of the utility of the cross, and cap. 9 invites to meditation on the future life. Lastly, cap. 10 clearly shows, as in no small degree conducive to this end, how we are to use this life and its comforts without abusing them. This sixth chapter consists of two parts

I. Connection between this treatise on the Christian Life and the doctrine of Regeneration and Repentance. Arrangement of the treatise, sec. 1-3.

II. Extremes to be avoided;

Outline:

1. False Christians denying Christ by their works condemned, sec. 4.

2. Christians should not despair, though they have not attained perfection, provided they make daily progress in piety and righteousness. Sections. 1. Connection between this chapter and the doctrine of Regeneration. Necessity of the doctrine concerning the Christian Life. The brevity of this treatise. The method of it. Plainness and unadorned simplicity of the Scripture system of morals. 2. Two divisions. First, Personal holiness. 1. Because God is holy. 2. Because of our communion with his saints.

3. Second division, relating to our Redemption. Admirable moral system of Scripture. Five special inducements or exhortations to a Christian Life.

4. False Christians who are opposed to this life censured. 1. They have not truly learned Christ. 2. The Gospel not the guide of their words or actions. 3. They do not imitate Christ the Master. 4. They would separate the Spirit from his word.

5. Christians ought not to despond: Provided 1. They take the word of God for their guide. 2. Sincerely cultivate righteousness. 3. Walk, according to their capacity, in the ways of the Lord. 4. Make some progress. 5. Persevere.

We have said that the object of regeneration is to bring the life of believers into concord and harmony with the righteousness of God, and so confirm the adoption by which they have been received as sons. But although the law comprehends within it that new life by which the image of God is restored in us, yet, as our sluggishness stands greatly in need both of helps and incentives it will be useful to collect out of Scripture a true account of this reformation, lest any who have a heartfelt desire of repentance should in their zeal go astray. Moreover, I am not unaware that, in undertaking to describe the life of the Christian, I am entering on a large and extensive subject, one which, when fully considered in all its parts, is sufficient to fill a large volume. We see the length to which the Fathers in treating of individual virtues extend their exhortations. This they do, not from mere loquaciousness; for whatever be the virtue which you undertake to recommend, your pen is spontaneously led by the copiousness of the matter so to amplify, that you seem not to have discussed it properly if you have not done it at length. My intention, however, in the plan of life which I now propose to give, is not to extend it so far as to treat of each virtue specially, and expatiate in exhortation. This must be sought in the writings of others, and particularly in the Homilies of the Fathers. For me it will be sufficient to point out the method by which a pious man may be taught how to frame his life aright, and briefly lay down some universal rule by which he may not improperly regulate his conduct. I shall one day possibly find time for more ample discourse, [or leave others to perform an office for which I am not so fit. I have a natural love of brevity, and, perhaps, any attempt of mine at copiousness would not succeed. Even if I could gain the highest applause by being more prolix, I would scarcely be disposed to attempt it], while the nature of my present work requires me to glance at simple doctrine with as much brevity as possible. As philosophers have certain definitions of rectitude and honesty, from which they derive particular duties and the whole train of virtues; so in this respect Scripture is not without order, but presents a most beautiful arrangement, one too which is every way much more certain than that of philosophers. The only difference is, that they, under the influence of ambition, constantly affect an exquisite perspicuity of arrangement, which may serve to display their genius, whereas the Spirit of God, teaching without affectation, is not so perpetually observant of exact method, and yet by observing it at times sufficiently intimates that it is not to be neglected.

2. The Scripture system of which we speak aims chiefly at two objects. The former is, that the love of righteousness, to which we are by no means naturally inclined, may be instilled and implanted into our minds. The latter is (see chap. 7), to prescribe a rule which will prevent us while in the pursuit of righteousness from going astray. It has numerous admirable methods of recommending righteousness. Many have been already pointed out in different parts of this work; but we shall here also briefly advert to some of them. With what better foundation can it begin than by reminding us that we must be holy, because "God is holy?" (Lev. 19:1; 1 Pet. 1:16). For when we were scattered abroad like lost sheep, wandering through the labyrinth of this world, he brought us back again to his own fold. When mention is made of our union with God, let us remember that holiness must be the bond; not that by the merit of holiness we come into communion with him (we ought rather first to cleave to him, in order that, pervaded with his holiness, we may follow whither he calls), but because it greatly concerns his glory not to have any fellowship with wickedness and impurity. Wherefore he tells us that this is the end of our calling, the end to which we ought ever to have respect, if we would answer the call of God. For to what end were we rescued from the iniquity and pollution of the world into which we were plunged, if we allow ourselves, during our whole lives, to wallow in them? Besides, we are at the same time admonished, that if we would be regarded as the Lord's people, we must inhabit the holy city Jerusalem (Isa. 35:8, et alibi); which, as he hath consecrated it to himself, it were impious for its inhabitants to profane by impurity. Hence the expressions, "Who shall abide in thy tabernacle? who shall dwell in thy holy hill? He that walketh uprightly, and worketh righteousness" (Ps. 15:1-2; 24:3-4); for the sanctuary in which he dwells certainly ought not to be like an unclean stall.

3. The better to arouse us, it exhibits God the Father, who, as he hath reconciled us to himself in his Anointed, has impressed his image upon us, to which he would have us to be conformed (Rom. 5:4).

Come, then, and let them show me a more excellent system among
philosophers, who think that they only have a moral philosophy duly
and orderly arranged. They, when they would give excellent exhortations to virtue, can only tell us to live agreeably to nature. Scripture
derives its exhortations from the true source, when it not only enjoins
us to regulate our lives with a view to God its author to whom it belongs; but after showing us that we have degenerated from our true
origin—viz. the law of our Creator, adds, that Christ, through whom
we have returned to favor with God, is set before us as a model, the
image of which our lives should express. What do you require more
effectual than this? Nay, what do you require beyond this? If the Lord
adopts us for his sons on the condition that our life be a representation of Christ, the bond of our adoption—then, unless we dedicate
and devote ourselves to righteousness, we not only, with the utmost
perfidy, revolt from our Creator, but also abjure the Savior himself.
Then, from an enumeration of all the blessings of God, and each part
of our salvation, it finds materials for exhortation. Ever since God exhibited himself to us as a Father, we must be convicted of extreme
ingratitude if we do not in turn exhibit ourselves as his sons. Ever
since Christ purified us by the laver of his blood, and communicated
this purification by baptism, it would ill become us to be defiled with
new pollution. Ever since he ingrafted us into his body, we, who are his
members, should anxiously beware of contracting any stain or taint.
Ever since he who is our head ascended to heaven, it is befitting in us
to withdraw our affections from the earth, and with our whole soul
aspire to heaven. Ever since the Holy Spirit dedicated us as temples to
the Lord, we should make it our endeavor to show forth the glory of
God, and guard against being profaned by the defilement of sin. Ever
since our soul and body were destined to heavenly incorruptibility and
an unfading crown, we should earnestly strive to keep them pure and
uncorrupted against the day of the Lord. These, I say, are the surest
foundations of a well-regulated life, and you will search in vain for

anything resembling them among philosophers, who, in their commendation of virtue, never rise higher than the natural dignity of man.

4. This is the place to address those who, having nothing of Christ
but the name and sign, would yet be called Christians. How dare they
boast of this sacred name? None have intercourse with Christ but
those who have acquired the true knowledge of him from the Gospel.
The Apostle denies that any man truly has learned Christ who has
not learned to put off "the old man, which is corrupt according to the
deceitful lusts, and put on Christ" (Eph. 4:22). They are convicted,
therefore, of falsely and unjustly pretending a knowledge of Christ,
whatever be the volubility and eloquence with which they can talk
of the Gospel. Doctrine is not an affair of the tongue, but of the life;
is not apprehended by the intellect and memory merely, like other
branches of learning; but is received only when it possesses the whole
soul, and finds its seat and habitation in the inmost recesses of the
heart. Let them, therefore, either cease to insult God, by boasting that
they are what they are not, or let them show themselves not unworthy
disciples of their divine Master. To doctrine in which our religion is
contained we have given the first place, since by it our salvation com-
mences; but it must be transfused into the breast, and pass into the
conduct, and so transform us into itself, as not to prove unfruitful. If
philosophers are justly offended, and banish from their company with
disgrace those who, while professing an art which ought to be the
mistress of their conduct, convert it into mere loquacious sophistry,
with how much better reason shall we detest those flimsy sophists
who are contented to let the Gospel play upon their lips, when, from
its efficacy, it ought to penetrate the inmost affections of the heart, fix
its seat in the soul, and pervade the whole man a hundred times more
than the frigid discourses of philosophers?

5. I insist not that the life of the Christian shall breathe nothing
but the perfect Gospel, though this is to be desired, and ought to be
attempted. I insist not so strictly on evangelical perfection, as to refuse

to acknowledge as a Christian any man who has not attained it. In this way all would be excluded from the Church, since there is no man who is not far removed from this perfection, while many, who have made but little progress, would be undeservedly rejected. What then? Let us set this before our eye as the end at which we ought constantly to aim. Let it be regarded as the goal towards which we are to run. For you cannot divide the matter with God, undertaking part of what his word enjoins, and omitting part at pleasure. For, in the first place, God uniformly recommends integrity as the principal part of his worship, meaning by integrity real singleness of mind, devoid of gloss and fiction, and to this is opposed a double mind; as if it had been said, that the spiritual commencement of a good life is when the internal affections are sincerely devoted to God, in the cultivation of holiness and justice. But seeing that, in this earthly prison of the body, no man is supplied with strength sufficient to hasten in his course with due alacrity, while the greater number are so oppressed with weakness, that hesitating, and halting, and even crawling on the ground, they make little progress, let every one of us go as far as his humble ability enables him, and prosecute the journey once begun. No one will travel so badly as not daily to make some degree of progress. This, therefore, let us never cease to do, that we may daily advance in the way of the Lord; and let us not despair because of the slender measure of success. How little soever the success may correspond with our wish, our labor is not lost when today is better than yesterday, provided with true singleness of mind we keep our aim, and aspire to the goal, not speaking flattering things to ourselves, nor indulging our vices, but making it our constant endeavor to become better, until we attain to goodness itself. If during the whole course of our life we seek and follow, we shall at length attain it, when relieved from the infirmity of flesh we are admitted to full fellowship with God.

Study Guide Questions

Section 1

1. What is the object of regeneration?

2. What is one danger for those who heartily repent?

3. What is different between the teaching of the Holy Spirit and the teaching of moral philosophers?

Section 2

1. What are the two main aspects of scriptural instruction?

2. What is the nature of our bond with God?

Section 3

1. What is the strongest motive to the Christian life?

2. Why must we not disfigure ourselves with sin?

Section 4

1. What group does Calvin upbraid in this section?

2. Who only has true intimacy with Christ?

Section 5

1. Why does Calvin not withhold the name "Christian" from those who have not attained to an evangelical perfection?

2. What should we not be discouraged by?

CHAPTER 7

A summary of the Christian life. Of self-denial.

The divisions of the chapter are
I. The rule which permits us not to go astray in the study of righteousness, requires two things—viz. that man, abandoning his own will, devote himself entirely to the service of God; whence it follows, that we must seek not our own things, but the things of God, sec. 1-2.

II. A description of this renovation or Christian life taken from the Epistle to Titus, and accurately explained under certain special heads, sec. 3 to end.

Outline:

1. Consideration of the second general division in regard to the Christian life. Its beginning and sum. A twofold respect. 1. We are not our own. Respect to both the fruit and the use. Unknown to philosophers, who have placed reason on the throne of the Holy Spirit.

2. Since we are not our own, we must seek the glory of God, and obey his will. Self-denial recommended to the disciples of Christ.

He who neglects it, deceived either by pride or hypocrisy, rushes on destruction.

3. Three things to be followed, and two to be shunned in life. Impiety and worldly lusts to be shunned. Sobriety, justice, and piety, to be followed. An inducement to right conduct.

4. Self-denial the sum of Paul's doctrine. Its difficulty. Qualities in us which make it difficult. Cures for these qualities. 1. Ambition to be suppressed. 2. Humility to be embraced. 3. Candor to be esteemed. 4. Mutual charity to be preserved. 5. Modesty to be sincerely cultivated.

5. The advantage of our neighbor to be promoted. Here self-denial most necessary, and yet most difficult. Here a double remedy. 1. The benefits bestowed upon us are for the common benefit of the Church. 2. We ought to do all we can for our neighbor. This illustrated by analogy from the members of the human body. This duty of charity founded on the divine command.

6. Charity ought to have for its attendants patience and kindness. We should consider the image of God in our neighbors, and especially in those who are of the household of faith. Hence a fourfold consideration which refutes all objections. A common objection refuted.

7. Christian life cannot exist without charity. Remedies for the vices opposed to charity. 1. Mercy. 2. Humility. 3. Modesty. 4. Diligence. 5. Perseverance.

8. Self-denial, in respect of God, should lead to equanimity and tolerance. 1. We are always subject to God. 2. We should shun avarice and ambition. 3. We should expect all prosperity from the blessing of God, and entirely depend on him.

9. We ought not to desire wealth or honors without the divine blessing, nor follow the arts of the wicked. We ought to cast all our care upon God, and never envy the prosperity of others.

10. We ought to commit ourselves entirely to God. The necessity of this doctrine. Various uses of affliction. Heathen abuse and corruption.

Although the Law of God contains a perfect rule of conduct admirably arranged, it has seemed proper to our divine Master to train his people by a more accurate method, to the rule which is enjoined in the Law; and the leading principle in the method is, that it is the duty of believers to present their "bodies a living sacrifice, holy and acceptable unto God, which is their reasonable service" (Rom. 12:1). Hence he draws the exhortation: "Be not conformed to this world: but be ye transformed by the renewing of your mind, that ye may prove what is that good, and acceptable, and perfect will of God." The great point, then, is, that we are consecrated and dedicated to God, and, therefore, should not henceforth think, speak, design, or act, without a view to his glory. What he hath made sacred cannot, without single insult to him, be applied to profane use. But if we are not our own, but the Lord's, it is plain both what error is to be shunned, and to what end the actions of our lives ought to be directed. We are not our own; therefore, neither is our own reason or will to rule our acts and counsels. We are not our own; therefore, let us not make it our end to seek what may be agreeable to our carnal nature. We are not our own; therefore, as far as possible, let us forget ourselves and the things that are ours. On the other hand, we are God's; let us, therefore, live and die to him (Rom. 14:8). We are God's; therefore, let his wisdom and will preside over all our actions. We are God's; to him, then, as the only legitimate end, let every part of our life be directed. O how great the proficiency of him who, taught that he is not his own, has withdrawn the dominion and government of himself from his own reason that he may give them to God! For as the surest source of destruction to men is to obey themselves, so the only haven of safety is to have no other will, no other wisdom, than to follow the Lord wherever he leads. Let this, then be the first step, to abandon ourselves, and devote the whole energy of our minds to the service of God. By service, I mean not only that which consists in verbal obedience, but that by which the mind, divested of its own carnal feelings, implicitly obeys the call of the Spirit of God. This transformation (which Paul calls the renewing of the mind, Rom. 12:2; Eph. 4:23), though it is the first entrance to life, was unknown to all the philosophers. They give the government of man to reason alone, thinking that she alone is to be listened to; in short, they assign to her the sole direction of the conduct. But Christian philosophy bids her give place, and yield complete submission to the Holy Spirit, so that the man himself no longer lives, but Christ lives and reigns in him (Gal. 2:20).

2. Hence follows the other principle, that we are not to seek our own, but the Lord's will, and act with a view to promote his glory. Great is our proficiency, when, almost forgetting ourselves, certainly postponing our own reason, we faithfully make it our study to obey God and his commandments. For when Scripture enjoins us to lay aside private regard to ourselves, it not only divests our minds of an excessive longing for wealth, or power, or human favor, but eradicates all ambition and thirst for worldly glory, and other more secret pests. The Christian ought, indeed, to be so trained and disposed as to consider, that during his whole life he has to do with God. For this reason, as he will bring all things to the disposal and estimate of God, so he will religiously direct his whole mind to him. For he who has learned to look to God in everything he does, is at the same time diverted from all vain thoughts. This is that self-denial which Christ so strongly enforces on his disciples from the very outset (Matt. 16:24), which, as soon as it takes hold of the mind, leaves no place either, first, for pride, show, and ostentation; or, secondly, for avarice, lust, luxury, effeminacy, or other vices which are engendered by self-love. On the contrary, wherever it reigns not, the foulest vices are indulged in without shame; or, if there is some appearance of virtue, it is vitiated by a depraved longing for applause. Show me, if you can, an individual who, unless he has renounced himself in obedience to the Lord's command, is disposed to do good for its own sake. Those who

have not so renounced themselves have followed virtue at least for the sake of praise. The philosophers who have contended most strongly that virtue is to be desired on her own account, were so inflated with arrogance as to make it apparent that they sought virtue for no other reason than as a ground for indulging in pride. So far, therefore, is God from being delighted with these hunters after popular applause with their swollen breasts, that he declares they have received their reward in this world (Matt. 6:2), and that harlots and publicans are nearer the kingdom of heaven than they (Matt. 21:31). We have not yet sufficiently explained how great and numerous are the obstacles by which a man is impeded in the pursuit of rectitude, so long as he has not renounced himself. The old saying is true, There is a world of iniquity treasured up in the human soul. Nor can you find any other remedy for this than to deny yourself, renounce your own reason, and direct your whole mind to the pursuit of those things which the Lord requires of you, and which you are to seek only because they are pleasing to Him.

3. In another passage, Paul gives a brief, indeed, but more distinct account of each of the parts of a well-ordered life: "The grace of God that bringeth salvation hath appeared to all men, teaching us that, denying ungodliness and worldly lusts, we should live soberly, righteously, and godly, in this present world; looking for that blessed hope, and the glorious appearance of the great God and our Savior Jesus Christ; who gave himself for us, that he might redeem us from all iniquity, and purify to himself a peculiar people, zealous of good works" (Tit. 2:11-14). After holding forth the grace of God to animate us, and pave the way for His true worship, he removes the two greatest obstacles which stand in the way—viz. ungodliness, to which we are by nature too prone, and worldly lusts, which are of still greater extent. Under ungodliness, he includes not merely superstition, but everything at variance with the true fear of God. Worldly lusts are equivalent to the lusts of the flesh. Thus he enjoins us, in regard to

both tables of the Law, to lay aside our own mind, and renounce whatever our own reason and will dictate. Then he reduces all the actions of our lives to three branches, sobriety, righteousness, and godliness. Sobriety undoubtedly denotes as well chastity and temperance as the pure and frugal use of temporal goods, and patient endurance of want. Righteousness comprehends all the duties of equity, in everyone his due. Next follows godliness, which separates us from the pollutions of the world, and connects us with God in true holiness. These, when connected together by an indissoluble chain, constitute complete perfection. But as nothing is more difficult than to bid adieu to the will of the flesh, subdue, nay, abjure our lusts, devote ourselves to God and our brethren, and lead an angelic life amid the pollutions of the world, Paul, to set our minds free from all entanglements, recalls us to the hope of a blessed immortality, justly urging us to contend, because as Christ has once appeared as our Redeemer, so on his final advent he will give full effect to the salvation obtained by him. And in this way he dispels all the allurements which becloud our path, and prevent us from aspiring as we ought to heavenly glory; nay, he tells us that we must be pilgrims in the world, that we may not fail of obtaining the heavenly inheritance.

4. Moreover, we see by these words that self-denial has respect partly to men and partly (more especially) to God (sec. 8-10). For when Scripture enjoins us, in regard to our fellow men, to prefer them in honor to ourselves, and sincerely labor to promote their advantages (Rom. 12:10; Phil. 2:3), he gives us commands which our mind is utterly incapable of obeying until its natural feelings are suppressed. For so blindly do we all rush in the direction of self-love, that everyone thinks he has a good reason for exalting himself and despising all others in comparison. If God has bestowed on us something not to be repented of, trusting to it, we immediately become elated, and not only swell, but almost burst with pride. The vices with which we abound we both carefully conceal from others, and flatteringly

represent to ourselves as minute and trivial, nay, sometimes hug them as virtues. When the same qualities which we admire in ourselves are seen in others, even though they should be superior, we, in order that we may not be forced to yield to them, maliciously lower and carp at them; in like manner, in the case of vices, not contented with severe and keen animadversion, we studiously exaggerate them. Hence the insolence with which each, as if exempted from the common lot, seeks to exalt himself above his neighbor, confidently and proudly despising others, or at least looking down upon them as his inferiors. The poor man yields to the rich, the plebeian to the noble, the servant to the master, the unlearned to the learned, and yet everyone inwardly cherishes some idea of his own superiority. Thus each flattering himself, sets up a kind of kingdom in his breast; the arrogant, to satisfy themselves, pass censure on the minds and manners of other men, and when contention arises, the full venom is displayed. Many bear about with them some measure of mildness so long as all things go smoothly and lovingly with them, but how few are there who, when stung and irritated, preserve the same tenor of moderation? For this there is no other remedy than to pluck up by the roots those most noxious pests, self-love and love of victory (φιλονεικια και φιλαυτια). This the doctrine of Scripture does. For it teaches us to remember, that the endowments which God has bestowed upon us are not our own, but His free gifts, and that those who plume themselves upon them betray their ingratitude. "Who maketh thee to differ," says Paul, "and what hast thou that thou didst not receive? Now if thou didst receive it, why dost thou glory, as if thou hadst not received it?" (1 Cor. 4:7). Then by a diligent examination of our faults let us keep ourselves humble. Thus while nothing will remain to swell our pride, there will be much to subdue it. Again, we are enjoined, whenever we behold the gifts of God in others, so to reverence and respect the gifts, as also to honor those in whom they reside. God having been pleased to bestow honor upon them, it would ill become us to deprive them of it. Then we are told to overlook their faults, not, indeed, to encourage by flattering them, but not because of them to insult those whom we ought to regard with honor and good will. In this way, with regard to all with whom we have intercourse, our behavior will be not only moderate and modest, but courteous and friendly. The only way by which you can ever attain to true meekness, is to have your heart imbued with a humble opinion of yourself and respect for others.

5. How difficult it is to perform the duty of seeking the good of our neighbor! Unless you leave off all thought of yourself and in a manner cease to be yourself, you will never accomplish it. How can you exhibit those works of charity which Paul describes unless you renounce yourself, and become wholly devoted to others? "Charity (says he, 1 Cor. 13:4) suffereth long, and is kind; charity envieth not; charity vaunteth not itself, is not puffed up, doth not behave itself unseemly, seeketh not her own, is not easily provoked," &c. Were it the only thing required of us to seek not our own, nature would not have the least power to comply: she so inclines us to love ourselves only, that she will not easily allow us carelessly to pass by ourselves and our own interests that we may watch over the interests of others, nay, spontaneously to yield our own rights and resign it to another. But Scripture, to conduct us to this, reminds us, that whatever we obtain from the Lord is granted on the condition of our employing it for the common good of the Church, and that, therefore, the legitimate use of all our gifts is a kind and liberal communication of them with others. There cannot be a surer rule, nor a stronger exhortation to the observance of it, than when we are taught that all the endowments which we possess are divine deposits entrusted to us for the very purpose of being distributed for the good of our neighbor. But Scripture proceeds still farther when it likens these endowments to the different members of the body (1 Cor. 12:12). No member has its function for itself, or applies it for its own private use, but transfers it to its fellow-members; nor does it derive any other advantage from

it than that which it receives in common with the whole body. Thus, whatever the pious man can do, he is bound to do for his brethren, not consulting his own interest in any other way than by striving earnestly for the common edification of the Church. Let this, then, be our method of showing good-will and kindness, considering that, in regard to everything which God has bestowed upon us, and by which we can aid our neighbor, we are his stewards, and are bound to give account of our stewardship; moreover, that the only right mode of administration is that which is regulated by love. In this way, we shall not only unite the study of our neighbor's advantage with a regard to our own, but make the latter subordinate to the former. And lest we should have omitted to perceive that this is the law for duly administering every gift which we receive from God, he of old applied that law to the minutest expressions of his own kindness. He commanded the firstfruits to be offered to him as an attestation by the people that it was impious to reap any advantage from goods not previously consecrated to him (Exod. 22:29; 23:19). But if the gifts of God are not sanctified to us until we have with our own hand dedicated them to the Giver, it must be a gross abuse that does not give signs of such dedication. It is in vain to contend that you cannot enrich the Lord by your offerings. Though, as the Psalmist says "Thou art my Lord: my goodness extendeth not unto thee," yet you can extend it "to the saints that are in the earth" (Ps. 16:2-3); and therefore a comparison is drawn between sacred oblations and alms as now corresponding to the offerings under the Law.

6. Moreover, that we may not weary in well-doing (as would otherwise forthwith and infallibly be the case), we must add the other quality in the Apostle's enumeration, "Charity suffereth long, and is kind, is not easily provoked" (1 Cor. 13:4). The Lord enjoins us to do good to all without exception, though the greater part, if estimated by their own merit, are most unworthy of it. But Scripture subjoins a most excellent reason, when it tells us that we are not to look to what

men in themselves deserve, but to attend to the image of God, which exists in all, and to which we owe all honor and love. But in those who are of the household of faith, the same rule is to be more carefully observed, inasmuch as that image is renewed and restored in them by the Spirit of Christ. Therefore, whoever be the man that is presented to you as needing your assistance, you have no ground for declining to give it to him. Say he is a stranger. The Lord has given him a mark which ought to be familiar to you: for which reason he forbids you to despise your own flesh (Gal. 6:10). Say he is mean and of no consideration. The Lord points him out as one whom he has distinguished by the luster of his own image (Isa. 58:7). Say that you are bound to him by no ties of duty. The Lord has substituted him as it were into his own place, that in him you may recognize the many great obligations under which the Lord has laid you to himself. Say that he is unworthy of your least exertion on his account; but the image of God, by which he is recommended to you, is worthy of yourself and all your exertions. But if he not only merits no good, but has provoked you by injury and mischief, still this is no good reason why you should not embrace him in love, and visit him with offices of love. He has deserved very differently from me, you will say. But what has the Lord deserved? Whatever injury he has done you, when he enjoins you to forgive him, he certainly means that it should be imputed to himself. In this way only we attain to what is not to say difficult but altogether against nature, to love those that hate us, render good for evil, and blessing for cursing, remembering that we are not to reflect on the wickedness of men, but look to the image of God in them, an image which, covering and obliterating their faults, should by its beauty and dignity allure us to love and embrace them.

7. We shall thus succeed in mortifying ourselves if we fulfill all the duties of charity. Those duties, however, are not fulfilled by the mere discharge of them, though none be omitted, unless it is done from a pure feeling of love. For it may happen that one may perform every

one of these offices, insofar as the external act is concerned, and be far from performing them aright. For you see some who would be thought very liberal, and yet accompany everything they give with insult, by the haughtiness of their looks, or the violence of their words. And to such a calamitous condition have we come in this unhappy age, that the greater part of men never almost give alms without contumely. Such conduct ought not to have been tolerated even among the heathen; but from Christians something more is required than to carry cheerfulness in their looks, and give attractiveness to the discharge of their duties by courteous language. First, they should put themselves in the place of him whom they see in need of their assistance, and pity his misfortune as if they felt and bore it, so that a feeling of pity and humanity should incline them to assist him just as they would themselves. He who is thus minded will go and give assistance to his brethren, and not only not taint his acts with arrogance or upbraiding but will neither look down upon the brother to whom he does a kindness, as one who needed his help, or keep him in subjection as under obligation to him, just as we do not insult a diseased member when the rest of the body labors for its recovery, nor think it under special obligation to the other members, because it has required more exertion than it has returned. A communication of offices between members is not regarded as at all gratuitous, but rather as the payment of that which being due by the law of nature it were monstrous to deny. For this reason, he who has performed one kind of duty will not think himself thereby discharged, as is usually the case when a rich man, after contributing somewhat of his substance, delegates remaining burdens to others as if he had nothing to do with them. Everyone should rather consider, that however great he is, he owes himself to his neighbors, and that the only limit to his beneficence is the failure of his means. The extent of these should regulate that of his charity.

8. The principal part of self-denial, that which as we have said has reference to God, let us again consider more fully. Many things have already been said with regard to it which it were superfluous to repeat; and, therefore, it will be sufficient to view it as forming us to equanimity and endurance. First, then, in seeking the convenience or tranquility of the present life, Scripture calls us to resign ourselves, and all we have, to the disposal of the Lord, to give him up the affections of our heart, that he may tame and subdue them. We have a frenzied desire, an infinite eagerness, to pursue wealth and honor, intrigue for power, accumulate riches, and collect all those frivolities which seem conducive to luxury and splendor. On the other hand, we have a remarkable dread, a remarkable hatred of poverty, mean birth, and a humble condition, and feel the strongest desire to guard against them. Hence, in regard to those who frame their life after their own counsel, we see how restless they are in mind, how many plans they try, to what fatigues they submit, in order that they may gain what avarice or ambition desires, or, on the other hand, escape poverty and meanness. To avoid similar entanglements, the course which Christian men must follow is this: first, they must not long for, or hope for, or think of any kind of prosperity apart from the blessing of God; on it they must cast themselves, and there safely and confidently recline. For, however much the carnal mind may seem sufficient for itself when in the pursuit of honor or wealth, it depends on its own industry and zeal, or is aided by the favor of men, it is certain that all this is nothing, and that neither intellect nor labor will be of the least avail, except insofar as the Lord prospers both. On the contrary, his blessing alone makes a way through all obstacles, and brings every thing to a joyful and favorable issue. Secondly, though without this blessing we may be able to acquire some degree of fame and opulence (as we daily see wicked men loaded with honors and riches), yet since those on whom the curse of God lies do not enjoy the least particle

of true happiness, whatever we obtain without his blessing must turn out ill. But surely men ought not to desire what adds to their misery. 9. Therefore, if we believe that all prosperous and desirable success depends entirely on the blessing of God, and that when it is wanting all kinds of misery and calamity await us, it follows that we should not eagerly contend for riches and honors, trusting to our own dexterity and assiduity, or leaning on the favor of men, or confiding in any empty imagination of fortune; but should always have respect to the Lord, that under his auspices we may be conducted to whatever lot he has provided for us. First, the result will be, that instead of rushing on regardless of right and wrong, by wiles and wicked arts, and with injury to our neighbors, to catch at wealth and seize upon honors, we will only follow such fortune as we may enjoy with innocence. Who can hope for the aid of the divine blessing amid fraud, rapine, and other iniquitous arts? As this blessing attends him only who thinks purely and acts uprightly, so it calls off all who long for it from sinister designs and evil actions. Secondly, a curb will be laid upon us, restraining a too eager desire of becoming rich, or an ambitious striving after honor. How can anyone have the effrontery to expect that God will aid him in accomplishing desires at variance with his word? What God with his own lips pronounces cursed, never can be prosecuted with his blessing. Lastly, if our success is not equal to our wish and hope, we shall, however, be kept from impatience and detestation of our condition, whatever it be, knowing that so to feel were to murmur against God, at whose pleasure riches and poverty, contempt and honors, are dispensed. In shorts he who leans on the divine blessing in the way which has been described, will not, in the pursuit of those things which men are wont most eagerly to desire, employ wicked arts which he knows would avail him nothing; nor when anything prosperous befalls him will he impute it to himself and his own diligence, or industry, or fortune, instead of ascribing it to God as its author. If, while the affairs of others flourish, his make little progress, or even retrograde, he will bear his humble lot with greater equanimity and moderation than any irreligious man does the moderate success which only falls short of what he wished; for he has a solace in which he can rest more tranquilly than at the very summit of wealth or power, because he considers that his affairs are ordered by the Lord in the manner most conducive to his salvation. This, we see, is the way in which David was affected, who, while he follows God and gives up himself to his guidance, declares, "Neither do I exercise myself in great matters, or in things too high for me. Surely I have behaved and quieted myself as a child that is weaned of his mother" (Ps. 131:1-2).

10. Nor is it in this respect only that pious minds ought to manifest this tranquility and endurance; it must be extended to all the accidents to which this present life is liable. He alone, therefore, has properly denied himself, who has resigned himself entirely to the Lord, placing all the course of his life entirely at his disposal. Happen what may, he whose mind is thus composed will neither deem himself wretched nor murmur against God because of his lot. How necessary this disposition is will appear, if you consider the many accidents to which we are liable. Various diseases ever and anon attack us: at one time pestilence rages; at another we are involved in all the calamities of war. Frost and hail, destroying the promise of the year, cause sterility, which reduces us to penury; wife, parents, children, relatives, are carried off by death; our house is destroyed by fire. These are the events which make men curse their life, detest the day of their birth, execrate the light of heaven, even censure God, and (as they are eloquent in blasphemy) charge him with cruelty and injustice. The believer must in these things also contemplate the mercy and truly paternal indulgence of God. Accordingly, should he see his house by the removal of kindred reduced to solitude even then he will not cease to bless the Lord; his thought will be, Still the grace of the Lord, which dwells within my house, will not leave it desolate. If his crops

are blasted, mildewed, or cut off by frost, or struck down by hail, and he sees famine before him, he will not however despond or murmur against God, but maintain his confidence in him; "We thy people, and sheep of thy pasture, will give thee thanks for ever" (Ps. 79:13); he will supply me with food, even in the extreme of sterility. If he is afflicted with disease, the sharpness of the pain will not so overcome him, as to make him break out with impatience, and expostulate with God; but, recognizing justice and lenity in the rod, will patiently endure. In short, whatever happens, knowing that it is ordered by the Lord, he will receive it with a placid and grateful mind, and will not contumaciously resist the government of him, at whose disposal he has placed himself and all that he has. Especially let the Christian breast eschew that foolish and most miserable consolation of the heathen, who, to strengthen their mind against adversity, imputed it to fortune, at which they deemed it absurd to feel indignant, as she was ασκοπος (aimless) and rash, and blindly wounded the good equally with the bad. On the contrary, the rule of piety is, that the hand of God is the ruler and arbiter of the fortunes of all, and, instead of rushing on with thoughtless violence, dispenses good and evil with perfect regularity.

Study Guide Questions

Section 1

1. What is the central principle to remember in Christian living?
2. To what must reason submit?

Section 2

1. What does godly self-denial lead to?
2. What happens when virtue is pursued for its own sake?

Section 3

1. According to Calvin, what three aspects of Christian living does Paul give to Titus?

Section 4

1. What relation does self-denial have to our fellow men and to God?
2. What happens when we rush into self-love?
3. What does each person find within his breast through self-flattery?

Section 5

1. What will keep you from accomplishing anything in this life?
2. What makes up the lawful use of all benefits to others?
3. What makes the acceptance of an enjoyment unlawful?

Section 6

1. Do our neighbors deserve to be loved by us?
2. How then may we love them?
3. When faced with the duty of loving someone unworthy, what should we do?

Section 7

1. For Calvin, are loving actions sufficient?
2. How can liberal actions be made reprehensible?
3. When we give to the downtrodden, what must we experience?

Section 8

1. When we learn self-denial, what two things form in us?
2. Our fear of what is wonderful to contemplate?
3. What must happen for true prosperity to occur?

Section 9

1. When we look for divine blessing on our labors, what is bridled in us?
2. If we rest in God, what outcomes will we be content in?

Section 10

1. What part of our lives must we entrust to God?

2. If we are confident in this, what will we do in adversity?

3. This firm resolve in adversity must not be confused with what pagan view?

4. How does God structure our lives?

CHAPTER 8

Of bearing the cross—one branch of self-denial.

The four divisions of this chapter are
I. The nature of the cross, its necessity and dignity, sec. 1-2.
II. The manifold advantages of the cross described, sec. 3-6.
III. The form of the cross the most excellent of all, and yet it by no means removes all sense of pain, sec. 7-8.
IV. A description of warfare under the cross, and of true patience (not that of philosophers), after the example of Christ, sec. 9-11.

Outline:

1. What the cross is. By whom, and on whom, and for what cause imposed. Its necessity and dignity. 2. The cross necessary. 1. To humble our pride. 2. To make us apply to God for aid. Example of David. 3. To give us experience of God's presence.

3. Manifold uses of the cross. 1. Produces patience, hope, and firm confidence in God, gives us victory and perseverance. Faith invincible.

4. 2. Frames us to obedience. Example of Abraham. This training how useful.

5. The cross necessary to subdue the wantonness of the flesh. This portrayed by an apposite simile. Various forms of the cross.

6. 3. God permits our infirmities, and corrects past faults, that he may keep us in obedience. This confirmed by a passage from Solomon and an Apostle.

7. Singular consolation under the cross, when we suffer persecution for righteousness. Some parts of this consolation.

8. This form of the cross most appropriate to believers, and should be borne willingly and cheerfully. This cheerfulness is not unfeeling hilarity, but, while groaning under the burden, waits patiently for the Lord.

9. A description of this conflict. Opposed to the vanity of the Stoics. Illustrated by the authority and example of Christ.

10. Proved by the testimony and uniform experience of the elect. Also by the special example of the Apostle Peter. The nature of the patience required of us.

11. Distinction between the patience of Christians and philosophers. The latter pretend a necessity which cannot be resisted. The former hold forth the justice of God and his care of our safety. A full exposition of this difference.

The pious mind must ascend still higher, namely, whither Christ calls his disciples when he says, that every one of them must "take up his cross" (Matt. 16:24). Those whom the Lord has chosen and honored with his intercourse must prepare for a hard, laborious, troubled life, a life full of many and various kinds of evils; it being the will of our heavenly Father to exercise his people in this way while putting them to the proof. Having begun this course with Christ the first-born, he continues it towards all his children. For though that Son was dear to him above others, the Son in whom he was "well pleased," yet we see, that far from being treated gently and indulgently, we may say, that not only was he subjected to a perpetual cross while he dwelt on earth, but his whole life was nothing else than a kind of perpetual cross. The Apostle assigns the reason, "Though he was a Son, yet learned he obedience by the things which he suffered" (Heb. 5:8). Why then should we exempt ourselves from that condition to which Christ our Head behooved to submit; especially since he submitted on our account, that he might in his own person exhibit a model of patience? Wherefore, the Apostle declares, that all the children of God are destined to be conformed to him. Hence it affords us great consolation in hard and difficult circumstances, which men deem evil and adverse, to think that we are holding fellowship with the sufferings of Christ; that as he passed to celestial glory through a labyrinth of many woes, so we too are conducted thither through various tribulations. For, in another passage, Paul himself thus speaks, "we must through much tribulation enter the kingdom of God" (Acts 14:22); and again, "that I may know him, and the power of his resurrection, and the fellowship of his sufferings, being made conformable unto his death" (Rom 8:29). How powerfully should it soften the bitterness of the cross, to think that the more we are afflicted with adversity, the surer we are made of our fellowship with Christ; by communion with whom our sufferings are not only blessed to us, but tend greatly to the furtherance of our salvation.

2. We may add, that the only thing which made it necessary for our Lord to undertake to bear the cross, was to testify and prove his obedience to the Father; whereas there are many reasons which make it necessary for us to live constantly under the cross. Feeble as we are by nature, and prone to ascribe all perfection to our flesh, unless we receive as it were ocular demonstration of our weakness, we readily estimate our virtue above its proper worth, and doubt not that, whatever happens, it will stand unimpaired and invincible against all difficulties. Hence we indulge a stupid and empty confidence in the flesh, and then trusting to it wax proud against the Lord himself; as if our own faculties were sufficient without his grace. This arrogance

cannot be better repressed than when He proves to us by experience, not only how great our weakness, but also our frailty is. Therefore, he visits us with disgrace, or poverty, or bereavement, or disease, or other afflictions. Feeling altogether unable to support them, we forthwith, insofar as regards ourselves, give way, and thus humbled learn to invoke his strength, which alone can enable us to bear up under a weight of affliction. Nay, even the holiest of men, however well aware that they stand not in their own strength, but by the grace of God, would feel too secure in their own fortitude and constancy, were they not brought to a more thorough knowledge of themselves by the trial of the cross. This feeling gained even upon David, "In my prosperity I said, I shall never be moved. Lord, by thy favor thou hast made my mountain to stand strong: thou didst hide thy face, and I was troubled" (Ps. 30:6-7). He confesses that in prosperity his feelings were dulled and blunted, so that, neglecting the grace of God, on which alone he ought to have depended, he leaned to himself, and promised himself perpetuity. If it so happened to this great prophet, who of us should not fear and study caution? Though in tranquility they flatter themselves with the idea of greater constancy and patience, yet, humbled by adversity, they learn the deception. Believers, I say, warned by such proofs of their diseases, make progress in humility, and, divesting themselves of a depraved confidence in the flesh, betake themselves to the grace of God, and, when they have so betaken themselves, experience the presence of the divine power, in which is ample protection.

3. This Paul teaches when he says that tribulation worketh patience, and patience experience. God having promised that he will be with believers in tribulation, they feel the truth of the promise; while supported by his hand, they endure patiently. This they could never do by their own strength. Patience, therefore, gives the saints an experimental proof that God in reality furnishes the aid which he has promised whenever there is need. Hence also their faith is confirmed, for it were very ungrateful not to expect that in future the truth of

God will be, as they have already found it, firm and constant. We now see how many advantages are at once produced by the cross. Overturning the overweening opinion we form of our own virtue, and detecting the hypocrisy in which we delight, it removes our pernicious carnal confidence, teaching us, when thus humbled, to recline on God alone, so that we neither are oppressed nor despond. Then victory is followed by hope, inasmuch as the Lord, by performing what he has promised, establishes his truth in regard to the future. Were these the only reasons, it is surely plain how necessary it is for us to bear the cross. It is of no little importance to be rid of your self-love, and made fully conscious of your weakness; so impressed with a sense of your weakness as to learn to distrust yourself—to distrust yourself so as to transfer your confidence to God, reclining on him with such heartfelt confidence as to trust in his aid, and continue invincible to the end, standing by his grace so as to perceive that he is true to his promises, and so assured of the certainty of his promises as to be strong in hope.

4. Another end which the Lord has in afflicting his people is to try their patience, and train them to obedience—not that they can yield obedience to him except insofar as he enables them; but he is pleased thus to attest and display striking proofs of the graces which he has conferred upon his saints, lest they should remain within unseen and unemployed. Accordingly, by bringing forward openly the strength and constancy of endurance with which he has provided his servants, he is said to try their patience. Hence the expressions that God tempted Abraham (Gen. 21:1, 12), and made proof of his piety by not declining to sacrifice his only son. Hence, too, Peter tells us that our faith is proved by tribulation, just as gold is tried in a furnace of fire. But who will say it is not expedient that the most excellent gift of patience which the believer has received from his God should be applied to uses by being made sure and manifest? Otherwise men would never value it according to its worth. But if God himself, to prevent the virtues which he has conferred upon believers from

lurking in obscurity, nay, lying useless and perishing, does aright in supplying materials for calling them forth, there is the best reason for the afflictions of the saints, since without them their patience could not exist. I say, that by the cross they are also trained to obedience, because they are thus taught to live not according to their own wish, but at the disposal of God. Indeed, did all things proceed as they wish, they would not know what it is to follow God. Seneca mentions (*De Vit. Beata*, cap. 15) that there was an old proverb when anyone was exhorted to endure adversity, "Follow God;" thereby intimating, that men truly submitted to the yoke of God only when they gave their back and hand to his rod. But if it is most right that we should in all things prove our obedience to our heavenly Father, certainly we ought not to decline any method by which he trains us to obedience.

5. Still, however, we see not how necessary that obedience is, unless we at the same time consider how prone our carnal nature is to shake off the yoke of God whenever it has been treated with some degree of gentleness and indulgence. It just happens to it as with refractory horses, which, if kept idle for a few days at hack and manger, become ungovernable, and no longer recognize the rider, whose command before they implicitly obeyed. And we invariably become what God complains of in the people of Israel—waxing gross and fat, we kick against him who reared and nursed us (Deut. 32:15). The kindness of God should allure us to ponder and love his goodness; but since such is our malignity, that we are invariably corrupted by his indulgence, it is more than necessary for us to be restrained by discipline from breaking forth into such petulance. Thus, lest we become emboldened by an overabundance of wealth; lest elated with honor, we grow proud; lest inflated with other advantages of body, or mind, or fortune, we grow insolent, the Lord himself interferes as he sees to be expedient by means of the cross, subduing and curbing the arrogance of our flesh, and that in various ways, as the advantage of each requires. For as we do not all equally labor under the same disease, so

we do not all need the same difficult cure. Hence we see that all are not exercised with the same kind of cross. While the heavenly Physician treats some more gently, in the case of others he employs harsher remedies, his purpose being to provide a cure for all. Still none is left free and untouched, because he knows that all, without a single exception, are diseased.

6. We may add, that our most merciful Father requires not only to prevent our weakness, but often to correct our past faults, that he may keep us in due obedience. Therefore, whenever we are afflicted we ought immediately to call to mind our past life. In this way we will find that the faults which we have committed are deserving of such castigation. And yet the exhortation to patience is not to be founded chiefly on the acknowledgment of sin. For Scripture supplies a far better consideration when it says, that in adversity "we are chastened of the Lord, that we should not be condemned with the world" (1 Cor. 11:32). Therefore, in the very bitterness of tribulation we ought to recognize the kindness and mercy of our Father, since even then he ceases not to further our salvation. For he afflicts, not that he may ruin or destroy but rather that he may deliver us from the condemnation of the world. Let this thought lead us to what Scripture elsewhere teaches: "My son, despise not the chastening of the Lord; neither be weary of his correction: For whom the Lord loveth he correcteth; even as a father the son in whom he delighteth" (Prov. 3:11-12). When we perceive our Father's rod, is it not our part to behave as obedient docile sons rather than rebelliously imitate desperate men, who are hardened in wickedness? God dooms us to destruction, if he does not, by correction, call us back when we have fallen off from him, so that it is truly said, "If ye be without chastisement," "then are ye bastards, and not sons" (Heb. 12:8). We are most perverse then if we cannot bear him while he is manifesting his good-will to us, and the care which he takes of our salvation. Scripture states the difference between believers and unbelievers to be, that the latter, as the slaves of inveterate and deep-seated iniquity, only become

worse and more obstinate under the lash; whereas the former, like free-born sons turn to repentance. Now, therefore, choose your class. But as I have already spoken of this subject, it is sufficient to have here briefly adverted to it.

7. There is singular consolation, moreover, when we are persecuted for righteousness' sake. For our thought should then be, How high the honor which God bestows upon us in distinguishing us by the special badge of his soldiers. By suffering persecution for righteousness' sake, I mean not only striving for the defense of the Gospel, but for the defense of righteousness in any way. Whether, therefore, in maintaining the truth of God against the lies of Satan, or defending the good and innocent against the injuries of the bad, we are obliged to incur the offence and hatred of the world, so as to endanger life, fortune, or honor, let us not grieve or decline so far to spend ourselves for God; let us not think ourselves wretched in those things in which he with his own lips has pronounced us blessed (Matt. 5:10). Poverty, indeed considered in itself, is misery; so are exile, contempt, imprisonment, ignominy: in fine, death itself is the last of all calamities. But when the favor of God breathes upon us, there is none of these things which may not turn out to our happiness. Let us then be contented with the testimony of Christ rather than with the false estimate of the flesh, and then, after the example of the Apostles, we will rejoice in being "counted worthy to suffer shame for his name" (Acts 5:41). For why? If, while conscious of our innocence, we are deprived of our substance by the wickedness of man, we are, no doubt, humanly speaking, reduced to poverty; but in truth our riches in heaven are increased: if driven from our homes we have a more welcome reception into the family of God; if vexed and despised, we are more firmly rooted in Christ; if stigmatized by disgrace and ignominy, we have a higher place in the kingdom of God; and if we are slain, entrance is thereby given us to eternal life. The Lord having set such a price upon

us, let us be ashamed to estimate ourselves at less than the shadowy and evanescent allurements of the present life.

8. Since by these, and similar considerations, Scripture abundantly solaces us for the ignominy or calamities which we endure in defense of righteousness, we are very ungrateful if we do not willingly and cheerfully receive them at the hand of the Lord, especially since this form of the cross is the most appropriate to believers, being that by which Christ desires to be glorified in us, as Peter also declares (1 Pet. 4:11, 14). But as to ingenuous natures, it is more bitter to suffer disgrace than a hundred deaths, Paul expressly reminds us that not only persecution, but also disgrace awaits us, "because we trust in the living God" (1 Tim. 4:10). So in another passage he bids us, after his example, walk "by evil report and good report" (2 Cor. 6:8). The cheerfulness required, however, does not imply a total insensibility to pain. The saints could show no patience under the cross if they were not both tortured with pain and grievously molested. Were there no hardship in poverty, no pain in disease, no sting in ignominy, no fear in death, where would be the fortitude and moderation in enduring them? But while every one of these, by its inherent bitterness, naturally vexes the mind, the believer in this displays his fortitude, that though fully sensible of the bitterness and laboring grievously, he still withstands and struggles boldly; in this displays his patience, that though sharply stung, he is however curbed by the fear of God from breaking forth into any excess; in this displays his alacrity, that though pressed with sorrow and sadness, he rests satisfied with spiritual consolation from God.

9. This conflict which believers maintain against the natural feeling of pain, while they study moderation and patience, Paul elegantly describes in these words: "We are troubled on every side, yet not distressed; we are perplexed, but not in despair; persecuted, but not forsaken; cast down, but not destroyed" (2 Cor. 4:8-9). You see that to bear the cross patiently is not to have your feelings altogether blunted, and

to be absolutely insensible to pain, according to the absurd description which the Stoics of old gave of their hero as one who, divested of humanity, was affected in the same way by adversity and prosperity, grief and joy; or rather, like a stone, was not affected by anything. And what did they gain by that sublime wisdom? they exhibited a shadow of patience, which never did, and never can, exist among men. Nay, rather by aiming at a too exact and rigid patience, they banished it altogether from human life. Now also we have among Christians a new kind of Stoics, who hold it vicious not only to groan and weep, but even to be sad and anxious. These paradoxes are usually started by indolent men who, employing themselves more in speculation than in action, can do nothing else for us than beget such paradoxes. But we have nothing to do with that iron philosophy which our Lord and Master condemned—not only in word, but also by his own example. For he both grieved and shed tears for his own and others' woes. Nor did he teach his disciples differently: "Ye shall weep and lament, but the world shall rejoice" (John 16:20). And lest anyone should regard this as vicious, he expressly declares, "Blessed are they that mourn" (Matt. 5:4). And no wonder. If all tears are condemned, what shall we think of our Lord himself, whose "sweat was as it were great drops of blood falling down to the ground?" (Luke 22:44; Matt. 26:38). If every kind of fear is a mark of unbelief, what place shall we assign to the dread which, it is said, in no slight degree amazed him; if all sadness is condemned, how shall we justify him when he confesses, "My soul is exceeding sorrowful, even unto death?"

10. I wished to make these observations to keep pious minds from despair, lest, from feeling it impossible to divest themselves of the natural feeling of grief, they might altogether abandon the study of patience. This must necessarily be the result with those who convert patience into stupor, and a brave and firm man into a block. Scripture gives saints the praise of endurance when, though afflicted by the hardships they endure, they are not crushed; though they feel bitterly, they are

at the same time filled with spiritual joy; though pressed with anxiety, breathe exhilarated by the consolation of God. Still there is a certain degree of repugnance in their hearts, because natural sense shuns and dreads what is adverse to it, while pious affection, even through these difficulties, tries to obey the divine will. This repugnance the Lord expressed when he thus addressed Peter: "Verily, verily, I say unto thee, When thou wast young, thou girdedst thyself and walkedst whither thou wouldst; but when thou shalt be old, thou shalt stretch forth thy hands, and another shall gird thee; and carry thee whither thou wouldst not" (John 21:18). It is not probable, indeed, that when it became necessary to glorify God by death he was driven to it unwilling and resisting; had it been so, little praise would have been due to his martyrdom. But though he obeyed the divine ordination with the greatest alacrity of heart, yet, as he had not divested himself of humanity, he was distracted by a double will. When he thought of the bloody death which he was to die, struck with horror, he would willingly have avoided it: on the other hand, when he considered that it was God who called him to it, his fear was vanquished and suppressed, and he met death cheerfully. It must therefore be our study, if we would be disciples of Christ, to imbue our minds with such reverence and obedience to God as may tame and subjugate all affections contrary to his appointment. In this way, whatever be the kind of cross to which we are subjected, we shall in the greatest straits firmly maintain our patience. Adversity will have its bitterness, and sting us. When afflicted with disease, we shall groan and be disquieted, and long for health; pressed with poverty, we shall feel the stings of anxiety and sadness, feel the pain of ignominy, contempt, and injury, and pay the tears due to nature at the death of our friends: but our conclusion will always be, The Lord so willed it, therefore let us follow his will. Nay, amid the pungency of grief, among groans and tears this thought will necessarily suggest itself and incline us cheerfully to endure the things for which we are so afflicted.

11. But since the chief reason for enduring the cross has been derived from a consideration of the divine will, we must in few words explain wherein lies the difference between philosophical and Christian patience. Indeed, very few of the philosophers advanced so far as to perceive that the hand of God tries us by means of affliction, and that we ought in this matter to obey God. The only reason which they adduce is, that so it must be. But is not this just to say, that we must yield to God, because it is in vain to contend against him? For if we obey God only because it is necessary, provided we can escape, we shall cease to obey him. But what Scripture calls us to consider in the will of God is very different, namely, first justice and equity, and then a regard to our own salvation. Hence Christian exhortations to patience are of this nature, Whether poverty, or exile, or imprisonment, or contumely, or disease, or bereavement, or any such evil affects us, we must think that none of them happens except by the will and providence of God; moreover, that everything he does is in the most perfect order. What! Do not our numberless daily faults deserve to be chastised, more severely, and with a heavier rod than his mercy lays upon us? Is it not most right that our flesh should be subdued, and be, as it were, accustomed to the yoke, so as not to rage and wanton as it lists? Are not the justice and the truth of God worthy of our suffering on their account? But if the equity of God is undoubtedly displayed in affliction, we cannot murmur or struggle against them without iniquity. We no longer hear the frigid cant, Yield, because it is necessary; but a living and energetic precept, Obey, because it is unlawful to resist; bear patiently, because impatience is rebellion against the justice of God. Then as that only seems to us attractive which we perceive to be for our own safety and advantage, here also our heavenly Father consoles us, by the assurance, that in the very cross with which he afflicts us he provides for our salvation. But if it is clear that tribulations are salutary to us, why should we not receive them with calm and grateful minds? In bearing them patiently we are not

submitting to necessity but resting satisfied with our own good. The effect of these thoughts is, that to whatever extent our minds are contracted by the bitterness which we naturally feel under the cross, to the same extent will they be expanded with spiritual joy. Hence arises thanksgiving, which cannot exist unless joy be felt. But if the praise of the Lord and thanksgiving can emanate only from a cheerful and gladdened breast, and there is nothing which ought to interrupt these feelings in us, it is clear how necessary it is to temper the bitterness of the cross with spiritual joy.

Study Guide Questions

Section 1

1. If we have been adopted by the Lord, what should we be prepared for?

2. Was the Lord exempt from this in His life?

Section 2

1. Why does God subject us to this kind of thing?

Section 3

1. What does the cross strike at?

2. Apart from trials given by God, could we learn these things?

Section 4

1. What is the testing function of trials?

Section 5

1. If different believers go through different kinds of trials, what does this mean?

Section 6

1. Does God want to destroy us?

2. If we don't receive this kind of chastisement, what does it mean?

Section 7
1. What is the special badge of God's soldiery?
2. What phrase makes you wonder about the American founders' familiarity with Calvin?

Section 8
1. Does the believer shrug suffering off as though it were nothing?
2. What does the believer do with his bitter troubles?

Section 9
1. What is the distinction between what Calvin urges here and Stoicism?
2. What does Calvin identify as the Stoic's problem?
3. What does Calvin call a contemporary form of neo-Stoicism?

Section 10
1. Why was the apostle Peter pulled apart by a double will at his martyrdom, according to Calvin?
2. What do we do at the funerals of our dear ones?

Section 11
1. What reason for submitting does fatalism give?
2. What reason does Calvin give?

CHAPTER 9

Of meditating on the future life.

The three divisions of this chapter are—

I. The principal use of the cross is, that it in various ways accustoms us to despise the present, and excites us to aspire to the future life, sec. 1-2.

II. In withdrawing from the present life we must neither shun it nor feel hatred for it; but desiring the future life, gladly quit the present at the command of our sovereign Master, sec. 3-4.

III. Our infirmity in dreading death described. The correction and safe remedy, sec. 6.

Outline:

1. The design of God in afflicting his people. 1. To accustom us to despise the present life. Our infatuated love of it. Afflictions employed as the cure. 2. To lead us to aspire to heaven.

2. Excessive love of the present life prevents us from duly aspiring to the other. Hence the disadvantages of prosperity. Blindness of the human judgment. Our philosophizing on the vanity of life only of momentary influence. The necessity of the cross.

3. The present life an evidence of the divine favor to his people; and therefore, not to be detested. On the contrary, should call forth thanksgiving. The crown of victory in heaven after the contest on earth.

4. Weariness of the present life how to be tempered. The believer's estimate of life. Comparison of the present and the future life. How far the present life should be hated.

5. Christians should not tremble at the fear of death. Two reasons. Objection. Answer. Other reasons.

6. Reasons continued. Conclusion.

Whatever be the kind of tribulation with which we are afflicted, we should always consider the end of it to be, that we may be trained to despise the present, and thereby stimulated to aspire to the future life. For since God well knows how strongly we are inclined by nature to a slavish love of this world, in order to prevent us from clinging too strongly to it, he employs the fittest reason for calling us back, and shaking off our lethargy. Every one of us, indeed, would be thought to aspire and aim at heavenly immortality during the whole course of his life. For we would be ashamed in no respect to excel the lower animals; whose condition would not be at all inferior to ours, had we not a hope of immortality beyond the grave. But when you attend to the plans, wishes, and actions of each, you see nothing in them but the earth. Hence our stupidity; our minds being dazzled with the glare of wealth, power, and honors, that they can see no farther. The heart also, engrossed with avarice, ambition, and lust, is weighed down and cannot rise above them. In short, the whole soul, ensnared by the allurements of the flesh, seeks its happiness on the earth. To meet this disease, the Lord makes his people sensible of the vanity of the present life, by a constant proof of its miseries. Thus, that they may not promise themselves deep and lasting peace in it, he often allows them to be assailed by war, tumult, or rapine, or to be disturbed by other injuries. That they may not long with too much eagerness after fleeting and fading riches, or rest in those which they already possess, he reduces them to want, or, at least, restricts them to a moderate allowance, at one time by exile, at another by sterility, at another by fire, or by other means. That they may not indulge too complacently in the advantages of married life, he either vexes them by the misconduct of their partners, or humbles them by the wickedness of their children, or afflicts them by bereavement. But if in all these he is indulgent to them, lest they should either swell with vain-glory, or be elated with confidence, by diseases and dangers he sets palpably before them how unstable and evanescent are all the advantages competent to mortals. We duly profit by the discipline of the cross, when we learn that this life, estimated in itself, is restless, troubled, in numberless ways wretched, and plainly in no respect happy; that what are estimated its blessings are uncertain, fleeting, vain, and vitiated by a great admixture of evil. From this we conclude, that all we have to seek or hope for here is contest; that when we think of the crown we must raise our eyes to heaven. For we must hold, that our mind never rises seriously to desire and aspire after the future, until it has learned to despise the present life.

2. For there is no medium between the two things: the earth must either be worthless in our estimation, or keep us enslaved by an intemperate love of it. Therefore, if we have any regard to eternity, we must carefully strive to disencumber ourselves of these fetters. Moreover, since the present life has many enticements to allure us, and great semblance of delight, grace, and sweetness to soothe us, it is of great consequence to us to be now and then called off from its fascinations. For what, pray, would happen, if we here enjoyed an uninterrupted course of honor and felicity, when even the constant stimulus of affliction cannot arouse us to a due sense of our misery? That human life is like smoke or a shadow, is not only known to the learned; there is not a more trite proverb among the vulgar. Considering it a

fact most useful to be known, they have recommended it in many well-known expressions. Still there is no fact which we ponder less carefully, or less frequently remember. For we form all our plans just as if we had fixed our immortality on the earth. If we see a funeral, or walk among graves, as the image of death is then present to the eye, I admit we philosophize admirably on the vanity of life. We do not indeed always do so, for those things often have no effect upon us at all. But, at the best, our philosophy is momentary. It vanishes as soon as we turn our back, and leaves not the vestige of remembrance behind; in short, it passes away, just like the applause of a theatre at some pleasant spectacle. Forgetful not only of death, but also of mortality itself, as if no rumor of it had ever reached us, we indulge in supine security as expecting a terrestrial immortality. Meanwhile, if anyone breaks in with the proverb, that man is the creature of a day, we indeed acknowledge its truth, but, so far from giving heed to it, the thought of perpetuity still keeps hold of our minds. Who then can deny that it is of the highest importance to us all, I say not, to be admonished by words, but convinced by all possible experience of the miserable condition of our earthly life; since even when convinced we scarcely cease to gaze upon it with vicious, stupid admiration, as if it contained within itself the sum of all that is good? But if God finds it necessary so to train us, it must be our duty to listen to him when he calls, and shakes us from our torpor, that we may hasten to despise the world, and aspire with our whole heart to the future life.

3. Still the contempt which believers should train themselves to feel for the present life, must not be of a kind to beget hatred of it or ingratitude to God. This life, though abounding in all kinds of wretchedness, is justly classed among divine blessings which are not to be despised. Wherefore, if we do not recognize the kindness of God in it, we are chargeable with no little ingratitude towards him. To believers, especially, it ought to be a proof of divine benevolence, since it is wholly destined to promote their salvation. Before openly

exhibiting the inheritance of eternal glory, God is pleased to manifest himself to us as a Father by minor proofs—viz. the blessings
which he daily bestows upon us. Therefore, while this life serves to
acquaint us with the goodness of God, shall we disdain it as if it did
not contain one particle of good? We ought, therefore, to feel and be
affected towards it in such a manner as to place it among those gifts
of the divine benignity which are by no means to be despised. Were
there no proofs in Scripture (they are most numerous and clear), yet
nature herself exhorts us to return thanks to God for having brought
us forth into light, granted us the use of it, and bestowed upon us all
the means necessary for its preservation. And there is a much higher
reason when we reflect that here we are in a manner prepared for the
glory of the heavenly kingdom. For the Lord hath ordained, that those
who are ultimately to be crowned in heaven must maintain a previous
warfare on the earth, that they may not triumph before they have
overcome the difficulties of war, and obtained the victory. Another
reason is, that we here begin to experience in various ways a foretaste
of the divine benignity, in order that our hope and desire may be
whetted for its full manifestation. When once we have concluded
that our earthly life is a gift of the divine mercy, of which, agreeably
to our obligation, it behooves us to have a grateful remembrance, we
shall then properly descend to consider its most wretched condition,
and thus escape from that excessive fondness for it, to which, as I have
said, we are naturally prone.

4. In proportion as this improper love diminishes, our desire of
a better life should increase. I confess, indeed, that a most accurate
opinion was formed by those who thought, that the best thing was
not to be born, the next best to die early. For, being destitute of the
light of God and of true religion, what could they see in it that was
not of dire and evil omen? Nor was it unreasonable for those who felt
sorrow and shed tears at the birth of their kindred, to keep holiday at
their deaths. But this they did without profit; because, devoid of the

true doctrine of faith, they saw not how that which in itself is neither happy nor desirable turns to the advantage of the righteous: and
hence their opinion issued in despair. Let believers, then, in forming
an estimate of this mortal life, and perceiving that in itself it is nothing but misery, make it their aim to exert themselves with greater
alacrity, and less hindrance, in aspiring to the future and eternal life.
When we contrast the two, the former may not only be securely neglected, but, in comparison of the latter, be disdained and contemned.
If heaven is our country, what can the earth be but a place of exile? If
departure from the world is entrance into life, what is the world but
a sepulcher, and what is residence in it but immersion in death? If to
be freed from the body is to gain full possession of freedom, what is
the body but a prison? If it is the very summit of happiness to enjoy
the presence of God, is it not miserable to want it? But "whilst we
are at home in the body, we are absent from the Lord" (2 Cor. 5:6).
Thus when the earthly is compared with the heavenly life, it may
undoubtedly be despised and trampled under foot. We ought never,
indeed, to regard it with hatred, except insofar as it keeps us subject
to sin; and even this hatred ought not to be directed against life itself. At all events, we must stand so affected towards it in regard to
weariness or hatred as, while longing for its termination, to be ready
at the Lord's will to continue in it, keeping far from everything like
murmuring and impatience. For it is as if the Lord had assigned us a
post, which we must maintain till he recalls us. Paul, indeed, laments
his condition, in being still bound with the fetters of the body, and
sighs earnestly for redemption (Rom. 7:24); nevertheless, he declared
that, in obedience to the command of God, he was prepared for both
courses, because he acknowledges it as his duty to God to glorify his
name whether by life or by death, while it belongs to God to determine what is most conducive to His glory (Phil. 1:20-24). Wherefore,
if it becomes us to live and die to the Lord, let us leave the period of
our life and death at his disposal. Still let us ardently long for death,

and constantly meditate upon it, and in comparison with future immortality, let us despise life, and, on account of the bondage of sin,
long to renounce it whenever it shall so please the Lord.

5. But, most strange to say, many who boast of being Christians,
instead of thus longing for death, are so afraid of it that they tremble
at the very mention of it as a thing ominous and dreadful. We cannot wonder, indeed, that our natural feelings should be somewhat
shocked at the mention of our dissolution. But it is altogether intolerable that the light of piety should not be so powerful in a Christian
breast as with greater consolation to overcome and suppress that fear.
For if we reflect that this our tabernacle, unstable, defective, corruptible, fading, pining, and putrid, is dissolved, in order that it may forthwith be renewed in sure, perfect, incorruptible, in fine, in heavenly
glory, will not faith compel us eagerly to desire what nature dreads?
If we reflect that by death we are recalled from exile to inhabit our
native country, a heavenly country, shall this give us no comfort? But
everything longs for permanent existence. I admit this, and therefore
contend that we ought to look to future immortality, where we may
obtain that fixed condition which nowhere appears on the earth. For
Paul admirably enjoins believers to hasten cheerfully to death, not because they "would be unclothed, but clothed upon" (2 Cor. 5:2). Shall
the lower animals, and inanimate creatures themselves even wood and
stone, as conscious of their present vanity, long for the final resurrection, that they may with the sons of God be delivered from vanity
(Rom. 8:19); and shall we, endued with the light of intellect, and more
than intellect, enlightened by the Spirit of God, when our essence is
in question, rise no higher than the corruption of this earth? But it is
not my purpose, nor is this the place, to plead against this great perverseness. At the outset, I declared that I had no wish to engage in a
diffuse discussion of commonplaces. My advice to those whose minds
are thus timid is to read the short treatise of Cyprian *De Mortalitate*,
unless it be more accordant with their deserts to send them to the

philosophers, that by inspecting what they say on the contempt of death, they may begin to blush. This, however, let us hold as fixed, that no man has made much progress in the school of Christ who does not look forward with joy to the day of death and final resurrection (2 Tim. 4:18; Tit. 2:13) for Paul distinguishes all believers by this mark; and the usual course of Scripture is to direct us thither whenever it would furnish us with an argument for substantial joy. "Look up," says our Lord, "and lift up your heads: for your redemption draweth nigh" (Luke 21:28). Is it reasonable, I ask, that what he intended to have a powerful effect in stirring us up to alacrity and exultation should produce nothing but sadness and consternation? If it is so, why do we still glory in him as our Master? Therefore, let us come to a sounder mind, and how repugnant soever the blind and stupid longing of the flesh may be, let us doubt not to desire the advent of the Lord not in wish only, but with earnest sighs, as the most propitious of all events. He will come as a Redeemer to deliver us from an immense abyss of evil and misery, and lead us to the blessed inheritance of his life and glory.

6. Thus, indeed, it is; the whole body of the faithful, so long as they live on the earth, must be like sheep for the slaughter, in order that they may be conformed to Christ their head (Rom. 8:36). Most deplorable, therefore, would their situation be did they not, by raising their mind to heaven, become superior to all that is in the world, and rise above the present aspect of affairs (1 Cor. 15:19). On the other hand, when once they have raised their head above all earthly objects, though they see the wicked flourishing in wealth and honor, and enjoying profound peace, indulging in luxury and splendor, and reveling in all kinds of delights, though they should moreover be wickedly assailed by them, suffer insult from their pride, be robbed by their avarice, or assailed by any other passion, they will have no difficulty in bearing up under these evils. They will turn their eye to that day (Isa. 25:8; Rev. 7:17), on which the Lord will receive his faithful servants, wipe away all tears from their eyes, clothe them in a robe of glory

and joy, feed them with the ineffable sweetness of his pleasures, exalt them to share with him in his greatness; in fine, admit them to a participation in his happiness. But the wicked who may have flourished on the earth, he will cast forth in extreme ignominy, will change their delights into torments, their laughter and joy into wailing and gnashing of teeth, their peace into the gnawing of conscience, and punish their luxury with unquenchable fire. He will also place their necks under the feet of the godly, whose patience they abused. For, as Paul declares, "it is a righteous thing with God to recompense tribulation to them that trouble you; and to you who are troubled rest with us, when the Lord Jesus shall be revealed from heaven" (2 Thess. 1:6-7). This, indeed, is our only consolation; deprived of it, we must either give way to despondency, or resort to our destruction to the vain solace of the world. The Psalmist confesses, "My feet were almost gone: my steps had well-nigh slipt: for I was envious at the foolish when I saw the prosperity of the wicked" (Ps. 73:3-4); and he found no resting place until he entered the sanctuary, and considered the latter end of the righteous and the wicked. To conclude in one word, the cross of Christ then only triumphs in the breasts of believers over the devil and the flesh, sin and sinners, when their eyes are directed to the power of his resurrection.

Study Guide Questions

Section 1

1. Where does our blockishness arise?
2. What is necessary before we are aroused to contemplate the life to come?

Section 2

1. There is no middle ground between what two options?
2. Do humans generally acknowledge the vanity of this life?

Section 3

1. Does contempt for this world mean ingratitude?

Section 4

1. If heaven is our homeland, then what must the earth be?

Section 5

1. What does Calvin say of the man who does not joyfully await the day of death and final resurrection?

Section 6

1. When we lift up our heads in hope, what are we enabled to see in right perspective?

CHAPTER 10

How to use the present life, and the comforts of it.

The divisions of this chapter are—
I. The necessity and usefulness of this doctrine. Extremes to be avoided, if we would rightly use the present life and its comforts, sec. 1-2.
II. One of these extremes—viz. the intemperance of the flesh—to be carefully avoided. Four methods of doing so described in order, sec. 3-6.

Outline:
1. Necessity of this doctrine. Use of the goods of the present life. Extremes to be avoided. 1. Excessive austerity. 2. Carnal intemperance and lasciviousness.

2. God, by creating so many mercies, consulted not only for our necessities, but also for our comfort and delight. Confirmation from a passage in the Psalms, and from experience.

3. Excessive austerity, therefore, to be avoided. So also must the wantonness of the flesh. 1. The creatures invite us to know, love, and

honor the Creator. 2. This not done by the wicked, who only abuse these temporal mercies.

4. All earthly blessings to be despised in comparison of the heavenly life. Aspiration after this life destroyed by an excessive love of created objects. First, Intemperance.

5. Second, Impatience and immoderate desire. Remedy of these evils. The creatures assigned to our use. Man still accountable for the use he makes of them.

6. God requires us in all our actions to look to his calling. Use of this doctrine. It is full of comfort.

By such rudiments we are at the same time well instructed by Scripture in the proper use of earthly blessings, a subject which, in forming a scheme of life, is by no means to be neglected. For if we are to live, we must use the necessary supports of life; nor can we even shun those things which seem more subservient to delight than to necessity. We must therefore observe a mean, that we may use them with a pure conscience, whether for necessity or for pleasure. This the Lord prescribes by his word, when he tells us that to his people the present life is a kind of pilgrimage by which they hasten to the heavenly kingdom. If we are only to pass through the earth, there can be no doubt that we are to use its blessings only insofar as they assist our progress, rather than retard it. Accordingly, Paul, not without cause, admonishes us to use this world without abusing it, and to buy possessions as if we were selling them (1 Cor. 7:30-31). But as this is a slippery place, and there is great danger of falling on either side, let us fix our feet where we can stand safely. There have been some good and holy men who, when they saw intemperance and luxury perpetually carried to excess, if not strictly curbed, and were desirous to correct so pernicious an evil, imagined that there was no other method than to allow man to use corporeal goods only insofar as they were necessaries: a counsel pious indeed, but unnecessarily austere; for it does the very dangerous thing of binding consciences in closer fetters than those in which they are bound by the word of God. Moreover, necessity, according to them, was abstinence from every thing which could be wanted, so that they held it scarcely lawful to make any addition to bread and water. Others were still more austere, as is related of Cratetes the Theban, who threw his riches into the sea, because he thought, that unless he destroyed them they would destroy him. Many also in the present day, while they seek a pretext for carnal intemperance in the use of external things, and at the same time would pave the way for licentiousness, assume for granted, what I by no means concede, that this liberty is not to be restrained by any modification, but that it is to be left to every man's conscience to use them as far as he thinks lawful. I indeed confess that here consciences neither can nor ought to be bound by fixed and definite laws; but that Scripture having laid down general rules for the legitimate uses we should keep within the limits which they prescribe.

2. Let this be our principle, that we err not in the use of the gifts of Providence when we refer them to the end for which their author made and destined them, since he created them for our good, and not for our destruction. No man will keep the true path better than he who shall have this end carefully in view. Now then, if we consider for what end he created food, we shall find that he consulted not only for our necessity, but also for our enjoyment and delight. Thus, in clothing, the end was, in addition to necessity, comeliness and honor; and in herbs, fruits, and trees, besides their various uses, gracefulness of appearance and sweetness of smell. Were it not so, the Prophet would not enumerate among the mercies of God "wine that maketh glad the heart of man, and oil to make his face to shine" (Ps. 104:15). The Scriptures would not everywhere mention, in commendation of his benignity, that he had given such things to men. The natural qualities of things themselves demonstrate to what end, and how far, they may be lawfully enjoyed. Has the Lord adorned flowers with all the beauty

which spontaneously presents itself to the eye, and the sweet odor which delights the sense of smell, and shall it be unlawful for us to enjoy that beauty and this odor? What? Has he not so distinguished colors as to make some more agreeable than others? Has he not given qualities to gold and silver, ivory and marble, thereby rendering them precious above other metals or stones? In short, has he not given many things a value without having any necessary use?

3. Have done, then, with that inhuman philosophy which, in allowing no use of the creatures but for necessity, not only maliciously deprives us of the lawful fruit of the divine beneficence, but cannot be realized without depriving man of all his senses, and reducing him to a block. But, on the other hand, let us with no less care guard against the lusts of the flesh, which, if not kept in order, break through all bounds, and are, as I have said, advocated by those who, under pretense of liberty, allow themselves every sort of license. First one restraint is imposed when we hold that the object of creating all things was to teach us to know their author, and feel grateful for his indulgence. Where is the gratitude if you so gorge or stupefy yourself with feasting and wine as to be unfit for offices of piety, or the duties of your calling? Where the recognition of God, if the flesh, boiling forth in lust through excessive indulgences infects the mind with its impurity, so as to lose the discernment of honor and rectitude? Where thankfulness to God for clothing, if on account of sumptuous raiment we both admire ourselves and disdain others? if, from a love of show and splendor, we pave the way for immodesty? Where our recognition of God, if the glare of these things captivates our minds? For many are so devoted to luxury in all their senses that their mind lies buried: many are so delighted with marble, gold, and pictures, that they become marble-hearted—are changed as it were into metal, and made like painted figures. The kitchen, with its savory smells, so engrosses them that they have no spiritual savor. The same thing may be seen in other matters. Wherefore, it is plain that there is here great

necessity for curbing licentious abuse, and conforming to the rule of Paul, "make not provision for the flesh to fulfill the lusts thereof" (Rom. 13:14). Where too much liberty is given to them, they break forth without measure or restraint.

4. There is no surer or quicker way of accomplishing this than by despising the present life and aspiring to celestial immortality. For hence two rules arise: First, "it remaineth, that both they that have wives be as though they had none;" "and they that use this world, as not abusing it" (1 Cor. 7:29, 31). Secondly, we must learn to be no less placid and patient in enduring penury, than moderate in enjoying abundance. He who makes it his rule to use this world as if he used it not, not only cuts off all gluttony in regard to meat and drink, and all effeminacy, ambition, pride, excessive shows and austerity, in regard to his table, his house, and his clothes, but removes every care and affection which might withdraw or hinder him from aspiring to the heavenly life, and cultivating the interest of his soul. It was well said by Cato: Luxury causes great care, and produces great carelessness as to virtue; and it is an old proverb—Those who are much occupied with the care of the body, usually give little care to the soul. Therefore while the liberty of the Christian in external matters is not to be tied down to a strict rule, it is, however, subject to this law—he must indulge as little as possible; on the other hand, it must be his constant aims not only to curb luxury, but to cut off all show of superfluous abundance, and carefully beware of converting a help into a hindrance.

5. Another rule is, that those in narrow and slender circumstances should learn to bear their wants patiently, that they may not become immoderately desirous of things, the moderate use of which implies no small progress in the school of Christ. For in addition to the many other vices which accompany a longing for earthly good, he who is impatient under poverty almost always betrays the contrary disease in abundance. By this I mean, that he who is ashamed of a sordid garment will be vain-glorious of a splendid one; he who not contented with a

slender, feels annoyed at the want of a more luxurious supper, will intemperately abuse his luxury if he obtains it; he who has a difficulty, and is dissatisfied in submitting to a private and humble condition, will be unable to refrain from pride if he attain to honor. Let it be the aim of all who have any unfeigned desire for piety to learn, after the example of the Apostle, "both to be full and to be hungry, both to abound and to suffer need" (Phil. 4:12). Scripture, moreover, has a third rule for modifying the use of earthly blessings. We have already adverted to it when considering the offices of charity. For it declares that they have all been given us by the kindness of God, and appointed for our use under the condition of being regarded as trusts, of which we must one day give account. We must, therefore, administer them as if we constantly heard the words sounding in our ears, "Give an account of your stewardship." At the same time, let us remember by whom the account is to be taken—viz. by him who, while he so highly commends abstinence, sobriety, frugality, and moderation, abominates luxury, pride, ostentation, and vanity; who approves of no administration but that which is combined with charity, who with his own lips has already condemned all those pleasures which withdraw the heart from chastity and purity, or darken the intellect.

6. The last thing to be observed is, that the Lord enjoins every one of us, in all the actions of life, to have respect to our own calling. He knows the boiling restlessness of the human mind, the fickleness with which it is borne hither and thither, its eagerness to hold opposites at one time in its grasp, its ambition. Therefore, lest all things should be thrown into confusion by our folly and rashness, he has assigned distinct duties to each in the different modes of life. And that no one may presume to overstep his proper limits, he has distinguished the different modes of life by the name of callings. Every man's mode of life, therefore, is a kind of station assigned him by the Lord, that he may not be always driven about at random. So necessary is this distinction, that all our actions are thereby estimated in his sight, and

often in a very different way from that in which human reason or philosophy would estimate them. There is no more illustrious deed even among philosophers than to free one's country from tyranny, and yet the private individual who stabs the tyrant is openly condemned by the voice of the heavenly Judge. But I am unwilling to dwell on particular examples; it is enough to know that in everything the call of the Lord is the foundation and beginning of right action. He who does not act with reference to it will never, in the discharge of duty, keep the right path. He will sometimes be able, perhaps, to give the semblance of something laudable, but whatever it may be in the sight of man, it will be rejected before the throne of God; and besides, there will be no harmony in the different parts of his life. Hence, he only who directs his life to this end will have it properly framed; because free from the impulse of rashness, he will not attempt more than his calling justifies, knowing that it is unlawful to overleap the prescribed bounds. He who is obscure will not decline to cultivate a private life, that he may not desert the post at which God has placed him. Again, in all our cares, toils, annoyances, and other burdens, it will be no small alleviation to know that all these are under the superintendence of God. The magistrate will more willingly perform his office, and the father of a family confine himself to his proper sphere. Everyone in his particular mode of life will, without repining, suffer its inconveniences, cares, uneasiness, and anxiety, persuaded that God has laid on the burden. This, too, will afford admirable consolation, that in following your proper calling, no work will be so mean and sordid as not to have a splendor and value in the eye of God.

Study Guide Questions

Section 1

1. What is the double danger Calvin warns against on material possessions?

2. Can this be governed by a fixed rule?

Section 2

1. What must we remember in the use of all things?

2. Does that include delight and pleasure?

Section 3

1. What does restriction to function do to a man?

2. And what does the sweet smell of the kitchen do to another kind of man?

Section 4

1. What Pauline principle does Calvin cite?

Section 5

1. How can we know if we can safely go with something?

2. What is the third rule that Calvin mentions?

Section 6

1. What else guides us in our use of things?

2. Is understanding our calling important?

CHAPTER 11

Of justification by faith. Both the name and the reality defined.

In this chapter and the seven which follow, the doctrine of Justification by Faith is expounded, and opposite errors refuted. The following may be regarded as the arrangement of these chapters:— Chapter 11 states the doctrine, and the four subsequent chapters, by destroying the righteousness of works, confirm the righteousness of faith, each in the order which appears in the respective titles of these chapters. In Chapter 12 the doctrine of Justification is confirmed by a description of perfect righteousness; in Chapter 13 by calling attention to two precautions; in Chapter 14 by a consideration of the commencement and progress of regeneration in the regenerate; and in Chapter 15 by two very pernicious effects which constantly accompany the righteousness of works. The three other chapters are devoted to refutation; Chapter 16 disposes of the objections of opponents; Chapter 17 replies to the arguments drawn from the promises of the Law or the Gospel; Chapter 18 refutes what is said in support of the righteousness of faith from the promise of reward.

There are three principal divisions in the Eleventh Chapter.

I. The terms used in this discussion are explained, sec. 1-4.

II. Osiander's dream as to essential righteousness impugned, sec. 5-13.

III. The righteousness of faith established in opposition to the righteousness of works.

Outline:

1. Connection between the doctrine of Justification and that of Regeneration. The knowledge of this doctrine very necessary for two reasons.

2. For the purpose of facilitating the exposition of it, the terms are explained. 1. What it is to be justified in the sight of God. 2. To be justified by works. 3. To be justified by faith. Definition.

3. Various meanings of the term "justification." 1. To give praise to God and truth. 2. To make a vain display of righteousness. 3. To impute righteousness by faith, by and on account of Christ. Confirmation from an expression of Paul, and another of our Lord.

4. Another confirmation from a comparison with other expressions, in which justification means free righteousness before God through faith in Jesus Christ. 1. Acceptance. 2. Imputation of righteousness. 3. Remission of sins. 4. Blessedness. 5. Reconciliation with God. 6. Righteousness by the obedience of Christ.

5. The second part of the chapter. Osiander's dream as to essential righteousness refuted. 1. Osiander's argument: Answer. 2. Osiander's second argument: Answer. Third argument: Answer.

6. Necessity of this refutation. Fourth argument: Answer. Confirmation: Another answer. Fifth and sixth arguments and answers.

7. Seventh and eighth arguments.

8. Ninth argument: Answer.

9. Tenth argument: Answer.

10. In what sense Christ is said to be our righteousness. Eleventh and twelfth arguments and answers.

11. Thirteenth and fourteenth arguments: Answers. An exception by Osiander. Imputed and begun righteousness to be distinguished. Osiander confounds them. Fifteenth argument: Answer.

12. Sixteenth argument, a dream of Osiander: Answer. Other four arguments and answers. Conclusion of the refutation of Osiander's errors.

13. Last part of the chapter. Refutation of the Sophists pretending a righteousness compounded partly of faith and partly of works.

14. Sophistical evasion by giving the same name to different things: Two answers.

15. Second evasion: Two answers. First answer. Pernicious consequences resulting from this evasion.

16. Second answer, showing wherein, according to Scripture, Justification consists.

17. In explanation of this doctrine of Justification, two passages of Scripture produced.

18. Another passage of Scripture.

19. Third evasion. Papistical objection to the doctrine of Justification by Faith alone: Three answers. Fourth evasion: Three answers.

20. Fifth evasion, founded on the application of the term "Righteousness" to good works, and also on their reward: Answer, confirmed by the invincible argument of Paul. Sixth evasion: Answer.

21. Osiander and the Sophists being thus refuted, the accuracy of the definition of Justification by Faith established.

22. Definition confirmed. 1. By passages of Scripture. 2. By the writings of the ancient Fathers.

23. Man justified by faith, not because by it he obtains the Spirit, and is thus made righteous, but because by faith he lays hold of the righteousness of Christ. An objection removed. An example of the doctrine of Justification by Faith from the works of Ambrose.

I trust I have now sufficiently shown how man's only resource for escaping from the curse of the law, and recovering salvation, lies in faith; and also what the nature of faith is, what the benefits which it confers, and the fruits which it produces. The whole may be thus summed up: Christ given to us by the kindness of God is apprehended and possessed by faith, by means of which we obtain in particular a twofold benefit; first, being reconciled by the righteousness of Christ, God becomes, instead of a judge, an indulgent Father; and, secondly, being sanctified by his Spirit, we aspire to integrity and purity of life. This second benefit—viz. regeneration, appears to have been already sufficiently discussed. On the other hand, the subject of justification was discussed more cursorily, because it seemed of more consequence first to explain that the faith by which alone, through the mercy of God, we obtain free justification, is not destitute of good works; and also to show the true nature of these good works on which this question partly turns. The doctrine of Justification is now to be fully discussed, and discussed under the conviction, that as it is the principal ground on which religion must be supported, so it requires greater care and attention. For unless you understand first of all what your position is before God, and what the judgment which he passes upon you, you have no foundation on which your salvation can be laid, or on which piety towards God can be reared. The necessity of thoroughly understanding this subject will become more apparent as we proceed with it.

2. Lest we should stumble at the very threshold (this we should do were we to begin the discussion without knowing what the subject is), let us first explain the meaning of the expressions, "To be justified in the sight of God," "to be Justified by faith or by works." A man is said to be justified in the sight of God when in the judgment of God he is deemed righteous, and is accepted on account of his righteousness; for as iniquity is abominable to God, so neither can the sinner find grace in his sight, so far as he is and so long as he is regarded as a

sinner. Hence, wherever sin is, there also are the wrath and vengeance of God. He, on the other hand, is justified who is regarded not as a sinner, but as righteous, and as such stands acquitted at the judgment seat of God, where all sinners are condemned. As an innocent man, when charged before an impartial judge, who decides according to his innocence, is said to be justified by the judge, as a man is said to be justified by God when, removed from the catalogue of sinners, he has God as the witness and asserter of his righteousness. In the same manner, a man will be said to be justified by works, if in his life there can be found a purity and holiness which merits an attestation of righteousness at the throne of God, or if by the perfection of his works he can answer and satisfy the divine justice. On the contrary, a man will be justified by faith when, excluded from the righteousness of works, he by faith lays hold of the righteousness of Christ, and clothed in it appears in the sight of God not as a sinner, but as righteous. Thus we simply interpret justification, as the acceptance with which God receives us into his favor as if we were righteous; and we say that this justification consists in the forgiveness of sins and the imputation of the righteousness of Christ (see sec. 21 and 23).

3. In confirmation of this there are many clear passages of Scripture. First, it cannot be denied that this is the proper and most usual signification of the term. But as it were too tedious to collect all the passages, and compare them with each other, let it suffice to have called the reader's attention to the fact: he will easily convince himself of its truth. I will only mention a few passages in which the justification of which we speak is expressly handled. First, when Luke relates that all the people that heard Christ "justified God" (Luke 7:29), and when Christ declares, that "Wisdom is justified of all her children" (Luke 7:35), Luke means not that they conferred righteousness which always dwells in perfection with God, although the whole world should attempt to wrest it from him, nor does Christ mean that the doctrine of salvation is made just: this it is in its own nature; but both modes

of expression are equivalent to attributing due praise to God and his doctrine. On the other hand, when Christ upbraids the Pharisees for justifying themselves (Luke 16:15), he means not that they acquired righteousness by acting properly, but that they ambitiously courted a reputation for righteousness of which they were destitute. Those acquainted with Hebrew understand the meaning better: for in that language the name of wicked is given not only to those who are conscious of wickedness, but to those who receive sentence of condemnation. Thus, when Bathsheba says, "I and my son Solomon shall be counted offenders," she does not acknowledge a crime, but complains that she and her son will be exposed to the disgrace of being numbered among reprobates and criminals (1 Kings 1:21). It is, indeed, plain from the context, that the term even in Latin must be thus understood—viz. relatively—and does not denote any quality. In regard to the use of the term with reference to the present subject, when Paul speaks of the Scripture, "foreseeing that God would justify the heathen through faith" (Gal. 3:8), what other meaning can you give it than that God imputes righteousness by faith? Again, when he says, "that he (God) might be just, and the justifier of him who believeth in Jesus" (Rom. 3:26), what can the meaning be, if not that God, in consideration of their faith, frees them from the condemnation which their wickedness deserves? This appears still more plainly at the conclusion, when he exclaims, "Who shall lay anything to the charge of God's elect? It is God that justifieth. Who is he that condemneth? It is Christ that died, yea rather, that is risen again, who is even at the right hand of God, who also maketh intercession for us" (Rom. 8:33-34). For it is just as if he had said, Who shall accuse those whom God has acquitted? Who shall condemn those for whom Christ pleads? To justify, therefore, is nothing else than to acquit from the charge of guilt, as if innocence were proved. Hence, when God justifies us through the intercession of Christ, he does not acquit us on a proof of our own innocence, but by an imputation of righteousness, so that though not righteous in ourselves, we are deemed righteous in Christ. Thus it is said, in Paul's discourse in the Acts, "Through this man is preached unto you the forgiveness of sins; and by him all that believe are justified from all things from which ye could not be justified by the law of Moses" (Acts 13:38-39). You see that after remission of sins justification is set down by way of explanation; you see plainly that it is used for acquittal; you see how it cannot be obtained by the works of the law; you see that it is entirely through the interposition of Christ; you see that it is obtained by faith; you see, in fine, that satisfaction intervenes, since it is said that we are justified from our sins by Christ. Thus when the publican is said to have gone down to his house "justified" (Luke 18:14), it cannot be held that he obtained this justification by any merit of works. All that is said is, that after obtaining the pardon of sins he was regarded in the sight of God as righteous. He was justified, therefore, not by any approval of works, but by gratuitous acquittal on the part of God. Hence Ambrose elegantly terms confession of sins "legal justification" (Ambrose on *Psalm 118*, Serm. 10).

4. Without saying more about the term, we shall have no doubt as to the thing meant if we attend to the description which is given of it. For Paul certainly designates justification by the term "acceptance," when he says to the Ephesians, "Having predestinated us unto the adoption of children by Jesus Christ to himself, according to the good pleasure of his will, to the praise of the glory of his grace, wherein he has made us accepted in the Beloved" (Eph. 1:5-6). His meaning is the very same as where he elsewhere says, "being justified freely by his grace" (Rom. 3:24). In the fourth chapter of the Epistle to the Romans, he first terms it "the imputation of righteousness," and hesitates not to place it in forgiveness of sins: "Even as David also describeth the blessedness of the man unto whom God imputeth righteousness without works, saying, Blessed are they whose iniquities are forgiven," &c. (Rom. 4:6-8). There, indeed, he is not speaking of a part

of justification, but of the whole. He declares, moreover, that a definition of it was given by David, when he pronounced him blessed who
has obtained the free pardon of his sins. Whence it appears that this
righteousness of which he speaks is simply opposed to judicial guilt.
But the most satisfactory passage on this subject is that in which he
declares the sum of the Gospel message to be reconciliation to God,
who is pleased, through Christ, to receive us into favor by not imputing our sins (2 Cor. 5:18-21). Let my readers carefully weigh the
whole context. For Paul shortly after adding, by way of explanation, in
order to designate the mode of reconciliation, that Christ who knew
no sin was made sin for us, undoubtedly understands by reconciliation nothing else than justification. Nor, indeed, could it be said, as
he elsewhere does, that we are made righteous "by the obedience" of
Christ (Rom. 5:19), were it not that we are deemed righteous in the
sight of God in him and not in ourselves.

5. But as Osiander has introduced a kind of monstrosity termed
"essential righteousness," by which, although he designed not to abolish free righteousness, he involves it in darkness, and by that darkness
deprives pious minds of a serious sense of divine grace; before I pass
to other matters, it may be proper to refute this delirious dream. And,
first, the whole speculation is mere empty curiosity. He indeed, heaps
together many passages of scripture showing that Christ is one with
us, and we likewise one with him, a point which needs no proof; but
he entangles himself by not attending to the bond of this unity. The
explanation of all difficulties is easy to us, who hold that we are united
to Christ by the secret agency of his Spirit, but he had formed some
idea akin to that of the Manichees, desiring to transfuse the divine
essence into men. Hence his other notion, that Adam was formed
in the image of God, because even before the fall Christ was destined to be the model of human nature. But as I study brevity, I will
confine myself to the matter in hand. He says, that we are one with
Christ. This we admit, but still we deny that the essence of Christ is

confounded with ours. Then we say that he absurdly endeavors to support his delusions by means of this principle: that Christ is our righteousness, because he is the eternal God, the fountain of righteousness, the very righteousness of God. My readers will pardon me for now only touching on matters which method requires me to defer to another place. But although he pretends that, by the term "essential righteousness," he merely means to oppose the sentiment that we are reputed righteous on account of Christ, he however clearly shows, that not contented with that righteousness, which was procured for us by the obedience and sacrificial death of Christ, he maintains that we are substantially righteous in God by an infused essence as well as quality. For this is the reason why he so vehemently contends that not only Christ but the Father and the Spirit dwell in us. The fact I admit to be true, but still I maintain it is wrested by him. He ought to have attended to the mode of dwelling—viz. that the Father and the Spirit are in Christ; and as in him the fullness of the Godhead dwells, so in him we possess God entire. Hence, whatever he says separately concerning the Father and the Spirit, has no other tendency than to lead away the simple from Christ. Then he introduces a substantial mixture, by which God, transfusing himself into us, makes us as it were a part of himself. Our being made one with Christ by the agency of the Spirit, he being the head and we the members, he regards as almost nothing unless his essence is mingled with us. But, as I have said, in the case of the Father and the Spirit, he more clearly betrays his views—namely, that we are not justified by the mere grace of the Mediator, and that righteousness is not simply or entirely offered to us in his person, but that we are made partakers of divine righteousness when God is essentially united to us.

6. Had he only said, that Christ by justifying us becomes ours by an essential union, and that he is our head not only insofar as he is man, but that as the essence of the divine nature is diffused into us, he might indulge his dreams with less harm, and, perhaps, it were less

necessary to contest the matter with him; but since this principle is like a cuttlefish, which, by the ejection of dark and inky blood, conceals its many tails, if we would not knowingly and willingly allow ourselves to be robbed of that righteousness which alone gives us full assurance of our salvation, we must strenuously resist. For, in the whole of this discussion, the noun "righteousness" and the verb "to justify," are extended by Osiander to two parts; to be justified being not only to be reconciled to God by a free pardon, but also to be made just; and righteousness being not a free imputation, but the holiness and integrity which the divine essence dwelling in us inspires. And he vehemently asserts (see sec. 8) that Christ is himself our righteousness, not insofar as he, by expiating sins, appeased the Father, but because he is the eternal God and life. To prove the first point—viz. that God justifies not only by pardoning but by regenerating, he asks, whether he leaves those whom he justifies as they were by nature, making no change upon their vices? The answer is very easy: as Christ cannot be divided into parts, so the two things, justification and sanctification, which we perceive to be united together in him, are inseparable. Whomsoever, therefore, God receives into his favor, he presents with the Spirit of adoption, whose agency forms them anew into his image. But if the brightness of the sun cannot be separated from its heat, are we therefore to say, that the earth is warmed by light and illumined by heat? Nothing can be more apposite to the matter in hand than this simile. The sun by its heat quickens and fertilizes the earth; by its rays enlightens and illumines it. Here is a mutual and undivided connection, and yet reason itself prohibits us from transferring the peculiar properties of the one to the other. In the confusion of a twofold grace, which Osiander obtrudes upon us, there is a similar absurdity. Because those whom God freely regards as righteous, he in fact renews to the cultivation of righteousness, Osiander confounds that free acceptance with this gift of regeneration, and contends that they are one and the same. But Scriptures while combining both, classes them separately, that it may the better display the manifold grace of God. Nor is Paul's statement superfluous, that Christ is made unto us "righteousness and sanctification" (1 Cor. 1:30). And whenever he argues from the salvation procured for us, from the paternal love of God and the grace of Christ, that we are called to purity and holiness, he plainly intimates, that to be justified is something else than to be made new creatures. Osiander on coming to Scripture corrupts every passage which he quotes. Thus when Paul says, "to him that worketh not, but believeth on him that justifieth the ungodly, his faith is counted for righteousness," he expounds justifying as making just. With the same rashness he perverts the whole of the fourth chapter to the Romans. He hesitates not to give a similar gloss to the passage which I lately quoted, "Who shall lay anything to the charge of God's elect? It is God that justifieth." Here it is plain that guilt and acquittal simply are considered, and that the Apostle's meaning depends on the antithesis. Therefore his futility is detected both in his argument and his quotations for support from Scripture. He is not a whit sounder in discussing the term "righteousness," when it is said, that faith was imputed to Abraham for righteousness after he had embraced Christ (who is the righteousness of God and God himself) and was distinguished by excellent virtues. Hence it appears that two things which are perfect are viciously converted by him into one which is corrupt. For the righteousness which is there mentioned pertains not to the whole course of life; or rather, the Spirit testifies, that though Abraham greatly excelled in virtue, and by long perseverance in it had made so much progress, the only way in which he pleased God was by receiving the grace which was offered by the promise, in faith. From this it follows, that, as Paul justly maintains, there is no room for works in justification.

7. When he objects that the power of justifying exists not in faith, considered in itself, but only as receiving Christ, I willingly admit it. For did faith justify of itself, or (as it is expressed) by its own intrinsic

virtue, as it is always weak and imperfect, its efficacy would be partial, and thus our righteousness being maimed would give us only a
portion of salvation. We indeed imagine nothing of the kind, but say,
that, properly speaking, God alone justifies. The same thing we likewise transfer to Christ, because he was given to us for righteousness;
while we compare faith to a kind of vessel, because we are incapable of
receiving Christ, unless we are emptied and come with open mouth
to receive his grace. Hence it follows, that we do not withdraw the
power of justifying from Christ, when we hold that, previous to his
righteousness, he himself is received by faith. Still, however, I admit
not the tortuous figure of the sophist, that faith is Christ; as if a vessel
of clay were a treasure, because gold is deposited in it. And yet this is
no reason why faith, though in itself of no dignity or value, should not
justify us by giving Christ; Just as such a vessel filled with coin may
give wealth. I say, therefore, that faith, which is only the instrument
for receiving justification, is ignorantly confounded with Christ, who
is the material cause, as well as the author and minister of this great
blessing. This disposes of the difficulty—viz. how the term "faith" is to
be understood when treating of justification.

8. Osiander goes still farther in regard to the mode of receiving
Christ, holding, that by the ministry of the external word the internal
word is received; that he may thus lead us away from the priesthood
of Christ, and his office of Mediator, to his eternal divinity. We, indeed, do not divide Christ, but hold that he who, reconciling us to
God in his flesh, bestowed righteousness upon us, is the eternal Word
of God; and that he could not perform the office of Mediator, nor
acquire righteousness for us, if he were not the eternal God. Osiander
will have it, that as Christ is God and man, he was made our righteousness in respect not of his human but of his divine nature. But if
this is a peculiar property of the Godhead, it will not be peculiar to
Christ, but common to him with the Father and the Spirit, since their
righteousness is one and the same. Thus it would be incongruous to

say, that that which existed naturally from eternity was made ours. But granting that God was made unto us righteousness, what are we to make of Paul's interposed statement, that he was so made by God? This certainly is peculiar to the office of mediator, for although he contains in himself the divine nature, yet he receives his own proper title, that he may be distinguished from the Father and the Spirit. But he makes a ridiculous boast of a single passage of Jeremiah, in which it is said, that Jehovah will be our righteousness (Jer. 23:6; 33:16). But all he can extract from this is, that Christ, who is our righteousness, was God manifest in the flesh. We have elsewhere quoted from Paul's discourse, that God purchased the Church with his own blood (Acts 20:28). Were anyone to infer from this that the blood by which sins were expiated was divine, and of a divine nature, who could endure so foul a heresy? But Osiander, thinking that he has gained the whole cause by this childish cavil, swells, exults, and stuffs whole pages with his bombast, whereas the solution is simple and obvious—viz. that Jehovah, when made of the seed of David, was indeed to be the righteousness of believers, but in what sense Isaiah declares, "By his knowledge shall my righteous servant justify many" (Isa. 53:11). Let us observe that it is the Father who speaks. He attributes the office of justifying to the Son, and adds the reason—because he is "righteous." He places the method, or medium (as it is called), in the doctrine by which Christ is known. For the word is more properly to be understood in a passive sense. Hence I infer, first, that Christ was made righteousness when he assumed the form of a servant; secondly, that he justified us by his obedience to the Father; and, accordingly that he does not perform this for us in respect of his divine nature, but according to the nature of the dispensation laid upon him. For though God alone is the fountain of righteousness, and the only way in which we are righteous is by participation with him, yet, as by our unhappy revolt we are alienated from his righteousness, it is necessary to descend to this lower remedy, that Christ may justify us by the power of his death and resurrection.

9. If he objects that this work by its excellence transcends human, and therefore can only be ascribed to the divine nature; I concede the former point, but maintain, that on the latter he is ignorantly deluded. For although Christ could neither purify our souls by his own blood, nor appease the Father by his sacrifice, nor acquit us from the charge of guilt, nor, in short, perform the office of priest, unless he had been very God, because no human ability was equal to such a burden, it is however certain, that he performed all these things in his human nature. If it is asked, in what way we are justified? Paul answers, by the obedience of Christ. Did he obey in any other way than by assuming the form of a servant? We infer, therefore, that righteousness was manifested to us in his flesh. In like manner, in another passage (which I greatly wonder that Osiander does not blush repeatedly to quote), he places the fountain of righteousness entirely in the incarnation of Christ, "He has made him to be sin for us who knew no sin, that we might be made the righteousness of God in him" (2 Cor. 5:21). Osiander in turgid sentences lays hold of the expression, righteousness of God, and shouts victory! as if he had proved it to be his own phantom of essential righteousness, though the words have a very different meaning—viz. that we are justified through the expiation made by Christ. That the righteousness of God is used for the righteousness which is approved by God, should be known to mere tyros, as in John, the praise of God is contrasted with the praise of men (John 12:43). I know that by the righteousness of God is sometimes meant that of which God is the author, and which he bestows upon us; but that here the only thing meant is, that being supported by the expiation of Christ, we are able to stand at the tribunal of God, sound readers perceive without any observation of mine. The word is not of so much importance, provided Osiander agrees with us in this, that we are justified by Christ in respect he was made an expiatory victim for us.

This he could not be in his divine nature. For which reason also, when Christ would seal the righteousness and salvation which he brought to us, he holds forth the sure pledge of it in his flesh. He indeed calls himself "living bread," but, in explanation of the mode, adds, "my flesh is meat indeed, and my blood is drink indeed" (John 6:55). The same doctrine is clearly seen in the sacraments; which, though they direct our faith to the whole, not to a part of Christ, yet, at the same time, declare that the materials of righteousness and salvation reside in his flesh; not that the mere man of himself justifies or quickens, but that God was pleased, by means of a Mediator, to manifest his own hidden and incomprehensible nature. Hence I often repeat, that Christ has been in a manner set before us as a fountain, whence we may draw what would otherwise lie without use in that deep and hidden abyss which streams forth to us in the person of the Mediator. In this way, and in this meaning, I deny not that Christ, as he is God and man, justifies us; that this work is common also to the Father and the Holy Spirit; in fine, that the righteousness of which God makes us partakers is the eternal righteousness of the eternal God, provided effect is given to the clear and valid reasons to which I have adverted.

10. Moreover, lest by his cavils he deceive the unwary, I acknowledge that we are devoid of this incomparable gift until Christ become ours. Therefore, to that union of the head and members, the residence of Christ in our hearts, in fine, the mystical union, we assign the highest rank, Christ when he becomes ours making us partners with him in the gifts with which he was endued. Hence we do not view him as at a distance and without us, but as we have put him on, and been ingrafted into his body, he deigns to make us one with himself, and, therefore, we glory in having a fellowship of righteousness with him. This disposes of Osiander's calumny, that we regard faith as righteousness; as if we were robbing Christ of his rights when we say, that, destitute in ourselves, we draw near to him by faith, to make way for his grace, that he alone may fill us. But Osiander, spurning

this spiritual union, insists on a gross mixture of Christ with believers; and, accordingly, to excite prejudice, gives the name of Zwinglians to all who subscribe not to his fanatical heresy of essential righteousness, because they do not hold that, in the supper, Christ is eaten substantially. For my part, I count it the highest honor to be thus assailed by a haughty man, devoted to his own impostures; though he assails not me only, but writers of known reputation throughout the world, and whom it became him modestly to venerate. This, however, does not concern me, as I plead not my own cause, and plead the more sincerely that I am free from every sinister feeling. In insisting so vehemently on essential righteousness, and an essential inhabitation of Christ within us, his meaning is, first, that God by a gross mixture transfuses himself into us, as he pretends that there is a carnal eating in the supper; And, secondly that by instilling his own righteousness into us, he makes us really righteous with himself since, according to him, this righteousness is as well God himself as the probity, or holiness, or integrity of God. I will not spend much time in disposing of the passages of Scripture which he adduces, and which, though used in reference to the heavenly life, he wrests to our present state. Peter says, that through the knowledge of Christ "are given unto us exceeding great and precious promises, that by them ye might be partakers of the divine nature" (2 Pet. 1:4); as if we now were what the gospel promises we shall be at the final advent of Christ; nay, John reminds us, that "when he shall appear we shall be like him, for we shall see him as he is" (1 John 3:2). I only wished to give my readers a slender specimen of Osiander, it being my intention to decline the discussion of his frivolities, not because there is any difficulty in disposing of them, but because I am unwilling to annoy the reader with superfluous labor.

11. But more poison lurks in the second branch, when he says that we are righteous together with God. I think I have already sufficiently proved, that although the dogma were not so pestiferous, yet because

it is frigid and jejune, and falls by its own vanity, it must justly be disrelished by all sound and pious readers. But it is impossible to tolerate the impiety which, under the pretense of a twofold righteousness, undermines our assurance of salvation, and hurrying us into the clouds, tries to prevent us from embracing the gift of expiation in faith, and invoking God with quiet minds. Osiander derides us for teaching, that to be justified is a forensic term, because it behaves us to be in reality just: there is nothing also to which he is more opposed than the idea of our being justified by a free imputation. Say, then, if God does not justify us by acquitting and pardoning, what does Paul mean when he says "God was in Christ reconciling the world unto himself, not imputing their trespasses unto them"? "He made him to be sin for us who knew no sin; that we might be made the righteousness of God in him" (2 Cor. 5:19, 21). Here I learn, first, that those who are reconciled to God are regarded as righteous: then the method is stated, God justifies by pardoning; and hence, in another place, justification is opposed to accusation (Rom. 8:33); this antithesis clearly demonstrating that the mode of expression is derived from forensic use. And, indeed, no man, moderately verdant in the Hebrew tongue (provided he is also of sedate brain), is ignorant that this phrase thus took its rise, and thereafter derived its tendency and force. Now, then, when Paul says that David "describeth the blessedness of the man unto whom God imputeth righteousness without works, saying, Blessed are they whose iniquities are forgiven" (Rom. 4:6-7; Ps. 32:1), let Osiander say whether this is a complete or only a partial definition. He certainly does not adduce the Psalmist as a witness that pardon of sins is a part of righteousness, or concurs with something else in justifying, but he includes the whole of righteousness in gratuitous forgiveness, declaring those to be blessed "whose iniquities are forgiven, and whose sins are covered," and "to whom the Lord will not impute sin." He estimates and judges of his happiness from this that in this way he is righteous not in reality, but by imputation.

Osiander objects that it would be insulting to God, and contrary to his nature, to justify those who still remain wicked. But it ought to be remembered, as I already observed, that the gift of justification is not separated from regeneration, though the two things are distinct. But as it is too well known by experience, that the remains of sin always exist in the righteous, it is necessary that justification should be something very different from reformation to newness of life. This latter God begins in his elect, and carries on during the whole course of life, gradually and sometimes slowly, so that if placed at his judgment seat they would always deserve sentence of death. He justifies not partially, but freely, so that they can appear in the heavens as if clothed with the purity of Christ. No portion of righteousness could pacify the conscience. It must be decided that we are pleasing to God, as being without exception righteous in his sight. Hence it follows that the doctrine of justification is perverted and completely overthrown whenever doubt is instilled into the mind, confidence in salvation is shaken, and free and intrepid prayer is retarded; yea, whenever rest and tranquility with spiritual joy are not established. Hence Paul argues against objectors, that "if the inheritance be of the law, it is no more of promise" (Gal. 3:18). that in this way faith would be made vain; for if respect be had to works it fails, the holiest of men in that case finding nothing in which they can confide. This distinction between justification and regeneration (Osiander confounding the two, calls them a twofold righteousness) is admirably expressed by Paul. Speaking of his real righteousness, or the integrity bestowed upon him (which Osiander terms his essential righteousness), he mournfully exclaims, "O wretched man that I am! who shall deliver me from the body of this death?" (Rom. 7:24); but retaking himself to the righteousness which is founded solely on the mercy of God, he breaks forth thus magnificently into the language of triumph: "Who shall lay anything to the charge of God's elect? It is God that justifieth." "Who shall separate us from the love of Christ? shall tribulation, or distress, or persecution, or famine, or nakedness, or peril, or sword?" (Rom. 8:33, 35). He clearly declares that the only righteousness for him is that which alone suffices for complete salvation in the presence of God, so that that miserable bondage, the consciousness of which made him a little before lament his lot, derogates not from his confidence, and is no obstacle in his way. This diversity is well known, and indeed is familiar to all the saints who groan under the burden of sin, and yet with victorious assurance rise above all fears. Osiander's objection as to its being inconsistent with the nature of God, falls back upon himself; for though he clothes the saints with a twofold righteousness as with a coat of skins, he is, however, forced to admit, that without forgiveness no man is pleasing to God. If this be so, let him at least admit, that with reference to what is called the proportion of imputation, those are regarded as righteous who are not so in reality. But how far shall the sinner extend this gratuitous acceptance, which is substituted in the room of righteousness? Will it amount to the whole pound, or will it be only an ounce? He will remain in doubt, vibrating to this side and to that, because he will be unable to assume to himself as much righteousness as will be necessary to give confidence. It is well that he who would prescribe a law to God is not the judge in this cause. But this saying will ever stand true, "That thou mightest be justified when thou speakest, and be clear when thou judges" (Ps. 51:4). What arrogance to condemn the Supreme Judge when he acquits freely, and try to prevent the response from taking affect: "I will have mercy on whom I will have mercy." And yet the intercession of Moses, which God calmed by this answer, was not for pardon to some individual, but to all alike, by wiping away the guilt to which all were liable. And we, indeed, say, that the lost are justified before God by the burial of their sins; for (as he hates sin) he can only love those whom he justifies. But herein is the wondrous method of justification, that, clothed with the righteousness of Christ, they dread not the

judgment of which they are worthy, and while they justly condemn
themselves, are yet deemed righteous out of themselves.

12. I must admonish the reader carefully to attend to the mystery
which he boasts he is unwilling to conceal from them. For after contending with great prolixity that we do not obtain favor with God
through the mere imputation of the righteousness of Christ, because
(to use his own words) it were impossible for God to hold those as
righteous who are not so, he at length concludes that Christ was giv-
en to us for righteousness, in respect not of his human, but of his
divine nature; and though this can only be found in the person of the
Mediator, it is, however, the righteousness not of man, but of God.
He does not now twist his rope of two righteousnesses, but plainly
deprives the human nature of Christ of the office of justifying. It is
worthwhile to understand what the nature of his argument is. It is
said in the same passage that Christ is made unto us wisdom (1 Cor.
1:30); but this is true only of the eternal Word, and, therefore, it is
not the man Christ that is made righteousness. I answer, that the
only begotten Son of God was indeed his eternal wisdom, but that
this title is applied to him by Paul in a different way—viz. because "in
him are hid all the treasures of wisdom and righteousness" (Col. 2:3).
That, therefore, which he had with the Father he manifested to us;
and thus Paul's expression refers not to the essence of the Son of God,
but to our use, and is fitly applied to the human nature of Christ;
for although the light shone in darkness before he was clothed with
flesh, yet he was a hidden light until he appeared in human nature
as the Sun of Righteousness, and hence he calls himself the light of
the world. It is also foolishly objected by Osiander, that justifying far
transcends the power both of men and angels, since it depends not on
the dignity of any creature, but on the ordination of God. Were angels
to attempt to give satisfaction to God, they could have no success, because they are not appointed for this purpose, it being the peculiar office of Christ, who "has redeemed us from the curse of the law, being

made a curse for us" (Gal. 3:13). Those who deny that Christ is our righteousness, in respect of his divine nature, are wickedly charged by Osiander with leaving only a part of Christ, and (what is worse) with making two Gods; because, while admitting that God dwells in us, they still insist that we are not justified by the righteousness of God. For though we call Christ the author of life, inasmuch as he endured death that he might destroy him who had the power of death (Heb. 2:14), we do not thereby rob him of this honor, in his whole character as God manifested in the flesh. We only make a distinction as to the manner in which the righteousness of God comes to us, and is enjoyed by us—a matter as to which Osiander shamefully erred. We deny not that that which was openly exhibited to us in Christ flowed from the secret grace and power of God; nor do we dispute that the righteousness which Christ confers upon us is the righteousness of God, and proceeds from him. What we constantly maintain is, that our righteousness and life are in the death and resurrection of Christ. I say nothing of that absurd accumulation of passages with which without selection or common understanding, he has loaded his readers, in endeavoring to show, that whenever mention is made of righteousness, this essential righteousness of his should be understood; as when David implores help from the righteousness of God. This David does more than a hundred times, and as often Osiander hesitates not to pervert his meaning. Not a whit more solid is his objection, that the name of righteousness is rightly and properly applied to that by which we are moved to act aright, but that it is God only that worketh in us both to will and to do (Phil. 2:13). For we deny not that God by his Spirit forms us anew to holiness and righteousness of life; but we must first see whether he does this of himself, immediately, or by the hand of his Son, with whom he has deposited all the fullness of the Holy Spirit, that out of his own abundance he may supply the wants of his members. When, although righteousness comes to us from the secret fountain of the Godhead, it does not follow that Christ, who sanctified himself in the flesh on our account, is our righteousness in respect of his divine nature (John 17:19). Not less frivolous is his observation, that the righteousness with which Christ himself was righteous was divine; for had not the will of the Father impelled him, he could not have fulfilled the office assigned him. For although it has been elsewhere said that all the merits of Christ flow from the mere good pleasure of God, this gives no countenance to the phantom by which Osiander fascinates both his own eyes and those of the simple. For who will allow him to infer, that because God is the source and commencement of our righteousness, we are essentially righteous, and the essence of the divine righteousness dwells in us? In redeeming us, says Isaiah, "he (God) put on righteousness as a breastplate, and an helmet of salvation upon his head" (Isa. 59:17), was this to deprive Christ of the armor which he had given him, and prevent him from being a perfect Redeemer? All that the Prophet meant was, that God borrowed nothing from an external quarter, that in redeeming us he received no external aid. The same thing is briefly expressed by Paul in different terms, when he says that God set him forth "to declare his righteousness for the remission of sins." This is not the least repugnant to his doctrine: in another place, that "by the obedience of one shall many be made righteous" (Rom. 5:19). In short, everyone who, by the entanglement of a twofold righteousness, prevents miserable souls from resting entirely on the mere mercy of God, mocks Christ by putting on him a crown of plaited thorns.

13. But since a great part of mankind imagine a righteousness compounded of faith and work, let us here show that there is so wide a difference between justification by faith and by works, that the establishment of the one necessarily overthrows the other. The Apostle says, "Yea doubtless, and I count all things but loss for the excellency of the knowledge of Christ Jesus my Lord: for whom I have suffered the loss of all things, and do count them but dung, that I may win Christ, and be found in him, not having mine own righteousness,

which is of the law, but that which is through the faith of Christ, the righteousness which is of God by faith" (Phil. 3:8-9). You here see a comparison of contraries, and an intimation that every one who would obtain the righteousness of Christ must renounce his own. Hence he elsewhere declares the cause of the rejection of the Jews to have been, that "they being ignorant of God's righteousness, and going about to establish their own righteousness, have not submitted themselves unto the righteousness of God" (Rom. 10:3). If we destroy the righteousness of God by establishing our own righteousness, then, in order to obtain his righteousness, our own must be entirely abandoned. This also he shows, when he declares that boasting is not excluded by the Law, but by faith (Rom. 3:27). Hence it follows, that so long as the minutest portion of our own righteousness remains, we have still some ground for boasting. Now if faith utterly excludes boasting, the righteousness of works cannot in any way be associated with the righteousness of faith. This meaning is so clearly expressed in the fourth chapter to the Romans as to leave no room for cavil or evasion. "If Abraham were justified by works he has whereof to glory;" and then it is added, "but not before God" (Rom. 4:2). The conclusion, therefore, is, that he was not justified by works. He then employs another argument from contraries—viz. when reward is paid to works, it is done of debt, not of grace; but the righteousness of faith is of grace: therefore it is not of the merit of works. Away, then, with the dream of those who invent a righteousness compounded of faith and works (see Calvin, *ad Concilium Tridentinum*).

14. The Sophists, who delight in sporting with Scripture and in empty cavils, think they have a subtle evasion when they expound works to mean, such as unregenerated men do literally, and by the effect of free will, without the grace of Christ, and deny that these have any reference to spiritual works. Thus according to them, man is justified by faith as well as by works, provided these are not his own works, but gifts of Christ and fruits of regeneration; Paul's only object

in so expressing himself being to convince the Jews, that in trusting
to their own strength they foolishly arrogated righteousness to themselves, whereas it is bestowed upon us by the Spirit of Christ alone,
and not by studied efforts of our own nature. But they observe not
that in the antithesis between Legal and Gospel righteousness, which
Paul elsewhere introduces, all kinds of works, with whatever name
adorned, are excluded (Gal. 3:11-12). For he says that the righteousness of the Law consists in obtaining salvation by doing what the
Law requires, but that the righteousness of faith consists in believing
that Christ died and rose again (Rom. 10:5-9). Moreover, we shall
afterwards see, at the proper place, that the blessings of sanctification
and justification, which we derive from Christ, are different. Hence
it follows, that not even spiritual works are taken into account when
the power of justifying is ascribed to faith. And, indeed, the passage
above quoted, in which Paul declares that Abraham had no ground
of glorying before God, because he was not justified by works, ought
not to be confined to a literal and external form of virtue, or to the
effort of free will. The meaning is, that though the life of the Patriarch
had been spiritual and almost angelic, yet he could not by the merit of
works have procured justification before God.

15. The Schoolmen treat the matter somewhat more grossly by
mingling their preparations with it; and yet the others instill into the
simple and unwary a no less pernicious dogma, when, under cover
of the Spirit and grace, they hide the divine mercy, which alone can
give peace to the trembling soul. We, indeed, hold with Paul, that
those who fulfill the Law are justified by God, but because we are all
far from observing the Law, we infer that the works which should
be most effectual to justification are of no avail to us, because we are
destitute of them. In regard to vulgar Papists or Schoolmen, they are
here doubly wrong, both in calling faith assurance of conscience while
waiting to receive from God the reward of merits, and in interpreting
divine grace to mean not the imputation of gratuitous righteousness,

but the assistance of the Spirit in the study of holiness. They quote from an Apostle: "He that comes to God must believe that he is, and that he is the rewarder of them that diligently seek him" (Heb. 11:6). But they observe not what the method of seeking is. Then in regard to the term "grace," it is plain from their writings that they labor under a delusion. For Lombard holds that justification is given to us by Christ in two ways. "First," says he (Lombard, *Sent.* Lib. 3, Dist. 16, chap. 11), "the death of Christ justifies us when by means of it the love by which we are made righteous is excited in our hearts; and, secondly, when by means of it sin is extinguished, sin by which the devil held us captive, but by which he cannot now procure our condemnation." You see here that the chief office of divine grace in our justification he considers to be its directing us to good works by the agency of the Holy Spirit. He intended, no doubt, to follow the opinion of Augustine, but he follows it at a distance, and even wanders far from a true imitation of him both obscuring what was clearly stated by Augustine, and making what in him was less pure more corrupt. The Schools have always gone from worse to worse, until at length, in their downward path, they have degenerated into a kind of Pelagianism. Even the sentiment of Augustine, or at least his mode of expressing it, cannot be entirely approved of. For although he is admirable in stripping man of all merit of righteousness, and transferring the whole praise of it to God, yet he classes the grace by which we are regenerated to newness of life under the head of sanctification.

16. Scripture, when it treats of justification by faith, leads us in a very different direction. Turning away our view from our own works, it bids us look only to the mercy of God and the perfection of Christ. The order of justification which it sets before us is this: first, God of his mere gratuitous goodness is pleased to embrace the sinner, in whom he sees nothing that can move him to mercy but wretchedness, because he sees him altogether naked and destitute of good works. He, therefore, seeks the cause of kindness in himself, that thus he

may affect the sinner by a sense of his goodness, and induce him, in distrust of his own works, to cast himself entirely upon his mercy for salvation. This is the meaning of faith by which the sinner comes into the possession of salvation, when, according to the doctrine of the Gospel, he perceives that he is reconciled by God; when, by the intercession of Christ, he obtains the pardon of his sins, and is justified; and, though renewed by the Spirit of God, considers that, instead of leaning on his own works, he must look solely to the righteousness which is treasured up for him in Christ. When these things are weighed separately, they will clearly explain our view, though they may be arranged in a better order than that in which they are here presented. But it is of little consequence, provided they are so connected with each other as to give us a full exposition and solid confirmation of the whole subject.

17. Here it is proper to remember the relation which we previously established between faith and the Gospel; faith being said to justify because it receives and embraces the righteousness offered in the Gospel. By the very fact of its being said to be offered by the Gospel, all consideration of works is excluded. This Paul repeatedly declares, and in two passages, in particular, most clearly demonstrates. In the Epistle to the Romans, comparing the Law and the Gospel, he says, "Moses describeth the righteousness which is of the law, That the man which does those things shall live by them. But the righteousness which is of faith speaketh on this wise—If thou shalt confess with thy mouth the Lord Jesus, and shalt believe in thine heart that God has raised him from the dead, thou shalt be saved" (Rom. 10:5, 6:9). Do you see how he makes the distinction between the Law and the Gospel to be, that the former gives justification to works, whereas the latter bestows it freely without any help from works? This is a notable passage, and may free us from many difficulties if we understand that the justification which is given us by the Gospel is free from any terms of Law. It is for this reason he more than once places the

promise in diametrical opposition to the Law. "If the inheritance be of the law, it is no more of promise" (Gal. 3:18). Expressions of similar import occur in the same chapter. Undoubtedly the Law also has its promises; and, therefore, between them and the Gospel promises there must be some distinction and difference, unless we are to hold that the comparison is inept. And in what can the difference consist unless in this that the promises of the Gospel are gratuitous, and founded on the mere mercy of God, whereas the promises of the Law depend on the condition of works? But let no prater here allege that only the righteousness which men would obtrude upon God of their own strength and free will is repudiated; since Paul declares, without exceptions that the Law gained nothing by its commands, being such as none, not only of mankind in general, but none even of the most perfect, are able to fulfill. Love assuredly is the chief commandment in the Law, and since the Spirit of God trains us to love, it cannot but be a cause of righteousness in us, though that righteousness even in the saints is defective, and therefore of no value as a ground of merit.

18. The second passage is, "That no man is justified by the law in the sight of God, it is evident: for, The just shall live by faith. And the law is not of faith: but, The man that does them shall live in them" (Gal. 3:11-12; Hab. 2:4). How could the argument hold unless it be true that works are not to be taken into account, but are to be altogether separated? The Law, he says, is different from faith. Why? Because to obtain justification by it, works are required; and hence it follows, that to obtain justification by the Gospel they are not required. From this statement, it appears that those who are justified by faith are justified independent of, nay, in the absence of, the merit of works, because faith receives that righteousness which the Gospel bestows. But the Gospel differs from the Law in this, that it does not confine justification to works, but places it entirely in the mercy of God. In like manner, Paul contends, in the Epistle to the Romans, that Abraham had no ground of glorying, because faith was imputed to him

for righteousness (Rom. 4:2); and he adds in confirmation, that the proper place for justification by faith is where there are no works to which reward is due. "To him that worketh is the reward not reckoned of grace, but of debt." What is given to faith is gratuitous, this being the force of the meaning of the words which he there employs. Shortly after he adds, "Therefore it is of faith, that it might be by grace" (Rom. 4:16); and hence infers that the inheritance is gratuitous because it is procured by faith. How so but just because faith, without the aid of works, leans entirely on the mercy of God? And in the same sense, doubtless, he elsewhere teaches, that the righteousness of God without the Law was manifested, being witnessed by the Law and the Prophets (Rom. 3:21); for excluding the Law, he declares that it is not aided by worlds, that we do not obtain it by working, but are destitute when we draw near to receive it.

19. The reader now perceives with what fairness the Sophists of the present day cavil at our doctrine, when we say that a man is justified by faith alone (Rom. 4:2). They dare not deny that he is justified by faith, seeing Scripture so often declares it; but as the word alone is nowhere expressly used they will not tolerate its being added. Is it so? What answer then will they give to the words of Paul, when he contends that righteousness is not of faith unless it be gratuitous? How can it be gratuitous, and yet by works? By what cavils, moreover, will they evade his declaration in another place, that in the Gospel the righteousness of God is manifested? (Rom. 1:17). If righteousness is manifested in the Gospel, it is certainly not a partial or mutilated, but a full and perfect righteousness. The Law, therefore, has no part in its and their objection to the exclusive word "alone" is not only unfounded, but is obviously absurd. Does he not plainly enough attribute everything to faith alone when he disconnects it with works? What I would ask, is meant by the expressions, "The righteousness of God without the law is manifested;" "Being justified freely by his grace;" "Justified by faith without the deeds of the law?" (Rom. 3:21, 24, 28).

Here they have an ingenious subterfuge, one which, though not of their own devising but taken from Origin and some ancient writers, is most childish. They pretend that the works excluded are ceremonial, not moral works. Such profit do they make by their constant wrangling, that they possess not even the first elements of logic. Do they think the Apostle was raving when he produced, in proof of his doctrine, these passages? "The man that does them shall live in them" (Gal. 3:12). "Cursed is everyone that continueth not in all things that are written in the book of the law to do them" (Gal. 3:10). Unless they are themselves raving, they will not say that life was promised to the observers of ceremonies, and the curse denounced only against the transgressors of them. If these passages are to be understood of the Moral Law, there cannot be a doubt that moral works also are excluded from the power of justifying. To the same effect are the arguments which he employs. "By the deeds of the law there shall no flesh be justified in his sight: for by the law is the knowledge of sin" (Rom. 3:20). "The law worketh wrath" (Rom. 4:15), and therefore not righteousness. "The law cannot pacify the conscience," and therefore cannot confer righteousness. "Faith is imputed for righteousness," and therefore righteousness is not the reward of works, but is given without being due. Because "we are justified by faith," boasting is excluded. "Had there been a law given which could have given life, verily righteousness should have been by the law. But the Scripture has concluded all under sin, that the promise by faith of Jesus Christ might be given to them that believe" (Gal. 3:21-22). Let them maintain, if they dare, that these things apply to ceremonies, and not to morals, and the very children will laugh at their effrontery. The true conclusion, therefore, is, that the whole Law is spoken of when the power of justifying is denied to it.

20. Should anyone wonder why the Apostle, not contented with having named works, employs this addition, the explanation is easy. However highly works may be estimated, they have their whole value

more from the approbation of God than from their own dignity. For who will presume to plume himself before God on the righteousness of works, unless insofar as He approves of them? Who will presume to demand of Him a reward except insofar as He has promised it? It is owing entirely to the goodness of God that works are deemed worthy of the honor and reward of righteousness; and, therefore, their whole value consists in this, that by means of them we endeavor to manifest obedience to God. Wherefore, in another passage, the Apostle, to prove that Abraham could not be justified by works, declares, "that the covenant, that was confirmed before of God in Christ, the law, which was four hundred and thirty years after, cannot disannul, that it should make the promise of none effect" (Gal. 3:17). The unskillful would ridicule the argument that there could be righteous works before the promulgation of the Law, but the Apostle, knowing that works could derive this value solely from the testimony and honor conferred on them by God, takes it for granted that, previous to the Law, they had no power of justifying. We see why he expressly terms them "works of Law" when he would deny the power of justifying to theme—viz. because it was only with regard to such works that a question could be raised; although he sometimes, without addition, excepts all kinds of works whatever, as when on the testimony of David he speaks of the man to whom the Lord imputeth righteousness without works (Rom. 4:5-6). No cavils, therefore, can enable them to prove that the exclusion of works is not general. In vain do they lay hold of the frivolous subtlety, that the faith alone, by which we are justified, "worketh by love," and that love, therefore, is the foundation of justification. We, indeed, acknowledge with Paul, that the only faith which justifies is that which works by love (Gal. 3:6); but love does not give it its justifying power. Nay, its only means of justifying consists in its bringing us into communication with the righteousness of Christ. Otherwise the whole argument, on which the Apostle insists with so much earnestness, would fall. "To him that worketh is the reward not reckoned of grace, but of debt. But to him that worketh not, but believeth on him that justifieth the ungodly, his faith is counted for righteousness." Could he express more clearly than in this word, that there is justification in faith only where there are no works to which reward is due, and that faith is imputed for righteousness only when righteousness is conferred freely without merit?

21. Let us now consider the truth of what was said in the definition—viz. that justification by faith is reconciliation with God, and that this consists solely in the remission of sins. We must always return to the axioms that the wrath of God lies upon all men so long as they continue sinners. This is elegantly expressed by Isaiah in these words: "Behold, the Lord's hand is not shortened, that it cannot save; neither his ear heavy, that it cannot hear: but your iniquities have separated between you and your God, and your sins have hid his face from you, that he will not hear" (Isa. 59:1-2). We are here told that sin is a separation between God and man; that His countenance is turned away from the sinner; and that it cannot be otherwise, since, to have any intercourse with sin is repugnant to his righteousness. Hence the Apostle shows that man is at enmity with God until he is restored to favor by Christ (Rom. 5:8-10). When the Lord, therefore, admits him to union, he is said to justify him, because he can neither receive him into favor, nor unite him to himself, without changing his condition from that of a sinner into that of a righteous man. We add, that this is done by remission of sins. For if those whom the Lord has reconciled to himself are estimated by works, they will still prove to be in reality sinners, while they ought to be pure and free from sin. It is evident therefore, that the only way in which those whom God embraces are made righteous, is by having their pollutions wiped away by the remission of sins, so that this justification may be termed in one word the remission of sins.

22. Both of these become perfectly clear from the words of Paul: "God was in Christ reconciling the world unto himself, not imputing

their trespasses unto them; and has committed unto us the word of reconciliation." He then subjoins the sum of his embassy: "He has made him to be sin for us who knew no sin; that we might be made the righteousness of God in him" (2 Cor. 5:19-21). He here uses righteousness and reconciliation indiscriminately, to make us understand that the one includes the other. The mode of obtaining this righteousness he explains to be, that our sins are not imputed to us. Wherefore, you cannot henceforth doubt how God justifies us when you hear that he reconciles us to himself by not imputing our faults. In the same manner, in the Epistle to the Romans, he proves, by the testimony of David, that righteousness is imputed without works, because he declares the man to be blessed "whose transgression is forgiven, whose sin is covered," and "unto whom the Lord imputeth not iniquity" (Rom. 4:6; Ps. 32:1-2). There he undoubtedly uses blessedness for righteousness; and as he declares that it consists in forgiveness of sins, there is no reason why we should define it otherwise. Accordingly, Zacharias, the father of John the Baptist, sings that the knowledge of salvation consists in the forgiveness of sins (Luke 1:77). The same course was followed by Paul when, in addressing the people of Antioch, he gave them a summary of salvation. Luke states that he concluded in this way: "Through this man is preached unto you the forgiveness of sins, and by him all that believe are justified from all things from which ye could not be justified by the law of Moses" (Acts 13:38-39). Thus the Apostle connects forgiveness of sins with justification in such a way as to show that they are altogether the same; and hence he properly argues that justification, which we owe to the indulgence of God, is gratuitous. Nor should it seem an unusual mode of expression to say that believers are justified before God not by works, but by gratuitous acceptance, seeing it is frequently used in Scripture, and sometimes also by ancient writers. Thus Augustine says: "The righteousness of the saints in this world consists more in the forgiveness of sins than the perfection of virtue" (August.

de Civitate Dei, lib. 19, cap. 27). To this corresponds the well-known sentiment of Bernard: "Not to sin is the righteousness of God, but the righteousness of man is the indulgence of God" (Bernard, *Serm.* 22-23 in *Cant*). He previously asserts that Christ is our righteousness in absolution, and, therefore, that those only are just who have obtained pardon through mercy.

23. Hence also it is proved, that it is entirely by the intervention of Christ's righteousness that we obtain justification before God. This is equivalent to saying that man is not just in himself, but that the righteousness of Christ is communicated to him by imputation, while he is strictly deserving of punishment. Thus vanishes the absurd dogma, that man is justified by faith, inasmuch as it brings him under the influence of the Spirit of God by whom he is rendered righteous. This is so repugnant to the above doctrine that it never can be reconciled with it. There can be no doubt that he who is taught to seek righteousness out of himself does not previously possess it in himself. This is most clearly declared by the Apostle, when he says, that he who knew no sin was made an expiatory victim for sin, that we might be made the righteousness of God in him (2 Cor. 5:21). You see that our righteousness is not in ourselves, but in Christ; that the only way in which we become possessed of it is by being made partakers with Christ, since with him we possess all riches. There is nothing repugnant to this in what he elsewhere says: "God sending his own Son in the likeness of sinful flesh, and for sin condemned sin in the flesh: that the righteousness of the law might be fulfilled in us" (Rom. 8:3-4). Here the only fulfillment to which he refers is that which we obtain by imputation. Our Lord Jesus Christ communicates his righteousness to us, and so by some wondrous ways insofar as pertains to the justice of God, transfuses its power into us. That this was the Apostle's view is abundantly clear from another sentiment which he had expressed a little before: "As by one man's disobedience many were made sinners, so by the obedience of one shall many be made righteous" (Rom.

5:19). To declare that we are deemed righteous, solely because the obedience of Christ is imputed to us as if it were our own, is just to place our righteousness in the obedience of Christ. Wherefore, Ambrose appears to me to have most elegantly adverted to the blessing of Jacob as an illustration of this righteousness, when he says that as he who did not merit the birthright in himself personated his brother, put on his garments which gave forth a most pleasant odor, and thus introduced himself to his father that he might receive a blessing to his own advantage, though under the person of another, so we conceal ourselves under the precious purity of Christ, our firstborn brother, that we may obtain an attestation of righteousness from the presence of God. The words of Ambrose are—"Isaac's smelling the odor of his garments, perhaps means that we are justified not by works, but by faith, since carnal infirmity is an impediment to works, but errors of conduct are covered by the brightness of faith, which merits the pardon of faults" (Ambrose, *de Jacobo et Vita Beata*, Lib. 2, cap. 2). And so indeed it is; for in order to appear in the presence of God for salvation, we must send forth that fragrant odor, having our vices covered and buried by his perfection.

Study Guide Questions

Section 1

1. Because Christ was given to us, what double grace have we received?
2. What is regeneration?
3. How important is justification to Calvin?

Section 2

1. Why do we need to get the concept of justification straight?
2. How do we appear in God's sight as righteous, since we are sinners?
3. What is justification?

Section 3

1. Do we need to be innocent to be acquitted?

Section 4

1. According to Calvin, does Scripture describe the reality of justification without using the word?

Section 5

1. What does Calvin call Osiander's doctrine of essential righteousness?
2. What was Osiander's error?

Section 6

1. What two things does Osiander confound?
2. What illustration does Calvin use of things that must be distinguished but which cannot be confused?

Section 7

1. What does Calvin compare faith to?
2. What is faith, and what is its relation to Christ?

Section 8

1. What is Osiander's view?

Section 9

1. What is the basis for our justification that does not comport with the divine nature alone?

Section 10

1. What slander does Calvin refute?
2. What does Calvin say is his highest glory?

Section 11

1. Does Osiander accept or reject "justification" as a legal term?

2. What happens if faith pays any attention to works?

3. What is the wonderful plan of salvation?

Section 12

1. What is impossible, according to Osiander?

2. To what end does Osiander heap up passages that talk about righteousness?

Section 13

1. What error does Calvin address next?

2. A man who wishes to obtain Christ's righteousness must do what?

3. As long as a particle of works-righteousness remains, what else remains?

Section 14

1. What work-around to this did the Sophists come up with?

2. How does Calvin reply?

Section 15

1. How do the Schoolmen interpret the grace of God?

2. What does Lombard do to Augustine?

Section 16

1. What does the regenerate man trust in?

Section 17

1. How is faith said to justify?

2. Why can the righteousness formed in us by the Spirit of God not be a cause of righteousness?

Section 18

1. What is Paul's argument on faith and works in a nutshell?
2. How must we come in order to receive righteousness?

Section 19

1. Does Calvin agree with Luther's translation of Romans 3:28?
2. What evasion does Calvin then deal with?

Section 20

1. Does Calvin agree that justifying faith has to be the kind of faith that works through love (Gal. 5:6)?

Section 21

1. What is the righteousness of faith equated with?
2. What is such righteousness called?

Section 22

1. What passages does Calvin cite in defense of this idea?
2. Augustine says what about the righteousness of the saints?

Section 23

1. How does this righteousness come to us?
2. What illustration does Ambrose use for this (an illustration that Calvin approves)?

CHAPTER 12

Necessity of contemplating the judgment seat of God, in order to
be seriously convinced of the doctrine of gratuitous justification.

The divisions of this chapter are
I. A consideration of the righteousness of God overturns the
righteousness of works, as is plain from passages of Scripture, and the
confession and example of the saints, sec. 1-3.

II. The same effect produced by a serious examination of the conscience, and a constant citation to the divine tribunal, sec. 4 and 5.

III. Hence arises, in the hearts of the godly, not hypocrisy, or a vain
opinion of merit, but true humility. This illustrated by the authority of
Scripture and the example of the Publican, sec. 6-7.

IV. Conclusion—arrogance and security must be discarded, every
man throwing an impediment in the way of the divine goodness in
proportion as he trusts to himself.

Outline:

1. Source of error on the subject of Justification. Sophists speak
as if the question were to be discussed before some human tribunal.
It relates to the majesty and justice of God. Hence nothing accepted without absolute perfection. Passages confirming this doctrine. If

we descend to the righteousness of the Law, the curse immediately appears.

2. Source of hypocritical confidence. Illustrated by a simile. Exhortation. Testimony of Job, David, and Paul.

3. Confession of Augustine and Bernard.

4. Another engine overthrowing the righteousness of works—viz. A serious examination of the conscience, and a comparison between the perfection of God and the imperfection of man.

5. How it is that we so indulge this imaginary opinion of our own works. The proper remedy to be found in a consideration of the majesty of God and our own misery. A description of this misery.

6. Christian humility consists in laying aside the imaginary idea of our own righteousness, and trusting entirely to the mercy of God, apprehended by faith in Christ. This humility described. Proved by passages of Scripture.

7. The parable of the Publican explained.

8. Arrogance, security, and self-confidence, must be renounced. General rule, or summary of the above doctrine.

Although the perfect truth of the above doctrine is proved by clear passages of Scripture, yet we cannot clearly see how necessary it is, before we bring distinctly into view the foundations on which the whole discussion ought to rest. First, then, let us remember that the righteousness which we are considering is not that of a human, but of a heavenly tribunal; and so beware of employing our own little standard to measure the perfection which is to satisfy the justice of God. It is strange with what rashness and presumption this is commonly defined. Nay, we see that none talk more confidently, or, so to speak, more blusteringly, of the righteousness of works than those whose diseases are most palpable, and blemishes most apparent. This they do because they reflect not on the righteousness of Christ, which, if they had the slightest perception of it, they would never treat with so much insult. It is certainly undervalued, if not recognized to be so perfect that nothing can be accepted that is not in every respect entire and absolute, and tainted by no impurity; such indeed as never has been, and never will be, found in man. It is easy for any man, within the precincts of the schools, to talk of the sufficiency of works for justification; but when we come into the presence of God there must be a truce to such talk. The matter is there discussed in earnest, and is no longer a theatrical logomachy. Hither must we turn our minds if we would inquire to any purpose concerning true righteousness; the question must be: How shall we answer the heavenly Judge when he calls us to account? Let us contemplate that Judge, not as our own unaided intellect conceives of him, but as he is portrayed to us in Scripture (see especially the Book of Job), with a brightness which obscures the stars, a strength which melts the mountains, an anger which shakes the earth, a wisdom which takes the wise in their own craftiness, a purity before which all things become impure, a righteousness to which not even angels are equal (so far is it from making the guilty innocent), a vengeance which once kindled burns to the lowest hell (Exod. 34:7; Nah. 1:3; Deut. 32:22). Let Him, I say, sit in judgment on the actions of men, and who will feel secure in sisting himself before his throne? "Who among us," says the prophets "shall dwell with the devouring fire? who among us shall dwell with ev- erlasting burnings? He that walketh righteously, and speaketh upright- ly," &c. (Isa. 33:14-15). Let whoso will come forth. Nay, the answer shows that no man can. For, on the other hand, we hear the dreadful voice: "If thou, Lord, shouldst mark our iniquities, O Lord, who shall stand?" (Ps. 130:3). All must immediately perish, as Job declares, "Shall mortal man be more just than God? shall a man be more pure than his Maker? Behold, he put no trust in his servants; and his angels he charged with folly: How much less in them that dwell in houses of clay, whose foundation is in the dust, which are crushed before the moth? They are destroyed from morning to evening" (Job 4:17-20). Again, "Behold, he putteth no trust in his saints; yea, the heavens are not clean in his sight. How much more abominable and filthy is man, which drinketh iniquity like water?" (Job 15:15-16). I confess, indeed, that in the Book of Job reference is made to a righteousness of a more exalted description than the observance of the Law. It is of importance to attend to this distinction; for even could a man satisfy the Law, he could not stand the scrutiny of that righteousness which transcends all our thoughts. Hence, although Job was not conscious of offending, he is still dumb with astonishment, because he sees that God could not be appeased even by the sanctity of angels, were their works weighed in that supreme balance. But to advert no farther to this righteousness, which is incomprehensible, I only say, that if our life is brought to the standard of the written law, we are lethargic indeed if we are not filled with dread at the many maledictions which God has employed for the purpose of arousing us, and among others, the following general one: "Cursed be he that confirmeth not all the words of this law to do them" (Deut. 27:26). In short, the whole discussion of this subject will be insipid and frivolous, unless we sist ourselves before the heavenly Judge, and anxious for our acquittal, voluntarily humble ourselves, confessing our nothingness.

2. Thus then must we raise our eyes that we may learn to tremble instead of vainly exulting. It is easy, indeed, when the comparison is made among men, for everyone to plume himself on some quality which others ought not to despise; but when we rise to God, that confidence instantly falls and dies away. The case of the soul with regard to God is very analogous to that of the body in regard to the visible firmament. The bodily eye, while employed in surveying adjacent objects, is pleased with its own perspicacity; but when directed to the sun, being dazzled and overwhelmed by the refulgence, it becomes no less convinced of its weakness than it formerly was of its power in viewing inferior objects. Therefore, lest we deceive ourselves by vain confidence, let us recollect that even though we deem ourselves equal or superior to other men, this is nothing to God, by whose judgment

the decision must be given. But if our presumption cannot be tamed by these considerations, he will answer us as he did the Pharisees, "Ye are they which justify yourselves before men; but God knoweth your hearts: for that which is highly esteemed among men is abomination in the sight of God" (Luke 16:15). Go now and make a proud boast of your righteousness among men, while God in heaven abhors it. But what are the feelings of the servants of God, of those who are truly taught by his Spirit? "Enter not into judgment with thy servant; for in thy sight shall no man living be justified" (Ps. 143:2). Another, though in a sense somewhat different, says, "How should man be just with God? If he will contend with him he cannot answer him one of a thousand" (Job 9:2-3). Here we are plainly told what the righteousness of God is, namely, a righteousness which no human works can satisfy which charges us with a thousand sins, while not one sin can be excused. Of this righteousness Paul, that chosen vessel of God, had formed a just idea, when he declared, "I know nothing by myself, yet am I not hereby justified" (1 Cor. 4:4).

3. Such examples exist not in the sacred volume only; all pious writers show that their sentiment was the same. Thus Augustine says, "Of all pious men groaning under this burden of corruptible flesh, and the infirmities of this life, the only hope is, that we have one Mediator Jesus Christ the righteous, and that he intercedes for our sins" (August. *ad Bonif.* lib. 3, cap. 5). What do we hear? If this is their only hope, where is their confidence in works? When he says only, he leaves no other. Bernard says, "And, indeed, where have the infirm firm security and safe rest, but in the wounds of the Savior? Hold it then the more securely, the more powerful he is to save. The world frowns, the body presses, the devil lays snares: I fall not, because I am founded on a firm rock. I have sinned a grievous sin: conscience is troubled, but it shall not be overwhelmed, for I will remember the wounds of the Lord." He afterwards concludes, "My merit, therefore, is the compassion of the Lord; plainly I am not devoid of merit so long as he is not devoid

of commiseration. But if the mercies of the Lord are many, equally many are my merits. Shall I sing of my own righteousness? O Lord, I will make mention of thy righteousness alone. That righteousness is mine also, being made mine by God" (Bernard, Serm. 61, in *Cantic.*). Again, in another passage, "Man's whole merit is to place his whole hope in him who makes the whole man safe" (in *Ps. Qui Habitat.* Serm. 15). In like manner, reserving peace to himself, he leaves the glory to God: "Let thy glory remain unimpaired: it is well with me if I have peace; I altogether abjure boasting, lest if I should usurp what is not mine, I lose also what is offered" (Serm. 13, in *Cantic*). He says still more plainly in another place: "Why is the Church solicitous about merits? God purposely supplies her with a firmer and more secure ground of boasting. There is no reason for asking by what merits may we hope for blessings, especially when you hear in the prophet, 'Thus saith the Lord God, I do not this for your sakes, O house of Israel, but for mine holy name's sake,' (Ezek. 36:22, 32). It is sufficient for merit to know that merits suffice not; but as it is sufficient for merit not to presume on merit, so to be without merits is sufficient for condemnation" (Bernard, Serm. 68). The free use of the term merits for good works must be pardoned to custom. Bernard's purpose was to alarm hypocrites, who turned the grace of God into licentiousness, as he shortly after explains: "Happy the church which neither wants merit without presumption, nor presumption without merit. It has ground to presume, but not merit. It has merit, merit to deserve, not presume. Is not the absence of presumption itself a merit? He, therefore, to whom the many mercies of the Lord furnish ample grounds of boasting, presumes the more securely that he presumes not" (Bernard, Serm. 68).

4. Thus, indeed, it is. Aroused consciences, when they have to do with God, feel this to be the only asylum in which they can breathe safely. For if the stars which shine most brightly by night lose their brightness on the appearance of the sun, what think we will be the

case with the highest purity of man when contrasted with the purity of God? For the scrutiny will be most strict, penetrating to the most hidden thoughts of the heart. As Paul says, it "will bring to light the hidden things of darkness and will make manifest the counsels of the heart" (1 Cor. 4:5); will compel the reluctant and dissembling conscience to bring forward everything, even things which have now escaped our memory. The devil, aware of all the iniquities which he has induced us to perpetrate, will appear as accuser; the external show of good works, the only thing now considered, will then be of no avail; the only thing demanded will be the true intent of the will. Hence hypocrisy, not only that by which a man, though consciously guilty before God, affects to make an ostentatious display before man, but that by which each imposes upon himself before God (so prone are we to soothe and flatter ourselves), will fall confounded, how much soever it may now swell with pride and presumption. Those who do not turn their thoughts to this scene may be able for the moment calmly and complacently to rear up a righteousness for themselves; but this the judgment of God will immediately overthrow, just as great wealth amassed in a dream vanishes the moment we awake. Those who, as in the presence of God, inquire seriously into the true standard of righteousness, will certainly find that all the works of men, if estimated by their own worth, are nothing but vileness and pollution, that what is commonly deemed justice is with God mere iniquity; what is deemed integrity is pollution; what deemed glory is ignominy.

5. Let us not decline to descend from this contemplation of the divine perfection, to look into ourselves without flattery or blind self-love. It is not strange that we are so deluded in this matter, seeing none of us can avoid that pestilential self-indulgence, which, as Scripture proclaims, is naturally inherent in all: "Every way of a man is right in his own eyes," says Solomon (Prov. 21:2). And again, "All the ways of a man are clean in his own eyes" (Prov. 16:2). What then? does this hallucination excuse him? No, indeed, as Solomon immediately

adds, "The Lord weigheth the spirits;" that is, while man flatters himself by wearing an external mask of righteousness, the Lord weighs the hidden impurity of the heart in his balance. Seeing, therefore, that nothing is gained by such flattery, let us not voluntarily delude ourselves to our own destruction. To examine ourselves properly, our conscience must be called to the judgment seat of God. His light is necessary to disclose the secret recesses of wickedness which otherwise lie too deeply hid. Then only shall we clearly perceive what the value of our works is; that man, so far from being just before God, is but rottenness and a worm, abominable and vain, drinking in "iniquity like water." For "who can bring a clean thing out of an unclean? not one" (Job 14:5). Then we shall experience the truth of what Job said of himself: "If I justify myself, mine own mouth shall condemn me: if I say I am perfect, it shall prove me perverse" (Job 9:20). Nor does the complaint which the prophet made concerning Israel apply to one age only. It is true of every age, that "all we like sheep have gone astray; we have turned every one to his own way" (Isa. 53:6). Indeed, he there comprehends all to whom the gift of redemption was to come. And the strictness of the examination ought to be continued until it have completely alarmed us, and in that way prepared us for receiving the grace of Christ. For he is deceived who thinks himself capable of enjoying it, until he have laid aside all loftiness of mind. There is a well-known declaration, "God resisteth the proud, but giveth grace to the humble" (1 Pet. 5:5).

6. But what means is there of humbling us if we do not make way for the mercy of God by our utter indigence and destitution? For I call it not humility, so long as we think there is any good remaining in us. Those who have joined together the two things, to think humbly of ourselves before God and yet hold our own righteousness in some estimation, have hitherto taught a pernicious hypocrisy. For if we confess to God contrary to what we feel, we wickedly lie to him; but we cannot feel as we ought without seeing that everything like a

ground of boasting is completely crushed. Therefore, when you hear from the prophets "thou wilt save the afflicted people; but wilt bring down high looks" (Ps. 18:27), consider, first, that there is no access to salvation unless all pride is laid aside and true humility embraced; secondly, that that humility is not a kind of moderation by which you yield to God some article of your right (thus men are called humble in regard to each other when they neither conduct themselves haughtily nor insult over other, though they may still entertain some consciousness of their own excellence), but that it is the unfeigned submission of a mind overwhelmed by a serious conviction of its want and misery. Such is the description everywhere given by the word of God. When in Zephaniah the Lord speaks thus, "I will take away out of the midst of thee them that rejoice in thy pride, and thou shalt no more be haughty because of my holy mountain. I will also leave in the midst of thee an afflicted and poor people, and they shall trust in the name of the Lord" (Zeph. 3:11-12), does he not plainly show who are the humble—viz. those who lie afflicted by a knowledge of their poverty? On the contrary, he describes the proud as rejoicing (*exultantes*), such being the mode in which men usually express their delight in prosperity. To the humble, whom he designs to save, he leaves nothing but hope in the Lord. Thus, also, in Isaiah, "To this man will I look, even to him that is poor and of a contrite spirit, and trembleth at my word" (Isa. 66:2). Again, "Thus saith the high and lofty One that inhabiteth eternity, whose name is Holy; I dwell in the high and holy place, with him also that is of a contrite and humble spirit, to revive the spirit of the humble, and to revive the heart of the contrite ones" (Isa. 57:15). By the term "contrition" which you so often hear, understand a wounded heart, which, humbling the individual to the earth, allows him not to rise. With such contrition must your heart be wounded, if you would, according to the declaration of God, be exalted with the humble. If this is not your case, you shall be humbled by the mighty hand of God to your shame and disgrace.

7. Our divine Master, not confining himself to words, has by a parable set before us, as in a picture, a representation of true humility. He brings forward a publican, who standing afar off, and not daring to lift up his eyes to heaven, smites upon his breast, laments aloud, and exclaims, "God be merciful to me a sinner" (Luke 18:13). Let us not suppose that he gives the signs of a fictitious modesty when he dares not come near or lift up his eyes to heaven, but, smiting upon his breast, confesses himself a sinner; let us know that these are the evidences of his internal feeling. With him our Lord contrasts the Pharisee, who thanks God "I am not as other men are, extortioners, unjust, adulterers, or even as this publican. I fast twice in the week, I give tithes of all that I possess." In this public confession he admits that the righteousness which he possesses is the gift of God; but because of his confidence that he is righteous, he departs from the presence of God unaccepted and abominated. The publican acknowledging his iniquity is justified. Hence we may see how highly our humility is valued by the Lord: our breast cannot receive his mercy until deprived completely of all opinion of its own worth. When such an opinion is entertained, the door of mercy is shut. That there might be no doubt on this matter, the mission on which Christ was sent into the world by his Father was "to preach good tidings to the meek," "to bind up the broken-hearted, to proclaim liberty to the captives, and the opening of the prison to them that are bound; to proclaim the acceptable year of the Lord, and the day of vengeance of our God; to comfort all that mourn; to appoint unto them that mourn in Zion to give unto them beauty for ashes, the oil of joy for mourning, the garment of praise for the spirit of heaviness" (Isa. 61:1-3). In fulfillment of that mission, the only persons whom he invites to share in his beneficence are the "weary and heavy laden." In another passage he says, " I am not come to call the righteous, but sinners to repentance" (Matt. 11:28; 9:13).

8. Therefore if we would make way for the call of Christ, we must put far from us all arrogance and confidence. The former is produced by a foolish persuasion of self-righteousness, when a man thinks that he has something in himself which deservedly recommends him to God; the latter may exist without any confidence in works. For many sinners, intoxicated with the pleasures of vice, think not of the judgment of God. Lying stupefied, as it were, by a kind of lethargy, they aspire not to the offered mercy. It is not less necessary to shake off torpor of this description than every kind of confidence in ourselves, in order that we may haste to Christ unencumbered, and while hungry and empty be filled with his blessings. Never shall we have sufficient confidence in him unless utterly distrustful of ourselves; never shall we take courage in him until we first despond of ourselves; never shall we have full consolation in him until we cease to have any in ourselves. When we have entirely discarded all self-confidence, and trust solely in the certainty of his goodness, we are fit to apprehend and obtain the grace of God. "When" (as Augustine says), "forgetting our own merits, we embrace the gifts of Christ, because if he should seek for merits in us we should not obtain his gifts" (August. *de Verb. Apost.* 8). With this Bernard admirably accords, comparing the proud who presume in the least on their merits, to unfaithful servants, who wickedly take the merit of a favor merely passing through them, just as if a wall were to boast of producing the ray which it receives through the window (Bernard, Serm. 13, in *Cant.*). Not to dwell longer here, let us lay down this short but sure and general rule, That he is prepared to reap the fruits of the divine mercy who has thoroughly emptied himself, I say not of righteousness (he has none), but of a vain and blustering show of righteousness; for to whatever extent any man rests in himself, to the same extent he impedes the beneficence of God.

Study Guide Questions

Section 1

1. What happens when we evaluate ourselves before an earthly tribunal?
2. What do we miss until we come into the presence of God?

Section 2

1. How may we come out ahead in moral comparisons of ourselves?

Section 3

1. Who are the two "pious writers" that Calvin cites?
2. According to Bernard, what is "my merit"?
3. What does Calvin excuse as "custom"?

Section 4

1. What do awakened consciences do?
2. What is the actual state of what is considered righteousness before God?

Section 5

1. We must consider ourselves without what two things?
2. What is there a need to strip bare?

Section 6

1. What does Calvin refuse to identify as humility?
2. What must you do if you want to be exalted with the humble?

Section 7

1. Why was the publican who prayed in the Temple a sincere man?

Section 8

1. What blocks the way to Christ?

2. What illustration does Calvin take from Bernard on the impossibility of taking credit for grace?

CHAPTER 13

Two things to be observed in gratuitous justification.

The divisions of this chapter are—
I. The glory of God, and peace of conscience, both secured by gratuitous justification. An insult to the glory of God to glory in ourselves and seek justification out of Christ, whose righteousness, apprehended by faith, is imputed to all the elect for reconciliation and eternal salvation, sec. 1-2.

II. Peace of conscience cannot be obtained in any other way than by gratuitous justification. This fully proved, sec. 3-5.

Outline:

1. The glory of God remains untarnished, when he alone is acknowledged to be just. This proved from Scripture.

2. Those who glory in themselves glory against God. Objection. Answer, confirmed by the authority of Paul and Peter.

3. Peace of conscience obtained by free justification only. Testimony of Solomon, of conscience itself, and the Apostle Paul, who contends that faith is made vain if righteousness come by the law.

4. The promise confirmed by faith in the mercy of Christ. This is confirmed by Augustine and Bernard, is in accordance with what has been above stated, and is illustrated by clear predictions of the prophets.

5. Farther demonstration by an Apostle. Refutation of a sophism.

Outline:

Here two ends must be kept specially in view, namely, that the glory of God be maintained unimpaired, and that our consciences, in the view of his tribunal, be secured in peaceful rest and calm tranquility. When the question relates to righteousness, we see how often and how anxiously Scripture exhorts us to give the whole praise of it to God. Accordingly, the Apostle testifies that the purpose of the Lord in conferring righteousness upon us in Christ, was to demonstrate his own righteousness. The nature of this demonstration he immediately subjoins—viz. "that he might be just, and the justifier of him which believeth in Jesus" (Rom. 3:25). Observe, that the righteousness of God is not sufficiently displayed, unless He alone is held to be righteous, and freely communicates righteousness to the undeserving. For this reason it is his will, that "every mouth may be stopped, and all the world may become guilty before God" (Rom. 3:19). For so long as a man has anything, however small, to say in his own defense, so long he deducts somewhat from the glory of God. Thus we are taught in Ezekiel how much we glorify his name by acknowledging our iniquity: "Then shall ye remember your ways and all your doings, wherein ye have been defiled; and ye shall loathe yourselves in your own sight, for all your evils that ye have committed. And ye shall know that I am the Lord, when I have wrought with you for my name's sake, not according to your wicked ways, nor according to your corrupt doings" (Ezek. 20:43-44). If part of the true knowledge of God consists in being oppressed by a consciousness of our own iniquity, and in recognizing him as doing good to those who are unworthy of it, why do we attempt, to our great injury, to steal from the Lord even one particle of the praise of unmerited kindness? In like manner, when Jeremiah exclaims, "Let not the wise man glory in his wisdom, neither let the mighty man glory in his might, let not the rich man glory in his riches: but let him that glorieth glory in the Lord" (Jer. 9:23-24), does he not intimate, that the glory of the Lord is infringed when man glories in himself? To this purpose, indeed, Paul accommodates the words when he says, that all the parts of our salvation are treasured up with Christ, that we may glory only in the Lord (1 Cor. 1:29). For he intimates, that whosoever imagines he has anything of his own, rebels against God, and obscures his glory.

2. Thus, indeed, it is: we never truly glory in him until we have utterly discarded our own glory. It must, therefore, be regarded as a universal proposition, that whoso glories in himself glories against God. Paul indeed considers, that the whole world is not made subject to God until every ground of glorying has been withdrawn from men (Rom. 3:19). Accordingly, Isaiah, when he declares that "in the Lord shall all the seed of Israel be justified" adds, "and shall glory" (Isa. 45:25), as if he had said that the elect are justified by the Lord, in order that they may glory in him, and in none else. The way in which we are to glory in the Lord he had explained in the preceding verse, "Unto me every knee shall bow, every tongue shall swear;" "Surely, shall one say, in the Lord have I righteousness and strength, even to him shall men come." Observe, that the thing required is not simple confession, but confession confirmed by an oath, that it might not be imagined that any kind of fictitious humility might suffice. And let no man here allege that he does not glory, when without arrogance he recognizes his own righteousness; such a recognition cannot take place without generating confidence, nor such confidence without begetting boasting. Let us remember, therefore, that in the whole discussion concerning justification the great thing to be attended to is, that God's glory be maintained entire and unimpaired; since as the

Apostle declares, it was in demonstration of his own righteousness that he shed his favor upon us; it was "that he might be just, and the justifier of him which believeth in Jesus" (Rom. 3:26). Hence, in another passage, having said that the Lord conferred salvation upon us, in order that he might show forth the glory of his name (Eph. 1:6), he afterwards, as if repeating the same thing, adds, "By grace are ye saved through faith; and that not of yourselves: it is the gift of God: not of works, lest any man should boast" (Eph. 2:8). And Peter, when he reminds us that we are called to the hope of salvation, "that ye should show forth the praises of him who has called you out of darkness into his marvelous light" (1 Pet. 2:9), doubtless intends thus to proclaim in the ears of believers only the praises of God, that they may bury in profound silence all arrogance of the flesh. The sum is, that man cannot claim a single particle of righteousness to himself, without at the same time detracting from the glory of the divine righteousness.

3. If we now inquire in what way the conscience can be quieted as in the view of God, we shall find that the only way is by having righteousness bestowed upon us freely by the gift of God. Let us always remember the words of Solomon, "Who can say I have made my heart clean, I am free from my sin?" (Prov. 20:9). Undoubtedly there is not one man who is not covered with infinite pollutions. Let the most perfect man descend into his own conscience, and bring his actions to account, and what will the result be? Will he feel calm and quiescent, as if all matters were well arranged between himself and God; or will he not rather be stung with dire torment, when he sees that the ground of condemnation is within him if he be estimated by his works? Conscience, when it beholds God, must either have sure peace with his justice, or be beset by the terrors of hell. We gain nothing, therefore, by discoursing of righteousness, unless we hold it to be a righteousness stable enough to support our souls before the tribunal of God. When the soul is able to appear intrepidly in the presence of God, and receive his sentence without dismay, then only

let us know that we have found a righteousness that is not fictitious. It is not, therefore, without cause, that the Apostle insists on this matter. I prefer giving it in his words rather than my own: "If they which are of the law be heirs, faith is made void, and the promise made of no effect" (Rom. 4:14). He first infers that faith is made void if the promise of righteousness has respect to the merit of our works, or depends on the observance of the law. Never could anyone rest securely in it, for never could he feel fully assured that he had fully satisfied the law; and it is certain that no man ever fully satisfied it by works. Not to go far for proof of this, every one who will use his eyes aright may be his own witness. Hence it appears how deep and dark the abyss is into which hypocrisy plunges the minds of men, when they indulge so securely as, without hesitations to oppose their flattery to the judgment of God, as if they were relieving him from his office as judge. Very different is the anxiety which fills the breasts of believers, who sincerely examine themselves. Every mind, therefore, would first begin to hesitate, and at length to despair, while each determined for itself with how great a load of debt it was still oppressed, and how far it was from coming up to the enjoined condition. Thus, then, faith would be oppressed and extinguished. To have faith is not to fluctuate, to vary, to be carried up and down, to hesitate, remain in suspense, vacillate, in fine, to despair; it is to possess sure certainty and complete security of mind, to have whereon to rest and fix your foot.

4. Paul, moreover, adds, that the promise itself would be rendered null and void. For if its fulfillment depends on our merits when pray, will we be able to come the length of meriting the favor of God? Nay, the second clause is a consequence of the former, since the promise will not be fulfilled unless to those who put faith in it. Faith therefore failing, no power will remain in the promise. "Therefore it is of faith, that it might be by grace, to the end the promise might be sure to all the seed" (Rom. 4:16). It was abundantly confirmed when made to rest on the mercy of God alone, for mercy and truth are united by

an indissoluble tie; that is, whatever God has mercifully promised he faithfully performs. Thus David, before he asks salvation according to the word of God, first places the source of it in his mercy. "Let, I pray thee, thy merciful kindness be for my comfort, according to thy word unto thy servant" (Ps. 119:76). And justly, for nothing but mere mercy induces God to promise. Here, then, we must place, and, as it were, firmly fix our whole hope, paying no respect to our works, and asking no assistance from them. And lest you should suppose that there is anything novel in what I say, Augustine also enjoins us so to act. "Christ," says he, "will reign forever among his servants. This God has promised, God has spoken; if this is not enough, God has sworn. Therefore, as the promise stands firm, not in respect of our merits, but in respect of his mercy, no one ought to tremble in announcing that of which he cannot doubt" (August. *in Ps. 88,* Tract. 50). Thus Bernard also, "Who can be saved? ask the disciples of Christ. He replies, With men it is impossible, but not with God. This is our whole confidence, this our only consolation; this the whole ground of our hope: but be-ing assured of the possibility, what are we to say as to his willingness? Who knows whether he is deserving of love or hatred? (Eccles. 9:1). Who has known the mind of the Lord that he may instruct him?' (1 Cor. 2:16). Here it is plain, faith must come to our aid: here we must have the assistance of truth, in order that the secret purpose of the Father respecting us may be revealed by the Spirit, and the Spirit tes-tifying may persuade our hearts that we are the sons of God. But let him persuade by calling and justifying freely by faith: in these there is a kind of transition from eternal predestination to future glory" (Bert. in *Dedica. Templi,* Serm. 5). Let us thus briefly conclude: Scrip-ture indicates that the promises of God are not sure, unless they are apprehended with full assurance of conscience; it declares that wher-ever there is doubt or uncertainty, the promises are made void; on the other hand, that they can only waver and fluctuate if they depend on our works. Therefore, either our righteousness must perish, or without any consideration of our works, place must be given to faith alone, whose nature it is to prick up the ear, and shut the eye; that is, to be intent on the promise only, to give up all idea of any dignity or merit in man. Thus is fulfilled the celebrated prophecy of Zechariah: "I will remove the iniquity of that land in one day. In that day, saith the Lord of hosts, shall ye call every man his neighbor under the vine, and under the fig tree" (Zech. 3:9-10). Here the prophet intimates that the only way in which believers can enjoy true peace, is by obtaining the remission of their sins. For we must attend to this peculiarity in the prophets, that when they discourse of the kingdom of Christ, they set forth the external mercies of God as types of spiritual blessings. Hence Christ is called the Prince of Peace, and our peace, Isa. 9:6; Eph. 2:14), because he calms all the agitations of conscience. If the method is asked, we must come to the sacrifice by which God was appeased, for no man will ever cease to tremble, until he hold that God is propitiated solely by that expiation in which Christ endured his anger. In short, peace must be sought nowhere but in the agonies of Christ our Redeemer.

5. But why employ a more obscure testimony? Paul uniformly declares that the conscience can have no peace or quiet joy until it is held for certain that we are justified by faith. And he at the same time declares whence this certainty is derived—viz. when "the love of God is shed abroad in our hearts by the Holy Ghost" (Rom. 5:5); as if he had said that our Souls cannot have peace until we are fully assured that we are pleasing to God. Hence he elsewhere exclaims in the person of believers in general, "Who shall separate us from the love of Christ?" (Rom. 8:35). Until we have reached that haven, the slightest breeze will make us tremble, but so long as the Lord is our Shepherd, we shall walk without fear in the valley of the shadow of death (Ps. 23). Thus those who pretend that justification by faith consists in being regenerated and made just, by living spiritually, have never tasted the sweetness of grace in trusting that God will be propitious. Hence

also, they know no more of praying aright than do the Turks or any other heathen people. For, as Paul declares, faith is not true, unless it suggest and dictate the delightful name of Father; nay, unless it open our mouths and enable us freely to cry, Abba, Father. This he expresses more clearly in another passage, "In whom we have boldness and access with confidence by the faith of him" (Eph. 3:12). This, certainly, is not obtained by the gift of regeneration, which, as it is always defective in the present state, contains within it many grounds of doubt. Wherefore, we must have recourse to this remedy; we must hold that the only hope which believers have of the heavenly inheritance is, that being engrafted into the body of Christ, they are justified freely. For, in regard to justification, faith is merely passive, bringing nothing of our own to procure the favor of God, but receiving from Christ everything that we want.

Study Guide Questions

Section 1
1. What two things does Calvin aim at in this section?
2. Who rises up against God?

Section 2
1. Where must the praise of righteousness remain?

Section 3
1. How may a guilty conscience be quieted before God?

Section 4
1. If we may depend upon works-righteousness at all, what else happens?
2. Why does Calvin cite Augustine at this point?

Section 5
1. What alone gives us peace of conscience and gladness in prayer?

CHAPTER 14

The beginning of justification. In what sense progressive.

To illustrate what has been already said, and show what kind of righteousness man can have during the whole course of his life, mankind are divided into four classes.

I. First class considered, sec. 1-6.

II. Second and third classes considered together, sec. 7-8.

III. Fourth class considered, sec. 9 to end.

Outline:

1. Men either idolatrous, profane, hypocritical, or regenerate. 1. Idolaters void of righteousness, full of unrighteousness, and hence in the sight of God altogether wretched and undone.

2. Still a great difference in the characters of men. This difference manifested. 1. In the gifts of God. 2. In the distinction between honorable and base. 3. In the blessings of he present life.

3. All human virtue, how praiseworthy soever it may appear, is corrupted. 1. By impurity of heart. 2. By the absence of a proper nature.

4. By the want of Christ, without whom there is no life.

5. Natural condition of man as described by Scripture. All men dead in sins before regeneration.

6. Passages of Scripture to this effect. Vulgar error confounding the righteousness of works with the redemption purchased by Christ.

7. The second and third classes of men, comprehending hypocrites and Christians in name only. Every action of theirs deserves condemnation. Passage from Haggai. Objection. Answer.

8. Other passages. Quotations from Augustine and Gregory.

9. The fourth class—viz. the regenerate. Though guided by the Spirit, corruption adheres to all they do, especially when brought to the bar of God.

10. One fault sufficient to efface all former righteousness. Hence they cannot possibly be justified by works.

11. In addition to the two former arguments, a third adduced against the Sophists, to show that whatever be the works of the regenerate, they are justified solely by faith and the free imputation of Christ's righteousness.

12. Sophism of the Schoolmen in opposition to the above doctrine. Answer.

13. Answer explained. Refutation of the fiction of partial righteousness, and compensation by works of supererogation. This fiction necessarily falls with that of satisfaction.

14. Statement of our Savior—viz. that after we have done all, we are still unprofitable servants.

15. Objection founded on Paul's boasting. Answer, showing the Apostle's meaning. Other answers, stating the general doctrine out of Chrysostom. Third answer, showing that supererogation is the merest vanity.

16. Fourth answer, showing how Scripture dissuades us from all confidence in works. Fifth answer, showing that we have no ground of boasting.

17. Sixth answer, showing, in regard to four different classes, that works have no part in procuring our salvation. 1. The efficient cause is the free love of the Father. 2. The material cause is Christ acquiring righteousness for us. 3. The instrumental cause is faith. 4. The final cause the display of the divine justice and praise of the divine goodness.

18. A second objection, founded on the glorying of saints. An answer, explaining these modes of expression. How the saints feel in regard to the certainty of salvation. The opinion they have of their own works as in the sight of God.

19. Another answer—viz. that the elect, by this kind of glorying, refer only to their adoption by the Father as proved by the fruits of their calling. The order of this glorying. Its foundation, structure, and parts.

20. Conclusion. The saints neither attribute anything to the merits of works, nor derogate in any degree from the righteousness which they obtain in Christ. Confirmation from a passage of Augustine, in which he gives two reasons why no believer will presume to boast before God of his works.

21. A third objection—viz. that the good works of believers are the causes of divine blessings. Answer. There are inferior causes, but these depend on free justification, which is the only true cause why God blesses us. These modes of expression designate the order of sequence rather than the cause.

Outline:

In farther illustration of the subject, let us consider what kind of righteousness man can have, during the whole course of his life, and for this purpose let us make a fourfold division. Mankind, either endued with no knowledge of God, are sunk in idolatry; or, initiated in the sacraments, but by the impurity of their lives denying him whom they confess with their mouths, are Christians in name only;

or they are hypocrites, who with empty glosses hide the iniquity of the heart; or they are regenerated by the Spirit of God, and aspire to true holiness. In the first place, when men are judged by their natural endowments, not an iota of good will be found from the crown of the head to the sole of the foot, unless we are to charge Scripture with falsehood, when it describes all the sons of Adam by such terms as these: "The heart is deceitful above all things, and desperately wicked." "The imagination of man's heart is evil from his youth." "The Lord knoweth the thoughts of man that they are vanity." "They are all gone aside: they are altogether become filthy; there is none that does good, no, not one." In short, that they are flesh, under which name are comprehended all those works which are enumerated by Paul: adultery, fornication, uncleanness, lasciviousness, idolatry, witchcraft, hatred, variance, emulation, wrath, strife, seditions, heresies, envyings, murders, drunkenness, revelings, and all kinds of pollution and abomination which it is possible to imagine. Such, then, is the worth on which men are to plume themselves. But if any among them possess an integrity of manners which presents some semblance of sanctity among men, yet because we know that God regards not the outward appearance, we must penetrate to the very source of action, if we would see how far works avail for righteousness. We must, I say, look within, and see from what affection of the heart these works proceed. This is a very wide field of discussion, but as the matter may be explained in few words, I will use as much brevity as I can.

2. First, then, I deny not, that whatever excellent endowments appear in unbelievers are divine gifts. Nor do I set myself so much in opposition to common sense, as to contend that there was no difference between the justice, moderation, and equity of Titus and Trojan, and the rage, intemperance, and cruelty of Caligula, Nero, and Domitian; between the continence of Vespasian, and the obscene lusts of Tiberius; and (not to dwell on single virtues and vices) between the observance of law and justice, and the contempt of them. So great is

the difference between justice and injustice, that it may be seen even where the former is only a lifeless image. For what order would remain in the world if we were to confound them? Hence this distinction between honorable and base actions God has not only engraven on the minds of each, but also often confirms in the administration of his providence. For we see how he visits those who cultivate virtue with many temporal blessings. Not that that external image of virtue in the least degree merits his favor, but he is pleased thus to show how much he delights in true righteousness, since he does not leave even the outward semblance of it to go unrewarded. Hence it follows, as we lately observed, that those virtues, or rather images of virtues, of whatever kind, are divine gifts, since there is nothing in any degree praiseworthy which proceeds not from him.

3. Still the observation of Augustine is true, that all who are strangers to the true God, however excellent they may be deemed on account of their virtues are more deserving of punishment than of reward, because, by the pollution of their heart, they contaminate the pure gifts of God (August. *contra Julia.* Lib. 4). For though they are instruments of God to preserve human society by justice, continence, friendship, temperance, fortitude, and prudence, yet they execute these good works of God in the worst manner, because they are kept from acting ill, not by a sincere love of goodness, but merely by ambition or self-love, or some other sinister affection. Seeing then that these actions are polluted as in their very source, by impurity of heart, they have no better title to be classed among virtues than vices, which impose upon us by their affinity or resemblance to virtue. In short, when we remember that the object at which righteousness always aims is the service of God, whatever is of a different tendency deservedly forfeits the name. Hence, as they have no regard to the end which the divine wisdom prescribes, although from the performance the act seems good, yet from the perverse motive it is sin. Augustine, therefore, concludes that all the Fabriciuses, the Scipios, and Catos, in

their illustrious deeds, sinned in this, that, wanting the light of faith, they did not refer them to the proper end, and that, therefore, there was no true righteousness in them, because duties are estimated not by acts but by motives.

4. Besides, if it is true, as John says, that there is no life without the Son of God (1 John 5:12), those who have no part in Christ, whoever they be, whatever they do or devise, are hastening on, during their whole career, to destruction and the judgment of eternal death. For this reason, Augustine says, "Our religion distinguishes the righteous from the wicked, by the law, not of works but of faith, without which works which seem good are converted into sins" (August. *ad Bonif.* Lib. 3, cap. 5). He finely expresses the same idea in another passage, when he compares the zeal of such men to those who in a race mistake the course (August. *Praef.* in Ps. 31). He who is off the course, the more swiftly he runs is the more distant from the goal and, therefore, the more unhappy. It is better to limp in the way than run out of the way. Lastly, as there is no sanctification without union with Christ, it is evident that they are bad trees which are beautiful and fair to look upon, and may even produce fruit, sweet to the taste, but are still very far from good. Hence we easily perceive that everything which man thinks, designs, and performs, before he is reconciled to God by faith, is cursed, and not only of no avail for justification, but merits certain damnation. And why do we talk of this as if it were doubtful, when it has already been proved by the testimony of an apostle, that "without faith it is impossible to please God?" (Heb. 11:6).

5. But the proof will be still clearer if divine grace is set in opposition to the natural condition of man. For Scripture everywhere proclaims that God finds nothing in man to induce him to show kindness, but that he prevents him by free liberality. What can a dead man do to obtain life? But when he enlightens us with the knowledge of himself, he is said to raise us from the dead, and make us new creatures (John 5:25). On this ground we see that the kindness of

God toward us is often commended, especially by the apostle: "God," says he, "who is rich in mercy, for his great love wherewith he loved us, even when we were dead in sins, has quickened us together with Christ" (Eph. 2:4). In another passage, when treating of the general call of believers under the type of Abraham, he says, "God quickeneth the dead, and calleth those things which be not as though they were" (Rom. 4:17). If we are nothing, what, pray, can we do? Wherefore, in the Book of Job the Lord sternly represses all arrogance in these words, "Who has prevented me, that I should repay him? whatsoever is under the whole heaven is mine" (Job 41:11). Paul explaining this sentence applies it in this way—Let us not imagine that we bring to the Lord anything but the mere disgrace of want and destitution (Rom. 11:35). Wherefore, in the passage above quoted, to prove that we attain to the hope of salvation, not by works but only by grace, he affirms that "we are his workmanship, created in Christ Jesus unto good works, which God has before ordained that we should walk in them" (Eph. 2:10); as if he had said, Who of us can boast of having challenged God by his righteousness, seeing our first power to act aright is derived from regeneration? For, as we are formed by nature, sooner shall oil be extracted from stone than good works from us. It is truly strange how man, convicted of such ignominy, dares still to claim anything as his own. Let us acknowledge, therefore, with that chosen vessel, that God "has called us with an holy calling, not according to our works, but according to his own purpose and grace;" and "that the kindness and love of God our Savior toward men appeared not by works of righteousness which we have done, but according to his mercy he saved us;" that being justified by his grace, we might become the heirs of everlasting life (2 Tim. 1:9; Tit. 3:4-5). By this confession we strip man of every particle of righteousness, until by mere mercy he is regenerated unto the hope of eternal life, since it is not true to say we are justified by grace, if works contribute in any degree to our justification. The apostle undoubtedly had not forgotten himself in declaring that justification is gratuitous, seeing he argues in another place, that if works are of any avail, "grace is no more grace" (Rom. 11:6). And what else does our Lord mean, when he declares, "I am not come to call the righteous, but sinners to repentance?" (Matt. 9:13). If sinners alone are admitted, why do we seek admission by means of fictitious righteousness?

6. The thought is ever and anon recurring to me, that I am in danger of insulting the mercy of God by laboring with so much anxiety to maintain it, as if it were doubtful or obscure. Such, however, is our malignity in refusing to concede to God what belongs to him until most strongly urged that I am obliged to insist at greater length. But as Scripture is clear enough on this subject, I shall contend in its words rather than my own. Isaiah, after describing the universal destruction of the human race, finely subjoins the method of restitution. "The Lord saw it, and it displeased him that there was no judgment. And he saw that there was no man, and wondered that there was no intercessor: therefore his arm brought salvation unto him; and his righteousness, it sustained him" (Isa. 59:15-16). Where is our righteousness, if the prophet says truly, that no man in recovering salvation gives any assistance to the Lord? Thus another prophet, introducing the Lord as treating concerning the reconciliation of sinners, says, "I will betroth thee unto me forever; yea, I will betroth thee unto me in righteousness, and in judgment, and in loving-kindness, and in mercies." "I will have mercy upon her that had not obtained mercy" (Hos. 2:19, 23). If a covenant of this kind, evidently forming our first union with God, depends on mercy, there is no foundation left for our righteousness. And, indeed, I would fain know, from those who pretend that man meets God with some righteousness of works, whether they imagine there is any kind of righteousness save that which is acceptable to Him. If it were insane to think so, can anything agreeable to God proceed from his enemies, whom he abominates with all their deeds? Truth declares that we are all the avowed and

inveterate enemies of God until we are justified and admitted to his friendship (Rom. 5:6; Col. 1:21). If justification is the beginning of love, how can the righteousness of works precede it? Hence John, to put down the arrogant idea, carefully reminds us that God first loved us (1 John 4:10). The Lord had formerly taught the same thing by his Prophet: "I will love them freely: for mine anger is turned away from him" (Hos. 14:4). Assuredly he is not influenced by works if his love turns to us spontaneously. But the rude and vulgar idea entertained is, that we did not merit the interposition of Christ for our redemption, but that we are aided by our works in obtaining possession of it. On the contrary, though we may be redeemed by Christ, still, until we are engrafted into union with him by the calling of the Father, we are darkness, the heirs of death, and the enemies of God. For Paul declares that we are not purged and washed from our impurities by the blood of Christ until the Spirit accomplishes that cleansing in us (1 Cor. 6:11). Peter, intending to say the same thing, declares that the sanctification of the Spirit avails "unto obedience and sprinkling of the blood of Jesus Christ" (1 Pet. 1:2). If the sprinkling of the blood of Christ by the Spirit gives us purification, let us not think that, previous to this sprinkling, we are anything but sinners without Christ. Let us, therefore, hold it as certain, that the beginning of our salvation is as it were a resurrection from death unto life, because, when it is given us on behalf of Christ to believe on him (Phil. 1:29), then only do we begin to pass from death unto life.

7. Under this head the second and third classes of men noted in the above division are comprehended. Impurity of conscience proves that as yet neither of these classes is regenerated by the Spirit of God. And, again, their not being regenerated proves their want of faith. Whence it is clear that they are not yet reconciled, not yet justified, since it is only by faith that these blessings are obtained. What can sinners, alienated from God, produce save that which is abominable in his sight? Such, however, is the stupid confidence entertained by

all the wicked, and especially by hypocrites, that however conscious that their whole heart teems with impurity, they yet deem any spurious works which they may perform as worthy of the approbation of God. Hence the pernicious consequence, that though convicted of a wicked and impious mind, they cannot be induced to confess that they are devoid of righteousness. Even acknowledging themselves to be unrighteous, because they cannot deny it, they yet arrogate to themselves some degree of righteousness. This vanity the Lord admirably refutes by the prophet: "Ask now the priests concerning the law, saying, If one bear holy flesh in the skirt of his garment, and with his skirt do touch bread, or pottage, or wine, or oil, or any meat, shall it be holy? And the priests answered and said, No. Then said Haggai, If one that is unclean by a dead body touch any of these, shall it be unclean? And the priests answered and said, It shall be unclean. Then answered Haggai, and said, So is this people, and so is this nation before me, saith the Lord; and so is every work of their hands; and that which they offer there is unclean" (Hag. 2:11-14). I wish these sentiments could obtain full credit with us, and be deeply fixed on our memories. For there is no man, however flagitous the whole tenor of his life may be, who will allow himself to be convinced of what the Lord here so clearly declares. As soon as any person, even the most wicked, has performed some one duty of the law, he hesitates not to impute it to himself for righteousness; but the Lord declares that no degree of holiness is thereby acquired, unless the heart has previously been made pure. And not contented with this, he declares that all the works performed by sinners are contaminated by impurity of heart. Let us cease then to give the name of righteousness to works which the mouth of the Lord condemns as polluted. How well is this shown by that elegant similitude? It might be objected, that what the Lord has commanded is inviolably holy. But he, on the contrary, replies, that it is not strange that those things which are sanctified in the law are contaminated by the impurity of the wicked, the unclean hand profaning that which is sacred by handling it.

8. The same argument is admirably followed out by Isaiah: "Bring no more vain oblations; incense is an abomination unto me; the new moons and Sabbaths, the calling of assemblies, I cannot away with; it is iniquity, even the solemn meeting. Your new moons and your appointed feasts my soul hateth: they are a trouble unto me; I am weary to bear them. And when ye spread forth your hands I will hide mine eyes from you; yea, when ye make many prayers, I will not hear: your hands are full of blood. Wash you, make you clean; put away the evil of your doings from before mine eyes" (Isa. 1:13-16, compared with chap. 58). What is meant by the Lord thus nauseating the observance of his law? Nay, indeed, he does not repudiate anything relating to the genuine observance of the law, the beginning of which is as he uniformly declares the sincere fear of his name. When this is wanting, all the services which are offered to him are not only nugatory but vile and abominable. Let hypocrites now go, and while keeping depravity wrapped up in their heart, study to lay God under obligation by their works. In this way they will only offend him more and more. "The sacrifice of the wicked is an abomination to the Lord; but the prayer of the upright is his delight" (Prov. 15:8). We hold it, therefore, as indubitable, indeed it should be notorious to all tolerably verdant with Scriptures that the most splendid works performed by men, who are not yet truly sanctified, are so far from being righteousness in the sight of the Lord, that he regards them as sins. And, therefore it is taught with perfect truth, that no man procures favor with God by means of works, but that, on the contrary, works are not pleasing to God unless the person has previously found favor in his sight. Here we should carefully observe the order which scripture sets before us. Moses says that "the Lord had respect unto Abel and to his offering" (Gen. 4:4). Observe how he says that the Lord was propitious (had respect) to Abel, before he had respect to his works. Wherefore,

purification of heart ought to precede, in order that the works performed by us may be graciously accepted by God: for the saying of Jeremiah is always true, "O Lord, are not thine eyes upon the truth?" (Jer. 5:3). Moreover the Holy Spirit declared by the mouth of Peter, that it is by faith alone the heart is purified (Acts 15:9). Hence it is evident, that the primary foundation is in true and living faith.

9. Let us now see what kind of righteousness belongs to those persons whom we have placed in the fourth class. We admit that when God reconciles us to himself by the intervention of the righteousness of Christ, and bestowing upon us the free pardon of sins regards us as righteous, his goodness is at the same time conjoined with mercy, so that he dwells in us by means of his Holy Spirit, by whose agency the lusts of our flesh are every day more and more mortified while that we ourselves are sanctified; that is consecrated to the Lord for true purity of life, our hearts being trained to the obedience of the law. It thus becomes our leading desire to obey his will, and in all things advance his glory only. Still, however, while we walk in the ways of the Lord, under the guidance of the Holy Spirit, lest we should become unduly elated, and forget ourselves, we have still remains of imperfection which serve to keep us humble: "There is no man that sinneth not," saith Scripture (1 Kings 8:46). What righteousness then can men obtain by their works? First, I say, that the best thing which can be produced by them is always tainted and corrupted by the impurity of the flesh, and has, as it were, some mixture of dross in it. Let the holy servant of God, I say, select from the whole course of his life the action which he deems most excellent, and let him ponder it in all its parts; he will doubtless find in it something that savors of the rottenness of the flesh, since our alacrity in well-doing is never what it ought to be, but our course is always retarded by much weakness. Although we see that the stains by which the works of the righteous are blemished, are by no means unapparent, still, granting that they are the minutest possible, will they give no offense to the eye of God,

before which even the stars are not clean? We thus see, that even saints cannot perform one work which, if judged on its own merits, is not deserving of condemnation.

10. Even were it possible for us to perform works absolutely pure, yet one sin is sufficient to efface and extinguish all remembrance of former righteousness, as the prophet says (Ezek. 18:24). With this James agrees, "Whosoever shall keep the whole law, and yet offend in one point, is guilty of all" (James 2:10). And since this mortal life is never entirely free from the taint of sin, whatever righteousness we could acquire would ever and anon be corrupted, overwhelmed, and destroyed, by subsequent sins, so that it could not stand the scrutiny of God, or be imputed to us for righteousness. In short, whenever we treat of the righteousness of works, we must look not to the legal work but to the command. Therefore, when righteousness is sought by the Law, it is in vain to produce one or two single works; we must show an uninterrupted obedience. God does not (as many foolishly imagine) impute that forgiveness of sins, once for all, as righteousness; so that having obtained the pardon of our past life we may afterwards seek righteousness in the Law. This were only to mock and delude us by the entertainment of false hopes. For since perfection is altogether unattainable by us, so long as we are clothed with flesh, and the Law denounces death and judgment against all who have not yielded a perfect righteousness, there will always be ground to accuse and convict us unless the mercy of God interpose, and ever and anon absolve us by the constant remission of sins. Wherefore the statement which we set out is always true, If we are estimated by our own worthiness, in everything that we think or devise, with all our studies and endeavors we deserve death and destruction.

11. We must strongly insist on these two things: That no believer ever performed one work which, if tested by the strict judgment of God, could escape condemnation; and, moreover, that were this granted to be possible (though it is not), yet the act being vitiated and polluted by

the sins of which it is certain that the author of it is guilty, it is deprived
of its merit. This is the cardinal point of the present discussion. There is
no controversy between us and the sounder Schoolmen as to the beginning of justification. They admit that the sinner, freely delivered from
condemnation, obtains justification, and that by forgiveness of sins;
but under the term "justification" they comprehend the renovation by
which the Spirit forms us anew to the obedience of the Law; and in describing the righteousness of the regenerate man, maintain that being
once reconciled to God by means of Christ, he is afterwards deemed
righteous by his good works, and is accepted in consideration of them.
The Lord, on the contrary, declares, that he imputed Abraham's faith
for righteousness (Rom. 4:3), not at the time when he was still a worshiper of idols, but after he had been many years distinguished for holiness. Abraham had long served God with a pure heart, and performed
that obedience of the Law which a mortal man is able to perform: yet
his righteousness still consisted in faith. Hence we infer, according to
the reasoning of Paul, that it was not of works. In like manners when
the prophet says, "The just shall live by his faith" (Hab. 2:4), he is not
speaking of the wicked and profane, whom the Lord justifies by converting them to the faith: his discourse is directed to believers, and life
is promised to them by faith. Paul also removes every doubt, when in
confirmation of this sentiment he quotes the words of David, "Blessed
is he whose transgression is forgiven, whose sin is covered" (Ps. 32:1).
It is certain that David is not speaking of the ungodly but of believers
such as he himself was, because he was giving utterance to the feelings
of his own mind. Therefore we must have this blessedness not once
only, but must hold it fast during our whole lives. Moreover, the message of free reconciliation with God is not promulgated for one or two
days, but is declared to be perpetual in the Church (2 Cor. 5:18-19).
Hence believers have not even to the end of life any other righteousness than that which is there described. Christ ever remains a Mediator
to reconcile the Father to us, and there is a perpetual efficacy in his

death—viz. ablution, satisfaction, expiation; in short, perfect obedience, by which all our iniquities are covered. In the Epistle to the Ephesians, Paul says not that the beginning of salvation is of grace, but "by grace are ye saved," "not of works, lest any man should boast" (Eph. 2:8-9).

12. The subterfuges by which the Schoolmen here endeavor to escape will not disentangle them. They say that good works are not of such intrinsic worth as to be sufficient to procure justification, but it is owing to accepting grace that they have this effect. Then because they are forced to confess that here the righteousness of works is always imperfect, they grant that so long as we are in this life we stand in need of the forgiveness of sin in order to supply the deficiency of works, but that the faults which are committed are compensated by works of supererogation. I answer, that the grace which they call accepting, is nothing else than the free goodness with which the Father embraces us in Christ when he clothes us with the innocence of Christ, and accepts it as ours, so that in consideration of it he regards us as holy, pure, and innocent. For the righteousness of Christ (as it alone is perfect, so it alone can stand the scrutiny of God) must be sisted for us, and as a surety represent us judicially. Provided with this righteousness, we constantly obtain the remission of sins through faith. Our imperfection and impurity, covered with this purity, are not imputed but are as it were buried, so as not to come under judgment until the hour arrive when the old man being destroyed, and plainly extinguished in us, the divine goodness shall receive us into beatific peace with the new Adam, there to await the day of the Lord, on which, being clothed with incorruptible bodies, we shall be translated to the glory of the heavenly kingdom.

13. If these things are so, it is certain that our works cannot in themselves make us agreeable and acceptable to God, and even cannot please God, except insofar as being covered with the righteousness of Christ we thereby please him and obtain forgiveness of sins. God has not promised life as the reward of certain works, but only

declares, "which if a man do, he shall live in them" (Lev. 18:5), denouncing the well-known curse against all who do not continue in all things that are written in the book of the Law to do them. In this way is completely refuted the fiction of a partial righteousness, the only righteousness acknowledged in heaven being the perfect observance of the Law. There is nothing more solid in their dogma of compensation by means of works of supererogation. For must they not always return to the proposition which has already been disproved—viz. that he who observes the Law in part is so far justified by works? This, which no man of sound judgment will concede to them, they are not ashamed to take for granted. The Lord having so often declared that he recognizes no justification by works unless they be works by which the Law is perfectly fulfilled—how perverse is it, while we are devoid of such works, to endeavor to secure some ground of glorying to ourselves; that is not to yield it entirely to God, by boasting of some kind of fragments of works, and trying to supply the deficiency by other satisfactions? Satisfactions have already been so completely disposed of, that we ought never again even to dream of them. Here all I say is, that those who thus trifle with sin do not at all consider how execrable it is in the sight of God; if they did, they would assuredly understand, that all the righteousness of men collected into one heap would be inadequate to compensate for a single sin. For we see that by one sin man was so cast off and forsaken by God, that he at the same time lost all power of recovering salvation. He was, therefore, deprived of the power of giving satisfaction. Those who flatter themselves with this idea will never satisfy God, who cannot possibly accept or be pleased with anything that proceeds from his enemies. But all to whom he imputes sin are enemies, and, therefore, our sins must be covered and forgiven before the Lord has respect to any of our works. From this it follows, that the forgiveness of sins is gratuitous, and this forgiveness is wickedly insulted by those who introduce the idea of satisfaction. Let us, therefore, after the example of the Apostle, "forgetting those things which are behind, and reaching forth unto those things which are before," "press toward the mark for the prize of the high calling of God in Jesus Christ" (Phil. 3:13-14).

14. How can boasting in works of supererogation agree with the command given to us: "When ye shall have done all those things which are commanded you, say, We are unprofitable servants: we have done that which was our duty to do?" (Luke 17:10). To say or speak in the presence of God is not to feign or lie, but to declare what we hold as certain. Our Lord, therefore, enjoins us sincerely to feel and consider with ourselves that we do not perform gratuitous duties, but pay him service which is due. And truly. For the obligations of service under which we lie are so numerous that we cannot discharge them though all our thoughts and members were devoted to the observance of the Law; and, therefore, when he says "When ye shall have done all those things which are commanded you," it is just as if he had said that all the righteousness of men would not amount to one of these things. Seeing, then, that everyone is very far distant from that goal, how can we presume to boast of having accumulated more than is due? It cannot be objected that a person, though failing in some measure in what is necessary, may yet in intention go beyond what is necessary. For it must ever be held that in whatever pertains to the worship of God, or to charity, nothing can ever be thought of that is not comprehended under the Law. But if it is part of the Law, let us not boast of voluntary liberality in matters of necessary obligation.

15. On this subject, they ceaselessly allege the boast of Paul, that among the Corinthians he spontaneously renounced a right which, if he had otherwise chosen, he might have exercised (1 Cor. 9:15); thus not only paying what he owed them in duty, but gratuitously bestowing upon them more than duty required. They ought to have attended to the reason there expressed, that his object was to avoid giving offense to the weak. For wicked and deceitful workmen employed this pretense of kindness that they might procure favor to their pernicious

dogmas, and excite hatred against the Gospel, so that it was necessary for Paul either to peril the doctrine of Christ, or to thwart their
schemes. Now, if it is a matter of indifference to a Christian man
whether or not he cause a scandal when it is in his power to avoid it,
then I admit that the Apostle performed a work of supererogation
to his Master; but if the thing which he did was justly required in a
prudent minister of the Gospel, then I say he did what he was bound
to do. In short, even when no such reason appears, yet the saying of
Chrysostom is always true, that everything which we have is held on
the same condition as the private property of slaves; it is always due
to our Master. Christ does not disguise this in the parable, for he asks
in regard to the master who, on return from his labor, requires his
servant to gird himself and serve him, "Does he thank that servant
because he did the things that were commanded him? I trow not"
(Luke 17:9). But possibly the servant was more industrious than the
master would have ventured to exact. Be it so: still he did nothing to
which his condition as a servant did not bind him, because his utmost
ability is his master's. I say nothing as to the kind of supererogations
on which these men would plume themselves before God. They are
frivolities which he never commanded, which he approves not, and
will not accept when they come to give in their account. The only
sense in which we admit works of supererogation is that expressed
by the prophet, when he says, "Who has required this at your hand?"
(Isa. 1:12). But let them remember what is elsewhere said of them:
"Wherefore do ye spend money for that which is not bread? and your
labor for that which satisfieth not?" (Isa. 55:2). It is, indeed, an easy
matter for these indolent Rabbis to carry on such discussions sitting
in their soft chairs under the shade, but when the Supreme Judge
shall sit on his tribunal, all these blustering dogmas will behave to
disappear. This, this I say, was the true question: not what we can fable
and talk in schools and corners, but what ground of defense we can
produce at his judgment seat.

16. In this matter the minds of men must be specially guarded against two pestiferous dogmas—viz. against putting any confidence in the righteousness of works, or ascribing any glory to them. From all such confidence the Scriptures uniformly dissuade us when they declare that our righteousness is offensive in the sight of God unless it derives a sweet odor from the purity of Christ: that it can have no other effect than to excite the divine vengeance unless sustained by his indulgent mercy. Accordingly, the only thing they leave to us is to deprecate our Judge with that confession of David: "Enter not into judgment with thy servant: for in thy sight shall no living be justified" (Ps. 143:2). And when Job says, "If I be wicked, woe unto me: and if I be righteous, yet will I not lift up my head" (Job 10:15). Although he refers to that spotless righteousness of God, before which even angels are not clean, he however shows, that when brought to the bar of God all that mortals can do is to stand dumb. He does not merely mean that he chooses rather to give way spontaneously than to risk a contest with the divine severity, but that he was not conscious of possessing any righteousness that would not fall the very first moment it was brought into the presence of God. Confidence being banished, all glorying must necessarily cease. For who can attribute any merit of righteousness to works, which instead of giving confidence, only make us tremble in the presence of God? We must, therefore, come to what Isaiah invites us: "In the Lord shall all the seed of Israel be justified, and shall glory" (Isa. 45:25); for it is most true, as he elsewhere says, that we are "the planting of the Lord, that he might be glorified" (Isa. 61:3). Our soul, therefore, will not be duly purified until it ceases to have any confidence, or feel any exultation in works. Foolish men are puffed up to this false and lying confidence by the erroneous idea that the cause of their salvation is in works.

17. But if we attend to the four kinds of causes which philosophers bring under our view in regard to effects, we shall find that not one of them is applicable to works as a cause of salvation. The efficient

cause of our eternal salvation the Scripture uniformly proclaims to be
the mercy and free love of the heavenly Father towards us; the material cause to be Christ, with the obedience by which he purchased
righteousness for us; and what can the formal or instrumental cause
be but faith? John includes the three-in-one sentence when he says,
"God so loved the world, that he gave his only begotten Son, that
whosoever believeth in him should not perish but have everlasting
life" (John 3:16). The Apostle, moreover, declares that the final cause
is the demonstration of the divine righteousness and the praise of his
goodness. There also he distinctly mentions the other three causes; for
he thus speaks to the Romans: "All have sinned, and come short of
the glory of God, being justified freely by his grace" (Rom. 3:23-24).
You have here the head and primary source—God has embraced us
with free mercy. The next words are, "through the redemption that is
in Christ Jesus;" this is as it were the material cause by which righteousness is procured for us. "Whom God has set forth to be a propitiation through faith." Faith is thus the instrumental cause by which
righteousness is applied to us. He lastly subjoins the final cause when
he says, "To declare at this time his righteousness; that he might be
just, and the justifier of him that believeth in Jesus." And to show by
the way that this righteousness consists in reconciliation, he says that
Christ was "set forth to be a propitiation." Thus also, in the Epistle
to the Ephesians, he tells us that we are received into the favor of
God by mere mercy; that this is done by the intervention of Christ;
that it is apprehended by faith; the end of all being that the glory of
the divine goodness may be fully displayed. When we see that all the
parts of our salvation thus exist without us, what ground can we have
for glorying or confiding in our works? Neither as to the efficient nor
the final cause can the most sworn enemies of divine grace raise any
controversy with us unless they would abjure the whole of Scripture.
In regard to the material or formal cause they make a gloss, as if they
held that our works divide the merit with faith and the righteousness

of Christ. But here also Scripture reclaims, simply affirming that Christ is both righteousness and life, and that the blessing of justification is possessed by faith alone.

18. When the saints repeatedly confirm and console themselves with the remembrance of their innocence and integrity, and sometimes even abstain not from proclaiming them, it is done in two ways: either because by comparing their good cause with the bad cause of the ungodly, they thence feel secure of victory, not so much from commendation of their own righteousness, as from the just and merited condemnation of their adversaries; or because, reviewing themselves before God, even without any comparison with others the purity of their conscience gives them some comfort and security. The former reason will afterwards be considered (chap. 17, sec. 14, and chap. 20, sec. 10); let us now briefly show, in regard to the latter, how it accords with what we have above said, that we can have no confidence in works before the bar of God, that we cannot glory in any opinion of their worth. The accordance lies here, that when the point considered is the constitution and foundation of salvation, believers, without paying any respect to works, direct their eyes to the goodness of God alone. Nor do they turn to it only in the first instance, as to the commencement of blessedness, but rest in it as the completion. Conscience being thus founded, built up, and established is farther established by the consideration of works, inasmuch as they are proofs of God dwelling and reigning in us. Since, then, this confidence in works has no place unless you have previously fixed your whole confidence on the mercy of God, it should not seem contrary to that on which it depends. Wherefore, when we exclude confidence in works, we merely mean, that the Christian mind must not turn back to the merit of works as an aid to salvation, but must dwell entirely on the free promise of justification. But we forbid no believer to confirm and support this faith by the signs of the divine favor towards him. For if when we call to mind the gifts which God has bestowed upon us, they

are like rays of the divine countenance, by which we are enabled to behold the highest light of his goodness; much more is this the case with the gift of good works, which shows that we have received the Spirit of adoption.

19. When believers therefore feel their faith strengthened by a consciousness of integrity, and entertain sentiments of exultation, it is just because the fruits of their calling convince them that the Lord has admitted them to a place among his children. Accordingly, when Solomon says, "In the fear of the Lord is strong confidence" (Prov. 14:26), and when the saints sometimes beseech the Lord to hear them, because they walked before his face in simplicity and integrity (Gen. 24:10; 2 Kings 20:3), these expressions apply not to laying the foundation of a firm conscience, but are of force only when taken *a posteriori*. For there is nowhere such a fear of God as can give full security, and the saints are always conscious that any integrity which they may possess is mingled with many remains of the flesh. But as the fruits of regeneration furnish them with a proof of the Holy Spirit dwelling in them, experiencing God to be a Father in a matter of so much moment, they are strengthened in no slight degree to wait for his assistance in all their necessities. Even this they could not do, had they not previously perceived that the goodness of God is sealed to them by nothing but the certainty of the promise. Should they begin to estimate it by their good works, nothing will be weaker or more uncertain; works, when estimated by themselves, no less proving the divine displeasure by their imperfection, than his good-will by their incipient purity. In short, while proclaiming the mercies of the Lord, they never lose sight of his free favor, with all its "breadth and length, and depth and height," testified by Paul (Eph. 3:18); as if he had said, Whithersoever the believer turns, however loftily he climbs, however far and wide his thoughts extend, he must not go farther than the love of Christ, but must be wholly occupied in meditating upon it, as including in itself all dimensions. Accordingly, he declares that it

"passeth knowledge," that "to know the love of Christ" is to "be filled with all the fullness of God" (Eph. 3:19). In another passage, where he glories that believers are victorious in every contest, he adds the reason, "through him that loved us" (Rom. 8:37).

20. We now see that believers have no such confidence in works as to attribute any merit to them (since they regard them only as divine gifts, in which they recognize his goodness, and signs of calling, in which they discern their election); nor such confidence as to derogate in any respect from the free righteousness of Christ; since on this it depends, and without this cannot subsist. The same thing is briefly but elegantly expressed by Augustine when he says, "I do not say to the Lord, Despise not the works of my hands; I have sought the Lord with my hands, and have not been deceived. But I commend not the works of my hands, for I fear that when thou examinest them thou wilt find more faults than merits. This only I say, this ask, this desire, Despise not the works of thy hands. See in me thy work, not mine. If thou sees mine, thou condemnest; if thou sees thine own, thou crownest. Whatever good works I have are of thee" (August. *in Ps. 137*). He gives two reasons for not venturing to boast of his works before God: first, that if he has any good works, he does not see in them anything of his own; and, secondly, that these works are overwhelmed by a multitude of sins. Whence it is, that the conscience derives from them more fear and alarm than security. Therefore, the only way in which he desires God to look at any work which he may have done aright is, that he may therein see the grace of his calling, and perfect the work which he has begun.

21. Moreover, when Scripture intimates that the good works of believers are causes why the Lord does them good, we must still understand the meaning so as to hold unshaken what has previously been said—viz. that the efficient cause of our salvation is placed in the love of God the Father; the material cause in the obedience of the Son; the instrumental cause in the illumination of the Spirit, that is, in faith;

and the final cause in the praise of the divine goodness. In this, however, there is nothing to prevent the Lord from embracing works as
inferior causes. But how so? In this way: Those whom in mercy he has
destined for the inheritance of eternal life, he, in his ordinary administration, introduces to the possession of it by means of good works.
What precedes in the order of administration is called the cause of
what follows. For this reason, he sometimes makes eternal life a consequent of works; not because it is to be ascribed to them, but because
those whom he has elected he justifies, that he may at length glorify
(Rom. 8:30); he makes the prior grace to be a kind of cause, because it
is a kind of step to that which follows. But whenever the true cause is
to be assigned, he enjoins us not to take refuge in works, but to keep
our thoughts entirely fixed on the mercy of God; "The wages of sin
is death; but the gift of God is eternal life" (Rom. 6:23). Why, as he
contrasts life with death, does he not also contrast righteousness with
sin? Why, when setting down sin as the cause of death, does he not
also set down righteousness as the cause of life? The antithesis which
would otherwise be complete is somewhat marred by this variation;
but the Apostle employed the comparison to express the fact, that
death is due to the deserts of men, but that life was treasured up
solely in the mercy of God. In short, by these expressions, the order
rather than the cause is noted. The Lord adding grace to grace, takes
occasion from a former to add a subsequent, so that he may omit no
means of enriching his servants. Still, in following out his liberality,
he would have us always look to free election as its source and beginning. For although he loves the gifts which he daily bestows upon us,
inasmuch as they proceed from that fountain, still our duty is to hold
fast by that gratuitous acceptance, which alone can support our souls;
and so to connect the gifts of the Spirit, which he afterwards bestows,
with their primary cause, as in no degree to detract from it.

Study Guide Questions

Section 1

1. What are the four classes of men outlined by Calvin?

Section 2

1. How does Calvin account for pagan virtues, where they exist?
2. Does he lump pagan vice and virtue all together?
3. What kind of blessing does God give such men?

Section 3

1. Does Calvin account these pagan virtues as true virtue?
2. What is necessary for something to be truly virtuous?

Section 4

1. What illustration does Calvin take from Augustine here?

Section 5

1. What must we set the grace of God against?
2. Where does our first capacity for well-doing come from?

Section 6

1. What were we before we were sprinkled through the Spirit with the blood of Christ?

Section 7

1. What do the two middle categories of Calvin's fourfold division have in common?

Section 8

1. What does the Lord abominate?
2. What is man in his highest moral splendor?
3. What is the first foundation?

Section 9

1. What happens in believers each day?
2. What are our best works mixed with?

Section 10

1. What will just one sin do?

Section 11

1. What is the believer's righteousness always to be considered?
2. What two reasons keep a believer's work from being considered pure righteousness?
3. What is the pivotal point of dispute with the Schoolmen?

Section 12

1. What are works of supererogation?
2. Does Calvin allow for them?

Section 13

1. What tendency does holding to works of supererogation have?
2. What position does Calvin reject with regard to those who keep the law partly?
3. What cannot overcome a single sin?

Section 14

1. Is it possible to go beyond what God requires?
2. What should we not boast of?

Section 15

1. What is the only kind of supererogation that Calvin allows?

Section 16

1. What are the two plagues that we must banish from our minds?

Section 17
1. What are the four causes of our salvation?
2. What is not included in this list?

Section 18
1. In what two ways can believers refer to their own works?

Section 19
1. What are the fruits of regeneration proof of?

Section 20
1. What was Augustine's prayer with regard to works?

Section 21
1. Does Scripture ever speak of good works in a causal way?

CHAPTER 15

The boasted merit of works subversive both of the glory of God,
in bestowing righteousness, and of the certainty of salvation.

The divisions of this chapter are—
I. To the doctrine of free justification is opposed the question,
Whether or not works merit favor with God, sec. 1. This question
answered, sec. 2 and 3.

II. An exposition of certain passages of Scripture produced in support of the erroneous doctrine of merit, sec. 4 and 5.

III. Sophisms of Semipelagian Schoolmen refuted, sec. 6 and 7.

IV. Conclusion, proving the sufficiency of the orthodox doctrine,
sec. 8.

Outline:

1. After a brief recapitulation, the question, Whether or not good
works merit favor with God, considered.

2. First answer, fixing the meaning of the term "merit." This term
improperly applied to works, but used in a good sense, as by Augustine, Chrysostom, Bernard.

3. A second answer to the question. First by a negative, then by a
concession. In the rewarding of works what to be attributed to God,

and what to man. Why good works please God, and are advantageous
to those who do them. The ingratitude of seeking righteousness by
works. This shown by a double similitude.

4. First objection taken from Ecclesiasticus. Second objection from
the Epistle to the Hebrews. Two answers to both objections. A weak
distinction refuted.

5. A third and most complete answer, calling us back to Christ as
the only foundation of salvation. How Christ is our righteousness.
Whence it is manifest that we have all things in Christ and he nothing in us.

6. We must abhor the sophistry which destroys the merit of Christ,
in order to establish that of man. This impiety refuted by clear passages of Scripture.

7. Errors, of the younger Sophists extracted from Lombard. Refuted by Augustine. Also by Scripture.

8. Conclusion, showing that the foundation which has been laid
is sufficient for doctrine, exhortation, and comfort. Summery of the
orthodox doctrine of Justification.

The principal point in this subject has been now explained: as
justification if dependent upon works, cannot possibly stand in
the sight of God, it must depend solely on the mercy of God and
communion with Christ, and therefore on faith alone. But let us carefully attend to the point on which the whole subject hinges, lest we
get entangled in the common delusion, not only of the vulgar, but of
the learned. For the moment the question is raised as to the justification by faith or works, they run off to those passages which seem
to ascribe some merit to works in the sight of God, just as if justification by works were proved whenever it is proved that works have
any value with God. Above we have clearly shown that justification
by works consists only in a perfect and absolute fulfillment of the
law, and that, therefore, no man is justified by works unless he has

reached the summit of perfection, and cannot be convicted of even the smallest transgression. But there is another and a separate question, Though works by no means suffice to justify, do they not merit favor with God?

2. First, I must premise with regard to the term "merit," that he, whoever he was, that first applied it to human works, viewed in reference to the divine tribunal, consulted very ill for the purity of the faith. I willingly abstain from disputes about words, but I could wish that Christian writers had always observed this soberness—that when there was no occasion for it, they had never thought of using terms foreign to the Scriptures—terms which might produce much offense, but very little fruit. I ask, what need was there to introduce the word "merit," when the value of works might have been fully expressed by another term, and without offense? The quantity of offense contained in it the world shows to its great loss. It is certain that, being a high-sounding term, it can only obscure the grace of God, and inspire men with pernicious pride. I admit it was used by ancient ecclesiastical writers, and I wish they had not by the abuse of one term furnished posterity with matter of heresy, although in some passages they themselves show that they had no wish to injure the truth. For Augustine says, "Let human merits, which perished by Adam, here be silent, and let the grace of God reign by Jesus Christ" (August. *de Praedest. Sanct.*). Again, "The saints ascribe nothing to their merits; every thing will they ascribe solely to thy mercy, O God" (August. *in Ps. 139*). Again, "And when a man sees that whatever good he has he has not of himself, but of his God, he sees that everything in him which is praised is not of his own merits, but of the divine mercy" (August. *in Ps. 88*). You see how he denies man the power of acting aright, and thus lays merit prostrate. Chrysostom says, "If any works of ours follow the free calling of God, they are return and debt; but the gifts of God are grace, and beneficence, and great liberality." But to say nothing more of the name, let us attend to the thing. I formerly

quoted a passage from Bernard: "As it is sufficient for merit not to presume on merit, so to be without merit is sufficient for condemnation" (Bernard in *Cantic.* Serm. 98). He immediately adds an explanation which softens the harshness of the expression, when he says, "Hence be careful to have merits; when you have them, know that they were given; hope for fruit from the divine mercy, and you have escaped all the perils of poverty, ingratitude, and presumption. Happy the Church which neither wants merit without presumption, nor presumption without merit." A little before he had abundantly shown that he used the words in a sound sense, saying, "Why is the Church anxious about merits? God has furnished her with a firmer and surer ground of boasting. God cannot deny himself; he will do what he has promised. Thus there is no reason for asking by what merits may we hope for blessings; especially when you hear, Thus saith the Lord God 'I do not this for your sakes, O house of Israel, but for mine holy name's sake,' (Ezek. 36:22). It suffices for merit to know that merits suffice not."

3. What all our works can merit Scripture shows when it declares that they cannot stand the view of God, because they are full of impurity; it next shows what the perfect observance of the law (if it can anywhere be found) will merit when it enjoins, "So likewise ye, when ye shall have done all those things which are commanded you, say, We are unprofitable servants, we have done that which was our duty to do" (Luke 17:10); because we make no free-offering to God, but only perform due service by which no favor is deserved. And yet those good works which the Lord has bestowed upon us he counts ours also, and declares, that they are not only acceptable to him, but that he will recompense them. It is ours in return to be animated by this great promise, and to keep up our courage, that we may not weary in well-doing, but feel duly grateful for the great kindness of God. There cannot be a doubt, that everything in our works which deserves praise is owing to divine grace, and that there is not a particle of it which we

can properly ascribe to ourselves. If we truly and seriously acknowledge this, not only confidence, but every idea of merit vanishes. I say we do not, like the Sophists share the praise of works between God and man, but we keep it entire and unimpaired for the Lord. All we assign to man is that, by his impurity he pollutes and contaminates the very works which were good. The most perfect thing which proceeds from man is always polluted by some stain. Should the Lord, therefore, bring to judgment the best of human works, he would indeed behold his own righteousness in them; but he would also behold man's dishonor and disgrace. Thus good works please God, and are not without fruit to their authors, since, by way of recompense, they obtain more ample blessings from God, not because they so deserve, but because the divine benignity is pleased of itself to set this value upon them. Such, however is our malignity, that not contented with this liberality on the part of God, which bestows rewards on works that do not at all deserve them, we with profane ambition maintain that that which is entirely due to the divine munificence is paid to the merit of works. Here I appeal to every man's common sense. If one who by another's liberality possesses the usufruct of a field, rear up a claim to the property of it, does he not by his ingratitude deserve to lose the possession formerly granted? In like manner, if a slave, who has been manumitted, conceals his humble condition of freedman, and gives out that he was free-born, does he not deserve to be reduced to his original slavery? A benefit can only be legitimately enjoyed when we neither arrogate more to ourselves than has been given, nor defraud the author of it of his due praise; nay, rather when we so conduct ourselves as to make it appear that the benefit conferred still in a manner resides with him who conferred it. But if this is the moderation to be observed towards men, let everyone reflect and consider for himself what is due to God.

4. I know that the Sophists abuse some passages in order to prove that the Scriptures use the term "merit" with reference to God. They

quote a passage from Ecclesiasticus: "Mercy will give place to every man according to the merit of his works" (Ecclesiasticus 16:14); and from the Epistle to the Hebrews: "To do good and communicate forget not; for with such sacrifices God is well pleased" (Heb. 13:16). I now renounce my right to repudiate the authority of Ecclesiasticus; but I deny that the words of Ecclesiasticus, whoever the writer may have been, are faithfully quoted. The Greek is as follows: Παση ελεημοσυνη ποιησει τοπον εκαστος γαρ κατα τα εργα αυτου ευρησει. "He will make room for all mercy: for each shall find according to his works." That this is the genuine reading, and has been corrupted in the Latin version, is plain, both from the very structure of the sentence, and from the previous context. In the Epistle to the Hebrews there is no room for their quibbling on one little word, for in the Greek the Apostle simply says, that such sacrifices are pleasing and acceptable to God. This alone should amply suffice to quell and beat down the insolence of our pride, and prevent us from attaching value to works beyond the rule of Scripture. It is the doctrine of Scripture, moreover, that our good works are constantly covered with numerous stains by which God is justly offended and made angry against us, so far are they from being able to conciliate him, and call forth his favor towards us; and yet because of his indulgence, he does not examine them with the utmost strictness, he accepts them just as if they were most pure; and therefore rewards them, though undeserving, with innumerable blessings, both present and future. For I admit not the distinction laid down by otherwise learned and pious men, that good works merit the favors which are conferred upon us in this life, whereas eternal life is the reward of faith only. The recompense of our toils, and crown of our contest, our Lord almost uniformly places in heaven. On the other hand, to attribute to the merit of works, so as to deny it to grace, that we are loaded with other gifts from the Lord, is contrary to the doctrine of Scripture. For though Christ says, "Unto everyone that has shall be given;" "thou hast been faithful over a few things, I will make thee ruler over many things" (Matt. 25:29, 21), he, at the same time, shows that all additional gifts to believers are of his free benignity: "Ho, everyone that thirsteth, come ye to the waters, and he that has no money, come ye, buy, and eat: yea, come, buy wine and milk, without money and without price" (Isa. 55:1). Therefore, every help to salvation bestowed upon believers, and blessedness itself, are entirely the gift of God, and yet in both the Lord testifies that he takes account of works, since to manifest the greatness of his love toward us, he thus highly honors not ourselves only, but the gifts, which he has bestowed upon us.

5. Had these points been duly handled and digested in past ages, never could so many tumults and dissensions have arisen. Paul says, that in the architecture of Christian doctrine, it is necessary to retain the foundation which he had laid with the Corinthians, "Other foundation can no man lay than that which is laid, which is Jesus Christ" (1 Cor. 3:11). What then is our foundation in Christ? Is it that he begins salvation and leaves us to complete it? Is it that he only opened up the way, and left us to follow it in our own strength? By no means, but as Paul had a little before declared, it is to acknowledge that he has been given us for righteousness. No man, therefore, is well founded in Christ who has not entire righteousness in him, since the Apostle says not that he was sent to assist us in procuring, but was himself to be our righteousness. Thus, it is said that God "has chosen us in him before the foundation of the world," not according to our merit, but "according to the good pleasure of his will;" that in him "we have redemption through his blood, even the forgiveness of sins;" that peace has been made "through the blood of his cross;" that we are reconciled by his blood; that, placed under his protection, we are delivered from the danger of finally perishing; that thus ingrafted into him we are made partakers of eternal life, and hope for admission into the kingdom of God. Nor is this all. Being admitted to participation in him, though we are still foolish, he is our wisdom; though we

are still sinners he is our righteousness; though we are unclean, he is our purity; though we are weak, unarmed, and exposed to Satan, yet ours is the power which has been given him in heaven and in earth, to bruise Satan under our feet, and burst the gates of hell (Matt. 28:18); though we still bear about with us a body of death, he is our life; in short, all things of his are ours, we have all things in him, he nothing in us. On this foundation, I say, we must be built, if we would grow up into a holy temple in the Lord.

6. For a long time the world has been taught very differently. A kind of good works called "moral" has been found out, by which men are rendered agreeable to God before they are engrafted into Christ; as if Scripture spoke falsely when it says, "He that has the Son has life, and he that has not the Son of God has not life" (1 John 5:12). How can they produce the materials of life if they are dead? Is there no meaning in its being said that "whatsoever is not of faith is sin?" (Rom. 14:23); or can good fruit be produced from a bad tree? What have these most pestilential Sophists left to Christ on which to exert his virtue? They say that he merited for us the first grace, that is, the occasion of meriting, and that it is our part not to let slip the occasion thus offered. O the daring effrontery of impiety! Who would have thought that men professing the name of Christ would thus strip him of his power, and all but trample him under foot? The testimony uniformly borne to him in Scripture is that whoso believeth in him is justified; the doctrine of these men is, that the only benefit which proceeds from him is to open up a way for each to justify himself. I wish they could get a taste of what is meant by these passages: "He that hath the Son hath life." "He that heareth my word, and believeth in him that sent me," "is passed from death unto life." Whoso believeth in him "is passed from death unto life." "Being justified freely by his grace, through the redemption that is in Christ Jesus." "He that keepeth his commandments dwelleth in him, and he in him." God "has raised us up together, and made us sit together in heavenly

places in Christ." "Who has delivered us from the power of darkness, and has translated us into the kingdom of his dear Son." There are similar passages without number. Their meaning is not, that by faith in Christ an opportunity is given us of procuring justifications or acquiring salvation, but that both are given us. Hence, so soon as you are engrafted into Christ by faith, you are made a son of God, an heir of heaven, a partaker of righteousness, a possessor of life, and (the better to manifest the false tenets of these men) you have not obtained an opportunity of meriting, but all the merits of Christ, since they are communicated to you.

7. In this way the schools of Sorbonne, the parents of all heresies, have deprived us of justification by faith, which lies at the root of all godliness. They confess, indeed, in word, that men are justified by a formed faith, but they afterwards explain this to mean that of faith they have good works which avail to justification, so that they almost seem to use the term "faith" in mockery, because they were unable, without incurring great obloquy, to pass it in silence, seeing it is so often repeated by Scripture. And yet not contented with this, they by the praise of good works transfer to man what they steal from God. And seeing that good works give little ground for exultation, and are not even properly called merits, if they are regarded as the fruits of divine grace, they derive them from the power of free-will; in other words, extract oil out of stone. They deny not that the principal cause is in grace; but they contend that there is no exclusion of free-will through which all merit comes. This is the doctrine, not only of the later Sophists, but of Lombard their Pythagoras (*Sent.* Lib. 2, Dist. 28), who, in comparison of them, may be called sound and sober. It was surely strange blindness, while he had Augustine so often in his mouth, not to see how cautiously he guarded against ascribing a single particle of praise to man because of good works. Above, when treating of free-will, we quoted some passages from him to this effect, and similar passages frequently occur in his writings (see in Ps. 104;

Ep. 105), as when he forbids us ever to boast of our merits, because they themselves also are the gifts of God, and when he says that all our merits are only of grace, are not provided by our sufficiency, but are entirely the production of grace, &c. It is less strange that Lombard was blind to the light of Scripture, in which it is obvious that he had not been a very successful student. Still there cannot be a stronger declaration against him and his disciples than the words of the Apostles who, after interdicting all Christians from glorying, subjoins the reason why glorying is unlawful: "For we are his workmanship, created in Christ Jesus unto good works, which God has before ordained that we should walk in them" (Eph. 2:10). Seeing, then, that no good proceeds from us unless insofar as we are regenerated—and our regeneration is without exception wholly of God—there is no ground for claiming to ourselves one iota in good works. Lastly, while these men constantly inculcate good works, they, at the same time, train the conscience in such a way as to prevent it from venturing to confide that works will render God favorable and propitious. We, on the contrary, without any mention of merit, give singular comfort to believers when we teach them that in their works they please, and doubtless are accepted of God. Nay, here we even insist that no man shall attempt or enter upon any work without faith, that is, unless he previously have a firm conviction that it will please God.

8. Wherefore, let us never on any account allow ourselves to be drawn away one nail's breadth from that only foundation. After it is laid, wise architects build upon it rightly and in order. For whether there is need of doctrine or exhortation, they remind us that "for this purpose the Son of God was manifested, that he might destroy the works of the devil;" that "whosoever is born of God does not commit sin;" that "the time past of our life may suffice us to have wrought the will of the Gentiles;" that the elect of God are vessels of mercy, appointed "to honor," purged, "sanctified, and meet for the Master's use, and prepared unto every good work." The whole is expressed at

once, when Christ thus describes his disciples, "If any man will come after me, let him deny himself, and take up his cross daily, and follow me." He who has denied himself has cut off the root of all evils so as no longer to seek his own; he who has taken up his cross has prepared himself for all meekness and endurance. The example of Christ includes this and all offices of piety and holiness. He obeyed his Father even unto death; his whole life was spent in doing the works of God; his whole soul was intent on the glory of his Father; he laid down his life for the brethren; he did good to his enemies, and prayed for them. And when there is need of comfort, it is admirably afforded in these words: "We are troubled on every side, yet not distressed; we are perplexed, but not in despair; persecuted but not forsaken; cast down, but not destroyed; always bearing about in the body the dying of the Lord Jesus, that the life also of Jesus might be made manifest in our body." "For if we be dead with him we shall also live with him; if we suffer, we shall also reign with him;" by means of "the fellowship of his sufferings, being made conformable unto his death;" the Father having predestinated us "to be conformed to the image of his Son, that he might be the firstborn among many brethren." Hence it is, that "neither death, nor life, nor angels, nor principalities, nor powers, nor things present, nor things to come, nor height, nor depth, nor any other creature, shall be able to separate us from the love of God which is in Christ Jesus our Lord;" nay, rather all things will work together for our good. See how it is that we do not justify men before God by works, but say, that all who are of God are regenerated and made new creatures, so that they pass from the kingdom of sin into the kingdom of righteousness. In this way they make their calling sure, and, like trees, are judged by their fruits.

Study Guide Questions

Section 1

1. For Calvin, what is justification by faith alone?

Section 2

1. What problem does Calvin have with the use of the word "merit"?
2. Can someone use it without corrupting the gospel?

Section 3

1. If we don't use the word "merit," what place is there for good works?
2. What don't we do like the Sophists?

Section 4

1. How does Calvin handle the appeal from Ecclesiasticus?
2. What is the problem with our good works?

Section 5

1. What is the sole foundation for our lives, according to Calvin?
2. What did Jesus not come to do?
3. If Christ is all, what follows?

Section 6

1. What are those in the state of death unable to do?

Section 7

1. What is the mother of all errors?
2. What is the sum of all piety?
3. What must happen in order for any good to proceed from us at all?
4. Does justification by faith alone prevent us from cheering the hearts of believers?

Section 8

1. What must we refuse to let happen?

CHAPTER 16

Refuutation of calumnies by which it is attempted to throw
odium on this doctrine.

The divisions of this chapter are—
I. The calumnies of the Papists against the orthodox doctrine
of Justification by Faith are reduced to two classes. The first class, with
its consequences, refuted, sec. 1-3.

II. The second class, which is dependent on the first, refuted in the
last section.

Outline:

1. Calumnies of the Papists. 1. That we destroy good works, and
give encouragement to sin. Refutation of the first calumny. 1. Character of those who censure us. 2. Justification by faith establishes the
necessity of good works.

2. Refutation of a consequent of the former calumny—viz. that men
are dissuaded from well-doing when we destroy merit. Two modes of
refutation. First mode confirmed by many invincible arguments.

3. The Apostles make no mention of merit, when they exhort us to
good works. On the contrary, excluding merit, they refer us entirely to
the mercy of God. Another mode of refutation.

4. Refutation of the second calumny and of an inference from it—viz. that the obtaining righteousness is made too easy, when it is made to consist in the free remission of sins.

Our last sentence may refute the impudent calumny of certain ungodly men, who charge us, first, with destroying good works and leading men away from the study of them, when we say, that men are not justified, and do not merit salvation by works; and, secondly, with making the means of justification too easy, when we say that it consists in the free remission of sins, and thus alluring men to sin to which they are already too much inclined. These calumnies, I say, are sufficiently refuted by that one sentence; however, I will briefly reply to both. The allegation is that justification by faith destroys good works. I will not describe what kind of zealots for good works the persons are who thus charge us. We leave them as much liberty to bring the charge, as they take license to taint the whole world with the pollution of their lives. They pretend to lament that when faith is so highly extolled, works are deprived of their proper place. But what if they are rather ennobled and established? We dream not of a faith which is devoid of good works, nor of a justification which can exist without them: the only difference is, that while we acknowledge that faith and works are necessarily connected, we, however, place justification in faith, not in works. How this is done is easily explained, if we turn to Christ only, to whom our faith is directed and from whom it derives all its power. Why, then, are we justified by faith? Because by faith we apprehend the righteousness of Christ, which alone reconciles us to God. This faith, however, you cannot apprehend without at the same time apprehending sanctification; for Christ "is made unto us wisdom, and righteousness, and sanctification, and redemption" (1 Cor. 1:30). Christ, therefore, justifies no man without also sanctifying him. These blessings are conjoined by a perpetual and inseparable tie. Those whom he enlightens by his wisdom he redeems;

whom he redeems he justifies; whom he justifies he sanctifies. But as the question relates only to justification and sanctification, to them let us confine ourselves. Though we distinguish between them, they are both inseparably comprehended in Christ. Would ye then obtain justification in Christ? You must previously possess Christ. But you cannot possess him without being made a partaker of his sanctification: for Christ cannot be divided. Since the Lord, therefore, does not grant us the enjoyment of these blessings without bestowing himself, he bestows both at once but never the one without the other. Thus it appears how true it is that we are justified not without, and yet not by works, since in the participation of Christ, by which we are justified, is contained not less sanctification than justification.

2. It is also most untrue that men's minds are withdrawn from the desire of well-doing when we deprive them of the idea of merit. Here, by the way, the reader must be told that those men absurdly infer merit from reward, as I will afterwards more clearly explain. They thus infer, because ignorant of the principle that God gives no less a display of his liberality when he assigns reward to works, than when he bestows the faculty of well-doing. This topic it will be better to defer to its own place. At present, let it be sufficient merely to advert to the weakness of their objection. This may be done in two ways. For, first, they are altogether in error when they say that, unless a hope of reward is held forth, no regard will be had to the right conduct of life. For if all that men do when they serve God is to look to the reward, and hire out or sell their labor to him, little is gained: he desires to be freely worshiped, freely loved: I say he approves the worshiper who, even if all hope of reward were cut off, would cease not to worship him. Moreover, when men are to be urged, there cannot be a stronger stimulus than that derived from the end of our redemption and calling, such as the word of God employs when it says, that it were the height of impiety and ingratitude not to "love him who first loved us;" that by "the blood of Christ" our conscience is purged "from dead

works to serve the living God;" that it were impious sacrilege in anyone to count "the blood of the covenant, wherewith he was sanctified,
an unholy thing;" that we have been "delivered out of the hands of
our enemies," that we "might serve him without fear, in holiness and
righteousness before him, all the days of our life;" that being "made
free from sin," we "become the servants of righteousness;" "that our
old man is crucified with him," in order that we might rise to newness of life. Again, "if ye then be risen with Christ (as becomes his
members), seek those things which are above," living as pilgrims in
the world, and aspiring to heaven, where our treasure is. "The grace
of God has appeared to all men, bringing salvation, teaching us that,
denying ungodliness and worldly lusts, we should live soberly, righteously, and godly in this present world; looking for that blessed hope,
and the glorious appearing of the great God and our Savior Jesus
Christ." "For God has not appointed us to wrath, but to obtain salvation through our Lord Jesus Christ." "Know ye not that ye are the
temples of the Holy Spirit," which it were impious to profane? "Ye
were sometimes darkness, but now are ye light in the Lord: walk as
the children of light." "God has not called us unto uncleanness, but
unto holiness." "For this is the will of God, even your sanctification,
that ye should abstain" from all illicit desires: ours is a "holy calling,"
and we respond not to it except by purity of life. "Being then made
free from sin, ye became the servants of righteousness." Can there
be a stronger argument in eliciting us to charity than that of John?
"If God so loved us, we ought also to love one another." "In this the
children of God are manifest, and the children of the devil: whosoever does not righteousness is not of God, neither he that loveth not
his brother." Similar is the argument of Paul, "Know ye not that your
bodies are the members of Christ?" "For as the body is one, and has
many members, and all the members of that one body being many, are
one body, so also is Christ." Can there be a stronger incentive to holiness than when we are told by John, "Every man that has this hope

in him purifieth himself; even as he is pure?" and by Paul, "Having, therefore, these promises, dearly beloved, cleanse yourselves from all filthiness of the flesh and spirit;" or when we hear our Savior hold forth himself as an example to us that we should follow his steps?

3. I have given these few passages merely as a specimen; for were I to go over them all, I should form a large volume. All the Apostles abound in exhortations, admonitions and rebukes, for the purpose of training the man of God to every good work, and that without any mention of merit. Nay, rather their chief exhortations are founded on the fact, that without any merit of ours, our salvation depends entirely on the mercy of God. Thus Paul, who during a whole Epistle had maintained that there was no hope of life for us save in the righteousness of Christ, when he comes to exhortations beseeches us by the mercy which God has bestowed upon us (Rom. 12:1). And indeed, this one reason ought to have been sufficient, that God may be glorified in us. But if any are not so ardently desirous to promote the glory of God, still the remembrance of his kindness is most sufficient to incite them to do good (see Chrysost. *Homily. in Genes.*). But those men, because, by introducing the idea of merit, they perhaps extract some forced and servile obedience of the Law, falsely allege, that as we do not adopt the same course, we have no means of exhorting to good works. As if God were well pleased with such services when he declares that he loves a cheerful giver, and forbids anything to be given him grudgingly or of necessity (2 Cor. 9:7). I say not that I would reject that or omit any kind of exhortation which Scripture employs, its object being not to leave any method of animating us untried. For it states, that the recompense which God will render to everyone is according to his deeds; but, first, I deny that that is the only, or, in many instances, the principal motive; and, secondly, I admit not that it is the motive with which we are to begin. Moreover, I maintain that it gives not the least countenance to those merits which these men are always preaching. This will afterwards be seen. Lastly, there is no use

in this recompense, unless we have previously embraced the doctrine that we are justified solely by the merits of Christ as apprehended by faith, and not by any merit of works; because the study of piety can be fitly prosecuted only by those by whom this doctrine has been previously imbibed. This is beautifully intimated by the Psalmist when he thus addresses God, "There is forgiveness with thee, that thou mayest be feared" (Ps. 130:4). For he shows that the worship of God cannot exist without acknowledging his mercy, on which it is founded and established. This is specially deserving of notice, as showing us not only that the beginning of the due worship of God is confidence in his mercy; but that the fear of God (which Papists will have to be meritorious) cannot be entitled to the name of merit, for this reason, that it is founded on the pardon and remission of sins.

4. But the most futile calumny of all is, that men are invited to sin when we affirm that the pardon in which we hold that justification consists is gratuitous. Our doctrine is, that justification is a thing of such value, that it cannot be put into the balance with any good quality of ours; and, therefore, could never be obtained unless it were gratuitous: moreover, that it is gratuitous to us, but not also to Christ, who paid so dearly for it; namely his own most sacred blood, out of which there was no price of sufficient value to pay what was due to the justice of God. When men are thus taught they are reminded that it is owing to no merit of theirs that the shedding of that most sacred blood is not repeated every time they sin. Moreover, we say that our pollution is so great, that it can never be washed away save in the fountain of his pure blood. Must not those who are thus addressed conceive a greater horror of sin than if it were said to be wiped off by a sprinkling of good works? If they have any reverence for God, how can they, after being once purified, avoid shuddering at the thought of again wallowing in the mire, and as much as in them lies troubling and polluting the purity of this fountain? "I have washed my feet" (says the believing soul in the Song of Solomon, 5:3), "how shall I

defile them?" It is now plain which of the two makes the forgiveness of sins of less value, and derogates from the dignity of justification. They pretend that God is appeased by their frivolous satisfactions; in other words, by mere dross. We maintain that the guilt of sin is too heinous to be so frivolously expiated; that the offense is too grave to be forgiven to such valueless satisfactions; and, therefore, that forgiveness is the prerogative of Christ's blood alone. They say that righteousness, wherever it is defective, is renewed and repaired by works of satisfaction. We think it too precious to be balanced by any compensation of works, and, therefore, in order to restore it, recourse must be had solely to the mercy of God. For the other points relating to the forgiveness of sins, see the following chapter.

Study Guide Questions

Section 1

1. What slanderous charge does Calvin answer next?

2. How does Calvin answer this?

3. So what is the relationship of our salvation to our works?

Section 2

1. Does Calvin acknowledge rewards?

2. What is our calling?

Section 3

1. Does Calvin acknowledge that God will render to each man according to his works?

2. What is necessary before men are fit to pursue holiness?

Section 4

1. Is free grace free all around?

2. Our salvation is therefore too precious for what?

CHAPTER 17

The promises of the law and the gospel reconciled.

In the following chapter, the arguments of Sophists, who would destroy or impair the doctrine of Justification by Faith, are reduced to two classes. The former is general, the latter special, and contains some arguments peculiar to itself.

I. The first class, which is general, and in a manner contains the foundation of all the arguments, draws an argument from the promises of the law. This is considered from sec. 1-3.

II. The second class following from the former, and containing special proofs. An argument drawn from the history of Cornelius explained, sec. 4-5.

III. A full exposition of those passages of Scripture which represent God as showing mercy and favor to the cultivators of righteousness, sec. 6.

IV. A third argument from the passages which distinguish good works by the name of righteousness, and declare that men are justified by them, sec. 7-8.

V. The adversaries of justification by faith placed in a dilemma. Their partial righteousness refuted, sec. 9-10.

VI. A fourth argument, setting the Apostle James in opposition to Paul, considered, sec. 11-12.

VII. Answer to a fifth argument, that, according to Paul, not the hearers but the doers of the law are justified, sec. 13.

VIII. Consideration of a sixth argument, drawn from those passages in which believers boldly submit their righteousness to the judgment of God, and ask him to decide according to it, sec. 14.

IX. Examination of the last argument, drawn from passages which ascribe righteousness and life to the ways of believers, sec. 15.

Outline:

1. Brief summary of Chapters 15 and 16. Why justification is denied to works. Argument of opponents founded on the promises of the law. The substance of this argument. Answer. Those who would be justified before God must be exempted from the power of the law. How this is done.

2. Confirmation of the answer *ab impossibili*, and from the testimony of an Apostle and of David.

3. Answer to the objection, by showing why these promises were given. Refutation of the sophistical distinction between the intrinsic value of works, and their value *ex pacto*.

4. Argument from the history of Cornelius. Answer, by distinguishing between two kinds of acceptance. Former kind. Sophistical objection refuted.

5. Latter kind. Plain from this distinction that Cornelius was accepted freely before his good works could be accepted. Similar explanations to be given of the passage in which God is represented as merciful and propitious to the cultivators of righteousness.

6. Exposition of these passages. Necessary to observe whether the promise is legal or evangelical. The legal promise always made under the condition that we "do," the evangelical under the condition that we "believe."

7. Argument from the passages which distinguish good works by the name of righteousness, and declare that man is justified by them. Answer to the former part of the argument respecting the name. Why the works of the saints called works of righteousness. Distinction to be observed.

8. Answer to the second part of the argument—viz. that man is justified by works. Works of no avail by themselves; we are justified by faith only. This kind of righteousness defined. Whence the value set on good works.

9. Answer confirmed and fortified by a dilemma.

10. In what sense the partial imperfect righteousness of believers accepted. Conclusion of the refutation.

11. Argument founded on the Epistle of James. First answer. One Apostle cannot be opposed to another. Second answer. Third answer, from the scope of James. A double paralogism in the term "faith." In James the faith said not to justify is a mere empty opinion; in Paul it is the instrument by which we apprehend Christ our righteousness.

12. Another paralogism on the word "justify." Paul speaks of the cause, James of the effects, of justification. Sum of the discussion.

13. Argument founded on Rom. 2:13. Answer, explaining the Apostle's meaning. Another argument, containing a *reductio ad impossibili*. Why Paul used the argument.

14. An argument founded on the passages in which believers confidently appeal to their righteousness. Answer, founded on a consideration of two circumstances. 1. They refer only to a special cause. 2. They claim righteousness in comparison with the wicked.

15. Last argument from those passages which ascribe righteousness and life to the ways of believers. Answer. This proceeds from the paternal kindness of God. What meant by the perfection of saints.

Let us now consider the other arguments which Satan by his satellites invents to destroy or impair the doctrine of Justification by

Faith. I think we have already put it out of the power of our calumniators to treat us as if we were the enemies of good works—justification
being denied to works not in order that no good works may be done
or that those which are done may be denied to be good; but only that
we may not trust or glory in them, or ascribe salvation to them. Our
only confidence and boasting, our only anchor of salvation is, that
Christ the Son of God is ours, and that we are in him sons of God
and heirs of the heavenly kingdom, being called, not by our worth, but
the kindness of God, to the hope of eternal blessedness. But since, as
has been said, they assail us with other engines, let us now proceed to
demolish them also. First, they recur to the legal promises which the
Lord proclaimed to the observers of the law, and they ask us whether
we hold them to be null or effectual. Since it were absurd and ridiculous to say they are null, they take it for granted that they have some
efficacy. Hence they infer that we are not justified by faith only. For
the Lord thus speaks: "Wherefore it shall come to pass, if ye hearken
to these judgments, and keep and do them, that the Lord thy God
shall keep unto thee the covenant and the mercy which he swore unto
thy fathers; and he will love thee, and bless thee and multiply thee"
(Deut. 7:12-13). Again, "If ye thoroughly amend your ways and your
doings; if ye thoroughly execute judgment between a man and his
neighbor; if ye oppress not the stranger, the fatherless, and the widow,
and shed not innocent blood in this place, neither walk after other
gods to your hurt: then will I cause you to dwell in this place, in the
land that I gave to your fathers, for ever and ever" (Jer. 7:5-7). It were
to no purpose to quote a thousand similar passages, which, as they are
not different in meaning, are to be explained on the same principle. In
substance, Moses declares that in the law is set down "a blessing and a
curse," life and death (Deut. 11:26); and hence they argue, either that
that blessing is become inactive and unfruitful, or that justification
is not by faith only. We have already shown, that if we cleave to the
law we are devoid of every blessing, and have nothing but the curse

denounced on all transgressors. The Lord does not promise anything except to the perfect observers of the law; and none such are any where to be found. The result, therefore, is that the whole human race is convicted by the law, and exposed to the wrath and curse of God: to be saved from this they must escape from the power of the law, and be, as it were, brought out of bondage into freedom—not that carnal freedom which indisposes us for the observance of the law, tends to licentiousness, and allows our passions to wanton unrestrained with loosened reins; but that spiritual freedom which consoles and raises up the alarmed and smitten conscience, proclaiming its freedom from the curse and condemnation under which it was formerly held bound. This freedom from subjection to the law, this manumission, if I may so express it, we obtain when by faith we apprehend the mercy of God in Christ, and are thereby assured of the pardon of sins, with a consciousness of which the law stung and tortured us.

2. For this reason, the promises offered in the law would all be null and ineffectual, did not God in his goodness send the gospel to our aid, since the condition on which they depend, and under which only they are to be performed—viz. the fulfillment of the law, will never be accomplished. Still, however, the aid which the Lord gives consists not in leaving part of justification to be obtained by works, and in supplying part out of his indulgence, but in giving us Christ as in himself alone the fulfillment of righteousness. For the Apostle, after premising that he and the other Jews, aware that "a man is not justified by the works of the law," had "believed in Jesus Christ," adds as the reason, not that they might be assisted to make up the sum of righteousness by faith in Christ, but that they "might be justified by the faith of Christ, and not by the works of the law" (Gal. 2:16). If believers withdraw from the law to faith, that in the latter they may find the justification which they see is not in the former, they certainly disclaim justification by the law. Therefore, whoso will, let him amplify the rewards which are said to await the observer of the law, provided

he at the same time understand, that owing to our depravity, we derive no benefit from them until we have obtained another righteousness by faith. Thus David after making mention of the reward which the Lord has prepared for his servants (Ps. 25 almost throughout), immediately descends to an acknowledgment of sins, by which the reward is made void. In Psalm 19, also, he loudly extols the benefits of the law; but immediately exclaims, "Who can understand his errors? cleanse thou me from secret faults" (Ps. 19:12). This passage perfectly accords with the former, when, after saying, "the paths of the Lord are mercy and truth unto such as keep his covenant and his testimonies," he adds, "For thy name's sake, O Lord, pardon mine iniquity: for it is great" (Ps. 25:10-11). Thus, too, we ought to acknowledge that the favor of God is offered to us in the law, provided by our works we can deserve it; but that it never actually reaches us through any such desert.

3. What then? Were the promises given that they might vanish away without fruit? I lately declared that this is not my opinion. I say, indeed, that their efficacy does not extend to us so long as they have respect to the merit of works, and, therefore, that, considered in themselves, they are in some sense abolished. Hence the Apostle shows, that the celebrated promise, "Ye shall therefore keep my statutes and my judgments: which if a man do, he shall live in them" (Lev. 18:5; Ezek. 20:10), will, if we stop at it, be of no avail, and will profit us not a whit more than if it were not given, being inaccessible even to the holiest servants of God, who are all far from fulfilling the law, being encompassed with many infirmities. But when the gospel promises are substituted, promises which announce the free pardon of sins, the result is not only that our persons are accepted of God, but his favor also is shown to our works, and that not only in respect that the Lord is pleased with them, but also because he visits them with the blessings which were due by agreement to the observance of his law. I admit, therefore, that the works of the faithful are rewarded

with the promises which God gave in his law to the cultivators of righteousness and holiness; but in this reward we should always attend to the cause which procures favor to works. This cause, then, appears to be threefold. First, God turning his eye away from the works of his servants which merit reproach more than praise, embraces them in Christ, and by the intervention of faith alone reconciles them to himself without the aid of works. Secondly the works not being estimated by their own worth, he, by his fatherly kindness and indulgence, honors so far as to give them some degree of value. Thirdly, he extends his pardon to them, not imputing the imperfection by which they are all polluted, and would deserve to be regarded as vices rather than virtues. Hence it appears how much Sophists were deluded in thinking they admirably escaped all absurdities when they said, that works are able to merit salvation, not from their intrinsic worth, but according to agreement, the Lord having, in his liberality, set this high value upon them. But, meanwhile, they observed not how far the works which they insisted on regarding as meritorious must be from fulfilling the condition of the promises, were they not preceded by a justification founded on faith alone, and on forgiveness of sins—a forgiveness necessary to cleanse even good works from their stains. Accordingly, of the three causes of divine liberality to which it is owing that good works are accepted, they attended only to one: the other two, though the principal causes, they suppressed.

4. They quote the saying of Peter as given by Luke in the Acts, "Of a truth I perceive that God is no respecter of persons: but in every nation he that feareth him, and worketh righteousness, is accepted with him" (Acts 10:34-35). And hence they infer, as a thing which seems to them beyond a doubt, that if man by right conduct procures the favor of God, his obtaining salvation is not entirely the gift of God. Nay, that when God in his mercy assists the sinner, he is inclined to mercy by works. There is no way of reconciling the passages of Scripture, unless you observe that man's acceptance with God is

twofold. As man is by nature, God finds nothing in him which can incline him to mercy, except merely big wretchedness. If it is clear then that man, when God first interposes for him, is naked and destitute of all good, and, on the other hand, loaded and filled with all kinds of evil—for what quality, pray, shall we say that he is worthy of the heavenly kingdom? Where God thus clearly displays free mercy, have done with that empty imagination of merit. Another passage in the same book—viz. where Cornelius hears from the lips of an angel, "Thy prayer and thine alms are come up for a memorial before God" (Acts 10:4), is miserably wrested to prove that man is prepared by the study of good works to receive the favor of God. Cornelius being endued with true wisdom, in other words, with the fear of God, must have been enlightened by the Spirit of wisdom, and being an observer of righteousness, must have been sanctified by the same Spirit; righteousness being, as the Apostle testifies, one of the most certain fruits of the Spirit (Gal. 5:5). Therefore, all those qualities by which he is said to have pleased God he owed to divine grace: so far was he from preparing himself by his own strength to receive it. Indeed, not a syllable of Scripture can be produced which does not accord with the doctrine, that the only reason why God receives man into his favor is, because he sees that he is in every respect lost when left to himself; lost, if he does not display his mercy in delivering him. We now see that in thus accepting, God looks not to the righteousness of the individual, but merely manifests the divine goodness towards miserable sinners, who are altogether undeserving of this great mercy.

5. But after the Lord has withdrawn the sinner from the abyss of perdition, and set him apart for himself by means of adoption, having begotten him again and formed him to newness of life, he embraces him as a new creature, and bestows the gifts of his Spirit. This is the acceptance to which Peter refers, and by which believers after their calling are approved by God even in respect of works; for the Lord cannot but love and delight in the good qualities which he

produces in them by means of his Spirit. But we must always bear in mind, that the only way in which men are accepted of God in respect of works is, that whatever good works he has conferred upon those whom he admits to favor, he by an increase of liberality honors with his acceptance. For whence their good works, but just that the Lord having chosen them as vessels of honor, is pleased to adorn them with true purity? And how are their actions deemed good as if there was no deficiency in them, but just that their merciful Father indulgently pardons the spots and blemishes which adhere to them? In one word, the only meaning of acceptance in this passage is, that God accepts and takes pleasure in his children, in whom he sees the traces and lineaments of his own countenance. We have elsewhere said, that regeneration is a renewal of the divine image in us. Since God, therefore, whenever he beholds his own face, justly loves it and holds it in honor, the life of believers, when formed to holiness and justice, is said, not without cause, to be pleasing to him. But because believers, while encompassed with mortal flesh, are still sinners, and their good works only begun savor of the corruption of the flesh, God cannot be propitious either to their persons or their works, unless he embraces them more in Christ than in themselves. In this way are we to understand the passages in which God declares that he is clement and merciful to the cultivators of righteousness. Moses said to the Israelites, "Know, therefore, that the Lord thy God, he is God, the faithful God, which keepeth covenant and mercy with them that love him and keep his commandments, to a thousand generations." These words afterwards became a common form of expression among the people. Thus Solomon in his prayer at the dedication says, "Lord God of Israel, there is no God like thee, in heaven above, or on earth beneath, who keepest covenant and mercy with thy servants that walk before thee with all their heart" (1 Kings 8:23). The same words are repeated by Nehemiah (Neh. 1:5). As the Lord in all covenants of mercy stipulates on his part for integrity and holiness of life in his servants (Deut. 29:18), lest his goodness might be held in derision, or anyone, puffed up with exultation in it, might speak flatteringly to his soul while walking in the depravity of his heart, so he is pleased that in this way those whom he admits to communion in the covenant should be kept to their duty. Still, however, the covenant was gratuitous at first, and such it ever remains. Accordingly, while David declares, "according to the cleanness of my hands has he recompensed me," yet does he not omit the fountain to which I have referred; "he delivered me, because he delighted in me" (2 Sam. 22:20-21). In commending the goodness of his cause, he derogates in no respect from the free mercy which takes precedence of all the gifts of which it is the origin.

6. Here, by the way, it is of importance to observe how those forms of expression differ from legal promises. By legal promises, I mean not those which lie scattered in the books of Moses (for there many Evangelical promises occur), but those which properly belong to the legal dispensation. All such promises, by whatever name they may be called, are made under the condition that the reward is to be paid on the things commanded being done. But when it is said that the Lord keeps a covenant of mercy with those who love him, the words rather demonstrate what kind of servants those are who have sincerely entered into the covenant, than express the reason why the Lord blesses them. The nature of the demonstration is this: As the end for which God bestows upon us the gift of eternal life is, that he may be loved, feared, and worshiped by us, so the end of all the promises of mercy contained in Scripture justly is that we may reverence and serve their author. Therefore, whenever we hear that he does good to those that observe his law, let us remember that the sons of God are designated by the duty which they ought perpetually to observe, that his reason for adopting us is, that we may reverence him as a father. Hence, if we would not deprive ourselves of the privilege of adoption, we must always strive in the direction of our calling. On the other hand, however, let us remember, that the completion of the Divine mercy depends

not on the works of believers, but that God himself fulfill the promise of salvation to those who by right conduct correspond to their calling, because he recognizes the true badges of sons in those only who are directed to good by his Spirit. To this we may refer what is said of the members of the Church, "Lord, who shall abide in thy tabernacle? who shall dwell in thy holy hill? He that walketh uprightly, and worketh righteousness, and speaketh the truth in his heart," &c. (Ps. 15:1-2). Again, in Isaiah, "Who among us shall dwell with the devouring fire? who among us shall dwell with everlasting burnings? He that walketh righteously," &c. (Isa. 33:14-15). For the thing described is not the strength with which believers can stand before the Lord, but the manner in which our most merciful Father introduces them into his fellowship, and defends and confirms them therein. For as he detests sin and loves righteousness, so those whom he unites to himself he purifies by his Spirit, that he may render them conformable to himself and to his kingdom. Therefore, if it be asked, What is the first cause which gives the saints free access to the kingdom of God, and a firm and permanent footing in it? the answer is easy. The Lord in his mercy once adopted and ever defends them. But if the question relates to the manner, we must descend to regeneration, and the fruits of it, as enumerated in the fifteenth Psalm.

7. There seems much more difficulty in those passages which distinguish good works by the name of righteousness, and declare that man is justified by them. The passages of the former class are very numerous, as when the observance of the commandments is termed "justification" or "righteousness." Of the other classes we have a description in the words of Moses, "It shall be our righteousness, if we observe to do all these commandments" (Deut. 6:25). But if you object, that it is a legal promise, which, having an impossible condition annexed to it, proves nothing, there are other passages to which the same answer cannot be made; for instance, "If the man be poor," "thou shalt deliver him the pledge again when the sun goes down:" "and it

shall be righteousness unto thee before the Lord thy God" (Deut. 24:13). Likewise the words of the prophet, "Then stood up Phineas, and executed judgment: and so the plague was stayed. And that was counted unto him for righteousness unto all generations for evermore" (Ps. 106:30-31). Accordingly the Pharisees of our day think they have here full scope for exultation. For, as we say, that when justification by faith is established, justification by works falls; they argue on the same principle, If there is a justification by works, it is false to say that we are justified by faith only. When I grant that the precepts of the law are termed "righteousness," I do nothing strange: for they are so in reality. I must, however, inform the reader, that the Hebrew word *miqh* has been rendered by the Septuagint, not very appropriately, *dikaiomata*, "justifications," instead of "edicts." But I readily give up any dispute as to the word. Nor do I deny that the Law of God contains a perfect righteousness. For although we are debtors to do all the things which it enjoins, and, therefore, even after a full obedience, are unprofitable servants; yet, as the Lord has deigned to give it the name of righteousness, it is not ours to take from it what he has given. We readily admit, therefore, that the perfect obedience of the law is righteousness, and the observance of any precept a part of righteousness, the whole substance of righteousness being contained in the remaining parts. But we deny that any such righteousness ever exists. Hence we discard the righteousness of the law, not as being in itself maimed and defective, but because of the weakness of our flesh it nowhere appears. But then Scripture does not merely call the precepts of the law righteousness, it also gives this name to the works of the saints: as when it states that Zacharias and his wife "were both righteous before God, walking in all the commandments and ordinances of the Lord blameless" (Luke 1:6). Surely when it thus speaks, it estimates works more according to the nature of the law than their own proper character. And here, again, I must repeat the observation which I lately made, that the law is not to be ascertained from a careless translation of the Greek interpreter. Still, as Luke chose not to make any change on the received version, I will not contend for this. The things contained in the law God enjoined upon man for righteousness but that righteousness we attain not unless by observing the whole law: every transgression whatever destroys it. While, therefore, the law commands nothing but righteousness, if we look to itself, every one of its precepts is righteousness: if we look to the men by whom they are performed, being transgressors in many things, they by no means merit the praise of righteousness for one work, and that a work which, through the imperfection adhering to it, is always in some respect vicious.

8. I come to the second class (sec. 1, 7, ad init.), in which the chief difficulty lies. Paul finds nothing stronger to prove justification by faith than that which is written of Abraham, he "believed God, and it was counted unto him for righteousness" (Rom. 4:3; Gal. 3:6). Therefore, when it is said that the achievement of Phineas "was counted unto him for righteousness" (Ps. 106:30-31), we may argue that what Paul contends for respecting faith applies also to works. Our opponents, accordingly, as if the point were proved, set it down that though we are not justified without faith, it is not by faith only; that our justification is completed by works. Here I beseech believers, as they know that the true standard of righteousness must be derived from Scripture alone, to consider with me seriously and religiously, how Scripture can be fairly reconciled with that view. Paul, knowing that justification by faith was the refuge of those who wanted righteousness of their own, confidently infers, that all who are justified by faith are excluded from the righteousness of works. But as it is clear that this justification is common to all believers, he with equal confidence infers that no man is justified by works; nay, more, that justification is without any help from works. But it is one thing to determine what power works have in themselves, and another to determine what place they are to hold after justification by faith has been established.

If a price is to be put upon works according to their own worth, we hold that they are unfit to appear in the presence of God: that man, accordingly, has no works in which he can glory before God, and that hence, deprived of all aid from works, he is justified by faith alone. Justification, moreover, we thus define: The sinner being admitted into communion with Christ is, for his sake, reconciled to God; when purged by his blood he obtains the remission of sins, and clothed with righteousness, just as if it were his own, stands secure before the judgment seat of heaven. Forgiveness of sins being previously given, the good works which follow have a value different from their merit, because whatever is imperfect in them is covered by the perfection of Christ, and all their blemishes and pollutions are wiped away by his purity, so as never to come under the cognizance of the divine tribunal. The guilt of all transgressions, by which men are prevented from offering God an acceptable service, being thus effaced, and the imperfection which is wont to sully even good works being buried, the good works which are done by believers are deemed righteous, or, which is the same thing, are imputed for righteousness.

9. Now, should anyone state this to me as an objection to justification by faith, I would first ask him, Whether a man is deemed righteous for one holy work or two, while in all the other acts of his life he is a transgressor of the law? This were, indeed, more than absurd. I would next ask, Whether he is deemed righteous on account of many good works if he is guilty of transgression in some one part? Even this he will not venture to maintain in opposition to the authority of the law, which pronounces, "Cursed be he that confirmeth not all the words of this law to do them" (Deut. 27:26). I would go still farther and ask, Whether there be any work which may not justly be convicted of impurity or imperfection? How, then, will it appear to that eye before which even the heavens are not clean, and angels are chargeable with folly? (Job 4:18). Thus he will be forced to confess that no good work exists that is not defiled, both by contrary transgression

and also by its own corruption, so that it cannot be honored as righteousness. But if it is certainly owing to justification by faith that works, otherwise impure, unclean, defective, unworthy of the sight, not to say of the love of God, are imputed for righteousness, why do they by boasting of this imputation aim at the destruction of that justification, but for which the boast were vain? Are they desirous of having a viper's birth? To this their ungodly language tends. They cannot deny that justification by faith is the beginning, the foundation, the cause, the subject, the substance, of works of righteousness, and yet they conclude that justification is not by faith, because good works are counted for righteousness. Let us have done then with this frivolity, and confess the fact as it stands; if any righteousness which works are supposed to possess depends on justification by faith, this doctrine is not only not impaired, but on the contrary confirmed, its power being thereby more brightly displayed. Nor let us suppose, that after free justification works are commended, as if they afterwards succeeded to the office of justifying, or shared the office with faith. For did not justification by faith always remain entire, the impurity of works would be disclosed. There is nothing absurd in the doctrine, that though man is justified by faith, he is himself not only not righteous, but the righteousness attributed to his works is beyond their own deserts.

10. In this way we can admit not only that there is a partial righteousness in works (as our adversaries maintain), but that they are approved by God as if they were absolutely perfect. If we remember on what foundation this is rested, every difficulty will be solved. The first time when a work begins to be acceptable is when it is received with pardon. And whence pardon, but just because God looks upon us and all that belongs to us as in Christ? Therefore, as we ourselves when engrafted into Christ appear righteous before God, because our iniquities are covered with his innocence; so our works are, and are deemed righteous, because everything otherwise defective in them

being buried by the purity of Christ is not imputed. Thus we may justly say, that not only ourselves, but our works also, are justified by faith alone. Now, if that righteousness of works, whatever it be, depends on faith and free justification, and is produced by it, it ought to be included under it and, so to speak, made subordinate to it, as the effect to its cause; so far is it from being entitled to be set up to impair or destroy the doctrine of justification. Thus Paul, to prove that our blessedness depends not on our works, but on the mercy of God, makes special use of the words of David, "Blessed is he whose transgression is forgiven, whose sin is covered;" "Blessed is the man unto whom the Lord imputeth not iniquity." Should anyone here obtrude the numberless passages in which blessedness seems to be attributed to works, as, "Blessed is the man that feareth the Lord;" "He that has mercy on the poor, happy is he;" "Blessed is the man that walketh not in the counsel of the ungodly," and "that endureth temptation;" "Blessed are they that keep judgment," that are "pure in heart," "meek," "merciful," &c., they cannot make out that Paul's doctrine is not true. For seeing that the qualities thus extolled never all so exist in man as to obtain for him the approbation of God, it follows, that man is always miserable until he is exempted from misery by the pardon of his sins. Since, then, all the kinds of blessedness extolled in the Scripture are vain so that man derives no benefit from them until he obtains blessedness by the forgiveness of sins, a forgiveness which makes way for them, it follows that this is not only the chief and highest, but the only blessedness, unless you are prepared to maintain that it is impaired by things which owe their entire existence to it. There is much less to trouble us in the name of righteous which is usually given to believers. I admit that they are so called from the holiness of their lives, but as they rather exert themselves in the study of righteousness than fulfill righteousness itself, any degree of it which they possess must yield to justification by faith, to which it is owing that it is what it is.

11. But they say that we have a still more serious business with James, who in express terms opposes us. For he asks, "Was not Abraham our father justified by works?" and adds "You see then how that by works a man is justified, and not by faith only" (James 2:21, 24). What then? Will they engage Paul in a quarrel with James? If they hold James to be a servant of Christ, his sentiments must be understood as not dissenting from Christ speaking by the mouth of Paul. By the mouth of Paul the Spirit declares that Abraham obtained justification by faith, not by works; we also teach that all are justified by faith without the works of the law. By James the same Spirit declares that both Abraham's justification and ours consists of works, and not of faith only. It is certain that the Spirit cannot be at variance with himself. Where, then, will be the agreement? It is enough for our opponents, provided they can tear up that justification by faith which we regard as fixed by the deepest roots: to restore peace to the conscience is to them a matter of no great concern. Hence you may see, that though they indeed carp at the doctrine of justification by faith, they meanwhile point out no goal of righteousness at which the conscience may rest. Let them triumph then as they will, so long as the only victory they can boast of is, that they have deprived righteousness of all its certainty. This miserable victory they will indeed obtain when the light of truth is extinguished, and the Lord permits them to darken it with their lies. But wherever the truth of God stands they cannot prevail. I deny, then, that the passage of James which they are constantly holding up before us as if it were the shield of Achilles, gives them the slightest countenance. To make this plain, let us first attend to the scope of the Apostle, and then show wherein their hallucination consists. As at that time (and the evil has existed in the Church ever since) there were many who, while they gave manifest proof of their infidelity, by neglecting and omitting all the works peculiar to believers, ceased not falsely to glory in the name of faith, James here dissipates their vain confidence. His intention therefore

is, not to derogate in any degree from the power of true faith, but to show how absurdly these triflers laid claim only to the empty name, and resting satisfied with it, felt secure in unrestrained indulgence in vice. This state of matters being understood, it will be easy to see where the error of our opponents lies. They fall into a double paralogism, the one in the term "faith," the other in the term "justifying." The Apostle, in giving the name of faith to an empty opinion altogether differing from true faith, makes a concession which derogates in no respect from his case. This he demonstrates at the outset by the words, "What does it profit, my brethren, though a man say he has faith, and have not works?" (James 2:14). He says not, "If a man have faith without works," but "if he say that he has." This becomes still clearer when a little after he derides this faith as worse than that of devils, and at last when he calls it "dead." You may easily ascertain his meaning by the explanation, "Thou believest that there is one God." Surely if all which is contained in that faith is a belief in the existence of God, there is no wonder that it does not justify. The denial of such a power to it cannot be supposed to derogate in any degree from Christian faith, which is of a very different description. For how does true faith justify unless by uniting us to Christ, so that being made one with him, we may be admitted to a participation in his righteousness? It does not justify because it forms an idea of the divine existence, but because it reclines with confidence on the divine mercy.

12. We have not made good our point until we dispose of the other paralogism: since James places a part of justification in works. If you would make James consistent with the other Scriptures and with himself, you must give the word "justify," as used by him, a different meaning from what it has with Paul. In the sense of Paul we are said to be justified when the remembrance of our unrighteousness is obliterated and we are counted righteous. Had James had the same meaning it would have been absurd for him to quote the words of Moses, "Abraham believed God," &c. The context runs thus: "Was

not Abraham our father justified by works when he had offered Isaac his son upon the altar? Seest thou how faith wrought with his works, and by works was faith made perfect? And the Scripture was fulfilled which saith, Abraham believed God, and it was imputed unto him for righteousness." If it is absurd to say that the effect was prior to its cause, either Moses falsely declares in that passage that Abraham's faith was imputed for righteousness or Abraham, by his obedience in offering up Isaac, did not merit righteousness. Before the existence of Ishmael, who was a grown youth at the birth of Isaac, Abraham was justified by his faith. How then can we say that he obtained justification by an obedience which followed long after? Wherefore, either James erroneously inverts the proper order (this it were impious to suppose), or he meant not to say that he was justified, as if he deserved to be deemed just. What then? It appears certain that he is speaking of the manifestation, not of the imputation of righteousness, as if he had said, Those who are justified by true faith prove their justification by obedience and good works, not by a bare and imaginary semblance of faith. In one word, he is not discussing the mode of justification, but requiring that the justification of believers shall be operative. And as Paul contends that men are justified without the aid of works, so James will not allow any to be regarded as justified who are destitute of good works. Due attention to the scope will thus disentangle every doubt; for the error of our opponents lies chiefly in this, that they think James is defining the mode of justification, whereas his only object is to destroy the depraved security of those who vainly pretended faith as an excuse for their contempt of good works. Therefore, let them twist the words of James as they may, they will never extract out of them more than the two propositions: That an empty phantom of faith does not justify, and that the believer, not contented with such an imagination, manifests his justification by good works.

13. They gain nothing by quoting from Paul to the same effect, that "not the hearers of the law are just before God, but the doers of the

law shall be justified" (Rom. 2:13). I am unwilling to evade the difficulty by the solution of Ambrose, that Paul spoke thus because faith in Christ is the fulfillment of the law. This I regard as a mere subterfuge, and one too for which there is no occasion, as the explanation is perfectly obvious. The Apostle's object is to suppress the absurd confidence of the Jews who gave out that they alone had a knowledge of the law, though at the very time they were its greatest despisers. That they might not plume themselves so much on a bare acquaintance with the law, he reminds them that when justification is sought by the law, the thing required is not the knowledge but the observance of it. We certainly mean not to dispute that the righteousness of the law consists in works, and not only so, but that justification consists in the dignity and merits of works. But this proves not that we are justified by works unless they can produce someone who has fulfilled the law. That Paul had no other meaning is abundantly obvious from the context. After charging Jews and Gentiles in common with unrighteousness, he descends to particulars and says, that "as many as have sinned without law shall also perish without law," referring to the Gentiles, and that "as many as have sinned in the law shall be judged by the law," referring to the Jews. Moreover, as they, winking at their transgressions, boasted merely of the law, he adds most appropriately, that the law was passed with the view of justifying not those who only heard it, but those only who obeyed it; as if he had said, Do you seek righteousness in the law? do not bring forward the mere hearing of it, which is in itself of little weight, but bring works by which you may show that the law has not been given to you in vain. Since in these they were all deficient, it followed that they had no ground of boasting in the law. Paul's meaning, therefore, rather leads to an opposite argument. The righteousness of the law consists in the perfection of works; but no man can boast of fulfilling the law by works, and, therefore, there is no righteousness by the law.

14. They now betake themselves to those passages in which believers boldly submit their righteousness to the judgment of God, and wish to be judged accordingly; as in the following passages: "Judge me, O Lord, according to my righteousness, and according to mine integrity that is in me." Again, "Hear the right, O Lord;" "Thou hast proved mine heart; thou hast visited me in the night; thou hast tried me, and shalt find nothing." Again, "The Lord regarded me according to my righteousness; according to the cleanness of my hands has he recompensed me. For I have kept the ways of the Lord, and have not wickedly departed from my God." "I was also upright before him, and I kept myself from mine iniquity." Again, "Judge me, O Lord; for I have walked in mine integrity;" "I have not sat with vain persons; neither will I go in with dissemblers;" "Gather not my soul with sinners, nor my life with bloody men; in whose hands is mischief, and their right hand is full of bribes. But as for me, I will walk in mine integrity." I have already spoken of the confidence which the saints seem to derive simply from works. The passages now quoted will not occasion much difficulty, if we attend to their περιστασις, their connection, or (as it is commonly called) special circumstances. These are of two kinds; for those who use them have no wish that their whole life should be brought to trial, so that they may be acquitted or condemned according to its tenor; all they wish is, that a decision should be given on the particular case; and even here the righteousness which they claim is not with reference to the divine perfection, but only by comparison with the wicked and profane. When the question relates to justification, the thing required is not that the individual have a good ground of acquittal in regard to some particular matter, but that his whole life be in accordance with righteousness. But when the saints implore the divine justice in vindication of their innocence, they do not present themselves as free from fault, and in every respect blameless but while placing their confidence of salvation in the divine goodness only, and trusting that he will vindicate his poor when they

are afflicted contrary to justice and equity, they truly commit to him
the cause in which the innocent are oppressed. And when they sist
themselves with their adversaries at the tribunal of God, they pretend
not to an innocence corresponding to the divine purity were inquiry
strictly made, but knowing that in comparison of the malice, dishon-
esty, craft, and iniquity of their enemies, their sincerity justice, simplicity, and purity, are ascertained and approved by God, they dread
not to call upon him to judge between them. Thus when David said
to Saul, "The Lord render to every man his righteousness and his
faithfulness" (1 Sam. 26:23), he meant not that the Lord should examine and reward everyone according to his deserts, but he took the
Lord to witness how great his innocence was in comparison of Saul's
injustice. Paul, too, when he indulges in the boast, "Our rejoicing is
this, the testimony of our conscience, that in simplicity and godly
sincerity, not with fleshly wisdom, but by the grace of God, we have
had our conversation in the world, and more abundantly to you-ward"
(2 Cor. 1:12), means not to call for the scrutiny of God, but compelled
by the calumnies of the wicked he appeals, in contradiction of all their
slanders, to his faith and probity, which he knew that God had indulgently accepted. For we see how he elsewhere says, "I know nothing
by myself; yet am I not hereby justified" (1 Cor. 4:4); in other words,
he was aware that the divine judgment far transcended the blind estimate of man. Therefore, however believers may, in defending their
integrity against the hypocrisy of the ungodly, appeal to God as their
witness and judge, still when the question is with God alone, they all
with one mouth exclaim, "If thou, Lord, should mark iniquities, O
Lord, who shall stand?" Again, "Enter not into judgment with thy
servant; for in thy sight shall no man living be justified." Distrusting
their own words, they gladly exclaim, "Thy loving-kindness is better
than life" (Ps. 130:3; 143:2; 63:3).

15. There are other passages not unlike those quoted above, at
which some may still demur. Solomon says, "The just man walketh

in his integrity" (Prov. 20:7). Again, "In the way of righteousness is life; and in the pathway thereof there is no death" (Prov. 12:28). For this reason Ezekiel says, He that "has walked in my statutes, and has kept my judgments, to deal truly; he is just, he shall surely live" (Ezek. 18:9, 21; 23:15). None of these declarations do we deny or obscure. But let one of the sons of Adam come forward with such integrity. If there is none, they must perish from the presence of God, or retake themselves to the asylum of mercy. Still we deny not that the integrity of believers, though partial and imperfect, is a step to immortality. How so, but just that the works of those whom the Lord has assumed into the covenant of grace, he tries not by their merit, but embraces with paternal indulgence. By this we understand not with the Schoolmen, that works derive their value from accepting grace. For their meaning is, that works otherwise unfit to obtain salvation in terms of law, are made fit for such a purpose by the divine acceptance. On the other hand, I maintain that these works being sullied both by other transgressions and by their own deficiencies, have no other value than this, that the Lord indulgently pardons them; in other words, that the righteousness which he bestows on man is gratuitous. Here they unseasonably obtrude those passages in which the Apostle prays for all perfection to believers, "To the end he may establish your hearts unblamable in holiness before God, even our Father" (1 Thess. 3:13, and elsewhere). These words were strongly urged by the Celestines of old, in maintaining the perfection of holiness in the present life. To this we deem it sufficient briefly to reply with Augustine, that the goal to which all the pious ought to aspire is, to appear in the presence of God without spot and blemish; but as the course of the present life is at best nothing more than progress, we shall never reach the goal until we have laid aside the body of sin, and been completely united to the Lord. If anyone choose to give the name of perfection to the saints, I shall not obstinately quarrel with him, provided he defines this perfection in the words of Augustine, "When we speak of the perfect virtue of the saints, part of this perfection consists in the recognition of our imperfection both in truth and in humility" (August. *ad Bonif.* lib. 3, cap. 7).

Study Guide Questions

Section 1

1. Justification is to be separated from good works for what three reasons?
2. What is another argument for justification by works that Calvin answers here?

Section 2

1. Why will we not attain to these promises through works?
2. What do we need in order to receive the promises?

Section 3

1. Have these promises been given for no reason then?
2. How are these promises fulfilled? What three conditions does Calvin set forth?

Section 4

1. How does Calvin explain the fact that Cornelius was accepted by God (Acts 10:31)?

Section 5

1. Why is the Lord pleased with the good works of the believer?
2. What is regeneration?
3. How does God embrace our good works?

Section 6

1. Does Calvin acknowledge more than one kind of promise in the Old Testament?

Section 7

1. Is conformity to the law sometimes called "righteousness"?

2. Does Calvin reject what he calls law-righteousness?

Section 8

1. How are good works appraised by God?

Section 9

1. What relationship does justification by faith have to genuine good works?

Section 10

1. What is necessary before works can be acceptable?

2. Does justification cover our persons only?

Section 11

1. What is the apparent conflict between James and Paul?

2. What is Calvin's starting assumption?

3. Those who set James against the doctrine of the Protestants are guilty of what?

4. What kind of "faith" is James talking about?

Section 12

1. Are Paul and James using the word "justify" in the same way?

Section 13

1. How does Calvin handle Romans 2:13?

Section 14

1. How does Calvin handle the multiple places where believers appeal to God on the basis of their innocence?

Section 15

1. Does Calvin allow believers to claim any kind of perfection?

CHAPTER 18

The righteousness of works improperly inferred from rewards.

There are three divisions in this chapter—

I. A solution of two general objections which are urged in support of justification by works. First, That God will render to every one according to his works, sec. 1. Second, That the reward of works is called eternal, sec. 2-6.

II. Answer to other special objections derived from the former, and a perversion of passages of Scripture, sec. 6-9.

III. Refutation of the sophism that faith itself is called a work, and, therefore, justification by it is by works, sec. 10.

Outline:

1. Two general objections. The former solved and explained. What meant by the term working.

2. Solution of the second general objection. 1. Works not the cause of salvation. This shown from the name and nature of inheritance. 2. A striking example that the Lord rewards the works of believers with blessings which he had promised before the works were thought of.

3. First reason why eternal life said to be the reward of works. This confirmed by passages of Scripture. The concurrence of Ambrose. A rule to be observed. Declarations of Christ and an Apostle.

4. Other four reasons. Holiness the way to the kingdom, not the cause of obtaining it. Proposition of the Sophists.

5. Objection that God crowns the works of his people. Three answers from Augustine. A fourth from Scripture.

6. First special objection—viz. that we are ordered to lay up treasure in heaven. Answer, showing in what way this can be done.

7. Second objection—viz. that the righteous enduring affliction are said to be worthy of the kingdom of heaven. Answer. What meant by righteousness.

8. A third objection founded on three passages of Paul. Answer.

9. Fourth objection founded on our Savior's words, "If ye would enter into life, keep the commandments." Answer, giving an exposition of the passage.

10. Last objection—viz. that faith itself is called a work. Answer— it is not as a work that faith justifies.

L et us now proceed to those passages which affirm that God will render to everyone according to his deeds. Of this description are the following: "We must all appear before the judgment seat of Christ; that everyone may receive the things done in his body, according to that he has done, whether it be good or bad;" "Who will render to every man according to his deeds: to them who by patient continuance in well-doing seek for glory, and honor, and immortality, eternal life;" but "tribulation and anguish upon every soul of man that does evil;" "They that have done good, unto the resurrection of life; and they that have done evil, unto the resurrection of damnation;" "Come, ye blessed of my Father;" "For I was an hungered, and ye gave me meat; I was thirsty, and ye gave me drink," &c. To these we may add the passages which describe eternal life as the reward of works, such as the following: "The recompense of a man's hands shall be rendered unto him;" "He that feareth the commandment shall be rewarded;" "Rejoice and be exceeding glad, for great is your reward in heaven;" "Every man shall receive his own rewards according to his own labor." The passages in which it is said that God will reward every man according to his works are easily disposed of. For that mode of expression indicates not the cause but the order of sequence. Now, it is beyond a doubt that the steps by which the Lord in his mercy consummates our salvation are these, "Whom he did predestinate, them he also called; and whom he called, them he also justified; and whom he justified, them he also glorified" (Rom. 8:30). But though it is by mercy alone that God admits his people to life, yet as he leads them into possession of it by the course of good works, that he may complete his work in them in the order which he has destined, it is not strange that they are said to be crowned according to their works, since by these doubtless they are prepared for receiving the crown of immortality. Nay, for this reason they are aptly said to work out their own salvation (Phil. 2:12), while by exerting themselves in good works they aspire to eternal life, just as they are elsewhere told to labor for the meat which perisheth not (John 6:27), while they acquire life for themselves by believing in Christ; and yet it is immediately added, that this meat "the Son of man shall give unto you." Hence it appears, that working is not at all opposed to grace, but refers to pursuit, and, therefore, it follows not that believers are the authors of their own salvation, or that it is the result of their works. What then? The moment they are admitted to fellowship with Christ, by the knowledge of the gospel, and the illumination of the Holy Spirit, their eternal life is begun, and then He which has begun a good work in them "will perform it until the day of Jesus Christ" (Phil. 1:6). And it is performed when in righteousness and holiness they bear a resemblance to their heavenly Father, and prove that they are not degenerate sons.

2. There is nothing in the term "reward" to justify the inference that our works are the cause of salvation. First, let it be a fixed principle in our hearts, that the kingdom of heaven is not the hire of servants, but the inheritance of sons (Eph. 1:18); an inheritance obtained by those only whom the Lord has adopted as sons, and obtained for no other cause than this adoption, "The son of the bond-women shall not be heir with the son of the free-woman" (Gal. 4:30). And hence in those very passages in which the Holy Spirit promises eternal glory as the reward of works, by expressly calling it an inheritance, he demonstrates that it comes to us from some other quarter. Thus Christ enumerates the works for which he bestows heaven as a recompense, while he is calling his elect to the possession of it, but he at the same time adds, that it is to be possessed by right of inheritance (Matt. 25:34). Paul, too, encourages servants, while faithfully doing their duty, to hope for reward from the Lord, but adds, "of the inheritance" (Col. 3:24). You see how, as it were, in formal terms they carefully caution us to attribute eternal blessedness not to works, but to the adoption of God. Why, then, do they at the same time make mention of works? This question will be elucidated by an example from Scripture (Gen. 15:5; 17:1). Before the birth of Isaac, Abraham had received promise of a seed in whom all the families of the earth should be blessed; the propagation of a seed that for number should equal the stars of heaven, and the sand of the sea, &c. Many years after he prepares, in obedience to a divine message, to sacrifice his son. Having done this act of obedience, he receives the promise, "By myself have I sworn, saith the Lord, for because thou hast done this thing, and hast not withheld thy son, thine only son; that in blessing I will bless thee, and in multiplying I will multiply thy seed as the stars of the heaven, and as the sand which is upon the seashore, and thy seed shall possess the gate of his enemies; and in thy seed shall all the nations of the earth be blessed, because thou hast obeyed my voice" (Gen. 22:16-18). What is it we hear? Did Abraham by his obedience

merit the blessing which had been promised him before the precept was given? Here assuredly we see without ambiguity that God rewards the works of believers with blessings which he had given them before the works were thought of, there still being no cause for the blessings which he bestows but his own mercy.

3. And yet the Lord does not act in vain, or delude us when he says, that he renders to works what he had freely given previous to works. As he would have us to be exercised in good works, while aspiring to the manifestation, or, if I may so speak, the fruition of the things which he has promised, and by means of them to hasten on to the blessed hope set before us in heaven, the fruit of the promises is justly ascribed to those things by which it is brought to maturity. Both things were elegantly expressed by the Apostle, when he told the Colossians to study the offices of charity, "for the hope which is laid up for you in heaven, whereof ye heard before in the word of the truth of the gospel" (Col. 1:5). For when he says that the gospel informed them of the hope which was treasured up for them in heaven, he declares that it depends on Christ alone, and not at all upon works. With this accords the saying of Peter, that believers "are kept by the power of God through faith unto salvation, ready to be revealed in the last time" (1 Pet. 1:5). When he says that they strive on account of it, he intimates that believers must continue running during the whole course of their lives in order that they may attain it. But to prevent us from supposing that the reward which is promised becomes a kind of merit, our Lord introduced a parable, in which he represented himself as a householder, who sent all the laborers whom he met to work in his vineyard, some at the first hour of the day, others at the second, others at the third, some even at the eleventh; at evening he paid them all alike. The interpretation of this parable is briefly and truly given by that ancient writer (whoever he was) who wrote the book *De Vocatione Gentium*, which goes under the name of Ambrose. I will give it in his words rather than my own: "By means of this comparison, our

Lord represented the many various modes of calling as pertaining to grace alone, where those who were introduced into the vineyard at the eleventh hour and made equal to those who had toiled the whole day, doubtless represent the case of those whom the indulgence of God, to commend the excellence of grace, has rewarded in the decline of the day and the conclusion of life; not paying the price of labor, but shedding the riches of his goodness on those whom he chose without works; in order that even those who bore the heat of the day, and yet received no more than those who came last, may understand that they received a gift of grace, not the hire of works" (Lib. 1, cap. 5). Lastly, it is also worthy of remark, that in those passages in which eternal life is called the reward of works, it is not taken simply for that communion which we have with God preparatory to a blessed immortality, when with paternal benevolence he embraces us in Christ, but for the possession, or, as it is called, the fruition of blessedness, as the very words of Christ express it, "in the world to come eternal life" (Mark 10:30), and elsewhere, "Come, ye blessed of my Father, inherit the kingdom," &c. (Matt. 25:34). For this reason also Paul gives the name of adoption to that revelation of adoption which shall be made at the resurrection; and which adoption he afterwards interprets to mean, the redemption of our body (Rom. 8:23). But, otherwise, as alienation from God is eternal death—so when man is received into favor by God that he may enjoy communion with him and become one with him, he passes from death unto life. This is owing to adoption alone. Although after their manner they pertinaciously urge the term "reward," we can always carry them back to the declaration of Peter, that eternal life is the reward of faith (1 Pet. 1:9).

4. Let us not suppose, then, that the Holy Spirit, by this promise, commends the dignity of our works, as if they were deserving of such a reward. For Scripture leaves us nothing of which we may glory in the sight of God. Nay, rather its whole object is to repress, humble, cast down, and completely crush our pride. But in this way help is given to

our weakness, which would immediately give way were it not sustained by this expectation, and soothed by this comfort. First, let every man reflect for himself how hard it is not only to leave all things, but to leave and abjure one's self. And yet this is the training by which Christ initiates his disciples, that is, all the godly. Secondly, he thus keeps them all their lifetime under the discipline of the cross, lest they should allow their heart to long for or confide in present good. In short, his treatment is usually such, that wherever they turn their eyes, as far as this world extends, they see nothing before them but despair; and hence Paul says "If in this life only we have hope in Christ, we are of all men most miserable" (1 Cor. 15:19). That they may not fail in these great straits, the Lord is present reminding them to lift their head higher and extend their view farther, that in him they may find a happiness which they see not in the world: to this happiness he gives the name of reward, hire, recompense, not as estimating the merit of works, but intimating that it is a compensation for their straits, sufferings, and affronts, &c. Wherefore, there is nothing to prevent us from calling eternal life a recompense after the example of Scripture, because in it the Lord brings his people from labor to quiet, from affliction to a prosperous and desirable condition, from sorrow to joy, from poverty to affluence, from ignominy to glory; in short, exchanges all the evils which they endured for blessings. Thus there will be no impropriety in considering holiness of life as the way, not indeed the way which gives access to the glory of the heavenly kingdom; but a way by which God conducts his elect to the manifestation of that kingdom, since his good pleasure is to glorify those whom he has sanctified (Rom. 8:30). Only let us not imagine that "merit" and "hire" are correlative terms, a point on which the Sophists absurdly insist, from not attending to the end to which we have adverted. How preposterous is it when the Lord calls us to one end to look to another? Nothing is clearer than that a reward is promised to good works, in order to support the weakness of our flesh by some degree of comfort; but not to inflate our minds with vain glory. He, therefore, who from merit infers reward, or weighs works and reward in the same balance, errs very widely from the end which God has in view.

5. Accordingly, when the Scripture speaks of "a crown of righteousness which God the righteous Judge shall give" "at that day" (2 Tim. 4:8), I not only say with Augustine, "To whom could the righteous Judge give the crown if the merciful Father had not given grace, and how could there have been righteousness but for the precedence of grace which justified the ungodly? how could these be paid as things due were not things not due previously given?" (August. *ad Valent. de Grat. et Lib. Art.*); but I also add, how could he impute righteousness to our works, did not his indulgence hide the unrighteousness that is in them? How could he deem them worthy of reward, did he not with boundless goodness destroy what is unworthy in them? Augustine is wont to give the name of grace to eternal life, because, while it is the recompense of works, it is bestowed by the gratuitous gifts of God. But Scripture humbles us more, and at the same time elevates us. For besides forbidding us to glory in works, because they are the gratuitous gifts of God, it tells us that they are always defiled by some degrees of impurity, so that they cannot satisfy God when they are tested by the standard of his justice; but that lest our activity should be destroyed, they please merely by pardon. But though Augustine speaks somewhat differently from us, it is plain from his words that the difference is more apparent than real. After drawing a contrast between two individuals the one with a life holy and perfect almost to a miracle; the other honest indeed, and of pure morals, yet not so perfect as not to leave much room for desiring better, he at length infers, "He who seems inferior in conduct, yet on account of the true faith in God by which he lives (Hab. 2:4), and in conformity to which he accuses himself in all his faults, praises God in all his good works, takes shame to himself, and ascribes glory to God, from whom he receives both forgiveness for his sins, and the love of well-doing, the moment he is set free from this life is translated into the society of

Christ. Why, but just on account of his faith? For though it saves no man without works (such faith being reprobate and not working by love), yet by means of it sins are forgiven; for the just lives by faith: without it works which seem good are converted into sins" (August. *ad Bonifac.*, Lib. 3, c. 5). Here he not obscurely acknowledges what we so strongly maintains that the righteousness of good works depends on their being approved by God in the way of pardon.

6. In a sense similar to the above passages our opponents quote the following: "Make to yourselves friends of the mammon of un-righteousness; that when ye fail, they may receive you into everlasting habitations" (Luke 16:9). "Charge them that are rich in this world, that they be not high-minded, nor trust in uncertain riches, but in the living God, who giveth us richly all things to enjoy: that they do good, that they be rich in good works, ready to distribute, willing to communicate; laying up in store for themselves a good foundation against the time to come, that they may lay hold on eternal life" (1 Tim. 6:17-19). For the good works which we enjoy in eternal bless-edness are compared to riches. I answer, that we shall never attain to the true knowledge of these passages unless we attend to the scope of the Spirit in uttering them. If it is true, as Christ says, "Where your treasure is, there will your heart be also" (Matt. 6:21), then, as the children of the world are intent on providing those things which form the delight of the present life, so it is the duty of believers, after they have learned that this life will shortly pass away like a dream, to take care that those things which they would truly enjoy be transmit-ted thither where their entire life is to be spent. We must, therefore, do like those who begin to remove to any place where they mean to fix their abode. As they send forward their effects, and grudge not to want them for a season, because they think the more they have in their future residence, the happier they are; so, if we think that heaven is our country, we should send our wealth thither rather than retain it here, where on our sudden departure it will be lost to us. But how

shall we transmit it? By contributing to the necessities of the poor, the Lord imputing to himself whatever is given to them. Hence that excellent promise, "He that has pity on the poor lendeth to the Lord" (Prov. 19:17; Matt. 25:40); and again, "He which soweth bountifully shall reap also bountifully" (2 Cor. 9:6). What we give to our brethren in the exercise of charity is a deposit with the Lord, who, as a faithful depositary, will ultimately restore it with abundant interest. Are our duties, then, of such value with God that they are as a kind of treasure placed in his hand? Who can hesitate to say so when Scripture so often and so plainly attests it? But if anyone would leap from the mere kindness of God to the merit of works, his error will receive no support from these passages. For all you can properly infer from them is the inclination on the part of God to treat us with indulgence. For, in order to animate us in well-doing, he allows no act of obedience, however unworthy of his eye, to pass unrewarded.

7. But they insist more strongly on the words of the apostle when, in consoling the Thessalonians under their tribulations, he tells them that these were sent, "that ye may be counted worthy of the kingdom of God, for which ye also suffer; seeing it is a righteous thing with God to recompense tribulation to them that trouble you; and to you who are troubled, rest with us, when the Lord Jesus shall be revealed from heaven with his mighty angels" (2 Thess. 1:6-7). The author of the Epistle to the Hebrews says, "God is not unrighteous to forget your work and labor of love, which ye have showed towards his name, in that ye have ministered to the saints, and do minister" (Heb. 6:10). To the former passage I answer, that the worthiness spoken of is not that of merit, but as God the Father would have those whom he has chosen for sons to be conformed to Christ the firstborn, and as it behooved him first to suffer, and then to enter into his glory, so we also, through much tribulation, enter the kingdom of heaven. Therefore, while we suffer tribulation for the name of Christ, we in a manner receive the marks with which God is wont to stamp the sheep of his

flock (Gal. 6:17). Hence we are counted worthy of the kingdom of God, because we bear in our body the marks of our Lord and Master, these being the insignia of the children of God. In this sense are we to understand the passages: "Always bearing about in the body the dying of the Lord Jesus, that the life also of Jesus might be made manifest in our body" (2 Cor. 4:10). "That I may know him and the power of his resurrection, and the fellowship of his sufferings, being made conformable unto his death" (Phil. 3:10). The reason which is subjoined is intended not to prove any merit, but to confirm our hope of the kingdom of God; as if he had said, As it is befitting the just judgment of God to take vengeance on your enemies for the tribulation which they have brought upon you, so it is also befitting to give you release and rest from these tribulations. The other passage, which speaks as if it were becoming the justice of God not to overlook the services of his people, and almost insinuates that it were unjust to forget them, is to be thus explained: God, to arouse us from sloth, assures us that every labor which we undertake for the glory of his name shall not be in vain. Let us always remember that this promise, like all other promises, will be of no avail unless it is preceded by the free covenant of mercy, on which the whole certainty of our salvation depends. Trusting to it, however, we ought to feel secure that however unworthy our services, the liberality of God will not allow them to pass unrewarded. To confirm us in this expectation, the Apostle declares that God is not unrighteous; but will act consistently with the promise once given. Righteousness, therefore, refers rather to the truth of the divine promise than to the equity of paying what is due. In this sense there is a celebrated saying of Augustine, which, as containing a memorable sentiment, that holy man declined not repeatedly to employ, and which I think not unworthy of being constantly remembered: "Faithful is the Lord, who has made himself our debtor, not by receiving anything from us, but by promising us all things" (August. *in Ps. 32, 109*, et alibi).

8. Our opponents also adduce the following passages from Paul: "Though I have all faith, so that I could remove mountains, and have not charity, I am nothing" (1 Cor. 13:2). Again, "Now abideth faith, hope, charity, these three; but the greatest of these is charity" (1 Cor. 13:13). "Above all these things put on charity, which is the bond of perfectness" (Col. 3:14). From the two first passages our Pharisees contend that we are justified by charity rather than by faith, charity being, as they say, the better virtue. This mode of arguing is easily disposed of. I have elsewhere shown that what is said in the first passage refers not to true faith. In the second passage we admit that charity is said to be greater than true faith, but not because charity is more meritorious, but because it is more fruitful, because it is of wider extent, of more general service, and always flourishes, whereas the use of faith is only for a time. If we look to excellence, the love of God undoubtedly holds the first place. Of it, however, Paul does not here speak; for the only thing he insists on is, that we should by mutual charity edify one another in the Lord. But let us suppose that charity is in every respect superior to faith, what man of sound judgment, nay, what man with any soundness in his brain, would argue that it therefore does more to justify? The power of justifying which belongs to faith consists not in its worth as a work. Our justification depends entirely on the mercy of God and the merits of Christ: when faith apprehends these, it is said to justify. Now, if you ask our opponents in what sense they ascribe justification to charity, they will answer, Being a duty acceptable to God, righteousness is in respect of its merit imputed to us by the acceptance of the divine goodness. Here you see how beautifully the argument proceeds. We say that faith justifies not because it merits justification for us by its own worth, but because it is an instrument by which we freely obtain the righteousness of Christ. They, overlooking the mercy of God, and passing by Christ, the sum of righteousness, maintain that we are justified by charity as being superior to faith; just as if one were to maintain that a king is fitter to make a shoe than a

shoemaker, because the king is infinitely the superior of the two. This one syllogism is ample proof that all the schools of Sorbonne have never had the slightest apprehension of what is meant by justification by faith. Should any disputant here interpose, and ask why we give different meanings to the term "faith" as used by Paul in passages so near each other, I can easily show that I have not slight grounds for so doing. For while those gifts which Paul enumerates are in some degree subordinate to faith and hope, because they relate to the knowledge of God, he by way of summary comprehends them all under the name of faith and hope; as if he had said, Prophecy and tongues, and the gift of interpreting, and knowledge, are all designed to lead us to the knowledge of God. But in this life it is only by faith and hope that we acknowledge God. Therefore, when I name faith and hope, I at the same time comprehend the whole. "Now abideth faith, hope, charity, these three;" that is, how great soever the number of the gifts, they are all to be referred to them; but "the greatest of these is charity." From the third passage they infer, If charity is the bond of perfection, it must be the bond of righteousness, which is nothing else than perfection. First, without objecting that the name of perfection is here given by Paul to proper union among the members of a rightly constituted church, and admitting that by charity we are perfected before God, what new result do they gain by it? I will always object in reply, that we never attain to that perfection unless we fulfill all the parts of charity; and will thence infer, that as all are most remote from such fulfillment, the hope of perfection is excluded.

9. I am unwilling to discuss all the things which the foolish Sorbonnists have rashly laid hold of in Scripture as it chanced to come in their way, and throw out against us. Some of them are so ridiculous, that I cannot mention them without laying myself open to a charge of trifling. I will, therefore, conclude with an exposition of one of our Savior's expressions with which they are wondrously pleased. When the lawyer asked him, "Good Master, what good thing shall I do, that

I may have eternal life?" he answers, "If thou wilt enter into life, keep the commandments" (Matt. 19:16-17). What more (they ask) would we have, when the very author of grace bids us acquire the kingdom of heaven by the observance of the commandments? As if it were not plain that Christ adapted his answers to the characters of those whom he addressed. Here he is questioned by a Doctor of the Law as to the means of obtaining eternal life; and the question is not put simply, but is, What can men do to attain it? Both the character of the speaker and his question induced our Lord to give this answer. Imbued with a persuasion of legal righteousness, the lawyer had a blind confidence in works. Then all he asked was, what are the works of righteousness by which salvation is obtained? Justly, therefore, is he referred to the law, in which there is a perfect mirror of righteousness. We also distinctly declare, that if life is sought in works, the commandments are to be observed. And the knowledge of this doctrine is necessary to Christians; for how should they retake themselves to Christ, unless they perceived that they had fallen from the path of life over the precipice of death? Or how could they understand how far they have wandered from the way of life unless they previously understand what that way is? Then only do they feel that the asylum of safety is in Christ when they see how much their conduct is at variance with the divine righteousness, which consists in the observance of the law. The sum of the whole is this, If salvation is sought in works, we must keep the commandments, by which we are instructed in perfect righteousness. But we cannot remain here unless we would stop short in the middle of our course; for none of us is able to keep the commandments. Being thus excluded from the righteousness of the law, we must retake ourselves to another remedy—viz. to the faith of Christ. Wherefore, as a teacher of the law, whom our Lord knew to be puffed up with a vain confidence in works, was here directed by him to the law, that he might learn he was a sinner exposed to the fearful sentence of eternal death; so others, who were already humbled with this knowledge, he elsewhere solaces with the promise of grace, without making any mention of the law. "Come unto me, all ye that labor and are heavy laden, and I will give you rest." "Take my yoke upon you, and learn of me; for I am meek and lowly in heart: and ye shall find rest unto your souls" (Matt. 11:28-29).

10. At length, after they have wearied themselves with perverting Scripture, they have recourse to subtleties and sophisms. One cavil is, that faith is somewhere called a work (John 6:29); hence they infer that we are in error in opposing faith to works; as if faith, regarded as obedience to the divine will, could by its own merit procure our justification, and did not rather, by embracing the mercy of God, thereby seal upon our hearts the righteousness of Christ, which is offered to us in the preaching of the gospel. My readers will pardon me if I stay not to dispose of such absurdities; their own weakness, without external assault, is sufficient to destroy them. One objection, however, which has some semblance of reason, it will be proper to dispose of in passing, lest it give any trouble to those less experienced. As common sense dictates that contraries must be tried by the same rule, and as each sin is charged against us as unrighteousness, so it is right (say our opponents) that each good work should receive the praise of righteousness. The answer which some give, that the condemnation of men proceeds on unbelief alone, and not on particular sins does not satisfy me. I agree with them, indeed, that infidelity is the fountain and root of all evil; for it is the first act of revolt from God, and is afterwards followed by particular transgressions of the law. But as they seem to hold, that in estimating righteousness and unrighteousness, the same rule is to be applied to good and bad works, in this I dissent from them. The righteousness of works consists in perfect obedience to the law. Hence you cannot be justified by works unless you follow this straight line (if I may so call it) during the whole course of your life. The moment you decline from it you have fallen into unrighteousness. Hence it appears, that righteousness is not obtained by a

few works, but by an indefatigable and inflexible observance of the divine will. But the rule with regard to unrighteousness is very different. The adulterer or the thief is by one act guilty of death, because he offends against the majesty of God. The blunder of these arguers of ours lies here: they attend not to the words of James, "Whosoever shall keep the whole law, and yet offend in one point, he is guilty of all. For he that said, Do not commit adultery, said also, Do not kill," &c. (James 2:10-11). Therefore, it should not seem absurd when we say that death is the just recompense of every sin, because each sin merits the just indignation and vengeance of God. But you reason absurdly if you infer the converse, that one good work will reconcile a man to God notwithstanding of his meriting wrath by many sins.

Study Guide Questions

Section 1

1. How does Calvin explain those passages which say that God will repay every man according to his works?
2. How do we know that our good works are not meritorious in themselves?

Section 2

1. How is the term "reward" to be understood?
2. How do we know that Abraham did not earn the promise by his obedience with Isaac?

Section 3

1. What trains us to meditate on the fruition of our lives?
2. Calvin quotes an early church writer to what effect?

Section 4

1. What is the whole end of Scripture?
2. What must we not deduce from the concept of reward?

Section 5

1. How can God impute righteousness to our works?
2. How does a faith that is not reprobate work?
3. The righteousness of good works depends upon what?

Section 6

1. How does one lend to the Lord?
2. Is this kind of generosity meritorious?
3. Why does God allow us to lay up treasures in heaven this way?

Section 7

1. What about tribulation? Doesn't God promise that He will not forget our sufferings?
2. According to Augustine, in what sense is the Lord our debtor?

Section 8

1. Is love greater than faith?
2. Does this mean that love can justify?
3. What illustration does Calvin use?
4. If we were justified by our love, who would be justified?

Section 9

1. How does Calvin understand Matthew 19:17?

Section 10

1. In relationship to other sins, what is unbelief?
2. For someone to be called righteous, what must their life be like?

CHAPTER 19

Of Christian Liberty.

The three divisions of this chapter are—

I. Necessity of the doctrine of Christian Liberty, sec. 1. The principal parts of this liberty explained, sec. 2-8.

II. The nature and efficacy of this liberty against the Epicureans and others who take no account whatever of the weak, sec. 9 and 10.

III. Of offense given and received. A lengthened and not unnecessary discussion of this subject, sec. 11-16.

Outline:

1. Connection of this chapter with the previous one on Justification. A true knowledge of Christian liberty useful and necessary. 1. It purifies the conscience. 2. It checks licentiousness. 3. It maintains the merits of Christ, the truth of the Gospel, and the peace of the soul.

2. This liberty consists of three parts. First, Believers renouncing the righteousness of the law, look only to Christ. Objection. Answer, distinguishing between Legal and Evangelical righteousness.

3. This first part clearly established by the whole Epistle to the Galatians.

4. The second part of Christian liberty—viz. that the conscience, freed from the yoke of the law, voluntarily obeys the will of God. This cannot be done so long as we are under the law. Reason.

5. When freed from the rigorous exactions of the law, we can cheerfully and with much alacrity answer the call of God.

6. Proof of this second part from an Apostle. The end of this liberty.

7. Third part of liberty—viz. the free rise of things indifferent. The knowledge of this part necessary to remove despair and superstition. Superstition described.

8. Proof of this third part from the Epistle to the Romans. Those who observe it not only use evasion. 1. Despisers of God. 2. The desperate. 3. The ungrateful. The end and scope of this third part.

9. Second part of the chapter, showing the nature and efficacy of Christian liberty, in opposition to the Epicureans. Their character described. Pretext and allegation. Use of things indifferent. Abuse detected. Mode of correcting it.

10. This liberty maintained in opposition to those who pay no regard to the weak. Error of this class of men refuted. A most pernicious error. Objection. Reply.

11. Application of the doctrine of Christian liberty to the subject of offenses. These of two kinds. Offense given. Offense received. Of offense given, a subject comprehended by few. Of Pharisaical offense, or offense received.

12. Who are to be regarded as weak and Pharisaical. Proved by examples and the doctrine of Paul. The just moderation of Christian liberty. Necessity of vindicating it. No regard to be paid to hypocrites. Duty of edifying our weak neighbors.

13. Application of the doctrine to things indifferent. Things necessary not to be omitted from any fear of offense.

14. Refutation of errors in regard to Christian liberty. The consciences of the godly not to be fettered by human traditions in matters of indifference.

15. Distinction to be made between Spiritual and Civil government. These must not be confounded. How far conscience can be bound by human constitutions. Definition of conscience. Definition explained by passages from the Apostolic writings.

16. The relation which conscience bears to external obedience; first, in things good and evil; secondly, in things indifferent.

We are now to treat of Christian Liberty, the explanation of which certainly ought not to be omitted by anyone proposing to give a compendious summary of Gospel doctrine. For it is a matter of primary necessity, one without the knowledge of which the conscience can scarcely attempt anything without hesitation, in many must demur and fluctuate, and in all proceed with fickleness and trepidation. In particular, it forms a proper appendix to Justification, and is of no little service in understanding its force. Nay, those who seriously fear God will hence perceive the incomparable advantages of a doctrine which wicked scoffers are constantly assailing with their jibes; the intoxication of mind under which they labor leaving their petulance without restraint. This, therefore, seems the proper place for considering the subject. Moreover, though it has already been occasionally adverted to, there was an advantage in deferring the fuller consideration of it till now, for the moment any mention is made of Christian liberty, lust begins to boil, or insane commotions arise, if a speedy restraint is not laid on those licentious spirits by whom the best things are perverted into the worst. For they either, under pretext of this liberty, shake off all obedience to God, and break out into unbridled licentiousness, or they feel indignant, thinking that all choice, order, and restraint, are abolished. What can we do when thus encompassed with straits? Are we to bid adieu to Christian liberty, in order that we may cut off all opportunity for such perilous consequences? But, as we have said, if the subject be not understood, neither Christ, nor the truth of the Gospel, nor the inward peace of

INSTITUTES OF THE CHRISTIAN RELIGION

the soul, is properly known. Our endeavor must rather be, while not suppressing this very necessary part of doctrine, to obviate the absurd objections to which it usually gives rise.

2. Christian liberty seems to me to consist of three parts. First, the consciences of believers, while seeking the assurance of their justification before God, must rise above the law, and think no more of obtaining justification by it. For while the law, as has already been demonstrated (supra, chap. 17, sec. 1), leaves not one man righteous, we are either excluded from all hope of justification, or we must be loosed from the law, and so loosed as that no account at all shall be taken of works. For he who imagines that in order to obtain justification he must bring any degree of works whatever, cannot fix any mode or limit, but makes himself debtor to the whole law. Therefore, laying aside all mention of the law, and all idea of works, we must in the matter of justification have recourse to the mercy of God only; turning away our regard from ourselves, we must look only to Christ. For the question is, not how we may be righteous, but how, though unworthy and unrighteous, we may be regarded as righteous. If consciences would obtain any assurance of this, they must give no place to the law. Still it cannot be rightly inferred from this that believers have no need of the law. It ceases not to teach, exhort, and urge them to good, although it is not recognized by their consciences before the judgment seat of God. The two things are very different, and should be well and carefully distinguished. The whole lives of Christians ought to be a kind of aspiration after piety, seeing they are called unto holiness (Eph. 1:4; 1 Thess. 4:5). The office of the law is to excite them to the study of purity and holiness, by reminding them of their duty. For when the conscience feels anxious as to how it may have the favor of God, as to the answer it could give, and the confidence it would feel, if brought to his judgment seat, in such a case the requirements of the law are not to be brought forward, but Christ, who surpasses all the perfection of the law, is alone to be held forth for righteousness.

3. On this almost the whole subject of the Epistle to the Galatians hinges; for it can be proved from express passages that those are absurd interpreters who teach that Paul there contends only for freedom from ceremonies. Of such passages are the following: "Christ has redeemed us from the curse of the law, being made a curse for us." "Stand fast, therefore, in the liberty wherewith Christ has made us free, and be not entangled again with the yoke of bondage. Behold, I Paul say unto you, that if ye be circumcised, Christ shall profit you nothing. For I testify again to every man that is circumcised, that he is a debtor to do the whole law. Christ is become of no effect unto you, whosoever of you are justified by the law; ye are fallen from grace" (Gal. 3:13; 5:1-4). These words certainly refer to something of a higher order than freedom from ceremonies. I confess, indeed, that Paul there treats of ceremonies, because he was contending with false apostles, who were plotting to bring back into the Christian Church those ancient shadows of the law which were abolished by the advent of Christ. But, in discussing this question, it was necessary to introduce higher matters, on which the whole controversy turns. First, because the brightness of the Gospel was obscured by those Jewish shadows, he shows that in Christ we have a full manifestation of all those things which were typified by Mosaic ceremonies. Secondly, as those impostors instilled into the people the most pernicious opinion, that this obedience was sufficient to merit the grace of God, he insists very strongly that believers shall not imagine that they can obtain justification before God by any works, far less by those paltry observances. At the same time, he shows that by the cross of Christ they are free from the condemnation of the law, to which otherwise all men are exposed, so that in Christ alone they can rest in full security. This argument is pertinent to the present subject (Gal. 4:5, 21, &c). Lastly, he asserts the right of believers to liberty of conscience, a liberty which may not be restrained without necessity.

4. Another point which depends on the former is, that consciences obey the law, not as if compelled by legal necessity; but being free from the yoke of the law itself, voluntarily obey the will of God. Being constantly in terror so long as they are under the dominion of the law, they are never disposed promptly to obey God, unless they have previously obtained this liberty. Our meaning shall be explained more briefly and clearly by an example. The command of the law is, "Thou shalt love the Lord thy God with all thine heart, and with all thy soul, and with all thy might" (Deut. 6:5). To accomplish this, the soul must previously be divested of every other thought and feeling, the heart purified from all its desires, all its powers collected and united on this one object. Those who, in comparison of others, have made much progress in the way of the Lord, are still very far from this goal. For although they love God in their mind, and with a sincere affection of heart, yet both are still in a great measure occupied with the lusts of the flesh, by which they are retarded and prevented from proceeding with quickened pace towards God. They indeed make many efforts, but the flesh partly enfeebles their strength, and partly binds them to itself. What can they do while they thus feel that there is nothing of which they are less capable than to fulfill the law? They wish, aspire, endeavor; but do nothing with the requisite perfection. If they look to the law, they see that every work which they attempt or design is accursed. Nor can anyone deceive himself by inferring that the work is not altogether bad, merely because it is imperfect, and, therefore, that any good which is in it is still accepted of God. For the law demanding perfect love condemns all imperfection, unless its rigor is mitigated. Let any man therefore consider his work which he wishes to be thought partly good, and he will find that it is a transgression of the law by the very circumstance of its being imperfect.

5. See how our works lie under the curse of the law if they are tested by the standard of the law. But how can unhappy souls set themselves with alacrity to a work from which they cannot hope to gain anything

in return but cursing? On the other hand, if freed from this severe exaction, or rather from the whole rigor of the law, they hear themselves
invited by God with paternal levity, they will cheerfully and alertly obey
the call, and follow his guidance. In one word, those who are bound by
the yoke of the law are like servants who have certain tasks daily assigned them by their masters. Such servants think that naught has been
done; and they dare not come into the presence of their masters until
the exact amount of labor has been performed. But sons who are treated in a more candid and liberal manner by their parents, hesitate not
to offer them works that are only begun or half finished, or even with
something faulty in them, trusting that their obedience and readiness
of mind will be accepted, although the performance be less exact than
was wished. Such should be our feelings, as we certainly trust that our
most indulgent Parent will approve our services, however small they
may be, and however rude and imperfect. Thus He declares to us by the
prophet, "I will spare them as a man spareth his own son that serveth
him" (Mal. 3:17); where the word "spare" evidently means indulgence,
or connivance at faults, while at the same time service is remembered.
This confidence is necessary in no slight degree, since without it every
thing should be attempted in vain; for God does not regard any work
of ours as done to himself, unless truly done from a desire to serve him.
But how can this be amidst these terrors, while we doubt whether God
is offended or served by our work?

6. This is the reason why the author of the Epistle to the Hebrews
ascribes to faith all the good works which the holy patriarchs are said
to have performed, and estimates them merely by faith (Heb. 11:2).
In regard to this liberty there is a remarkable passage in the Epistle
to the Romans, where Paul argues, "Sin shall not have dominion over
you; for ye are not under the law, but under grace" (Rom. 6:14). For
after he had exhorted believers, "Let not sin therefore reign in your
mortal body, that ye should obey it in the lusts thereof: Neither yield
ye your members as instruments of unrighteousness unto sin; but

yield yourselves unto God, as those that are alive from the dead, and your members as instruments of righteousness unto God;" they might have objected that they still bore about with them a body full of lust, that sin still dwelt in them. He therefore comforts them by adding, that they are freed from the law; as if he had said, Although you feel that sin is not yet extinguished, and that righteousness does not plainly live in you, you have no cause for fear and dejection, as if God were always offended because of the remains of sin, since by grace you are freed from the law, and your works are not tried by its standard. Let those, however, who infer that they may sin because they are not under the law, understand that they have no right to this liberty, the end of which is to encourage us in well-doing.

7. The third part of this liberty is that we are not bound before God to any observance of external things which are in themselves indifferent (αδιαφορα), but that we are now at full liberty either to use or omit them. The knowledge of this liberty is very necessary to us; where it is wanting our consciences will have no rest, there will be no end of superstition. In the present day many think us absurd in raising a question as to the free eating of flesh, the free use of dress and holidays, and similar frivolous trifles, as they think them; but they are of more importance than is commonly supposed. For when once the conscience is entangled in the net, it enters a long and inextricable labyrinth, from which it is afterwards most difficult to escape. When a man begins to doubt whether it is lawful for him to use linen for sheets, shirts, napkins, and handkerchiefs, he will not long be secure as to hemp, and will at last have doubts as to tow; for he will revolve in his mind whether he cannot sup without napkins, or dispense with handkerchiefs. Should he deem a daintier food unlawful, he will afterwards feel uneasy for using loafbread and common eatables, because he will think that his body might possibly be supported on a still meaner food. If he hesitates as to a more genial wine, he will scarcely drink the worst with a good conscience; at last he will not

dare to touch water if more than usually sweet and pure. In fine, he will come to this, that he will deem it criminal to trample on a straw lying in his way. For it is no trivial dispute that is here commenced, the point in debate being, whether the use of this thing or that is in accordance with the divine will, which ought to take precedence of all our acts and counsels. Here some must by despair be hurried into an abyss, while others, despising God and casting off his fear, will not be able to make a way for themselves without ruin. When men are involved in such doubts whatever be the direction in which they turn, everything they see must offend their conscience.

8. "I know," says Paul, "that there is nothing unclean of itself" (by unclean meaning unholy); "but to him that esteemeth anything to be unclean, to him it is unclean" (Rom. 14:14). By these words he makes all external things subject to our liberty, provided the nature of that liberty approves itself to our minds as before God. But if any superstitious idea suggests scruples, those things which in their own nature were pure are to us contaminated. Wherefore the apostle adds, "Happy is he that condemneth not himself in that which he alloweth. And he that doubteth is damned if he eat, because he eateth not of faith: for whatsoever is not of faith is sin" (Rom. 14:22-23). When men, amid such difficulties, proceed with greater confidence, securely doing whatever pleases them, do they not insofar revolt from God? Those who are thoroughly impressed with some fear of God, if forced to do many things repugnant to their consciences are discouraged and filled with dread. All such persons receive none of the gifts of God with thanksgiving, by which alone Paul declares that all things are sanctified for our use (1 Tim. 4:5). By "thanksgiving" I understand that which proceeds from a mind recognizing the kindness and goodness of God in his gifts. For many, indeed, understand that the blessings which they enjoy are the gifts of God, and praise God in their works; but not being persuaded that these have been given to them, how can they give thanks to God as the giver? In one word,

we see whither this liberty tends—viz. that we are to use the gifts of God without any scruple of conscience, without any perturbation of mind, for the purpose for which he gave them: in this way our souls may both have peace with him, and recognize his liberality towards us. For here are comprehended all ceremonies of free observance, so that while our consciences are not to be laid under the necessity of observing them, we are also to remember that, by the kindness of God, the use of them is made subservient to edification.

9. It is, however, to be carefully observed, that Christian liberty is in all its parts a spiritual matter, the whole force of which consists in giving peace to trembling consciences, whether they are anxious and disquieted as to the forgiveness of sins, or as to whether their imperfect works, polluted by the infirmities of the flesh, are pleasing to God, or are perplexed as to the use of things indifferent. It is, therefore, perversely interpreted by those who use it as a cloak for their lusts, that they may licentiously abuse the good gifts of God, or who think there is no liberty unless it is used in the presence of men, and, accordingly, in using it pay no regard to their weak brethren. Under this head, the sins of the present age are more numerous. For there is scarcely anyone whose means allow him to live sumptuously, who does not delight in feasting, and dress, and the luxurious grandeur of his house, who wishes not to surpass his neighbor in every kind of delicacy, and does not plume himself amazingly on his splendor. And all these things are defended under the pretext of Christian liberty. They say they are things indifferent: I admit it, provided they are used indifferently. But when they are too eagerly longed for, when they are proudly boasted of, when they are indulged in luxurious profusion, things which otherwise were in themselves lawful are certainly defiled by these vices. Paul makes an admirable distinction in regard to things indifferent: "Unto the pure all things are pure: but unto them that are defiled and unbelieving is nothing pure; but even their mind and conscience is defiled" (Tit. 1:15). For why is a woe pronounced upon the rich who have received their

consolation? (Luke 6:24), who are full, who laugh now, who "lie upon beds of ivory and stretch themselves upon their couches;" "join house to house," and "lay field to field;" "and the harp and the viol, the tablet and pipe, and wine, are in their feasts" (Amos 6:6; Isa. 5:8, 10). Certainly ivory and gold, and riches, are the good creatures of God, permitted, nay, destined, by divine providence for the use of man; nor was it ever forbidden to laugh, or to be full, or to add new to old and hereditary possessions, or to be delighted with music, or to drink wine. This is true, but when the means are supplied to roll and wallow in luxury, to intoxicate the mind and soul with the present and be always hunting after new pleasures, is very far from a legitimate use of the gifts of God. Let them, therefore, suppress immoderate desire, immoderate profusion, vanity, and arrogance, that they may use the gifts of God purely with a pure conscience. When their mind is brought to this state of soberness, they will be able to regulate the legitimate use. On the other hand, when this moderation is wanting, even plebeian and ordinary delicacies are excessive. For it is a true saying, that a haughty mind often dwells in a coarse and homely garb, while true humility lurks under fine linen and purple. Let everyone then live in his own station, poorly or moderately, or in splendor; but let all remember that the nourishment which God gives is for life, not luxury, and let them regard it as the law of Christian liberty, to learn with Paul in whatever state they are, "therewith to be content," to know "both how to be abased," and "how to abound," "to be full and to be hungry, both to abound and to suffer need" (Phil. 4:11).

10. Very many also err in this: as if their liberty were not safe and entire, without having men to witness it, they use it indiscriminately and imprudently, and in this way often give offense to weak brethren. You may see some in the present day who cannot think they possess their liberty unless they come into possession of it by eating flesh on Friday. Their eating I blame not, but this false notion must be driven from their minds: for they ought to think that their liberty gains

nothing new by the sight of men, but is to be enjoyed before God, and consists as much in abstaining as in using. If they understand that it is of no consequence in the sight of God whether they eat flesh or eggs, whether they are clothed in red or in black, this is amply sufficient. The conscience to which the benefit of this liberty was due is loosed. Therefore, though they should afterwards, during their whole life, abstain from flesh, and constantly wear one color, they are not less free. Nay, just because they are free, they abstain with a free conscience. But they err most egregiously in paying no regard to the infirmity of their brethren, with which it becomes us to bear, so as not rashly to give them offense. But it is sometimes also of consequence that we should assert our liberty before men. This I admit: yet must we use great caution in the mode, lest we should cast off the care of the weak whom God has specially committed to us.

11. I will here make some observations on offenses, what distinctions are to be made between them, what kind are to be avoided and what disregarded. This will afterwards enable us to determine what scope there is for our liberty among men. We are pleased with the common division into offense given and offense taken, since it has the plain sanction of Scripture, and not improperly expresses what is meant. If from unseasonable levity or wantonness, or rashness, you do anything out of order or not in its own place, by which the weak or unskillful are offended, it may be said that offense has been given by you, since the ground of offense is owing to your fault. And in general, offense is said to be given in any matter where the person from whom it has proceeded is in fault. Offense is said to be taken when a thing otherwise done, not wickedly or unseasonably, is made an occasion of offense from malevolence or some sinister feeling. For here offense was not given, but sinister interpreters ceaselessly take offense. By the former kind, the weak only, by the latter, the ill-tempered and Pharisaical are offended. Wherefore, we shall call the one the offense of the weak, the other the offense of Pharisees, and we will so temper the

use of our liberty as to make it yield to the ignorance of weak brethren, but not to the austerity of Pharisees. What is due to infirmity is fully shown by Paul in many passages. "Him that is weak in the faith receive ye." Again, "Let us not judge one another any more: but judge this rather, that no man put a stumbling-block, or an occasion to fall, in his brother's way;" and many others to the same effect in the same place, to which, instead of quoting them here, we refer the reader. The sum is, "We then that are strong ought to bear the infirmities of the weak, and not to please ourselves. Let every one of us please his neighbor for his good to edification." Elsewhere he says, "Take heed lest by any means this liberty of yours become a stumbling-block to them that are weak." Again "Whatsoever is sold in the shambles, that eat, asking no question for conscience sake." "Conscience, I say, not thine own, but of the other." Finally, "Give none offense, neither to the Jews nor to the Gentiles nor to the Church of God." Also in another passage, "Brethren, ye have been called into liberty, only use not liberty for an occasion to the flesh, but by love serve one another." Thus, indeed, it is: our liberty was not given us against our weak neighbors, whom charity enjoins us to serve in all things, but rather that, having peace with God in our minds, we should live peaceably among men. What value is to be set upon the offense of the Pharisees we learn from the words of our Lord, in which he says, "Let them alone: they be blind leaders of the blind" (Matt. 15:14). The disciples had intimated that the Pharisees were offended at his words. He answers that they are to be let alone that their offense is not to be regarded.

12. The matter still remains uncertain, unless we understand who are the weak and who the Pharisees: for if this distinction is destroyed, I see not how, in regard to offenses, any liberty at all would remain without being constantly in the greatest danger. But Paul seems to me to have marked out most clearly, as well by example as by doctrine, how far our liberty, in the case of offense, is to be modified or maintained. When he adopts Timothy as his companion, he circumcises

him: nothing can induce him to circumcise Titus (Acts 16:3; Gal. 2:3). The acts are different, but there is no difference in the purpose or intention; in circumcising Timothy, as he was free from all men, he made himself the servant of all: "Unto the Jews I became as a Jew, that I might gain the Jews; to them that are under the law, as under the law, that I might gain them that are under the law; to them that are without law, as without law (being not without law to God, but under the law to Christ), that I might gain them that are without law. To the weak became I as weak that I might gain the weak: I am made all things to all men, that I might by all means save some" (1 Cor. 9:20-22). We have here the proper modification of liberty, when in things indifferent it can be restrained with some advantage. What he had in view in firmly resisting the circumcision of Titus, he himself testifies when he thus writes: "But neither Titus, who was with me, being a Greek, was compelled to be circumcised: and that because of false brethren unawares brought in, who came in privily to spy out our liberty which we have in Christ Jesus, that they might bring us into bondage: to whom we gave place by subjection, no, not for an hour, that the truth of the gospel might continue with you" (Gal. 2:3-5). We here see the necessity of vindicating our liberty when, by the unjust exactions of false apostles, it is brought into danger with weak consciences. In all cases we must study charity, and look to the edification of our neighbor. "All things are lawful for me," says he, "but all things are not expedient; all things are lawful for me, but all things edify not. Let no man seek his own, but every man another's wealth" (1 Cor. 10:23-24). There is nothing plainer than this rule, that we are to use our liberty if it tends to the edification of our neighbor, but if inexpedient for our neighbor, we are to abstain from it. There are some who pretend to imitate this prudence of Paul by abstinence from liberty, while there is nothing for which they less employ it than for purposes of charity. Consulting their own ease, they would have all mention of liberty buried, though it is not less for the interest of our neighbor to use liberty for their good and edification, than to modify it occasionally for their advantage. It is the part of a pious man to think, that the free power conceded to him in external things is to make him the readier in all offices of charity.

13. Whatever I have said about avoiding offenses, I wish to be referred to things indifferent. Things which are necessary to be done cannot be omitted from any fear of offense. For as our liberty is to be made subservient to charity, so charity must in its turn be subordinate to purity of faith. Here, too, regard must be had to charity, but it must go as far as the altar; that is, we must not offend God for the sake of our neighbor. We approve not of the intemperance of those who do everything tumultuously, and would rather burst through every restraint at once than proceed step by step. But neither are those to be listened to who, while they take the lead in a thousand forms of impiety, pretend that they act thus to avoid giving offense to their neighbor, as if in the meantime they did not train the consciences of their neighbors to evil, especially when they always stick in the same mire without any hope of escape. When a neighbor is to be instructed, whether by doctrine or by example, then smooth-tongued men say that he is to be fed with milk, while they are instilling into him the worst and most pernicious opinions. Paul says to the Corinthians, "I have fed you with milk, and not with meat" (1 Cor. 3:2); but had there then been a Popish mass among them, would he have sacrificed as one of the modes of giving them milk? By no means: milk is not poison. It is false then to say they nourish those whom, under a semblance of soothing they cruelly murder. But granting that such dissimulation may be used for a time, how long are they to make their pupils drink that kind of milk? If they never grow up so as to be able to bear at least some gentle food, it is certain that they have never been reared on milk. Two reasons prevent me from now entering farther into contest with these people, first, their follies are scarcely worthy of refutation, seeing all men of sense must nauseate them;

and, secondly, having already amply refuted them in special treatises, I am unwilling to do it over again. Let my readers only bear in mind, first, that whatever be the offenses by which Satan and the world attempt to lead us away from the law of God, we must, nevertheless, strenuously proceed in the course which he prescribes; and, secondly, that whatever dangers impend, we are not at liberty to deviate one nail's breadth from the command of God, that on no pretext is it lawful to attempt anything but what he permits.

14. Since by means of this privilege of liberty which we have described, believers have derived authority from Christ not to entangle themselves by the observance of things in which he wished them to be free, we conclude that their consciences are exempted from all human authority. For it were unbecoming that the gratitude due to Christ for his liberal gift should perish or that the consciences of believers should derive no benefit from it. We must not regard it as a trivial matter when we see how much it cost our Savior, being purchased not with silver or gold, but with his own blood (1 Pet. 1:18-19); so that Paul hesitates not to say that Christ has died in vain, if we place our souls under subjection to men (Gal. 5:1, 4; 1 Cor. 7:23). Several chapters of the Epistle to the Galatians are wholly occupied with showing that Christ is obscured, or rather extinguished to us, unless our consciences maintain their liberty; from which they have certainly fallen, if they can be bound with the chains of laws and constitutions at the pleasure of men. But as the knowledge of this subject is of the greatest importance, so it demands a longer and clearer exposition. For the moment the abolition of human constitutions is mentioned, the greatest disturbances are excited, partly by the seditious, and partly by calumniators, as if obedience of every kind were at the same time abolished and overthrown.

15. Therefore, lest this prove a stumbling-block to any, let us observe that in man government is twofold: the one spiritual, by which the conscience is trained to piety and divine worship; the other civil, by

which the individual is instructed in those duties which, as men and citizens, we are bold to performs (see Book 4, chap. 10, sec. 3-6). To these two forms are commonly given the not inappropriate names of spiritual and temporal jurisdiction, intimating that the former species has reference to the life of the soul, while the latter relates to matters of the present life, not only to food and clothing, but to the enacting of laws which require a man to live among his fellows purely, honorably, and modestly. The former has its seat within the soul, the latter only regulates the external conduct. We may call the one the spiritual, the other the civil kingdom. Now, these two, as we have divided them, are always to be viewed apart from each other. When the one is considered, we should call off our minds, and not allow them to think of the other. For there exists in man a kind of two worlds, over which different kings and different laws can preside. By attending to this distinction, we will not erroneously transfer the doctrine of the gospel concerning spiritual liberty to civil order, as if in regard to external government Christians were less subject to human laws, because their consciences are unbound before God, as if they were exempted from all carnal service, because in regard to the Spirit they are free. Again, because even in those constitutions which seem to relate to the spiritual kingdom, there may be some delusion, it is necessary to distinguish between those which are to be held legitimate as being agreeable to the Word of God, and those, on the other hand, which ought to have no place among the pious. We shall elsewhere have an opportunity of speaking of civil government (see Book 4, chap. 20). For the present, also, I defer speaking of ecclesiastical laws, because that subject will be more fully discussed in the Fourth Book when we come to treat of the Power of the Church. We would thus conclude the present discussion. The question, as I have said, though not very obscure, or perplexing in itself, occasions difficulty to many, because they do not distinguish with sufficient accuracy between what is called the external forum, and the forum of conscience. What increases the difficulty is, that Paul commands us to obey the magistrate, "not only for wrath, but also for conscience's sake" (Rom. 13:1, 5). Whence it follows that civil laws also bind the conscience. Were this so, then what we said a little ago, and are still to say of spiritual governments would fall. To solve this difficulty, the first thing of importance is to understand what is meant by "conscience." The definition must be sought in the etymology of the word. For as men, when they apprehend the knowledge of things by the mind and intellects are said to know, and hence arises the term "knowledge" or "science," so when they have a sense of the divine justice added as a witness which allows them not to conceal their sins, but drags them forward as culprits to the bar of God, that sense is called "conscience." For it stands as it were between God and man, not suffering man to suppress what he knows in himself; but following him on even to conviction. It is this that Paul means when he says, "Their conscience also bearing witness, and their thoughts the meanwhile accusing, or else excusing one another" (Rom. 2:15). Simple knowledge may exist in man, as it were shut up; therefore this sense, which sists man before the bar of God, is set over him as a kind of sentinel to observe and spy out all his secrets, that nothing may remain buried in darkness. Hence the ancient proverb, Conscience is a thousand witnesses. For the same reason, Peter also employs the expression, "the answer of a good conscience" (1 Pet. 3:21), for tranquility of mind; when persuaded of the grace of Christ, we boldly present ourselves before God. And the author of the Epistle to the Hebrews says, that we have "no more conscience of sins" (Heb. 10:2), that we are held as freed or acquitted, so that sin no longer accuses us.

16. Wherefore, as works have respect to men, so conscience bears reference to God, a good conscience being nothing else than inward integrity of heart. In this sense, Paul says that "the end of the commandment is charity, out of a pure heart, and of a good consciences, and of faith unfeigned" (1 Tim. 1:5). He afterwards, in the same chapter, shows how much it differs from intellect when he speaks of

"holding faith, and a good conscience; which some having put away, have made shipwreck" (1 Tim. 1:19). For by these words he intimates, that it is a lively inclination to serve God, a sincere desire to live in piety and holiness. Sometimes, indeed, it is even extended to men, as when Paul testifies, "Herein do I exercise myself, to have always a conscience void of offense toward God, and toward men" (Acts 24:16). He speaks thus, because the fruits of a good conscience go forth and reach even to men. But, as I have said, properly speaking, it refers to God only. Hence a law is said to bind the conscience, because it simply binds the individual, without looking at men, or taking any account of them. For example, God not only commands us to keep our mind chaste and pure from lust, but prohibits all external lasciviousness or obscenity of language. My conscience is subjected to the observance of this law, though there were not another man in the world, and he who violates it sins not only by setting a bad example to his brethren, but stands convicted in his conscience before God. The same rule does not hold in things indifferent. We ought to abstain from everything that produces offense, but with a free conscience. Thus Paul, speaking of meat consecrated to idols, says, "If any man say unto you, This is offered in sacrifice unto idols, eat not for his sake that showed it, and for conscience's sake:" "Conscience, I say, not thine own, but of the other" (1 Cor. 10:28-29). A believer, after being previously admonished, would sin were he still to eat meat so offered. But though abstinence, on his part, is necessary, in respect of a brother, as it is prescribed by God, still he ceases not to retain liberty of conscience. We see how the law, while binding the external act, leaves the conscience unbound.

Study Guide Questions

Section 1

1. How many aspects to Christian freedom are there?
2. Is Christian liberty important?

3. What are the two errors he describes with regard to Christian liberty?

Section 2
1. What is the first error he addresses?

Section 3
1. Is the letter to the Galatians simply about freedom from ceremonies?
2. What is that loftier something?

Section 4
1. What is true obedience?
2. Does anyone do this fully?

Section 5
1. What two kinds of obedience does Calvin compare here?
2. What passage does Calvin cite to justify his statement of how God receives our labors?

Section 6
1. What do we need not fear now that we have been emancipated by grace?

Section 7
1. Why do we need to really understand the importance of what is "indifferent" and what is not?
2. What does Calvin understand about the nature of "scruples"?

Section 8
1. How should we use God's gifts?

Section 9
1. Are luxuries a thing indifferent?

2. Has God forbidden us to use lovely things?

Section 10

1. What other key element must we remember in using our liberty?

Section 11

1. What fundamental distinction does Calvin make between different kinds of offenses?
2. Who takes offense with each kind?

Section 12

1. What two situations did Paul handle differently, but with "no difference in the purpose or intention"?

Section 13

1. What limit is placed on our use of freedom?

Section 14

1. From what is the believing human conscience freed by Christ?

Section 15

1. What are the two kingdoms among men?
2. In which forum do we find each respectively?

Section 16

1. What is a good conscience?

CHAPTER 20

Of prayer—A perpetual exercise of faith. The daily benefits
derived from it.

The principal divisions of this chapter are—
I. Connection of the subject of prayer with the previous
chapters. The nature of prayer, and its necessity as a Christian exercise, sec. 1-2.

II. To whom prayer is to be offered. Refutation of an objection
which is too apt to present itself to the mind, sec. 3.

III. Rules to be observed in prayer, sec. 4-16.

IV. Through whom prayer is to be made, sec. 17-19.

V. Refutation of an error as to the doctrine of our Mediator and
Intercessor, with answers to the leading arguments urged in support
of the intercession of saints, sec. 20-27.

VI. The nature of prayer, and some of its accidents, sec. 28-33.

VII. A perfect form of invocation, or an exposition of the Lord's
Prayer, sec. 34-50.

VIII. Some rules to be observed with regard to prayer, as time,
perseverance, the feeling of the mind, and the assurance of faith, sec.
50-52.

Outline:

1. A general summary of what is contained in the previous part of the work. A transition to the doctrine of prayer. Its connection with the subject of faith.

2. Prayer defined. Its necessity and use.

3. Objection, that prayer seems useless, because God already knows our wants. Answer, from the institution and end of prayer. Confirmation by example. Its necessity and propriety. Perpetually reminds us of our duty, and leads to meditation on divine providence. Conclusion. Prayer a most useful exercise. This proved by three passages of Scripture.

4. Rules to be observed in prayer. First, reverence to God. How the mind ought to be composed.

5. All giddiness of mind must be excluded, and all our feelings seriously engaged. This confirmed by the form of lifting the hand in prayer. We must ask only insofar as God permits. To help our weakness, God gives the Spirit to be our guide in prayer. What the office of the Spirit in this respect. We must still pray both with the heart and the lips.

6. Second rule of prayer, a sense of our want. This rule violated, 1. By perfunctory and formal prayer 2. By hypocrites who have no sense of their sins. 3. By giddiness in prayer. Remedies.

7. Objection, that we are not always under the same necessity of praying. Answer, we must pray always. This answer confirmed by an examination of the dangers by which both our life and our salvation are every moment threatened. Confirmed farther by the command and permission of God, by the nature of true repentance, and a consideration of impenitence. Conclusion.

8. Third rule, the suppression of all pride. Examples. Daniel, David, Isaiah, Jeremiah, Baruch.

9. Advantage of thus suppressing pride. It leads to earnest entreaty for pardon, accompanied with humble confession and sure confidence

in the Divine mercy. This may not always be expressed in words. It is peculiar to pious penitents. A general introduction to procure favor to our prayers never to be omitted.

10. Objection to the third rule of prayer. Of the glorying of the saints. Answer. Confirmation of the answer.

11. Fourth rule of prayer—a sure confidence of being heard animating us to prayer. The kind of confidence required—viz. a serious conviction of our misery, joined with sure hope. From these true prayer springs. How diffidence impairs prayer. In general, faith is required.

12. This faith and sure hope regarded by our opponents as most absurd. Their error described and refuted by various passages of Scripture, which show that acceptable prayer is accompanied with these qualities. No repugnance between this certainty and an acknowledgment of our destitution.

13. To our unworthiness we oppose, 1. The command of God. 2. The promise. Rebels and hypocrites completely condemned. Passages of Scripture confirming the command to pray.

14. Other passages respecting the promises which belong to the pious when they invoke God. These realized though we are not possessed of the same holiness as other distinguished servants of God, provided we indulge no vain confidence, and sincerely betake ourselves to the mercy of God. Those who do not invoke God under urgent necessity are no better than idolaters. This concurrence of fear and confidence reconciles the different passages of Scripture, as to humbling ourselves in prayer, and causing our prayers to ascend.

15. Objection founded on some examples—viz. that prayers have proved effectual, though not according to the form prescribed. Answer. Such examples, though not given for our imitation, are of the greatest use. Objection, the prayers of the faithful sometimes not effectual. Answer confirmed by a noble passage of Augustine. Rule for right prayer.

16. The above four rules of prayer not so rigidly exacted, as that every prayer deficient in them in any respect is rejected by God. This shown by examples. Conclusion, or summary of this section.

17. Through whom God is to be invoked—viz. Jesus Christ. This founded on a consideration of the divine majesty, and the precept and promise of God himself. God therefore to be invoked only in the name of Christ.

18. From the first all believers were heard through him only: yet this specially restricted to the period subsequent to his ascension. The ground of this restriction.

19. The wrath of God lies on those who reject Christ as a Mediator. This excludes not the mutual intercession of saints on the earth.

20. Refutation of errors interfering with the intercession of Christ. 1. Christ the Mediator of redemption; the saints mediators of intercession. Answer confirmed by the clear testimony of Scripture, and by a passage from Augustine. The nature of Christ's intercession.

21. Of the intercession of saints living with Christ in heaven. Fiction of the Papists in regard to it. Refuted. 1. Its absurdity. 2. It is no where mentioned by Scripture. 3. Appeal to the conscience of the superstitious. 4. Its blasphemy. Exception. Answers.

22. Monstrous errors resulting from this fiction. Refutation. Exception by the advocates of this fiction. Answer.

23. Arguments of the Papists for the intercession of saints. 1. From the duty and office of angels. Answer. 2. From an expression of Jeremiah respecting Moses and Samuel. Answer, retorting the argument. 3. The meaning of the prophet confirmed by a similar passage in Ezekiel, and the testimony of an apostle.

24. 4. Fourth Papistical argument from the nature of charity, which is more perfect in the saints in glory. Answer.

25. Argument founded on a passage in Moses. Answer.

26. Argument from its being said that the prayers of saints are heard. Answer, confirmed by Scripture, and illustrated by examples.

27. Conclusion, that the saints cannot be invoked without impiety. 1. It robs God of his glory. 2. Destroys the intercession of Christ. 3. Is repugnant to the word of God. 4. Is opposed to the due method of prayer. 5. Is without approved example. 6. Springs from distrust. Last objection. Answer.

28. Kinds of prayer. Vows. Supplications. Petitions. Thanksgiving. Connection of these, their constant use and necessity. Particular explanation confirmed by reason, Scripture, and example. Rule as to supplication and thanksgiving.

29. The accidents of prayer—viz. private and public, constant, at stated seasons, &c. Exception in time of necessity. Prayer without ceasing. Its nature. Garrulity of Papists and hypocrites refuted. The scope and parts of prayer. Secret prayer. Prayer at all places. Private and public prayer.

30. Of public places or churches in which common prayers are offered up. Right use of churches. Abuse.

31. Of utterance and singing. These of no avail if not from the heart. The use of the voice refers more to public than private prayer.

32. Singing of the greatest antiquity, but not universal. How to be performed.

33. Public prayers should be in the vulgar, not in a foreign tongue. Reason, 1. The nature of the Church. 2. Authority of an apostle. Sincere affection always necessary. The tongue not always necessary. Bending of the knee, and uncovering of the head.

34. The form of prayer delivered by Christ displays the boundless goodness of our heavenly Father. The great comfort thereby afforded.

35. Lord's Prayer divided into six petitions. Subdivision into two principal parts, the former referring to the glory of God, the latter to our salvation.

36. The use of the term "Father" implies, 1. That we pray to God in the name of Christ alone. 2. That we lay aside all distrust. 3. That we expect everything that is for our good.

37. Objection, that our sins exclude us from the presence of him whom we have made a Judge, not a Father. Answer, from the nature of God, as described by an apostle, the parable of the prodigal son, and from the expression, "Our Father." Christ the earnest, the Holy Spirit the witness, of our adoption.

38. Why God is called generally, Our Father.

39. We may pray specially for ourselves and certain others, provided we have in our mind a general reference to all.

40. In what sense God is said to be in heaven. A threefold use of this doctrine for our consolation. Three cautions. Summary of the preface to the Lord's Prayer.

41. The necessity of the first petition a proof of our unrighteousness. What meant by the name of God. How it is hallowed. Parts of this hallowing. A deprecation of the sins by which the name of God is profaned.

42. Distinction between the first and second petitions. The kingdom of God, what. How said to come. Special exposition of this petition. It reminds us of three things. Advent of the kingdom of God in the world.

43. Distinction between the second and third petitions. The will here meant not the secret will or good pleasure of God, but that manifested in the word. Conclusion of the three first petitions.

44. A summary of the second part of the Lord's Prayer. Three petitions. What contained in the first. Declares the exceeding kindness of God, and our distrust. What meant by bread. Why the petition for bread precedes that for the forgiveness of sins. Why it is called ours. Why to be sought this day, or daily. The doctrine resulting from this petition, illustrated by an example. Two classes of men sin in regard to this petition. In what sense it is called, our bread. Why we ask God to give it to us.

45. Close connection between this and the subsequent petition. Why our sins are called debts. This petition violated, 1. By those who

think they can satisfy God by their own merits, or those of others. 2. By those who dream of a perfection which makes pardon unnecessary. Why the elect cannot attain perfection in this life. Refutation of the libertine dreamers of perfection. Objection refuted. In what sense we are said to forgive those who have sinned against us. How the condition is to be understood.

46. The sixth petition reduced to three heads. 1. The various forms of temptation. The depraved conceptions of our minds. The wiles of Satan, on the right hand and on the left. 2. What it is to be led into temptation. We do not ask not to be tempted of God. What meant by evil, or the evil one. Summary of this petition. How necessary it is. Condemns the pride of the superstitious. Includes many excellent properties. In what sense God may be said to lead us into temptation.

47. The three last petitions show that the prayers of Christians ought to be public. The conclusion of the Lord's Prayer. Why the word "Amen" is added.

48. The Lord's Prayer contains everything that we can or ought to ask of God. Those who go beyond it sin in three ways.

49. We may, after the example of the saints, frame our prayers in different words, provided there is no difference in meaning.

50. Some circumstances to be observed. Of appointing special hours of prayer. What to be aimed at, what avoided. The will of God, the rule of our prayers.

51. Perseverance in prayer especially recommended, both by precept and example. Condemnatory of those who assign to God a time and mode of hearing.

52. Of the dignity of faith, through which we always obtain, in answer to prayer, whatever is most expedient for us. The knowledge of this most necessary.

From the previous part of the work we clearly see how completely destitute man is of all good, how devoid of every means of procuring his own salvation. Hence, if he would obtain succor in his necessity, he must go beyond himself, and procure it in some other quarter. It has farther been shown that the Lord kindly and spontaneously manifests himself in Christ, in whom he offers all happiness for our misery, all abundance for our want, opening up the treasures of heaven to us, so that we may turn with full faith to his beloved Son, depend upon him with full expectation, rest in him, and cleave to him with full hope. This, indeed, is that secret and hidden philosophy which cannot be learned by syllogisms: a philosophy thoroughly understood by those whose eyes God has so opened as to see light in his light (Ps. 36:9). But after we have learned by faith to know that whatever is necessary for us or defective in us is supplied in God and in our Lord Jesus Christ, in whom it hath pleased the Father that all fullness should dwell, that we may thence draw as from an inexhaustible fountain, it remains for us to seek and in prayer implore of him what we have learned to be in him. To know God as the sovereign disposer of all good, inviting us to present our requests, and yet not to approach or ask of him, were so far from availing us, that it were just as if one told of a treasure were to allow it to remain buried in the ground. Hence the Apostle, to show that a faith unaccompanied with prayer to God cannot be genuine, states this to be the order: As faith springs from the Gospel, so by faith our hearts are framed to call upon the name of God (Rom. 10:14). And this is the very thing which he had expressed some time before—viz. that the Spirit of adoption, which seals the testimony of the Gospel on our hearts, gives us courage to make our requests known unto God, calls forth groanings which cannot be uttered, and enables us to cry, Abba, Father (Rom. 8:26). This last point, as we have hitherto only touched upon it slightly in passing, must now be treated more fully.

2. To prayer, then, are we indebted for penetrating to those riches which are treasured up for us with our heavenly Father. For there is a kind of intercourse between God and men, by which, having entered

the upper sanctuary, they appear before Him and appeal to his promises, that when necessity requires they may learn by experiences that what they believed merely on the authority of his word was not in vain. Accordingly, we see that nothing is set before us as an object of expectation from the Lord which we are not enjoined to ask of Him in prayer, so true it is that prayer digs up those treasures which the Gospel of our Lord discovers to the eye of faith. The necessity and utility of this exercise of prayer no words can sufficiently express. Assuredly it is not without cause our heavenly Father declares that our only safety is in calling upon his name, since by it we invoke the presence of his providence to watch over our interests, of his power to sustain us when weak and almost fainting, of his goodness to receive us into favor, though miserably loaded with sin; in fine, call upon him to manifest himself to us in all his perfections. Hence, admirable peace and tranquility are given to our consciences; for the straits by which we were pressed being laid before the Lord, we rest fully satisfied with the assurance that none of our evils are unknown to him, and that he is both able and willing to make the best provision for us.

3. But someone will say, Does he not know without a monitor both what our difficulties are, and what is meet for our interest, so that it seems in some measure superfluous to solicit him by our prayers, as if he were winking, or even sleeping, until aroused by the sound of our voice? Those who argue thus attend not to the end for which the Lord taught us to pray. It was not so much for his sake as for ours. He wills indeed, as is just, that due honor be paid him by acknowledging that all which men desire or feel to be useful, and pray to obtain, is derived from him. But even the benefit of the homage which we thus pay him redounds to ourselves. Hence the holy patriarchs, the more confidently they proclaimed the mercies of God to themselves and others felt the stronger incitement to prayer. It will be sufficient to refer to the example of Elijah, who being assured of the purpose of God had good ground for the promise of rain which he gives to Ahab,

and yet prays anxiously upon his knees, and sends his servant seven
times to inquire (1 Kings 18:42); not that he discredits the oracle, but
because he knows it to be his duty to lay his desires before God, lest
his faith should become drowsy or torpid. Wherefore, although it is
true that while we are listless or insensible to our wretchedness, he
wakes and watches for use and sometimes even assists us unasked; it
is very much for our interest to be constantly supplicating him; first,
that our heart may always be inflamed with a serious and ardent desire of seeking, loving and serving him, while we accustom ourselves
to have recourse to him as a sacred anchor in every necessity; secondly, that no desires, no longing whatever, of which we are ashamed to
make him the witness, may enter our minds, while we learn to place
all our wishes in his sight, and thus pour out our heart before him;
and, lastly, that we may be prepared to receive all his benefits with true
gratitude and thanksgiving, while our prayers remind us that they
proceed from his hand. Moreover, having obtained what we asked,
being persuaded that he has answered our prayers, we are led to long
more earnestly for his favor, and at the same time have greater pleasure in welcoming the blessings which we perceive to have been obtained by our prayers. Lastly, use and experience confirm the thought
of his providence in our minds in a manner adapted to our weakness,
when we understand that he not only promises that he will never fail
us, and spontaneously gives us access to approach him in every time
of need, but has his hand always stretched out to assist his people, not
amusing them with words, but proving himself to be a present aid.
For these reasons, though our most merciful Father never slumbers
nor sleeps, he very often seems to do so, that thus he may exercise us,
when we might otherwise be listless and slothful, in asking, entreating, and earnestly beseeching him to our great good. It is very absurd,
therefore, to dissuade men from prayer, by pretending that Divine
Providence, which is always watching over the government of the
universes is in vain importuned by our supplications, when, on the

contrary, the Lord himself declares, that he is "nigh unto all that call upon him, to all that call upon him in truth" (Ps. 145:18). No better is the frivolous allegation of others, that it is superfluous to pray for things which the Lord is ready of his own accord to bestow; since it is his pleasure that those very things which flow from his spontaneous liberality should be acknowledged as conceded to our prayers. This is testified by that memorable sentence in the psalms to which many others corresponds: "The eyes of the Lord are upon the righteous, and his ears are open unto their cry" (Ps. 34:15). This passage, while extolling the care which Divine Providence spontaneously exercises over the safety of believers, omits not the exercise of faith by which the mind is aroused from sloth. The eyes of God are awake to assist the blind in their necessity, but he is likewise pleased to listen to our groans, that he may give us the better proof of his love. And thus both things are true, "He that keepeth Israel shall neither slumber nor sleep" (Ps. 121:4); and yet whenever he sees us dumb and torpid, he withdraws as if he had forgotten us.

4. Let the first rule of right prayer then be, to have our heart and mind framed as becomes those who are entering into converse with God. This we shall accomplish in regard to the mind, if, laying aside carnal thoughts and cares which might interfere with the direct and pure contemplation of God, it not only be wholly intent on prayer, but also, as far as possible, be borne and raised above itself. I do not here insist on a mind so disengaged as to feel none of the gnawings of anxiety; on the contrary, it is by much anxiety that the fervor of prayer is inflamed. Thus we see that the holy servants of God betray great anguish, not to say solicitude, when they cause the voice of complaint to ascend to the Lord from the deep abyss and the jaws of death. What I say is, that all foreign and extraneous cares must be dispelled by which the mind might be driven to and fro in vague suspense, be drawn down from heaven, and kept groveling on the earth. When I say it must be raised above itself, I mean that it must not bring into

the presence of God any of those things which our blind and stupid reason is wont to devise, nor keep itself confined within the little measure of its own vanity, but rise to a purity worthy of God.

5. Both things are specially worthy of notice. First, let every one in professing to pray turn thither all his thoughts and feelings, and be not (as is usual) distracted by wandering thoughts; because nothing is more contrary to the reverence due to God than that levity which bespeaks a mind too much given to license and devoid of fear. In this matter we ought to labor the more earnestly the more difficult we experience it to be; for no man is so intent on prayer as not to feel many thoughts creeping in, and either breaking off the tenor of his prayer, or retarding it by some turning or digression. Here let us consider how unbecoming it is when God admits us to familiar intercourse to abuse his great condescension by mingling things sacred and profane, reverence for him not keeping our minds under restraint; but just as if in prayer we were conversing with one like ourselves forgetting him, and allowing our thoughts to run to and fro. Let us know, then, that none duly prepare themselves for prayer but those who are so impressed with the majesty of God that they engage in it free from all earthly cares and affections. The ceremony of lifting up our hands in prayer is designed to remind us that we are far removed from God, unless our thoughts rise upward: as it is said in the psalm, "Unto thee, O Lord, do I lift up my soul" (Ps. 25:1). And Scripture repeatedly uses the expression "to raise our prayer," meaning that those who would be heard by God must not grovel in the mire. The sum is, that the more liberally God deals with us, condescendingly inviting us to disburden our cares into his bosom, the less excusable we are if this admirable and incomparable blessing does not in our estimation outweigh all other things, and win our affection, that prayer may seriously engage our every thought and feeling. This cannot be unless our mind, strenuously exerting itself against all impediments, rise upward. Our second proposition was, that we are to ask only insofar as God

permits. For though he bids us pour out our hearts (Ps. 62:8) he does not indiscriminately give loose reins to foolish and depraved affections; and when he promises that he will grant believers their wish, his indulgence does not proceed so far as to submit to their caprice. In both matters grievous delinquencies are everywhere committed. For not only do many without modesty, without reverence, presume to invoke God concerning their frivolities, but impudently bring forward their dreams, whatever they may be, before the tribunal of God. Such is the folly or stupidity under which they labor, that they have the hardihood to obtrude upon God desires so vile, that they would blush exceedingly to impart them to their fellow men. Profane writers have derided and even expressed their detestation of this presumption, and yet the vice has always prevailed. Hence, as the ambitious adopted Jupiter as their patron; the avaricious, Mercury; the literary aspirants, Apollo and Minerva; the warlike, Mars; the licentious, Venus: so in the present day, as I lately observed, men in prayer give greater license to their unlawful desires than if they were telling jocular tales among their equals. God does not suffer his condescension to be thus mocked, but vindicating his own light, places our wishes under the restraint of his authority. We must, therefore, attend to the observation of John, "This is the confidence that we have in him, that if we ask anything according to his will, he heareth us" (1 John 5:14). But as our faculties are far from being able to attain to such high perfection, we must seek for some means to assist them. As the eye of our mind should be intent upon God, so the affection of our heart ought to follow in the same course. But both fall far beneath this, or rather, they faint and fail, and are carried in a contrary direction. To assist this weakness, God gives us the guidance of the Spirit in our prayers to dictate what is right, and regulate our affections. For seeing "we know not what we should pray for as we ought," "the Spirit itself maketh intercession for us with groanings which cannot be uttered" (Rom. 8:26) not that he actually prays or groans, but he excites in us sighs, and wishes, and confidence, which our natural powers are not at all able to conceive. Nor is it without cause Paul gives the name of groanings which cannot be uttered to the prayers which believers send forth under the guidance of the Spirit. For those who are truly exercised in prayer are not unaware that blind anxieties so restrain and perplex them, that they can scarcely find what it becomes them to utter; nay, in attempting to lisp they halt and hesitate. Hence it appears that to pray aright is a special gift. We do not speak thus in indulgence to our sloth, as if we were to leave the office of prayer to the Holy Spirit, and give way to that carelessness to which we are too prone. Thus we sometimes hear the impious expression, that we are to wait in suspense until he take possession of our minds while otherwise occupied. Our meaning is, that, weary of our own heartlessness and sloth, we are to long for the aid of the Spirit. Nor, indeed, does Paul, when he enjoins us to pray in the Spirit (1 Cor. 14:15), cease to exhort us to vigilance, intimating, that while the inspiration of the Spirit is effectual to the formation of prayer, it by no means impedes or retards our own endeavors; since in this matter God is pleased to try how efficiently faith influences our hearts.

6. Another rule of prayer is, that in asking we must always truly feel our wants, and seriously considering that we need all the things which we ask, accompany the prayer with a sincere, nay, ardent desire of obtaining them. Many repeat prayers in a perfunctory manner from a set form, as if they were performing a task to God, and though they confess that this is a necessary remedy for the evils of their condition, because it were fatal to be left without the divine aid which they implore, it still appears that they perform the duty from custom, because their minds are meanwhile cold, and they ponder not what they ask. A general and confused feeling of their necessity leads them to pray, but it does not make them solicitous as in a matter of present consequence, that they may obtain the supply of their need. Moreover, can we suppose anything more hateful or even more execrable to

God than this fiction of asking the pardon of sins, while he who asks at the very time either thinks that he is not a sinner, or, at least, is not thinking that he is a sinner; in other words, a fiction by which God is plainly held in derision? But mankind, as I have lately said, are full of depravity, so that in the way of perfunctory service they often ask many things of God which they think come to them without his beneficence, or from some other quarter, or are already certainly in their possession. There is another fault which seems less heinous, but is not to be tolerated. Some murmur out prayers without meditation, their only principle being that God is to be propitiated by prayer. Believers ought to be specially on their guard never to appear in the presence of God with the intention of presenting a request unless they are under some serious impression, and are, at the same time, desirous to obtain it. Nay, although in these things which we ask only for the glory of God, we seem not at first sight to consult for our necessity, yet we ought not to ask with less fervor and vehemence of desire. For instance, when we pray that his name be hallowed—that hallowing must, so to speak, be earnestly hungered and thirsted after.

7. If it is objected, that the necessity which urges us to pray is not always equal, I admit it, and this distinction is profitably taught us by James: "Is any among you afflicted? let him pray. Is any merry? let him sing psalms" (James 5:13). Therefore, common sense itself dictates, that as we are too sluggish, we must be stimulated by God to pray earnestly whenever the occasion requires. This David calls a time when God "may be found" (a seasonable time); because, as he declares in several other passages, that the more hardly grievances, annoyances, fears, and other kinds of trial press us, the freer is our access to God, as if he were inviting us to himself. Still not less true is the injunction of Paul to pray "always" (Eph. 6:18); because, however prosperously according to our view, things proceed, and however we may be surrounded on all sides with grounds of joy, there is not an instant of time during which our want does not exhort us to prayer.

A man abounds in wheat and wine; but as he cannot enjoy a morsel of bread, unless by the continual bounty of God, his granaries or cellars will not prevent him from asking for daily bread. Then, if we consider how many dangers impend every moment, fear itself will teach us that no time ought to be without prayer. This, however, may be better known in spiritual matters. For when will the many sins of which we are conscious allow us to sit secure without suppliantly entreating freedom from guilt and punishment? When will temptation give us a truce, making it unnecessary to hasten for help? Moreover, zeal for the kingdom and glory of God ought not to seize us by starts, but urge us without intermission, so that every time should appear seasonable. It is not without cause, therefore, that assiduity in prayer is so often enjoined. I am not now speaking of perseverance, which shall afterwards be considered; but Scripture, by reminding us of the necessity of constant prayer, charges us with sloth, because we feel not how much we stand in need of this care and assiduity. By this rule hypocrisy and the device of lying to God are restrained, nay, altogether banished from prayer. God promises that he will be near to those who call upon him in truth, and declares that those who seek him with their whole heart will find him: those, therefore, who delight in their own pollution cannot surely aspire to him. One of the requisites of legitimate prayer is repentance. Hence the common declaration of Scripture, that God does not listen to the wicked; that their prayers, as well as their sacrifices, are an abomination to him. For it is right that those who seal up their hearts should find the ears of God closed against them, that those who, by their hardheartedness, provoke his severity should find him inflexible. In Isaiah he thus threatens: "When ye make many prayers, I will not hear: your hands are full of blood" (Isa. 1:15). In like manner, in Jeremiah, "Though they shall cry unto me, I will not hearken unto them" (Jer. 11:7-8, 11); because he regards it as the highest insult for the wicked to boast of his covenant while profaning his sacred name by their whole lives.

Hence he complains in Isaiah: "This people draw near to me with their mouth, and with their lips do honor me; but have removed their heart far from me" (Isa. 29:13). Indeed, he does not confine this to prayers alone, but declares that he abominates pretense in every part of his service. Hence the words of James, "Ye ask and receive not, because ye ask amiss, that ye may consume it upon your lusts" (James 4:3). It is true, indeed (as we shall again see in a little), that the pious, in the prayers which they utter, trust not to their own worth; still the admonition of John is not superfluous: "Whatsoever we ask, we receive of him, because we keep his commandments" (1 John 3:22); an evil conscience shuts the door against us. Hence it follows, that none but the sincere worshipers of God pray aright, or are listened to. Let everyone, therefore, who prepares to pray feel dissatisfied with what is wrong in his condition, and assume, which he cannot do without repentance, the character and feelings of a poor suppliant.

8. The third rule to be added is: that he who comes into the presence of God to pray must divest himself of all vainglorious thoughts, lay aside all idea of worth; in short, discard all self-confidence, humbly giving God the whole glory, lest by arrogating anything, however little, to himself, vain pride cause him to turn away his face. Of this submission, which casts down all haughtiness, we have numerous examples in the servants of God. The holier they are, the more humbly they prostrate themselves when they come into the presence of the Lord. Thus Daniel, on whom the Lord himself bestowed such high commendation, says, "We do not present our supplications before thee for our righteousness but for thy great mercies. O Lord, hear; O Lord, forgive; O Lord, hearken and do; defer not, for thine own sake, O my God: for thy city and thy people are called by thy name." This he does not indirectly in the usual manner, as if he were one of the individuals in a crowd: he rather confesses his guilt apart, and as a suppliant betaking himself to the asylum of pardon, he distinctly declares that he was confessing his own sin, and the sin of his people

Israel (Dan. 9:18-20). David also sets us an example of this humility: "Enter not into judgment with thy servant: for in thy sight shall
no man living be justified" (Ps. 143:2). In like manner, Isaiah prays,
"Behold, thou art wroth; for we have sinned: in those is continuance,
and we shall be saved. But we are all as an unclean thing, and all our
righteousnesses are as filthy rags; and we all do fade as a leaf; and our
iniquities, like the wind, have taken us away. And there is none that
calleth upon thy name, that stirreth up himself to take hold of thee:
for thou hast hid thy face from us, and hast consumed us, because
of our iniquities. But now, O Lord, thou art our Father; we are the
clay, and thou our potter; and we all are the work of thy hand. Be not
wroth very sore, O Lord, neither remember iniquity for ever: Behold,
see, we beseech thee, we are all thy people." (Isa. 64:5-9). You see how
they put no confidence in anything but this: considering that they
are the Lord's, they despair not of being the objects of his care. In
the same way, Jeremiah says, "O Lord, though our iniquities testify
against us, do thou it for thy name's sake" (Jer. 14:7). For it was most
truly and piously written by the uncertain author (whoever he may
have been) that wrote the book which is attributed to the prophet
Baruch, "But the soul that is greatly vexed, which goeth stooping and
feeble, and the eyes that fail, and the hungry soul, will give thee praise
and righteousness, O Lord. Therefore, we do not make our humble
supplication before thee, O Lord our God, for the righteousness of
our fathers, and of our kings." "Hear, O Lord, and have mercy; for
thou art merciful: and have pity upon us, because we have sinned
before thee" (Baruch 2:18-19; 3:2).

9. In fine, supplication for pardon, with humble and ingenuous
confession of guilt, forms both the preparation and commencement
of right prayer. For the holiest of men cannot hope to obtain anything
from God until he has been freely reconciled to him. God cannot be
propitious to any but those whom he pardons. Hence it is not strange
that this is the key by which believers open the door of prayer, as we

learn from several passages in The Psalms. David, when presenting a request on a different subject, says, "Remember not the sins of my youth, nor my transgressions; according to thy mercy remember me, for thy goodness sake, O Lord" (Ps. 25:7). Again, "Look upon my affliction and my pain, and forgive my sins" (Ps. 25:18). Here also we see that it is not sufficient to call ourselves to account for the sins of each passing day; we must also call to mind those which might seem to have been long before buried in oblivion. For in another passage the same prophet, confessing one grievous crime, takes occasion to go back to his very birth, "I was shapen in iniquity, and in sin did my mother conceive me" (Ps. 51:5); not to extenuate the fault by the corruption of his nature, but as it were to accumulate the sins of his whole life, that the stricter he was in condemning himself, the more placable God might be. But although the saints do not always in express terms ask forgiveness of sins, yet if we carefully ponder those prayers as given in Scripture, the truth of what I say will readily appear; namely, that their courage to pray was derived solely from the mercy of God, and that they always began with appeasing him. For when a man interrogates his conscience, so far is he from presuming to lay his cares familiarly before God, that if he did not trust to mercy and pardon, he would tremble at the very thought of approaching him. There is, indeed, another special confession. When believers long for deliverance from punishment, they at the same time pray that their sins may be pardoned; for it were absurd to wish that the effect should be taken away while the cause remains. For we must beware of imitating foolish patients who, anxious only about curing accidental symptoms, neglect the root of the disease. Nay, our endeavor must be to have God propitious even before he attests his favor by external signs, both because this is the order which he himself chooses, and it were of little avail to experience his kindness, did not conscience feel that he is appeased, and thus enable us to regard him as altogether lovely. Of this we are even reminded by our Savior's reply. Having determined to cure the paralytic, he says, "Thy sins are forgiven thee;" in other words, he raises our thoughts to the object which is especially to be desired—viz. admission into the favor of God, and then gives the fruit of reconciliation by bringing assistance to us. But besides that special confession of present guilt which believers employ, in supplicating for pardon of every fault and punishment, that general introduction which procures favor for our prayers must never be omitted, because prayers will never reach God unless they are founded on free mercy. To this we may refer the words of John, "If we confess our sins, he is faithful and just to forgive us our sins and to cleanse us from all unrighteousness" (1 John 1:9). Hence, under the law it was necessary to consecrate prayers by the expiation of blood, both that they might be accepted, and that the people might be warned that they were unworthy of the high privilege until, being purged from their defilements, they founded their confidence in prayer entirely on the mercy of God.

10. Sometimes, however, the saints in supplicating God, seem to appeal to their own righteousness, as when David says, "Preserve my soul; for I am holy" (Ps. 86:2). Also Hezekiah, "Remember now, O Lord, I beseech thee how I have walked before thee in truth, and with a perfect heart, and have done that which is good in thy sight" (Isa. 38:2). All they mean by such expressions is, that regeneration declares them to be among the servants and children to whom God engages that he will show favor. We have already seen how he declares by the Psalmist that his eyes "are upon the righteous, and his ears are open unto their cry" (Ps. 34:16) and again by the apostle, that "whatsoever we ask of him we obtain, because we keep his commandments" (John 3:22). In these passages he does not fix a value on prayer as a meritorious work, but designs to establish the confidence of those who are conscious of an unfeigned integrity and innocence, such as all believers should possess. For the saying of the blind man who had received his sight is in perfect accordance with divine truth, "And God

heareth not sinners" (John 9:31); provided we take the term "sinners" in the sense commonly used by Scripture to mean those who, without any desire for righteousness, are sleeping secure in their sins; since no heart will ever rise to genuine prayer that does not at the same time long for holiness. Those supplications in which the saints allude to their purity and integrity correspond to such promises, that they may thus have, in their own experience, a manifestation of that which all the servants of God are made to expect. Thus they almost always use this mode of prayer when before God they compare themselves with their enemies, from whose injustice they long to be delivered by his hand. When making such comparisons, there is no wonder that they bring forward their integrity and simplicity of heart, that thus, by the justice of their cause, the Lord may be the more disposed to give them succor. We rob not the pious breast of the privilege of enjoying a consciousness of purity before the Lord, and thus feeling assured of the promises with which he comforts and supports his true worshipers, but we would have them to lay aside all thought of their own merits and found their confidence of success in prayer solely on the divine mercy.

11. The fourth rule of prayer is, that notwithstanding of our being thus abased and truly humbled, we should be animated to pray with the sure hope of succeeding. There is, indeed, an appearance of contradiction between the two things, between a sense of the just vengeance of God and firm confidence in his favor, and yet they are perfectly accordant, if it is the mere goodness of God that raises up those who are overwhelmed by their own sins. For, as we have formerly shown (chap. 3, sec. 1-2) that repentance and faith go hand in hand, being united by an indissoluble tie, the one causing terror, the other joy, so in prayer they must both be present. This concurrence David expresses in a few words: "But as for me, I will come into thy house in the multitude of thy mercy, and in thy fear will I worship toward thy holy temple" (Ps. 5:7). Under the goodness of God he

comprehends faith, at the same time not excluding fear; for not only does his majesty compel our reverence, but our own unworthiness also divests us of all pride and confidence, and keeps us in fear. The confidence of which I speak is not one which frees the mind from all anxiety, and soothes it with sweet and perfect rest; such rest is peculiar to those who, while all their affairs are flowing to a wish are annoyed by no care, stung with no regret, agitated by no fear. But the best stimulus which the saints have to prayer is when, in consequence of their own necessities, they feel the greatest disquietude, and are all but driven to despair, until faith seasonably comes to their aid; because in such straits the goodness of God so shines upon them, that while they groan, burdened by the weight of present calamities, and tormented with the fear of greater, they yet trust to this goodness, and in this way both lighten the difficulty of endurance, and take comfort in the hope of final deliverance. It is necessary, therefore, that the prayer of the believer should be the result of both feelings, and exhibit the influence of both; namely, that while he groans under present and anxiously dreads new evils, he should, at the same time, have recourse to God, not at all doubting that God is ready to stretch out a helping hand to him. For it is not easy to say how much God is irritated by our distrust, when we ask what we expect not of his goodness. Hence, nothing is more accordant to the nature of prayer than to lay it down as a fixed rule, that it is not to come forth at random, but is to follow in the footsteps of faith. To this principle Christ directs all of us in these words, "Therefore, I say unto you, What things soever ye desire, when ye pray, believe that ye receive them, and ye shall have them" (Mark 11:24). The same thing he declares in another passage, "All things, whatsoever ye shall ask in prayer, believing, ye shall receive" (Matt. 21:22). In accordance with this are the words of James, "If any of you lack wisdom, let him ask of God, that giveth to all men liberally, and upbraideth not, and it shall be given him. But let him ask in faith, nothing wavering" (James 1:5). He most aptly expresses the power of faith by opposing it to wavering. No less worthy of notice is his additional statement, that those who approach God with a doubting, hesitating mind, without feeling assured whether they are to be heard or not, gain nothing by their prayers. Such persons he compares to a wave of the sea, driven with the wind and tossed. Hence, in another passage he terms genuine prayer "the prayer of faith" (James 5:15). Again, since God so often declares that he will give to every man according to his faith he intimates that we cannot obtain anything without faith. In short, it is faith which obtains everything that is granted to prayer. This is the meaning of Paul in the well known passage to which dull men give too little heed, "How then shall they call upon him in whom they have not believed? and how shall they believe in him of whom they have not heard?" "So then faith cometh by hearing, and hearing by the word of God" (Rom. 10:14, 17). Gradually deducing the origin of prayer from faith, he distinctly maintains that God cannot be invoked sincerely except by those to whom, by the preaching of the Gospel, his mercy and willingness have been made known, nay, familiarly explained.

12. This necessity our opponents do not at all consider. Therefore, when we say that believers ought to feel firmly assured, they think we are saying the absurdest thing in the world. But if they had any experience in true prayer, they would assuredly understand that God cannot be duly invoked without this firm sense of the Divine benevolence. But as no man can well perceive the power of faith, without at the same time feeling it in his heart, what profit is there in disputing with men of this character, who plainly show that they have never had more than a vain imagination? The value and necessity of that assurance for which we contend is learned chiefly from prayer. Everyone who does not see this gives proof of a very stupid conscience. Therefore, leaving those who are thus blinded, let us fix our thoughts on the words of Paul, that God can only be invoked by such as have obtained a knowledge of his mercy from the Gospel, and feel firmly

assured that that mercy is ready to be bestowed upon them. What kind of prayer would this be? "O Lord, I am indeed doubtful whether or not thou art inclined to hear me; but being oppressed with anxiety I fly to thee that if I am worthy, thou mayest assist me." None of the saints whose prayers are given in Scripture thus supplicated. Nor are we thus taught by the Holy Spirit, who tells us to "come boldly unto the throne of grace, that we may obtain mercy, and find grace to help in time of need" (Heb. 4:16); and elsewhere teaches us to "have boldness and access with confidence by the faith of Christ" (Eph. 3:12). This confidence of obtaining what we ask, a confidence which the Lord commands, and all the saints teach by their example, we must therefore hold fast with both hands, if we would pray to any advantage. The only prayer acceptable to God is that which springs (if I may so express it) from this presumption of faith, and is founded on the full assurance of hope. He might have been contented to use the simple name of faith, but he adds not only confidence, but liberty or boldness, that by this mark he might distinguish us from unbelievers, who indeed like us pray to God, but pray at random. Hence, the whole Church thus prays "Let thy mercy O Lord, be upon us, according as we hope in thee" (Ps. 33:22). The same condition is set down by the Psalmist in another passage, "When I cry unto thee, then shall mine enemies turn back: this I know, for God is for me" (Ps. 56:9). Again, "In the morning will I direct my prayer unto thee, and will look up" (Ps. 5:3). From these words we gather, that prayers are vainly poured out into the air unless accompanied with faith, in which, as from a watchtower, we may quietly wait for God. With this agrees the order of Paul's exhortation. For before urging believers to pray in the Spirit always, with vigilance and assiduity, he enjoins them to take "the shield of faith," "the helmet of salvation, and the sword of the Spirit, which is the word of God" (Eph. 6:16-18). Let the reader here call to mind what I formerly observed, that faith by no means fails though accompanied with a recognition of our wretchedness, poverty, and pollution. How much soever believers may feel that they are oppressed by a heavy load of iniquity, and are not only devoid of everything which can procure the favor of God for them, but justly burdened with many sins which make him an object of dread, yet they cease not to present themselves, this feeling not deterring them from appearing in his presence, because there is no other access to him. Genuine prayer is not that by which we arrogantly extol ourselves before God, or set a great value on anything of our own, but that by which, while confessing our guilt, we utter our sorrows before God, just as children familiarly lay their complaints before their parents. Nay, the immense accumulation of our sins should rather spur us on and incite us to prayer. Of this the Psalmist gives us an example, "Heal my soul: for I have sinned against thee" (Ps. 41:4). I confess, indeed, that these stings would prove mortal darts, did not God give succor; but our heavenly Father has, in ineffable kindness, added a remedy, by which, calming all perturbation, soothing our cares, and dispelling our fears he condescendingly allures us to himself; nay, removing all doubts, not to say obstacles, makes the way smooth before us.

13. And first, indeed in enjoining us to pray, he by the very injunction convicts us of impious contumacy if we obey not. He could not give a more precise command than that which is contained in the psalms: "Call upon me in the day of trouble" (Ps. 50:15). But as there is no office of piety more frequently enjoined by Scripture, there is no occasion for here dwelling longer upon it. "Ask," says our Divine Master, "and it shall be given you; seek, and ye shall find; knock, and it shall be opened unto you" (Matt. 7:7). Here, indeed, a promise is added to the precept, and this is necessary. For though all confess that we must obey the precept, yet the greater part would shun the invitation of God, did he not promise that he would listen and be ready to answer. These two positions being laid down, it is certain that all who cavillingly allege that they are not to come to God directly, are not only rebellious and disobedient but are also convicted of unbelief,

inasmuch as they distrust the promises. There is the more occasion to attend to this, because hypocrites, under a pretense of humility and modesty, proudly contemn the precept, as well as deny all credit to the gracious invitation of God; nay, rob him of a principal part of his worship. For when he rejected sacrifices, in which all holiness seemed then to consist, he declared that the chief thing, that which above all others is precious in his sight, is to be invoked in the day of necessity. Therefore, when he demands that which is his own, and urges us to alacrity in obeying, no pretexts for doubt, how specious soever they may be, can excuse us. Hence, all the passages throughout Scripture in which we are commanded to pray, are set up before our eyes as so many banners, to inspire us with confidence. It were presumption to go forward into the presence of God, did he not anticipate us by his invitation. Accordingly, he opens up the way for us by his own voice, "I will say, It is my people: and they shall say, The Lord is my God" (Zech. 13:9). We see how he anticipates his worshipers, and desires them to follow, and therefore we cannot fear that the melody which he himself dictates will prove unpleasing. Especially let us call to mind that noble description of the divine character, by trusting to which we shall easily overcome every obstacle: "O thou that hearest prayer, unto thee shall all flesh come" (Ps. 65:2). What can be more lovely or soothing than to see God invested with a title which assures us that nothing is more proper to his nature than to listen to the prayers of suppliants? Hence the Psalmist infers, that free access is given not to a few individuals, but to all men, since God addresses all in these terms, "Call upon me in the day of trouble: I will deliver thee, and thou shalt glorify me" (Ps. 50:15). David, accordingly, appeals to the promise thus given in order to obtain what he asks: "Thou, O Lord of hosts, God of Israel, hast revealed to thy servant, saying, I will build thee an house: therefore hath thy servant found in his heart to pray this prayer unto thee" (2 Sam. 7:27). Here we infer, that he would have been afraid but for the promise which emboldened him. So in another passage he fortifies himself with the general doctrine, "He will fulfill the desire of them that fear him" (Ps. 145:19). Nay, we may observe in The Psalms how the continuity of prayer is broken, and a transition is made at one time to the power of God, at another to his goodness, at another to the faithfulness of his promises. It might seem that David, by introducing these sentiments, unseasonably mutilates his prayers; but believers well know by experience, that their ardor grows languid unless new fuel be added, and, therefore, that meditation as well on the nature as on the word of God during prayer, is by no means superfluous. Let us not decline to imitate the example of David, and introduce thoughts which may reanimate our languid minds with new vigor.

14. It is strange that these delightful promises affect us coldly, or scarcely at all, so that the generality of men prefer to wander up and down, forsaking the fountain of living waters, and hewing out to themselves broken cisterns, rather than embrace the divine liberality voluntarily offered to them. "The name of the Lord," says Solomon, "is a strong tower; the righteous runneth into it, and is safe." Joel, after predicting the fearful disaster which was at hand, subjoins the following memorable sentence: "And it shall come to pass, that whosoever shall call on the name of the Lord shall be delivered." This we know properly refers to the course of the Gospel. Scarcely one in a hundred is moved to come into the presence of God, though he himself exclaims by Isaiah, "And it shall come to pass, that before they call, I will answer; and while they are yet speaking, I will hear." This honor he elsewhere bestows upon the whole Church in general, as belonging to all the members of Christ: "He shall call upon me, and I will answer him: I will be with him in trouble; I will deliver him, and honor him." My intention, however, as I already observed, is not to enumerate all, but only select some admirable passages as a specimen how kindly God allures us to himself, and how extreme our ingratitude must be when with such powerful motives our sluggishness still retards us.

Wherefore, let these words always resound in our ears: "The Lord is nigh unto all them that call upon him, to all that call upon him in truth" (Ps. 145:18). Likewise those passages which we have quoted from Isaiah and Joel, in which God declares that his ear is open to our prayers, and that he is delighted as with a sacrifice of sweet savor when we cast our cares upon him. The special benefit of these promises we receive when we frame our prayer, not timorously or doubtingly, but when trusting to his word whose majesty might otherwise deter us, we are bold to call him Father, he himself deigning to suggest this most delightful name. Fortified by such invitations it remains for us to know that we have therein sufficient materials for prayer, since our prayers depend on no merit of our own, but all their worth and hope of success are founded and depend on the promises of God, so that they need no other support, and require not to look up and down on this hand and on that. It must therefore be fixed in our minds, that though we equal not the lauded sanctity of patriarchs, prophets, and apostles, yet as the command to pray is common to us as well as them, and faith is common, so if we lean on the word of God, we are in respect of this privilege their associates. For God declaring, as has already been seen, that he will listen and be favorable to all, encourages the most wretched to hope that they shall obtain what they ask; and, accordingly, we should attend to the general forms of expression, which, as it is commonly expressed, exclude none from first to last; only let there be sincerity of heart, self-dissatisfaction, humility, and faith, that we may not, by the hypocrisy of a deceitful prayer, profane the name of God. Our most merciful Father will not reject those whom he not only encourages to come, but urges in every possible way. Hence David's method of prayer to which I lately referred: "And now, O Lord God, thou art that God, and thy words be true, and thou hast promised this goodness unto thy servant, that it may continue for ever before thee" (2 Sam. 7:28). So also, in another passage, "Let, I pray thee, thy merciful kindness be for my comfort, according to thy word unto thy servant" (Ps. 119:76). And the whole body of the Israelites, whenever they fortify themselves with the remembrance of the covenant, plainly declare, that since God thus prescribes they are not to pray timorously (Gen. 32:13). In this they imitated the example of the patriarchs, particularly Jacob, who, after confessing that he was unworthy of the many mercies which he had received of the Lord's hand, says, that he is encouraged to make still larger requests, because God had promised that he would grant them. But whatever be the pretexts which unbelievers employ, when they do not flee to God as often as necessity urges, nor seek after him, nor implore his aid, they defraud him of his due honor just as much as if they were fabricating to themselves new gods and idols, since in this way they deny that God is the author of all their blessings. On the contrary, nothing more effectually frees pious minds from every doubt, than to be armed with the thought that no obstacle should impede them while they are obeying the command of God, who declares that nothing is more grateful to him than obedience. Hence, again, what I have previously said becomes still more clear, namely, that a bold spirit in prayer well accords with fear, reverence, and anxiety, and that there is no inconsistency when God raises up those who had fallen prostrate. In this way forms of expression apparently inconsistent admirably harmonize. Jeremiah and David speak of humbly laying their supplications before God. In another passage Jeremiah says "Let, we beseech thee, our supplication be accepted before thee, and pray for us unto the Lord thy God, even for all this remnant." On the other hand, believers are often said to lift up prayer. Thus Hezekiah speaks, when asking the prophet to undertake the office of interceding. And David says, "Let my prayer be set forth before thee as incense; and the lifting up of my hands as the evening sacrifice." The explanation is, that though believers, persuaded of the paternal love of God, cheerfully rely on his faithfulness, and have no hesitation in imploring the aid which he voluntarily offers, they are not elated with supine or presumptuous security; but climbing up by the ladder of the promises, still remain humble and abased suppliants.

15. Here, by way of objection, several questions are raised. Scripture relates that God sometimes complied with certain prayers which had been dictated by minds not duly calmed or regulated. It is true, that the cause for which Jotham imprecated on the inhabitants of Shechem the disaster which afterwards befell them was well founded; but still he was inflamed with anger and revenge (Judges 9:20); and hence God, by complying with the execration, seems to approve of passionate impulses. Similar fervor also seized Samson, when he prayed, "Strengthen me, I pray thee, only this once, O God, that I may be at once avenged of the Philistines for my two eyes" (Judges 16:28). For although there was some mixture of good zeal, yet his ruling feeling was a fervid, and therefore vicious longing for vengeance. God assents, and hence apparently it might be inferred that prayers are effectual, though not framed in conformity to the rule of the word. But I answer, first, that a perpetual law is not abrogated by singular examples; and, secondly, that special suggestions have sometimes been made to a few individuals, whose case thus becomes different from that of the generality of men. For we should attend to the answer which our Savior gave to his disciples when they inconsiderately wished to imitate the example of Elias, "Ye know not what manner of spirit ye are of" (Luke 9:55). We must, however, go farther and say, that the wishes to which God assents are not always pleasing to him; but he assents, because it is necessary, by way of example, to give clear evidence of the doctrine of Scripture—viz. that he assists the miserable, and hears the groans of those who unjustly afflicted implore his aid: and, accordingly, he executes his judgments when the complaints of the needy, though in themselves unworthy of attention, ascend to him. For how often, in inflicting punishment on the ungodly for cruelty, rapine, violence, lust, and other crimes, in curbing audacity and fury, and also in overthrowing tyrannical power, has he declared that

he gives assistance to those who are unworthily oppressed though they by addressing an unknown deity only beat the air? There is one psalm which clearly teaches that prayers are not without effect, though they do not penetrate to heaven by faith (Ps. 107:6, 13, 19). For it enumerates the prayers which, by natural instinct, necessity extorts from unbelievers not less than from believers, and to which it shows by the event, that God is, notwithstanding, propitious. Is it to testify by such readiness to hear that their prayers are agreeable to him? Nay; it is, first, to magnify or display his mercy by the circumstance, that even the wishes of unbelievers are not denied; and, secondly, to stimulate his true worshipers to more urgent prayer, when they see that sometimes even the wailings of the ungodly are not without avail. This, however, is no reason why believers should deviate from the law divinely imposed upon them, or envy unbelievers, as if they gained much in obtaining what they wished. We have observed (chap. 3, sec. 25), that in this way God yielded to the feigned repentance of Ahab, that he might show how ready he is to listen to his elect when, with true contrition, they seek his favor. Accordingly, he upbraids the Jews, that shortly after experiencing his readiness to listen to their prayers, they returned to their own perverse inclinations. It is also plain from the Book of Judges that, whenever they wept, though their tears were deceitful, they were delivered from the hands of their enemies. Therefore, as God sends his sun indiscriminately on the evil and on the good, so he despises not the tears of those who have a good cause, and whose sorrows are deserving of relief. Meanwhile, though he hears them, it has no more to do with salvation than the supply of food which he gives to other despisers of his goodness. There seems to be a more difficult question concerning Abraham and Samuel, the one of whom, without any instruction from the word of God, prayed in behalf of the people of Sodom, and the other, contrary to an express prohibition, prayed in behalf of Saul (Gen. 18:23; 1 Sam. 15:11). Similar is the case of Jeremiah, who prayed that the city might not be destroyed (Jer. 32:16). It is true their prayers were refused, but it seems harsh to affirm that they prayed without faith. Modest readers will, I hope, be satisfied with this solution—viz. that leaning to the general principle on which God enjoins us to be merciful even to the unworthy, they were not altogether devoid of faith, though in this particular instance their wish was disappointed. Augustine shrewdly remarks, "How do the saints pray in faith when they ask from God contrary to what he has decreed? Namely, because they pray according to his will, not his hidden and immutable will, but that which he suggests to them, that he may hear them in another manner; as he wisely distinguishes" (August. *de Civit. Dei*, Lib. 22 cap. 2). This is truly said: for, in his incomprehensible counsel, he so regulates events, that the prayers of the saints, though involving a mixture of faith and error, are not in vain. And yet this no more sanctions imitation than it excuses the saints themselves, who I deny not exceeded due bounds. Wherefore, whenever no certain promise exists, our request to God must have a condition annexed to it. Here we may refer to the prayer of David, "Awake for me to the judgment that thou hast commanded" (Ps. 7:6); for he reminds us that he had received special instruction to pray for a temporal blessing.

16. It is also of importance to observe, that the four laws of prayer of which I have treated are not so rigorously enforced, as that God rejects the prayers in which he does not find perfect faith or repentance, accompanied with fervent zeal and wishes duly framed. We have said (sec. 4), that though prayer is the familiar intercourse of believers with God, yet reverence and modesty must be observed: we must not give loose reins to our wishes, nor long for anything farther than God permits; and, moreover, lest the majesty of God should be despised, our minds must be elevated to pure and chaste veneration. This no man ever performed with due perfection. For, not to speak of the generality of men, how often do David's complaints savor of intemperance? Not that he actually means to expostulate with God,

or murmur at his judgments, but failing, through infirmity, he finds no better solace than to pour his griefs into the bosom of his heavenly Father. Nay, even our stammering is tolerated by God, and pardon is granted to our ignorance as often as anything rashly escapes us: indeed, without this indulgence, we should have no freedom to pray. But although it was David's intention to submit himself entirely to the will of God, and he prayed with no less patience than fervor, yet irregular emotions appear, nay, sometimes burst forth—emotions not a little at variance with the first law which we laid down. In particular, we may see in a clause of the thirty-ninth Psalm, how this saint was carried away by the vehemence of his grief, and unable to keep within bounds. "O spare me, that I may recover strength, before I go hence, and be no more" (Ps. 39:13). You would call this the language of a desperate man, who had no other desire than that God should withdraw and leave him to relish in his distresses. Not that his devout mind rushes into such intemperance, or that, as the reprobate are wont, he wishes to have done with God; he only complains that the divine anger is more than he can bear. During those trials, wishes often escape which are not in accordance with the rule of the word, and in which the saints do not duly consider what is lawful and expedient. Prayers contaminated by such faults, indeed, deserve to be rejected; yet provided the saints lament, administer self-correction and return to themselves, God pardons. Similar faults are committed in regard to the second law (as to which, see sec. 6), for the saints have often to struggle with their own coldness, their want and misery not urging them sufficiently to serious prayer. It often happens, also, that their minds wander, and are almost lost; hence in this matter also there is need of pardon, lest their prayers, from being languid or mutilated, or interrupted and wandering, should meet with a refusal. One of the natural feelings which God has imprinted on our mind is, that prayer is not genuine unless the thoughts are turned upward. Hence the ceremony of raising the hands, to which we have adverted, a ceremony known to all ages and nations, and still in common use. But who, in lifting up his hands, is not conscious of sluggishness, the heart cleaving to the earth? In regard to the petition for remission of sins (sec. 8), though no believer omits it, yet all who are truly exercised in prayer feel that they bring scarcely a tenth of the sacrifice of which David speaks, "The sacrifices of God are a broken spirit: a broken and a contrite heart, O God, thou wilt not despise" (Ps. 51:17). Thus a twofold pardon is always to be asked; first, because they are conscious of many faults the sense of which, however, does not touch them so as to make them feel dissatisfied with themselves as they ought; and, secondly, insofar as they have been enabled to profit in repentance and the fear of God, they are humbled with just sorrow for their offenses, and pray for the remission of punishment by the judge. The thing which most of all vitiates prayer, did not God indulgently interpose, is weakness or imperfection of faith; but it is not wonderful that this defect is pardoned by God, who often exercises his people with severe trials, as if he actually wished to extinguish their faith. The hardest of such trials is when believers are forced to exclaim, "O Lord God of hosts, how long wilt thou be angry against the prayer of thy people?" (Ps. 80:4), as if their very prayers offended him. In like manner, when Jeremiah says "Also when I cry and shout, he shutteth out my prayers" (Lam. 3:8), there cannot be a doubt that he was in the greatest perturbation. Innumerable examples of the same kind occur in the Scriptures, from which it is manifest that the faith of the saints was often mingled with doubts and fears, so that while believing and hoping, they, however, betrayed some degree of unbelief, But because they do not come so far as were to be wished, that is only an additional reason for their exerting themselves to correct their faults, that they may daily approach nearer to the perfect law of prayer, and at the same time feel into what an abyss of evils those are plunged, who, in the very cures they use, bring new diseases upon themselves: since there is no prayer which God would not deservedly disdain, did he not overlook the blemishes with which all of them are polluted. I do not mention these things that believers may securely pardon themselves in any faults which they commit, but that they may call themselves to strict account, and thereby endeavor to surmount these obstacles; and though Satan endeavors to block up all the paths in order to prevent them from praying, they may, nevertheless, break through, being firmly persuaded that though not disencumbered of all hindrances, their attempts are pleasing to God, and their wishes are approved, provided they hasten on and keep their aim, though without immediately reaching it.

17. But since no man is worthy to come forward in his own name, and appear in the presence of God, our heavenly Father, to relieve us at once from fear and shame, with which all must feel oppressed, has given us his Son, Jesus Christ our Lord, to be our Advocate and Mediator, that under his guidance we may approach securely, confiding that with him for our Intercessor nothing which we ask in his name will be denied to us, as there is nothing which the Father can deny to him (1 Tim. 2:5; 1 John 2:1; see sec. 36-37). To this it is necessary to refer all that we have previously taught concerning faith; because, as the promise gives us Christ as our Mediator, so, unless our hope of obtaining what we ask is founded on him, it deprives us of the privilege of prayer. For it is impossible to think of the dread majesty of God without being filled with alarm; and hence the sense of our own unworthiness must keep us far away, until Christ interpose, and convert a throne of dreadful glory into a throne of grace, as the Apostle teaches that thus we can "come boldly unto the throne of grace, that we may obtain mercy, and find grace to help in time of need" (Heb. 4:16). And as a rule has been laid down as to prayer, as a promise has been given that those who pray will be heard, so we are specially enjoined to pray in the name of Christ, the promise being that we shall obtain what we ask in his name. "Whatsoever ye shall ask in my name," says our Savior, "that will I do; that the Father may be glorified

in the Son;" "Hitherto ye have asked nothing in my name; ask, and ye shall receive, that your joy may be full" (John 14:13; 16:24). Hence it is incontrovertibly clear that those who pray to God in any other name than that of Christ contumaciously falsify his orders, and regard his will as nothing, while they have no promise that they shall obtain. For, as Paul says "All the promises of God in him are yea, and in him amen;" (2 Cor. 1:20), that is, are confirmed and fulfilled in him.

18. And we must carefully attend to the circumstance of time. Christ enjoins his disciples to have recourse to his intercession after he shall have ascended to heaven: "At that day ye shall ask in my name" (John 16:26). It is certain, indeed, that from the very first all who ever prayed were heard only for the sake of the Mediator. For this reason God had commanded in the Law, that the priest alone should enter the sanctuary, bearing the names of the twelve tribes of Israel on his shoulders, and as many precious stones on his breast, while the people were to stand at a distance in the outer court, and thereafter unite their prayers with the priest. Nay, the sacrifice had even the effect of ratifying and confirming their prayers. That shadowy ceremony of the Law therefore taught, first, that we are all excluded from the face of God, and, therefore, that there is need of a Mediator to appear in our name, and carry us on his shoulders and keep us bound upon his breast, that we may be heard in his person; And secondly, that our prayers, which, as has been said, would otherwise never be free from impurity, are cleansed by the sprinkling of his blood. And we see that the saints, when they desired to obtain anything, founded their hopes on sacrifices, because they knew that by sacrifice all prayers were ratified: "Remember all thy offerings," says David, "and accept thy burnt sacrifice" (Ps. 20:3). Hence we infer, that in receiving the prayers of his people, God was from the very first appeased by the intercession of Christ. Why then does Christ speak of a new period ("at that day") when the disciples were to begin to pray in his name, unless it be that this grace, being now more brightly displayed, ought

also to be in higher estimation with us? In this sense he had said a little before, "Hitherto ye have asked nothing in my name; ask." Not that they were altogether ignorant of the office of Mediator (all the Jews were instructed in these first rudiments), but they did not clearly understand that Christ by his ascent to heaven would be more the advocate of the Church than before. Therefore, to solace their grief for his absence by some more than ordinary result, he asserts his office of advocate, and says, that hitherto they had been without the special benefit which it would be their privilege to enjoy, when aided by his intercession they should invoke God with greater freedom. In this sense the Apostle says that we have "boldness to enter into the holiest by the blood of Jesus, by a new and living way, which he hath consecrated for us" (Heb. 10:19-20). Therefore, the more inexcusable we are, if we do not with both hands (as it is said) embrace the inestimable gift which is properly destined for us.

19. Moreover since he himself is the only way and the only access by which we can draw near to God, those who deviate from this way, and decline this access, have no other remaining; his throne presents nothing but wrath, judgment, and terror. In short, as the Father has consecrated him our guide and head, those who abandon or turn aside from him in any way endeavor, as much as in them lies, to sully and efface the stamp which God has impressed. Christ, therefore, is the only Mediator by whose intercession the Father is rendered propitious and exorable (1 Tim. 2:5). For though the saints are still permitted to use intercessions, by which they mutually beseech God in behalf of each other's salvation, and of which the Apostle makes mention (Eph. 6:18-19; 1 Tim. 2:1); yet these depend on that one intercession, so far are they from derogating from it. For as the intercessions which, as members of one body we offer up for each other, spring from the feeling of love, so they have reference to this one head. Being thus also made in the name of Christ, what more do they than declare that no man can derive the least benefit from any prayers

without the intercession of Christ? As there is nothing in the intercession of Christ to prevent the different members of the Church from offering up prayers for each other, so let it be held as a fixed principle, that all the intercessions thus used in the Church must have reference to that one intercession. Nay, we must be specially careful to show our gratitude on this very account, that God pardoning our unworthiness, not only allows each individual to pray for himself, but allows all to intercede mutually for each other. God having given a place in his Church to intercessors who would deserve to be rejected when praying privately on their own account, how presumptuous were it to abuse this kindness by employing it to obscure the honor of Christ?

20. Moreover, the Sophists are guilty of the merest trifling when they allege that Christ is the Mediator of redemption, but that believers are mediators of intercession; as if Christ had only performed a temporary mediation, and left an eternal and imperishable mediation to his servants. Such, forsooth, is the treatment which he receives from those who pretend only to take from him a minute portion of honor. Very different is the language of Scripture, with whose simplicity every pious man will be satisfied, without paying any regard to those importers. For when John says, "If any man sin, we have an advocate with the Father, Jesus Christ the righteous" (1 John 2:1), does he mean merely that we once had an advocate; does he not rather ascribe to him a perpetual intercession? What does Paul mean when he declares that he "is even at the right hand of God, who also maketh intercession for us"? (Rom. 8:32). But when in another passage he declares that he is the only Mediator between God and man (1 Tim. 2:5), is he not referring to the supplications which he had mentioned a little before? Having previously said that prayers were to be offered up for all men, he immediately adds, in confirmation of that statement, that there is one God, and one Mediator between God and man. Nor does Augustine give a different interpretation

when he says, "Christian men mutually recommend each other in their prayers. But he for whom none intercedes, while he himself intercedes for all, is the only true Mediator. Though the Apostle Paul was under the head a principal member, yet because he was a member of the body of Christ, and knew that the most true and High Priest of the Church had entered not by figure into the inner veil to the holy of holies, but by firm and express truth into the inner sanctuary of heaven to holiness, holiness not imaginary, but eternal, he also commends himself to the prayers of the faithful. He does not make himself a mediator between God and the people, but asks that all the members of the body of Christ should pray mutually for each other, since the members are mutually sympathetic: if one member suffers, the others suffer with it. And thus the mutual prayers of all the members still laboring on the earth ascend to the Head, who has gone before into heaven, and in whom there is propitiation for our sins. For if Paul were a mediator, so would also the other apostles, and thus there would be many mediators, and Paul's statement could not stand, 'There is one God, and one Mediator between God and men, the man Christ Jesus;' in whom we also are one if we keep the unity of the faith in the bond of peace" (August. *Contra Parmenian*, Lib. 2 cap. 8). Likewise in another passage Augustine says, "If thou requirest a priest, he is above the heavens, where he intercedes for those who on earth died for thee" (August. *in Ps. 94*) imagine not that he throws himself before his Father's knees, and suppliantly intercedes for us; but we understand with the Apostle, that he appears in the presence of God, and that the power of his death has the effect of a perpetual intercession for us; that having entered into the upper sanctuary, he alone continues to the end of the world to present the prayers of his people, who are standing far off in the outer court.

21. In regard to the saints who having died in the body live in Christ, if we attribute prayer to them, let us not imagine that they have any other way of supplicating God than through Christ who

alone is the way, or that their prayers are accepted by God in any other name. Wherefore, since the Scripture calls us away from all others to Christ alone, since our heavenly Father is pleased to gather together all things in him, it were the extreme of stupidity, not to say madness, to attempt to obtain access by means of others, so as to be drawn away from him without whom access cannot be obtained. But who can deny that this was the practice for several ages, and is still the practice, wherever Popery prevails? To procure the favor of God, human merits are ever and anon obtruded, and very frequently while Christ is passed by, God is supplicated in their name. I ask if this is not to transfer to them that office of sole intercession which we have above claimed for Christ? Then what angel or devil ever announced one syllable to any human being concerning that fancied intercession of theirs? There is not a word on the subject in Scripture. What ground then was there for the fiction? Certainly, while the human mind thus seeks help for itself in which it is not sanctioned by the word of God, it plainly manifests its distrust (see sec. 27). But if we appeal to the consciences of all who take pleasure in the intercession of saints, we shall find that their only reason for it is, that they are filled with anxiety, as if they supposed that Christ were insufficient or too rigorous. By this anxiety they dishonor Christ, and rob him of his title of sole Mediator, a title which being given him by the Father as his special privilege, ought not to be transferred to any other. By so doing they obscure the glory of his nativity and make void his cross; in short, divest and defraud of due praise everything which he did or suffered, since all which he did and suffered goes to show that he is and ought to be deemed sole Mediator. At the same time, they reject the kindness of God in manifesting himself to them as a Father, for he is not their Father if they do not recognize Christ as their brother. This they plainly refuse to do if they think not that he feels for them a brother's affection; affection than which none can be more gentle or tender. Wherefore Scripture offers him alone, sends us to him, and establishes us in him. "He," says Ambrose, "is our mouth by which we speak to the Father; our eye by which we see the Father; our right hand by which we offer ourselves to the Father. Save by his intercession neither we nor any saints have any intercourse with God" (Ambros. *Lib. de Isaac et Anima*). If they object that the public prayers which are offered up in churches conclude with the words, "through Jesus Christ our Lord," it is a frivolous evasion; because no less insult is offered to the intercession of Christ by confounding it with the prayers and merits of the dead, than by omitting it altogether, and making mention only of the dead. Then, in all their litanies, hymns, and proses where every kind of honor is paid to dead saints, there is no mention of Christ.

22. But here stupidity has proceeded to such a length as to give a manifestation of the genius of superstition, which, when once it has shaken off the rein, is wont to wanton without limit. After men began to look to the intercession of saints, a peculiar administration was gradually assigned to each, so that, according to diversity of business, now one, now another, intercessor was invoked. Then individuals adopted particular saints, and put their faith in them, just as if they had been tutelar deities. And thus not only were gods set up according to the number of the cities (the charge which the prophet brought against Israel of old, Jer. 2:28; 11:13), but according to the number of individuals. But while the saints in all their desires refer to the will of God alone, look to it, and acquiesce in it, yet to assign to them any other prayer than that of longing for the arrival of the kingdom of God, is to think of them stupidly, carnally, and even insultingly. Nothing can be farther from such a view than to imagine that each, under the influence of private feeling, is disposed to be most favorable to his own worshipers. At length vast numbers have fallen into the horrid blasphemy of invoking them not merely as helping but presiding over their salvation. See the depth to which miserable men fall when they forsake their proper station, that is, the word of

God. I say nothing of the more monstrous specimens of impiety in which, though detestable to God, angels, and men, they themselves feel no pain or shame. Prostrated at a statue or picture of Barbara or Catherine, and the like, they mutter a *Pater Noster*; and so far are their pastors from curing or curbing this frantic course, that, allured by the scent of gain, they approve and applaud it. But while seeking to relieve themselves of the odium of this vile and criminal procedure, with what pretext can they defend the practice of calling upon Eloy (Eligius) or Medard to look upon their servants, and send them help from heaven, or the Holy Virgin to order her Son to do what they ask? The Council of Carthage forbade direct prayer to be made at the altar to saints. It is probable that these holy men, unable entirely to suppress the force of depraved custom, had recourse to this check, that public prayers might not be vitiated with such forms of expression as *Sancte Petre, ora pro nobis*—St Peter, pray for us. But how much farther has this devilish extravagance proceeded when men hesitate not to transfer to the dead the peculiar attributes of Christ and God?

23. In endeavoring to prove that such intercession derives some support from Scripture they labor in vain. We frequently read (they say) of the prayers of angels, and not only so, but the prayers of believers are said to be carried into the presence of God by their hands. But if they would compare saints who have departed this life with angels, it will be necessary to prove that saints are ministering spirits, to whom has been delegated the office of superintending our salvation, to whom has been assigned the province of guiding us in all our ways, of encompassing, admonishing, and comforting us, of keeping watch over us. All these are assigned to angels, but none of them to saints. How preposterously they confound departed saints with angels is sufficiently apparent from the many different offices by which Scripture distinguishes the one from the other. No one unless admitted will presume to perform the office of pleader before an earthly judge; whence then have worms such license as to obtrude themselves

on God as intercessors, while no such office has been assigned them? God has been pleased to give angels the charge of our safety. Hence they attend our sacred meetings, and the Church is to them a theatre in which they behold the manifold wisdom of God (Eph. 3:10). Those who transfer to others this office which is peculiar to them, certainly pervert and confound the order which has been established by God and ought to be inviolable. With similar dexterity they proceed to quote other passages. God said to Jeremiah, "Though Moses and Samuel stood before me, yet my mind could not be toward this people" (Jer. 15:1). How (they ask) could he have spoken thus of the dead but because he knew that they interceded for the living? My inference, on the contrary, is this: since it thus appears that neither Moses nor Samuel interceded for the people of Israel, there was then no intercession for the dead. For who of the saints can be supposed to labor for the salvation of the peoples while Moses who, when in life, far surpassed all others in this matter, does nothing? Therefore, if they persist in the paltry quibble, that the dead intercede for the living, because the Lord said, "If they stood before me" (*intercesserint*), I will argue far more speciously in this way: Moses, of whom it is said, "if he interceded," did not intercede for the people in their extreme necessity: it is probable, therefore, that no other saint intercedes, all being far behind Moses in humanity, goodness, and paternal solicitude. Thus all they gain by their caviling is to be wounded by the very arms with which they deem themselves admirably protected. But it is very ridiculous to wrest this simple sentence in this manner; for the Lord only declares that he would not spare the iniquities of the people, though some Moses or Samuel, to whose prayers he had shown himself so indulgent, should intercede for them. This meaning is most clearly elicited from a similar passage in Ezekiel: "Though these three men, Noah, Daniel, and Job, were in it, they should deliver but their own souls by their righteousness, saith the Lord God" (Ezek. 14:14). Here there can be no doubt that we are to understand the words as if it had been said, If two of the persons named were again to come alive; for the third was still living, namely, Daniel, who it is well known had then in the bloom of youth given an incomparable display of piety. Let us therefore leave out those whom Scripture declares to have completed their course. Accordingly, when Paul speaks of David, he says not that by his prayers he assisted posterity, but only that he "served his own generation" (Acts 13:36).

24. They again object, Are those, then, to be deprived of every pious wish, who, during the whole course of their lives, breathed nothing but piety and mercy? I have no wish curiously to pry into what they do or meditate; but the probability is, that instead of being subject to the impulse of various and particular desires, they, with one fixed and immovable will, long for the kingdom of God, which consists not less in the destruction of the ungodly than in the salvation of believers. If this be so, there cannot be a doubt that their charity is confined to the communion of Christ's body, and extends no farther than is compatible with the nature of that communion. But though I grant that in this way they pray for us, they do not, however, lose their quiescence so as to be distracted with earthly cares: far less are they, therefore, to be invoked by us. Nor does it follow that such invocation is to be used because, while men are alive upon the earth, they can mutually commend themselves to each other's prayers. It serves to keep alive a feeling of charity when they, as it were, share each other's wants, and bear each other's burdens. This they do by the command of the Lord, and not without a promise, the two things of primary importance in prayer. But all such reasons are inapplicable to the dead, with whom the Lord, in withdrawing them from our society, has left us no means of intercourse (Eccles. 9:5-6), and to whom, so far as we can conjecture, he has left no means of intercourse with us. But if anyone allege that they certainly must retain the same charity for us, as they are united with us in one faith, who has revealed to us that they have ears capable of listening to the sounds of our voice, or eyes clear enough to

discern our necessities? Our opponents, indeed, talk in the shade of their schools of some kind of light which beams upon departed saints from the divine countenance, and in which, as in a mirror, they, from their lofty abode, behold the affairs of men; but to affirm this with the confidence which these men presume to use, is just to desire, by means of the extravagant dreams of our own brain, and without any authority, to pry and penetrate into the hidden judgments of God, and trample upon Scripture, which so often declares that the wisdom of our flesh is at enmity with the wisdom of God, utterly condemns the vanity of our mind, and humbling our reason, bids us look only to the will of God.

25. The other passages of Scripture which they employ to defend their error are miserably wrested. Jacob (they say) asks for the sons of Joseph, "Let my name be named on them, and the name of my fathers, Abraham and Isaac" (Gen. 48:16). First, let us see what the nature of this invocation was among the Israelites. They do not implore their fathers to bring succor to them, but they beseech God to remember his servants, Abraham, Isaac, and Jacob. Their example, therefore, gives no countenance to those who use addresses to the saints themselves. But such being the dullness of these blocks, that they comprehend not what it is to invoke the name of Jacob, nor why it is to be invoked, it is not strange that they blunder thus childishly as to the mode of doing it. The expression repeatedly occurs in Scripture. Isaiah speaks of women being called by the name of men, when they have them for husbands and live under their protection (Isa. 4:1). The calling of the name of Abraham over the Israelites consists in referring the origin of their race to him, and holding him in distinguished remembrance as their author and parent. Jacob does not do so from any anxiety to extend the celebrity of his name, but because he knows that all the happiness of his posterity consisted in the inheritance of the covenant which God had made with them. Seeing that this would give them the sum of all blessings, he prays that they may be regarded

as of his race, this being nothing else than to transmit the succession of the covenant to them. They again, when they make mention of this subject in their prayers, do not betake themselves to the intercession of the dead, but call to remembrance that covenant in which their most merciful Father undertakes to be kind and propitious to them for the sake of Abraham, Isaac, and Jacob. How little, in other respects, the saints trusted to the merits of their fathers, the public voice of the Church declares in the prophets "Doubtless thou art our Father, though Abraham be ignorant of us, and Israel acknowledge us not; thou, O Lord, art our Father, our Redeemer" (Isa. 63:16). And while the Church thus speaks, she at the same time adds, "Return for thy servants' sake," not thinking of anything like intercession, but adverting only to the benefit of the covenant. Now, indeed, when we have the Lord Jesus, in whose hand the eternal covenant of mercy was not only made but confirmed, what better name can we bear before us in our prayers? And since those good Doctors would make out by these words that the Patriarchs are intercessors, I should like them to tell me why, in so great a multitude, no place whatever is given to Abraham, the father of the Church? We know well from what a crew they select their intercessors. Let them then tell me what consistency there is in neglecting and rejecting Abraham, whom God preferred to all others, and raised to the highest degree of honor. The only reason is, that as it was plain there was no such practice in the ancient Church, they thought proper to conceal the novelty of the practice by saying nothing of the Patriarchs: as if by a mere diversity of names they could excuse a practice at once novel and impure. They sometimes, also, object that God is entreated to have mercy on his people "for David's sake" (Ps. 132:10; see *Calv. Com.*). This is so far from supporting their error, that it is the strongest refutation of it. We must consider the character which David bore. He is set apart from the whole body of the faithful to establish the covenant which God made in his hand. Thus regard is had to the covenant rather than to the individual. Under him as a type the sole intercession of Christ is asserted. But what was peculiar to David as a type of Christ is certainly inapplicable to others.

26. But some seem to be moved by the fact, that the prayers of saints are often said to have been heard. Why? Because they prayed. "They cried unto thee" (says the Psalmist), "and were delivered: they trusted in thee, and were not confounded" (Ps. 22:5). Let us also pray after their example, that like them we too may be heard. Those men, on the contrary, absurdly argue that none will be heard but those who have been heard already. How much better does James argue, "Elias was a man subject to like passions as we are, and he prayed earnestly that it might not rain: and it rained not on the earth by the space of three years and six months. And he prayed again and the heaven gave rain, and the earth brought forth her fruit." (James 5:17-18). What? Does he infer that Elias possessed some peculiar privilege, and that we must have recourse to him for the use of it? By no means. He shows the perpetual efficacy of a pure and pious prayer, that we may be induced in like manner to pray. For the kindness and readiness of God to hear others is malignantly interpreted, if their example does not inspire us with stronger confidence in his promise, since his declaration is not that he will incline his ear to one or two, or a few individuals, but to all who call upon his name. In this ignorance they are the less excusable, because they seem as it were avowedly to contemn the many admonitions of Scripture. David was repeatedly delivered by the power of God. Was this to give that power to him that we might be delivered on his application? Very different is his affirmation: "The righteous shall compass me about; for thou shalt deal bountifully with me" (Ps. 142:7). Again, "The righteous also shall see, and fear, and shall laugh at him" (Ps. 52:6). "This poor man cried, and the Lord heard him, and saved him out of all his troubles" (Ps. 34:6). In The Psalms are many similar prayers, in which David calls upon God to give him what he asks, for this reason—viz. that the righteous

may not be put to shame, but by his example encouraged to hope. Here let one passage suffice, "For this shall everyone that is godly pray unto thee in a time when thou mayest be found" (Ps. 32:6, *Calv. Com.*). This passage I have quoted the more readily, because those ravers who employ their hireling tongues in defense of the Papacy, are not ashamed to adduce it in proof of the intercession of the dead. As if David intended anything more than to show the benefit which he shall obtain from the divine clemency and condescension when he shall have been heard. In general, we must hold that the experience of the grace of God, as well towards ourselves as towards others, tends in no slight degree to confirm our faith in his promises. I do not quote the many passages in which David sets forth the loving-kindness of God to him as a ground of confidence, as they will readily occur to every reader of The Psalms. Jacob had previously taught the same thing by his own example, "I am not worthy of the least of all thy mercies, and of all the truth which thou hast showed unto thy servant: for with my staff I passed over this Jordan; and now I am become two bands" (Gen. 32:10). He indeed alleges the promise, but not the promise only; for he at the same time adds the effect, to animate him with greater confidence in the future kindness of God. God is not like men who grow weary of their liberality, or whose means of exercising it become exhausted; but he is to be estimated by his own nature, as David properly does when he says, "Thou hast redeemed me, O Lord God of truth" (Ps 31:5). After ascribing the praise of his salvation to God, he adds that he is true: for were he not ever like himself, his past favor would not be an infallible ground for confidence and prayer. But when we know that as often as he assists us, he gives us a specimen and proof of his goodness and faithfulness, there is no reason to fear that our hope will be ashamed or frustrated.

27. On the whole, since Scripture places the principal part of worship in the invocation of God (this being the office of piety which he requires of us in preference to all sacrifices), it is manifest sacrilege to

offer prayer to others. Hence it is said in the psalm: "If we have forgotten the name of our God, or stretched out our hands to a strange god, shall not God search this out?" (Ps. 44:20-21). Again, since it is only in faith that God desires to be invoked, and he distinctly enjoins us to frame our prayers according to the rule of his word: in fine, since faith is founded on the word, and is the parent of right prayer, the moment we decline from the word, our prayers are impure. But we have already shown, that if we consult the whole volume of Scripture, we shall find that God claims this honor to himself alone. In regard to the office of intercession, we have also seen that it is peculiar to Christ, and that no prayer is agreeable to God which he as Mediator does not sanctify. And though believers mutually offer up prayers to God in behalf of their brethren, we have shown that this derogates in no respect from the sole intercession of Christ, because all trust to that intercession in commending themselves as well as others to God. Moreover, we have shown that this is ignorantly transferred to the dead, of whom we nowhere read that they were commanded to pray for us. The Scripture often exhorts us to offer up mutual prayers; but says not one syllable concerning the dead; nay, James tacitly excludes the dead when he combines the two things, to "confess our sins one to another, and to pray one for another" (James 5:16). Hence it is sufficient to condemn this error, that the beginning of right prayer springs from faith, and that faith comes by the hearing of the word of God, in which there is no mention of fictitious intercession, superstition having rashly adopted intercessors who have not been divinely appointed. While the Scripture abounds in various forms of prayer, we find no example of this intercession, without which Papists think there is no prayer. Moreover, it is evident that this superstition is the result of distrust, because they are either not contented with Christ as an intercessor, or have altogether robbed him of this honor. This last is easily proved by their effrontery in maintaining, as the strongest of all their arguments for the intercession of the saints, that we are unworthy of familiar access to God. This, indeed, we acknowledge to be most true, but we thence infer that they leave nothing to Christ, because they consider his intercession as nothing, unless it is supplemented by that of George and Hypolyte, and similar phantoms.

28. But though prayer is properly confined to vows and supplications, yet so strong is the affinity between petition and thanksgiving, that both may be conveniently comprehended under one name. For the forms which Paul enumerates (1 Tim. 2:1) fall under the first member of this division. By prayer and supplication we pour out our desires before God, asking as well those things which tend to promote his glory and display his name, as the benefits which contribute to our advantage. By thanksgiving we duly celebrate his kindnesses toward us, ascribing to his liberality every blessing which enters into our lot. David accordingly includes both in one sentence, "Call upon me in the day of trouble: I will deliver thee, and thou shalt glorify me" (Ps. 50:15). Scripture, not without reason, commands us to use both continually. We have already described the greatness of our want, while experience itself proclaims the straits which press us on every side to be so numerous and so great, that all have sufficient ground to send forth sighs and groans to God without intermission, and suppliantly implore him. For even should they be exempt from adversity, still the holiest ought to be stimulated first by their sins, and, secondly, by the innumerable assaults of temptation, to long for a remedy. The sacrifice of praise and thanksgiving can never be interrupted without guilt, since God never ceases to load us with favor upon favor, so as to force us to gratitude, however slow and sluggish we may be. In short, so great and widely diffused are the riches of his liberality towards us, so marvelous and wondrous the miracles which we behold on every side, that we never can want a subject and materials for praise and thanksgiving. To make this somewhat clearer: since all our hopes and resources are placed in God (this has already been fully proved), so that neither our persons nor our interests can prosper without his blessing,

we must constantly submit ourselves and our all to him. Then whatever we deliberate, speak, or do, should be deliberated, spoken, and done under his hand and will; in fine, under the hope of his assistance. God has pronounced a curse upon all who, confiding in themselves or others, form plans and resolutions, who, without regarding his will, or invoking his aid, either plan or attempt to execute (James 4:14; Isa. 30:1; 31:1). And since, as has already been observed, he receives the honor which is due when he is acknowledged to be the author of all good, it follows that, in deriving all good from his hand, we ought continually to express our thankfulness, and that we have no right to use the benefits which proceed from his liberality, if we do not assiduously proclaim his praise, and give him thanks, these being the ends for which they are given. When Paul declares that every creature of God "is sanctified by the word of God and prayers" (1 Tim. 4:5), he intimates that without the word and prayers none of them are holy and pure, word being used metonymically for faith. Hence David, on experiencing the loving-kindness of the Lord, elegantly declares, "He hath put a new song in my mouth" (Ps. 40:3); intimating, that our silence is malignant when we leave his blessings unpraised, seeing every blessing he bestows is a new ground of thanksgiving. Thus Isaiah, proclaiming the singular mercies of God, says, "Sing unto the Lord a new song (Isa. 42:10)." In the same sense David says in another passage, "O Lord, open thou my lips; and my mouth shall show forth thy praise" (Ps. 51:15). In like manner, Hezekiah and Jonah declare that they will regard it as the end of their deliverance "to celebrate the goodness of God with songs in his temple" (Isa. 38:20; Jonah 2:10). David lays down a general rule for all believers in these words, "What shall I render unto the Lord for all his benefits toward me? I will take the cup of salvation, and call upon the name of the Lord" (Ps. 116:12-13). This rule the Church follows in another psalm, "Save us, O Lord our God, and gather us from among the heathen, to give thanks unto thy holy name, and to triumph in thy praise" (Ps. 106:47).

Again, "He will regard the prayer of the destitute, and not despise their prayer. This shall be written for the generation to come: and the people which shall be created shall praise the Lord." "To declare the name of the Lord in Zion, and his praise in Jerusalem" (Ps. 102:18, 21). Nay, whenever believers beseech the Lord to do anything for his own name's sake, as they declare themselves unworthy of obtaining it in their own name, so they oblige themselves to give thanks, and promise to make the right use of his lovingkindness by being the heralds of it. Thus Hosea, speaking of the future redemption of the Church, says, "Take away all iniquity, and receive us graciously; so will we render the calves of our lips" (Hos. 14:2). Not only do our tongues proclaim the kindness of God, but they naturally inspire us with love to him. "I love the Lord, because he hath heard my voice and my supplications" (Ps. 116:1). In another passage, speaking of the help which he had experienced, he says, "I will love thee, O Lord, my strength" (Ps. 18:1). No praise will ever please God that does not flow from this feeling of love. Nay, we must attend to the declaration of Paul, that all wishes are vicious and perverse which are not accompanied with thanksgiving. His words are, "In everything by prayer and supplication with thanksgiving let your requests be made known unto God" (Phil. 4:6). Because many, under the influence of moroseness, weariness, impatience, bitter grief and fear, use murmuring in their prayers, he enjoins us so to regulate our feelings as cheerfully to bless God even before obtaining what we ask. But if this connection ought always to subsist in full vigor between things that are almost contrary, the more sacred is the tie which binds us to celebrate the praises of God whenever he grants our requests. And as we have already shown that our prayers, which otherwise would be polluted) are sanctified by the intercession of Christ, so the Apostle, by enjoining us "to offer the sacrifice of praise to God continually" by Christ (Heb. 13:15), reminds us, that without the intervention of his priesthood our lips are not pure enough to celebrate the name of God. Hence we infer that a monstrous delusion prevails among Papists, the great majority of whom wonder when Christ is called an intercessor. The reason why Paul enjoins, "Pray without ceasing; in everything give thanks" (1 Thess. 5:17-18), is, because he would have us with the utmost assiduity, at all times, in every place, in all things, and under all circumstances, direct our prayers to God, to expect all the things which we desire from him, and when obtained ascribe them to him; thus furnishing perpetual grounds for prayer and praise.

29. This assiduity in prayer, though it specially refers to the peculiar private prayers of individuals, extends also in some measure to the public prayers of the Church. These, it may be said, cannot be continual, and ought not to be made, except in the manner which, for the sake of order, has been established by public consent. This I admit, and hence certain hours are fixed beforehand, hours which, though indifferent in regard to God, are necessary for the use of man, that the general convenience may be consulted, and all things be done in the Church, as Paul enjoins, "decently and in order" (1 Cor. 14:40). But there is nothing in this to prevent each church from being now and then stirred up to a more frequent use of prayer and being more zealously affected under the impulse of some greater necessity. Of perseverance in prayer, which is much akin to assiduity, we shall speak towards the close of the chapter (sec. 51-52). This assiduity, moreover, is very different from the Βαττολογια, vain speaking, which our Savior has prohibited (Matt. 6:7). For he does not there forbid us to pray long or frequently, or with great fervor, but warns us against supposing that we can extort anything from God by importuning him with garrulous loquacity, as if he were to be persuaded after the manner of men. We know that hypocrites, because they consider not that they have to do with God, offer up their prayers as pompously as if it were part of a triumphal show. The Pharisee, who thanked God that he was not as other men, no doubt proclaimed his praises before men, as if he had wished to gain a reputation for sanctity by his

prayers. Hence that vain speaking, which for a similar reason prevails so much in the Papacy in the present day, some vainly spinning out the time by a reiteration of the same frivolous prayers, and others employing a long series of verbiage for vulgar display. This childish garrulity being a mockery of God, it is not strange that it is prohibited in the Church, in order that every feeling there expressed may be sincere, proceeding from the inmost heart. Akin to this abuse is another which our Savior also condemns, namely, when hypocrites for the sake of ostentation court the presence of many witnesses, and would sooner pray in the marketplace than pray without applause. The true object of prayer being, as we have already said (sec. 4-5), to carry our thoughts directly to God, whether to celebrate his praise or implore his aid, we can easily see that its primary seat is in the mind and heart, or rather that prayer itself is properly an effusion and manifestation of internal feeling before Him who is the searcher of hearts. Hence (as has been said), when our divine Master was pleased to lay down the best rule for prayer, his injunction was, "Enter into thy closet, and when thou hast shut thy door, pray to thy Father which is in secret, and thy Father which seeth in secret shall reward thee openly" (Matt. 6:6). Dissuading us from the example of hypocrites, who sought the applause of men by an ambitious ostentation in prayer, he adds the better course—enter thy chamber, shut thy door, and there pray. By these words (as I understand them) he taught us to seek a place of retirement which might enable us to turn all our thoughts inwards and enter deeply into our hearts, promising that God would hold converse with the feelings of our mind, of which the body ought to be the temple. He meant not to deny that it may be expedient to pray in other places also, but he shows that prayer is somewhat of a secret nature, having its chief seat in the mind, and requiring a tranquility far removed from the turmoil of ordinary cares. And hence it was not without cause that our Lord himself, when he would engage more earnestly in prayer, withdrew into a retired spot beyond the bustle of the world, thus reminding us by his example that we are not to neglect those helps which enable the mind, in itself too much disposed to wander, to become sincerely intent on prayer. Meanwhile, as he abstained not from prayer when the occasion required it, though he were in the midst of a crowd, so must we, whenever there is need, lift up "pure hands" (1 Tim. 2:8) at all places. And hence we must hold that he who declines to pray in the public meeting of the saints, knows not what it is to pray apart, in retirement, or at home. On the other hand, he who neglects to pray alone and in private, however sedulously he frequents public meetings, there gives his prayers to the wind, because he defers more to the opinion of man than to the secret judgment of God. Still, lest the public prayers of the Church should be held in contempt, the Lord anciently bestowed upon them the most honorable appellation, especially when he called the temple the "house of prayer" (Isa. 56:7). For by this expression he both showed that the duty of prayer is a principal part of his worship, and that to enable believers to engage in it with one consent his temple is set up before them as a kind of banner. A noble promise was also added, "Praise waiteth for thee, O God, in Zion: and unto thee shall the vow be performed" (Ps. 65:1). By these words the Psalmist reminds us that the prayers of the Church are never in vain; because God always furnishes his people with materials for a song of joy. But although the shadows of the law have ceased, yet because God was pleased by this ordinance to foster the unity of the faith among us also, there can be no doubt that the same promise belongs to us—a promise which Christ sanctioned with his own lips, and which Paul declares to be perpetually in force.

30. As God in his word enjoins common prayer, so public temples are the places destined for the performance of them, and hence those who refuse to join with the people of God in this observance have no ground for the pretext, that they enter their chamber in order that they may obey the command of the Lord. For he who promises to

grant whatsoever two or three assembled in his name shall ask (Matt. 18:20), declares, that he by no means despises the prayers which are publicly offered up, provided there be no ostentation, or catching at human applause, and provided there be a true and sincere affection in the secret recesses of the heart. If this is the legitimate use of churches (and it certainly is), we must, on the other hand, beware of imitating the practice which commenced some centuries ago, of imagining that churches are the proper dwellings of God, where he is more ready to listen to us, or of attaching to them some kind of secret sanctity, which makes prayer there more holy. For seeing we are the true temples of God, we must pray in ourselves if we would invoke God in his holy temple. Let us leave such gross ideas to the Jews or the heathen, knowing that we have a command to pray without distinction of place, "in spirit and in truth" (John 4:23). It is true that by the order of God the temple was anciently dedicated for the offering of prayers and sacrifices, but this was at a time when the truth (which being now fully manifested, we are not permitted to confine to any material temple) lay hid under the figure of shadows. Even the temple was not represented to the Jews as confining the presence of God within its walls, but was meant to train them to contemplate the image of the true temple. Accordingly, a severe rebuke is administered both by Isaiah and Stephen, to those who thought that God could in any way dwell in temples made with hands (Isa. 66:2; Acts 7:48).

31. Hence it is perfectly clear that neither words nor singing (if used in prayer) are of the least consequence, or avail one iota with God, unless they proceed from deep feeling in the heart. Nay, rather they provoke his anger against us, if they come from the lips and throat only, since this is to abuse his sacred name, and hold his majesty in derision. This we infer from the words of Isaiah, which, though their meaning is of wider extent, go to rebuke this vice also: "Forasmuch as this people draw near me with their mouth, and with their lips do honor me, but have removed their heart far from me, and

their fear toward me is taught by the precept of men: therefore, be-hold, I will proceed to do a marvelous work among this people, even a marvelous work and a wonder: for the wisdom of their wise men shall perish, and the understanding of their prudent men shall be hid" (Isa. 29:13). Still we do not condemn words or singing, but rather greatly commend them, provided the feeling of the mind goes along with them. For in this way the thought of God is kept alive on our minds, which, from their fickle and versatile nature, soon relax, and are distracted by various objects, unless various means are used to support them. Besides, since the glory of God ought in a manner to be displayed in each part of our body, the special service to which the tongue should be devoted is that of singing and speaking, inasmuch as it has been expressly created to declare and proclaim the praise of God. This employment of the tongue is chiefly in the public services which are performed in the meeting of the saints. In this way the God whom we serve in one spirit and one faith, we glorify together as it were with one voice and one mouth; and that openly, so that each may in turn receive the confession of his brother's faith, and be invited and incited to imitate it.

32. It is certain that the use of singing in churches (which I may mention in passing) is not only very ancient, but was also used by the Apostles, as we may gather from the words of Paul, "I will sing with the spirit, and I will sing with the understanding also" (1 Cor. 14:15). In like manner he says to the Colossians, "Teaching and admonishing one another in psalms, and hymns, and spiritual songs, singing with grace in your hearts to the Lord" (Col. 3:16). In the former passage, he enjoins us to sing with the voice and the heart; in the latter, he commends spiritual Songs, by which the pious mutually edify each other. That it was not an universal practice, however, is attested by Augustine (*Confess.* Lib. 9 cap. 7), who states that the church of Milan first began to use singing in the time of Ambrose, when the orthodox faith being persecuted by Justina, the mother of Valentinian, the vigils

of the people were more frequent than usual; and that the practice was afterwards followed by the other Western churches. He had said a little before that the custom came from the East. He also intimates (*Retract.* Lib. 2) that it was received in Africa in his own time. His words are, "Hilarius, a man of tribunitial rank, assailed with the bitterest invectives he could use the custom which then began to exist at Carthage, of singing hymns from the book of Psalms at the altar, either before the oblation, or when it was distributed to the people; I answered him, at the request of my brethren." And certainly if singing is tempered to a gravity befitting the presence of God and angels, it both gives dignity and grace to sacred actions, and has a very powerful tendency to stir up the mind to true zeal and ardor in prayer. We must, however, carefully beware, lest our ears be more intent on the music than our minds on the spiritual meaning of the words. Augustine confesses (*Confess.* Lib. 10 cap. 33) that the fear of this danger sometimes made him wish for the introduction of a practice observed by Athanasius, who ordered the reader to use only a gentle inflection of the voice, more akin to recitation than singing. But on again considering how many advantages were derived from singing, he inclined to the other side. If this moderation is used, there cannot be a doubt that the practice is most sacred and salutary. On the other hand, songs composed merely to tickle and delight the ear are unbecoming the majesty of the Church, and cannot but be most displeasing to God.

33. It is also plain that the public prayers are not to be couched in Greek among the Latins, nor in Latin among the French or English (as hitherto has been everywhere practiced), but in the vulgar tongue, so that all present may understand them, since they ought to be used for the edification of the whole Church, which cannot be in the least degree benefited by a sound not understood. Those who are not moved by any reason of humanity or charity, ought at least to be somewhat moved by the authority of Paul, whose words are by no means ambiguous: "When thou shalt bless with the spirit, how shall

he that occupieth the room of the unlearned say, Amen, at thy giving of thanks, seeing he understandeth not what thou sayest? For thou verily givest thanks, but the other is not edified" (1 Cor. 14:16-17). How then can one sufficiently admire the unbridled license of the Papists, who, while the Apostle publicly protests against it, hesitate not to bawl out the most verbose prayers in a foreign tongue, prayers of which they themselves sometimes do not understand one syllable, and which they have no wish that others should understand? Different is the course which Paul prescribes, "What is it then? I will pray with the spirit, and I will pray with the understanding also; I will sing with the spirit, and I will sing with the understanding also:" meaning by the spirit the special gift of tongues, which some who had received it abused when they dissevered it from the mind, that is, the understanding. The principle we must always hold is, that in all prayer, public and private, the tongue without the mind must be displeasing to God. Moreover, the mind must be so incited, as in ardor of thought far to surpass what the tongue is able to express. Lastly, the tongue is not even necessary to private prayer, unless insofar as the internal feeling is insufficient for incitement, or the vehemence of the incitement carries the utterance of the tongue along with it. For although the best prayers are sometimes without utterance, yet when the feeling of the mind is overpowering, the tongue spontaneously breaks forth into utterance, and our other members into gesture. Hence that dubious muttering of Hannah (1 Sam. 1:13), something similar to which is experienced by all the saints when concise and abrupt expressions escape from them. The bodily gestures usually observed in prayer, such as kneeling and uncovering of the head (*Calv. in Acts 20:36*), are exercises by which we attempt to rise to higher veneration of God.

34. We must now attend not only to a surer method, but also form of prayer, that, namely, which our heavenly Father has delivered to us by his beloved Son, and in which we may recognize his boundless

goodness and condescension (Matt. 6:9; Luke 11:2). Besides admonishing and exhorting us to seek him in our every necessity (as children are wont to betake themselves to the protection of their parents when oppressed with any anxiety), seeing that we were not fully aware how great our poverty was, or what was right or for our interest to ask, he has provided for this ignorance; that wherein our capacity failed he has sufficiently supplied. For he has given us a form in which is set before us as in a picture everything which it is lawful to wish, everything which is conducive to our interest, everything which it is necessary to demand. From his goodness in this respect we derive the great comfort of knowing, that as we ask almost in his words, we ask nothing that is absurd, or foreign, or unseasonable; nothing, in short, that is not agreeable to him. Plato, seeing the ignorance of men in presenting their desires to God, desires which if granted would often be most injurious to them, declares the best form of prayer to be that which an ancient poet has furnished: "O king Jupiter, give what is best, whether we wish it or wish it not; but avert from us what is evil even though we ask it" (Plato, *Alcibiad.* 2). This heathen shows his wisdom in discerning how dangerous it is to ask of God what our own passion dictates; while, at the same time, he reminds us of our unhappy condition in not being able to open our lips before God without dangers unless his Spirit instruct us how to pray aright (Rom. 8:26). The higher value, therefore, ought we to set on the privilege, when the only begotten Son of God puts words into our lips, and thus relieves our minds of all hesitation.

35. This form or rule of prayer is composed of six petitions. For I am prevented from agreeing with those who divide it into seven by the adversative mode of diction used by the Evangelist, who appears to have intended to unite the two members together; as if he had said, Do not allow us to be overcome by temptation, but rather bring assistance to our frailty, and deliver us that we may not fall. Ancient writers also agree with us, that what is added by Matthew as

a seventh head is to be considered as explanatory of the sixth petition. But though in every part of the prayer the first place is assigned to the glory of God, still this is more especially the object of the three first petitions, in which we are to look to the glory of God alone, without any reference to what is called our own advantage. The three remaining petitions are devoted to our interest, and properly relate to things which it is useful for us to ask. When we ask that the name of God may be hallowed, as God wishes to prove whether we love and serve him freely, or from the hope of reward, we are not to think at all of our own interest; we must set his glory before our eyes, and keep them intent upon it alone. In the other similar petitions, this is the only manner in which we ought to be affected. It is true, that in this way our own interest is greatly promoted, because, when the name of God is hallowed in the way we ask, our own sanctification also is thereby promoted. But in regard to this advantage, we must, as I have said, shut our eyes, and be in a manner blind, so as not even to see it; and hence were all hope of our private advantage cut off, we still should never cease to wish and pray for this hallowing, and everything else which pertains to the glory of God. We have examples in Moses and Paul, who did not count it grievous to turn away their eyes and minds from themselves, and with intense and fervent zeal long for death, if by their loss the kingdom and glory of God might be promoted (Exod. 32:32; Rom. 9:3). On the other hand, when we ask for daily bread, although we desire what is advantageous for ourselves, we ought also especially to seek the glory of God, so much so that we would not ask at all unless it were to turn to his glory. Let us now proceed to an exposition of the Prayer.

OUR FATHER WHICH ART IN HEAVEN.

36. The first thing suggested at the very outset is, as we have already said (sec. 17-19), that all our prayers to God ought only to be presented in the name of Christ, as there is no other name which can recommend them. In calling God our Father, we certainly plead the

name of Christ. For with what confidence could any man call God his Father? Who would have the presumption to arrogate to himself the honor of a son of God were we not gratuitously adopted as his sons in Christ? He being the true Son, has been given to us as a brother, so that that which he possesses as his own by nature becomes ours by adoption, if we embrace this great mercy with firm faith. As John says, "As many as received him, to them gave he power to become the sons of God, even to them that believe in his name" (John 1:12). Hence he both calls himself our Father, and is pleased to be so called by us, by this delightful name relieving us of all distrust, since nowhere can a stronger affection be found than in a father. Hence, too, he could not have given us a stronger testimony of his boundless love than in calling us his sons. But his love towards us is so much the greater and more excellent than that of earthly parents, the farther he surpasses all men in goodness and mercy (Isa. 63:16). Earthly parents, laying aside all paternal affection, might abandon their offspring; he will never abandon us (Ps. 27:10), seeing he cannot deny himself. For we have his promise, "If ye then, being evil, know how to give good gifts unto your children, how much more shall your Father which is in heaven give good things to them that ask him?" (Matt. 7:11). In like manner in the prophet, "Can a woman forget her sucking child, that she should not have compassion on the son of her womb? Yea, they may forget, yet will not I forget thee" (Isa. 49:15). But if we are his sons, then as a son cannot betake himself to the protection of a stranger and a foreigner without at the same time complaining of his father's cruelty or poverty, so we cannot ask assistance from any other quarter than from him, unless we would upbraid him with poverty, or want of means, or cruelty and excessive austerity.

37. Nor let us allege that we are justly rendered timid by a consciousness of sin, by which our Father, though mild and merciful, is daily offended. For if among men a son cannot have a better advocate to plead his cause with his father, and cannot employ a better

intercessor to regain his lost favor, than if he come himself suppliant and downcast, acknowledging his fault, to implore the mercy of his father, whose paternal feelings cannot but be moved by such entreaties, what will that "Father of all mercies, and God of all comfort," do? (2 Cor. 1:3). Will he not rather listen to the tears and groans of his children, when supplicating for themselves (especially seeing he invites and exhorts us to do so), than to any advocacy of others to whom the timid have recourse, not without some semblance of despair, because they are distrustful of their father's mildness and clemency? The exuberance of his paternal kindness he sets before us in the parable (Luke 15:20; see *Calv. Comm.*). when the father with open arms receives the son who had gone away from him, wasted his substance in riotous living, and in all ways grievously sinned against him. He waits not till pardon is asked in words, but, anticipating the request, recognizes him afar off, runs to meet him, consoles him, and restores him to favor. By setting before us this admirable example of mildness in a man, he designed to show in how much greater abundance we may expect it from him who is not only a Father, but the best and most merciful of all fathers, however ungrateful, rebellious, and wicked sons we may be, provided only we throw ourselves upon his mercy. And the better to assure us that he is such a Father if we are Christians, he has been pleased to be called not only a Father, but our Father, as if we were pleading with him after this manner, O Father, who art possessed of so much affection for thy children, and art so ready to forgive, we thy children approach thee and present our requests, fully persuaded that thou hast no other feelings towards us than those of a father, though we are unworthy of such a parent. But as our narrow hearts are incapable of comprehending such boundless favor, Christ is not only the earnest and pledge of our adoption, but also gives us the Spirit as a witness of this adoption, that through him we may freely cry aloud, Abba, Father. Whenever, therefore, we are restrained by any feeling of hesitation, let us remember to ask of him that he may correct our timidity, and placing us under the magnanimous guidance of the Spirit, enable us to pray boldly.

38. The instruction given us, however, is not that every individual in particular is to call him Father, but rather that we are all in common to call him Our Father. By this we are reminded how strong the feeling of brotherly love between us ought to be, since we are all alike, by the same mercy and free kindness, the children of such a Father. For if He from whom we all obtain whatever is good is our common Father (Matt. 23:9), everything which has been distributed to us we should be prepared to communicate to each other, as far as occasion demands. But if we are thus desirous as we ought, to stretch out our hands and give assistance to each other, there is nothing by which we can more benefit our brethren than by committing them to the care and protection of the best of parents, since if He is propitious and favorable nothing more can be desired. And, indeed, we owe this also to our Father. For as he who truly and from the heart loves the father of a family, extends the same love and good-will to all his household, so the zeal and affection which we feel for our heavenly Parent it becomes us to extend towards his people, his family, and, in fine, his heritage, which he has honored so highly as to give them the appellation of the "fullness" of his only begotten Son (Eph. 1:23). Let the Christian, then, so regulate his prayers as to make them common, and embrace all who are his brethren in Christ; not only those whom at present he sees and knows to be such, but all men who are alive upon the earth. What God has determined with regard to them is beyond our knowledge, but to wish and hope the best concerning them is both pious and humane. Still it becomes us to regard with special affection those who are of the household of faith, and whom the Apostle has in express terms recommended to our care in everything (Gal. 6:10). In short, all our prayers ought to bear reference to that community which our Lord has established in his kingdom and family.

39. This, however, does not prevent us from praying specially for ourselves, and certain others, provided our mind is not withdrawn from the view of this community, does not deviate from it, but constantly refers to it. For prayers, though couched in special terms, keeping that object still in view, cease not to be common. All this may easily be understood by analogy. There is a general command from God to relieve the necessities of all the poor, and yet this command is obeyed by those who with that view give succor to all whom they see or know to be in distress, although they pass by many whose wants are not less urgent, either because they cannot know or are unable to give supply to all. In this way there is nothing repugnant to the will of God in those who, giving heed to this common society of the Church, yet offer up particular prayers, in which, with a public mind, though in special terms, they commend to God themselves or others, with whose necessity he has been pleased to make them more familiarly acquainted. It is true that prayer and the giving of our substance are not in all respects alike. We can only bestow the kindness of our liberality on those of whose wants we are aware, whereas in prayer we can assist the greatest strangers, how wide soever the space which may separate them from us. This is done by that general form of prayer which, including all the sons of God, includes them also. To this we may refer the exhortation which Paul gave to the believers of his age, to lift up "holy hands without wrath and doubting" (1 Tim. 2:8). By reminding them that dissension is a bar to prayer, he shows it to be his wish that they should with one accord present their prayers in common.

40. The next words are, WHICH ART IN HEAVEN. From this we are not to infer that he is enclosed and confined within the circumference of heaven, as by a kind of boundaries. Hence Solomon confesses, "The heaven of heavens cannot contain thee" (1 Kings 8:27); and he himself says by the Prophet, "The heaven is my throne, and the earth is my footstool" (Isa. 66:1); thereby intimating, that his

presence, not confined to any region, is diffused over all space. But as our gross minds are unable to conceive of his ineffable glory, it is designated to us by heaven, nothing which our eyes can behold being so full of splendor and majesty. While, then, we are accustomed to regard every object as confined to the place where our senses discern it, no place can be assigned to God; and hence, if we would seek him, we must rise higher than all corporeal or mental discernment. Again, this form of expression reminds us that he is far beyond the reach of change or corruption, that he holds the whole universe in his grasp, and rules it by his power. The effect of the expressions therefore, is the same as if it had been said, that he is of infinite majesty, incomprehensible essence, boundless power, and eternal duration. When we thus speak of God, our thoughts must be raised to their highest pitch; we must not ascribe to him anything of a terrestrial or carnal nature, must not measure him by our little standards, or suppose his will to be like ours. At the same time, we must put our confidence in him, understanding that heaven and earth are governed by his providence and power. In short, under the name of Father is set before us that God, who hath appeared to us in his own image, that we may invoke him with sure faith; the familiar name of Father being given not only to inspire confidence, but also to curb our minds, and prevent them from going astray after doubtful or fictitious gods. We thus ascend from the only begotten Son to the supreme Father of angels and of the Church. Then when his throne is fixed in heaven, we are reminded that he governs the world, and, therefore, that it is not in vain to approach him whose present care we actually experience. "He that cometh to God," says the Apostle, "must believe that he is, and that he is a rewarder of them that diligently seek him" (Heb. 11:6). Here Christ makes both claims for his Father, first, that we place our faith in him; and, secondly, that we feel assured that our salvation is not neglected by him, inasmuch as he condescends to extend his providence to us. By these elementary principles Paul prepares us to pray aright; for before enjoining us to make our requests known unto God, he premises in this way, "The Lord is at hand. Be careful for nothing" (Phil. 4:5-6). Whence it appears that doubt and perplexity hang over the prayers of those in whose minds the belief is not firmly seated, that "the eyes of the Lord are upon the righteous" (Ps. 34:15).

41. The first petition is, HALLOWED BE THY NAME. The necessity of presenting it bespeaks our great disgrace. For what can be more unbecoming than that our ingratitude and malice should impair, our audacity and petulance should as much as in them lies destroy, the glory of God? But though all the ungodly should burst with sacrilegious rage, the holiness of God's name still shines forth. Justly does the Psalmist exclaim, "According to thy name, O God, so is thy praise unto the ends of the earth" (Ps. 48:10). For wherever God hath made himself known, his perfections must be displayed, his power, goodness, wisdom, justice, mercy, and truth, which fill us with admiration, and incite us to show forth his praise. Therefore, as the name of God is not duly hallowed on the earth, and we are otherwise unable to assert it, it is at least our duty to make it the subject of our prayers. The sum of the whole is, It must be our desire that God may receive the honor which is his due: that men may never think or speak of him without the greatest reverence. The opposite of this reverence is profanity, which has always been too common in the world, and is very prevalent in the present day. Hence the necessity of the petition, which, if piety had any proper existence among us, would be superfluous. But if the name of God is duly hallowed only when separated from all other names it alone is glorified, we are in the petition enjoined to ask not only that God would vindicate his sacred name from all contempt and insult, but also that he would compel the whole human race to reverence it. Then since God manifests himself to us partly by his word, and partly by his works, he is not sanctified unless in regard to both of these we ascribe to him what is due, and thus embrace whatever has proceeded from him, giving no less

praise to his justice than to his mercy. On the manifold diversity of his works he has inscribed the marks of his glory, and these ought to call forth from every tongue an ascription of praise. Thus Scripture will obtain its due authority with us, and no event will hinder us from celebrating the praises of God, in regard to every part of his government. On the other hand, the petition implies a wish that all impiety which pollutes this sacred name may perish and be extinguished, that every thing which obscures or impairs his glory, all detraction and insult, may cease; that all blasphemy being suppressed, the divine majesty may be more and more signally displayed.

42. The second petition is, THY KINGDOM COME. This contains nothing new, and yet there is good reason for distinguishing it from the first. For if we consider our lethargy in the greatest of all matters, we shall see how necessary it is that what ought to be in itself perfectly known should be inculcated at greater length. Therefore, after the injunction to pray that God would reduce to order, and at length completely efface every stain which is thrown on his sacred name, another petition, containing almost the same wish, is added—viz. Thy kingdom come. Although a definition of this kingdom has already been given, I now briefly repeat that God reigns when men, in denial of themselves and contempt of the world and this earthly life, devote themselves to righteousness and aspire to heaven (see Calvin, *Harm.* Matt. 6). Thus this kingdom consists of two parts; the first is, when God by the agency of his Spirit corrects all the depraved lusts of the flesh, which in bands war against Him; and the second, when he brings all our thoughts into obedience to his authority. This petition, therefore, is duly presented only by those who begin with themselves; in other words, who pray that they may be purified from all the corruptions which disturb the tranquility and impair the purity of God's kingdom. Then as the word of God is like his royal scepter, we are here enjoined to pray that he would subdue all minds and hearts to voluntary obedience. This is done when by

the secret inspiration of his Spirit he displays the efficacy of his word, and raises it to the place of honor which it deserves. We must next descend to the wicked, who perversely and with desperate madness resist his authority. God, therefore, sets up his kingdom, by humbling the whole world, though in different ways, taming the wantonness of some, and breaking the ungovernable pride of others. We should desire this to be done every day, in order that God may gather churches to himself from all quarters of the world, may extend and increase their numbers, enrich them with his gifts, establish due order among them; on the other hand, beat down all the enemies of pure doctrine and religion, dissipate their counsels, defeat their attempts. Hence it appears that there is good ground for the precept which enjoins daily progress, for human affairs are never so prosperous as when the impurities of vice are purged away, and integrity flourishes in full vigor. The completion, however, is deferred to the final advent of Christ, when, as Paul declares, "God will be all in all" (1 Cor. 15:28). This prayer, therefore, ought to withdraw us from the corruptions of the world which separate us from God, and prevent his kingdom from flourishing within us; secondly, it ought to inflame us with an ardent desire for the mortification of the flesh; and, lastly, it ought to train us to the endurance of the cross; since this is the way in which God would have his kingdom to be advanced. It ought not to grieve us that the outward man decays provided the inner man is renewed. For such is the nature of the kingdom of God, that while we submit to his righteousness he makes us partakers of his glory. This is the case when continually adding to his light and truth, by which the lies and the darkness of Satan and his kingdom are dissipated, extinguished, and destroyed, he protects his people, guides them aright by the agency of his Spirit, and confirms them in perseverance; while, on the other hand, he frustrates the impious conspiracies of his enemies, dissipates their wiles and frauds, prevents their malice and curbs their petulance, until at length he consume Antichrist "with the spirit of his mouth," and destroy all impiety "with the brightness of his coming" (2 Thess. 2:8, *Calv. Com.*).

43. The third petition is, THY WILL BE DONE ON EARTH AS IT IS IN HEAVEN. Though this depends on his kingdom, and cannot be disjoined from it, yet a separate place is not improperly given to it on account of our ignorance, which does not at once or easily apprehend what is meant by God reigning in the world. This, therefore, may not improperly be taken as the explanation, that God will be King in the world when all shall subject themselves to his will. We are not here treating of that secret will by which he governs all things, and destines them to their end (see chap. 24, sec. 17). For although devils and men rise in tumult against him, he is able by his incomprehensible counsel not only to turn aside their violence, but make it subservient to the execution of his decrees. What we here speak of is another will of God, namely, that of which voluntary obedience is the counterpart; and, therefore, heaven is expressly contrasted with earth, because, as is said in The Psalms, the angels "do his commandments, hearkening unto the voice of his word" (Ps. 103:20). We are, therefore, enjoined to pray that as everything done in heaven is at the command of God, and the angels are calmly disposed to do all that is right, so the earth may be brought under his authority, all rebellion and depravity having been extinguished. In presenting this request we renounce the desires of the flesh, because he who does not entirely resign his affections to God, does as much as in him lies to oppose the divine will, since everything which proceeds from us is vicious. Again, by this prayer we are taught to deny ourselves, that God may rule us according to his pleasure; and not only so, but also having annihilated our own may create new thoughts and new minds so that we shall have no desire save that of entire agreement with his will; in short, wish nothing of ourselves, but have our hearts governed by his Spirit, under whose inward teaching we may learn to love those things which please and hate those things which displease him. Hence also

we must desire that he would nullify and suppress all affections which are repugnant to his will. Such are the three first heads of the prayer, in presenting which we should have the glory of God only in view, taking no account of ourselves, and paying no respect to our own advantage, which, though it is thereby greatly promoted, is not here to be the subject of request. And though all the events prayed for must happen in their own time, without being either thought of, wished, or asked by us, it is still our duty to wish and ask for them. And it is of no slight importance to do so, that we may testify and profess that we are the servants and children of God, desirous by every means in our power to promote the honor due to him as our Lord and Father, and truly and thoroughly devoted to his service. Hence if men, in praying that the name of God may be hallowed, that his kingdom may come, and his will be done, are not influenced by this zeal for the promotion of his glory, they are not to be accounted among the servants and children of God; and as all these things will take place against their will, so they will turn out to their confusion and destruction.

44. Now comes the second part of the prayer, in which we descend to our own interests, not, indeed, that we are to lose sight of the glory of God (to which, as Paul declares, we must have respect even in meat and drink, 1 Cor. 10:31), and ask only what is expedient for ourselves; but the distinction, as we have already observed, is this: God claiming the three first petitions as specially his own, carries us entirely to himself, that in this way he may prove our piety. Next he permits us to look to our own advantage, but still on the condition, that when we ask anything for ourselves it must be in order that all the benefits which he confers may show forth his glory, there being nothing more incumbent on us than to live and die to him. By the first petition of the second part, GIVE US THIS DAY OUR DAILY BREAD, we pray in general that God would give us all things which the body requires in this sublunary state, not only food and clothing, but everything which he knows will assist us to eat our bread in peace. In this

way we briefly cast our care upon him, and commit ourselves to his providence, that he may feed, foster, and preserve us. For our heavenly Father disdains not to take our body under his charge and protection, that he may exercise our faith in those minute matters, while we look to him for everything, even to a morsel of bread and a drop of water. For since, owing to some strange inequality, we feel more concern for the body than for the soul, many who can trust the latter to God still continue anxious about the former, still hesitate as to what they are to eat, as to how they are to be clothed, and are in trepidation whenever their hands are not filled with corn, and wine, and oil, so much more value do we set on this shadowy, fleeting life, than on a blessed immortality. But those who, trusting to God, have once cast away that anxiety about the flesh, immediately look to him for greater gifts, even salvation and eternal life. It is no slight exercise of faith, therefore, to hope in God for things which would otherwise give us so much concern; nor have we made little progress when we get quit of this unbelief, which cleaves, as it were, to our very bones. The speculations of some concerning supersubstantial bread seem to be very little accordant with our Savior's meaning; for our prayer would be defective were we not to ascribe to God the nourishment even of this fading life. The reason which they give is heathenish—viz. that it is inconsistent with the character of sons of God, who ought to be spiritual, not only to occupy their mind with earthly cares, but to suppose God also occupied with them. As if his blessing and paternal favor were not eminently displayed in giving us food, or as if there were nothing in the declaration that godliness hath "the promise of the life that now is, and of that which is to come" (1 Tim. 4:8). But although the forgiveness of sins is of far more importance than the nourishment of the body, yet Christ has set down the inferior in the prior place, in order that he might gradually raise us to the other two petitions, which properly belong to the heavenly life—in this providing for our sluggishness. We are enjoined to ask our bread, that we may

be contented with the measure which our heavenly Father is pleased
to dispense, and not strive to make gain by illicit arts. Meanwhile, we
must hold that the title by which it is ours is donation, because, as
Moses says (Lev. 26:20, Deut. 8:17), neither our industry, nor labor,
nor hands, acquire anything for us, unless the blessing of God be
present; nay, not even would abundance of bread be of the least avail
were it not divinely converted into nourishment. And hence this liberality of God is not less necessary to the rich than the poor, because,
though their cellars and barns were full, they would be parched and
pine with want did they not enjoy his favor along with their bread.
The terms "this day," or, as it is in another Evangelist, "daily," and also
the epithet "daily," lay a restraint on our immoderate desire of fleeting
good—a desire which we are extremely apt to indulge to excess, and
from which other evils ensue: for when our supply is in richer abundance we ambitiously squander it in pleasure, luxury, ostentation, or
other kinds of extravagance. Wherefore, we are only enjoined to ask
as much as our necessity requires, and as it were for each day, confiding that our heavenly Father, who gives us the supply of today, will
not fail us on the morrow. How great soever our abundance may be,
however well filled our cellars and granaries, we must still always ask
for daily bread, for we must feel assured that all substance is nothing,
unless insofar as the Lord, by pouring out his blessing, make it fruitful during its whole progress; for even that which is in our hand is not
ours except insofar as he every hour portions it out, and permits us to
use it. As nothing is more difficult to human pride than the admission of this truth, the Lord declares that he gave a special proof for
all ages, when he fed his people with manna in the desert (Deut. 8:3),
that he might remind us that "man shall not live by bread alone, but
by every word that proceedeth out of the mouth of God" (Matt. 4:4).
It is thus intimated, that by his power alone our life and strength are
sustained, though he ministers supply to us by bodily instruments. In
like manner, whenever it so pleases, he gives us a proof of an opposite

description, by breaking the strength, or, as he himself calls it, the staff of bread (Lev. 26:26), and leaving us even while eating to pine with hunger, and while drinking to be parched with thirst. Those who, not contented with daily bread, indulge an unrestrained insatiable cupidity, or those who are full of their own abundance, and trust in their own riches, only mock God by offering up this prayer. For the former ask what they would be unwilling to obtain, nay, what they most of all abominate, namely, daily bread only, and as much as in them lies disguise their avarice from God, whereas true prayer should pour out the whole soul and every inward feeling before him. The latter, again, ask what they do not at all expect to obtain, namely, what they imagine that they in themselves already possess. In its being called "ours," God, as we have already said, gives a striking display of his kindness, making that to be ours to which we have no just claim. Nor must we reject the view to which I have already adverted—viz. that this name is given to what is obtained by just and honest labor, as contrasted with what is obtained by fraud and rapine, nothing being our own which we obtain with injury to others. When we ask God to give us, the meaning is, that the thing asked is simply and freely the gift of God, whatever be the quarter from which it comes to us, even when it seems to have been specially prepared by our own art and industry, and procured by our hands, since it is to his blessing alone that all our labors owe their success.

45. The next petition is, FORGIVE US OUR DEBTS. In this and the following petition our Savior has briefly comprehended whatever is conducive to the heavenly life, as these two members contain the spiritual covenant which God made for the salvation of his Church, "I will put my law in their inward parts, and write it on their hearts." "I will pardon all their iniquities" (Jer. 31:33; 33:8). Here our Savior begins with the forgiveness of sins, and then adds the subsequent blessing—viz. that God would protect us by the power, and support us by the aid of his Spirit, so that we may stand invincible against

all temptations. To sins he gives the name of debts, because we owe the punishment due to them, a debt which we could not possibly pay were we not discharged by this remission, the result of his free mercy, when he freely expunges the debt, accepting nothing in return; but of his own mercy receiving satisfaction in Christ, who gave himself a ransom for us (Rom. 3:24). Hence, those who expect to satisfy God by merits of their own or of others, or to compensate and purchase forgiveness by means of satisfactions, have no share in this free pardon, and while they address God in this petition, do nothing more than subscribe their own accusation, and seal their condemnation by their own testimony. For they confess that they are debtors, unless they are discharged by means of forgiveness. This forgiveness, however, they do not receive, but rather reject, when they obtrude their merits and satisfactions upon God, since by so doing they do not implore his mercy, but appeal to his justice. Let those, again, who dream of a perfection which makes it unnecessary to seek pardon, find their disciples among those whose itching ears incline them to imposture (see *Calv. on Dan. 9:20*); only let them understand that those whom they thus acquire have been carried away from Christ, since he, by instructing all to confess their guilt, receives none but sinners, not that he may soothe, and so encourage them in their sins, but because he knows that believers are never so divested of the sins of the flesh as not to remain subject to the justice of God. It is, indeed, to be wished, it ought even to be our strenuous endeavor, to perform all the parts of our duty, so as truly to congratulate ourselves before God as being pure from every stain; but as God is pleased to renew his image in us by degrees, so that to some extent there is always a residue of corruption in our flesh, we ought by no means to neglect the remedy. But if Christ, according to the authority given him by his Father, enjoins us, during the whole course of our lives, to implore pardon, who can tolerate those new teachers who, by the phantom of perfect innocence, endeavor to dazzle the simple, and make them believe that they can render themselves completely free from guilt? This, as John declares, is nothing else than to make God a liar (1 John 1:10). In like manner, those foolish men mutilate the covenant in which we have seen that our salvation is contained by concealing one head of it, and so destroying it entirely; being guilty not only of profanity in that they separate things which ought to be indissolubly connected; but also of wickedness and cruelty in overwhelming wretched souls with despair—of treachery also to themselves and their followers, in that they encourage themselves in a carelessness diametrically opposed to the mercy of God. It is excessively childish to object, that when they long for the advent of the kingdom of God, they at the same time pray for the abolition of sin. In the former division of the prayer absolute perfection is set before us; but in the latter our own weakness. Thus the two fitly correspond to each other—we strive for the goal, and at the same time neglect not the remedies which our necessities require. In the next part of the petition we pray to be forgiven, "as we forgive our debtors;" that is, as we spare and pardon all by whom we are in any way offended, either in deed by unjust, or in word by contumelious treatment. Not that we can forgive the guilt of a fault or offense; this belongs to God only; but we can forgive to this extent: we can voluntarily divest our minds of wrath, hatred, and revenge, and efface the remembrance of injuries by a voluntary oblivion. Wherefore, we are not to ask the forgiveness of our sins from God, unless we forgive the offenses of all who are or have been injurious to us. If we retain any hatred in our minds, if we meditate revenge, and devise the means of hurting; nay, if we do not return to a good understanding with our enemies, perform every kind of friendly office, and endeavor to effect a reconciliation with them, we by this petition beseech God not to grant us forgiveness. For we ask him to do to us as we do to others. This is the same as asking him not to do unless we do also. What, then, do such persons obtain by this petition but a heavier judgment? Lastly, it is to be observed that the condition of being forgiven as we forgive our debtors, is not added because by forgiving others we deserve forgiveness, as if the cause of forgiveness were expressed; but by the use of this expression the Lord has been pleased partly to solace the weakness of our faith, using it as a sign to assure us that our sins are as certainly forgiven as we are certainly conscious of having forgiven others, when our mind is completely purged from all envy, hatred, and malice; and partly using as a badge by which he excludes from the number of his children all who, prone to revenge and reluctant to forgive, obstinately keep up their enmity, cherishing against others that indignation which they deprecate from themselves; so that they should not venture to invoke him as a Father. In the Gospel of Luke, we have this distinctly stated in the words of Christ.

46. The sixth petition corresponds (as we have observed) to the promise of writing the law upon our hearts; but because we do not obey God without a continual warfare, without sharp and arduous contests, we here pray that he would furnish us with armor, and defend us by his protection, that we may be able to obtain the victory. By this we are reminded that we not only have need of the gift of the Spirit inwardly to soften our hearts, and turn and direct them to the obedience of God, but also of his assistance, to render us invincible by all the wiles and violent assaults of Satan. The forms of temptation are many and various. The depraved conceptions of our minds provoking us to transgress the law—conceptions which our concupiscence suggests or the devil excites, are temptations; and things which in their own nature are not evil, become temptations by the wiles of the devil, when they are presented to our eyes in such a way that the view of them makes us withdraw or decline from God. These temptations are both on the right hand and on the left. On the right, when riches, power, and honors, which by their glare, and the semblance of good which they present, generally dazzle the eyes of men, and so entice by their blandishments, that, caught by their snares, and intoxicated by their sweetness, they forget their God: on the left, when offended by

the hardship and bitterness of poverty, disgrace, contempt, afflictions, and other things of that description, they despond, cast away their confidence and hope, and are at length totally estranged from God. In regard to both kinds of temptation, which either enkindled in us by concupiscence or presented by the craft of Satan's war against us, we pray God the Father not to allow us to be overcome, but rather to raise and support us by his hand, that strengthened by his mighty power we may stand firm against all the assaults of our malignant enemy, whatever be the thoughts which he sends into our minds; next we pray that whatever of either description is allotted us, we may turn to good, that is, may neither be inflated with prosperity, nor cast down by adversity. Here, however, we do not ask to be altogether exempted from temptation, which is very necessary to excite, stimulate, and urge us on, that we may not become too lethargic. It was not without reason that David wished to be tried, nor is it without cause that the Lord daily tries his elect, chastising them by disgrace, poverty, tribulation, and other kinds of cross. But the temptations of God and Satan are very different: Satan tempts, that he may destroy, condemn, confound, throw headlong; God, that by proving his people he may make trial of their sincerity, and by exercising their strength confirm it; may mortify, tame, and cauterize their flesh, which, if not curbed in this manner, would wanton and exult above measure. Besides, Satan attacks those who are unarmed and unprepared, that he may destroy them unawares; whereas whatever God sends, he "will with the temptation also make a way to escape, that ye may be able to bear it." Whether by the term "evil" we understand the devil or sin, is not of the least consequence. Satan is indeed the very enemy who lays snares for our life, but it is by sin that he is armed for our destruction. Our petition, therefore, is, that we may not be overcome or overwhelmed with temptation, but in the strength of the Lord may stand firm against all the powers by which we are assailed; in other words, may not fall under temptation: that being thus taken under his charge and protection, we may remain invincible by sin, death, the gates of hell, and the whole power of the devil; in other words, be delivered from evil. Here it is carefully to be observed, that we have no strength to contend with such a combatant as the devil, or to sustain the violence of his assault. Were it otherwise, it would be mockery of God to ask of him what we already possess in ourselves. Assuredly those who in self-confidence prepare for such a fight, do not understand how bold and well-equipped the enemy is with whom they have to do. Now we ask to be delivered from his power, as from the mouth of some furious raging lion, who would instantly tear us with his teeth and claws, and swallow us up, did not the Lord rescue us from the midst of death; at the same time knowing that if the Lord is present and will fight for us while we stand by, through him "we shall do valiantly" (Ps. 60:12). Let others if they will confide in the powers and resources of their free will which they think they possess; enough for us that we stand and are strong in the power of God alone. But the prayer comprehends more than at first sight it seems to do. For if the Spirit of God is our strength in waging the contest with Satan, we cannot gain the victory unless we are filled with him, and thereby freed from all infirmity of the flesh. Therefore, when we pray to be delivered from sin and Satan, we at the same time desire to be enriched with new supplies of divine grace, until completely replenished with them, we triumph over every evil. To some it seems rude and harsh to ask God not to lead us into temptation, since, as James declares (James 1:13), it is contrary to his nature to do so. This difficulty has already been partly solved by the fact that our concupiscence is the cause, and therefore properly bears the blame of all the temptations by which we are overcome. All that James means is, that it is vain and unjust to ascribe to God vices which our own consciousness compels us to impute to ourselves. But this is no reason why God may not when he sees it meet bring us into bondage to Satan, give us up to a reprobate mind and shameful lusts, and so by a just, indeed, but often hidden judgment, lead us into

temptation. Though the cause is often concealed from men, it is well
known to him. Hence we may see that the expression is not improper,
if we are persuaded that it is not without cause he so often threatens
to give sure signs of his vengeance, by blinding the reprobate, and
hardening their hearts.

47. These three petitions, in which we specially commend ourselves
and all that we have to God, clearly show what we formerly observed
(sec. 38-39), that the prayers of Christians should be public, and have
respect to the public edification of the Church and the advancement
of believers in spiritual communion. For no one requests that anything should be given to him as an individual, but we all ask in common for daily bread and the forgiveness of sins, not to be led into
temptation, but delivered from evil. Moreover, there is subjoined the
reason for our great boldness in asking and confidence of obtaining
(sec. 11, 36). Although this does not exist in the Latin copies, yet as
it accords so well with the whole, we cannot think of omitting it. The
words are, THINE IS THE KINGDOM, AND THE POWER,
AND THE GLORY, FOR EVER. Here is the calm and firm assurance of our faith. For were our prayers to be commended to God
by our own worth, who would venture even to whisper before him?
Now, however wretched we may be, however unworthy, however devoid of commendation, we shall never want a reason for prayer, nor a
ground of confidence, since the kingdom, power, and glory, can never
be wrested from our Father. The last word is AMEN, by which is
expressed the eagerness of our desire to obtain the things which we
ask, while our hope is confirmed, that all things have already been
obtained and will assuredly be granted to us, seeing they have been
promised by God, who cannot deceive. This accords with the form of
expression to which we have already adverted: "Grant, O Lord, for
thy name's sake, not on account of us or of our righteousness." By this
the saints not only express the end of their prayers, but confess that

they are unworthy of obtaining did not God find the cause in himself and were not their confidence founded entirely on his nature.

48. All things that we ought, indeed all that we are able, to ask of God, are contained in this formula, and as it were rule, of prayer delivered by Christ, our divine Master, whom the Father has appointed to be our teacher, and to whom alone he would have us to listen (Matt. 17:5). For he ever was the eternal wisdom of the Father, and being made man, was manifested as the Wonderful, the Counselor (Isa. 11:2). Accordingly, this prayer is complete in all its parts, so complete, that whatever is extraneous and foreign to it, whatever cannot be referred to it, is impious and unworthy of the approbation of God. For he has here summarily prescribed what is worthy of him, what is acceptable to him, and what is necessary for us; in short, whatever he is pleased to grant. Those, therefore, who presume to go further and ask something more from God, first seek to add of their own to the wisdom of God (this it is insane blasphemy to do); secondly, refusing to confine themselves within the will of God, and despising it, they wander as their cupidity directs; lastly, they will never obtain anything, seeing they pray without faith. For there cannot be a doubt that all such prayers are made without faith, because at variance with the word of God, on which if faith do not always lean it cannot possibly stand. Those who, disregarding the Master's rule, indulge their own wishes, not only have not the word of God, but as much as in them lies oppose it. Hence Tertullian (*De Fuga in Persequutione*) has not less truly than elegantly termed it "Lawful Prayer," tacitly intimating that all other prayers are lawless and illicit.

49. By this, however, we would not have it understood that we are so restricted to this form of prayer as to make it unlawful to change a word or syllable of it. For in Scripture we meet with many prayers differing greatly from it in word, yet written by the same Spirit, and capable of being used by us with the greatest advantage. Many prayers also are continually suggested to believers by the same Spirit, though

in expression they bear no great resemblance to it. All we mean to say is, that no man should wish, expect, or ask anything which is not summarily comprehended in this prayer. Though the words may be very different, there must be no difference in the sense. In this way, all prayers, both those which are contained in the Scripture, and those which come forth from pious breasts, must be referred to it, certainly none can ever equal it, far less surpass it in perfection. It omits nothing which we can conceive in praise of God, nothing which we can imagine advantageous to man, and the whole is so exact that all hope of improving it may well be renounced. In short, let us remember that we have here the doctrine of heavenly wisdom. God has taught what he willed; he willed what was necessary.

50. But although it has been said above (sec. 7, 27, &c.), that we ought always to raise our minds upwards towards God, and pray without ceasing, yet such is our weakness, which requires to be supported, such our torpor, which requires to be stimulated, that it is requisite for us to appoint special hours for this exercise, hours which are not to pass away without prayer, and during which the whole affections of our minds are to be completely occupied; namely, when we rise in the morning, before we commence our daily work, when we sit down to food, when by the blessing of God we have taken it, and when we retire to rest. This, however, must not be a superstitious observance of hours, by which, as it were, performing a task to God, we think we are discharged as to other hours; it should rather be considered as a discipline by which our weakness is exercised, and ever and anon stimulated. In particular, it must be our anxious care, whenever we are ourselves pressed, or see others pressed by any strait, instantly to have recourse to him not only with quickened pace, but with quickened minds; and again, we must not in any prosperity of ourselves or others omit to testify our recognition of his hand by praise and thanksgiving. Lastly, we must in all our prayers carefully avoid wishing to confine God to certain circumstances, or prescribe to him the time, place, or

mode of action. In like manner, we are taught by this prayer not to fix any law or impose any condition upon him, but leave it entirely to him to adopt whatever course of procedure seems to him best, in respect of method, time, and place. For before we offer up any petition for ourselves, we ask that his will may be done, and by so doing place our will in subordination to his, just as if we had laid a curb upon it, that, instead of presuming to give law to God, it may regard him as the ruler and disposer of all its wishes.

51. If, with minds thus framed to obedience, we allow ourselves to be governed by the laws of Divine Providence, we shall easily learn to persevere in prayer, and suspending our own desires wait patiently for the Lord, certain, however little the appearance of it may be, that he is always present with us, and will in his own time show how very far he was from turning a deaf ear to prayers, though to the eyes of men they may seem to be disregarded. This will be a very present consolation, if at any time God does not grant an immediate answer to our prayers, preventing us from fainting or giving way to despondency, as those are wont to do who, in invoking God, are so borne away by their own fervor, that unless he yield on their first importunity and give present help, they immediately imagine that he is angry and offended with them and abandoning all hope of success cease from prayer. On the contrary, deferring our hope with well-tempered equanimity, let us insist with that perseverance which is so strongly recommended to us in Scripture. We may often see in The Psalms how David and other believers, after they are almost weary of praying, and seem to have been beating the air by addressing a God who would not hear, yet cease not to pray because due authority is not given to the word of God, unless the faith placed in it is superior to all events. Again, let us not tempt God, and by wearying him with our importunity provoke his anger against us. Many have a practice of formally bargaining with God on certain conditions, and, as if he were the servant of their lust, binding him to certain stipulations; with which if he do not

immediately comply, they are indignant and fretful, murmur, complain, and make a noise. Thus offended, he often in his anger grants to such persons what in mercy he kindly denies to others. Of this we have a proof in the children of Israel, for whom it had been better not to have been heard by the Lord, than to swallow his indignation with their flesh (Num. 11:18, 33).

52. But if our sense is not able till after long expectation to perceive what the result of prayer is, or experience any benefit from it, still our faith will assure us of that which cannot be perceived by sense—viz. that we have obtained what was fit for us, the Lord having so often and so surely engaged to take an interest in all our troubles from the moment they have been deposited in his bosom. In this way we shall possess abundance in poverty, and comfort in affliction. For though all things fail, God will never abandon us, and he cannot frustrate the expectation and patience of his people. He alone will suffice for all, since in himself he comprehends all good, and will at last reveal it to us on the day of judgment, when his kingdom shall be plainly manifested. We may add, that although God complies with our request, he does not always give an answer in the very terms of our prayers but while apparently holding us in suspense, yet in an unknown way, shows that our prayers have not been in vain. This is the meaning of the words of John, "If we know that he hear us, whatsoever we ask, we know that we have the petitions that we desired of him" (1 John 5:15). It might seem that there is here a great superfluity of words, but the declaration is most useful, namely, that God, even when he does not comply with our requests, yet listens and is favorable to our prayers, so that our hope founded on his word is never disappointed. But believers have always need of being supported by this patience, as they could not stand long if they did not lean upon it. For the trials by which the Lord proves and exercises us are severe, nay, he often drives us to extremes, and when driven allows us long to stick fast in the mire before he gives us any taste of his sweetness. As Hannah says,

"The Lord killeth, and maketh alive; he bringeth down to the grave, and bringeth up" (1 Sam. 2:6). What could they here do but become dispirited and rush on despair, were they not, when afflicted, desolate, and half dead, comforted with the thought that they are regarded by God, and that there will be an end to their present evils. But however secure their hopes may stand, they in the meantime cease not to pray, since prayer unaccompanied by perseverance leads to no result.

Study Guide Questions

Section 1

1. How can the treasures of the Christian philosophy not be obtained?
2. Once we have learned what we are in Christ, what are we to do?

Section 2

1. What are we to do when God promises us something?
2. What is the result of prayer offered by burdened sinners?

Section 3

1. Calvin gives six motives to prayer. What are they?

Section 4

1. What is the first rule for framing prayer?
2. What model should we follow in prayer?
3. What is the mind, when left to itself?

Section 5

1. What is most contrary to reverence for God?
2. Why do we lift our hands in prayer?
3. What are we not to ask?

Section 6

1. What is the second rule for framing prayer?

2. How does Calvin describe cold-hearted prayer?

3. What do men do, stuffed with depravity?

4. What is another fault, less serious, but no less tolerable?

Section 7

1. Do we pray according to the occasion?

2. Does this mean there are times when we need not pray?

3. What does lawful prayer demand?

Section 8

1. What is the third rule for prayer?

2. Which Apocryphal book does Calvin quote with some approval?

Section 9

1. What is the most important part of prayer?

2. Can we seek forgiveness without seeking deliverance?

Section 10

1. What is meant when various saints in Scripture plead their own righteousness?

Section 11

1. What is the fourth rule for prayer?

2. What does lack of trust in prayer do?

3. What is our guide in prayer?

Section 12

1. What comparison does Calvin use for us unburdening ourselves in prayer?

Section 13

1. What should be our basic motive in praying this way?

Section 14

1. What demeanor should we have in prayer instead of terror?

2. Is this consistent with confidence?

3. Upon what does this confidence rest?

Section 15

1. Why does God answer prayers from unbelievers that are clearly defective?

2. What are the prayers of the saints a mixture of?

Section 16

1. How can our prayers obtain an answer?

2. Does Calvin give any examples of intemperate prayers that are answered?

3. Should the defects in these prayers be repudiated?

4. Is it legitimate to raise hands in prayer?

Section 17

1. What two offices of Christ are assumed when we pray in Jesus' name?

Section 18

1. In what way is Christ like the high priest of the Old Testament?

Section 19

1. If Christ were removed, what would remain for us at the throne of God?

2. As we intercede for one another, what should we be careful to do?

Section 20

1. What error of the Sophists does Calvin address next?

2. Who alone bears the petitions of God's people to God?

Section 21

1. How would departed saints need to petition God?

2. What is the import of this observation?

3. Why do people feel a need to enlist the saints?

Section 22

1. What church council forbade directing prayers to the saints from the altar?

Section 23

1. What confusion is used by those who urge veneration of the saints?

Section 24

1. What would prayers to the departed saints do to their rest or "quiescence"?

2. And what do such prayers presuppose about the saints' abilities?

Section 25

1. What did invocation of the patriarchs mean?

2. Whose name should we rather put forward rather than Christ's? Anyone's?

Section 26

1. When the Bible tells us the saints were heard by God, what did this not mean?

2. What did it mean?

Section 27

1. What is the mother of right prayer?

Section 28

1. What should accompany our reception of all the blessings God gives?

2. If we fail to offer Him praise for His blessings, what is our silence?

3. Why do some mumble as they pray?

Section 29

1. Does God appoint public hours for prayer?

2. What are two kinds of corruption in public prayer?

Section 30

1. What do we need to have since there needs to be common prayers for believers?

2. Public prayer is lawful, provided what?

3. Do the buildings make prayers more holy?

Section 31

1. Does Calvin condemn speaking and singing in church?

Section 32

1. What does music lend to sacred actions?

Section 33

1. What language should public prayers be in?

2. What is the tongue without the mind?

3. What gestures does Calvin approve for prayer?

Section 34

1. The Lord's Prayer is a table of what?

Section 35

1. How many petitions does Calvin divide the Lord's Prayer into?

2. How are those six divided?

Section 36
1. What are we doing when we call God Father?
2. How does Calvin describe the name of Father?

Section 37
1. What should encourage us about our use of the name Father?

Section 38
1. What is significant in the word "our"?
2. If you love the Father, what follows?

Section 39
1. How is prayer like almsgiving?
2. What shuts the gate to prayers?

Section 40
1. Though God is in heaven, what does Calvin want us to recognize?

Section 41
1. What is the first petition of the Lord's Prayer?
2. What are we always bidden to be concerned for in our prayers?

Section 42
1. What is the second petition?
2. What relation does the second petition have to the first?
3. How does God set up His kingdom?

Section 43
1. What is the third petition?
2. What does this tell us about God's kingdom?

3. What can be said about those who do not pray for these things?

Section 44

1. What do we do in the second half of the prayer?
2. What is the fourth petition?
3. What do some who entrust their souls to God still struggle with?
4. When our storehouses are stuffed and our cellars full, what should we still do?

Section 45

1. What is the fifth petition?
2. Why does He call sins debts?
3. What do people who offer their own merits to God do?

Section 46

1. What sort of gain should we pursue?
2. What do greedy men look like?
3. What should we do if we have to contend with faithless and deceitful men?

Section 47

1. What should the prayers of Christians be?
2. What is signified by the "amen"?

Section 48

1. What is the Lord's Prayer a summary of?

Section 49

1. Must we be entirely limited to the words of the Lord's Prayer?
2. What should no man ask for?

Section 50

1. What is necessary because of our weakness in prayer?

2. What is one such aid and support?

3. And at the same time, what should be avoided?

Section 51

1. What do our prayers sometimes appear to be?

Section 52

1. When God refuses to comply with our wishes, what is His disposition toward us?

CHAPTER 21

Of the eternal election, by which God has predestinated some to
salvation, and others to destruction.

The divisions of this chapter are—
    I. The necessity and utility of the doctrine of eternal Election
explained. Excessive curiosity restrained, sec. 1-2.

    II. Explanation to those who through false modesty shun the doctrine of Predestination, sec. 3-4.

    III. The orthodox doctrine expounded.

Outline:

1. The doctrine of Election and Predestination. It is useful, necessary, and most sweet. Ignorance of it impairs the glory of God, plucks up humility by the roots, begets and fosters pride. The doctrine establishes the certainty of salvation, peace of conscience, and the true origin of the Church. Answer to two classes of men: 1. The curious.

2. A sentiment of Augustine confirmed by an admonition of our Savior and a passage of Solomon.

3. An answer to a second class—viz. those who are unwilling that the doctrine should be adverted to. An objection founded on a passage of Solomon, solved by the words of Moses.

4. A second objection—viz. That this doctrine is a stumbling-block to the profane. Answer 1. The same may be said of many other heads of doctrine. 2. The truth of God will always defend itself. Third objection—viz. That this doctrine is dangerous even to believers. Answer 1. The same objection made to Augustine. 2. We must not despise anything that God has revealed. Arrogance and blasphemy of such objections.

5. Certain cavils against the doctrine. 1. Prescience regarded as the cause of predestination. Prescience and predestination explained. Not prescience, but the good pleasure of God the cause of predestination. This apparent from the gratuitous election of the posterity of Abraham and the rejection of all others.

6. Even of the posterity of Abraham some elected and others rejected by special grace.

7. The Apostle shows that the same thing has been done in regard to individuals under the Christian dispensation.

The covenant of life is not preached equally to all, and among those to whom it is preached, does not always meet with the same reception. This diversity displays the unsearchable depth of the divine judgment, and is without doubt subordinate to God's purpose of eternal election. But if it is plainly owing to the mere pleasure of God that salvation is spontaneously offered to some, while others have no access to it, great and difficult questions immediately arise, questions which are inexplicable, when just views are not entertained concerning election and predestination. To many this seems a perplexing subject, because they deem it most incongruous that of the great body of mankind some should be predestinated to salvation, and others to destruction. How ceaselessly they entangle themselves will appear as we proceed. We may add, that in the very obscurity which deters them, we may see not only the utility of this doctrine, but also its most pleasant fruits. We shall never feel persuaded as we

ought that our salvation flows from the free mercy of God as its fountain, until we are made acquainted with his eternal election, the grace
of God being illustrated by the contrast—viz. that he does not adopt
all promiscuously to the hope of salvation, but gives to some what he
denies to others. It is plain how greatly ignorance of this principle de-
tracts from the glory of God, and impairs true humility. But though
thus necessary to be known, Paul declares that it cannot be known
unless God, throwing works entirely out of view, elect those whom
he has predestined. His words are, "Even so then at this present time
also, there is a remnant according to the election of grace. And if by
grace, then it is no more of works: otherwise grace is no more grace.
But if it be of works, then it is no more grace: otherwise work is no
more work" (Rom. 11:6). If to make it appear that our salvation flows
entirely from the good mercy of God, we must be carried back to the
origin of election, then those who would extinguish it, wickedly do as
much as in them lies to obscure what they ought most loudly to extol,
and pluck up humility by the very roots. Paul clearly declares that
it is only when the salvation of a remnant is ascribed to gratuitous
election, we arrive at the knowledge that God saves whom he wills of
his mere good pleasure, and does not pay a debt, a debt which never
can be due. Those who preclude access, and would not have anyone
to obtain a taste of this doctrine, are equally unjust to God and men,
there being no other means of humbling us as we ought, or making
us feel how much we are bound to him. Nor, indeed, have we elsewhere any sure ground of confidence. This we say on the authority of
Christ, who, to deliver us from all fear, and render us invincible amid
our many dangers, snares and mortal conflicts, promises safety to all
that the Father has taken under his protection (John 10:26). From
this we infer, that all who know not that they are the peculiar people
of God, must be wretched from perpetual trepidation, and that those
therefore, who, by overlooking the three advantages which we have
noted, would destroy the very foundation of our safety, consult ill for

themselves and for all the faithful. What? Do we not here find the
very origin of the Church, which, as Bernard rightly teaches (Serm.
in *Cantic.*) could not be found or recognized among the creatures,
because it lies hid (in both cases wondrously) within the lap of blessed
predestination, and the mass of wretched condemnation?

But before I enter on the subject, I have some remarks to address
to two classes of men. The subject of predestination, which in itself
is attended with considerable difficulty, is rendered very perplexed
and hence perilous by human curiosity, which cannot be restrained
from wandering into forbidden paths and climbing to the clouds determined if it can that none of the secret things of God shall remain
unexplored. When we see many, some of them in other respects not
bad men, everywhere rushing into this audacity and wickedness, it is
necessary to remind them of the course of duty in this matter. First,
then, when they inquire into predestination, let then remember that
they are penetrating into the recesses of the divine wisdom, where he
who rushes forward securely and confidently, instead of satisfying his
curiosity will enter in inextricable labyrinth. For it is not right that
man should with impunity pry into things which the Lord has been
pleased to conceal within himself, and scan that sublime eternal wisdom which it is his pleasure that we should not apprehend but adore,
that therein also his perfections may appear. Those secrets of his will,
which he has seen it meet to manifest, are revealed in his word—revealed insofar as he knew to be conducive to our interest and welfare.

2. "We have come into the way of faith," says Augustine: "let us
constantly adhere to it. It leads to the chambers of the king, in which
are hidden all the treasures of wisdom and knowledge. For our Lord
Jesus Christ did not speak invidiously to his great and most select
disciples when he said, 'I have yet many things to say unto you, but
ye cannot bear them now,' (John 16:12). We must walk, advance, increase, that our hearts may be able to comprehend those things which
they cannot now comprehend. But if the last day shall find us making

progress, we shall there learn what here we could not" (August. *Hom. in Joann.*). If we give due weight to the consideration, that the word of the Lord is the only way which can conduct us to the investigation of whatever it is lawful for us to hold with regard to him—is the only light which can enable us to discern what we ought to see with regard to him—it will curb and restrain all presumption. For it will show us that the moment we go beyond the bounds of the word we are out of the course, in darkness, and must every now and then stumble, go astray, and fall. Let it, therefore, be our first principle that to desire any other knowledge of predestination than that which is expounded by the word of God, is no less infatuated than to walk where there is no path, or to seek light in darkness. Let us not be ashamed to be ignorant in a matter in which ignorance is learning. Rather let us willingly abstain from the search after knowledge, to which it is both foolish as well as perilous, and even fatal to aspire. If an unrestrained imagination urges us, our proper course is to oppose it with these words, "It is not good to eat much honey: so for men to search their own glory is not glory" (Prov. 25:27). There is good reason to dread a presumption which can only plunge us headlong into ruin.

3. There are others who, when they would cure this disease, recommend that the subject of predestination should scarcely if ever be mentioned, and tell us to shun every question concerning it as we would a rock. Although their moderation is justly commendable in thinking that such mysteries should be treated with moderation, yet because they keep too far within the proper measure, they have little influence over the human mind, which does not readily allow itself to be curbed. Therefore, in order to keep the legitimate course in this matter, we must return to the word of God, in which we are furnished with the right rule of understanding. For Scripture is the school of the Holy Spirit, in which as nothing useful and necessary to be known has been omitted, so nothing is taught but what it is of importance to know. Everything, therefore delivered in Scripture on the subject of

predestination, we must beware of keeping from the faithful, lest we seem either maliciously to deprive them of the blessing of God, or to accuse and scoff at the Spirit, as having divulged what ought on any account to be suppressed. Let us, I say, allow the Christian to unlock his mind and ears to all the words of God which are addressed to him, provided he do it with this moderation—viz. that whenever the Lord shuts his sacred mouth, he also desists from inquiry. The best rule of sobriety is, not only in learning to follow wherever God leads, but also when he makes an end of teaching, to cease also from wishing to be wise. The danger which they dread is not so great that we ought on account of it to turn away our minds from the oracles of God. There is a celebrated saying of Solomon, "It is the glory of God to conceal a thing" (Prov. 25:2). But since both piety and common sense dictate that this is not to be understood of everything, we must look for a distinction, lest under the pretense of modesty and sobriety we be satisfied with a brutish ignorance. This is clearly expressed by Moses in a few words, "The secret things belong unto the Lord our God: but those things which are revealed belong unto us, and to our children for ever" (Deut. 29:29). We see how he exhorts the people to study the doctrine of the law in accordance with a heavenly decree, because God has been pleased to promulgate it, while he at the same time confines them within these boundaries, for the simple reason that it is not lawful for men to pry into the secret things of God.

4. I admit that profane men lay hold of the subject of predestination to carp, or cavil, or snarl, or scoff. But if their petulance frightens us, it will be necessary to conceal all the principal articles of faith, because they and their fellows leave scarcely one of them unassailed with blasphemy. A rebellious spirit will display itself no less insolently when it hears that there are three persons in the divine essence, than when it hears that God when he created man foresaw everything that was to happen to him. Nor will they abstain from their jeers when told that little more than five thousand years have elapsed since the

creation of the world. For they will ask, Why did the power of God slumber so long in idleness? In short, nothing can be stated that they will not assail with derision. To quell their blasphemies, must we say nothing concerning the divinity of the Son and Spirit? Must the creation of the world be passed over in silence? No! The truth of God is too powerful, both here and everywhere, to dread the slanders of the ungodly, as Augustine powerfully maintains in his treatise, *De Bono Perseverantiae* (cap. 14-20). For we see that the false apostles were unable, by defaming and accusing the true doctrine of Paul, to make him ashamed of it. There is nothing in the allegation that the whole subject is fraught with danger to pious minds, as tending to destroy exhortation, shake faith, disturb and dispirit the heart. Augustine disguises not that on these grounds he was often charged with preaching the doctrine of predestination too freely, but, as it was easy for him to do, he abundantly refutes the charge. As a great variety of absurd objections are here stated, we have thought it best to dispose of each of them in its proper place (see chap. 23). Only I wish it to be received as a general rule, that the secret things of God are not to be scrutinized, and that those which he has revealed are not to be overlooked, lest we may, on the one hand, be chargeable with curiosity, and, on the other, with ingratitude. For it has been shrewdly observed by Augustine (*de Genesi ad Literam*, Lib. 5), that we can safely follow Scripture, which walks softly, as with a mother's step, in accommodation to our weakness. Those, however, who are so cautious and timid, that they would bury all mention of predestination in order that it may not trouble weak minds, with what color, pray, will they cloak their arrogance, when they indirectly charge God with a want of due consideration, in not having foreseen a danger for which they imagine that they prudently provide? Whoever, therefore, throws obloquy on the doctrine of predestination, openly brings a charge against God, as having inconsiderately allowed something to escape from him which is injurious to the Church.

5. The predestination by which God adopts some to the hope of life, and adjudges others to eternal death, no man who would be thought pious ventures simply to deny; but it is greatly caviled at, especially by those who make prescience its cause. We, indeed, ascribe both prescience and predestination to God; but we say, that it is absurd to make the latter subordinate to the former (see chap. 22, sec. 1). When we attribute prescience to God, we mean that all things always were, and ever continue, under his eye; that to his knowledge there is no past or future, but all things are present, and indeed so present, that it is not merely the idea of them that is before him (as those objects are which we retain in our memory), but that he truly sees and contemplates them as actually under his immediate inspection. This prescience extends to the whole circuit of the world, and to all creatures. By predestination we mean the eternal decree of God, by which he determined with himself whatever he wished to happen with regard to every man. All are not created on equal terms, but some are preordained to eternal life, others to eternal damnation; and, accordingly, as each has been created for one or other of these ends, we say that he has been predestinated to life or to death. This God has testified, not only in the case of single individuals; he has also given a specimen of it in the whole posterity of Abraham, to make it plain that the future condition of each nation lives entirely at his disposal: "When the Most High divided to the nations their inheritance, when he separated the sons of Adam, he set the bounds of the people according to the number of the children of Israel. For the Lord's portion is his people; Jacob is the lot of his inheritance" (Deut. 32:8-9). The separation is before the eyes of all; in the person of Abraham, as in a withered stock, one people is specially chosen, while the others are rejected; but the cause does not appear, except that Moses, to deprive posterity of any handle for glorying, tells them that their superiority was owing entirely to the free love of God. The cause which he assigns for their deliverance is, "Because he loved thy fathers, therefore he chose their

seed after them" (Deut. 4:37); or more explicitly in another chapter, "The Lord did not set his love upon you, nor choose you, because you were more in number than any people: for ye were the fewest of all people: but because the Lord loved you" (Deut. 7:7-8). He repeatedly makes the same intimations, "Behold, the heaven, and the heaven of heavens is the Lord's thy God, the earth also, with all that therein is. Only the Lord had a delight in thy fathers to love them, and he chose their seed after them" (Deut. 10:14-15). Again, in another passage, holiness is enjoined upon them, because they have been chosen to be a peculiar people; while in another, love is declared to be the cause of their protection (Deut. 23:5). This, too, believers with one voice proclaim, "He shall choose our inheritance for us, the excellency of Jacob, whom he loved" (Ps. 47:4). The endowments with which God had adorned them, they all ascribe to gratuitous love, not only because they knew that they had not obtained them by any merit, but that not even was the holy patriarch endued with a virtue that could procure such distinguished honor for himself and his posterity. And the more completely to crush all pride, he upbraids them with having merited nothing of the kind, seeing they were a rebellious and stiff-necked people (Deut. 9:6). Often, also, do the prophets remind the Jews of this election by way of disparagement and opprobrium, because they had shamefully revolted from it. Be this as it may, let those who would ascribe the election of God to human worth or merit come forward. When they see that one nation is preferred to all others, when they hear that it was no feeling of respect that induced God to show more favor to a small and ignoble body, nay, even to the wicked and rebellious, will they plead against him for having chosen to give such a manifestation of mercy? But neither will their obstreperous words hinder his work, nor will their invectives, like stones thrown against heaven, strike or hurt his righteousness; nay, rather they will fall back on their own heads. To this principle of a free covenant, moreover, the Israelites are recalled whenever thanks are to be returned to God, or their hopes of the future to be animated. "The Lord he is God," says the Psalmist; "it is he that has made us, and not we ourselves: we are his people, and the sheep of his pasture" (Ps. 100:3; 95:7). The negation which is added, "not we ourselves," is not superfluous, to teach us that God is not only the author of all the good qualities in which men excel, but that they originate in himself, there being nothing in them worthy of so much honor. In the following words also they are enjoined to rest satisfied with the mere good pleasure of God: "O ye seed of Abraham, his servant; ye children of Jacob, his chosen" (Ps. 105:6). And after an enumeration of the continual mercies of God as fruits of election, the conclusion is, that he acted thus kindly because he remembered his covenant. With this doctrine accords the song of the whole Church, "They got not the land in possession by their own sword, neither did their own arm save them; but thy right hand, and thine arm, and the light of thy countenance, because thou hadst a favor unto them" (Ps. 44:3). It is to be observed, that when the land is mentioned, it is a visible symbol of the secret election in which adoption is comprehended. To like gratitude David elsewhere exhorts the people, "Blessed is the nation whose God is the Lord, and the people whom he has chosen for his own inheritance" (Ps. 33:12). Samuel thus animates their hopes, "The Lord will not forsake his people for his great name's sake: because it has pleased the Lord to make you his people" (1 Sam. 12:22). And when David's faith is assailed, how does he arm himself for the battle? "Blessed is the man whom thou choosest, and causes to approach unto thee, that he may dwell in thy courts" (Ps. 65:4). But as the hidden election of God was confirmed both by a first and second election, and by other intermediate mercies, Isaiah thus applies the terms "The Lord will have mercy on Jacob, and will yet choose Israel" (Isa. 14:1). Referring to a future period, the gathering together of the dispersion, who seemed to have been abandoned, he says, that it will be a sign of a firm and stable election, notwithstanding of the apparent abandonment. When it is elsewhere said, "I have chosen thee, and not cast thee away" (Isa. 41:9), the continual course of his great liberality is ascribed to paternal kindness. This is stated more explicitly in Zechariah by the angel, the Lord "shall choose Jerusalem again," as if the severity of his chastisements had amounted to reprobation, or the captivity had been an interruption of election, which, however, remains inviolable, though the signs of it do not always appear.

6. We must add a second step of a more limited nature, or one in which the grace of God was displayed in a more special form, when of the same family of Abraham God rejected some, and by keeping others within his Church showed that he retained them among his sons. At first Ishmael had obtained the same rank with his brother Isaac, because the spiritual covenant was equally sealed in him by the symbol of circumcision. He is first cut off, then Esau, at last an innumerable multitude, almost the whole of Israel. In Isaac was the seed called. The same calling held good in the case of Jacob. God gave a similar example in the rejection of Saul. This is also celebrated in the psalm, "Moreover he refused the tabernacle of Joseph, and chose not the tribe of Ephraim: but chose the tribe of Judah" (Ps. 78:67, 68). This the sacred history sometimes repeats that the secret grace of God may be more admirably displayed in that change. I admit that it was by their own fault Ishmael, Esau, and others, fell from their adoption; for the condition annexed was, that they should faithfully keep the covenant of God, whereas they perfidiously violated it. The singular kindness of God consisted in this, that he had been pleased to prefer them to other nations; as it is said in the psalm, "He has not dealt so with any nation: and as for his judgments, they have not known them" (Ps. 147:20). But I had good reason for saying that two steps are here to be observed; for in the election of the whole nation, God had already shown that in the exercise of his mere liberality he was under no law but was free, so that he was by no means to be restricted to an equal division of grace, its very inequality proving it

to be gratuitous. Accordingly, Malachi enlarges on the ingratitude of Israel, in that being not only selected from the whole human race, but set peculiarly apart from a sacred household; they perfidiously and impiously spurn God their beneficent parent. "Was not Esau Jacob's brother? saith the Lord: yet I loved Jacob, and I hated Esau" (Mal. 1:2-3). For God takes it for granted, that as both were the sons of a holy father, and successors of the covenant, in short, branches from a sacred root, the sons of Jacob were under no ordinary obligation for having been admitted to that dignity; but when by the rejection of Esau the firstborn, their progenitor though inferior in birth was made heir, he charges them with double ingratitude, in not being restrained by a double tie.

7. Although it is now sufficiently plain that God by his secret counsel chooses whom he will while he rejects others, his gratuitous election has only been partially explained until we come to the case of single individuals, to whom God not only offers salvation, but so assigns it, that the certainty of the result remains not dubious or suspended. These are considered as belonging to that one seed of which Paul makes mention (Rom. 9:8; Gal. 3:16, &c). For although adoption was deposited in the hand of Abraham, yet as many of his posterity were cut off as rotten members, in order that election may stand and be effectual, it is necessary to ascend to the head in whom the heavenly Father has connected his elect with each other, and bound them to himself by an indissoluble tie. Thus in the adoption of the family of Abraham, God gave them a liberal display of favor which he has denied to others; but in the members of Christ there is a far more excellent display of grace, because those ingrafted into him as their head never fail to obtain salvation. Hence Paul skillfully argues from the passage of Malachi which I quoted (Rom. 9:13; Mal. 1:2), that when God, after making a covenant of eternal life, invites any people to himself, a special mode of election is in part understood, so that he does not with promiscuous grace effectually elect all of them.

The words, "Jacob have I loved," refer to the whole progeny of the patriarch, which the prophet there opposes to the posterity of Esau. But there is nothing in this repugnant to the fact, that in the person of one man is set before us a specimen of election, which cannot fail of accomplishing its object. It is not without cause Paul observes, that these are called a remnant (Rom. 9:27; 11:5); because experience shows that of the general body many fall away and are lost, so that often a small portion only remains. The reason why the general election of the people is not always firmly ratified, readily presents itself—viz. that on those with whom God makes the covenant, he does not immediately bestow the Spirit of regeneration, by whose power they persevere in the covenant even to the end. The external invitation, without the internal efficacy of grace which would have the effect of retaining them, holds a kind of middle place between the rejection of the human race and the election of a small number of believers. The whole people of Israel are called the Lord's inheritance, and yet there were many foreigners among them. Still, because the covenant which God had made to be their Father and Redeemer was not altogether null, he has respect to that free favor rather than to the perfidious defection of many; even by them his truth was not abolished, since by preserving some residue to himself, it appeared that his calling was without repentance. When God ever and anon gathered his Church from among the sons of Abraham rather than from profane nations, he had respect to his covenant, which, when violated by the great body, he restricted to a few, that it might not entirely fail. In short, that common adoption of the seed of Abraham was a kind of visible image of a greater benefit which God deigned to bestow on some out of many. This is the reason why Paul so carefully distinguishes between the sons of Abraham according to the flesh and the spiritual sons who are called after the example of Isaac. Not that simply to be a son of Abraham was a vain or useless privilege (this could not be said without insult to the covenant), but that the immutable counsel of God, by which he predestinated to himself whomsoever he would, was alone effectual for their salvation. But until the proper view is made clear by the production of passages of Scripture, I advise my readers not to prejudge the question. We say, then, that Scripture clearly proves this much, that God by his eternal and immutable counsel determined once for all those whom it was his pleasure one day to admit to salvation, and those whom, on the other hand, it was his pleasure to doom to destruction. We maintain that this counsel, as regards the elect, is founded on his free mercy, without any respect to human worth, while those whom he dooms to destruction are excluded from access to life by a just and blameless, but at the same time incomprehensible, judgment. In regard to the elect, we regard calling as the evidence of election, and justification as another symbol of its manifestation, until it is fully accomplished by the attainment of glory. But as the Lord seals his elect by calling and justification, so by excluding the reprobate either from the knowledge of his name or the sanctification of his Spirit, he by these marks in a manner discloses the judgment which awaits them. I will here omit many of the fictions which foolish men have devised to overthrow predestination. There is no need of refuting objections which the moment they are produced abundantly betray their hollowness. I will dwell only on those points which either form the subject of dispute among the learned, or may occasion any difficulty to the simple, or may be employed by impiety as specious pretexts for assailing the justice of God.

Study Guide Questions

Section 1
1. What reveals the wonderful depth of God's judgment?
2. What are two characteristics of the doctrine?
3. What tears humility up by the roots?
4. What are the three benefits?
5. What happens if men pry too deeply into the subject?

Section 2

1. Where do we learn about predestination?
2. What sort of result comes from this?

Section 3

1. What do some men do with the subject?
2. What is Scripture?
3. So how far may we go in discussion of this topic?

Section 4

1. What will obstinate people do with the doctrine of predestination?
2. Should this prevent us from teaching it?
3. What are several of these other doctrines?
4. Why can we safely follow Scripture in this?
5. In what way do opponents of this doctrine accuse God of stupid thoughtlessness?

Section 5

1. Considering foreknowledge and predestination, what is to subject one to the other?
2. How does Calvin define predestination?
3. Arguments against God's sovereignty will not strike or hurt His righteousness—why?

Section 6

1. What is the second, more limited degree of election?
2. What then are the two degrees?

Section 7

1. What is only half explained?
2. How does Calvin explain what makes up this individual election?
3. What enables the elect to persevere to the very end?

CHAPTER 22

This doctrine confirmed by proofs from Scripture.

The divisions of this chapter are—

I. A confirmation of the orthodox doctrine in opposition to two classes of individuals. This confirmation founded on a careful exposition of our Savior's words, and passages in the writings of Paul, sec. 1-7.

II. A refutation of some objections taken from ancient writers, Thomas Aquinas, and more modern writers, sec. 8-10.

III. Of reprobation, which is founded entirely on the righteous will of God, sec. 11.

Outline:

1. Some imagine that God elects or reprobates according to a foreknowledge of merit. Others make it a charge against God that he elects some and passes by others. Both refuted, 1. By invincible arguments; 2. By the testimony of Augustine.

2. Who are elected, when, in whom, to what, for what reason.

3. The reason is the good pleasure of God, which so reigns in election that no works, either past or future, are taken into consideration. This proved by notable declarations of one Savior and passages of Paul.

4. Proved by a striking discussion in the Epistle to the Romans. Its scope and method explained. The advocates of foreknowledge refuted by the Apostle, when he maintains that election is special and wholly of grace.

5. Evasion refuted. A summary and analysis of the Apostle's discussion.

6. An exception, with three answers to it. The efficacy of gratuitous election extends only to believers, who are said to be elected according to foreknowledge. This foreknowledge or prescience is not speculative but active.

7. This proved from the words of Christ. Conclusion of the answer, and solution of the objection with regard to Judas.

8. An objection taken from the ancient fathers. Answer from Augustine, from Ambrose, as quoted by Augustine, and an invincible argument by an Apostle. Summary of this argument.

9. Objection from Thomas Aquinas. Answer.

10. Objection of more modern writers. Answers. Passages in which there is a semblance of contradiction reconciled. Why many called and few chosen. An objection founded on mutual consent between the word and faith. Solution confirmed by the words of Paul, Augustine, and Bernard. A clear declaration by our Savior.

11. The view to be taken of reprobation. It is founded on the righteous will of God.

M any controvert all the positions which we have laid down, especially the gratuitous election of believers, which, however, cannot be overthrown. For they commonly imagine that God distinguishes between men according to the merits which he foresees that each individual is to have, giving the adoption of sons to those whom he foreknows will not be unworthy of his grace, and dooming those to destruction whose dispositions he perceives will be prone to mischief and wickedness. Thus by interposing foreknowledge as a veil, they not only obscure election, but pretend to give it a different origin. Nor is this the commonly received opinion of the vulgar merely, for it has in all ages had great supporters (see sec. 8). This I candidly confess, lest anyone should expect greatly to prejudice our cause by opposing it with their names. The truth of God is here too certain to be shaken, too clear to be overborne by human authority. Others who are neither versed in Scripture, nor entitled to any weight, assail sound doctrine with a petulance and improbity which it is impossible to tolerate. Because God of his mere good pleasure electing some passes by others, they raise a plea against him. But if the fact is certain, what can they gain by quarreling with God? We teach nothing but what experience proves to be true—viz. that God has always been at liberty to bestow his grace on whom he would. Not to ask in what respect the posterity of Abraham excelled others if it be not in a worth, the cause of which has no existence out of God, let them tell why men are better than oxen or asses. God might have made them dogs when he formed them in his own image. Will they allow the lower animals to expostulate with God, as if the inferiority of their condition were unjust? It is certainly not more equitable that men should enjoy the privilege which they have not acquired by any merit, than that he should variously distribute favors as seems to him meet. If they pass to the case of individuals where inequality is more offensive to them, they ought at least, in regard to the example of our Savior, to be restrained by feelings of awe from talking so confidently of this sublime mystery. He is conceived a mortal man of the seed of David; what, I would ask them, are the virtues by which he deserved to become in the very womb, the head of angels the only begotten Son of God, the image and glory of the Father, the light, righteousness, and salvation of the world? It is wisely observed by Augustine that in the very head of the

Church we have a bright mirror of free election, lest it should give any trouble to us the members—viz. that he did not become the Son of God by living righteously, but was freely presented with this great honor, that he might afterwards make others partakers of his gifts. Should anyone here ask, why others are not what he was, or why we are all at so great a distance from him, why we are all corrupt while he is purity, he would not only betray his madness, but his effrontery also. But if they are bent on depriving God of the free right of electing and reprobating, let them at the same time take away what has been given to Christ. It will now be proper to attend to what Scripture declares concerning each. When Paul declares that we were chosen in Christ before the foundation of the world (Eph. 1:4), he certainly shows that no regard is had to our own worth; for it is just as if he had said, since in the whole seed of Adam our heavenly Father found nothing worthy of his election, he turned his eye upon his own Anointed, that he might select as members of his body those whom he was to assume into the fellowship of life. Let believers, then, give full effect to this reason—viz. that we were in Christ adopted unto the heavenly inheritance, because in ourselves we were incapable of such excellence. This he elsewhere observes in another passage in which he exhorts the Colossians to give thanks that they had been made meet to be partakers of the inheritance of the saints (Col. 1:12). If election precedes that divine grace by which we are made fit to obtain immortal life, what can God find in us to induce him to elect us? What I mean is still more clearly explained in another passage: God, says he, "has chosen us in him before the foundation of the world, that we might be holy and without blame before him in love: having predestinated us unto the adoption of children by Jesus Christ to himself, according to the good pleasure of his will" (Eph. 1:4-5). Here he opposes the good pleasure of God to our merits of every description. Holiness of life springs from election, and is the object of it.

2. That the proof may be more complete, it is of importance to attend to the separate clauses of that passage. When they are connected together they leave no doubt. From giving them the name of elect, it is clear that he is addressing believers, as indeed he shortly after declares. It is, therefore, a complete perversion of the name to confine it to the age in which the gospel was published. By saying they were elected before the foundation of the world, he takes away all reference to worth. For what ground of distinction was there between persons who as yet existed not, and persons who were afterwards like them to exist in Adam? But if they were elected in Christ, it follows not only that each was elected on some extrinsic ground, but that some were placed on a different footing from others, since we see that all are not members of Christ. In the additional statement that they were elected that they might be holy, the apostle openly refutes the error of those who deduce election from prescience, since he declares that whatever virtue appears in men is the result of election. Then, if a higher cause is asked, Paul answers that God so predestined, and predestined according to the good pleasure of his will. By these words, he overturns all the grounds of election which men imagine to exist in themselves. For he shows that whatever favors God bestows in reference to the spiritual life flow from this one fountain, because God chose whom he would, and before they were born had the grace which he designed to bestow upon them set apart for their use.

3. Wherever this good pleasure of God reigns, no good works are taken into account. The Apostle, indeed, does not follow out the antithesis, but it is to be understood, as he himself explains it in another passage, "Who has called us with a holy calling, not according to our works, but according to his own purpose and grace, which was given us in Christ Jesus before the world began" (2 Tim. 1:9). We have already shown that the additional words, "that we might be holy," remove every doubt. If you say that he foresaw they would be holy, and therefore elected them, you invert the order of Paul. You may, therefore, safely

infer if he elected us that we might be holy, he did not elect us because he foresaw that we would be holy. The two things are evidently inconsistent—viz. that the pious owe it to election that they are holy, and yet attain to election by means of works. There is no force in the cavil to which they are ever recurring, that the Lord does not bestow election in recompense of preceding, but bestows it in consideration of future merits. For when it is said that believers were elected that they might be holy, it is at the same time intimated that the holiness which was to be in them has its origin in election. And how can it be consistently said that things derived from election are the cause of election? The very thing which the Apostle had said, he seems afterwards to confirm by adding, "According to his good pleasure which he has purposed in himself" (Eph. 1:9); for the expression that God "purposed in himself" is the same as if it had been said that in forming his decree he considered nothing external to himself; and, accordingly, it is immediately subjoined that the whole object contemplated in our election is that "we should be to the praise of his glory." Assuredly divine grace would not deserve all the praise of election, were not election gratuitous; and it would not be gratuitous did God in electing any individual pay regard to his future works. Hence, what Christ said to his disciples is found to be universally applicable to all believers, "Ye have not chosen me, but I have chosen you" (John 15:16). Here he not only excludes past merits, but declares that they had nothing in themselves for which they could be chosen except insofar as his mercy anticipated. And how are we to understand the words of Paul, "Who has first given to him, and it shall be recompensed unto him again?" (Rom. 11:35). His meaning obviously is that men are altogether indebted to the preventing goodness of God, there being nothing in them, either past or future, to conciliate his favor.

4. In the Epistle to the Romans (Rom. 9:6), in which he again treats this subject more reconditely and at greater length, he declares that "they are not all Israel which are of Israel;" for though all were

blessed in respect of hereditary rights yet all did not equally obtain the succession. The whole discussion was occasioned by the pride and vain-glorying of the Jews, who, by claiming the name of the Church for themselves, would have made the faith of the Gospel dependent on their pleasure; just as in the present day the Papists would fain under this pretext substitute themselves in place of God. Paul, while he concedes that in respect of the covenant they were the holy off-spring of Abraham, yet contends that the greater part of them were strangers to it, and that not only because they were degenerate, and so had become bastards instead of sons, but because the principal point to be considered was the special election of God, by which alone his adoption was ratified. If the piety of some established them in the hope of salvation, and the revolt of others was the sole cause of their being rejected, it would have been foolish and absurd in Paul to carry his readers back to a secret election. But if the will of God (no cause of which external to him either appears or is to be looked for) distinguishes some from others, so that all the sons of Israel are not true Israelites, it is vain for anyone to seek the origin of his condition in himself. He afterwards prosecutes the subject at greater length by contrasting the cases of Jacob and Esau. Both being sons of Abraham, both having been at the same time in the womb of their mother, there was something very strange in the change by which the honor of the birthright was transferred to Jacob, and yet Paul declares that the change was an attestation to the election of the one and the reprobation of the other.

The question considered is the origin and cause of election. The advocates of foreknowledge insist that it is to be found in the virtues and vices of men. For they take the short and easy method of asserting that God showed in the person of Jacob that he elects those who are worthy of his grace; and in the person of Esau, that he rejects those whom he foresees to be unworthy. Such is their confident assertion; but what does Paul say? "For the children being not yet born, neither having done any good or evil, that the purpose of God according to election might stand, not of works, but of him that calleth; it was said unto her, [Rebecca] 'The elder shall serve the younger,' As it is written, 'Jacob have I loved, but Esau have I hated'" (Rom. 9:11-13). If foreknowledge had anything to do with this distinction of the brothers, the mention of time would have been out of place. Granting that Jacob was elected for a worth to be obtained by future virtues, to what end did Paul say that he was not yet born? Nor would there have been any occasion for adding that as yet he had done no good, because the answer was always ready that nothing is hid from God, and that therefore the piety of Jacob was present before him. If works procure favor, a value ought to have been put upon them before Jacob was born, just as if he had been of full age. But in explaining the difficulty, the Apostle goes on to show that the adoption of Jacob proceeded not on works but on the calling of God. In works he makes no mention of past or future, but distinctly opposes them to the calling of God, intimating that when place is given to the one the other is overthrown; as if he had said, the only thing to be considered is what pleased God, not what men furnished of themselves. Lastly, it is certain that all the causes which men are wont to devise as external to the secret counsel of God are excluded by the use of the terms "purpose" and "election."

5. Why should men attempt to darken these statements by assigning some place in election to past or future works? This is altogether to evade what the Apostle contends for—viz. that the distinction between the brothers is not founded on any ground of works, but on the mere calling of God, inasmuch as it was fixed before the children were born. Had there been any solidity in this subtlety, it would not have escaped the notice of the Apostle, but being perfectly aware that God foresaw no good in man, save that which he had already previously determined to bestow by means of his election, he does not employ a preposterous arrangement which would make good works antecedent to their cause. We learn from the Apostle's words that the salvation of believers is

founded entirely on the decree of divine election, that the privilege is procured not by works but free calling. We have also a specimen of the thing itself set before us. Esau and Jacob are brothers, begotten of the same parents, within the same womb, not yet born. In them all things are equal, and yet the judgment of God with regard to them is different. He adopts the one and rejects the other. The only right of precedence was that of primogeniture; but that is disregarded, and the younger is preferred to the elder. Nay, in the case of others, God seems to have disregarded primogeniture for the express purpose of excluding the flesh from all ground of boasting. Rejecting Ishmael he gives his favor to Isaac, postponing Manasseh he honors Ephraim.

6. Should anyone object that these minute and inferior favors do not enable us to decide with regard to the future life, that it is not to be supposed that he who received the honor of primogeniture was thereby adopted to the inheritance of heaven (many objectors do not even spare Paul, but accuse him of having in the quotation of these passages wrested Scripture from its proper meaning), I answer as before that the Apostle has not erred through inconsideration, or spontaneously misapplied the passages of Scripture; but he saw (what these men cannot be brought to consider) that God purposed under an earthly sign to declare the spiritual election of Jacob, which otherwise lay hidden at his inaccessible tribunal. For unless we refer the primogeniture bestowed upon him to the future world, the form of blessing would be altogether vain and ridiculous, inasmuch as he gained nothing by it but a multitude of toils and annoyances, exile, sharp sorrows, and bitter cares. Therefore, when Paul knew beyond a doubt that by the external, God manifested the spiritual and unfading blessings, which he had prepared for his servant in his kingdom, he hesitated not in proving the latter to draw an argument from the former. For we must remember that the land of Canaan was given in pledge of the heavenly inheritance; and that therefore there cannot be a doubt that Jacob was like the angels engrafted into the body of

Christ, that he might be a partaker of the same life. Jacob, therefore, is chosen, while Esau is rejected; the predestination of God makes a distinction where none existed in respect of merit. If you ask the reason the Apostle gives it, "For he saith to Moses, I will have mercy on whom I will have mercy, and I will have compassion on whom I will have compassion" (Rom. 9:15). And what pray, does this mean? It is just a clear declaration by the Lord that he finds nothing in men themselves to induce him to show kindness, that it is owing entirely to his own mercy, and, accordingly, that their salvation is his own work. Since God places your salvation in himself alone, why should you descend to yourself? Since he assigns you his own mercy alone, why will you recur to your own merits? Since he confines your thoughts to his own mercy why do you turn partly to the view of your own works?

We must therefore come to that smaller number whom Paul elsewhere describes as foreknown of God (Rom. 11:2); not foreknown, as these men imagine, by idle, inactive contemplations but in the sense which it often bears. For surely when Peter says that Christ was "delivered by the determinate counsel and foreknowledge of God" (Acts 2:23), he does not represent God as contemplating merely, but as actually accomplishing our salvation. Thus also Peter, in saying that the believers to whom he writes are elect "according to the foreknowledge of God" (1 Pet. 1:2), properly expresses that secret predestination by which God has sealed those whom he has been pleased to adopt as sons. In using the term "purpose" as synonymous with a term which uniformly denotes what is called a fixed determination, he undoubtedly shows that God, in being the author of our salvation, does not go beyond himself. In this sense he says in the same chapters that Christ as "a lamb" "was foreordained before the creation of the world" (1 Pet. 1:19-20). What could have been more frigid or absurd than to have represented God as looking from the height of heaven to see whence the salvation of the human race was to come? By a people foreknown, Peter means the same thing as Paul does by a remnant selected from a multitude falsely assuming the name of God. In another passage, to suppress the vain boasting of those who, while only covered with a mask, claim for themselves in the view of the world a first place among the godly, Paul says, "The Lord knoweth them that are his" (2 Tim. 2:19). In short, by that term he designates two classes of people, the one consisting of the whole race of Abraham, the other a people separated from that race, and though hidden from human view, yet open to the eye of God. And there is no doubt that he took the passage from Moses, who declares that God would be merciful to whomsoever he pleased (although he was speaking of an elect people whose condition was apparently equal); just as if he had said that in a common adoption was included a special grace which he bestows on some as a holier treasure, and that there is nothing in the common covenant to prevent this number from being exempted from the common order. God being pleased in this matter to act as a free dispenser and disposer, distinctly declares that the only ground on which he will show mercy to one rather than to another is his sovereign pleasure; for when mercy is bestowed on him who asks it, though he indeed does not suffer a refusal, he, however, either anticipates or partly acquires a favor, the whole merit of which God claims for himself.

7. Now, let the supreme Judge and Master decide on the whole case. Seeing such obduracy in his hearers, that his words fell upon the multitude almost without fruit, he to remove this stumbling-block exclaims, "All that the Father giveth me shall come to me." "And this is the Father's will which has sent me, that of all which he has given me I should lose nothing" (John 6:37, 39). Observe that the donation of the Father is the first step in our delivery into the charge and protection of Christ. Someone, perhaps, will here turn round and object that those only peculiarly belong to the Father who make a voluntary surrender by faith. But the only thing which Christ maintains is that though the defections of vast multitudes should shake the world, yet the counsel of God would stand firm, more stable than heaven itself,

that his election would never fail. The elect are said to have belonged to the Father before he bestowed them on his only begotten Son. It is asked if they were his by nature? Nay, they were aliens, but he makes them his by delivering them. The words of Christ are too clear to be rendered obscure by any of the mists of caviling. "No man can come to me except the Father which has sent me draw him." "Every man, therefore, that has heard and learned of the Father comes unto me" (John 6:44-45). Did all promiscuously bend the knee to Christ, election would be common; whereas now in the small number of believers a manifest diversity appears. Accordingly our Savior, shortly after declaring that the disciples who were given to him were the common property of the Father, adds, "I pray not for the world, but for them which thou hast given me; for they are thine" (John 17:9). Hence it is that the whole world no longer belongs to its Creator, except insofar as grace rescues from malediction, divine wrath, and eternal death, some, not many, who would otherwise perish, while he leaves the world to the destruction to which it is doomed. Meanwhile, though Christ interpose as a Mediator, yet he claims the right of electing in common with the Father, "I speak not of you all: I know whom I have chosen" (John 13:18). If it is asked whence he has chosen them, he answers in another passages "Out of the world;" which he excludes from his prayers when he commits his disciples to the Father (John 15:19). We must, indeed, hold, when he affirms that he knows whom he has chosen, first, that some individuals of the human race are denoted; and, secondly, that they are not distinguished by the quality of their virtues, but by a heavenly decree. Hence it follows that since Christ makes himself the author of election, none excel by their own strength or industry. In elsewhere numbering Judas among the elect, though he was a devil (John 6:70), he refers only to the apostolical office, which though a bright manifestation of divine favor (as Paul so often acknowledges it to be in his own person), does not, however, contain within itself the hope of eternal salvation. Judas, therefore, when he discharged the office of Apostle perfidiously, might have been worse than a devil; but not one of those whom Christ has once engrafted into his body will he ever permit to perish, for in securing their salvation, he will perform what he has promised; that is, exert a divine power greater than all (John 10:28). For when he says, "Those that thou gavest me I have kept, and none of them is lost but the son of perdition" (John 17:12), the expression, though there is a catachresis in it, is not at all ambiguous. The sum is that God by gratuitous adoption forms those whom he wishes to have for sons; but that the intrinsic cause is in himself, because he is contented with his secret pleasure.

8. But Ambrose, Origin, and Jerome were of opinion that God dispenses his grace among men according to the use which he foresees that each will make of it. It may be added that Augustine also was for some time of this opinion; but after he had made greater progress in the knowledge of Scripture, he not only retracted it as evidently false, but powerfully confuted it (August. *Retract.* Lib. 1, c. 13). Nay, even after the retractation, glancing at the Pelagians who still persisted in that error, he says, "Who does not wonder that the Apostle failed to make this most acute observation? For after stating a most startling proposition concerning those who were not yet born, and afterwards putting the question to himself by way of objection, 'What then? Is there unrighteousness with God?' he had an opportunity of answering that God foresaw the merits of both, he does not say so, but has recourse to the justice and mercy of God" (August. Epist. 106, *ad Sixtum*). And in another passage, after excluding all merit before election, he says, "Here, certainly, there is no place for the vain argument of those who defend the foreknowledge of God against the grace of God, and accordingly maintain that we were elected before the foundation of the world, because God foreknew that we would be good, not that he himself would make us good. This is not the language of him who says, 'Ye have not chosen me, but I have chosen you' (John

15:16). For had he chosen us because he foreknow that we would be good, he would at the same time also have foreknown that we were to choose him" (August. *in Joann. 8*, see also what follows to the same effect). Let the testimony of Augustine prevail with those who willingly acquiesce in the authority of the Fathers: although Augustine allows not that he differs from the others, but shows by clear evidence that the difference which the Pelagians invidiously objected to him is unfounded. For he quotes from Ambrose (*Lib. de Praedest. Sanct.* cap. 19), "Christ calls whom he pities." Again, "Had he pleased he could have made them devout instead of undevout; but God calls whom he deigns to call, and makes religious whom he will." Were we disposed to frame an entire volume out of Augustine, it would be easy to show the reader that I have no occasion to use any other words than his: but I am unwilling to burden him with a prolix statement. But assuming that the fathers did not speak thus, let us attend to the thing itself. A difficult question had been raised—viz. did God do justly in bestowing his grace on certain individuals? Paul might have disencumbered himself of this question at once by saying that God had respect to works. Why does he not do so? Why does he rather continue to use a language which leaves him exposed to the same difficulty? Why, but just because it would not have been right to say it? There was no obliviousness on the part of the Holy Spirit, who was speaking by his mouth. He, therefore, answers without ambiguity that God favors his elect, because he is pleased to do so, and shows mercy because he is pleased to do so. For the words, "I will be gracious to whom I will be gracious, and show mercy on whom I will show mercy" (Exod. 33:19), are the same in effect as if it had been said, God is moved to mercy by no other reason than that he is pleased to show mercy. Augustine's declaration, therefore, remains true. The grace of God does not find, but makes persons fit to be chosen.

9. Nor let us be detained by the subtlety of Thomas, that the foreknowledge of merit is the cause of predestination, not, indeed, in

respect of the predestinating act, but that on our part it may in some sense be so called, namely, in respect of a particular estimate of predestination; as when it is said that God predestinates man to glory according to his merit, inasmuch as he decreed to bestow upon him the grace by which he merits glory. For while the Lord would have us to see nothing more in election than his mere goodness, for anyone to desire to see more is preposterous affectation. But were we to make a trial of subtlety, it would not be difficult to refute the sophistry of Thomas. He maintains that the elect are in a manner predestinated to glory on account of their merits, because God predestines to give them the grace by which they merit glory. What if I should, on the contrary, object that predestination to grace is subservient to election unto life, and follows as its handmaid; that grace is predestined to those to whom the possession of glory was previously assigned, the Lord being pleased to bring his sons by election to justification? For it will hence follow that the predestination to glory is the cause of the predestination to grace, and not the converse. But let us have done with these disputes as superfluous among those who think that there is enough of wisdom for them in the word of God. For it has been truly said by an old ecclesiastical writer, those who ascribe the election of God to merits are wise above what they ought to be (Ambrose, *de Vocat. Gentium*, lib. 1, c. 2).

10. Some object that God would be inconsistent with himself, in inviting all without distinction while he elects only a few. Thus, according to them, the universality of the promise destroys the distinction of special grace. Some moderate men speak in this way, not so much for the purpose of suppressing the truth as to get quit of puzzling questions, and curb excessive curiosity. The intention is laudable, but the design is by no means to be approved, dissimulation being at no time excusable. In those, again, who display their petulance, we see only a vile cavil or a disgraceful error. The mode in which Scripture reconciles the two things—viz. that by external preaching

all are called to faith and repentance, and that yet the Spirit of faith and repentance is not given to all, I have already explained, and will again shortly repeat. But the point which they assume I deny as false in two respects: for he who threatens that when it shall rain on one city there will be drought in another (Amos 4:7); and declares in another passage that there will be a famine of the word (Amos 8:11), does not lay himself under a fixed obligation to call all equally. And he who, forbidding Paul to preach in Asia, and leading him away from Bithynia, carries him over to Macedonia (Acts 16:6), shows that it belongs to him to distribute the treasure in what way he pleases. But it is by Isaiah he more clearly demonstrates how he destines the promises of salvation specially to the elect (Isa. 8:16); for he declares that his disciples would consist of them only, and not indiscriminately of the whole human race. Whence it is evident that the doctrine of salvation, which is said to be set apart for the sons of the Church only, is abused when it is represented as effectually available to all. For the present let it suffice to observe that though the word of the gospel is addressed generally to all, yet the gift of faith is rare. Isaiah assigns the cause when he says that the arm of the Lord is not revealed to all (Isa. 53:1). Had he said that the gospel is malignantly and perversely condemned, because many obstinately refuse to hear, there might perhaps be some color for this universal call. It is not the purpose of the Prophet, however, to extenuate the guilt of men, when he states the source of their blindness to be that God deigns not to reveal his arm to them; he only reminds us that since faith is a special gift, it is in vain that external doctrine sounds in the ear. But I would fain know from those doctors whether it is mere preaching or faith that makes men sons of God. Certainly when it is said, "As many as received him, to them gave he power to become the sons of God, even to them that believe on his name" (John 1:12), a confused mass is not set before us, but a special order is assigned to believers, who are "born not of blood, nor of the will of the flesh, nor of the will of man, but of God."

But it is said, there is a mutual agreement between faith and the word. That must be wherever there is faith. But it is no new thing for the seed to fall among thorns or in stony places; not only because the majority appear in fact to be rebellious against God, but because all are not gifted with eyes and ears. How, then, can it consistently be said that God calls while he knows that the called will not come? Let Augustine answer for me: "Would you dispute with me? Wonder with me, and exclaim, O the depth! Let us both agree in dread, lest we perish in error" (August. *de Verb. Apost.* Serm. 11). Moreover, if election is, as Paul declares, the parent of faith, I retort the argument, and maintain that faith is not general, since election is special. For it is easily inferred from the series of causes and effects, when Paul says, that the Father "has blessed us with all spiritual blessings in heavenly places in Christ, according as he has chosen us in him before the foundation of the world" (Eph. 1:3-4), that these riches are not common to all, because God has chosen only whom he would. And the reason why in another passage he commends the faith of the elect is to prevent anyone from supposing that he acquires faith of his own nature, since to God alone belongs the glory of freely illuminating those whom he had previously chosen (Tit. 1:1). For it is well said by Bernard, "His friend hear apart when he says to them, Fear not, little flock: to you it is given to know the mysteries of the kingdom. Who are these? Those whom he foreknew and predestinated to be conformed to the image of his Son. He has made known his great and secret counsel. The Lord knoweth them that are his, but that which was known to God was manifested to men; nor, indeed, does he deign to give a participation in this great mystery to any but those whom he foreknew and predestinated to be his own" (Bernard, *ad Thomas Praepos. Benerlae.* Epist. 107). Shortly after he concludes, "The mercy of the Lord is from everlasting to everlasting upon them that fear him; from everlasting through predestination, to everlasting through glorification: the one knows no beginning, the other no end."

But why cite Bernard as a witness, when we hear from the lips of our Master, "Not that any man has seen the Father, save he which is of God" (John 6:46)? By these words he intimates that all who are not regenerated by God are amazed at the brightness of his countenance. And, indeed, faith is aptly conjoined with election, provided it hold the second place. This order is clearly expressed by our Savior in these words, "This is the Father's will which has sent me, that of all which he has given me I should lose nothing;" "And this is the will of him that sent me, that everyone which sees the Son, and believes on him, may have everlasting life" (John 6:39-40). If he would have all to be saved, he would appoint his Son their guardian, and would engraft them all into his body by the sacred bond of faith. It is now clear that faith is a singular pledge of paternal love, treasured up for the sons whom he has adopted. Hence Christ elsewhere says that the sheep follow the shepherd because they know his voice, but that they will not follow a stranger, because they know not the voice of strangers (John 10:4). But whence that distinction, unless that their ears have been divinely bored? For no man makes himself a sheep, but is formed by heavenly grace. And why does the Lord declare that our salvation will always be sure and certain, but just because it is guarded by the invincible power of God (John 10:29)? Accordingly, he concludes that unbelievers are not of his sheep (John 10:16). The reason is, because they are not of the number of those who, as the Lord promised by Isaiah, were to be his disciples. Moreover, as the passages which I have quoted imply perseverance, they are also attestations to the inflexible constancy of election.

11. We come now to the reprobate, to whom the Apostle at the same time refers (Rom. 9:13). For as Jacob, who as yet had merited nothing by good works, is assumed into favor; so Esau, while as yet unpolluted by any crime, is hated. If we turn our view to works, we do injustice to the Apostle, as if he had failed to see the very thing which is clear to us. Moreover, there is complete proof of his not

having seen it, since he expressly insists that when as yet they had done neither good nor evil, the one was elected, the other rejected, in order to prove that the foundation of divine predestination is not in works. Then after starting the objection, Is God unjust? instead of employing what would have been the surest and plainest defense of his justice—viz. that God had recompensed Esau according to his wickedness, he is contented with a different solution—viz. that the reprobate are expressly raised up, in order that the glory of God may thereby be displayed. At last, he concludes that God has mercy on whom he will have mercy, and whom he will he hardeneth (Rom. 9:18). You see how he refers both to the mere pleasure of God. Therefore, if we cannot assign any reason for his bestowing mercy on his people, but just that it so pleases him, neither can we have any reason for his reprobating others but his will. When God is said to visit in mercy or harden whom he will, men are reminded that they are not to seek for any cause beyond his will.

Study Guide Questions

Section 1

1. What do some do because God chooses some and passes over others?
2. What do Calvin's opponents need to explain and answer?
3. Who is the principal beneficiary of election?

Section 2

1. What distinction can be made among those who do not yet exist?

Section 3

1. Why are we not elect because of our holiness?

Section 4

1. In what way are all the children of Abraham holy?

2. Why do some of the "holy offspring" degenerate from legitimate children to bastards?

3. If Jacob were chosen on the basis of foreseen worth, what did Paul say to no purpose?

Section 5

1. What good can God foresee in us?

Section 6

1. Why was Jacob's blessing not to be considered as merely to earthly prosperity?

2. What does it mean that God has mercy on whom He will have mercy?

3. From what vantage does God not watch the future?

Section 7

1. What is the beginning of our reception into the surety and protection of Christ?

2. What is not the reason that some excel?

Section 8

1. Which church fathers appealed to God's foreknowledge of grace used well?

2. What is Calvin's "the dog that did not bark" argument against this view?

3. What is the relationship between God's grace and our fitness?

Section 9

1. What does Calvin do with Thomas' argument that merit is not the cause of predestination on God's side, but it may be spoken of that way on our side?

2. These observations would be amply sufficient for the pious and modest, and such as remember that they are men. But because many are the species of blasphemy which these virulent dogs utter against God, we shall, as far as the case admits, give an answer to each. Foolish men raise many grounds of quarrel with God, as if they held him subject to their accusations. First, they ask why God is offended with his creatures who have not provoked him by any previous offense; for to devote to destruction whomsoever he pleases more resembles the caprice of a tyrant than the legal sentence of a judge; and, therefore, there is reason to expostulate with God, if at his mere pleasure men are, without any desert of their own, predestinated to eternal death. If at any time thoughts of this kind come into the minds of the pious, they will be sufficiently armed to repress them by considering how sinful it is to insist on knowing the causes of the divine will, since it is itself, and justly ought to be, the cause of all that exists. For if his will has any cause, there must be something antecedent to it, and to which it is annexed; this it would be impious to imagine. The will of God is the supreme rule of righteousness, so that everything which he wills must be held to be righteous by the mere fact of his willing it. Therefore, when it is asked why the Lord did so, we must answer, because he pleased. But if you proceed farther to ask why he pleased, you ask for something greater and more sublime than the will of God, and nothing such can be found. Let human temerity then be quiet, and cease to inquire after what exists not, lest perhaps it fails to find what does exist. This, I say, will be sufficient to restrain anyone who would reverently contemplate the secret things of God. Against the audacity of the wicked, who hesitate not openly to blaspheme, God will sufficiently defend himself by his own righteousness, without our assistance, when depriving their consciences of all means of evasion, he shall hold them under conviction, and make them feel their guilt. We, however, give no countenance to the fiction of absolute power, which, as it is heathenish, so it ought justly to be held in detestation

by us. We do not imagine God to be lawless. He is a law to himself; because, as Plato says, men laboring under the influence of concupiscence need law; but the will of God is not only free from all vice, but is the supreme standard of perfection, the law of all laws. But we deny that he is bound to give an account of his procedure; and we moreover deny that we are fit of our own ability to give judgment in such a case. Wherefore, when we are tempted to go farther than we ought, let this consideration deter us: Thou shalt be "justified when thou speakest, and be clear when thou judgest" (Ps. 51:4).

3. God may thus quell his enemies by silence. But lest we should allow them with impunity to hold his sacred name in derision, he supplies us with weapons against them from his word. Accordingly, when we are accosted in such terms as these, why did God from the first predestine some to death, when, as they were not yet in existence, they could not have merited sentence of death?, let us by way of reply ask in our turn, what do you imagine that God owes to man, if he is pleased to estimate him by his own nature? As we are all vitiated by sin, we cannot but be hateful to God, and that not from tyrannical cruelty, but the strictest justice. But if all whom the Lord predestines to death are naturally liable to sentence of death, of what injustice, pray, do they complain? Should all the sons of Adam come to dispute and contend with their Creator, because by his eternal providence they were before their birth doomed to perpetual destruction, when God comes to reckon with them, what will they be able to mutter against this defense? If all are taken from a corrupt mass, it is not strange that all are subject to condemnation. Let them not, therefore, charge God with injustice, if by his eternal judgment they are doomed to a death to which they themselves feel that whether they will or not they are drawn spontaneously by their own nature. Hence it appears how perverse is this affectation of murmuring, when of set purpose they suppress the cause of condemnation which they are compelled to recognize in themselves, that they may lay the blame upon God. But

though I should confess a hundred times that God is the author (and it is most certain that he is), they do not, however, thereby efface their own guilt, which, engraven on their own consciences, is ever and anon presenting itself to their view.

4. They again object, were not men predestinated by the ordination of God to that corruption which is now held forth as the cause of condemnation? If so, when they perish in their corruptions they do nothing else than suffer punishment for that calamity, into which, by the predestination of God, Adam fell, and dragged all his posterity headlong with him. Is not he, therefore, unjust in thus cruelly mocking his creatures? I admit that by the will of God all the sons of Adam fell into that state of wretchedness in which they are now involved; and this is just what I said at the first, that we must always return to the mere pleasure of the divine will, the cause of which is hidden in himself. But it does not forthwith follow that God lies open to this charge. For we will answer with Paul in these words, "Nay but, O man, who art thou that repliest against God? Shall the thing formed say to him that formed it, why hast thou made me thus? Has not the potter power over the clay, of the same lump to make one vessel unto honor, and another unto dishonor?" (Rom. 9:20-21). They will deny that the justice of God is thus truly defended, and will allege that we seek an evasion, such as those are wont to employ who have no good excuse. For what more seems to be said here than just that the power of God is such as cannot be hindered, so that he can do whatsoever he pleases? But it is far otherwise. For what stronger reason can be given than when we are ordered to reflect who God is? How could he who is the Judge of the world commit any unrighteousness? If it properly belongs to the nature of God to do judgment, he must naturally love justice and abhor injustice. Wherefore, the Apostle did not, as if he had been caught in a difficulty, have recourse to evasion; he only intimated that the procedure of divine justice is too high to be scanned by human measure, or comprehended by the feebleness

of human intellect. The Apostle, indeed, confesses that in the divine judgments there is a depth in which all the minds of men must be engulfed if they attempt to penetrate into it. But he also shows how unbecoming it is to reduce the works of God to such a law as that we can presume to condemn them the moment they accord not with our reason. There is a well-known saying of Solomon (which, however, few properly understand), "The great God that formed all things both rewardeth the fool and rewardeth transgressors" (Prov. 26:10). For he is speaking of the greatness of God, whose pleasure it is to inflict punishment on fools and transgressors though he is not pleased to bestow his Spirit upon them. It is a monstrous infatuation in men to seek to subject that which has no bounds to the little measure of their reason. Paul gives the name of elect to the angels who maintained their integrity. If their steadfastness was owing to the good pleasure of God, the revolt of the others proves that they were abandoned. Of this no other cause can be adduced than reprobation, which is hidden in the secret counsel of God.

5. Now, should some Manes or Coelestinus come forward to arraign Divine Providence (see sec. 8), I say with Paul that no account of it can be given, because by its magnitude it far surpasses our understanding. Is there anything strange or absurd in this? Would we have the power of God so limited as to be unable to do more than our mind can comprehend? I say with Augustine that the Lord has created those who, as he certainly foreknew, were to go to destruction, and he did so because he so willed. Why he willed it is not ours to ask, as we cannot comprehend, nor can it become us even to raise a controversy as to the justice of the divine will. Whenever we speak of it, we are speaking of the supreme standard of justice (see August. Ep. 106). But when justice clearly appears, why should we raise any question of injustice? Let us not, therefore, be ashamed to stop their mouths after the example of Paul. Whenever they presume to carp, let us begin to repeat: Who are ye, miserable men, that bring an accusation

against God, and bring it because he does not adapt the greatness of his works to your meager capacity? As if every thing must be perverse that is hidden from the flesh. The immensity of the divine judgments is known to you by clear experience. You know that they are called "a great deep" (Ps. 36:6). Now, look at the narrowness of your own minds and say whether it can comprehend the decrees of God. Why then should you, by infatuated inquisitiveness, plunge yourselves into an abyss which reason itself tells you will prove your destruction? Why are you not deterred, in some degree at least, by what the Book of Job, as well as the Prophetical books declare concerning the incomprehensible wisdom and dreadful power of God? If your mind is troubled, decline not to embrace the counsel of Augustine, "You a man expect an answer from me: I also am a man. Wherefore, let us both listen to him who says, 'O man, who art thou?' Believing ignorance is better than presumptuous knowledge. Seek merits; you will find naught but punishment. O the height! Peter denies, a thief believes. O the height! Do you ask the reason? I will tremble at the height. Reason you, I will wonder; dispute you, I will believe. I see the height; I cannot sound the depth. Paul found rest, because he found wonder. He calls the judgments of God 'unsearchable;' and have you come to search them? He says that 'his ways are past finding out,' and do you seek to find them out?" (August. *de Verb. Apost.* Serm. 20). We shall gain nothing by proceeding farther. For neither will the Lord satisfy the petulance of these men, nor does he need any other defense than that which he used by his Spirit, who spoke by the mouth of Paul. We unlearn the art of speaking well when we cease to speak with God.

6. Impiety starts another objection, which, however, seeks not so much to criminate God as to excuse the sinner; though he who is condemned by God as a sinner cannot ultimately be acquitted without impugning the judge. This, then, is the scoffing language which profane tongues employ. Why should God blame men for things the necessity of which he has imposed by his own predestination? What

could they do? Could they struggle with his decrees? It would be vain for them to do it, since they could not possibly succeed. It is not just, therefore, to punish them for things the principal cause of which is in the predestination of God. Here I will abstain from a defense to which ecclesiastical writers usually recur, that there is nothing in the prescience of God to prevent him from regarding man as a sinner, since the evils which he foresees are man's, not his. This would not stop the caviler, who would still insist that God might, if he had pleased, have prevented the evils which he foresaw, and not having done so, must with determinate counsel have created man for the very purpose of so acting on the earth. But if by the providence of God man was created on the condition of afterwards doing whatever he does, then that which he cannot escape, and which he is constrained by the will of God to do, cannot be charged upon him as a crime. Let us, therefore, see what is the proper method of solving the difficulty. First, all must admit what Solomon says, "The Lord has made all things for himself; yea, even the wicked for the day of evil" (Prov. 16:4). Now, since the arrangement of all things is in the hand of God, since to him belongs the disposal of life and death, he arranges all things by his sovereign counsel, in such a way that individuals are born, who are doomed from the womb to certain death, and are to glorify him by their destruction. If anyone alleges that no necessity is laid upon them by the providence of God, but rather that they are created by him in that condition, because he foresaw their future depravity, he says something, but does not say enough. Ancient writers, indeed, occasionally employ this solution, though with some degree of hesitation. The Schoolmen, again, rest in it as if it could not be gainsaid. I, for my part, am willing to admit that mere prescience lays no necessity on the creatures, though some do not assent to this, but hold that it is itself the cause of things. But Valla, though otherwise not greatly skilled in sacred matters, seems to me to have taken a shrewder and more acute view, when he shows that the dispute is superfluous since life and death are acts of the divine will rather than of prescience. If God merely foresaw human events, and did not also arrange and dispose of them at his pleasure, there might be room for agitating the question, how far his foreknowledge amounts to necessity; but since he foresees the things which are to happen, simply because he has decreed that they are so to happen, it is vain to debate about prescience, while it is clear that all events take place by his sovereign appointment.

7. They deny that it is ever said in distinct terms, God decreed that Adam should perish by his revolt. As if the same God, who is declared in Scripture to do whatsoever he pleases, could have made the noblest of his creatures without any special purpose. They say that, in accordance with free-will, he was to be the architect of his own fortune, that God had decreed nothing but to treat him according to his desert. If this frigid fiction is received, where will be the omnipotence of God, by which, according to his secret counsel on which everything depends, he rules over all? But whether they will allow it or not, predestination is manifest in Adam's posterity. It was not owing to nature that they all lost salvation by the fault of one parent. Why should they refuse to admit with regard to one man that which against their will they admit with regard to the whole human race? Why should they in caviling lose their labor? Scripture proclaims that all were, in the person of one, made liable to eternal death. As this cannot be ascribed to nature, it is plain that it is owing to the wonderful counsel of God. It is very absurd in these worthy defenders of the justice of God to strain at a gnat and swallow a camel. I again ask how it is that the fall of Adam involves so many nations with their infant children in eternal death without remedy unless that it so seemed meet to God? Here the most loquacious tongues must be dumb. The decree, I admit, is, dreadful; and yet it is impossible to deny that God foreknew what the end of man was to be before he made him, and foreknew, because he had so ordained by his decree. Should anyone here inveigh against

the prescience of God, he does it rashly and unadvisedly. For why, pray, should it be made a charge against the heavenly Judge that he was not ignorant of what was to happen? Thus, if there is any just or plausible complaint, it must be directed against predestination. Nor ought it to seem absurd when I say that God not only foresaw the fall of the first man, and in him the ruin of his posterity; but also at his own pleasure arranged it. For as it belongs to his wisdom to foreknow all future events, so it belongs to his power to rule and govern them by his hand. This question, like others, is skillfully explained by Augustine: "Let us confess with the greatest benefit what we believe with the greatest truth: that the God and Lord of all things who made all things very good both foreknow that evil was to arise out of good, and knew that it belonged to his most omnipotent goodness to bring good out of evil, rather than not permit evil to be, and so ordained the life of angels and men as to show in it, first, what free-will could do; and, secondly, what the benefit of his grace and his righteous judgment could do" (August. *Enchir. ad Laurent.*).

8. Here they recur to the distinction between will and permission, the object being to prove that the wicked perish only by the permission, but not by the will of God. But why do we say that he permits, but just because he wills? Nor, indeed, is there any probability in the thing itself—viz. that man brought death upon himself merely by the permission, and not by the ordination of God; as if God had not determined what he wished the condition of the chief of his creatures to be. I will not hesitate, therefore, simply to confess with Augustine that the will of God is necessity, and that everything is necessary which he has willed; just as those things will certainly happen which he has foreseen (August. *de Gen. ad Lit.*, Lib. 6, cap. 15). Now, if in excuse of themselves and the ungodly, either the Pelagians, or Manichees, or Anabaptists, or Epicureans (for it is with these four sects we have to discuss this matter) should object the necessity by which they are constrained, in consequence of the divine predestination,

they do nothing that is relevant to the cause. For if predestination is nothing else than a dispensation of divine justice, secret indeed, but unblamable, because it is certain that those predestinated to that condition were not unworthy of it, it is equally certain that the destruction consequent upon predestination is also most just. Moreover, though their perdition depends on the predestination of God, the cause and matter of it is in themselves. The first man fell because the Lord deemed it meet that he should: why he deemed it meet, we know not. It is certain, however, that it was just, because he saw that his own glory would thereby be displayed. When you hear the glory of God mentioned, understand that his justice is included. For that which deserves praise must be just. Man therefore falls, divine providence so ordaining, but he falls by his own fault. The Lord had a little before declared that all the things which he had made were very good (Gen. 1:31). Whence then the depravity of man, which made him revolt from God? Lest it should be supposed that it was from his creation, God had expressly approved what proceeded from himself. Therefore man's own wickedness corrupted the pure nature which he had received from God, and his ruin brought with it the destruction of all his posterity. Wherefore, let us in the corruption of human nature contemplate the evident cause of condemnation (a cause which comes more closely home to us), rather than inquire into a cause hidden and almost incomprehensible in the predestination of God. Nor let us decline to submit our judgment to the boundless wisdom of God, so far as to confess its insufficiency to comprehend many of his secrets. Ignorance of things which we are not able, or which it is not lawful to know, is learning, while the desire to know them is a species of madness.

9. Someone, perhaps, will say that I have not yet stated enough to refute this blasphemous excuse. I confess that it is impossible to prevent impiety from murmuring and objecting; but I think I have said enough not only to remove the ground, but also the pretext for

throwing blame upon God. The reprobate would excuse their sins by alleging that they are unable to escape the necessity of sinning, especially because a necessity of this nature is laid upon them by the ordination of God. We deny that they can thus be validly excused, since the ordination of God, by which they complain that they are doomed to destruction, is consistent with equity—an equity, indeed, unknown to us, but most certain. Hence we conclude that every evil which they bear is inflicted by the most just judgment of God. Next we have shown that they act preposterously when, in seeking the origin of their condemnation, they turn their view to the hidden recesses of the divine counsel, and wink at the corruption of nature, which is the true source. They cannot impute this corruption to God, because he bears testimony to the goodness of his creation. For though, by the eternal providence of God, man was formed for the calamity under which he lies, he took the matter of it from himself, not from God, since the only cause of his destruction was his degenerating from the purity of his creation into a state of vice and impurity.

10. There is a third absurdity by which the adversaries of predestination defame it. As we ascribe it entirely to the counsel of the divine will that those whom God adopts as the heirs of his kingdom are exempted from universal destruction, they infer that he is an acceptor of persons; but this Scripture uniformly denies, and, therefore Scripture is either at variance with itself, or respect is had to merit in election. First, the sense in which Scripture declares that God is not an acceptor of persons is different from that which they suppose, since the term person means not man, but those things which when conspicuous in a man, either procure favor, grace, and dignity, or, on the contrary, produce hatred, contempt, and disgrace. Among these are, on the one hand, riches, wealth, power, rank, office, country, beauty, &c.; and, on the other hand, poverty, want, mean birth, sordidness, contempt, and the like. Thus Peter and Paul say that the Lord is no acceptor of persons, because he makes no distinction between the Jew

and the Greek; does not make the mere circumstance of country the ground for rejecting one or embracing the other (Acts 10:34; Rom. 2:10, Gal. 3:28). Thus James also uses the same words, when he would declare that God has no respect to riches in his judgment (James 2:5). Paul also says in another passage that in judging God has no respect to slavery or freedom (Eph. 6:9; Col. 3:25). There is nothing inconsistent with this when we say that God, according to the good pleasure of his will, without any regard to merit, elects those whom he chooses for sons, while he rejects and reprobates others. For fuller satisfaction the matter may be thus explained (see August. Epist. 115, et *ad Bonif.*, Lib. 2, cap. 7). It is asked how it happens that of two, between whom there is no difference of merit, God in his election adopts the one, and passes by the other? I, in my turn, ask, is there anything in him who is adopted to incline God towards him? If it must be confessed that there is nothing, it will follow that God looks not to the man, but is influenced entirely by his own goodness to do him good. Therefore, when God elects one and rejects another, it is owing not to any respect to the individual, but entirely to his own mercy which is free to display and exert itself when and where he pleases. For we have elsewhere seen that in order to humble the pride of the flesh, "not many wise men after the flesh, not many mighty, not many noble, are called" (1 Cor. 1:26); so far is God in the exercise of his favor from showing any respect to persons.

11. Wherefore it is false and most wicked to charge God with dispensing justice unequally, because in this predestination he does not observe the same course towards all. If (say they) he finds all guilty, let him punish all alike: if he finds them innocent, let him relieve all from the severity of judgment. But they plead with God as if he were either interdicted from showing mercy, or were obliged, if he show mercy, entirely to renounce judgment. What is it that they demand? That if all are guilty all shall receive the same punishment. We admit that the guilt is common, but we say that God in mercy succors some. Let

him (they say) succor all. We object, that it is right for him to show by punishing that he is a just judge. When they cannot tolerate this, what else are they attempting than to deprive God of the power of showing mercy; or, at least, to allow it to him only on the condition of altogether renouncing judgment? Here the words of Augustine most admirably apply: "Since in the first man the whole human race fell under condemnation, those vessels which are made of it unto honor are not vessels of self-righteousness, but of divine mercy. When other vessels are made unto dishonor, it must be imputed not to injustice, but to judgment" (August. Epist. 106, *De Praedest. et Gratia; De Bone Persever.*, cap. 12). Since God inflicts due punishment on those whom he reprobates, and bestows unmerited favor on those whom he calls, he is free from every accusation; just as it belongs to the creditor to forgive the debt to one, and exact it of another. The Lord therefore may show favor to whom he will, because he is merciful; not show it to all, because he is a just judge. In giving to some what they do not merit, he shows his free favor; in not giving to all, he declares what all deserve. For when Paul says, "God has concluded them all in unbelief, that he might have mercy upon all," it ought also to be added that he is debtor to none; for "who has first given to him and it shall be recompensed unto him again?" (Rom. 11:32-33).

12. Another argument which they employ to overthrow predestination is that if it stand, all care and study of well doing must cease. For what man can hear (say they) that life and death are fixed by an eternal and immutable decree of God, without immediately concluding that it is of no consequence how he acts, since no work of his can either hinder or further the predestination of God? Thus all will rush on, and like desperate men plunge headlong wherever lust inclines. And it is true that this is not altogether a fiction; for there are multitudes of a swinish nature who defile the doctrine of predestination by their profane blasphemies, and employ them as a cloak to evade all admonition and censure. "God knows what he has determined to

do with regard to us: if he has decreed our salvation, he will bring us to it in his own time; if he has doomed us to death, it is vain for us to fight against it." But Scripture, while it enjoins us to think of this high mystery with much greater reverence and religion, gives very different instruction to the pious, and justly condemns the accursed license of the ungodly. For it does not remind us of predestination to increase our audacity, and tempt us to pry with impious presumption into the inscrutable counsels of God, but rather to humble and abase us that we may tremble at his judgment and learn to look up to his mercy. This is the mark at which believers will aim. The grunt of these filthy swine is duly silenced by Paul. They say that they feel secure in vices because, if they are of the number of the elect, their vices will be no obstacle to the ultimate attainment of life. But Paul reminds us that the end for which we are elected is "that we should be holy, and without blame before him" (Eph. 1:4). If the end of election is holiness of life, it ought to arouse and stimulate us strenuously to aspire to it, instead of serving as a pretext for sloth. How wide the difference between the two things, between ceasing from well-doing because election is sufficient for salvation, and its being the very end of election, that we should devote ourselves to the study of good works. Have done, then, with blasphemies which wickedly invert the whole order of election. When they extend their blasphemies farther, and say that he who is reprobated by God will lose his pains if he studies to approve himself to him by innocence and probity of life, they are convicted of the most impudent falsehood. For whence can any such study arise but from election? As all who are of the number of the reprobate are vessels formed unto dishonor, so they cease not by their perpetual crimes to provoke the anger of God against them, and give evident signs of the judgment which God has already passed upon them; so far is it from being true that they vainly contend against it.

13. Another impudent and malicious calumny against this doctrine is that it destroys all exhortations to a pious life. The great odium to

which Augustine was at one time subjected on this head he wiped away in his treatise *De Correptione et Gratia*, to Valentinus, a perusal of which will easily satisfy the pious and docile. Here, however, I may touch on a few points, which will, I hope, be sufficient for those who are honest and not contentious. We have already seen how plainly and audibly Paul preaches the doctrine of free election: is he, therefore, cold in admonishing and exhorting? Let those good zealots compare his vehemence with theirs and they will find that they are ice, while he is all fervor. And surely every doubt on this subject should be removed by the principles which he lays down, that God has not called us to uncleanness; that every one should possess his vessel in honor; that we are the workmanship of God, "created in Christ Jesus unto good works, which God has before ordained that we should walk in them" (1 Thess. 4:4, 7; Eph. 2:10). In one word, those who have any tolerable acquaintance with the writings of Paul will understand, without a long demonstration, how well he reconciles the two things which those men pretend to be contradictory to each other. Christ commands us to believe in him, and yet there is nothing false or contrary to this command in the statement which he afterwards makes: "No man can come unto me, except it were given him of my Father" (John 6:65). Let preaching then have its free course, that it may lead men to faith, and dispose them to persevere with uninterrupted progress. Nor, at the same time, let there be any obstacle to the knowledge of predestination, so that those who obey may not plume themselves on anything of their own, but glory only in the Lord. It is not without cause our Savior says, "Who has ears to hear, let him hear" (Matt. 13:9). Therefore, while we exhort and preach, those who have ears willingly obey: in those again, who have no ears is fulfilled what is written: "Hear ye indeed, but understand not" (Isa. 6:9). "But why (says Augustine) have some ears, and others not? Who has known the mind of the Lord? Are we, therefore, to deny what is plain because we cannot comprehend what is hid?" This is a faithful quotation from

Augustine; but because his words will perhaps have more authority than mine, let us adduce the following passage from his treatise, *De Bone Persever.*, cap. 15.

"Should some on hearing this turn to indolence and sloth, and leaving off all exertion, rush headlong into lust, are we therefore to suppose that what has been said of the foreknowledge of God is not true? If God foreknew that they would be good, will they not be good, however great their present wickedness? And if God foreknow that they would be wicked, will they not be wicked, how great soever the goodness now seen in them? For reasons of this description, must the truth which has been stated on the subject of divine foreknowledge be denied or not mentioned? And more especially when, if it is not stated, other errors will arise?" In the sixteenth chapter he says, "The reason for not mentioning the truth is one thing, the necessity for telling the truth is another. It were tedious to inquire into all the reasons for silence. One, however, is, lest those who understand not become worse, while we are desirous to make those who understand better informed. Now such persons, when we say anything of this kind, do not indeed become better informed, but neither do they become worse. But when the truth is of such a nature that he who cannot comprehend it becomes worse by our telling it, and he who can comprehend it becomes worse by our not telling it, what think ye ought we to do? Are we not to tell the truth, that he who can comprehend may comprehend, rather than not tell it, and thereby not only prevent both from comprehending, but also make the more intelligent of the two to become worse, whereas if he heard and comprehended others might learn through him? And we are unwilling to say what, on the testimony of Scripture, it is lawful to say. For we fear lest, when we speak, he who cannot comprehend may be offended; but we have no fear lest while we are silent, he who can comprehend the truth be involved in falsehood." In chapter twentieth, glancing again at the same view, he more clearly confirms it. "Wherefore, if the apostles and teachers of the Church who came after them did both; if they discoursed piously of the eternal election of God, and at the same time kept believers under the discipline of a pious life, how can those men of our day, when shut up by the invincible force of truth, think they are right in saying that what is said of predestination, though it is true, must not be preached to the people? Nay, it ought indeed to be preached, that whoso has ears to hear may hear. And who has ears if he has not received them from him who has promised to give them? Certainly, let him who receives not, reject. Let him who receives, take and drink, drink and live. For as piety is to be preached, that God may be duly worshiped, so predestination also is to be preached, that he who has ears to hear may, in regard to divine grace, glory not in himself, but in God."

14. And yet as that holy man had a singular desire to edify, he so regulates his method of teaching as carefully, and as far as in him lay, to avoid giving offense. For he reminds us that those things which are truly should also be fitly spoken. Were any one to address the people thus: If you do not believe, the reason is, because God has already doomed you to destruction: he would not only encourage sloth, but also give countenance to wickedness. Were anyone to give utterance to the sentiment in the future tense, and say that those who hear will not believe because they are reprobates, it were imprecation rather than doctrine. Wherefore, Augustine not undeservedly orders such, as senseless teachers or ministers and ill-omened prophets, to retire from the Church. He, indeed, elsewhere truly contends that "a man profits by correction only when He who causes those whom He pleases to profit without correction pities and assists. But why is it thus with some, and differently with others? Far be it from us to say that it belongs to the clay and not to the potter to decide." He afterwards says, "When men by correction either come or return to the way of righteousness, who is it that works salvation in their hearts but he who gives the increase, whoever it be that plants and waters?

When he is pleased to save, there is no free-will in man to resist. Wherefore, it cannot be doubted that the will of God (who has done whatever he has pleased in heaven and in earth, and who has even done things which are to be) cannot be resisted by the human will, or prevented from doing what he pleases, since with the very wills of men he does so." Again, "When he would bring men to himself, does he bind them with corporeal fetters? He acts inwardly, inwardly holds, inwardly moves their hearts, and draws them by the will, which he has wrought in them." What he immediately adds must not be omitted: "because we know not who belongs to the number of the predestinated, or does not belong, our desire ought to be that all may be saved; and hence every person we meet, we will desire to be with us a partaker of peace. But our peace will rest upon the sons of peace. Wherefore, on our part, let correction be used as a harsh yet salutary medicine for all, that they may neither perish, nor destroy others. To God it will belong to make it available to those whom he has fore-known and predestinated."

Study Guide Questions

Section 1

1. What does human understanding do when it hears the truths of election?
2. If God passes over someone instead of electing him, what does that amount to?
3. Is hardening in the hand of God?
4. Is the relationship of God to good and evil the same?
5. So what is the cause of the hardening?

Section 2

1. What do the pious and moderate remember?
2. What is the highest rule of righteousness?
3. What cannot be found?

4. Is God therefore lawless and a law unto Himself?

Section 3
1. What does Calvin invite the sons of Adam to do?
2. As they attempt it, what do they deliberately suppress?

Section 4
1. What argument do these people then resort to?
2. Does Calvin agree that we are fallen in accordance with the will of God?
3. How does Calvin answer this?
4. What may we not do if we fail to understand something of God's will?

Section 5
1. Can we know that God has willed these things?
2. Can we know why?
3. How does Augustine answer when challenged on this point?
4. What should we do with these things?

Section 6
1. What is the next objection to election that Calvin answers?
2. Does Calvin agree that foreknowledge by itself is not deterministic?

Section 7
1. Does Calvin grant that the decree is dreadful?
2. If there were a legitimate complaint, where would it have lodged?

Section 8
1. Does Calvin grant a distinction between the will of God and the permission of God?
2. What must be just?

3. Where should we focus our attention when contemplating the cause of our condemnation?

4. What is it to stay out of God's decrees, and what is it to pry?

Section 9

1. Does Calvin think he is able to silence the objectors?

2. What is it to act perversely in this?

Section 10

1. What is a third objection that Calvin must answer?

2. How does Calvin answer this?

Section 11

1. When God chooses some for life and others not, why is He free from accusation?

Section 12

1. What is the next objection to this teaching?

2. Does Calvin acknowledge that some distort the doctrine this way?

3. But what does Paul say we have been chosen to?

Section 13

1. What is another related objection?

2. How does Calvin answer this?

Section 14

1. What example of balance does Calvin point to?

CHAPTER 24

Election confirmed by the calling of God. The reprobate bring
upon themselves the righteous destruction to which they are
doomed.

The title of this chapter shows that it consists of two parts—
I. The case of the Elect, from sec. 1-11.
II. The case of the Reprobate, from sec. 12-17.

Outline:

1. The election of God is secret, but is manifested by effectual calling. The nature of this effectual calling. How election and effectual calling are founded on the free mercy of God. A cavil of certain expositors refuted by the words of Augustine. An exception disposed of.

2. Calling proved to be free, 1. By its nature and the mode in which it is dispensed. 2. By the word of God. 3. By the calling of Abraham, the father of the faithful. 4. By the testimony of John. 5. By the example of those who have been called.

3. The pure doctrine of the calling of the elect misunderstood, 1. By those who attribute too much to the human will. 2. By those who make election dependent on faith. This error amply refuted.

4. In this and the five following sections the certainty of election vindicated from the assaults of Satan. The leading arguments are: 1. Effectual calling. 2. Christ apprehended by faith. 3. The protection of Christ, the guardian of the elect. We must not attempt to penetrate to the hidden recesses of the divine wisdom in order to learn what is decreed with regard to us at the judgment seat. We must begin and end with the call of God. This confirmed by an apposite saying of Bernard.

5. Christ the foundation of this calling and election. He who does not lean on him alone cannot be certain of his election. He is the faithful interpreter of the eternal counsel in regard to our salvation.

6. Another security of our election is the protection of Christ our Shepherd. How it is manifested to us. Objection 1. As to the future state. 2. As to perseverance. Both objections refuted.

7. Objection, that those who seem elected sometimes fall away. Answer. A passage of Paul dissuading us from security explained. The kind of fear required in the elect.

8. Explanation of the saying, that many are called, but few chosen. A twofold call.

9. Explanation of the passage, that none is lost but the son of perdition. Refutation of an objection to the certainty of election.

10. Explanation of the passages urged against the certainty of election. Examples by which some attempt to prove that the seed of election is sown in the hearts of the elect from their very birth. Answer. 1. One or two examples do not make the rule. 2. This view opposed to Scripture. 3. Is expressly opposed by an apostle.

11. An explanation and confirmation of the third answer.

12. Second part of the chapter, which treats of the reprobate. Some of them God deprives of the opportunity of hearing his word. Others he blinds and stupefies the more by the preaching of it.

13. Of this no other account can be given than that the reprobate are vessels fitted for destruction. This confirmed by the case of the

elect; of Pharaoh and of the Jewish people both before and after the manifestation of Christ.

14. Question, why does God blind the reprobate? Two answers. These confirmed by different passages of Scripture. Objection of the reprobate. Answer.

15. Objection to this doctrine of the righteous rejection of the reprobate. The first founded on a passage in Ezekiel. The passage explained.

16. A second objection founded on a passage in Paul. The apostle's meaning explained. A third objection and fourth objection answered.

17. A fifth objection—viz. that there seems to be a twofold will in God. Answer. Other objections and answers. Conclusion.

B ut that the subject may be more fully illustrated, we must treat both of the calling of the elect, and of the blinding and hardening of the ungodly. The former I have already in some measure discussed (chap. 22, sec. 10-11), when refuting the error of those who think that the general terms in which the promises are made place the whole human race on a level. The special election which otherwise would remain hidden in God, he at length manifests by his calling. "For whom he did foreknow, he also did predestinate to be conformed to the image of his Son." Moreover, "whom he did predestinate, them he also called; and whom he called, them he also justified," that he may one day glorify (Rom. 8:29-30). Though the Lord, by electing his people, adopted them as his sons, we, however, see that they do not come into possession of this great good until they are called; but when called, the enjoyment of their election is in some measure communicated to them. For which reason the Spirit which they receive is termed by Paul both the "Spirit of adoption," and the "seal" and "earnest" of the future inheritance, because by his testimony he confirms and seals the certainty of future adoption on their hearts. For although the preaching of the gospel springs from the fountain of election, yet being common to them with the reprobate, it would not be in itself a solid proof. God, however, teaches his elect effectually when he brings them to faith, as we formerly quoted from the words of our Savior, "Not that any man has seen the Father, save he which is of God, he has seen the Father" (John 6:46). Again, "I have manifested thy name unto the men which thou gavest me out of the world" (John 17:6). He says in another passage, "No man can come to me, except the Father which has sent me draw him" (John 6:44). This passage Augustine ably expounds in these words: "If (as Truth says) everyone who has learned comes, then everyone who does not come has not learned. It does not therefore follow that he who can come does come, unless he have willed and done it; but everyone who has learned of the Father, not only can come, but also comes; the antecedence of possibility the affection of will, and the effect of action being now present" (August. *de Grat. Chr. Cont. Pelag.*, Lib. 1, c. 14, 31). In another passage, he says still more clearly, "What means, everyone that has heard and learned of the Father comes unto me, but just that there is no one who hears and learns of the Father that does not come to me? For if everyone who has heard and learned, comes; assuredly everyone who does not come has neither heard nor learned of the Father: for if he had heard and learned, he would come. Far removed from carnal sense is this school in which the Father is heard and teaches us to come to the Son" (August. *de Praedes. Sanct.* c. 8). Shortly after, he says, "This grace, which is secretly imparted to the hearts of men, is not received by any hard heart; for the reason for which it is given is that the hardness of the heart may first be taken away. Hence, when the Father is heard within, he takes away the stony heart, and gives a heart of flesh. Thus he makes them sons of promise and vessels of mercy, which he has prepared for glory. Why then does he not teach all to come to Christ, but just because all whom he teaches he teaches in mercy, while those whom he teaches not he teaches not in judgment? For he pities whom he will, and hardens whom he will." Those, therefore, whom God has chosen he adopts as sons, while he becomes to them a Father. By calling, moreover, he admits them to his family, and unites them to himself, that they may be one with him. When calling is thus added to election, the Scripture plainly intimates that nothing is to be looked for in it but the free mercy of God. For if we ask whom it is he calls, and for what reason, he answers, it is those whom he had chosen. When we come to election, mercy alone everywhere appears; and, accordingly, in this the saying of Paul is truly realized, "So then, it is not of him that willeth, nor of him that runneth, but of God that showeth mercy" (Rom. 9:16); and that not as is commonly understood by those who share the result between the grace of God and the will and agency of man. For their exposition is that the desire and endeavor of sinners are of no avail by themselves, unless accompanied by the grace of God, but that when aided by his blessing, they also do their part in procuring salvation. This cavil I prefer refuting in the words of Augustine rather than my own: "If all that the apostle meant is that it is not alone of him that willeth, or of him that runneth, unless the Lord be present in mercy, we may retort and hold the converse, that it is not of mercy alone, unless willing and running be present" (August. *Enchir. ad Laurent.*, c. 31). But if this is manifestly impious, let us have no doubt that the apostle attributes all to the mercy of the Lord, and leaves nothing to our wills or exertions. Such were the sentiments of that holy man. I set not the value of a straw on the subtlety to which they have recourse—viz. that Paul would not have spoken thus had there not been some will and effort on our part. For he considered not what might be in man; but seeing that certain persons ascribed a part of salvation to the industry of man, he simply condemned their error in the former clause, and then claimed the whole substance of salvation for the divine mercy. And what else do the prophets than perpetually proclaim the free calling of God?

2. Moreover, this is clearly demonstrated by the nature and dispensation of calling, which consists not merely of the preaching of the word, but also of the illumination of the Spirit. Who those are to whom God offers his word is explained by the prophet, "I am sought of them that asked not for me: I am found of them that sought me not: I said, Behold me, behold me, unto a nation that was not called by my name" (Isa. 65:1). And lest the Jews should think that that mercy applied only to the Gentiles, he calls to their remembrance whence it was he took their father Abraham when he condescended to be his friend (Isa. 41:8); namely, from the midst of idolatry, in which he was plunged with all his people. When he first shines with the light of his word on the undeserving, he gives a sufficiently clear proof of his free goodness. Here, therefore, boundless goodness is displayed, but not so as to bring all to salvation, since a heavier judgment awaits the reprobate for rejecting the evidence of his love. God also, to display his own glory, withholds from them the effectual agency of his Spirit. Therefore, this inward calling is an infallible pledge of salvation. Hence the words of John, "Hereby we know that he abideth in us by the Spirit which he has given us" (1 John 3:24). And lest the flesh should glory, in at least responding to him, when he calls and spontaneously offers himself, he affirms that there would be no ears to hear, no eyes to see, did not he give them. And he acts not according to the gratitude of each, but according to his election. Of this you have a striking example in Luke, when the Jews and Gentiles in common heard the discourse of Paul and Barnabas. Though they were all instructed in the same word, it is said that "as many as were ordained to eternal life believed" (Acts 13:48). How can we deny that calling is gratuitous, when election alone reigns in it even to its conclusion?

3. Two errors are here to be avoided. Some make man a fellow-worker with God in such a sense that man's suffrage ratifies election, so that, according to them, the will of man is superior to the counsel of God. As if Scripture taught that only the power of being able to

believe is given us, and not rather faith itself. Others, although they do not so much impair the grace of the Holy Spirit, yet, induced by what means I know not, make election dependent on faith, as if it were doubtful and ineffectual till confirmed by faith. There can be no doubt, indeed, that in regard to us it is so confirmed. Moreover, we have already seen that the secret counsel of God, which lay concealed, is thus brought to light, by this nothing more being understood than that that which was unknown is proved, and as it were sealed. But it is false to say that election is then only effectual after we have embraced the gospel, and that it thence derives its vigor. It is true that we must there look for its certainty, because, if we attempt to penetrate to the secret ordination of God, we shall be engulfed in that profound abyss. But when the Lord has manifested it to us, we must ascend higher in order that the effect may not bury the cause. For what can be more absurd and unbecoming than while Scripture teaches that we are illuminated as God has chosen us, our eyes should be so dazzled with the brightness of this light as to refuse to attend to election? Meanwhile, I deny not that, in order to be assured of our salvation, we must begin with the word, and that our confidence ought to go no farther than the word when we invoke God the Father. For some to obtain more certainty of the counsel of God (which is nigh us in our mouth, and in our heart, Deut. 30:14), absurdly desire to fly above the clouds. We must, therefore, curb that temerity by the soberness of faith, and be satisfied to have God as the witness of his hidden grace in the external word; provided always that the channel in which the water flows, and out of which we may freely drink, does not prevent us from paying due honor to the fountain.

4. Therefore as those are in error who make the power of election dependent on the faith by which we perceive that we are elected, so we shall follow the best order if, in seeking the certainty of our election, we cleave to those posterior signs which are sure attestations to it. Among the temptations with which Satan assaults believers, none

is greater or more perilous than when disquieting them with doubts as to their election, he at the same time stimulates them with a depraved desire of inquiring after it out of the proper way (see Luther in *Genes.* cap. 26). By inquiring out of the proper way, I mean when puny man endeavors to penetrate to the hidden recesses of the divine wisdom, and goes back even to the remotest eternity, in order that he may understand what final determination God has made with regard to him. In this way he plunges headlong into an immense abyss, involves himself in numberless inextricable snares, and buries himself in the thickest darkness. For it is right that the stupidity of the human mind should be punished with fearful destruction whenever it attempts to rise in its own strength to the height of divine wisdom. And this temptation is the more fatal that it is the temptation to which of all others almost all of us are most prone. For there is scarcely a mind in which the thought does not sometimes rise, whence your salvation but from the election of God? But what proof have you of your election? When once this thought has taken possession of any individual, it keeps him perpetually miserable, subjects him to dire torment, or throws him into a state of complete stupor. I cannot wish a stronger proof of the depraved ideas which men of this description form of predestination than experience itself furnishes, since the mind cannot be infected by a more pestilential error than that which disturbs the conscience, and deprives it of peace and tranquility in regard to God. Therefore, as we dread shipwreck, we must avoid this rock, which is fatal to everyone who strikes upon it. And though the discussion of predestination is regarded as a perilous sea, yet in sailing over it the navigation is calm and safe, nay pleasant, provided we do not voluntarily court danger. For as a fatal abyss engulfs those who, to be assured of their election, pry into the eternal counsel of God without the word, yet those who investigate it rightly, and in the order in which it is exhibited in the word, reap from it rich fruits of consolation.

Let our method of inquiry then be to begin with the calling of God and to end with it. Although there is nothing in this to prevent believers from feeling that the blessings which they daily receive from the hand of God originate in that secret adoption, as they themselves express it in Isaiah, "Thou hast done wonderful things; thy counsels of old are faithfulness and truth" (Isa. 25:1). For with this as a pledge, God is pleased to assure us of as much of his counsel as can be lawfully known. But lest any should think that testimony weak, let us consider what clearness and certainty it gives us. On this subject there is an apposite passage in Bernard. After speaking of the reprobate, he says, "The purpose of God stands, the sentence of peace on those that fear him also stands, a sentence concealing their bad and recompensing their good qualities; so that, in a wondrous manner, not only their good but their bad qualities work together for good. Who will lay anything to the charge of God's elect? It is completely sufficient for my justification to have him propitious against whom only I have sinned. Everything which he has decreed not to impute to me is as if it had never been." A little after he says, "O the place of true rest, a place which I consider not unworthy of the name of inner-chamber, where God is seen, not as if disturbed with anger, or distracted by care, but where his will is proved to be good, and acceptable, and perfect. That vision does not terrify but soothes, does not excite restless curiosity but calms it, does not fatigue but tranquilizes the senses. Here is true rest. A tranquil God tranquilizes all things; and to see him at rest is to be at rest" (Bernard, super *Cantic.* Serm. 14).

5. First, if we seek for the paternal mercy and favor of God, we must turn our eyes to Christ, in whom alone the Father is well pleased (Matt. 3:17). When we seek for salvation, life, and a blessed immortality, to him also must we retake ourselves, since he alone is the fountain of life and the anchor of salvation, and the heir of the kingdom of heaven. Then what is the end of election, but just that being adopted as sons by the heavenly Father, we may by his favor obtain salvation

and immortality? How much soever you may speculate and discuss you will perceive that in its ultimate object it goes no farther. Hence, those whom God has adopted as sons, he is said to have elected, not in themselves, but in Christ Jesus (Eph. 1:4); because he could love them only in him, and only as being previously made partakers with him, honor them with the inheritance of his kingdom. But if we are elected in him, we cannot find the certainty of our election in ourselves; and not even in God the Father, if we look at him apart from the Son. Christ, then, is the mirror in which we ought, and in which, without deception, we may contemplate our election. For since it is into his body that the Father has decreed to engraft those whom from eternity he wished to be his, that he may regard as sons all whom he acknowledges to be his members, if we are in communion with Christ, we have proof sufficiently clear and strong that we are written in the Book of Life. Moreover, he admitted us to sure communion with himself, when, by the preaching of the gospel, he declared that he was given us by the Father, to be ours with all his blessings (Rom. 8:32). We are said to be clothed with him, to be one with him, that we may live, because he himself lives. The doctrine is often repeated, "God so loved the world, that he gave his only begotten Son, that whosoever believeth in him should not perish, but have everlasting life" (John 3:16). He who believes in him is said to have passed from death unto life (John 5:24). In this sense he calls himself the bread of life, of which if a man eat, he shall never die (John 6:35). He, I say, was our witness, that all by whom he is received in faith will be regarded by our heavenly Father as sons. If we long for more than to be regarded as sons of God and heirs, we must ascend above Christ. But if this is our final goal, how infatuated is it to seek out of him what we have already obtained in him, and can only find in him? Besides, as he is the Eternal Wisdom, the Immutable Truth, the Determinate Counsel of the Father, there is no room for fear that anything which he tells us will vary in the minutest degree from that will of the

Father after which we inquire. Nay, rather he faithfully discloses it to us as it was from the beginning, and always will be. The practical influence of this doctrine ought also to be exhibited in our prayers. For though a belief of our election animates us to involve God, yet when we frame our prayers, it would be preposterous to obtrude it upon God, or to stipulate in this way, "O Lord, if I am elected, hear me." He would have us to rest satisfied with his promises, and not to inquire elsewhere whether or not he is disposed to hear us. We shall thus be disentangled from many snares, if we know how to make a right use of what is rightly written; but let us not inconsiderately wrest it to purposes different from that to which it ought to be confined.

6. Another confirmation tending to establish our confidence is that our election is connected with our calling. For those whom Christ enlightens with the knowledge of his name, and admits into the bosom of his Church, he is said to take under his guardianship and protection. All whom he thus receives are said to be committed and entrusted to him by the Father, that they may be kept unto life eternal. What would we have? Christ proclaims aloud that all whom the Father is pleased to save he has delivered into his protection (John 6:37-39, 17:6, 12). Therefore, if we would know whether God cares for our salvation, let us ask whether he has committed us to Christ, whom he has appointed to be the only Savior of all his people. Then, if we doubt whether we are received into the protection of Christ, he obviates the doubt when he spontaneously offers himself as our Shepherd, and declares that we are of the number of his sheep if we hear his voice (John 10:3, 16). Let us, therefore, embrace Christ, who is kindly offered to us, and comes forth to meet us: he will number us among his flock, and keep us within his fold. But anxiety arises as to our future state. For as Paul teaches, that those are called who were previously elected, so our Savior shows that many are called, but few chosen (Matt. 22:14). Nay, even Paul himself dissuades us from security, when he says, "Let him that thinketh he standeth take heed

lest he fall" (1 Cor. 10:12). And again, "Well, because of unbelief they were broken off, and thou standest by faith. Be not high-minded, but fear: for if God spared not the natural branches, take heed lest he also spare not thee" (Rom. 11:20-21). In fine, we are sufficiently taught by experience itself, that calling and faith are of little value without per-severance, which, however, is not the gift of all. But Christ has freed us from anxiety on this head; for the following promises undoubtedly have respect to the future: "All that the Father giveth me shall come to me, and him that comes to me I will in no wise cast out." Again, "This is the will of him that sent me, that of all which he has giv-en me I should lose nothing; but should raise it up at the last day" (John 6:37, 39). Again "My sheep hear my voice, and I know them, and they follow me, and I give unto them eternal life, and they shall never perish, neither shall any man pluck them out of my hand. My Father which gave them me is greater than all, and no man is able to pluck them out of my Father's hand" (John 10:27-28). Again, when he declares, "Every plant which my heavenly Father has not planted shall be rooted up" (Matt. 15:13), he intimates conversely that those who have their root in God can never be deprived of their salvation. Agreeable to this are the words of John, "If they had been of us, they would no doubt have continued with us" (1 John 2:19). Hence, also, the magnificent triumph of Paul over life and death, things present, and things to come (Rom. 8:38). This must be founded on the gift of perseverance. There is no doubt that he employs the sentiment as ap-plicable to all the elect. Paul elsewhere says, "Being confident of this very thing, that he who has begun a good work in you will perform it until the day of Jesus Christ" (Phil. 1:6). David, also, when his faith threatened to fail, leaned on this support, "Forsake not the works of thy hands." Moreover, it cannot be doubted that since Christ prays for all the elect, he asks the same thing for them as he asked for Peter—viz. that their faith fail not (Luke 22:32). Hence we infer that there is no danger of their falling away, since the Son of God, who asks that their piety may prove constant, never meets with a refusal. What then did our Savior intend to teach us by this prayer, but just to confide that whenever we are his our eternal salvation is secure?

7. But it daily happens that those who seemed to belong to Christ revolt from him and fall away: Nay, in the very passage where he declares that none of those whom the Father has given to him have perished, he excepts the son of perdition. This, indeed, is true; but it is equally true that such persons never adhered to Christ with that heartfelt confidence by which I say that the certainty of our election is established: "They went out from us," says John, "but they were not of us; for if they had been of us, they would, no doubt, have continued with us" (1 John 2:19). I deny not that they have signs of calling similar to those given to the elect; but I do not at all admit that they have that sure confirmation of election which I desire believers to seek from the word of the gospel. Wherefore, let not examples of this kind move us away from tranquil confidence in the promise of the Lord, when he declares that all by whom he is received in true faith have been given him by the Father, and that none of them, while he is their Guardian and Shepherd, will perish (John 3:16; 6:39). Of Judas we shall shortly speak (sec. 9). Paul does not dissuade Christians from security simply, but from careless, carnal security, which is accompanied with pride, arrogance, and contempt of others, which extinguishes humility and reverence for God, and produces a forgetfulness of grace received (Rom. 11:20). For he is addressing the Gentiles, and showing them that they ought not to exult proudly and cruelly over the Jews, in consequence of whose rejection they had been substituted in their stead. He also enjoins fear, not a fear under which they may waver in alarm, but a fear which, teaching us to receive the grace of God in humility, does not impair our confidence in it, as has elsewhere been said. We may add that he is not speaking to individuals, but to sects in general (see 1 Cor. 10:12). The Church having been divided into two parties, and rivalship producing dissension, Paul reminds the Gentiles

that their having been substituted in the place of a peculiar and holy people was a reason for modesty and fear. For there were many vainglorious persons among them, whose empty boasting it was expedient to repress. But we have elsewhere seen that our hope extends into the future, even beyond death, and that nothing is more contrary to its nature than to be in doubt as to our future destiny.

8. The expression of our Savior, "Many are called, but few are chosen" (Matt. 22:14) is also very improperly interpreted (see Book 3, chap. 2, sec. 11-12). There will be no ambiguity in it, if we attend to what our former remarks ought to have made clear—viz. that there are two species of calling: for there is an universal call, by which God, through the external preaching of the word, invites all men alike, even those for whom he designs the call to be a savor of death, and the ground of a severer condemnation. Besides this there is a special call which, for the most part, God bestows on believers only, when by the internal illumination of the Spirit he causes the word preached to take deep root in their hearts. Sometimes, however, he communicates it also to those whom he enlightens only for a time, and whom afterwards, in just punishment for their ingratitude, he abandons and smites with greater blindness. Now, our Lord seeing that the gospel was published far and wide, was despised by multitudes, and justly valued by few, describes God under the character of a King, who, preparing a great feast, sends his servants all around to invite a great multitude, but can only obtain the presence of a very few, because almost all allege causes of excuse; at length, in consequence of their refusal, he is obliged to send his servants out into the highways to invite everyone they meet. It is perfectly clear that thus far the parable is to be understood of external calling. He afterwards adds that God acts the part of a kind entertainer, who goes round his table and affably receives his guests; but still if he finds anyone not adorned with the nuptial garment, he will by no means allow him to insult the festivity by his sordid dress. I admit that this branch of the parable

is to be understood of those who, by a profession of faith, enter the Church, but are not at all invested with the sanctification of Christ. Such disgraces to his Church, such cankers God will not always tolerate, but will cast them forth as their turpitude deserves. Few, then, out of the great number of called are chosen; the calling, however, not being of that kind which enables believers to judge of their election. The former call is common to the wicked, the latter brings with it the spirit of regeneration, which is the earnest and seal of the future inheritance by which our hearts are sealed unto the day of the Lord (Eph. 1:13-14). In one word, while hypocrites pretend to piety, just as if they were true worshipers of God, Christ declares that they will ultimately be ejected from the place which they improperly occupy, as it is said in the psalm, "Lord, who shall abide in thy tabernacle? who shall dwell in thy holy hill? He that walketh uprightly, and worketh righteousness, and speaketh the truth in his heart" (Psalm 15:1-2). Again in another passage, "This is the generation of them that seek him, that seek thy face, O Jacob" (Psalm 24:6). And thus the Spirit exhorts believers to patience, and not to murmur because Ishmaelites are mingled with them in the Church since the mask will at length be torn off, and they will be ejected with disgrace.

9. The same account is to be given of the passage lately quoted, in which Christ says that none is lost but the son of perdition (John 17:12). The expression is not strictly proper; but it is by no means obscure: for Judas was not numbered among the sheep of Christ, because he was one truly, but because he held a place among them. Then, in another passage, where the Lord says that he was elected with the apostles, reference is made only to the office, "Have I not chosen you twelve," says he, "and one of you is a devil?" (John 6:70). That is, he had chosen him to the office of apostle. But when he speaks of election to salvation, he altogether excludes him from the number of the elect, "I speak not of you all: I know whom I have chosen" (John 13:18). Should anyone confound the term "election" in the two passages, he

will miserably entangle himself; whereas if he distinguish between them, nothing can be plainer. Gregory, therefore, is most grievously and perniciously in error when he says that we are conscious only of our calling, but are uncertain of our election; and hence he exhorts all to fear and trembling, giving this as the reason, that though we know what we are today, yet we know not what we are to be (Gregor. Hom. 38). But in that passage he clearly shows how he stumbled on that stone. By suspending election on the merit of works, he had too good a reason for dispiriting the minds of his readers, while, at the same time, as he did not lead them away from themselves to confidence in the divine goodness, he was unable to confirm them. Hence believers may in some measure perceive the truth of what we said at the outset—viz. predestination duly considered does not shake faith, but rather affords the best confirmation of it. I deny not, however, that the Spirit sometimes accommodates his language to our feeble capacity; as when he says, "They shall not be in the assembly of my people, neither shall they be written in the writing of the house of Israel" (Ezek. 13:9). As if God were beginning to write the names of those whom he counts among his people in the Book of Life; whereas we know, even on the testimony of Christ, that the names of the children of God were written in the Book of Life from the beginning (Luke 10:20). The words simply indicate the abandonment of those who seemed to have a chief place among the elect, as is said in the psalm, "Let them be blotted out of the Book of the Living, and not be written with the righteous" (Psalm 69:28).

10. For the elect are brought by calling into the fold of Christ, not from the very womb, nor all at the same time, but according as God sees it meet to dispense his grace. Before they are gathered to the supreme Shepherd they wander dispersed in a common desert, and in no respect differ from others, except that by the special mercy of God they are kept from rushing to final destruction. Therefore, if you look to themselves, you will see the offspring of Adam giving

token of the common corruption of the mass. That they proceed not to extreme and desperate impiety is not owing to any innate goodness in them, but because the eye of God watches for their safety, and his hand is stretched over them. Those who dream of some seed of election implanted in their hearts from their birth, by the agency of which they are ever inclined to piety and the fear of God, are not supported by the authority of Scripture, but refuted by experience. They, indeed, produce a few examples to prove that the elect before they were enlightened were not aliens from religion; for instance, that Paul led an unblemished life during his Pharisaism, that Cornelius was accepted for his prayers and alms, and so forth (Phil. 3:5; Acts 10:2). The case of Paul we admit, but we hold that they are in error as to Cornelius; for it appears that he was already enlightened and regenerated, so that all which he wanted was a clear revelation of the Gospel. But what are they to extract from these few examples? Is it that all the elect were always endued with the spirit of piety? Just as well might anyone, after pointing to the integrity of Aristides, Socrates, Xenocrates, Scipio, Curios, Camillus, and others (see Book 2, c. 4, sec. 4) infer that all who are left in the blindness of idolatry are studious of virtue and holiness. Nay, even Scripture is plainly opposed to them in more passages than one. The description which Paul gives of the state of the Ephesians before regeneration shows not one grain of this seed. His words are, "You has he quickened, who were dead in trespasses and sins; wherein in time past ye walked according to the course of this world, according to the prince of the power of the air, the spirit that now worketh in the children of disobedience, among whom also we all had our conversation in times past in the lusts of our flesh, fulfilling the desires of the flesh and of the mind; and were by nature the children of wrath, even as others" (Eph. 2:1-3). And again, "At that time ye were without Christ," "having no hope, and without God in the world" (Eph. 2:12). Again, "Ye were sometimes darkness, but now are ye light in the Lord: walk as children of light" (Eph. 5:8).

But perhaps they will insist that in this last passage reference is made to that ignorance of the true God, in which they deny not that the elect lived before they were called. Though this is grossly inconsistent with the Apostle's inference that they were no longer to lie or steal (Eph. 4:28). What answer will they give to other passages; such as that in which, after declaring to the Corinthians that "neither fornicators, nor idolaters, nor adulterers, nor effeminate, nor abusers of themselves with mankind, nor thieves, nor covetous, nor drunkards, nor revilers, nor extortioners shall inherit the kingdom of God," he immediately adds, "Such were some of you: but ye are washed, but ye are sanctified, but ye are justified in the name of the Lord Jesus, and by the Spirit of our God"? (1 Cor. 6:9-11). Again he says to the Romans, "As ye have yielded your members servants to uncleanness and to iniquity unto iniquity; even so now yield your members servants to righteousness unto holiness. For when ye were the servants of sin, ye were free from righteousness. What fruit had ye then in those things whereof ye are now ashamed?" (Rom. 6:19-21).

11. Say, then, what seed of election germinated in those who, contaminated in various ways during their whole lives, indulged as with desperate wickedness in every kind of abomination? Had Paul meant to express this view, he ought to have shown how much they then owed to the kindness of God, by which they had been preserved from falling into such pollution. Thus, too, Peter ought to have exhorted his countrymen to gratitude for a perpetual seed of election. On the contrary, his admonition is, "The time past of our life may suffice us to have wrought the will of the Gentiles" (1 Pet. 4:3). What if we come to examples? Was there any germ of righteousness in Rahab the harlot before she believed? (Josh. 2:4); in Manasseh when Jerusalem was dyed and almost deluged with the blood of the prophets? (2 Kings 23:16); in the thief who only with his last breath thought of repentance? (Luke 23:42). Have done, then, with those arguments which curious men of themselves rashly devise without any authority from Scripture. But let

us hold fast what Scripture states—viz. that "All we like sheep have gone astray, we have turned everyone to his own way" (Isa. 53:6); that is to perdition. In this gulf of perdition God leaves those whom he has determined one day to deliver until his own time arrive; he only preserves them from plunging into irremediable blasphemy.

12. As the Lord by the efficacy of his calling accomplishes towards his elect the salvation to which he had by his eternal counsel destined them, so he has judgments against the reprobate, by which he executes his counsel concerning them. Those, therefore, whom he has created for dishonor during life and destruction at death that they may be vessels of wrath and examples of severity, in bringing to their doom, he at one time deprives of the means of hearing his word, at another by the preaching of it blinds and stupefies them the more. The examples of the former case are innumerable, but let us select one of the most remarkable of all. Before the advent of Christ, about four thousand years passed away, during which he hid the light of saving doctrine from all nations. If anyone answer that he did not put them in possession of the great blessing, because he judged them unworthy, then their posterity will be in no respect more worthy. Of this in addition to experience, Malachi is a sufficient witness; for while charging them with mixed unbelief and blasphemy, he yet declares that the Redeemer will come. Why then is he given to the latter rather than to the former? They will in vain torment themselves in seeking for a deeper cause than the secret and inscrutable counsel of God. And there is no occasion to fear lest some disciple of Porphyry with impunity arraign the justice of God, while we say nothing in its defense. For while we maintain that none perish without deserving it, and that it is owing to the free goodness of God that some are delivered, enough has been said for the display of his glory; there is not the least occasion for our caviling. The supreme Disposer then makes way for his own predestination, when depriving those whom he has reprobated of the communication of his light, he leaves them in blindness.

Everyday furnishes instances of the latter case, and many of them are set before us in Scripture. Among a hundred to whom the same discourse is delivered, twenty, perhaps, receive it with the prompt obedience of faith; the others set no value upon it, or deride, or spurn, or abominate it. If it is said that this diversity is owing to the malice and perversity of the latter, the answer is not satisfactory: for the same wickedness would possess the minds of the former, did not God in his goodness correct it. And hence we will always be entangled until we call in the aid of Paul's question, "Who maketh thee to differ?" (1 Cor. 4:7), intimating that some excel others, not by their own virtue, but by the mere favor of God.

13. Why, then, while bestowing grace on the one, does he pass by the other? In regard to the former, Luke gives the reason, because they "were ordained to eternal life" (Acts 13:48). What, then, shall we think of the latter, but that they are vessels of wrath unto dishonor? Wherefore, let us not decline to say with Augustine, "God could change the will of the wicked into good, because he is omnipotent. Clearly he could. Why, then, does he not do it? Because he is unwilling. Why he is unwilling remains with himself" (August. *de Genes. ad Lit.* Lib. 2). We should not attempt to be wise above what is meet, and it is much better to take Augustine's explanation than to quibble with Chrysostom "that he draws him who is willing, and stretching forth his hand" (Chrysost. *Hom. de Convers. Pauli*), lest the difference should seem to lie in the judgment of God, and not in the mere will of man. So far is it, indeed, from being placed in the mere will of man that we may add that even the pious, and those who fear God, need this special inspiration of the Spirit. Lydia, a seller of purple, feared God, and yet it was necessary that her heart should be opened that she might attend to the doctrine of Paul, and profit in it (Acts 16:14). This was not said of one woman only but to teach us that all progress in piety is the secret work of the Spirit. Nor can it be questioned that God sends his word to many whose blindness he is pleased to

aggravate. For why does he order so many messages to be taken to Pharaoh? Was it because he hoped that he might be softened by the repetition? Nay, before he began he both knew and had foretold the result: "The Lord said unto Moses, When thou goest to return into Egypt see that thou do all those wonders before Pharaoh, which I have put in thine hand: but I will harden his heart, that he will not let the people go" (Exod. 4:21). So when he raises up Ezekiel, he forewarns him, "I send thee to the children of Israel, to a rebellious nation that has rebelled against me." "Be not afraid of their words." "Thou dwellest in the midst of a rebellious house, which has eyes to see, and see not; they have ears to hear, and hear not" (Ezek. 2:3, 6; 12:2). Thus he foretells to Jeremiah that the effect of his doctrine would be, "to root out, and pull down, and to destroy" (Jer. 1:10). But the prophecy of Isaiah presses still more closely; for he is thus commissioned by the Lord, "Go and tell this people, Hear ye indeed, but understand not, and see ye indeed but perceive not. Make the heart of this people fat, and make their ears heavy, and shut their eyes; lest they see with their eyes, and hear with their ears, and understand with their heart, and convert and be healed" (Isa. 6:9-10). Here he directs his voice to them, but it is that they may turn a deafer ear; he kindles a light, but it is that they may become more blind; he produces a doctrine, but it is that they may be more stupid; he employs a remedy, but it is that they may not be cured. And John, referring to this prophecy, declares that the Jews could not believe the doctrine of Christ, because this curse from God lay upon them. It is also incontrovertible, that to those whom God is not pleased to illumine, he delivers his doctrine wrapt up in enigmas, so that they may not profit by it, but be given over to greater blindness. Hence our Savior declares that the parables in which he had spoken to the multitude he expounded to the Apostles only, "because it is given unto you to know the mysteries of the kingdom of heaven, but to them it is not given" (Matt. 13:11). What, you will ask, does our Lord mean, by teaching those by whom he is careful

not to be understood? Consider where the fault lies, and then cease
to ask. How obscure soever the word may be, there is always sufficient
light in it to convince the consciences of the ungodly.

14. It now remains to see why the Lord acts in the manner in
which it is plain that he does. If the answer be given that it is because
men deserve this by their impiety, wickedness, and ingratitude, it is
indeed well and truly said; but still, because it does not yet appear
what the cause of the difference is why some are turned to obedience
and others remain obdurate we must, in discussing it, pass to the passage from Moses, on which Paul has commented, namely, "Even for
this same purpose have I raised thee up, that I might show my power
in thee, and that my name might be declared throughout all the earth"
(Rom. 9:17). The refusal of the reprobate to obey the word of God
when manifested to them will be properly ascribed to the malice and
depravity of their hearts, provided it be at the same time added that
they were adjudged to this depravity, because they were raised up by
the just but inscrutable judgment of God, to show forth his glory
by their condemnation. In like manner, when it is said of the sons
of Eli that they would not listen to salutary admonitions "because
the Lord would slay them" (1 Sam. 2:25), it is not denied that their
stubbornness was the result of their own iniquity; but it is at the same
time stated why they were left to their stubbornness, when the Lord
might have softened their hearts: namely, because his immutable decree had once for all doomed them to destruction. Hence the words
of John, "Though he had done so many miracles before them, yet they
believed not on him; that the saying of Isaiah the prophet might be
fulfilled which he spake, Lord, who has believed our report?" (John
12:37-38); for though he does not exculpate their perverseness, he is
satisfied with the reason that the grace of God is insipid to men, until
the Holy Spirit gives it its savor. And Christ, in quoting the prophecy
of Isaiah, "They shall be all taught of God" (John 6:45), designs only
to show that the Jews were reprobates and aliens from the Church,

because they would not be taught, and gives no other reason than that the promise of God does not belong to them. Confirmatory of this are the words of Paul, "Christ crucified" was "unto the Jews a stumbling block, and unto the Greeks foolishness; but unto them which are called, both Jews and Greeks, Christ the power of God, and the wisdom of God" (1 Cor. 1:23). For after mentioning the usual result wherever the gospel is preached, that it exasperates some, and is despised by others, he says that it is precious to them only who are called. A little before he had given them the name of believers, but he was unwilling to refuse the proper rank to divine grace, which precedes faith; or rather, he added the second term by way of correction, that those who had embraced the gospel might ascribe the merit of their faith to the calling of God. Thus, also, he shortly after shows that they were elected by God. When the wicked hear these things, they complain that God abuses his inordinate power, to make cruel sport with the miseries of his creatures. But let us, who know that all men are liable on so many grounds to the judgment of God, that they cannot answer for one in a thousand of their transgressions (Job 9:3), confess that the reprobate suffer nothing which is not accordant with the most perfect justice. When unable clearly to ascertain the reason, let us not decline to be somewhat in ignorance in regard to the depths of the divine wisdom.

15. But since an objection is often founded on a few passages of Scripture, in which God seems to deny that the wicked perish through his ordination, except insofar as they spontaneously bring death upon themselves in opposition to his warning, let us briefly explain these passages, and demonstrate that they are not adverse to the above view. One of the passages adduced is, "have I any pleasure at all that the wicked should die? saith the Lord God; and not that he should return from his ways and live?" (Ezek. 18:23). If we are to extend this to the whole human race, why are not the very many whose minds might be more easily bent to obey urged to repentance, rather than those

who by his invitations become daily more and more hardened? Our Lord declares that the preaching of the gospel and miracles would have produced more fruit among the people of Nineveh and Sodom than in Judea (Matt. 13:23). How comes it, then, that if God would have all to be saved he does not open a door of repentance for the wretched, who would more readily have received grace? Hence we may see that the passage is violently wrested, if the will of God, which the prophet mentions, is opposed to his eternal counsel, by which he separated the elect from the reprobate. Now, if the genuine meaning of the prophet is inquired into, it will be found that he only means to give the hope of pardon to them who repent. The sum is that God is undoubtedly ready to pardon whenever the sinner turns. Therefore, he does not will his death, insofar as he wills repentance. But experience shows that this will, for the repentance of those whom he invites to himself, is not such as to make him touch all their hearts. Still, it cannot be said that he acts deceitfully; for though the external word only renders those who hear it and do not obey it inexcusable, it is still truly regarded as an evidence of the grace by which he reconciles men to himself. Let us therefore hold the doctrine of the prophet, that God has no pleasure in the death of the sinner; that the godly may feel confident that whenever they repent God is ready to pardon them; and that the wicked may feel that their guilt is doubled, when they respond not to the great mercy and condescension of God. The mercy of God, therefore, will ever be ready to meet the penitent; but all the prophets, and apostles, and Ezekiel himself clearly tell us who they are to whom repentance is given.

16. The second passage adduced is that in which Paul says that "God will have all men to be saved" (1 Tim. 2:4). Though the reason here differs from the former, they have somewhat in common. I answer, first, that the mode in which God thus wills is plain from the context; for Paul connects two things, a will to be saved, and to come to the knowledge of the truth. If by this they will have it to be fixed by

the eternal counsel of God that they are to receive the doctrine of salvation, what is meant by Moses in these words, "What nation is there so great, who has God so nigh unto them?" (Deut. 4:7). How comes it that many nations are deprived of that light of the Gospel which others enjoy? How comes it that the pure knowledge of the doctrine of godliness has never reached some, and others have scarcely tasted some obscure rudiments of it? It will now be easy to extract the purport of Paul's statement. He had commanded Timothy that prayers should be regularly offered up in the church for kings and princes; but as it seemed somewhat absurd that prayer should be offered up for a class of men who were almost hopeless (all of them being not only aliens from the body of Christ, but doing their utmost to overthrow his kingdom), he adds that it was acceptable to God, who will have all men to be saved. By this he assuredly means nothing more than that the way of salvation was not shut against any order of men; that, on the contrary, he had manifested his mercy in such a way that he would have none debarred from it. Other passages do not declare what God has, in his secret judgment, determined with regard to all, but declare that pardon is prepared for all sinners who only turn to seek after it. For if they persist in urging the words, "God has concluded all in unbelief, that he might have mercy upon all" (Rom. 11:32), I will, on the contrary, urge what is elsewhere written, "Our God is in the heavens: he has done whatsoever he has pleased" (Ps. 115:3). We must, therefore, expound the passage so as to reconcile it with another, "I will be gracious to whom I will be gracious, and will show mercy on whom I will show mercy" (Exod. 33:19). He who selects those whom he is to visit in mercy does not impart it to all. But since it clearly appears that he is there speaking not of individuals, but of orders of men, let us have done with a longer discussion. At the same time, we ought to observe that Paul does not assert what God does always, everywhere, and in all circumstances, but leaves it free to him to make kings and magistrates partakers of heavenly doctrine, though in their blindness they rage against it. A stronger objection seems to be founded on the passage in Peter; the Lord is "not willing that any should perish, but that all should come to repentance" (2 Pet. 3:9). But the solution of the difficulty is to be found in the second branch of the sentence, for his will that they should come to repentance cannot be used in any other sense than that which is uniformly employed. Conversion is undoubtedly in the hand of God, whether he designs to convert all can be learned from himself, when he promises that he will give some a heart of flesh, and leave to others a heart of stone (Ezek. 36:26). It is true that if he were not disposed to receive those who implore his mercy, it could not have been said, "Turn ye unto me, saith the Lord of Hosts, and I will turn unto you, saith the Lord of Hosts" (Zech. 1:3); but I hold that no man approaches God unless previously influenced from above. And if repentance were placed at the will of man, Paul would not say, "If God peradventure will give them repentance" (2 Tim. 2:25). Nay, did not God at the very time when he is verbally exhorting all to repentance, influence the elect by the secret movement of his Spirit, Jeremiah would not say, "Turn thou me, and I shall be turned; for thou art the Lord my God. Surely after that I was turned, I repented" (Jer. 31:18).

17. But if it is so (you will say), little faith can be put in the Gospel promises, which, in testifying concerning the will of God, declare that he wills what is contrary to his inviolable decree. Not at all; for however universal the promises of salvation may be, there is no discrepancy between them and the predestination of the reprobate, provided we attend to their effect. We know that the promises are effectual only when we receive them in faith, but, on the contrary, when faith is made void, the promise is of no effect. If this is the nature of the promises, let us now see whether there be any inconsistency between the two things—viz. that God, by an eternal decree, fixed the number of those whom he is pleased to embrace in love, and on whom he is pleased to display his wrath, and that he offers salvation

indiscriminately to all. I hold that they are perfectly consistent, for all that is meant by the promise is just that his mercy is offered to all who desire and implore it, and this none do, save those whom he has enlightened. Moreover, he enlightens those whom he has predestinated to salvation. Thus the truth of the promises remains firm and unshaken, so that it cannot be said there is any disagreement between the eternal election of God and the testimony of his grace which he offers to believers. But why does he mention all men? Namely that the consciences of the righteous may rest the more secure when they understand that there is no difference between sinners, provided they have faith, and that the ungodly may not be able to allege that they have not an asylum to which they may retake themselves from the bondage of sin, while they ungratefully reject the offer which is made to them. Therefore, since by the Gospel the mercy of God is offered to both, it is faith, in other words, the illumination of God, which distinguishes between the righteous and the wicked, the former feeling the efficacy of the Gospel, the latter obtaining no benefit from it. Illumination itself has eternal election for its rule.

Another passage quoted is the lamentation of our Savior, "O Jerusalem Jerusalem, how often would I have gathered thy children together, even as a hen gathereth her chickens under her wings, and ye would not!" (Matt. 23:37); but it gives them no support. I admit that here Christ speaks not only in the character of man, but upbraids them with having, in every age, rejected his grace. But this will of God, of which we speak, must be defined. For it is well known what exertions the Lord made to retain that people, and how perversely from the highest to the lowest they followed their own wayward desires, and refused to be gathered together. But it does not follow that by the wickedness of men the counsel of God was frustrated. They object that nothing is less accordant with the nature of God than that he should have a double will. This I concede, provided they are sound interpreters. But why do they not attend to the many passages in which God clothes himself with human affections, and descends beneath his proper majesty? He says, "I have spread out my hands all the day unto a rebellious people" (Isa. 65:1), exerting himself early and late to bring them back. Were they to apply these qualities without regarding the figure, many unnecessary disputes would arise which are quashed by the simple solution, that what is human is here transferred to God. Indeed, the solution which we have given elsewhere (see Book 1, c. 18, sec. 3; and Book 3, c. 20, sec. 43) is amply sufficient—viz. that though to our apprehension the will of God is manifold, yet he does not in himself will opposites, but, according to his manifold wisdom (so Paul styles it, Eph. 3:10), transcends our senses, until such time as it shall be given us to know how he mysteriously wills what now seems to be adverse to his will. They also amuse themselves with the cavil, that since God is the Father of all, it is unjust to discard any one before he has by his misconduct merited such a punishment. As if the kindness of God did not extend even to dogs and swine. But if we confine our view to the human race, let them tell why God selected one people for himself and became their father, and why, from that one people, he plucked only a small number as if they were the flower. But those who thus charge God are so blinded by their love of evil speaking that they consider not that as God "maketh his sun to rise on the evil and on the good" (Matt. 5:45), so the inheritance is treasured up for a few to whom it shall one day be said, "Come, ye blessed of my Father, inherit the kingdom," &c. (Matt. 25:34). They object, moreover, that God does not hate any of the things which he has made. This I concede, but it does not affect the doctrine which I maintain, that the reprobate are hateful to God, and that with perfect justice, since those destitute of his Spirit cannot produce anything that does not deserve cursing. They add that there is no distinction of Jew and Gentile, and that, therefore, the grace of God is held forth to all indiscriminately: true, provided they admit (as Paul declares) that God calls as well Jews as Gentiles, according to his good pleasure, without being astricted to any. This disposes of their gloss upon another passage,

"God has concluded all in unbelief, that he might have mercy upon all" (Rom. 11:32); in other words, he wills that all who are saved should ascribe their salvation to his mercy, although the blessing of salvation is not common to all. Finally, after all that has been adduced on this side and on that, let it be our conclusion to feel overawed with Paul at the great depth, and if petulant tongues will still murmur, let us not be ashamed to join in his exclamation, "Nay, but, O man, who art thou that replies against God?" (Rom. 9:20). Truly does Augustine maintain that it is perverse to measure divine by the standard of human justice (*De Praedest. et Gra.* c. 2).

Study Guide Questions

Section 1

1. Why does God teach His elect?
2. Can grace be received by a hard heart?
3. What does Scripture couple together so that we know that free mercy is to be sought?
4. How does Augustine turn around the view that "willing and running" are useless unless mercy is present?

Section 2

1. What is a pledge of salvation that cannot deceive us?

Section 3

1. Does grace merely give us the ability to believe or not?
2. Does election take effect only after we believe?
3. Can we take assurance from the fact that we believe?
4. What do some men do in order to make sure about God's plan?

Section 4

1. What is a grievous error concerning election, one that Satan loves?
2. What question must we avoid?

3. What is the greatest and most pestilential error?
4. Where should we begin and end?

Section 5
1. Where is election alone to be found?
2. Who alone is the fountain of life?
3. If we have been chosen in Christ, where will we not find assurance?
4. If we want more than to be sons and heirs, what would we have to do?
5. What would be a preposterous prayer?
6. Instead of praying this way, what should we be content with?

Section 6
1. Where does Christ bring those that He has truly illumined with the knowledge of His name?
2. If we want assurance, what should we embrace?
3. What does Paul magnificently lord it over?
4. What gift does this kind of boasting depend on?

Section 7
1. How then do we account for various apostasies that we have all seen?
2. What must we have instead of "careless, carnal security"?

Section 8
1. How are we to understand Christ's statement that many are called but few are chosen?
2. What is the first kind of call?
3. What is the second kind of call?
4. Is this special call for the true believer alone?
5. Can anyone apostatize from this special call?
6. Putting this together, who then cannot fall away?

Section 9

1. Was Judas one of Christ's sheep?
2. Did Jesus know this when He chose him to be an apostle?
3. When predestination is rightly understood, does it shake our faith?

Section 10

1. Before one of the elect is called, is there any difference between him and any of the nonelect?
2. How does Calvin show this?

Section 11

1. How does Calvin describe what happens to the elect?

Section 12

1. If the same sermon is preached to a hundred, and twenty believe, what needs to be explained?

Section 13

1. According to Augustine, could God have turned the will of evil men to good?
2. Why, then, does He not?

Section 14

1. What do the impious do when they hear of God's sovereignty in salvation?
2. In contrast, what should we be willing to admit?

Section 15

1. What problem does Calvin address next?
2. How does Calvin answer?

Section 16

1. How does Calvin handle 1 Timothy 2:3–4?
2. What is the second way he responds?

Section 17

1. What two elements of the problem does Calvin grant?
2. What is his final conclusion?

CHAPTER 25

Of the last resurrection.

There are four principal heads in this chapter—
I. The utility, necessity, truth, and irrefragable evidence of the orthodox doctrine of a final resurrection—a doctrine unknown to philosophers, sec. 1-4.

II. Refutation of the objections to this doctrine by Atheists, Sadducees, Chiliasts, and other fanatics, sec. 5-7.

III. The nature of the final resurrection explained, sec. 8-9.

IV. Of the eternal felicity of the elect, and the everlasting misery of the reprobate.

Outline:

1. For invincible perseverance in our calling, it is necessary to be animated with the blessed hope of our Savior's final advent.

2. The perfect happiness reserved for the elect at the final resurrection unknown to philosophers.

3. The truth and necessity of this doctrine of a final resurrection. To confirm our belief in it we have, 1. The example of Christ; and, 2. The omnipotence of God. There is an inseparable connection between us

and our risen Savior. The bodies of the elect must be conformed to the body of their Head. It is now in heaven. Therefore, our bodies also must rise, and, reanimated by their souls, reign with Christ in heaven. The resurrection of Christ a pledge of ours.

4. As God is omnipotent, he can raise the dead. Resurrection explained by a natural process. The vision of dry bones.

5. Second part of the chapter, refuting objections to the doctrine of resurrection. 1. Atheists. 2. Sadducees. 3. Chiliasts. Their evasion. Various answers. 4. Universalists. Answer.

6. Objections continued. 5. Some speculators who imagine that death destroys the whole man. Refutation. The condition and abode of souls from death till the last day. What meant by the bosom of Abraham.

7. Refutation of some weak men and Manichees, pretending that new bodies are to be given. Refutation confirmed by various arguments and passages of Scripture.

8. Refutation of the fiction of new bodies continued.

9. Shall the wicked rise again? Answer in the affirmative. Why the wicked shall rise again. Why resurrection promised to the elect only.

10. The last part of the chapter, treating of eternal felicity; its excellence transcends our capacity. Rules to be observed. The glory of all the saints will not be equal.

11. Without rewarding questions which merely puzzle, an answer given to some which are not without use.

12. As the happiness of the elect, so the misery of the reprobate will be without measure, and without end.

Although Christ, the Sun of righteousness, shining upon us through the gospel, has, as Paul declares, after conquering death, given us the light of life; and hence on believing we are said to have passed from "death unto life," being no longer strangers and pilgrims, but fellow citizens with the saints, and of the household of

God, who has made us sit with his only begotten Son in heavenly places, so that nothing is wanting to our complete felicity; yet, lest we should feel it grievous to be exercised under a hard warfare, as if the victory obtained by Christ had produced no fruit, we must attend to what is elsewhere taught concerning the nature of hope. For since we hope for what we see not, and faith, as is said in another passage, is "the evidence of things not seen" so long as we are imprisoned in the body we are absent from the Lord. For which reason Paul says, "Ye are dead, and your life is hid with Christ in God. When Christ, who is our life, shall appear, then shall ye also appear with him in glory." Our present condition, therefore, requires us to "live soberly, righteously, and godly;" "looking for that blessed hope, and the glorious appearing of the great God and our Savior Jesus Christ." Here there is need of no ordinary patience, lest, worn out with fatigue, we either turn backwards or abandon our post. Wherefore, all that has hitherto been said of our salvation calls upon us to raise our minds towards heaven, that, as Peter exhorts, though we now see not Christ, "yet believing," we may "rejoice with joy unspeakable and full of glory," receiving the end of our faith, even the salvation of our souls. For this reason Paul says that the faith and charity of the saints have respect to the faith and hope which is laid up for them in heaven (Col. 1:5). When we thus keep our eyes fixed upon Christ in heaven, and nothing on earth prevents us from directing them to the promised blessedness, there is a true fulfillment of the saying, "where your treasure is, there will your heart be also" (Matt. 6:21). Hence the reason why faith is so rare in the world; nothing being more difficult for our sluggishness than to surmount innumerable obstacles in striving for the prize of our high calling. To the immense load of miseries which almost overwhelm us are added the jeers of profane men, who assail us for our simplicity, when spontaneously renouncing the allurements of the present life we seem, in seeking a happiness which lies hid from us, to catch at a fleeting shadow. In short, we are beset above and below, behind and before, with violent temptations, which our minds would be altogether unable to withstand, were they not set free from earthly objects and devoted to the heavenly life, though apparently remote from us. Wherefore, he alone has made solid progress in the Gospel who has acquired the habit of meditating continually on a blessed resurrection.

2. In ancient times philosophers discoursed, and even debated with each other, concerning the chief good: none, however, except Plato acknowledged that it consisted in union with God. He could not, however, form even an imperfect idea of its true nature; nor is this strange, as he had learned nothing of the sacred bond of that union. We even in this our earthly pilgrimage know wherein our perfect and only felicity consists—a felicity which, while we long for it, daily inflames our hearts more and more, until we attain to full fruition. Therefore I said that none participate in the benefits of Christ save those who raise their minds to the resurrection. This, accordingly, is the mark which Paul sets before believers, and at which he says they are to aim, forgetting everything until they reach its (Phil. 3:8). The more strenuously, therefore, must we contend for it, lest if the world engross us we be severely punished for our sloth. Accordingly, he in another passage distinguishes believers by this mark, that their conversation is in heaven, from whence they look for the Savior (Phil. 3:20). And that they may not faint in their course, he associates all the other creatures with them. As shapeless ruins are everywhere seen, he says that all things in heaven and earth struggle for renovation. For since Adam by his fall destroyed the proper order of nature, the creatures groan under the servitude to which they have been subjected through his sin; not that they are at all endued with sense, but that they naturally long for the state of perfection from which they have fallen. Paul therefore describes them as groaning and travailing in pain (Rom. 8:19); so that we who have received the firstfruits of the Spirit may be ashamed to grovel in our corruption, instead of at least imitating the inanimate elements which are bearing the punishment

of another's sin. And in order that he may stimulate us the more powerfully, he terms the final advent of Christ our redemption. It is true, indeed, that all the parts of our redemption are already accomplished; but as Christ was once offered for sins (Heb. 9:28), so he shall again appear without sin unto salvation. Whatever, then, be the afflictions by which we are pressed, let this redemption sustain us until its final accomplishment.

3. The very importance of the subject ought to increase our ardor. Paul justly contends that if Christ rise not the whole gospel is delusive and vain (1 Cor. 15:13-17); for our condition would be more miserable than that of other mortals, because we are exposed to much hatred and insult, and incur danger every hour; nay, are like sheep destined for slaughter; and hence the authority of the gospel would fail, not in one part merely, but in its very essence, including both our adoption and the accomplishment of our salvation. Let us, therefore, give heed to a matter of all others the most serious, so that no length of time may produce weariness. I have deferred the brief consideration to be given of it to this place, that my readers may learn, when they have received Christ, the author of perfect salvation, to rise higher, and know that he is clothed with heavenly immortality and glory in order that the whole body may be rendered conformable to the Head. For thus the Holy Spirit is ever setting before us in his person an example of the resurrection. It is difficult to believe that after our bodies have been consumed with rottenness, they will rise again at their appointed time. And hence, while many of the philosophers maintained the immortality of the soul, few of them assented to the resurrection of the body. Although in this they were inexcusable, we are thereby reminded that the subject is too difficult for human apprehension to reach it. To enable faith to surmount the great difficulty, Scripture furnishes two auxiliary proofs: the one the likeness of Christ's resurrection, and the other the omnipotence of God. Therefore, whenever the subject of the resurrection is considered, let us think of the case of our Savior,

who, having completed his mortal course in our nature which he had assumed, obtained immortality, and is now the pledge of our future resurrection. For in the miseries by which we are beset, we always bear "about in the body the dying of the Lord Jesus, that the life also of Jesus might be made manifest in our mortal flesh" (2 Cor. 4:10). It is not lawful, it is not even possible to separate him from us without dividing him. Hence Paul's argument, "If there be no resurrection of the dead, then is Christ not risen" (1 Cor. 15:13); for he assumes it as an acknowledged principle that when Christ was subjected to death, and by rising gained a victory over death, it was not on his own account, but in the Head was begun what must necessarily be fulfilled in all the members, according to the degree and order of each. For it would not be proper to be made equal to him in all respects. It is said in the psalm, "Neither wilt thou suffer thine Holy One to see corruption" (Ps. 16:10). Although a portion of this confidence appertain to us according to the measure bestowed on us, yet the full effect appeared only in Christ, who, free from all corruption, resumed a spotless body. Then, that there may be no doubt as to our fellowship with Christ in a blessed resurrection, and that we may be contented with this pledge, Paul distinctly affirms that he sits in the heavens, and will come as a judge on the last day for the express purpose of changing our vile body, "that it may be fashioned like unto his glorious body" (Phil. 3:21). For he elsewhere says that God did not raise up his Son from death to give an isolated specimen of his mighty power, but that the Spirit exerts the same efficacy in regard to them that believe; and accordingly he says that the Spirit when he dwells in us is life, because the end for which he was given is to quicken our mortal body (Rom. 8:10-11; Col. 3:4). I briefly glance at subjects which might be treated more copiously, and deserve to be adorned more splendidly, and yet in the little I have said I trust pious readers will find sufficient materials for building up their faith. Christ rose again that he might have us as partakers with him of future life. He was raised up by the Father, inasmuch as he was the Head of the Church, from which he cannot possibly be dissevered. He was raised up by the power of the Spirit, who also in us performs the office of quickening. In fine, he was raised up to be the resurrection and the life. But as we have said, that in this mirror we behold a living image of the resurrection, so it furnishes a sure evidence to support our minds, provided we faint not, nor grow weary at the long delay, because it is not ours to measure the periods of time at our own pleasure; but to rest patiently till God in his own time renew his kingdom. To this Paul refers when he says, "But every man in his own order: Christ the firstfruits; afterward they that are Christ's at his coming" (1 Cor. 15:23).

But lest any question should be raised as to the resurrection of Christ on which ours is founded, we see how often and in what various ways he has borne testimony to it. Scoffing men will deride the narrative which is given by the Evangelist as a childish fable. For what importance will they attach to a message which timid women bring, and the disciples almost dead with fear, afterwards confirm? Why does not Christ rather place the illustrious trophies of his victory in the midst of the temple and the forum? Why does he not come forth, and in the presence of Pilate strike terror? Why does he not show himself alive again to the priests and all Jerusalem? Profane men will scarcely admit that the witnesses whom he selects are well qualified. I answer that though at the commencement their infirmity was contemptible, yet the whole was directed by the admirable providence of God, so that partly from love to Christ and religious zeal, partly from incredulity, those who were lately overcome with fear now hurry to the sepulcher, not only that they might be eyewitnesses of the fact, but that they might hear angels announce what they actually saw. How can we question the veracity of those who regarded what the women told them as a fable, until they saw the reality? It is not strange that the whole people and also the governor, after they were furnished with sufficient evidence for conviction, were not allowed to see Christ or the other signs (Matt. 27:66; 28:11). The sepulcher is sealed, sentinels keep watch, on the third day the body is not found. The soldiers are bribed to spread the report that his disciples had stolen the body. As if they had had the means of deforming a band of soldiers, or been supplied with weapons, or been trained so as to make such a daring attempt. But if the soldiers had not courage enough to repel them, why did they not follow and apprehend some of them by the aid of the populace? Pilate, therefore, in fact, put his signet to the resurrection of Christ, and the guards who were placed at the sepulcher by their silence or falsehood also became heralds of his resurrection. Meanwhile, the voice of angels was heard, "He is not here, but is risen" (Luke 24:6). The celestial splendor plainly shows that they were not men but angels. Afterwards, if any doubt still remained, Christ himself removed it. The disciples saw him frequently; they even touched his hands and his feet, and their unbelief is of no little avail in confirming our faith. He discoursed to them of the mysteries of the kingdom of God, and at length, while they beheld, ascended to heaven. This spectacle was exhibited not to eleven apostles only, but was seen by more than five hundred brethren at once (1 Cor. 15:6). Then by sending the Holy Spirit he gave a proof not only of life but also of supreme power, as he had foretold, "It is expedient for you that I go away: for if I go not away, the Comforter will not come unto you" (John 16:7). Paul was not thrown down on the way by the power of a dead man, but felt that he whom he was opposing was possessed of sovereign authority. To Stephen he appeared for another purpose— viz. that he might overcome the fear of death by the certainty of life. To refuse assent to these numerous and authentic proofs is not diffidence, but depraved and therefore infatuated obstinacy.

4. We have said that in proving the resurrection our thoughts must be directed to the immense power of God. This Paul briefly teaches, when he says that the Lord Jesus Christ "shall change our vile body, that it may be fashioned like unto his glorious body, according to the

working of that mighty power whereby he is able even to subdue all things unto himself" (Phil. 3:21). Wherefore, nothing can be more incongruous than to look here at what can be done naturally when the subject presented to us is an inestimable miracle, which by its magnitude absorbs our senses. Paul, however, by producing a proof from nature, confutes the senselessness of those who deny the resurrection. "Thou fool, that which thou sowest is not quickened except it die," &c. (1 Cor. 15:36). He says that in seed there is a species of resurrection, because the crop is produced from corruption. Nor would the thing be so difficult of belief were we as attentive as we ought to be to the wonders which meet our eye in every quarter of the world. But let us remember that none is truly persuaded of the future resurrection save he who carried away with admiration gives God the glory.

Elated with this conviction, Isaiah exclaims, "Thy dead men shall live, together with my dead body shall they arise. Awake and sing, ye that dwell in dust" (Isaiah 26:19). In desperate circumstances he rises to God, the author of life, in whose hand are "the issues from death" (Psalm 68:20). Job also, when liker a dead body than a living being, trusting to the power of God, hesitates not as if in full vigor to rise to that day: "I know that my Redeemer liveth, and that he will stand at the latter day upon the earth" (that is, that he will there exert his power) "and though after my skin worms destroy this body, yet in my flesh shall I see God; whom I shall see for myself, and mine eyes shall behold, and not another" (Job 19:25-27). For though some have recourse to a more subtle interpretation, by which they wrest these passages, as if they were not to be understood of the resurrection, they only confirm what they are desirous to overthrow; for holy men, in seeking consolation in their misfortunes, have recourse for alleviation merely to the similitude of a resurrection. This is better learned from a passage in Ezekiel. When the Jews scouted the promise of return, and objected that the probability of it was not greater than that of the dead coming forth from the tomb, there is presented to the prophet in vision a field covered with dry bones, which at the command of God recover sinews and flesh. Though under that figure he encourages the people to hope for return, yet the ground of hope is taken from the resurrection, as it is the special type of all the deliverances which believers experience in this world. Thus Christ declares that the voice of the Gospel gives life; but because the Jews did not receive it, he immediately adds, "Marvel not at this; for the hour is coming in which all that are in the grave shall hear his voice, and shall come forth" (John 5:28-29). Wherefore, amid all our conflicts let us exult after the example of Paul, that he who has promised us future life "is able to keep that which is committed unto him," and thus glory that there is laid up for us "a crown of righteousness, which the Lord, the righteous judge, shall give" (2 Tim. 1:12; 4:8). Thus all the hardships which we may endure will be a demonstration of our future life, "seeing it is a righteous thing with God to recompense tribulation to them that trouble you; and to you who are troubled rest with us, when the Lord Jesus shall be revealed from heaven with his mighty angels, in flaming fire" (2 Thess. 1:6-8). But we must attend to what he shortly after adds—viz. that he "shall come to be glorified in his saints, and to be admired in all them that believe," by receiving the Gospel.

5. Although the minds of men ought to be perpetually occupied with this pursuit, yet, as if they actually resolved to banish all remembrance of the resurrection, they have called death the end of all things, the extinction of man. For Solomon certainly expresses the commonly received opinion when he says "A living dog is better than a dead lion" (Eccl. 9:4). And again, "Who knoweth the spirit of man that goes upward, and the spirit of the beast that goes downward to the earth?" In all ages a brutish stupor has prevailed, and, accordingly, it has made its way into the very Church; for the Sadducees had the hardihood openly to profess that there was no resurrection, nay, that the soul was mortal (Mark 12:18; Luke 20:27). But that this gross

ignorance might be no excuse, unbelievers have always by natural instinct had an image of the resurrection before their eyes. For why the sacred and inviolable custom of burying, but that it might be the earnest of a new life? Nor can it be said that it had its origin in error, for the solemnity of sepulture always prevailed among the holy patriarchs, and God was pleased that the same custom should continue among the Gentiles, in order that the image of the resurrection thus presented might shake off their torpor. But although that ceremony was without profit, yet it is useful to us if we prudently consider its end; because it is no feeble refutation of infidelity that all men agreed in professing what none of them believed. But not only did Satan stupefy the senses of mankind, so that with their bodies they buried the remembrance of the resurrection; but he also managed by various fictions so to corrupt this branch of doctrine that it at length was lost. Not to mention that even in the days of Paul he began to assail it (1 Cor. 15), shortly after the Chiliasts arose, who limited the reign of Christ to a thousand years. This fiction is too puerile to need or to deserve refutation. Nor do they receive any countenance from the Apocalypse, from which it is known that they extracted a gloss for their error (Rev. 20:4), since the thousand years there mentioned refer not to the eternal blessedness of the Church, but only to the various troubles which await the Church militant in this world. The whole Scripture proclaims that there will be no end either to the happiness of the elect, or the punishment of the reprobate. Moreover, in regard to all things which lie beyond our sight, and far transcend the reach of our intellect, belief must either be founded on the sure oracles of God, or altogether renounced. Those who assign only a thousand years to the children of God to enjoy the inheritance of future life, observe not how great an insult they offer to Christ and his kingdom. If they are not to be clothed with immortality, then Christ himself, into whose glory they shall be transformed, has not been received into immortal glory; if their blessedness is to have an end, the kingdom of Christ, on whose solid structure it rests, is temporary. In short, they are either most ignorant of all divine things or they maliciously aim at subverting the whole grace of God and power of Christ, which cannot have their full effects unless sin is obliterated, death swallowed up, and eternal life fully renewed. How stupid and frivolous their fear that too much severity will be ascribed to God, if the reprobate are doomed to eternal punishment, even the blind may see. The Lord, forsooth, will be unjust if he exclude from his kingdom those who, by their ingratitude shall have rendered themselves unworthy of it. But their sins are temporary (see Bernard, Epist. 254). I admit it; but then the majesty of God, and also the justice which they have violated by their sins, are eternal. Justly, therefore, the memory of their iniquity does not perish. But in this way the punishment will exceed the measure of the fault. It is intolerable blasphemy to hold the majesty of God in so little estimation as not to regard the contempt of it as of greater consequence than the destruction of a single soul. But let us have done with these triflers, that we may not seem (contrary to what we first observed) to think their dreams deserving of refutation.

6. Besides these, other two dreams have been invented by men who indulge a wicked curiosity. Some, under the idea that the whole man perishes, have thought that the soul will rise again with the body; while others, admitting that spirits are immortal, hold that they will be clothed with new bodies, and thus deny the resurrection of the flesh. Having already adverted to the former point when speaking of the creation of man, it will be sufficient again to remind the reader how groveling an error it is to convert a spirit, formed after the image of God, into an evanescent breath, which animates the body only during this fading life, and to reduce the temple of the Holy Spirit to nothing; in short, to rob of the badge of immortality that part of ourselves in which the divinity is most Refulgent and the marks of immortality conspicuous, so as to make the condition of the body better and more excellent than that of the soul. Very different is the course taken

by Scripture, which compares the body to a tabernacle, from which it describes us as migrating when we die, because it estimates us by that part which distinguishes us from the lower animals. Thus Peter, in reference to his approaching death, says, "Knowing that shortly I must put off this my tabernacle" (2 Pet. 1:14). Paul, again, speaking of believers, after saying, "If our earthly house of this tabernacle were dissolved, we have a building of God," adds, "Whilst we are at home in the body, we are absent from the Lord" (2 Cor. 5:1, 6). Did not the soul survive the body, how could it be present with the Lord on being separated from the body? But an Apostle removes all doubt when he says that we go "to the spirits of just men made perfect" (Heb. 12:23); by these words meaning that we are associated with the holy patriarchs, who even when dead cultivate the same piety, so that we cannot be the members of Christ unless we unite with them. And did not the soul, when unclothed from the body, retain its essence, and be capable of beatific glory, our Savior would not have said to the thief, "Today shalt thou be with me in paradise" (Luke 23:43). Trusting to these clear proofs, let us doubt not, after the example of our Savior, to commend our spirits to God when we come to die, or after the example of Stephen to commit ourselves to the protection of Christ, who with good reason is called "The Shepherd and Bishop" of our souls (Acts 7:59; 1 Pet. 2:25). Moreover, to pry curiously into their intermediate state is neither lawful nor expedient (see Calvin, *Psychopannychia*). Many greatly torment themselves with discussing what place they occupy, and whether or not they already enjoy celestial glory. It is foolish and rash to inquire into hidden things, farther than God permits us to know. Scripture, after telling that Christ is present with them, and receives them into paradise (John 12:32), and that they are comforted, while the souls of the reprobate suffer the torments which they have merited goes no farther. What teacher or doctor will reveal to us what God has concealed? As to the place of abode, the question is not less futile and inept, since we know that the dimension of the soul is not the same as that of the body. When the abode of blessed spirits is designated as the bosom of Abraham, it is plain that, on quitting this pilgrimage, they are received by the common father of the faithful, who imparts to them the fruit of his faith. Still, since Scripture uniformly enjoins us to look with expectation to the advent of Christ, and delays the crown of glory till that period, let us be contented with the limits divinely prescribed to us—viz. that the souls of the righteous, after their warfare is ended, obtain blessed rest where in joy they wait for the fruition of promised glory, and that thus the final result is suspended till Christ the Redeemer appear. There can be no doubt that the reprobate have the same doom as that which Jude assigns to the devils, they are "reserved in everlasting chains under darkness unto the judgment of the great day" (Jude ver. 6).

7. Equally monstrous is the error of those who imagine that the soul, instead of resuming the body with which it is now clothed, will obtain a new and different body. Nothing can be more futile than the reason given by the Manichees—viz. that it were incongruous for impure flesh to rise again: as if there were no impurity in the soul; and yet this does not exclude it from the hope of heavenly life. It is just as if they were to say that what is infected by the taint of sin cannot be divinely purified; for I now say nothing to the delirious dream that flesh is naturally impure as having been created by the devil. I only maintain that nothing in us at present which is unworthy of heaven is any obstacle to the resurrection. But, first, Paul enjoins believers to purify themselves from "all filthiness of the flesh and spirit" (2 Cor. 7:1), and then denounces the judgment which is to follow, that everyone shall "receive the things done in his body, according to that he has done, whether it be good or bad" (2 Cor. 5:10). With this accords what he says to the Corinthians, "That the life also of Jesus might be made manifest in our body" (2 Cor. 4:10). For which reason he elsewhere says, "I pray God your whole spirit and soul and body be preserved blameless unto the coming of our Lord Jesus Christ"

(1 Thess. 5:23). He says "body" as well as "spirit and soul," and no wonder; for it were most absurd that bodies which God has dedicated to himself as temples should fall into corruption without hope of resurrection. What? Are they not also the members of Christ? Does he not pray that God would sanctify every part of them, and enjoin them to celebrate his name with their tongues, lift up pure hands, and offer sacrifices? That part of man, therefore, which the heavenly Judge so highly honors, what madness is it for any mortal man to reduce to dust without hope of revival? In like manner, when Paul exhorts, "glorify God in your body, and in your spirit, which are God's," he certainly does not allow that that which he claims for God as sacred is to be adjudged to eternal corruption. Nor, indeed, on any subject does Scripture furnish clearer explanation than on the resurrection of our flesh. "This corruptible (says Paul) must put on incorruption, and this mortal must put on immortality" (1 Cor. 15:53). If God formed new bodies, where would be this change of quality? If it were said that we must be renewed, the ambiguity of the expression might, perhaps, afford room for cavil; but here pointing with the finger to the bodies with which we are clothed, and promising that they shall be incorruptible, he very plainly affirms that no new bodies are to be fabricated. "Nay," as Tertullian says, "he could not have spoken more expressly, if he had held his skin in his hands" (Tertull. *de Resurrect. Carnis*). Nor can any cavil enable them to evade the force of another passage, in which saying that Christ will be the Judge of the world, he quotes from Isaiah, "As I live, saith the Lord, every knee shall bow to me" (Rom. 14:11; Isa. 45:23), since he openly declares that those whom he was addressing will have to give an account of their lives. This could not be true if new bodies were to be sisted to the tribunal. Moreover, there is no ambiguity in the words of Daniel, "Many of them that sleep in the dust of the earth shall awake, some to everlasting life, and some to shame and everlasting contempt" (Dan. 12:2), since he does not bring new matter from the four elements to

compose men, but calls forth the dead from their graves. And the reason which dictates this is plain. For if death, which originated in the fall of man, is adventitious, the renewal produced by Christ must be in the same body which began to be mortal. And, certainly, since the Athenians mocked Paul for asserting the resurrection (Acts 17:32), we may infer what his preaching was: their derision is of no small force to confirm our faith. The saying of our Savior also is worthy of observation, "Fear not them which kill the body, but are not able to kill the soul: but rather fear him which is able to destroy both soul and body in hell" (Matt. 10:28). Here there would be no ground for fear, were not the body which we now have liable to punishment. Nor is another saying of our Savior less obscure, "The hour is coming, in the which all that are in the graves shall hear his voice, and shall come forth; they that have done good, unto the resurrection of life; and they that have done evil, unto the resurrection of damnation" (John 5:28-29). Shall we say that the soul rests in the grave that it may there hear the voice of Christ, and not rather that the body shall at his command resume the vigor which it had lost? Moreover, if we are to receive new bodies, where will be the conformity of the Head and the members? Christ rose again. Was it by forming for himself a new body? Nay, he had foretold, "Destroy this temple, and in three days I will raise it up" (John 2:19). The mortal body which he had formerly carried he again received; for it would not have availed us much if a new body had been substituted, and that which had been offered in expiatory sacrifice been destroyed. We must, therefore, attend to that connection which the Apostle celebrates, that we rise because Christ rose (1 Cor. 15:12); nothing being less probable than that the flesh in which we bear about the dying of Christ shall have no share in the resurrection of Christ. This was even manifested by a striking example, when, at the resurrection of Christ, many bodies of the saints came forth from their graves. For it cannot be denied that this was a prelude, or rather earnest, of the final resurrection for which we hope, such as already existed in Enoch and Elijah, whom Tertullian calls candidates for resurrection, because, exempted from corruption, both in body and soul, they were received into the custody of God.

8. I am ashamed to waste so many words on so clear a matter; but my readers will kindly submit to the annoyance, in order that perverse and presumptuous minds may not be able to avail themselves of any flaw to deceive the simple. The volatile spirits with whom I now dispute adduce the fiction of their own brain, that in the resurrection there will be a creation of new bodies. Their only reason for thinking so is that it seems to them incredible that a dead body, long wasted by corruption, should return to its former state. Therefore, mere unbelief is the parent of their opinion. The Spirit of God, on the contrary, uniformly exhorts us in Scripture to hope for the resurrection of our flesh. For this reason Baptism is, according to Paul, a seal of our future resurrection; and in like manner the holy Supper invites us confidently to expect it, when with our mouths we receive the symbols of spiritual grace. And certainly the whole exhortation of Paul, "Yield ye your members as instruments of righteousness unto God" (Rom. 6:13), would be frigid, did he not add, as he does in another passage, "He that raised up Christ from the dead shall also quicken your mortal bodies" (Rom. 8:11). For what would it avail to apply feet, hands, eyes, and tongues to the service of God, did not these afterwards participate in the benefit and reward? This Paul expressly confirms when he says, "The body is not for fornication, but for the Lord; and the Lord for the body. And God has both raised up the Lord, and will also raise up us by his own power" (1 Cor. 6:13-14). The words which follow are still clearer, "Know ye not that your bodies are the members of Christ?" "Know ye not that your body is the temple of the Holy Ghost?" (1 Cor. 6:15, 19). Meanwhile, we see how he connects the resurrection with chastity and holiness, as he shortly after includes our bodies in the purchase of redemption. It would be inconsistent with reason that the body, in which Paul bore the marks

of his Savior, and in which he magnificently extolled him (Gal. 6:17), should lose the reward of the crown. Hence he glories thus, "Our conversation is in heaven; from whence also we look for the Savior, the Lord Jesus Christ, who shall change our vile body, that it may be fashioned like unto his glorious body" (Phil. 3:20-21). As it is true, "That we must through much tribulation enter into the kingdom of God" (Acts 14:22), so it would be unreasonable that this entrance should be denied to the bodies which God exercises under the banner of the cross and adorns with the palm of victory.

Accordingly, the saints never entertained any doubt that they would one day be the companions of Christ, who transfers to his own person all the afflictions by which we are tried, that he may show their quickening power. Nay, under the law, God trained the holy patriarch in this belief, by means of an external ceremony. For to what end was the rite of burial, as we have already seen, unless to teach that new life was prepared for the bodies thus deposited? Hence, also, the spices and other symbols of immortality, by which under the law the obscurity of the doctrine was illustrated in the same way as by sacrifices. That custom was not the offspring of superstition, since we see that the Spirit is not less careful in narrating burials than in stating the principal mysteries of the faith. Christ commends these last offices as of no trivial importance (Matt. 16:10), and that, certainly, for no other reason than just that they raise our eyes from the view of the tombs which corrupts and destroys all things, to the prospect of renovation. Besides, that careful observance of the ceremony for which the patriarchs are praised sufficiently proves that they found in it a special and valuable help to their faith. Nor would Abraham have been so anxious about the burial of his wife (Gen. 23:4, 19), had not the religious views and something superior to any worldly advantage been present to his mind; in other words, by adorning her dead body with the insignia of the resurrection, he confirmed his own faith, and that of his family. A clearer proof of this appears in the example of Jacob, who, to testify to his posterity that even death did not destroy the hope of the promised land, orders his bones to be carried thither. Had he been to be clothed with a new body would it not have been ridiculous in him to give commands concerning a dust which was to be reduced to nothing? Wherefore, if Scripture has any authority with us, we cannot desire a clearer or stronger proof of any doctrine. Even novices understand this to be the meaning of the words, "resurrection," and "raising up." A thing which is created for the first time cannot be said to rise again; nor could our Savior have said, "This is the Father's will which has sent me, that of all which he has given me I should lose nothing, but should raise it up again at the last day" (John 6:39). The same is implied in the word "sleeping," which is applicable only to the body. Hence, too, the name of cemetery, applied to burying-grounds.

It remains to make a passing remark on the mode of resurrection. I speak thus because Paul, by styling it a mystery, exhorts us to soberness, in order that he may curb a licentious indulgence in free and subtle speculation. First, we must hold, as has already been observed, that the body in which we shall rise will be the same as at present in respect of substance, but that the quality will be different; just as the body of Christ which was raised up was the same as that which had been offered in sacrifice, and yet excelled in other qualities, as if it had been altogether different. This Paul declares by familiar examples (1 Cor. 15:39). For as the flesh of man and of beasts is the same in substance, but not in quality; as all the stars are made of the same matter, but have different degrees of brightness; so he shows that though we shall retain the substance of the body, there will be a change, by which its condition will become much more excellent. The corruptible body, therefore, in order that we may be raised, will not perish or vanish away, but, divested of corruption, will be clothed with incorruption. Since God has all the elements at his disposal, no difficulty can prevent him from commanding the earth, the fire, and the water, to give up what they seem to have destroyed. This, also, though not without figure, Isaiah testifies, "Behold, the Lord comes out of his place to punish the inhabitants of the earth for their iniquity: the earth also shall disclose her blood, and shall no more cover her slain" (Isa. 26:21). But a distinction must be made between those who died long ago, and those who on that day shall be found alive. For as Paul declares, "We shall not all sleep, but we shall all be changed" (1 Cor. 15:51); that is, it will not be necessary that a period should elapse between death and the beginning of the second life, for in a moment of time, in the twinkling of an eye, the trumpet shall sound, raising up the dead incorruptible, and, by a sudden change, fitting those who are alive for the same glory. So, in another passage, he comforts believers who were to undergo death, telling them that those who are then alive shall not take precedence of the dead, because those who have fallen asleep in Christ shall rise first (1 Thess. 4:15). Should anyone urge the Apostle's declaration, "It is appointed unto all men once to die" (Heb. 9:27), the solution is easy, that when the natural state is changed there is an appearance of death, which is fitly so denominated, and, therefore, there is no inconsistency in the two things—viz. that all when divested of their mortal body shall be renewed by death; and yet that where the change is sudden, there will be no necessary separation between the soul and the body.

9. But a more difficult question here arises: how can the resurrection, which is a special benefit of Christ, be common to the ungodly, who are lying under the curse of God? We know that in Adam all died. Christ has come to be the resurrection and the life (John 11:25). Is it to revive the whole human race indiscriminately? But what more incongruous than that the ungodly in their obstinate blindness should obtain what the pious worshipers of God receive by faith only? It is certain, therefore, that there will be one resurrection to judgment, and another to life, and that Christ will come to separate the kids from the goats (Matt. 25:32). I observe that this ought not to seem very strange, seeing something resembling it occurs every day. We know

that in Adam we were deprived of the inheritance of the whole world, and that the same reason which excludes us from eating of the tree of life excludes us also from common food. How comes it, then, that God not only makes his sun to rise on the evil and on the good, but that, in regard to the uses of the present life, his inestimable liberality is constantly flowing forth in rich abundance? Hence we certainly perceive that things which are proper to Christ and his members abound to the wicked also; not that their possession is legitimate, but that they may thus be rendered more inexcusable. Thus the wicked often experience the beneficence of God, not in ordinary measures, but such as sometimes throw all the blessings of the godly into the shade, though they eventually lead to greater damnation. Should it be objected that the resurrection is not properly compared to fading and earthly blessings, I again answer, that when the devils were first alienated from God, the fountain of life, they deserved to be utterly destroyed; yet, by the admirable counsel of God, an intermediate state was prepared, where without life they might live in death. It ought not to seem in any respect more absurd that there is to be an adventitious resurrection of the ungodly which will drag them against their will before the tribunal of Christ, whom they now refuse to receive as their master and teacher. To be consumed by death would be a light punishment were they not, in order to the punishment of their rebellion, to be sisted before the Judge whom they have provoked to a vengeance without measure and without end. But although we are to hold, as already observed and as is contained in the celebrated confession of Paul to Felix, "That there shall be a resurrection of the dead, both of the just and unjust" (Acts 24:15), yet Scripture more frequently sets forth the resurrection as intended, along with celestial glory, for the children of God only, because, properly speaking, Christ comes not for the destruction, but for the salvation of the world, and, therefore, in the Creed the life of blessedness only is mentioned.

10. But since the prophecy that death shall be swallowed up in victory (Hosea 13:14) will then only be completed, let us always remember that the end of the resurrection is eternal happiness, of whose excellence scarcely the minutest part can be described by all that human tongues can say. For though we are truly told that the kingdom of God will be full of light, and gladness, and felicity, and glory, yet the things meant by these words remain most remote from sense, and as it were involved in enigma, until the day arrive on which he will manifest his glory to us face to face (1 Cor. 15:54). "Now" says John, "are we the sons of God; and it does not yet appear what we shall be: but we know that, when he shall appear, we shall be like him; for we shall see him as he is" (1 John 3:2). Hence, as the prophets were unable to give a verbal description of that spiritual blessedness, they usually delineated it by corporeal objects. On the other hand, because the fervor of desire must be kindled in us by some taste of its sweetness, let us specially dwell upon this thought, if God contains in himself as an inexhaustible fountain all fullness of blessing, those who aspire to the supreme good and perfect happiness must not long for anything beyond him. This we are taught in several passages, "Fear not, Abraham; I am thy shield, and thy exceeding great reward" (Gen. 15:1). With this accords David's sentiment, "The Lord is the portion of mine inheritance, and of my cup: thou maintainest my lot. The lines are fallen unto me in pleasant places" (Ps. 16:5-6). Again, "I shall be satisfied when I awake with thy likeness" (Ps. 17:15). Peter declares that the purpose for which believers are called is that they may be "partakers of the divine nature" (2 Pet. 1:4). How so? Because "he shall come to be glorified in his saints and to be admired in all them that believe" (2 Thess. 1:10). If our Lord will share his glory, power, and righteousness, with the elect, nay, will give himself to be enjoyed by them; and what is better still, will in a manner become one with them, let us remember that every kind of happiness is herein included. But when we have made great progress in thus meditating,

let us understand that if the conceptions of our minds be contrasted with the sublimity of the mystery, we are still halting at the very
entrance. The more necessary is it for us to cultivate sobriety in this
matter, lest unmindful of our feeble capacity we presume to take too
lofty a flight, and be overwhelmed by the brightness of the celestial
glory. We feel how much we are stimulated by an excessive desire
of knowing more than is given us to know, and hence frivolous and
noxious questions are ever and anon springing forth: by frivolous, I
mean questions from which no advantage can be extracted. But there
is a second class which is worse than frivolous; because those who
indulge in them involve themselves in hurtful speculations. Hence I
call them noxious. The doctrine of Scripture on the subject ought not
to be made the ground of any controversy, and it is that as God, in
the varied distribution of gifts to his saints in this world, gives them
unequal degrees of light, so when he shall crown his gifts, their degrees of glory in heaven will also be unequal. When Paul says, "Ye are
our glory and our joy" (1 Thess. 2:20), his words do not apply indiscriminately to all; nor do those of our Savior to his apostles, "Ye also
shall sit on twelve thrones judging the twelve tribes of Israel" (Matt.
19:28). But Paul, who knew that as God enriches the saints with spiritual gifts in this world, he will in like manner adorn them with glory
in heaven, hesitates not to say that a special crown is laid up for him
in proportion to his labors. Our Savior, also, to commend the dignity
of the office which he had conferred on the apostles, reminds them
that the fruit of it is laid up in heaven. This, too, Daniel says, "They
that be wise shall shine as the brightness of the firmament; and they
that turn many to righteousness as the stars for ever and ever" (Dan.
12:3). Anyone who attentively considers the Scriptures will see not
only that they promise eternal life to believers, but a special reward
to each. Hence the expression of Paul, "The Lord grant unto him
that he may find mercy of the Lord in that day" (2 Tim. 1:18; 4:14).
This is confirmed by our Savior's promise that they "shall receive an

hundredfold and shall inherit everlasting life" (Matt. 19:29). In short, as Christ, by the manifold variety of his gifts, begins the glory of his body in this world, and gradually increases it, so he will complete it in heaven.

11. While all the godly with one consent will admit this, because it is sufficiently attested by the word of God, they will, on the other hand, avoid perplexing questions which they feel to be a hindrance in their way, and thus keep within the prescribed limits. In regard to myself, I not only individually refrain from a superfluous investigation of useless matters, but also think myself bound to take care that I do not encourage the levity of others by answering them. Men puffed up with vain science are often inquiring how great the difference will be between prophets and apostles, and again, between apostles and martyrs; by how many degrees virgins will surpass those who are married; in short, they leave not a corner of heaven untouched by their speculations. Next it occurs to them to inquire to what end the world is to be repaired, since the children of God will not be in want of any part of this great and incomparable abundance, but will be like the angels, whose abstinence from food is a symbol of eternal blessedness. I answer that independent of use, there will be so much pleasantness in the very sight, so much delight in the very knowledge, that this happiness will far surpass all the means of enjoyment which are now afforded. Let us suppose ourselves placed in the richest quarter of the globe, where no kind of pleasure is wanting, who is there that is not ever and anon hindered and excluded by disease from enjoying the gifts of God? Who does not oftentimes interrupt the course of enjoyment by intemperance? Hence it follows that fruition, pure and free from all defect, though it be of no use to a corruptible life, is the summit of happiness. Others go further, and ask whether dross and other impurities in metals will have no existence at the restitution, and are inconsistent with it. Though I should go so far as to concede this to them, yet I expect with Paul a reparation of those defects which first

began with sin, and on account of which the whole creation groaneth and travaileth with pain (Rom. 8:22). Others go a step further, and ask, what better condition can await the human race, since the blessing of offspring shall then have an end? The solution of this difficulty also is easy. When Scripture so highly extols the blessing of offspring, it refers to the progress by which God is constantly urging nature forward to its goal; in perfection itself we know that the case is different. But as such alluring speculations instantly captivate the unwary, who are afterwards led farther into the labyrinth, until at length, everyone becoming pleased with his own views there is no limit to disputation, the best and shortest course for us will be to rest contented with seeing through a glass darkly until we shall see face to face. Few out of the vast multitude of mankind feel concerned how they are to get to heaven; all would fain know before the time what is done in heaven. Almost all, while slow and sluggish in entering upon the contest, are already depicting to themselves imaginary triumphs.

12. Moreover, as language cannot describe the severity of the divine vengeance on the reprobate, their pains and torments are figured to us by corporeal things, such as darkness, wailing and gnashing of teeth, inextinguishable fire, the ever-gnawing worm (Matt. 8:12; 22:13; Mark 9:43; Isa. 66:24). It is certain that by such modes of expression the Holy Spirit designed to impress all our senses with dread, as when it is said, "Tophet is ordained of old; yea, for the king it is prepared: he has made it deep and large; the pile thereof is fire and much wood; the breath of the Lord, like a stream of brimstone, does kindle it" (Isa. 30:33). As we thus require to be assisted to conceive the miserable doom of the reprobate, so the consideration on which we ought chiefly to dwell is the fearful consequence of being estranged from all fellowship with God, and not only so, but of feeling that his majesty is adverse to us, while we cannot possibly escape from it. For, first, his indignation is like a raging fire, by whose touch all things are devoured and annihilated. Next, all the creatures are

the instruments of his judgment, so that those to whom the Lord will thus publicly manifest his anger will feel that heaven, and earth, and sea, all beings, animate and inanimate, are, as it were, inflamed with dire indignation against them, and armed for their destruction. Wherefore, the Apostle made no trivial declaration, when he said that unbelievers shall be "punished with everlasting destruction from the presence of the Lord, and from the glory of his power" (2 Thess. 1:9). And whenever the prophets strike terror by means of corporeal figures, although in respect of our dull understanding there is no extravagance in their language, yet they give preludes of the future judgment in the sun and the moon, and the whole fabric of the world. Hence unhappy consciences find no rest, but are vexed and driven about by a dire whirlwind, feeling as if torn by an angry God, pierced through with deadly darts, terrified by his thunderbolts and crushed by the weight of his hand, so that it would be easier to plunge into abysses and whirlpools than to endure these terrors for a moment. How fearful, then, must it be to be thus beset throughout eternity! On this subject there is a memorable passage in the ninetieth Psalm: Although God by a mere look scatters all mortals, and brings them to naught, yet as his worshipers are more timid in this world, he urges them the more, that he may stimulate then, while burdened with the cross to press onward until he himself shall be all in all.

Study Guide Questions

Section 1

1. Why is it hard for us to hope and trust in the coming resurrection?

Section 2

1. Who alone receives the fruit of Christ's benefits?

Section 3

1. Does Calvin acknowledge the difficulty of believing in the resurrection?

2. What are the two main helps that God gives to us?

3. What do scorners do with the Evangelists' history?

Section 4

1. Why does Calvin argue that faith in the resurrection depends on faith in God's omnipotence?

Section 5

1. How does Calvin answer pagan unbelievers who deny the resurrection?

Section 6

1. What does Calvin teach about the intermediate state?

Section 7

1. What does Calvin do with the idea that God gives us a completely new body, made from scratch?

2. Why is the promised "change of quality" important in this?

3. What is Calvin's argument from headship on this?

Section 8

1. What is the mother of this notion?

2. How does Calvin answer?

3. Does Calvin think burial rites are superstitious?

Section 9

1. Does Calvin hold to a resurrection of the ungodly?

2. How can resurrection, a benefit of Christ's resurrection, be extended to the ungodly?

Section 10

1. How did the prophets describe our eternal state?

2. What must we not be titillated by?

3. Does Calvin believe that everyone will have equal measures of glory in heaven?

Section 11

1. Who inquires into the different glory rankings between apostle and prophet, apostle and martyr, and so on?
2. What faults in the creation are repaired in the resurrection?

Section 12

1. How are the torments of the lost described for us in Scripture?
2. What are these images intended to do?
3. For Calvin, what is the heart of damnation?

ANSWERS FOR STUDY GUIDE QUESTIONS

Chapter One

Section 1

1. **What has to happen before all Christ's benefits become ours?**
    We have to grow up into one body with Him.
2. **What is the bond that unites us to Christ?**
    The Holy Spirit.

Section 2

1. **What does the Spirit do for all living creatures?**
    He quickens and nourishes them in what we call their natural life.
2. **But what does He do for the believers?**
    He is also the root and seed of heavenly life in us.
3. **Does the Spirit belong to the Father or the Son?**
    Both. He is sometimes called the Spirit of the Father, sometimes the Spirit of the Son.

Section 3

1. **What are some of the titles or names given to the Spirit that Calvin records here?**
    Spirit of adoption, guarantee and seal, life, water, oil, fire, and more.

Section 4

1. **What is the principal work of the Holy Spirit?**

   Faith is the principal work of the Holy Spirit.

Chapter Two

Section 1

1. **Is it hard for us to keep the law?**

   Not only hard, but beyond our strength entirely.

2. **What inadequate notion of faith does Calvin address first?**

   Nothing deeper than a common assent to the gospel history.

3. **What two things must we know?**

   Our destination and the way to it.

4. **How does Christ the God/man help us in this?**

   As God He is the destination; as man He is the way.

Section 2

1. **What fiction does Calvin reject?**

   The idea of implicit faith, faith in whatever the church teaches.

Section 3

1. **Does Calvin believe that ignorance should be tempered by humility?**

   Yes, but it would be absurd to call this faith.

2. **What does Scripture regularly teach about this?**

   That understanding is joined with faith.

Section 4

1. **Does Calvin believe that there is such a thing as implicit faith?**

   Yes, but only to the extent that certain things are hidden from us.

Section 5

1. **Is there something else that we may call implicit faith?**

   Yes. There is a demeanor that is actually preparation for faith. It is a good thing, but it is not yet faith.

2. **Are there believers who are not yet believers in an exact sense?**

   Yes. They are in the process of being drawn in.

Section 6

1. **How must we receive Christ?**

   As He is offered by the Father, that is, clothed in the gospel.

2. **How does Paul define faith?**

   As the obedience that is given to the gospel.

Section 7

1. **Does the word of God automatically build faith?**

   No. Some statements from God will do nothing but shake our faith.

2. **Should we decide that God is well disposed toward us?**

   Not unless He gives us a witness of Himself.

Section 8

1. **What does Calvin think of the scholastic distinction between formed and unformed faith?**

   He calls it worthless.

2. **How does the assent of faith work?**

   It comes more from the heart than from the brain and is called the obedience of faith.

3. **What can faith not be separated from?**

   A devout disposition.

Section 9

1. **How does Calvin answer the proof from 1 Corinthians 13 that argues that if faith is described as being without love, there must be something like unformed faith?**

   Calvin shows that "faith" in that passage is talking about miraculous powers.

2. **What mistake is made by Calvin's adversaries here?**

   They argue as though the definition of a word must be the same everywhere in Scripture.

Section 10

1. What common explanation of Simon Magus' behavior does Calvin reject?

He rejects the idea that Simon Magus pretended with words to have a faith he did not actually have in his heart.

2. What kind of faith did he have then?

He had a temporary faith, one that resembles the real thing in many ways.

3. What is the human heart like, such that it makes self-deception possible?

The heart has "so many recesses for vanity, so many lurking places for falsehood" and is "so shrouded by fraud and hypocrisy." It often "deceives itself."

Section 11

1. What is hard to some?

The idea that the reprobate can have faith.

2. Yet what do the reprobate sometimes experience?

A feeling that is almost the same as that experienced by the elect.

3. What does Calvin call the effecting of this kind of transitory faith?

He calls it the "inferior operation of the Spirit." Nothing prevents God from doing a temporary work in some.

Section 12

1. In what way are the reprobate in this sense compared to a tree?

They are like a tree not planted deep enough, a tree that may for a time put forth blossoms and leaves, and even fruit. But they don't have what Calvin calls living roots.

2. What is common faith?

The faith that both the elect and reprobate have—there is great likeness and affinity between them. And yet they differ because one is transitory and the other is living and permanent.

Section 13

1. **What must we understand about the meaning of the word "faith"?**

   That the meaning of the word is ambiguous.

2. **Does the Bible use the word in ways that allow the reprobate to have "faith"?**

   Yes. Some "defection of certain ones from the faith" for example (1 Tim. 6:20–21).

Section 14

1. **Does faith comprehend what it knows?**

   No. What our mind embraces by faith is in every way infinite.

Section 15

1. **According to Calvin, what does genuine faith require?**

   It requires full and fixed certainty.

2. **What is God's intention with regard to us?**

   To uproot perverse doubts from our hearts.

Section 16

3. **What does the man who hopes in the Lord do?**

   He confidently glories in his heavenly inheritance.

Section 17

1. **If faith is essentially certain, then what must we explain in the believer's experience?**

   The fact that believers are in "perpetual struggle with their own distrust."

2. **Who does Calvin use as a prime example of this?**

   David, a man of faith, describes his unsettled emotional condition in numerous Psalms.

Section 18

1. **How does this variation arise within us?**

   It arises because of the imperfection of faith.

2. **What does this imperfect faith do?**

   Even though imperfect, it ultimately triumphs.

Section 19

1. What illustration of weak but real faith does Calvin use?

A prisoner in a dungeon cannot see the full light of the sun, but only a slanting ray of light. Nevertheless he does see the sun.

Section 20

1. In this life, what must we put up with?

The fact that faith and unbelief get jumbled up together.

Section 21

1. Although believers have to deal with unbelief, where does it come from?

Unbelief does not arise from within, but assails believers from without.

2. What illustration of shaken faith does Calvin give?

It is like a soldier forced to give way for a moment, and so he moves his foot, giving ground a little. But he fights on.

Section 22

1. What are the two kinds of fear?

One diminishes assurance of faith, while the right kind firmly establishes it.

2. What might happen among the Gentiles that had happened among the Jews?

Some covenant members might arise without true faith and abuse God's generosity.

Section 23

1. What kind of man does Solomon pronounce a blessing on?

The man who is always afraid in his own heart, that is, a man constantly cautious about his possible sin.

Section 24

1. What does Calvin call those who believe that we have assurance so long as we look to Christ (over there)?

He calls them half-papists.

2. What is the basis for our assurance in Christ?

The fact that He has joined Himself to us. We have assurance because we have been made members with Him.

Section 25

1. What medieval father does Calvin quote extensively and with approval on this subject of faith?

Bernard of Clairvaux.

Section 26

1. What do our duties of fear and honor relate to?

Honor is the obedience we render to God as Father, and fear is the service that is offered to Him as Lord.

Section 27

1. What distinguishes childlike and servile fear?

Believers fear offending God, while unbelievers only fear offending God because of what He can do to them.

Section 28

1. Does God guarantee believers earthly prosperity?

No, according to Calvin.

2. What does He promise then?

However many things fail us, God will never fail us.

Section 29

1. What is the foundation of faith?

The freely given promise of God.

Section 30

1. What must a man attain to in the first place to have faith?

The freely given promise.

2. What must also happen in order for this faith to reconcile us to God?

It must join us to Christ.

Section 31

1. Can faith latch on to nothing?

No. Faith needs to be according to the word.

2. What must God do to bring about faith?

He must illumine the word by the testimony of His grace.

Section 32

1. What is the testimony of God's love toward us?

Any promise whatever.

2. Did the ancient Jews know of Christ?

Obscurely, but yes.

Section 33

1. How do the Schoolmen go completely astray on the question of faith?

By considering assent to knowledge as faith, leaving out confidence and assurance of heart.

Section 34

1. Can we find our way unless someone leads us?

No. The Spirit must bring us to the promises of Christ.

2. What does Calvin compare the word to?

He compares it to the sun which, when it shines on a blind man, does not bring light.

Section 35

1. What does our corruption of nature do to our capacity for faith?

It renders us unfit to believe.

2. Can man initiate faith?

No.

3. What then is necessary for belief?

The Spirit of faith must be given.

Section 36

1. What is not true faith?

When the word flits about in the top of the brain instead of taking root in the heart.

2. What is greater than the mind's blindness?

The heart's distrust.

Section 37

1. **Can true faith be shaken?**

    Yes, according to Calvin's earlier argument. But it cannot be toppled.

Section 38

1. **According to the Schoolmen, how do we discern the grace of God toward us?**

    By moral conjecture. That is, when men determine that they are not unworthy of it.

2. **What does Calvin say faith should correspond to?**

    To a simple and free promise.

Section 39

1. **Is it a small error the Schoolmen have fallen into?**

    No. They trip over the first rudiments of the Christian faith.

2. **Do the Schoolmen deny that we have the Spirit?**

    No, but they think it modest and humble to be unsure of it.

3. **What is to charge with arrogance those Christians who dare to glory in the presence of the Holy Spirit?**

    It is miserable blindness.

Section 40

1. **What other argument against assurance is brought?**

    The argument that knowledge of our final perseverance remains in suspense.

2. **Did Paul say what he did in Romans 8:38–39 by special revelation in his own case?**

    No, Paul is talking about what all believers share in common.

3. **What does doubt about our future reveal instead of modesty?**

    Ingratitude.

Section 41

1. **What translation of *hypostasis* in Hebrews 11:1 does Calvin prefer?**

    He prefers "substance," but he can live with "confidence."

2. **What teaching of the Schoolmen does Calvin dismiss as mere madness?**

   The idea that love is prior to faith and hope.

3. **What three things does Bernard teach about the glory of the pious?**

   That there is no forgiveness apart from mercy, that we can do no good works unless God gives it, and that we cannot merit eternal life by any works unless they are also given.

4. **Does Calvin approve of this?**

   Strongly.

Section 42

1. **What is the foundation of hope?**

   Faith.

2. **How does faith look forward to our future blessedness?**

   In hope.

Section 43

1. **What common foundation do faith and hope share?**

   The mercy of God.

Chapter Three

Section 1

1. **According to Calvin, does true repentance follow faith or precede it?**

   It follows faith, arising from it.

Section 2

1. **How does he deal with the objection that in Scripture, the command to repent comes first?**

   He says that people are superstitiously clinging to the joining of syllables without considering the meaning that ties those words together.

Section 3

1. **What two aspects of repentance does Calvin discuss?**

   Mortification and vivification.

2. **How does Calvin define them?**

Mortification is contrition—hatred and loathing for the sin. Calvin defines vivification as the positive desire to live a holy and devout life.

Section 4

1. **What are the two kinds of repentance?**

Repentance of the law and repentance of the gospel.

2. **Unless it comes to the latter, what does repentance of the law accomplish?**

It serves as an entryway to hell.

Section 5

1. **What is the relationship of faith and repentance?**

They can be distinguished, but not separated.

2. **What does Calvin draw from the Hebrew and Greek meanings of their words for repentance?**

He derives the sense of conversion from the Hebrew, and a change of mind or intention from the Greek.

Section 6

1. **What is the first of three heads in Calvin's understanding of repentance?**

He defines it as a turning of the life to God, inner life included.

Section 7

1. **What is the second of these three heads?**

An earnest fear of God, knowing that He will bring everything into judgment.

Section 8

1. **What simple expression of mortification and vivification is used by the prophets?**

Turn from evil and do good.

2. **Is mortification easy?**

No. The word itself indicates how difficult it is to forget our previous nature.

Section 9

1. **How does Calvin sum up his understanding of repentance?**

    He defines it as regeneration.

2. **Does this regeneration take place at one moment in time?**

    No. It occurs throughout the course of our lives.

3. **How does Calvin interpret the image of God?**

    As true holiness and righteousness.

Section 10

1. **In this life, do we receive entire freedom from sin?**

    No. We do not receive "full possession of freedom."

2. **What remains within every believer?**

    A "depraved concupiscence."

3. **Where does Calvin differ with Augustine on this point?**

    Calvin calls this smoldering ember sin proper, while Augustine identifies it as a corrupt weakness.

Section 11

1. **What is the believer's relation to sin?**

    Sin remains within him, but it is not to reign in him.

2. **Do we have to worry about our salvation because of this remaining sin?**

    No. Through the mercy of God we are freed from this guilt.

Section 12

1. **Did God create these corruptions?**

    No. All that God created was good. Sin was our contribution.

Section 13

1. **Does Calvin think there is a substantive difference between himself and Augustine on this?**

    No. He thinks that Augustine was too wary about using the word "sin" because of his controversy with the Pelagians, but Calvin shows that Augustine knew that our remaining weaknesses are in fact sinful.

Section 14

1. **According to Calvin, what is the cause of certain Anabaptists claiming an antinomian perfection?**

   They are blinded by the madness of lusts and have put off common sense.

2. **What does the Spirit not do in leading us?**

   He is not giddy, and He does not run headlong through right and wrong.

Section 15

1. **How many aspects of repentance does Paul outline in 2 Corinthians 7:11?**

   Seven—earnestness, excuse, indignation, fear, longing, zeal, and avenging.

2. **In repentance, what must we exercise?**

   Restraint, lest sorrow engulf us.

Section 16

1. **In order to keep the signs of repentance sure, what must a man measure his life by?**

   By the standard of God's law.

2. **What are the two dangers of "exercises" to aid repentance?**

   They obscure internal repentance, and they tend to make the church severe when the church should be gentle.

Section 17

1. **When fasting is necessary, what proviso does Calvin urge pastors to teach?**

   That the people remember the principal point and rend their hearts, not their garments.

Section 18

1. **What is the difference between special repentance and ordinary repentance?**

   Special repentance is only required of some, when open sin makes public repentance necessary. Ordinary repentance is heart repentance and is required of all, in that corruption of nature requires our attention throughout our lives.

Section 19

1. Under what two headings is the whole gospel contained?
Repentance and forgiveness of sins.

2. Where do these two things come from?
They are the gift of God, and both are received by faith.

Section 20

1. Is repentance the *basis* for our receiving pardon?
No. The Lord already determined to have pity on men, and He wanted them to know what direction to look. That is the reason we are called to repentance.

Section 21

1. Why does Calvin believe that repentance is a gift of God?
Because of Acts 11:18; 2 Corinthians 7:10; and 2 Timothy 2:25–26.

2. What does the efficacy of this gift depend on?
On the Spirit of regeneration.

3. In passing, who does Calvin believe to be the author of Hebrews?
Paul.

Section 22

1. Where does Calvin differ with Augustine on the unpardonable sin?
He points out that it must be committed in the present life.

2. How does Calvin define the unpardonable sin?
The sin is committed when one, with evil intention, resists the illumination of God, knowing it to be the illumination of God.

3. What is a brief way of summarizing this sin?
Mixing knowledge with unbelief.

Section 23

1. Is this a sin that a man can fall into accidentally one day?

No. It is a complete turning away from God. It is apostasy of the whole man.

Section 24

1. Is this teaching consistent with the tender mercies of God?

Yes. The point is not that men who have done this seek forgiveness but are denied. Rather it is that because they have turned away from God, they never repent. They have passed the point of no return, and they do not attempt to return.

Section 25

1. Does God ever show mercy short of eternal mercy?

Yes. God shows mercy that is commensurate with the repentance. Temporal repentance can result in a temporal "stay of judgment." Calvin cites the examples of Ahab and Esau.

Chapter Four

Section 1

1. What are the three elements of repentance, according to the Scholastics?

Contrition, confession, and satisfaction.

2. And according to Calvin, how do they heal all the bitterness?

With a light sprinkling of ceremonies.

Section 2

1. Why does Calvin say that this is not a dispute about a "matter of no consequence"?

Because it revolves around forgiveness of sin.

Section 3

1. When someone follows the Scholastics in this, what are the two possible responses?

Desperation on the one hand, and pretended rather than true sorrow on the other.

INSTITUTES OF THE CHRISTIAN RELIGION

Section 4

1. How does Calvin respond to the Scholastics' allegorical argument from the ten lepers?

    By pointing to Christ. The "all the rights and honors of the priesthood have been transferred."

2. And how does Calvin explain why Christ sent the lepers to the priests?

    In order to make the Jews witnesses of Christ's miraculous power.

Section 5

1. What does Calvin say about allegorical interpretation and dogma?

    He says that allegories are of no great value in confirming any dogma.

Section 6

1. How does Calvin handle the argument for confession from the baptism of John the Baptist?

    By saying that it was a baptism of repentance, which made confession necessary given the nature of the case.

2. What about James' requirement that we confess our sins to one another (Jas. 5:16)?

    Calvin points out that a priest is not involved—we do this for one another. The passage proves too much.

Section 7

1. When was auricular confession made a matter of canon law?

    At the time of Innocent III, twelve hundred years after the resurrection of Christ.

2. What other historical argument does Calvin use?

    That it is not practiced in the east.

Section 8

1. What did Chrysostom teach on the subject of confession of sin?

    According to Calvin, he repeatedly urged his parishioners to confess their sins privately to God.

Section 9

1. **What mistake in interpretation did the defenders of auricular confession make?**

   They took passages that translated "praise" as "confess" and treated them as though they were talking about confession of sin.

2. **Calvin then cites a number of passages to prove what?**

   That we should confess our sins to the Lord.

Section 10

1. **If we have confessed to God, what are the two circumstances that would require confession to men?**

   If the divine glory or our humiliation demands it.

2. **What passage in the Old Testament urges public confession?**

   Leviticus 16:21.

Section 11

1. **When should people confess all together?**

   When they have sinned all together.

2. **What other circumstance should lead us to confess our sins corporately?**

   Whenever there is war, pestilence, barrenness, or any other sort of calamity. These are all signs of our guilt.

Section 12

1. **Scripture approves two forms of private confession to others. What are they?**

   When we confess for our own sake (Jas. 5:16), and when we confess for the sake of a brother whom we have offended.

2. **What role do ministers have in this?**

   They are to counsel those who need it and declare assurance of pardon.

3. **To whom do we commend private confession?**

   To those who know they have need of it.

Section 13

1. **What does Calvin ardently wish was observed everywhere?**

    The sheep coming to the shepherd "whenever they would partake of the Holy Spirit."

2. **If this were observed, Calvin would desire two things to be avoided. What are they?**

    Tyranny and superstition.

Section 14

1. **What are the three occasions, according to Calvin, when the power of the keys is to be used?**

    When the whole church has offended, when one man has been disciplined by the church, and in private counsel.

2. **What must we not "dream up" with regard to the power of the keys?**

    Some power separate from the preaching of the gospel.

Section 15

1. **What Roman practice is Calvin opposing?**

    The requirement that every Catholic make confession at least once a year, with all sins enumerated, and with the intent to confess.

Section 16

1. **What does Calvin see as one problem with this?**

    The enumeration of our sins for one day is impossible; how could we do it for a year?

Section 17

1. **What does Calvin call this requirement?**

    Butchery of souls.

2. **How do Roman theologians categorize sins?**

    Into arms, branches, twigs, and leaves, according to their formulas.

3. **And what did they discover when they were done?**

    That they had put out to open sea, with no port or anchorage anywhere, and no refuge possible.

Section 18

1. Does Calvin agree that sins should be confessed singly?

Yes, but only as possible—and to God, not "some priest."

2. What promise from the prophet Ezekiel does he quote?

"When the wicked shall turn away from all his sins that he has committed, and keep all my statutes, and do that which is lawful and right, he shall surely live, he shall not die," (Ezek. 18:21).

Section 19

1. What is the problem with the requirement that Catholics make confession once a year?

They "get rid of them all at once" and are careless throughout the year in between confessions.

Section 20

1. According to Calvin, what is necessary in order to hold the power of the keys?

"I deny, therefore, that any man, who has not previously received the Holy Spirit, is competent to possess the power of the keys."

Section 21

1. What is the central problem with auricular confession?

It can bring no assurance. The system is biased against assurance.

Section 22

1. Why is the Protestant practice free of "these absurdities"?

Because the Protestant minister makes his declaration conditionally. Each person hears according to their faith.

Section 23

1. Why do passages like Matthew 18:15–18 have nothing to do with auricular confession?

Because they relate to the discipline of the church and have nothing to do with secret sins.

Section 24

1. **What are the twin errors that arise when the Roman doctrine is practiced?**

    Where people fear God, they fall into despair; where they do not, they become sluggish.

Section 25

1. **What doctrine was Calvin countering here?**

    The idea that baptism washes all sins away, but sins committed after baptism must be dealt with in part by penance.

Section 26

1. **What do our duties of fear and honor relate to?**

    Honor is the obedience we render to God as Father, and fear is the service that is offered to Him as Lord.

Section 27

1. **What two things is Calvin concerned to press home in this section?**

    First, that we must be zealous for Christ's honor, and second, that assurance of pardon is something that should really assure the conscience, not torment it.

Section 28

1. **What does Calvin do with the distinction between venial and mortal sin?**

    He rejects it, holding that all sin is mortal.

2. **What objection does he dismiss?**

    That this means he must be saying that all sin is the same. But he does not hold to the equality of all sin—he holds that all unequal sins are mortal.

Section 29

1. **What distinction does the Roman position attempt?**

    A distinction between the penalty for sin and the guilt of sin. They say God's mercy deals with the guilt, but that we must merit remission of the penalty.

2. How does Calvin respond?

"How ridiculous this levity!" Forgiveness is forgiveness, all the way down.

Section 30

1. What must a man attain to in the first place to have faith?

The freely given promise.

2. What must also happen in order for this faith to reconcile us to God?

It must join us to Christ.

Section 31

1. What are the two kinds of judgment, according to Calvin?

They are a judgment of teaching and a judgment of vengeance.

2. What role does God have in each?

That of father and judge, respectively.

Section 32

1. What is characteristic of the judgment of vengeance?

Correction and instruction are not in view, only justice.

2. What is the characteristic of the judgment of teaching?

We learn to receive the admonition and receive the correction.

3. What is the difference between how two classes of people receive these respective judgments?

The ungodly respond with fury, and the godly are suppliants for pardon.

Section 33

1. What is the difference between discipline and punishment with respect to time?

Discipline is oriented to the future; punishment to the past.

2. When we as children of God are afflicted, what is it for?

It is not a penalty to confound us; it is a chastisement to instruct us.

Section 34

1. **Why must believers be exhorted not to lose heart?**
    Because the discipline, even though it is only discipline, can be severe.

Section 35

1. **Why was David disciplined with various calamities?**
    Because he was a beloved and faithful servant.

Section 36

1. **What is Solomon referring to when he says that love covers a multitude of sins?**
    This is not before God, but among men.

Section 37

1. **How does Calvin prove that the woman who was forgiven much because she loved much did not earn her forgiveness?**
    By looking at Christ's illustration for it. The man who had been forgiven the debt of many denarii loved for that reason. He was not forgiven the debt because he loved.

Sections 38–39

1. **What is Calvin's view of the church fathers on this subject?**
    He says that they were sound in the main. In places, they spoke poorly but were nowhere near as bad as the Schoolmen made them out to be.

Chapter Five

Section 1

1. **From which doctrine does the practice of granting indulgences flow?**
    From the doctrine of satisfaction.

2. **Does Calvin want to argue with the men who advance these notions?**
    No, he would rather administer drugs for insanity.

Section 2

1. What do many people see, and what do they miss?

They see the corrupt practices, but they do not see the root from which it all flows.

2. What do indulgences establish?

Another purchase price for the saints in the blood of the martyrs.

Section 3

1. What two fathers does Calvin cite against the practice?

Leo and Augustine.

2. According to this doctrine, does the merit of Christ mingle with the merit of the saints in the treasury of the church?

Yes, and according to Calvin, this makes Christ one of a throng.

Section 4

1. What then does the apostle Paul mean in Colossians 1:24?

Calvin shows that this does not refer to propitiation or redemption, but rather to the filling up of Christ's sufferings in His extended body, the Church.

Section 5

1. What does the practice of offering indulgences do to the redemption of Christ?

It divvies it up into pieces and destroys the unity of that redemption.

Section 6

1. What destroys the notion of purgatory before it is even discussed?

The biblical idea of satisfaction in Christ alone, which Calvin has already established. This is the "ax" that overturns the doctrine of purgatory.

2. Could the idea of purgatory be a trifle not worth discussing at all?

Yes, but not if it is linked to the atonement. When expiation of sins is sought anywhere other than in the blood of Christ, the issue is very important.

Sections 7–8

1. **What proofs of purgatory were offered from the gospels?**

    For example, if a certain sin was not to be remitted in the age to come, does this not hint that others might be? Calvin dismisses this kind of argumentation as trifling.

2. **What proofs are offered from Philippians and Revelation?**

    The references there to the netherworld. But Calvin points out that they say nothing about human inhabitants suffering there for their sins.

3. **How does he handle the proof from Maccabees?**

    By rejecting that book from the canon, citing Augustine, Jerome, and Cyprian. He also points out in passing that Maccabees does not teach the existence of purgatory.

Section 9

1. **What passage in Paul was considered by Calvin to be crucial to the purgatory debate?**

    First Corinthians 3:12–15. What fire could this be, they ask, but the fire of purgatory?

2. **How does Calvin handle this passage?**

    The fire is the hour of the Holy Spirit's testing of each man's work.

3. **And what class of men does this testing come upon?**

    Builders of the church who build on a lawful foundation with unsuitable materials.

Section 10

1. **Does Calvin acknowledge that many of the fathers went along with prayers for the dead?**

    Yes, he does. But he draws a distinction between the zealous heat his adversaries display for purgatory on the one hand, and the nervous coldness shown by the fathers on the other.

Chapter Three

Section 1

1. **What is the object of regeneration?**

    That there be harmony between God's righteousness and our obedience.

2. **What is one danger for those who heartily repent?**

    That they err in their zeal.

3. **What is different between the teaching of the Holy Spirit and the teaching of moral philosophers?**

    The Spirit teaches without affectation.

Section 2

1. **What are the two main aspects of scriptural instruction?**

    One is the inculcation of a love for righteousness; the second is that bounds are set so that we don't wander aimlessly in a misguided zeal for righteousness.

2. **What is the nature of our bond with God?**

    It is holiness, but not because we come to Him by virtue of our holiness.

Section 3

1. **What is the strongest motive to the Christian life?**

    It is Christ Himself.

2. **Why must we not disfigure ourselves with sin?**

    Because we are engrafted into His body.

Section 4

1. **What group does Calvin upbraid in this section?**

    Those who have nothing but the name and badge of Christ.

2. **Who only has true intimacy with Christ?**

    Those who have a right understanding of Christ from the word of the gospel.

Section 5

1. **Why does Calvin not withhold the name "Christian" from those who have not attained to an evangelical perfection?**

    Because then there would be no Christians.

2. What should we not be discouraged by?

Our slow progress. We should be able to see true progress in holiness without pretending we are already there.

Chapter Seven
Section 1

1. What is the central principle to remember in Christian living?

That we are consecrated and dedicated to God; that we belong to Him.

2. To what must reason submit?

Reason must subject itself to the Holy Spirit.

Section 2

1. What does godly self-denial lead to?

Devotion to the glory of God and loss of all craving for human glory.

2. What happens when virtue is pursued for its own sake?

It leads to a puffed-up arrogance.

Section 3

1. According to Calvin, what three aspects of Christian living does Paul give to Titus?

Soberness, righteousness, and godliness.

Section 4

1. What relation does self-denial have to our fellow men and to God?

It has regard partly to men, but chiefly to God.

2. What happens when we rush into self-love?

We believe we have just cause to be proud of ourselves, despising all others in comparison.

3. What does each person find within his breast through self-flattery?

A kind of kingdom which comes in conflict with others easily.

Section 5

1. **What will keep you from accomplishing anything in this life?**
   Failure to give up thoughts of self; failure to get out of yourself.

2. **What makes up the lawful use of all benefits to others?**
   A liberal and kindly sharing of those benefits.

3. **What makes the acceptance of an enjoyment unlawful?**
   Failure to consecrate that enjoyment to God in the first place.

Section 6

1. **Do our neighbors deserve to be loved by us?**
   No, not if we judge by merit.

2. **How then may we love them?**
   By considering the image of God in them.

3. **When faced with the duty of loving someone unworthy, what should we do?**
   We should treat that person as a placeholder for the Lord and ask what the Lord deserved from us. If the person has sinned against us, we should charge it to the Lord's account.

Section 7

1. **For Calvin, are loving actions sufficient?**
   No, they must also proceed from a sincere feeling of love.

2. **How can liberal actions be made reprehensible?**
   With a proud countenance or even insolent words.

3. **When we give to the downtrodden, what must we experience?**
   We must identify with them, thinking of ourselves in that position.

Section 8

1. **When we learn self-denial, what two things form in us?**
   Fair-mindedness and tolerance.

2. **Our fear of what is wonderful to contemplate?**
   Poverty, lowly birth, and humble condition.

3. **What must happen for true prosperity to occur?**
   God must bless.

Section 9

1. **When we look for divine blessing on our labors, what is bridled in us?**

    The desire to grow rich or ambitiously pant after honors.

2. **If we rest in God, what outcomes will we be content in?**

    We will be content in either blessing or want.

Section 10

1. **What part of our lives must we entrust to God?**

    Every part. God is master over all of it.

2. **If we are confident in this, what will we do in adversity?**

    We will remain firm in our trust.

3. **This firm resolve in adversity must not be confused with what pagan view?**

    The stoic resolve not to complain against fortune since fortune is blind.

4. **How does God structure our lives?**

    With a most orderly justice.

Chapter Eight

Section 1

1. **If we have been adopted by the Lord, what should we be prepared for?**

    A life that is hard, toilsome, and unquiet, crammed with various kinds of evil.

2. **Was the Lord exempt from this in His life?**

    No, He had the same kind of troubles as He lived His life as a perfect example.

Section 2

1. **Why does God subject us to this kind of thing?**

    So that our feebleness might be revealed to us. When in prosperity, we draw the wrong conclusions entirely.

Section 3

1. **What does the cross strike at?**

   Our perilous confidence in the flesh.

2. **Apart from trials given by God, could we learn these things?**

   No, endurance is quite unattainable by our own efforts.

Section 4

1. **What is the testing function of trials?**

   They reveal the difference between true faith and spurious faith.

Section 5

1. **If different believers go through different kinds of trials, what does this mean?**

   It means that we are diseased in different ways, requiring different treatments.

Section 6

1. **Does God want to destroy us?**

   No, He is simply delivering us from the condemnation of the world.

2. **If we don't receive this kind of chastisement, what does it mean?**

   It means we are not true sons.

Section 7

1. **What is the special badge of God's soldiery?**

   Persecution.

2. **What phrase makes you wonder about the American founders' familiarity with Calvin?**

   "Life, fortune, or honor" is reminiscent of "our lives, our fortunes, our sacred honor" in the Declaration.

Section 8

1. **Does the believer shrug suffering off as though it were nothing?**

   No, Calvin says. What fortitude or moderation would there be in bearing such things with indifference?

2. **What does the believer do with his bitter troubles?**

   Valiantly resisting, he surmounts them.

Section 9

1. **What is the distinction between what Calvin urges here and Stoicism?**

   The Christian gives expression to his pain and sorrow. He is not a stone.

2. **What does Calvin identify as the Stoic's problem?**

   He is a perfectionist, "too exact and rigid."

3. **What does Calvin call a contemporary form of neo-Stoicism?**

   This iron philosophy.

Section 10

1. **Why was the apostle Peter pulled apart by a double will at his martyrdom, according to Calvin?**

   Because he had not put off his human nature.

2. **What do we do at the funerals of our dear ones?**

   We weep the tears that are owed to our nature.

Section 11

1. **What reason for submitting does fatalism give?**

   That it is useless to resist.

2. **What reason does Calvin give?**

   That God does nothing that does not proceed from a well-ordered justice, and that He intends our good and our benefit.

Chapter Nine

Section 1

1. **Where does our blockishness arise?**

   From the empty dazzlement of riches, power, and honors.

2. **What is necessary before we are aroused to contemplate the life to come?**

   Contempt for the present life.

Section 2

1. **There is no middle ground between what two options?**

   Considering the world as worthless and having an intemperate love for it.

2. Do humans generally acknowledge the vanity of this life?

Yes, but they never remember it.

Section 3

1. Does contempt for this world mean ingratitude?

No. Calvin is careful to teach that our recognition of the vanity of this world must not lead to hatred of the world or ingratitude against God.

Section 4

2. If heaven is our homeland, then what must the earth be?

It must be a place of exile.

Section 5

1. What does Calvin say of the man who does not joyfully await the day of death and final resurrection?

He says he has made no progress in the school of Christ.

Section 6

1. When we lift up our heads in hope, what are we enabled to see in right perspective?

The wicked who take pride in the splendor and luxury of all their possessions.

Chapter Ten

Section 1

1. What is the double danger Calvin warns against on material possessions?

We have to guard against excessive strictness and excessive laxity both.

2. Can this be governed by a fixed rule?

No, there is no definite or precise legal formula to bind the conscience.

Section 2

1. What must we remember in the use of all things?

The point God intended in giving them.

2. Did that include delight and pleasure?

Yes. God clearly did not limit His gifts to mere function.

Section 3

1. **What does restriction to function do to a man?**

    It reduces him to a block.

2. **And what does the sweet smell of the kitchen do to another kind of man?**

    It makes him unable to smell anything spiritual.

Section 4

1. **What Pauline principle does Calvin cite?**

    From 1 Corinthians 7:29–31, he tells us that we should use things while sitting loose to them—those who buy, as if they had not bought, and so forth.

Section 5

1. **How can we know if we can safely go with something?**

    If we could safely go without it.

2. **What is the third rule that Calvin mentions?**

    Remembering that we must render an account of what we do; we are stewards.

Section 6

1. **What else guides us in our use of things?**

    Each man should look to his calling.

2. **Is understanding our calling important?**

    Yes—it is the beginning and foundation of well-doing.

Chapter Eleven

Section 1

1. **Because Christ was given to us, what double grace have we received?**

    We are reconciled to God through Christ's blamelessness, and we are sanctified by Christ's Spirit. In short, we are justified and sanctified.

2. **What is regeneration?**

    The gift of being able to cultivate blamelessness and purity of life.

3. How important is justification to Calvin?

It is the hinge on which religion turns.

Section 2

1. Why do we need to get the concept of justification straight?

So that we don't stumble at the very threshold.

2. How do we appear in God's sight as righteous, since we are sinners?

We grasp the righteousness of Christ through faith and appear before God clothed in it.

3. What is justification?

The acceptance with which God receives us into His favor as righteous men.

Section 3

1. Do we need to be innocent to be acquitted?

No, because Christ is righteous. Justification is nothing other than to acquit one who was accused, as if his innocence were confirmed. It is a judicial declaration.

Section 4

1. According to Calvin, does Scripture describe the reality of justification without using the word?

Yes. God has counted us acceptable and beloved (Eph. 1:5–6).
And in 2 Corinthians 5, the word reconciled means justified.

Section 5

1. What does Calvin call Osiander's doctrine of essential righteousness?

He calls it "a kind of monstrosity."

2. What was Osiander's error?

He wanted justification to consist of the impartation of God's essential righteousness to us, and not Christ's obedience on the cross.

Section 6

1. What two things does Osiander confound?

Forgiveness of sins with rebirth.

2. **What illustration does Calvin use of things that must be distinguished but which cannot be confused?**

   The light and heat from the sun. We can say they are inseparable, but we cannot say that heat lights the earth or that light heats it.

Section 7

1. **What does Calvin compare faith to?**

   A vessel that holds something of much greater value.

2. **What is faith, and what is its relation to Christ?**

   Faith is the instrumental cause of our justification; Christ is the material cause.

Section 8

1. **What is Osiander's view?**

   That Christ, both God and man, is made righteousness for us with respect to His divine nature, and not His human nature.

Section 9

1. **What is the basis for our justification that does not comport with the divine nature alone?**

   Christ's atoning sacrifice. He died as a man.

Section 10

1. **What slander does Calvin refute?**

   Osiander's accusation that Calvin and those with him reckon faith as righteousness.

2. **What does Calvin say is his highest glory?**

   To be insulted by a proud man.

Section 11

1. **Does Osiander accept or reject "justification" as a legal term?**

   He rejects it, maintaining that in order to be declared righteous, one must be righteous.

2. **What happens if faith pays any attention to works?**

   Faith totters.

3. **What is the wonderful plan of salvation?**

   That covered by the righteousness of Christ, we do not tremble at the judgment we deserve.

Section 12

1. **What is impossible, according to Osiander?**

   For God to regard as just any who are not just.

2. **To what end does Osiander heap up passages that talk about righteousness?**

   To try to persuade his readers that whenever righteousness is mentioned, it means "essentially righteousness."

Section 13

1. **What error does Calvin address next?**

   The notion that righteousness is composed of faith and works.

2. **A man who wishes to obtain Christ's righteousness must do what?**

   Abandon his own righteousness.

3. **As long as a particle of works-righteousness remains, what else remains?**

   Some occasion for boasting.

Section 14

1. **What work-around to this did the Sophists come up with?**

   They suggest that we are justified by faith and works, provided they are the works given by grace after regeneration.

2. **How does Calvin reply?**

   That Scripture says that the righteousness of faith is to believe that Christ died and rose again.

Section 15

1. **How do the Schoolmen interpret the grace of God?**

   As the Spirit helping in the pursuit of holiness, and not as the imputation of free righteousness.

2. **What does Lombard do to Augustine?**

   Where Augustine is clear, Lombard muddles it. Where Augustine is slightly contaminated, Lombard corrupts it.

Section 16

1. **What does the regenerate man trust in?**

   In the sole righteousness of Christ, and not in the good works toward which he inclines.

Section 17

1. **How is faith said to justify?**

   Because it receives and embraces the righteousness offered in the gospel.

2. **Why can the righteousness formed in us by the Spirit of God not be a cause of righteousness?**

   Because it is still imperfect.

Section 18

1. **What is Paul's argument on faith and works in a nutshell?**

   That if works are required for law righteousness, they must not be required for faith righteousness.

2. **How must we come in order to receive righteousness?**

   We must come empty.

Section 19

1. **Does Calvin agree with Luther's translation of Romans 3:28?**

   Yes, contextually.

2. **What evasion does Calvin then deal with?**

   The idea that Paul is only excluding reliance on ceremonial works, not moral works.

Section 20

1. **Does Calvin agree that justifying faith has to be the kind of faith that works through love (Gal. 5:6)?**

   Yes, but faith does not take its justifying power from that working.

Section 21

1. **What is the righteousness of faith equated with?**

   Calvin equates it with forgiveness of sins.

2. **What is such righteousness called?**

   Remission of sins.

Section 22

1. **What passages does Calvin cite in defense of this idea?**
   He cites 2 Corinthians 5:21 and Romans 4:6–8.

2. **Augustine says what about the righteousness of the saints?**
   He says it consists more of forgiveness than in perfection of virtues.

Section 23

1. **How does this righteousness come to us?**
   By imputation, Calvin notes carefully.

2. **What illustration does Ambrose use for this (an illustration that Calvin approves)?**
   That Jacob came in the clothing of another, smelling like another, in order to receive the blessing.

Chapter Twelve

Section 1

1. **What happens when we evaluate ourselves before an earthly tribunal?**
   We think too highly of ourselves.

2. **What do we miss until we come into the presence of God?**
   We miss that we are monstrously plagued with manifest diseases, and creak with defects beneath the skin.

Section 2

1. **How may we come out ahead in moral comparisons of ourselves?**
   By making sure the comparison stops with men.

Section 3

1. **Who are the two "pious writers" that Calvin cites?**
   Augustine and Bernard.

2. **According to Bernard, what is "my merit"?**
   The Lord's compassion.

3. **What does Calvin excuse as "custom"?**
   The use of "merits" for "good works."

Section 4

1. **What do awakened consciences do?**

   Take safe refuge in God's truth, which is the only safe haven.

2. **What is the actual state of what is considered righteousness before God?**

   It is sheer iniquity.

Section 5

1. **We must consider ourselves without what two things?**

   Without flattery and without blind self-love.

2. **What is there a need to strip bare?**

   The secret places of our depravity.

Section 6

1. **What does Calvin refuse to identify as humility?**

   Any demeanor that leaves anything to ourselves.

2. **What must you do if you want to be exalted with the humble?**

   Your heart must be wounded with the same contrition as theirs.

Section 7

1. **Why was the publican who prayed in the Temple a sincere man?**

   Because he spoke testimonies of inner feeling.

Section 8

1. **What blocks the way to Christ?**

   Arrogance and/or complacency.

2. **What illustration does Calvin take from Bernard on the impossibility of taking credit for grace?**

   It is like a wall saying it gave birth to a sunbeam that passed through one of its windows.

Chapter Thirteen

Section 1

1. **What two things does Calvin aim at in this section?**

   To see that God's glory remains undiminished, and that we can have consciences at rest.

2. Who rises up against God?

He who thinks he has anything at all of his own.

Section 2

1. Where must the praise of righteousness remain?

It must remain perfect and whole in the Lord's possession.

Section 3

1. How may a guilty conscience be quieted before God?

By receiving unmerited righteousness.

Section 4

1. If we may depend upon works-righteousness at all, what else happens?

We make the promise void and without force.

2. Why does Calvin cite Augustine at this point?

Lest anyone think he is saying something new.

Section 5

1. What alone gives us peace of conscience and gladness in prayer?

God's free grace alone.

Chapter Fourteen

Section 1

1. What are the four classes of men outlined by Calvin?

Those outside the Church entirely, those inside the Church who don't live it (both low-livers and hypocrites), and true Christians.

Section 2

1. How does Calvin account for pagan virtues, where they exist?

He says they are the gift of God.

2. Does he lump pagan vice and virtue all together?

No, he says that would remove all order from the world.

3. What kind of blessing does God give such men?

External blessing for a mere external conformity to His law.

Section 3

1. Does Calvin account these pagan virtues as true virtue?

No, because they proceed from perverse motives.

2. What is necessary for something to be truly virtuous?

It has to be directed to the right end, that of serving God.

Section 4

1. What illustration does Calvin take from Augustine here?

That men of virtuous ability who do not serve Christ are men who can run fast, but they are not on the right road. And it is better to limp on the road than to run fast off of it.

Section 5

1. What must we set the grace of God against?

The natural condition of man.

2. Where does our first capacity for well-doing come from?

From regeneration.

Section 6

1. What were we before we were sprinkled through the Spirit with the blood of Christ?

We were nothing other than sinners without Christ.

Section 7

1. 1. What do the two middle categories of Calvin's fourfold division have in common?

Neither have been regenerated by the Spirit of God.

Section 8

1. What does the Lord abominate?

The observance of His law when linked to personal iniquity.

2. What is man in his highest moral splendor?

Still so far away from righteousness before the Lord that his virtues are reckoned sins.

3. What is the first foundation?

True and living faith.

Section 9

1. **What happens in believers each day?**

   Their lusts are more and more mortified.

2. **What are our best works mixed with?**

   Some dregs are always mixed with them.

Section 10

1. **What will just one sin do?**

   Wipe out and extinguish every memory of previous righteousness.

Section 11

1. **What is the believer's righteousness always to be considered?**

   As faith righteousness, not works righteousness.

2. **What two reasons keep a believer's work from being considered pure righteousness?**

   First, it is corrupted in itself, and second, even if perfect, it would be corrupted by the surrounding sins.

3. **What is the pivotal point of dispute with the Schoolmen?**

   Whether renewal is to be considered as a part of justification.

Section 12

1. **What are works of supererogation?**

   Works that rack up a surplus of merit.

2. **Does Calvin allow for them?**

   No, not at all.

Section 13

1. **What tendency does holding to works of supererogation have?**

   It tends to diminish the sharpness of God's demands and minimize the gravity of sin.

2. **What position does Calvin reject with regard to those who keep the law partly?**

   He rejects the idea that partial law-keeping results in righteousness by works to that extent.

3. **What cannot overcome a single sin?**

   Men's whole righteousness, gathered together in one heap.

Section 14

1. Is it possible to go beyond what God requires?

No, after we have done everything, we still call ourselves "unprofitable servants."

2. What should we not boast of?

Voluntary liberality when we are actually constrained by necessity.

Section 15

1. What is the only kind of supererogation that Calvin allows?

The kind spoken of by the prophet—"Who has required this at your hands?"

Section 16

1. What are the two plagues that we must banish from our minds?

There must be no trust in works, and there must be no glory in works.

Section 17

1. What are the four causes of our salvation?

The efficient cause is the Father's love. The material cause is the Son's obedience. The instrumental cause is the Spirit's illumination in our hearts. The final cause is the glory of God's generosity.

2. What is not included in this list?

Human works of any kind.

Section 18

1. In what two ways can believers refer to their own works?

When contrasting them with the works of evil men, and when encouraging themselves in this evidence of God's election.

Section 19

1. What are the fruits of regeneration proof of?

They are proof of the indwelling of the Holy Spirit.

Section 20

1. What was Augustine's prayer with regard to works?

That God see His works in Augustine's works—because if He saw Augustine's He would condemn it, and if He saw His own, He would crown it.

Section 21

1. Does Scripture ever speak of good works in a causal way?

Yes, Calvin acknowledges. But this is simply to speak of the "ordinary administration" of events, and not of ultimate causes which are entirely from God.

Chapter Fifteen

Section 1

1. For Calvin, what is justification by faith alone?

It is the chief turning point.

Section 2

1. What problem does Calvin have with the use of the word "merit"?

When applied to men's works over against God's judgment, it tends to mislead people.

2. Can someone use it without corrupting the gospel?

Certainly. Calvin gives some examples of Augustine and Chrysostom.

Section 3

1. If we don't use the word "merit," what place is there for good works?

We have good works that God gives to us, and anything praiseworthy about them is due to God's grace.

2. What don't we do like the Sophists?

We don't divide the credit for good works between God and man.

Section 4

1. How does Calvin handle the appeal from Ecclesiasticus?

He forgoes his right to reject the authority of that book and mildly points out that if translated correctly, it loses its value to them as a proof text.

2. What is the problem with our good works?

They are always spattered with much uncleanness.

Section 5

1. **What is the sole foundation for our lives, according to Calvin?**
    Jesus Christ.

2. **What did Jesus not come to do?**
    He did not come to help us attain righteousness but to be our
    righteousness.

3. **If Christ is all, what follows?**
    That we in ourselves have nothing.

Section 6

1. **What are those in the state of death unable to do?**
    They are unable to beget the substance of life.

Section 7

1. **What is the mother of all errors?**
    The schools of the Sorbonne.

2. **What is the sum of all piety?**
    Justification by faith alone.

3. **What must happen in order for any good to proceed from us
    at all?**
    We must be regenerated.

4. **Does justification by faith alone prevent us from cheering the
    hearts of believers?**
    No, not at all. But we do so without reference to our own merit,
    which would only unsettle everything.

Section 8

1. **What must we refuse to let happen?**
    We must not allow ourselves to be drawn so much as a fin-
    ger-breadth from this sole foundation.

Chapter Sixteen

Section 1

1. **What slanderous charge does Calvin answer next?**
    That justification by faith alone abolishes any need for good
    works.

2. How does Calvin answer this?

By pointing out that our justification is Christ, and we cannot receive Him without receiving all of Him. And He brings holiness of life with Him as well.

3. So what is the relationship of our salvation to our works?

It is not without works, yet not through works.

Section 2

1. Does Calvin acknowledge rewards?

Yes, and chides his opponents for not being able to separate rewards from merit.

2. What is our calling?

Ours is a holy calling, one that demands purity of life and nothing less.

Section 3

1. Does Calvin acknowledge that God will render to each man according to his works?

Yes. But he denies that it is the principal thing.

2. What is necessary before men are fit to pursue holiness?

They must imbibe the doctrine of righteousness through Christ alone.

Section 4

1. Is free grace free all around?

No. What is free for us cost Christ a great deal.

2. Our salvation is therefore too precious for what?

It is too precious to be matched by any compensation of works. We take refuge in God's mercy alone.

Chapter Seventeen

Section 1

1. Justification is to be separated from good works for what three reasons?

That we might not rely on them, glory in them, or ascribe salvation to them.

2. What is another argument for justification by works that Calvin answers here?

That promises for faithful good works are attached to the commands of the law, and that justification by sheer grace would nullify those promises.

Section 2

1. Why will we not attain to these promises through works?

Because the promises have conditions, and we never meet those conditions.

2. What do we need in order to receive the promises?

Another kind of righteousness, obtained through faith.

Section 3

1. Have these promises been given for no reason then?

No, not at all. They are just fulfilled by a means other than works.

2. How are these promises fulfilled? What three conditions does Calvin set forth?

First, that God justifies His servants apart from works. Second, God raises our works to a place of honor, doing so by grace, apart from the inherent value of these works. And third, He receives these works while pardoning their imperfections.

Section 4

1. How does Calvin explain the fact that Cornelius was accepted by God (Acts 10:31)?

By pointing out that Cornelius was already a converted man.

Section 5

1. Why is the Lord pleased with the good works of the believer?

Because He cannot fail to love the good things He is doing in us.

2. What is regeneration?

A renewal of the divine image in us.

3. How does God embrace our good works?

In Christ.

Section 6

1. **Does Calvin acknowledge more than one kind of promise in the Old Testament?**

   Yes. Some are promises of the law ("Do this and you will live"), while others are promises of grace.

Section 7

1. **Is conformity to the law sometimes called "righteousness"?**

   Yes, as when someone returns a pledge to a poor man (Deut. 24:13).

2. **Does Calvin reject what he calls law righteousness?**

   No. He says he would accept it if it existed. But it doesn't; it "nowhere appears."

Section 8

1. **How are good works appraised by God?**

   After forgiveness of sins, our good works are evaluated on a basis other than their own merits.

Section 9

1. **What relationship does justification by faith have to genuine good works?**

   Justification by faith is the "beginning, the foundation, the cause, the subject, the substance" of godly good works.

Section 10

1. **What is necessary before works can be acceptable?**

   Sins have to be pardoned.

2. **Does justification cover our persons only?**

   No, our works are justified as well as our persons.

Section 11

1. **What is the apparent conflict between James and Paul?**

   Paul says we are justified by faith alone, and James seems to say we are not.

2. **What is Calvin's starting assumption?**

   That the two biblical writers do not conflict.

3. **Those who set James against the doctrine of the Protestants are guilty of what?**

   A "double paralogism" or error in reasoning. They misunderstand the word "faith" and the word "justify."

4. **What kind of "faith" is James talking about?**

   A boasting faith, a dead faith, a devil's knowledge. No surprise that it does not justify.

Section 12

1. **Are Paul and James using the word "justify" in the same way?**

   No, because Abraham was justified by faith before the birth of Ishmael, long before the sacrifice of Isaac. This means that James is speaking of the declaration of righteousness, not the imputation of it.

Section 13

1. **How does Calvin handle Romans 2:13?**

   As a hypothetical situation, designed to convict those Jews who thought they were keeping the law simply by hearing it.

Section 14

1. **How does Calvin handle the multiple places where believers appeal to God on the basis of their innocence?**

   He points to two particulars. The first is that sinful men may certainly protest their innocence with regard to a particular accusation (a theft, a murder, etc). This is a contextual plea. Secondly, they may protest their innocence in comparison to their accusers. This is a comparative plea. But in neither case is the believer claiming an absolute innocence.

Section 15

1. **Does Calvin allow believers to claim any kind of perfection?**

   Only if they follow Augustine's definition, where he insists that any claim of perfection must recognize in truth and in humility the reality of the continuing imperfections.

Chapter Eighteen

Section 1

1. How does Calvin explain those passages which say that God will repay every man according to his works?

By saying it refers to an order of sequence rather than causation.

2. How do we know that our good works are not meritorious in themselves?

Because the grace of God is conjoined to them (Jn. 6:27).

Section 2

1. How is the term "reward" to be understood?

As the inheritance of a son, not the wages of a servant.

2. How do we know that Abraham did not earn the promise by his obedience with Isaac?

Because the promise was given to him years before.

Section 3

1. What trains us to meditate on the fruition of our lives?

Our good works have that training function.

2. Calvin quotes an early church writer to what effect?

He quotes Pseudo-Ambrose who interpreted the parable of the workers in the vineyard as showing that those who had worked all day were as much recipients of grace as those who worked only the last part of the day.

Section 4

1. What is the whole end of Scripture?

To restrain our pride, to humble us, to cast us down, and to utterly crush us.

2. What must we not deduce from the concept of reward?

We must not deduce merit. To do so wanders very far from God's plan.

Section 5

1. How can God impute righteousness to our works?

Only by having His compassion cover over the unrighteousness that remains within them.

2. How does a faith that is not reprobate work?

It works through love.

3. The righteousness of good works depends upon what?

It depends upon God pardoning them.

Section 6

1. How does one lend to the Lord?

By giving to the poor.

2. Is this kind of generosity meritorious?

No.

3. Why does God allow us to lay up treasures in heaven this way?

Even though such gifts are unworthy even of His glance, He permits none of them to be lost.

Section 7

1. What about tribulation? Doesn't God promise that He will not forget our sufferings?

Yes, He does. But this promise, like all God's promises, would mean nothing unless God's mercies had gone before.

2. According to Augustine, in what sense is the Lord our debtor?

The Lord made Himself our debtor, not by accepting anything from us, but by promising us all things.

Section 8

1. Is love greater than faith?

Yes.

2. Does this mean that love can justify?

No.

3. What illustration does Calvin use?

The fact that a king is much greater than a cobbler does not mean he can make shoes better than a cobbler can.

4. If we were justified by our love, who would be justified?

No one.

Section 9

1. **How does Calvin understand Matthew 19:17?**

   Christ points the lawyer back to the law because he was not yet aware of his sinfulness.

Section 10

1. **In relationship to other sins, what is unbelief?**

   It is the first defection from God.

2. **For someone to be called righteous, what must their life be like?**

   It must be a life that follows the divine will with unwavering and unwearying observance.

Chapter Nineteen

Section 1

1. **How many aspects to Christian freedom are there?**

   Calvin describes three.

2. **Is Christian liberty important?**

   Calvin says it is a "primary necessity."

3. **What are the two errors he describes with regard to Christian liberty?**

   Those who abuse it and those who reject it.

Section 2

1. **What is the first error he addresses?**

   Tying our justification to performance of the law in any way.

Section 3

1. **Is the letter to the Galatians simply about freedom from ceremonies?**

   No. That is included, but the topic discussed is much loftier than that.

2. **What is that loftier something?**

   Freedom from the condemnation of the law in all things and in every respect.

Section 4

1. **What is true obedience?**

    To love the Lord with all our hearts, apart from any concern about self-justification or law righteousness.

2. **Does anyone do this fully?**

    No. Those who have progressed farther than all others are still far away from this goal.

Section 5

1. **What two kinds of obedience does Calvin compare here?**

    The obedience of servants and the obedience of sons.

2. **What passage does Calvin cite to justify his statement of how God receives our labors?**

    Malachi 3:17.

Section 6

1. **What do we need not fear now that we have been emancipated by grace?**

    The remnants of sin.

Section 7

1. **Why do we need to really understand the importance of what is "indifferent" and what is not?**

    Because if we don't, there will be no end of superstitions.

2. **What does Calvin understand about the nature of "scruples"?**

    He knows they never end—a man "will not dare to touch water if more than usually sweet and pure."

Section 8

1. **How should we use God's gifts?**

    We should use them for the purpose for which He gave them.

Section 9

1. **Are luxuries a thing indifferent?**

    Yes, but only if they are used indifferently.

2. **Has God forbidden us to use lovely things?**

    Not at all. But we are not to wallow in them. We are not to luxuriate in them.

Section 10

1. What other key element must we remember in using our liberty?

We must never use it in a way that stumbles the weak.

Section 11

1. What fundamental distinction does Calvin make between different kinds of offenses?

Between offenses given and offenses taken.

2. Who takes offense with each kind?

Weak brothers and Pharisees respectively.

Section 12

1. What two situations did Paul handle differently, but with "no difference in the purpose or intention"?

The circumcision of Timothy and the refusal to circumcise Titus.

Section 13

1. What limit is placed on our use of freedom?

We must never use our freedom to offend against God.

Section 14

1. From what is the believing human conscience freed by Christ?

From the power of all men.

Section 15

1. What are the two kingdoms among men?

Spiritual and temporal.

2. In which forum do we find each respectively?

The inner and outer forum.

Section 16

1. What is a good conscience?

Inward integrity of heart.

Chapter Twenty

Section 1

1. How can the treasures of the Christian philosophy not be obtained?

They cannot be wrested from a syllogism.

2. Once we have learned what we are in Christ, what are we to do?

In prayer we are to ask of Him that we might be in Him what we are in Him.

Section 2

1. What are we to do when God promises us something?

We are to ask for it in prayer.

2. What is the result of prayer offered by burdened sinners?

Extraordinary peace and repose.

Section 3

1. Calvin gives six motives to prayer. What are they?

First, to fire our hearts with love. Second, to keep sin out. Third, that we might receive our benefits with gratitude. Fourth, that we might meditate upon His kindness. Fifth, that we may enjoy what we have received with delight. And last, that we might confirm His providence.

Section 4

1. What is the first rule for framing prayer?

That we approach God with suitable reverence.

2. What model should we follow in prayer?

The prayers of God's saintly servants in the Psalms.

3. What is the mind, when left to itself?

A wanderer.

Section 5

1. What is most contrary to reverence for God?

Levity devoid of awe.

2. Why do we lift our hands in prayer?

To remind us that we are far removed from God unless we raise our thoughts on high.

3. **What are we not to ask?**
We are not to ask more than God allows.

Section 6

1. **What is the second rule for framing prayer?**
That we always sense our own insufficiency.

2. **How does Calvin describe cold-hearted prayer?**
That which does not ponder what it asks.

3. **What do men do, stuffed with depravity?**
They ask for what they believe they already have, apart from God.

4. **What is another fault, less serious, but no less tolerable?**
Mumbling prayers without meditation.

Section 7

1. **Do we pray according to the occasion?**
Yes, Calvin says, within limits.

2. **Does this mean there are times when we need not pray?**
No. Calvin points out "there is not an instant of time during which our want does not exhort us to prayer."

3. **What does lawful prayer demand?**
Repentance.

Section 8

1. **What is the third rule for prayer?**
Rejecting all self-confidence and seeking pardon and mercy.

2. **Which Apocryphal book does Calvin quote with some approval?**
Baruch.

Section 9

1. **What is the most important part of prayer?**
The plea for forgiveness.

2. **Can we seek forgiveness without seeking deliverance?**
No. It would be absurd to want the effect to be removed without also removing the cause.

Section 10

1. **What is meant when various saints in Scripture plead their own righteousness?**

   As Calvin covered earlier, they are referring to their regeneration (itself a gift). Their purity is seen in contrast with the impurity of their enemies.

Section 11

1. **What is the fourth rule for prayer?**

   That we should pray with a sure hope of answer.

2. **What does lack of trust in prayer do?**

   It provokes God.

3. **What is our guide in prayer?**

   Faith is our guide.

Section 12

1. **What comparison does Calvin use for us unburdening ourselves in prayer?**

   We are like children unburdening themselves to their parents.

Section 13

1. **What should be our basic motive in praying this way?**

   That God commands us to and promises a response.

Section 14

1. **What demeanor should we have in prayer instead of terror?**

   Reverential fear.

2. **Is this consistent with confidence?**

   Yes, fully consistent.

3. **Upon what does this confidence rest?**

   Our prayers rest, not upon our own merit, but upon God's promises.

Section 15

1. **Why does God answer prayers from unbelievers that are clearly defective?**

   To prove to His elect how easily entreated He is.

2. **What are the prayers of the saints a mixture of?**

   Faith and error.

Section 16

1. **How can our prayers obtain an answer?**
    Only through God's forgiveness.

2. **Does Calvin give any examples of intemperate prayers that are answered?**
    Yes. Some of David's prayers, and one of Jeremiah's.

3. **Should the defects in these prayers be repudiated?**
    Yes, according to Calvin. But God pardons and receives them.

4. **Is it legitimate to raise hands in prayer?**
    Certainly, but not if you leave your heart on the ground.

Section 17

1. **What two offices of Christ are assumed when we pray in Jesus' name?**
    The offices of advocate and mediator.

Section 18

1. **In what way is Christ like the high priest of the Old Testament?**
    He bears us into the presence of God, carrying us on His shoulders and breastplate.

Section 19

1. **If Christ were removed, what would remain for us at the throne of God?**
    Wrath, judgment, and terror.

2. **As we intercede for one another, what should we be careful to do?**
    We should direct all our intercessions to the sole intercession of Christ.

Section 20

1. **What error of the Sophists does Calvin address next?**
    That Christ is the mediator of redemption, but believers are the mediators of intercession.

2. **Who alone bears the petitions of God's people to God?**
    Christ alone.

Section 21

1. **How would departed saints need to petition God?**

   They would need to pray in Jesus' name also.

2. **What is the import of this observation?**

   If departed saints have to pray through Christ, then why should
   we not pray through Christ directly?

3. **Why do people feel a need to enlist the saints?**

   They are burdened by anxiety and believe Christ to be insufficient.

Section 22

1. **What church council forbade directing prayers to the saints
   from the altar?**

   The Council of Carthage.

Section 23

1. **What confusion is used by those who urge veneration of the
   saints?**

   A confusion of departed spirits with angels. If that were true,
   then departed saints would be appointed to minister to us (Heb.
   1:14).

Section 24

1. **What would prayers to the departed saints do to their rest or
   "quiescence"?**

   The saints would have to be drawn back into earthly cares.

2. **And what do such prayers presuppose about the saints'
   abilities?**

   That they have eyes keen enough to see our needs. In short, such
   prayer presupposes the saints have the attributes of deity.

Section 25

1. **What did invocation of the patriarchs mean?**

   Not that Israel was calling upon the patriarchs, but rather that
   God was being called upon to remember Abraham, Isaac, and
   Jacob.

2. **Whose name should we rather put forward rather than Christ's? Anyone's?**

No one's.

Section 26

1. **When the Bible tells us the saints were heard by God, what did this not mean?**

It did not mean that only they would be heard.

2. **What did it mean?**

It meant we should follow their example of faith.

Section 27

1. **What is the mother of right prayer?**

Faith grounded upon the word.

Section 28

1. **What should accompany our reception of all the blessings God gives?**

Continual thanksgiving.

2. **If we fail to offer Him praise for His blessings, what is our silence?**

Our silence is spiteful.

3. **Why do some mumble as they pray?**

Because of peevishness, boredom, impatience, bitter grief, and fear.

Section 29

1. **Does God appoint public hours for prayer?**

No. The times are indifferent to God but are agreed upon by us for our convenience.

2. **What are two kinds of corruption in public prayer?**

Saying over and over again the same little prayers and swelling up with a great mass of words.

Section 30

1. **What do we need to have since there needs to be common prayers for believers?**

There ought to be public temples.

2. **Public prayer is lawful, provided what?**

Provided ostentation and chasing after paltry human glory are banished.

3. **Do the buildings make prayers more holy?**

No, because we are the true temple.

Section 31

1. **Does Calvin condemn speaking and singing in church?**

No, he commends them, provided it comes from the heart.

Section 32

1. **What does music lend to sacred actions?**

It lends dignity and grace to them and has great value in kindling our hearts to zeal.

Section 33

1. **What language should public prayers be in?**

They should be in the common tongue.

2. **What is the tongue without the mind?**

Highly displeasing to God.

3. **What gestures does Calvin approve for prayer?**

Kneeling and uncovering the head.

Section 34

1. **The Lord's Prayer is a table of what?**

It is a table of all that the Lord allows us to request of Him.

Section 35

1. **How many petitions does Calvin divide the Lord's Prayer into?**

He divides it into six instead of seven.

2. **How are those six divided?**

Like the Ten Commandments. The first three concern God directly, the last three concern ourselves.

Section 36

1. **What are we doing when we call God Father?**

We are putting the name of Christ forward.

2. **How does Calvin describe the name of Father?**

As a name of great sweetness.

Section 37

1. What should encourage us about our use of the name Father?

We should be encouraged that God the Father is compassionate, as was the father in Christ's parable.

Section 38

1. What is significant in the word "our"?

This means that we have brothers, and that there should be brotherly love among us.

2. If you love the Father, what follows?

You love His children.

Section 39

1. How is prayer like almsgiving?

Just as you can't give alms to every poor person in the world, so you can't pray for everybody.

2. What shuts the gate to prayers?

Strife.

Section 40

1. Though God is in heaven, what does Calvin want us to recognize?

That He is not bound there.

Section 41

1. What is the first petition of the Lord's Prayer?

That God's name be hallowed.

2. What are we always bidden to be concerned for in our prayers?

God's holiness.

Section 42

1. What is the second petition?

That God's kingdom come.

2. What relation does the second petition have to the first?

They are almost identical.

3. How does God set up His kingdom?

By humbling the whole world in different ways.

Section 43

1. **What is the third petition?**

   That God's will be done on earth as it is in heaven.

2. **What does this tell us about God's kingdom?**

   It tells us that God will be king of the world when all submit to His will.

3. **What can be said about those who do not pray for these things?**

   That they are not to be reckoned among God's children and servants.

Section 44

1. **What do we do in the second half of the prayer?**

   We descend to our own affairs.

2. **What is the fourth petition?**

   Our request for our daily bread.

3. **What do some who entrust their souls to God still struggle with?**

   They are still troubled about the flesh.

4. **When our storehouses are stuffed and our cellars full, what should we still do?**

   We must still seek our daily bread.

Section 45

1. **What is the fifth petition?**

   That God forgive our debts.

2. **Why does He call sins debts?**

   Because we owe penalty for them.

3. **What do people who offer their own merits to God do?**

   They call for His judgment, instead of entreating mercy.

Section 46

1. **What sort of gain should we pursue?**

   Only that which is lawful and honest.

2. **What do greedy men look like?**

   They madly scrape together from everywhere, by fair means or foul.

3. **What should we do if we have to contend with faithless and deceitful men?**
   Give up something rather than contend with them.

Section 47

1. **What should the prayers of Christians be?**
   They should be public.

2. **What is signified by the "amen"?**
   The warmth of our desire.

Section 48

1. **What is the Lord's Prayer a summary of?**
   It is a summary of all that is acceptable in prayer.

Section 49

1. **Must we be entirely limited to the words of the Lord's Prayer?**
   No. We may pray for these things in our own words.

2. **What should no man ask for?**
   "Anything which is not summarily comprehended in this prayer."

Section 50

1. **What is necessary because of our weakness in prayer?**
   Many aids and supports.

2. **What is one such aid and support?**
   Prayer at regular times—before work, before meals, etc.

3. **And at the same time, what should be avoided?**
   Superstitious observance of hours.

Section 51

1. **What do our prayers sometimes appear to be?**
   Our prayers sometimes appear to be beating the air.

Section 52

1. **When God refuses to comply with our wishes, what is His disposition toward us?**
   He is still attentive and kindly to our prayers.

Chapter Twenty-Two

Section 1

1. **What reveals the wonderful depth of God's judgment?**
    The variations in the preaching of the gospel, and the varied responses among those to whom it is preached.

2. **What are two characteristics of the doctrine?**
    It is useful, and it is sweet fruit.

3. **What tears humility up by the roots?**
    Getting rid of the doctrine of predestination.

4. **What are the three benefits?**
    God's free mercy, God's glory, and sincere humility.

5. **What happens if men pry too deeply into the subject?**
    They get lost in a labyrinth.

Section 2

1. **Where do we learn about predestination?**
    We should learn from Scripture alone.

2. **What sort of result comes from this?**
    We achieve a learned ignorance.

Section 3

1. **What do some men do with the subject?**
    They avoid it, as mariners would a reef.

2. **What is Scripture?**
    It is the school of the Holy Spirit.

3. **So how far may we go in discussion of this topic?**
    As far as this curriculum takes us.

Section 4

1. **What will obstinate people do with the doctrine of predestination?**
    They will mock it.

2. **Should this prevent us from teaching it?**
    No, because the same thing can be done with other basic doctrines.

3. **What are several of these other doctrines?**

   The doctrine of the Trinity and that of young-earth creation.

4. **Why can we safely follow Scripture in this?**

   Because Scripture proceeds as a mother stooping so that her child can keep up—as Augustine put it.

5. **In what way do opponents of this doctrine accuse God of stupid thoughtlessness?**

   They talk as though God had not seen the peril that they have so wisely met.

Section 5

1. **Considering foreknowledge and predestination, what is to subject one to the other?**

   Absurd.

2. **How does Calvin define predestination?**

   As God's eternal decree, "by which he determined with himself whatever he wished to happen with regard to every man."

3. **Arguments against God's sovereignty will not strike or hurt His righteousness—why?**

   Because arguing this way is like throwing rocks at heaven. They only fall back on you.

Section 6

1. **What is the second, more limited degree of election?**

   God's special grace for those who will be eternally saved.

2. **What then are the two degrees?**

   An election to national or corporate grace is the first, and personal election to salvation the second.

Section 7

1. **What is only half explained?**

   Election, until we come to individual persons.

2. **How does Calvin explain what makes up this individual election?**

   He calls it "to ascend to the Head," which creates an indissoluble bond.

3. **What enables the elect to persevere to the very end?**

The spirit of regeneration.

Chapter Twenty-Two
Section 1

1. **What do some do because God chooses some and passes over others?**

They bring an action against Him.

2. **What do Calvin's opponents need to explain and answer?**

Why they are men rather than oxen or asses.

3. **Who is the principal beneficiary of election?**

The man, the Lord Jesus Himself, who was not made Son of God by righteousness living.

Section 2

1. **What distinction can be made among those who do not yet exist?**

None.

Section 3

1. **Why are we not elect because of our holiness?**

Because we were elected to holiness.

Section 4

1. **In what way are all the children of Abraham holy?**

By virtue of the covenant.

2. **Why do some of the "holy offspring" degenerate from legitimate children to bastards?**

Because God's special election towers and rules over all.

3. **If Jacob were chosen on the basis of foreseen worth, what did Paul say to no purpose?**

That Jacob had not yet been born when the choice was made.

Section 5

1. **What good can God foresee in us?**

Only the good that He Himself has determined to bestow.

Section 6

1. **Why was Jacob's blessing not to be considered as merely to earthly prosperity?**

    Because his election obtained for him a great deal of earthly troubles.

2. **What does it mean that God has mercy on whom He will have mercy?**

    It means that God finds in men themselves no reason to bless them.

3. **From what vantage does God not watch the future?**

    From an idle watchtower.

Section 7

1. **What is the beginning of our reception into the surety and protection of Christ?**

    The Father's gift.

2. **What is not the reason that some excel?**

    Their own effort or diligence.

Section 8

1. **Which church fathers appealed to God's foreknowledge of grace used well?**

    Ambrose, Origen, Jerome, and the early Augustine.

2. **What is Calvin's "the dog that did not bark" argument against this view?**

    That if this were the case, Paul should have presented that answer in Romans 9 after raising the objection, "Is there unrighteousness with God?"

3. **What is the relationship between God's grace and our fitness?**

    As Augustine said, "The grace of God does not find, but makes persons fit to be chosen."

Section 9

1. **What does Calvin do with Thomas' argument that merit is not the cause of predestination on God's side, but it may be spoken of that way on our side?**

    He dismisses it as an evasion. And he answers it by saying that predestination to grace could be made subordinate to predestination to glory, which would make Thomas's argument fall apart.

Section 10

1. **What is Calvin's basic answer to those who say the universality of the promise nullifies special election?**

    Calvin cites Scripture that shows God's distribution of grace not being conducted on egalitarian grounds (e.g., Acts 16:7ff).

2. **What is the mother of faith?**

    Election.

Section 11

1. **In what way do we wrong and patronize the apostle Paul?**

    By pretending that what is obvious to us was invisible to him.

2. **What central argument does Calvin repeat here?**

    If those who want our merits considered are in the right, then why did Paul not give this answer in Romans 9?

Chapter Twenty-Three

Section 1

1. **What does human understanding do when it hears the truths of election?**

    It breaks forth into "boils and rages as if aroused by the sound of a trumpet."

2. **If God passes over someone instead of electing him, what does that amount to?**

    It amounts to condemnation.

3. **Is hardening in the hand of God?**

    Absolutely.

4. Is the relationship of God to good and evil the same?

No. Calvin points out that Paul softens the expression when talking about hardening, but not in a way that moves the ultimate outcome away from the will of God.

5. So what is the cause of the hardening?

The secret plan of God.

Section 2

1. What do the pious and moderate remember?

That they are but men.

2. What is the highest rule of righteousness?

The will of God.

3. What cannot be found?

Anything higher than God's will.

4. Is God therefore lawless and a law unto Himself?

No. He is free of all fault. But He still owes an accounting to no one.

Section 3

1. What does Calvin invite the sons of Adam to do?

To come forward and quarrel with God.

2. As they attempt it, what do they deliberately suppress?

The cause of their condemnation, which is in themselves.

Section 4

1. What argument do these people then resort to?

They say yes, but the condemnation which they fall under was also foreordained for them.

2. Does Calvin agree that we are fallen in accordance with the will of God?

Yes.

3. How does Calvin answer this?

The same way Paul does—by appealing to the prerogatives of God. And he denies that he is resorting to a loophole. What stronger reason can be brought forward "than when we are ordered to reflect who God is"?

4. **What may we not do if we fail to understand something of God's will?**

    We may not condemn Him just because we are ignorant.

Section 5

1. **Can we know that God has willed these things?**

    Yes. He has revealed so much.

2. **Can we know why?**

    "No account of it can be given."

3. **How does Augustine answer when challenged on this point?**

    He said that he too is a man. Therefore we should both listen to
    the one who says, "O man, who art thou?"

4. **What should we do with these things?**

    We should imitate the apostle Paul and rest in the wonder.

Section 6

1. **What is the next objection to election that Calvin answers?**

    The idea that election removes man's responsibility.

2. **Does Calvin agree that foreknowledge by itself is not
    deterministic?**

    By itself, yes. But he notes dryly that God foreknows "by reason
    of the fact that he decreed."

Section 7

1. **Does Calvin grant that the decree is dreadful?**

    Yes, he calls it decretum horribile.

2. **If there were a legitimate complaint, where would it have
    lodged?**

    Against predestination.

Section 8

1. **Does Calvin grant a distinction between the will of God and
    the permission of God?**

    No. There is no distinction.

2. **What must be just?**

    That which deserves praise.

3. **Where should we focus our attention when contemplating the cause of our condemnation?**

    In the corrupt nature of humanity, which is closer to home.

4. **What is it to stay out of God's decrees, and what is it to pry?**

    Ignorance is learned, and the craving to know is a "species of madness."

Section 9

1. **Does Calvin think he is able to silence the objectors?**

    No, because impiety will always have something to growl and mutter about.

2. **What is it to act perversely in this?**

    To seek out the source of your own condemnation by looking at the "hidden recesses of the divine counsel."

Section 10

1. **What is a third objection that Calvin must answer?**

    It is that election makes God a respecter of persons, contrary to what Scripture says about Him.

2. **How does Calvin answer this?**

    By saying that if the cause for the distinction is not found in man, then the respecting must not be of man.

Section 11

1. **When God chooses some for life and others not, why is He free from accusation?**

    He does not owe forgiveness. He is like a lender who has the authority of remitting payment for one and not for another.

Section 12

1. **What is the next objection to this teaching?**

    That if it is taught, then zeal for doing good disappears.

2. **Does Calvin acknowledge that some distort the doctrine this way?**

    Yes, he says, "for there are multitudes of a swinish nature who defile the doctrine of predestination."

3. But what does Paul say we have been chosen to?

To a holy and blameless life.

Section 13

1. What is another related objection?

That it discourages teachers from moral admonition.

2. How does Calvin answer this?

He points to Paul, who taught this doctrine, and asks if Paul was cold in his admonitions and exhortations.

Section 14

1. What example of balance does Calvin point to?

Augustine, who taught this doctrine clearly, but in ways that would not give unnecessary offense.

Chapter Twenty-Four

Section 1

1. Why does God teach His elect?

In order to lead them to faith.

2. Can grace be received by a hard heart?

No. Grace is given first to take that hardness away.

3. What does Scripture couple together so that we know that free mercy is to be sought?

The call and election.

4. How does Augustine turn around the view that "willing and running" are useless unless mercy is present?

By pointing out that this means that mercy is useless unless willing and running are present. And that is manifestly impious.

Section 2

1. What is a pledge of salvation that cannot deceive us?

The inner call.

Section 3

1. Does grace merely give us the ability to believe or not?

No. Grace gives us faith itself.

2. Does election take effect only after we believe?
No, not at all.

3. Can we take assurance from the fact that we believe?
Certainly, for if we try to penetrate God's eternal ordination, we will be swallowed by an abyss.

4. What do some men do in order to make sure about God's plan?
They flit above the clouds, instead of heeding the word which is near us, in our hearts and mouths.

Section 4

1. What is a grievous error concerning election, one that Satan loves?
The error of trying break into the inner recesses of divine wisdom.

2. What question must we avoid?
What revelation do you have of your election?

3. What is the greatest and most pestilential error?
Investigating God's eternal plan apart from His word.

4. Where should we begin and end?
With the call of God, that comes through the word.

Section 5

1. Where is election alone to be found?
In Christ alone.

2. Who alone is the fountain of life?
Christ.

3. If we have been chosen in Christ, where will we not find assurance?
We will not find assurance in ourselves.

4. If we want more than to be sons and heirs, what would we have to do?
We would have to rise above Christ, which is impossible.

5. What would be a preposterous prayer?
"O Lord, if I am elected, hear me."

6. Instead of praying this way, what should we be content with?
The promises of the word.

Section 6

1. **Where does Christ bring those that He has truly illumined with the knowledge of His name?**

   Into the bosom of His Church.

2. **If we want assurance, what should we embrace?**

   Christ.

3. **What does Paul magnificently lord it over?**

   Life and death, things present and to come.

4. **What gift does this kind of boasting depend on?**

   The gift of perseverance.

Section 7

1. **How then do we account for various apostasies that we have all seen?**

   Those who fall away never cleaved to Christ "with that heartfelt confidence" that the certainty of election provides.

2. **What must we have instead of "careless, carnal security"?**

   We must have simple confidence, responding to the word.

Section 8

1. **How are we to understand Christ's statement that many are called but few are chosen?**

   By realizing that there are two kinds of calls.

2. **What is the first kind of call?**

   The general call which God extends to all indiscriminately through the preached word. This even includes those for whom that word is the savor of death.

3. **What is the second kind of call?**

   The special call, which is accompanied by the inward illumination of the Spirit.

4. **Is this special call for the true believer alone?**

   Calvin says "for the most part."

5. **Can anyone apostatize from this special call?**

   A few. God illumines some temporarily but then abandons them "in just punishment for their ingratitude."

6. **Putting this together, who then cannot fall away?**

    The one who has received this special call along with the gift of
    perseverance.

Section 9

1. **Was Judas one of Christ's sheep?**

    No, but he occupied the place of one.

2. **Did Jesus know this when He chose him to be an apostle?**

    Yes (Jn. 6:70; 13:18).

3. **When predestination is rightly understood, does it shake our
    faith?**

    No. Rather it provides its best confirmation.

Section 10

1. **Before one of the elect is called, is there any difference between
    him and any of the nonelect?**

    None at all.

2. **How does Calvin show this?**

    By citing multiple Scripture texts.

Section 11

1. **How does Calvin describe what happens to the elect?**

    As deliverance from evil, instead of maturation into a good that
    they had in seed form.

Section 12

1. **If the same sermon is preached to a hundred, and twenty be-
    lieve, what needs to be explained?**

    Not the eighty. They remain in unbelief according to their nature.
    What needs to be explained is the belief of the twenty, and the
    only explanation is the intervention of God.

Section 13

1. **According to Augustine, could God have turned the will of evil
    men to good?**

    Of course.

2. **Why, then, does He not?**

    Because, as Augustine put it, "Because he is unwilling."

Section 14

1. **What do the impious do when they hear of God's sovereignty in salvation?**

    They "complain that God abuses his inordinate power, to make cruel sport with the miseries of his creatures."

2. **In contrast, what should we be willing to admit?**

    Ignorance where God's wisdom rises to its height.

Section 15

1. **What problem does Calvin address next?**

    The problem of passages that seem to contradict what he has been saying, like Ezekiel 33:11.

2. **How does Calvin answer?**

    By showing that if God wills the wicked to live, without exception, this is not consistent with His behavior elsewhere (Matt. 11:23). If the inhabitants of Sodom would have responded more favorably to more grace than they got, then why did they not get more?

Section 16

1. **How does Calvin handle 1 Timothy 2:3–4?**

    The first way is the same as in the previous section—if God wants everyone saved equally, why doesn't He act like it?

2. **What is the second way he responds?**

    He points out that such passages are talking about classes of people, kings and such.

Section 17

1. **What two elements of the problem does Calvin grant?**

    He grants that God has a will that divides the human race into elect and reprobate, and he grants that God causes the gospel to be preached indiscriminately to all.

2. **What is his final conclusion?**

    That we should tremble with Paul at so great a mystery.

Chapter Twenty-Five

Section 1

1. **Why is it hard for us to hope and trust in the coming resurrection?**

   Because we are slow and must climb over innumerable obstacles.

Section 2

1. **Who alone receives the fruit of Christ's benefits?**

   Those who raise their minds to the resurrection.

Section 3

1. **Does Calvin acknowledge the difficulty of believing in the resurrection?**

   Yes, he does.

2. **What are the two main helps that God gives to us?**

   The first is the parallel of Christ's resurrection; the second is the omnipotence of God.

3. **What do scorners do with the Evangelists' history?**

   They treat it as a fairy tale.

Section 4

1. **Why does Calvin argue that faith in the resurrection depends on faith in God's omnipotence?**

   Because that is what Paul says in Philippians 3:21.

Section 5

1. **How does Calvin answer pagan unbelievers who deny the resurrection?**

   By pointing out that their universal custom of burial makes them profess what no one admits to believing.

Section 6

1. **What does Calvin teach about the intermediate state?**

   Not very much, because it is important not to go beyond what is written. But he says we know enough to say that we will be received by the Father of the faithful.

Section 7

1. **What does Calvin do with the idea that God gives us a completely new body, made from scratch?**

   He rejects it as a monstrosity.

2. **Why is the promised "change of quality" important in this?**

   If we had completely new bodies, there would be no transformation. But transformation is what is promised.

3. **What is Calvin's argument from headship on this?**

   If we get new bodies, and not our old bodies raised and transformed, then head and body do not match. Christ's old body was raised and transformed.

Section 8

1. **What is the mother of this notion?**

   Unbelief. Unbelief cannot handle the idea that bodies, exposed so long to corruption, could be restored.

2. **How does Calvin answer?**

   With Scripture. For example, Romans 8:11 says that God will give life to our mortal bodies.

3. **Does Calvin think burial rites are superstitious?**

   No. He thinks they are a testament to the reality of the resurrection.

Section 9

1. **Does Calvin hold to a resurrection of the ungodly?**

   Yes, on the basis of numerous scriptural statements.

2. **How can resurrection, a benefit of Christ's resurrection, be extended to the ungodly?**

   It extends to them, not to become their lawful possession, but rather "thus be rendered more inexcusable."

Section 10

1. **How did the prophets describe our eternal state?**

   Because of our limitations, they describe our blessedness under physical terms.

2. **What must we not be titillated by?**

   An immoderate desire to know more than is lawful.

3. **Does Calvin believe that everyone will have equal measures of glory in heaven?**

No, and he cites Scripture to this effect. Two jars can be completely full of happiness, full to capacity, and be differently sized jars.

Section 11

1. **Who inquires into the different glory rankings between apostle and prophet, apostle and martyr, and so on?**

Men hungry for empty learning.

2. **What faults in the creation are repaired in the resurrection?**

Those which took their beginning from sin.

Section 12

1. **How are the torments of the lost described for us in Scripture?**

Again, as with the saved, by means of physical images.

2. **What are these images intended to do?**

To confound all our senses with dread.

3. **For Calvin, what is the heart of damnation?**

Being excluded from the presence of the Lord and from the glory of His might (2 Thes. 1:9).

Made in the USA
Monee, IL
09 July 2024

61129911R00403